Sport, Society and Politi

General editors   Stephen Wagg and John Williams

Liberation cricket

Of the global community of cricketers, the West Indians are arguably the most well known and feared. Their hegemony has proven durable and shows no serious signs of being over-turned. This pioneering and ground-breaking book explains how this tradition of cricketing excellence and leadership emerged, and how it contributed to the rise of West Indian nation-alism and independence.

The essayists argue that cricket mirrors the anti-colonial tensions and ideological and social conflicts over race and class that have shaped West Indian society. In consequence, it has helped promote the region's democratic ethos and fragmented nationalism.

Liberation Cricket connects and embraces the diversity of West Indies social and political life, and suggests the relevance of cricket research for an understanding of the making of the modern West Indies.

Dedication

For
C.L.R. James

To
Biko Beckles and his generation of West Indian cricketers
and
Kirsten and Laura Stoddart who love the game

Liberation cricket

West Indies cricket culture

edited by

Hilary McD. Beckles and Brian Stoddart

Manchester University Press
Manchester and New York

distributed exclusively in the USA and Canada by St. Martin's Press

Published by Manchester University Press
Oxford Road, Manchester M13 9NR, UK
and Room 400, 175 Fifth Avenue, New York, NY 10010, USA

Distributed exclusively in the USA and Canada
by St. Martin's Press, Inc., 175 Fifth Avenue, New York,
NY 10010, USA

British Library Cataloguing-in-Publication Data
A catalogue record for this book is available from the British Library

Library of Congress Cataloging-in-Publication Data
    Liberation cricket: West Indies cricket culture / edited by Hilary
    McD. Beckles and Brian Stoddart.
        p.   cm. — (Sport, society, and politics)
        ISBN 0-7190-4314-X. — ISBN 0-7190-4315-8 (pbk.)
        1. Cricket—Social aspects—West Indies.   2. West Indies—Social
    conditions.   I. Beckles, Hilary, 1955–   .   II. Stoddart, Brian.
    III. Series.
    GV928.W47L53   1995
    796.358'09729—dc20   94-11595
                                                                          CIP

ISBN 0 7190 4314 X *hardback*
ISBN 0 7190 4315 8 *paperback*

Typeset in Great Britain
by Servis Filmsetting Ltd, Manchester

Printed in Great Britain
by Biddles Ltd, Guildford and King's Lynn

245782

Contents

v

Contents

Plates 1–10 appear between pages 140 and 141
Plates 11–20 appear between pages 268 and 269

Foreword

Viv Richards

Liberation cricket: West Indies cricket culture

In July, 1992, Hilary Beckles and Don Charles arranged an open seminar at the University of the West Indies – Cave Hill Campus, to launch in the Caribbean my just published autobiography – *Hitting across the Line*. I was unable to attend the launching on account of commitments to Glamorgan CCC in the UK but was most delighted to learn of the announcements that were made at this event. Cricket goes way beyond the boundary and the announcement of the UWI History Department's decision to offer a course on West Indies cricket history as part of its degree programme as well as to prepare texts that would make such a course viable in the long term, was of historic proportions. The course has since been offered and this book is the first of the texts planned.

As a former West Indies player and captain, I consider myself a citizen of the West Indies and welcomed this initiative by the University of the West Indies. For most of my own lifetime the UWI and the WI cricket team have been the two leading institutions in the struggle to unite our people and to maximise the use of our resources. There is much that I have learnt about the West Indian world through my role as a cricketer. I have always emphasised that cricket is more than a sport, it is a political and social process that requires detailed investigation. Indeed in my autobiography, I stated that cricket 'gets to the root' of societies and for this reason I welcome this text as a sociological study of the West Indies.

The title of the text is quite interesting. In the West Indies our cricketers have had to struggle against all kinds of injustices. Colonisation and the racism it bred, were not easily uprooted from the region. Cricketers, like all other West Indians, had little choice but to resist efforts to suppress their talents and their rights. In some instances cricketers were at the vanguard of West Indian liberation and in others they were used by backward interests. In my own way, I would like to think that I carried my bat for the liberation of African and other oppressed people every-where. The principle of fair play so deeply rooted within cricket values must be fought for and defended at all times.

Foreword

I am honoured, therefore, to be asked to provide the foreword to this academic landmark and hope that this text will serve as enlightenment for all those who use it as well as to provide them with the guidance and courage to continue the struggle for liberation within their own boundaries.

Acknowledgements

The authors thank the following for permission to publish the articles as noted:

Random House for C.L.R. James's 'The proof of the pudding' which appeared in *Beyond a Boundary* (London, Hutchinson, 1963).

Human Kinetics Publishers for Brian Stoddart, 'C.L.R. James: a remembrance', *Sociology of Sport Journal*, 7, 1 (1990).

North American Society for Sport History for Brian Stoddart, 'Cricket, social formation and cultural continuity in Barbados: a preliminary ethnohistory', *Journal of Sport History*, 14, 3 (1987).

American Anthropological Society for Frank E. Manning, 'Celebrating cricket: the symbolic construction of Caribbean politics', *American Ethnologist*, 8, 3 (1981).

Canadian Institute of International Affairs for Brian Stoddart, 'Caribbean cricket: the role of sport in emerging small-nation politics', *International Journal*, 43, 4 (1988).

Center for the Study of Sport in Society for Kevin Yelvington, 'Ethnicity "not out": the Indian cricket tour of the West Indies and the 1976 elections in Trinidad and Tobago', *Arena Review*, 14, 1 (1990).

University of New South Wales Press for Helen Tiffin, 'Cricket, literature and the Politics of de-colonisation: the case of C.L.R. James' in Richard Cashman and Michael McKernan (eds), *Sport, Money, Morality and the Media* (1981).

Institute of Jamaica for Orlando Patterson, 'The ritual of cricket', *Jamaica Journal*, 3 (1969).

MacMillan for Kenneth Surin, 'C.L.R. James' material aesthetic of cricket' in Alistair Hennessy (ed.), *Intellectuals in the Twentieth Century Caribbean* (1992).

Frank Cass for Keith Sandiford and Brian Stoddart, 'The elite schools and cricket in Barbados: a study in colonial continuity', *International Journal of the History of Sport*, 4 (1987).

—for R.D.E. Burton, 'Cricket, carnival and street culture in the Caribbean', *British Journal of Sport History*, 2 (1985).

—for Brian Stoddart, 'Cricket and colonialism in the English-speaking Caribbean to 1914: towards a cultural analysis' in J.A. Mangan (ed.), *Pleasure, Profit, Proselytism*.

Caribbean Quarterly for Maurice St Pierre, 'West Indian cricket', Parts I and II.

The authors would further like to thank all those friends and scholars who offered support and encouragement, the players and cricketing public (especially in the Caribbean) who provided the inspiration, and the team-mates with whom we have lived out the Caribbean cricketing heritage.

To Sue Wright, of the Faculty of Communication in the University of Canberra, our very great thanks for her skills in getting assorted texts up to manuscript status.

Finally, we thank our families who have had to live not only with us but also the game and now a book about the game – luckily for us, they share the sense of history, its social significance, and the sheer beauty and power of Caribbean cricket.

Contributors

Hilary Beckles   Professor of History, University of the West Indies, Barbados. Graduate of the University of Hull, and the author of several books on Caribbean history with special reference to the economic and social history of slavery. A keen and accomplished cricketer. Also, founder and coordinator of the Centre for Cricket Research, U.W.I., Cave Hill Campus.

Brian Stoddart   Professor of Cultural Studies and Dean of the Faculty of Communication, University of Canberra, Australia. An international authority on sports culture. Played cricket in several countries, including a year with the Maple Club in Barbados.

Richard Burton   Teaches in the French Department at the University of Sussex, and has done extensive work on Caribbean literature and social culture.

Hubert Devonish   Guyanese linguist, and Reader in socio-linguistics at the University of the West Indies, Mona Campus, Kingston, Jamaica.

C.L.R. James   The intellectual starting point for this book – see Brian Stoddart's remembrance of him.

Neil Lazarus   Associate Professor in English and Media at Brown University, Providence, Rhode Island. Author of a major work on resistance themes in post-colonial African fiction.

Frank Manning   Professor of Anthropology at the University of Western Ontario, London, Ontario, Canada, until his regrettably early death. His paper here arose from his major ethnography on popular culture in Bermuda. One of the pioneers of modern work into the relationship of play and culture.

Orlando Patterson   A distinguished Jamaican intellectual who is Professor of Sociology at Harvard University, and the author of several acclaimed works on the dynamics of slavery. Has also written works of fiction and been involved as a political activist.

Keith Sandiford   Professor of History at the University of Manitoba, Winnipeg, Manitoba and the author of several articles on cricket history. A graduate of Combermere, the University of the West Indies and the University of London.

June Soomer   PhD candidate in West Indian political history at the University of the West Indies, Barbados, investigating the experiences of the British West Indies Federation.

Maurice St Pierre   Professor of Sociology at Morgan State University, Baltimore, Maryland, and formerly Research Fellow at the Institute of Social and Economic Research in the University of the West Indies where he established his reputation as a leading analyst of Caribbean life.

Kenneth Surin   Formerly a theologian, he is now at Duke University, Durham, North

Carolina, where he teaches in the Marxism and Society Program, including a course on the work of C.L.R. James.

L. O'Brien Thompson   Teaches sociology at West Virginia State College Institute, West Virginia, and a well known analyst of Caribbean society and culture.

Helen Tiffin   Associate Professor of English at the University of Queensland, Brisbane, Australia, and has written extensively on post-colonial literature.

Harclyde Walcott   A Barbadian poet, photographer and director who is Director of Dramatic Studies at the Creative Arts Centre, University of the West Indies, Mona Campus, Kingston, Jamaica.

Kevin Yelvington   Graduated in social anthropology from the University of Sussex, and is now Associate Professor of Sociology at Florida International University, Miami, Florida. Works on race and gender relations in the modern West Indies.

Introduction

Hilary McD. Beckles

'Cricket is We!', West Indians are fond of proclaiming to the world – an expression laden with ontological significance that is richly supported by the writings of their most gifted intellectuals. Edward Kamau Brathwaite, for example, sets the tone for an evaluative discourse on cricket as 'life' in that famous passage from 'Rites', a poem that explores the predicaments of the West Indian personality:[1]

> this isn't no time for playing
> the fool nor making' no sport;
> this is cricket!

V.S. Naipaul indicates what is perhaps a serious pathological condition when he recorded parts of a discussion, on which he eavesdropped, between two West Indian spectators at the 1963 West Indies vs England test at the Oval:[2]

> 'You hear the latest from British Guiana?'
> 'What, the strike still on?'
> 'Things really bad out there.'
> 'Man, go away eh. We facing defeat, and you want to talk politics.'

C.L.R. James, always one to strip away the scaffold leaving the structure to stand or fall on the integrity or insincerity of its own weight, leads us by the nose when he stated that "West Indians crowding to tests bring with them the whole past history and future hopes of the islands."[3] Cricket, he maintained, represents our most sophisticated and sensitive cultural lens through which to view the sociological development of the West Indies from the Emancipation era of the 1830s to the Independence era of the 1950s and beyond.

While Caribbean social scientists have long accepted James's argument in a general sort of way, in 1992 the University of the West Indies (Barbados Campus) embarked upon an academic mission to test its specificity with the introduction of a cricket course in the History degree programme. Faculty members believed that they were batting on a good wicket when they decided to test Jamesian concepts by

1

introducing cricket studies into the intellectual environs of their prestigious academy.

The semester course, West Indies Cricket History since 1870, has proven very popular with students and has excited the curiosity of the cricket loving public who now wish to know much more. The principal objectives behind this compilation of essays, therefore, are to provide historiographical focus for these and future students, and to indicate to the wider public the central themes and issues that have emerged from social science research on West Indies cricket culture. In many respects this is a pioneering work, though many essays included have already been published.

Popular writers of cricket have succeeded in establishing a literary hegemony that emphasises the exciting, flamboyant, aggressive, artful and energetic aspect of the West Indies styles and methods. This text, however, does none of these things. Rather, it seeks to analyse the historical evolution of the social features and ideological expressions of the region's cricket by indicating its specific colonial and anti-colonial cultural imperatives. It takes as its point of departure the central paradigm around which an impressive body of recent literature revolves. That is, the debate which seeks to explore the extent to which West Indies cricket has strengthened the reproductive capacity of a colonised mentality or has functioned as an ideological weapon of a subversive, anti-colonial, creole nationalism.

In seeking out the central ideological pulse of West Indies cricket culture, the question is asked in many essays: what did the imported/imposed Victorian cricket ethic do to or for West Indians – white and black, and what in turn did these ethnic groups do to or for it? Answers address the specific forms of cricket domestication by colonials, and indicate that whites and blacks established their own different traditions within the indigenisation process.

The hegemonic tradition was that of the white, elite, planter-merchant communities that expressed a distinct subservient ideological stance in relation to Empire, and was fully committed to the importance of white supremacy attitudes within it. The initially subordinate black tradition emitted all the cultural characteristics of an alienated, marginalised sub-type seeking to establish itself in the little space made available to it. Both indigenous forms developed simultaneously, but were kept apart by the potency of an officially enforced social policy of racial segregation.

West Indies cricket, then, like all other aspects of socio-cultural life, eventually displayed the consequences of a racially fractured nationalism that threatened the movement towards nationhood in the era of dying English colonialism. Not everyone agrees with this view. It has been suggested, for example, that by the end of the nineteenth century when cricket became the region's leading expression of popular culture, its inner logic, methods, moral codes and aesthetics, were no longer shaped by the political ideologies of ethnic relations. The truth of the matter, however, is that by this time cricket, unlike any other form of community interaction, reflected the deepest ideological thoughts of colonials, and suggested the conflicting nature of ethnic interests. This meant, of course, that from its early days cricket in the West

Indies functioned as an agency of colonial oppression and at the same time provided an area in which the socially oppressed majority ventilated endemic anti-systemic attitudes and ideals.

Dialectical analysis best explains the dichotomous development of the social culture of West Indies cricket. The elite colonial community saw in cricket a zone of exclusive cultural activity consistent with its social and ideological outlook. Blacks and coloureds in turn saw this space as one on which they could gradually encroach without incurring severe penalties, but at the same time promote actions of a powerful symbolic nature designed to further the cause of the democratic revolution initiated by anti-slavery legislation.

West Indies cricket, then, was born, raised and socialised within the fiery cauldron of colonial oppression and liberation struggle. In its matured form it is essentially an ideological and politicised species and knows no world better than that of liberation struggle. No one has written about this process with as much intellectual rigour and literary sophistication as C.L.R. James. Which is why he was able to beautifully disguise his masterful examination of West Indies cricket culture as a semi-autobiography and political history of the modern region.

The text is divided into five discrete conceptual categories that constitute the critical elements of the structure established to discuss our central paradigm.

Part I, 'Colonisation and cultural imperialism', sets out the historical background against which the overall analysis departs. When, how and why cricket found its way into the West Indies is fully examined in order to discover the ideological luggage and the nature of the mission. The richly researched, pioneering work of Stoddart and Sandiford, and the survey analysis by Beckles establish the nineteenth century 'moment' of cricket's intervention as the latest, and perhaps most sophisticated, imperialist cultural technology.

Part II, 'Creolisation, ideology and popular culture', examines the process whereby the imported cricket culture was domesticated and transformed into a vehicle of the nascent democratising nationalist order. The infusion into cricket of a range of afro-cultural expressions and expectations, resulted in the 'carnivalisation' of crowd responses, which in turn became a barometer of political consciousness and a promoter of anti-systemic ideology. Burton, Patterson, St Pierre, and Beckles in their respective essays provide detailed sociological insights into the process whereby cricket was creolised, politicised, and ritualised within the context of the region's radical anti-colonial tradition.

Part III, 'Ethnicity, social ideology and politics', descends into the social and ideological mechanics of Caribbean race relations and indicates the manner in which the cricket culture, already a carrier of imperialistic attitudes and values about 'natives' – black and white – was further contaminated by ideologies whose historic origins and reproductive environments were to be found 'beyond the boundary'. Cricket was both a mirror and an arena that allowed ethnic groups to display, defend and define differences and similarities within the format of civic respectability and non-violent protest. Thompson, Devonish, Beckles and Yelvington explore how cricket

3

reflected the racial differences that divided West Indian nationalism, in spite of a concerted effort to promote a non-racial meritocracy.

Part IV, 'Nationalism and liberation', brings together the main currents in the fascinating historiographic diversity that characterises investigations into the politics of modern West Indies cricket. That cricket constitutes the first and most popular forum in which West Indies human resources were brought together for regional promotion remains a powerful historical fact that cannot be minimised. James' classic explanation of how the struggle for popular leadership under Frank Worrell in 1958/59 was organised, and Soomer's survey of the integrationist ideology of cricket, demonstrates with clarity the political seductiveness of the game within the democratic ethos. Stoddart and Manning outline with great skill the reasons why within these small nation-states cricket transcends institutional politics in the process of deepening nationalist self-perceptions.

Finally, Part V, 'Philosophy, art and literature', explores in an archaeological sort of way, the cultural materials embedded within the cricket world that, when excavated by sensitive artists, yield fascinating evidence for the creative imagination. In the West Indies the term 'cricket' is, perhaps, more appropriate than 'metaphor' – certainly in terms of the influence of the game upon language, popular art and literature. In this context C.L.R. James stands as a monument to the 'intellectualisation' of popular culture. This section constitutes, in an eclectic way, a tribute to James in which a celebration of cricket as art, politics and philosophy is excitingly articulated. Surin and Tiffin both ask some serious questions of the nature of James's work, and in the process establish the beginning of a critical evaluation. If James had overstated the impact of the Graeco-Roman literary and theatrical tradition upon West Indies cricket, Beckles goes in search of its African derived social ideology by examining the nature of the 'crowd' and its relationship to the literary and performing arts. Stoddart, batting at No. 11, comes in, takes guard, and says, thank you C.L.R.!

Richard Cashman has suggested: 'The task of analysing the colonial domestication of games, and of interpreting whether this represents adaptation, resistance, and/or subversion, has only just begun'.[4] We like to think that, with this modest contribution, the task is slightly advanced.

H. Beckles
B. Stoddart

Notes

1 Edward Kamau Brathwaite, *The Arrivants: a New World Trilogy* (Oxford University Press, Oxford, 1981) p. 198.
2 V.S. Naipaul, 'England v. West Indies, 1963', in Michael and Simon Davie (eds), *The Faber Book of Cricket* (Faber & Faber, London, 1987), p. 189.

3 Cited in *Time for Action: Report of the West Indies Commission* (University of the West Indies Press, Kingston, 1993, 2nd edn), p. 327.
4 Richard Cashman, 'Cricket and Colonialism: Colonial Hegemony and Indigenous Subversion?', in J.A. Mangan (ed.), *Pleasure, Profit and Proselytism: British Culture and Sport at Home and Abroad, 1700–1914* (Frank Cass, London, 1988), p. 271.

Part I

Colonisation and cultural imperialism

1

✳ Cricket and colonialism in the English-speaking Caribbean to 1914: towards a cultural analysis

Brian Stoddart

In 1929 the American writer T.S. Stribling set an intriguing detective story in the world of Barbadian cricket.[1] The son of a prominent Bridgetown banker was found dead in the Wanderers Cricket Club pavilion shortly after helping that team win its toughest match of the season. Murder was suspected, a club professional the prime suspect. Bumbling investigations by an American university psychology professor, enjoying a Caribbean sabbatical, eventually revealed the villain as a respectable amateur member of the club. The story appears trivial. In its detail, however, it sets the foundations for what Michel Foucault might have termed an archaeology of Caribbean cricket.[2] Stribling located both the playing and the sociological conditions of cricket deep in Barbadian civic culture, seeing the game constituted by its social context rather than arising merely as an adjunct to it.

Stribling's insights were left at the superficial and unexplored level, but still provide invaluable clues for a social unravelling of Barbadian cricket history in particular and, by extension, of the English-speaking Caribbean in general. To his American eye, cricket in Barbados was an integral part of local culture, prestige and power. That set him apart from earlier cricket-steeped writers like Pelham Warner and Lord Hawke; although both referred passingly to unique features of the Caribbean condition, neither provoke the analytical responses invited by Stribling.[3] (As C. Wright Mills pointed out, the unindoctrinated observer frequently seizes the possibilities of everyday material more readily than one socialized into the culture, be it national or sectional).[4] There is, then, a direct if curious link between Stribling and C.L.R. James who, in his magisterial 1963 work *Beyond a Boundary,* sought to reconcile a life dedicated to Marxism with a concurrent and contradictory obeisance to cricket and English literature, the antithesis of his radical ideology.[5] Since then a number of writers have essayed extensions to the James conclusions, but few if any have attempted an explanation of the construction process by which the conditions pointed to by Stribling and James came about.[6]

The purpose here, then, through a concentration on Barbados and with reference to the other major pre-1914 cricketing islands, is to isolate the underlying principles of the environmental culture of Caribbean cricket; the building of its social authority systems; the elaboration of its social classification process; the origins and growth of its peculiar professional tradition; and the development of its ideological acceptance and resistance practices. From this analysis, cricket emerges not simply as an agency for colonial recreation, but as an arena where players in the imperial and colonial 'game' struggled to decide the results of social proselytism and cultural power through sport.

By concentrating on Barbadian (or Bajan, as it is often referred to locally) cricket, Stribling confirmed the term 'West Indies' as a useful shorthand but a misguiding principle for social and historical investigation. Caribbean cricket is analysed most profitably through its specific components. There was certainly talk of West Indian cricket, political and other types of federation before 1914, but its non-arrival underlined the differences which distinguished the territories from their geographical and demographic conditions upwards.[7] British Guiana, at the southern end of the Caribbean, occupied an area the size of Great Britain located on the South American mainland, much of it reachable only by water.[8] By 1891 East Indians (the regional term for indentured labourers from India and their descendants) outnumbered blacks, 122,000 to 113,000 with Portuguese 11,000 and other Europeans a slight 4,000. This varied population produced minerals, coffee, cotton and sugar. The island of Trinidad occupied about 1,900 square miles of very different country, had one of the most diverse populations on earth, as revealed beautifully in Edgar Mittelholzer's novel *A Morning At The Office,* and produced sugar, cocoa and oil. At the northern end of the region was Jamaica, over 4,000 square miles of mostly steep hill country and small coastal plains. By 1891 blacks there numbered 488,000, coloureds (the result of European and black intermixing, there being no significant East Indian population) 121,000 and whites 14,000. Its main crop was sugar with strong contributions from coffee and pimento. Apart from a heritage in slavery and an acquired British governance, these states varied considerably in economic and cultural composition which, along with the weather, produced distinctive cricket traditions.

From the beginning of inter-colonial competition in 1865 Jamaican cricket was sealed off from that in the other islands because of both distance and the irregularity and prohibitive cost of inter-island transport.[9] In the years to 1914 Jamaica saw more English touring teams than it did those from other colonies. Physical separation led to a deep seated psychological one so that there were frequent disputes over the organization of tournaments and, from 1900, the selection of combined teams to visit England.[10] In Trinidad with weather conditions and attacks upon the soil by (ironically enough!) the mole, cricket combined to encourage the use of coconut matting as a substitute for traditional turf pitches. Until 1935, when an Australian coach introduced jute matting, Trinidadian playing conditions were said to develop batsmen who were excellent cutters and hookers but not drivers, because the ball did not 'come on' to the bat.[11] In British Guiana, two wet and two dry seasons made co-ordinating a common playing time with the other islands difficult. By 1895 the playing rules for inter-colonial matches stipulated that they be completed between

1 August and 31 October, but experience showed even that to be impractical.[12] Among other things the intersection of these geographical, climatic and social statistics put home teams at a substantial advantage, and a win away was always a source of particular jubilation. The local specificity produced by these varying circumstances of environment is demonstrated especially well by the Barbadian case.

By the later nineteenth century the tiny, 166 square-mile island, popularly known as 'Little England', was crammed with over 180,000 inhabitants creating one of the highest population densities in the world.[13] Just over 15,000 were white, the rest largely black with a small but significant coloured community known, most commonly, as 'brownskins'. Unlike its cricketing partners, Barbados had known no other political allegiance but to Britain since the first settlers landed early in the seventeenth century, and one result was a representative government different from that in the other islands.[14] Representation itself was based directly on a unique political economy because Barbados, under imperial rule, had known nothing but the production of sugar; it had remained 'faithful to the cane'.[15] 'Crop', as sugar cane harvesting is still known, defined Bajan life as production requirements provided the impetus for slavery and, after abolition, the need to maintain cheap 'free' labour in the face of increasing industrial inefficiency, faltering prices and growing competition for a static market. Tough legislation such as the 1840 Contract Act which created a located estate tenantry, determined that by the later nineteenth century 'working-class' had replaced 'slavery' in Bajan parlance.[16] But sugar went beyond even that. Its *idea*, its permeation of all aspects of island culture was as important as its economic fact. Every plane of Barbadian life was touched by sugar, cricket prominently included.[17]

Logically the game should have been played during the dry season but that was in 'crop', so matches took place during the unpredictable wet months. Many 1877 games played by the newly formed Wanderers Club were disrupted by rain.[18] In 1895 the Barbados side routed the first touring English team for 48 runs in its first innings on a damp wicket, then won the match convincingly.[19] In a local cup match in 1896 the Pickwick Club made only 45 but still beat Leeward by 4 runs – over five inches of rain had fallen the previous day.[20] In 1905, another English touring team was dismissed for 95 in its second innings leaving Barbados just 20 to win, rain again the determinant.[21] Calls for reform of the season received little support because of the sugar culture, and from 1909 onwards local matches became even more unpredictable when their playing time was stretched from one Saturday to three.[22] Barbadians turned this uncertainty into a virtue, claiming it gave them experience of differing conditions unlike British Guiana players who, it was claimed, never played on wet pitches.[23] More important even than the impact of sugar upon playing conditions, however, was its determination of who was placed where in the social hierarchy of Bajan cricket.

Plantation owners, merchants, bankers, clerks, and civil servants came to competition matches categorized by their place in the hierarchy of sugar production, and cricket was a powerful instrument in the preservation and promotion of that hierarchy. Cricketers, for example, were conspicuously prominent in the Voters Lists until 1914 and beyond.[24] The significance is that for most of the period under review less than 2 per cent of the population qualified for a vote, the stipulations for which required either a substantial yearly income, the freehold of land, the payment of substantial parish taxes or the possession of a university degree. By definition these people were planters, professionals, merchants, bankers or senior clerks. Their influence was accentuated by constituency imbalances: in 1900, for example, the city of Bridgetown (which contained most of the emergent middle-class blacks) had 407 voters to return its two representatives while St Lucy (a rural seat dominated by white planters) had just 47 voters to return its two. The aristocracy of cricket, then, was the aristocracy of sugar, but even that masks an important structural point.

By 1892, when the Barbados Challenge Cup competition was formalized, power within the sugar hierarchy was shifting rapidly from traditional plantation owners to a smaller group of merchants and associated service castes such as lawyers. As prices faltered and production costs climbed, owners unable to sustain operations were assisted by legislation such as the Agricultural Aids Act of 1889 under which merchants advanced loans against the imminent crop. By the early twentieth century sugar conditions were so poor that many planters were heavily indebted to merchants, and an increasing number were foreclosed by the lending institutions. Similarly, many estates changed hands in the Court of Chancery, basically an institution designed to pass properties from those who could not support them economically to those who could in order to keep the industry and, of course, the social economy going. Merchants were prominent purchasers, and towards 1914 the process was widespread.[25] In 1908, for example, a foreclosed planter who lost land held by his family for over 200 years attracted much sympathy, and the following year another traditional and influential planter severed his island connections.[26]

Cricket players and administrators (frequently one and the same) were prominent in this activity, men like[27] J.O. Wright (merchant, company director, planter, politician, Barbados Cricket Committee member and long-serving Wanderers President); D.C. da Costa (director of a family merchant firm, active cricket administrator and whose son, an excellent wicket-keeper, followed him into the business); A.S. Bryden (merchant, travelling agent and property dealer whose son, a Wanderers player, also took over the business); J. Gardiner Austin (founding member of Wanderers, merchant, politician and one of whose sons, H.B.G. Austin, became the doyen of Barbadian and Caribbean cricket as well as director of the reconstituted family company); and R.G. Challenor (a merchant whose son, George, became one of the greatest ever Caribbean batsmen as well as junior partner in the family firm which emerged at the end of the First World War as one of Barbados's largest trading conglomerates). These men were assisted by lawyers such as H.M. Cummins (long-serving secretary and player for the Spartan Club) whose practices thrived on the conveyancing of large property transfers. To speak of the 'plantocracy' dominating cricket, then, is imprecise. Although that group certainly provided numerous players and administrators, in the years down to 1914, the merchant-based emergent upper middle class became increasingly influential. And for them, cricket became a social bulwark in the midst of alarming change which sprang from two inter-related conditions: a shaken faith in the British political as opposed to cultural connection, and a fear of the proletariat based on economic uncertainty.

In 1876 the so-called Federation Riots sprang from reactions to the British government's apparent intention to alter the time-honoured Barbados constitution.[28] In the rioting, the elite divined that the 'working class', encouraged by the Governor, was beginning to demand greater rights.[29] Along with the urban growth of Bridgetown, this was interpreted as the old rural relationships breaking down along with the economic base of stability and good order. From the 1870s onwards there were endless complaints from 'respectable' society members, cricketers prominently among them, about the growing numbers of 'idlers and loafers' on the island, about the rise of youth gangs who terrorized and abused respectable citizens, about the insults and lewd suggestions offered to society women as they went through the streets, about the growing evils of grog shops and prostitution, and about the general increase in begging and lawlessness.[30]

One response to this unwelcome development was tough action by the lawyers and the judiciary.[31] In 1877 a field labourer received 12 months' imprisonment with hard labour for 'conspiring' to raise the wage of a cane-cutting contract. Setting fire to cane (among the gravest of anti-social acts) fetched up to 14 years with hard labour, and early in the twentieth century was thought in some quarters to warrant the recall of the cat-o'-nine-tails. In 1880 the Governor regretted a legal imprecision which seemed to prevent him from ordering female prisoners to have their hair cropped for breaches of discipline. In 1892 a woman received three months with hard labour for stealing two hens. By 1899 the Attorney-General thought 36 lashes not unreasonable for assault on girls under ten years. In 1909 an estate manager arbitrarily stopped wages for alleged worker indiscretions. When his employees disputed the decision with his bookkeeper, they were convicted on assault charges.

Among the judges and lawyers upholding this system were numerous cricket players and administrators: Sir Conrad Reeves (an extremely tough-minded Chief Justice and, from its foundation until his death, President of Spartan); G.A. Goodman (long-time Solicitor-General then Attorney-General, Barbados player and Pickwick President); Sir W.K. Chandler (Court of Appeal and Court of Chancery, President of Wanderers); H.S. Thorne (Police Magistrate and Barbados player); H.M. Seon (son of a Police Magistrate, court clerk, and Spartan player); Stephen Rudder (court clerk, Barbados and Spartan player); G.H. Corbin (solicitor and Spartan official) and E.C. Jackman (lawyer, planter, Barbados and Wanderers player). Cricket, then, had strong links with the legal arm of respectable society which was seeking to maintain civic order against what it considered massive social change.

A more subtle and, indeed, more influential defence against change than legal repression lay in cultural formation.[32] When Wanderers club was created in 1877, at least three of its officials had been key members of the Defence Association formed the previous year to oppose constitutional change: J. Gardiner Austin (sacked as a Governor's aide-de-camp for his actions); J.W. Carrington (a leading lawyer and politician), and T.B. Evelyn (attorney for the Bay estate from which the first Wanderers ground came).[33] D.C. da Costa and R. Challenor were other prominent Defence Association members also significant in early cricket circles. Cricket rapidly became a civilizing mechanism for this group, a source of both recreation and reaffirmation of social standards for its players and a display of civilized behaviour for spectators, especially those of the 'working class'. Cricket pitches were prominent in fashionable new housing developments like Belleville and Strathclyde which, from the 1880s, became monuments to the exclusivity of 'proper' society.[34] For the rising merchant group, in particular, this cultural style was an important means of maintaining social standards when older conventions were weakening. From these suburbs emanated hopes that 'propriety and decorum' might improve among the lower orders, preferably through 'an appreciation of the example which is set them by the higher classes'.[35] With the emerging popularity of cricket arose illusions of social unity which suggested the game transcended normal divisions of colour, class and status, even though it quite clearly preserved careful social distances within its organizational structures.

C.L.R. James is an invaluable analyst on this point as well as on the political role of Caribbean cricket more broadly, not least because he indicates both the relevance and power of Gramsci's theory of hegemony in such a context.[36] Gramsci argued, in general, that in many societies the ruled share with the rulers a belief in cultural values which over-ride economic and social inequalities. Consequently, opportunities for change are often lost because, for the ruled, to seize them would mean a rejection of those powerful shared cultural beliefs. James, who became a Marxist in spite of English literature and cricket, is the 'exception that proves the rule'. Before 1914 in Barbados, cricket was established as a major shared cultural value with the players being drawn from the elite, respectable section of the community, their exploits cheered on by the lower orders who themselves had few opportunities to play. These groups were part of a cultural authority system whose ideological model was drawn directly from the British heritage and its attendant ethical idealism through which cricket became as much moral metaphor as physical activity.

In the Stribling story Wanderers Cricket Club possessed a heritage dating to 1712 and a charter from the Prince of Wales. Historically the account is inaccurate but sentimentally Stribling was right, because the foundations of club cricket throughout the Caribbean were set upon a concern for British cultural continuity and social respectability. The social connotations of cricket reached far beyond the fences surrounding the Georgetown Cricket Club formed in British Guiana during 1852, the Kingston Cricket Club established in Jamaica during 1863 and Queen's Park Cricket Club in Trinidad, especially after its transfer to the Park from the Savannah early in the 1890s. In 1904 it was said that a 'respectable' visitor could *generally* be put up for temporary membership of Queen's Park, while a year later the Kingston Cricket Club was named 'one of the established institutions of the city'.[37] These clubs provided a cultural focus for the ruling elite which endeavoured to have its cricket and related values, themselves prized for their British role modelling, accepted by the rest of society.

As elsewhere in the British Empire, Caribbean cricket was based consciously on the reformed English game following the start of the county championship in 1873.[38] From at least the 1890s in Barbados, English and Australian scores and affairs were reported regularly and in detail by the newspapers. English manuals invariably were the authorities on technique, demeanour and conventions.[39] One concern was to demonstrate, through cricket, that English stock had not degenerated in the tropics.[40] Even though many cricketers came from Bajan families with island histories of 200 years or older, they still considered themselves British; cricket prowess was a yardstick of their success in remaining British, so victories against English teams produced great celebration.

The British attitudes aroused by cricket were far more important than its mere physical activities. There was simple loyalty to the Mother Country, an emphasized feature when any English team visited. Cricket symbolized wider unity. In 1895, for example, the affectionate farewell to the first England team was thought to reveal a bond 'other than a common enthusiasm for cricket'. G.A. Goodman noted simply that Barbadians were 'the sons of old England'.[41] In 1899 a spectator at Queen's Park Oval said that although Barbados had lost against Trinidad 'she would not give up because her sons were from old British stock'.[42] The extent and persistence of this sentiment was revealed in a 1923 speech by H.B.G. Austin to a Belfast cricket dinner during the West Indies tour of Great Britain. He hoped the tour would prove the West Indies worthy of the Empire; they did not want to lose their birthright and imperial privileges, he said.[43]

Then there was the symbolism of British statecraft through cricket. After Barbados beat British Guiana in 1891, one editorial comment offered as the social message of cricket which all citizens should imbibe: 'be loyal and obedient to constituted authority'.[44] A cricket team always 'elected' its captain, it was noted, then gave him undivided support even if he made mistakes. This replicated the British political system's democratic creation of authority and, like democracy, cricket created *esprit de corps* because team members entered a solemn contract to serve each other with maximum effort. This bred honourable behaviour because team members would not let each other down on or off the field. Consequently, 'respect for truth and right and fairplay is held in highest esteem'. So, when in 1909 against British Guiana a Barbados player ran himself out rather than the in-form George Challenor, the lawyer E.C. Jackman congratulated him publicly that 'In the true spirit of the game . . . he elected to sacrifice his own wicket.'[45] Conversely, lapses from the solemn, co-operative contract were most unwelcome. When the 1905 English tourists showed annoyance at losing their return match against Barbados, and when a team member criticized Barbadian crowds, their attitudes were received coolly.[46]

One heartland for the growth of this ideology lay in the prestigious schools on the island: Harrison College, The Lodge and, to a lesser extent, Combermere.[47] By 1900 over 24,000 island students were receiving education, but these high schools were exclusive: Harrison had 154 students, Combermere 122 and The Lodge just 51.[48] Harrison was largely the preserve of the white plantation and mercantile elite: Combermere that of the growing black middle class although a few of these sent their children to Harrison, while Lodge, the only boarding school, tended to be less exclusive than Harrison. Harrison and Lodge both had teams in the Cup competition, although Lodge withdrew briefly early in the twentieth century - after a reformation early in the 1880s a string of headmasters and financial worries undercut it as a cricket power.[49] For most of the period its cricket fame rested upon the Goodman brothers until the appearance in the late 1890s of P.H. (Tim) Tarilton, one of the Caribbean's most technically correct and high-scoring batsmen of all time. Harrison College, meanwhile, grew considerably in strength.

It originated in 1733 as a school for poor and indigent boys, but was rejuvenated by an 1870 Act which established it as a grammar school for the benefit of the better classes.[50] Horace Deighton was appointed headmaster in 1872 and, before his 1905 retirement, set the academic standard along with an English emphasis on the moral, social and cultural power of the playing field, especially the cricket ground. Dr Herbert Dalton then ran the school until 1922. He introduced the English school 'set' or 'house' system, and did much to raise school spirit on English public school lines. Both men were active on the Barbados Cricket Committee, their cricket influence in the school being boosted by their long service and by the presence of G.B.Y. Cox and A.S. Somers Cocks as masters from the 1890s until the 1920s.[51] These last were both outstanding players for Barbados, and both subscribed fully to the English public school ideology. Harrison College poured out great cricketers, schooled also in the game's social code, such as H.B.G. Austin and George Challenor who made his first tour for the West Indies to England in 1906 while still a student. Victories by Harrison and, indeed, by Lodge over teams of grown men were greeted warmly and as evidence of the power of cricket as a social training ground for adult life.[52] School cricket was central to a cultural reproduction system which maintained and boosted the code of respectability and which in itself was a major contributor to the classed nature of Barbadian cricket organization.[53]

Stribling's initial murder suspect attached great importance to being 'a gentleman in a gentlemen's cricket club'. As a Barbadian professional he could never have been a gentleman, of course, but the important point is that he *thought* he was. Barbadian cricket created the illusion of social equality but, at the same time, preserved rigid and complex social distinctions. Sport in most cultures has been reckoned to ignore normal class and status divisions but in reality it cannot; like any social institution it is constituted by the attitudes and prejudices of its host community.[54] Caribbean cricket was certainly not egalitarian, being predicated on class and colour.

Few passages in *Beyond a Boundary* are so rich as James's description of his dilemma about which Port of Spain club he might join after leaving Queen's Royal College, the Trinidad equivalent of Harrison College. As an educated dark-skinned man, he could not or would not join certain clubs: Queen's Park catered mainly for wealthy whites and established mulattos, Shamrock had an almost exclusively white Catholic clientele, and Stingo was a lower-class black preserve. His choice lay between Shannon, a black lower middle-class club, and Maple, a brownskin middle-class club. Such distinctions were repeated throughout the English-speaking Caribbean, varied only by the specifics of the population mix – Chinese and East Indian teams, even competitions, appeared in British Guiana and Trinidad. Class and status wrought similar distinctions within all cricket competitions.

Around 1900 in British Guiana the Georgetown Cricket Club was dominated by the white elite drawn mostly from the top civil service echelons; the expensive $10 entrance fee and $10 annual subscription helped maintain its exclusiveness. The British Guiana Cricket Club attracted more junior civil servants and merchant clerks who could afford the 10 shillings entrance fee and $5 annual subscription. The British Guiana Churchmen's Union Cricket Club (evidence of the 'muscular Christian' strain in cricket at the time) drew upon clerics and school teachers for the most part although J.T. Chung, one of its captains, was a clerk on a Chinese-owned estate. Up country in Berbice the County Cricket Club was run by the regional Commissioner of Taxation assisted by an auctioneer, a clerk, a copyist and an accountant.[55] Over in Jamaica the Kingston Cricket Club was for the colonial white elite; the Kensington Cricket Club began in 1879 among lower-status school products; the Melbourne Club was formed with an educated black leavening early in the 1890s; Lucas, a poor black club, emerged after the 1895 English tour and took its name from Slade-Lucas, the touring captain.[56] These clubs preserved and boosted their social limits well after 1914 and so it was in Barbados where there were eight competition teams for much of the period under review.[57]

Harrison College and Lodge never won a championship before 1914 and were often chopping boards for more powerful sides. Although there were no immutable rules, Harrison boys leaving school generally moved to Wanderers, those from Lodge to Pickwick. There were exceptions, of course, generally based upon social or occupational position, geographical location, or skin colour – until 1915 black school-leavers had Spartan as their only club choice. Then there was the Garrison, a team drawn from the white British troops stationed in Barbados until the early twentieth century. Leeward and Windward were two 'country' clubs, drawing their members from the white planting and managerial community at opposite ends of the island. Their matches against each other were traditionally the occasions for great celebration, the reaffirmation of the planting faith, so their high teas were legendary.[58] The social nature of their matches often meant scores were never relayed to Bridgetown, but the purity of their play and devotion to the higher cricket traditions were admired widely. The remaining clubs were in reality the 'big three': Wanderers, Pickwick and Spartan.

From its 1877 foundation until 1914 Wanderers was the most prestigious club in Barbados. During that time it had strong planting connections: among its captains were D.C.A. Ince whose family was connected with estates in the Christ Church parish; E.A. Hinkson who inherited the 340-acre Coconut Hall in St George and who married a daughter of Horace Deighton;[59] and Kenneth Mason whose family also held property in St George, the district for which he became Parochial Treasurer in 1903. Many other planters were prominent Wanderers players. Then there were the influential and respectable merchants: da Costa, father and son; Robert Arthur who inherited his father's business; the Collymores, the Austins and the Challenors. Other players were sometimes senior employees of these firms. Respectable English arrivals invariably gravitated to Wanderers. William Bowring arrived in the late 1890s, was a prominent player for Barbados and West Indies, married a da Costa, became a director of the firm and first President of the Barbados Cricket Association established in the 1930s. M.L. Horne arrived as a bank clerk and became a fast-bowling hero early in the twentieth century, taking 8 for 39 against the 1902 English tourists. A.S. Bryden junior joined the club after being educated at Tonbridge School in England, and later married the daughter of club President and legal luminary W.K. Chandler. Numerous senior civil servants were members. F.B. Smith entered the service in 1859 to become Inspector-General of Prisons and Provost Marshall among other posts; he batted through the Barbados innings in the first inter-colonial match in 1865, and influenced Wanderers considerably as secretary. W.H. 'Billy' Allder, the son of a cleric, succeeded Smith as secretary and was chief registers clerk in the Colonial Secretary's Office. Beyond that were lawyers like E.C. Jackman and C.E. Yearwood (who married J. Gardiner Austin's daughter), medical men like Dr John Hutson and clergymen like the lively Reverend C. King-Gill. Wanderers, then, drew on the leading quarters of Barbadian society throughout the period.

Pickwick rivalled Wanderers on the field but not in the social stakes where it lacked the same prestigious profile. There were few, if any, major planters although the Goodman brothers came from a family in the industry, and two of them (Clifford and Percy) married into planting interests while Aubrey, the lawyer, became a landholder in St John. The merchants were generally less important or newer to wealth than those in Wanderers. J.R. Bancroft, for example, worked for Challenors after leaving Harrison College, later became a partner in a smaller firm then moved into directorships as well as property.[60] One of his sons married a da Costa and another, a Barbados Scholar, was wicket-keeper for the 1906 West Indies tour of England. J.C. Hoad, an early secretary, ran a provisions business and the Hoad name was prominent in Pickwick circles until the 1960s. J.H. Emptage, an accountant, was an early secretary, and others of the same name and similar occupations followed. Lawyers were few, and G.O.D. Walton, who struggled for years to receive a permanent position on the bench, finally received one on the island of St Kitts, and was later knighted for his services to the Caribbean judiciary, was the most successful. There were numerous lower-level clerks both in business and the civil service, and some teachers: Percy Goodman became principal of Christ Church Foundation School, while L.A. Walcott, son of an accountant, an Island Scholar and Barbados player, was games master at both Harrison and Lodge between the wars and after. The touch of respectability was there in Pickwick but did not match that of Wanderers as the case of that magnificent player Tim Tarilton suggests. His father was Poor Law Inspector in St Johns and sent his boys to Lodge. Tim joined the Customs service, married the daughter of a veterinary surgeon and, in 1919, was appointed Parochial Treasurer of St James. He was clearly great friends with George Challenor (with whom he set many opening partnership records for Barbados and West Indies) and H.B.G. Austin (his captain in those teams). Just as clearly, he was from a different social world from the one inhabited by his playing colleagues, and in Barbados such different social circles very rarely mixed. In that difference, perhaps, originated the fierce Pickwick competitive spirit and club loyalty which appeared during 1895, for example, when some members refused to play for Barbados because other clubmates were not selected.[61]

The Spartan spirit lay in its representation of the emerging urban coloured middle and upper middle class (it is said that lightness of colour was an important admission criterion).[62] The club joined the Cup competition in 1893 playing on the ground in Belleville, the new respectable suburb. Sir Conrad Reeves, son of a white father, was its first President and a long serving Vice-President was J. Challenor Lynch. Lynch was a coloured, non-practising lawyer who inherited his father's merchant business and who, like his father, became a prominent politician. The firm was deeply involved in plantation transfer. As early as 1891, for example, Lynch bought in Chancery the major 454-acre Pine Estate, and he lived on another excellent property, Friendship. Then, the Rudder family was prominent in both playing and administration: Stephen and George, for example, were the sons of W.A. Rudder who was in planting as early as the 1860s and who gave evidence against Federation rioters. Stephen (who played for Barbados) reached senior civil service positions while his brother became Poor Law Inspector in St Thomas. There were medical men like Dr C.W. St John, lawyers like H.M. Cummins and G.H. Corbin. C.A. (Johnny) Browne was a well-to-do jeweller, brother of P.N. Browne who established the business, then moved to British Guiana where he moved into politics. He was joined there, at the end of this period, by another brother, C.R. (Snuffie) Browne who trained as a lawyer in England. The Brownes' father was among the first non-whites to enter Bridgetown politics. Snuffie established an excellent record as a West Indian all-rounder while Johnny played for Barbados as a stylish, hard-hitting batsman. A prominent founding player, captain and club power was Graham Trent Cumberbatch, son of a successful bootmaker. He took a degree through Codrington College and became Assistant Inspector of Schools but, like others in his social position, found progress difficult. When in 1901 he applied for the position of Inspector of Schools in the Leeward Islands, the Governor thought it necessary to inform the Colonial Office that he was 'a man of colour' and, by implication, inappropriate for the post.[63] Two general reactions to such discrimination emerged in Spartan. On the one hand, men like Cumberbatch and Cummins became ardent enthusiasts of the cricket ideology, attempting to share the cultural values of the whites with whom they competed both in cricket and in society. On the other hand, they developed a strong desire to win, to beat the representatives of those who displayed the prejudice. The essential paradox in this dual position is clear. While trying to emulate the ruling cricket and social values, Spartan members had also to deal with the inequalities contained in those ruling values. On the whole, Spartan men resolved to accept the inequalities, an excellent demonstration of Gramsci's theory of hegemony.

Given this general background, then, it was scarcely surprising that some Barbados club fixtures became exceptionally competitive, attracting large and partisan crowds. The most famous series was between Wanderers and Pickwick, usually the talk of the town for weeks beforehand.[64] But the inter-school matches always had an extra edge to them, Spartan singled out Harrison for particular attention,[65] and Pickwick versus Spartan also attracted notoriety. While the Barbados Cricket Committee for the period (manned by lawyers, merchants, senior civil servants but scarcely a coloured or black representative) promoted the idea of social unity through cricket, in reality there developed a clearly defined and stoutly defended social hierarchy based on caste and colour, and which could not always be hidden. As early as 1891, one commentator asked that the Barbados team be selected on grounds other than caste or creed.[66] But it was the 'Fitzy Lilly' affair of 1899 and after which showed how closely guarded social rankings became.

Fitzy Lilly, real name Fitz Hinds, was a painter by trade but more importantly, during the early and mid-1890s he was a prominent net bowler in the little layered world of the Bridgetown cricket clubs.[67] From the first appearance of organized clubs, a large number of lower-class blacks became skilled cricketers, especially bowlers, simply by giving practice to competition players. All clubs had them and Fitz Hinds was attached officially to Pickwick. By the late 1890s, however, he had decided upon a club–playing rather than service career so dropped out of Pickwick for a year; he put up for membership at Spartan where Cumberbatch and Cummins were his chief supporters. At the first ballot he was rejected by 4 out of the 16 voters, his inferior social status clearly counting against him. Only some smart committee work won him membership a few weeks later.[68]

By then, of course, the matter had reached the attention of other clubs, particularly Pickwick with its keen sense of social position (and where Hinds had been a servant) and Windward which contained a particularly conservative planter element.[69] Leading players in both teams refused to meet Hinds on the field so that the man suffered on all sides – one report had it that he was snubbed at Spartan practice sessions by those opposed to his membership. [70] His reply against Pickwick (where Clifford Goodman led a fight to recognize the ex-pro) was to topscore with 24, then take 8 wickets for 31 to give Spartan a rare victory. With the two rebel clubs refusing to field strong teams, Spartan swept to its first Cup win and Hinds did so well as to tour England with the 1900 West Indies side (one Pickwick player refused to go because Hinds was selected).[71] He remained a prominent Barbados player until he shifted to the United States in 1905 where he continued to play well, appearing against an Australian team there in 1913.[72] His was a stirring achievement under intense pressure which arose from the social layering of Barbadian cricket, itself produced by the island's sugar culture which allocated all members of the community a rank in its elaborately defined production hierarchy. It is important to note that colour was not the sole, or even the important, issue in the Hinds case; it was social position, as his rough treatment inside Spartan indicated. Barbadian cricket ideology and its imperial model demanded a minimum status for admission to its organized ranks. For that reason, the other importance of Fitz Hinds is that he indicated the presence, both formal and informal, of a substantial cricketing body outside Barbados Cricket Committee auspices. This sub-culture, as it might be called, is important because its fortunes, until 1914, indicate indirectly the power and success of the elite traditions and practices.

Stribling erred again in having his professional cricketer and murder suspect come from the poor white class; in Barbados such players were always black (the demographic variations of Trinidad and British Guiana meant that there a few emerged from the East Indian and Chinese communities).[73] But Stribling was right in his depiction of the professional's dependent social and economic position. By 1895 in Barbados there were at least 14 ground staff attached officially to six of the competition clubs, and earlier than that Wanderers and Pickwick alone supplied enough talented professionals to test an Island XI practising for an inter-colonial.[74] Many professionals had long club residencies: William Shepherd was with Spartan from the start until well into the twentieth century (in the off-season he frequently took his talents to New York), while Germain was a long stayer at Pickwick as was Oliver Layne at Wanderers. Their duties were twofold: to bowl to club members in the nets, and to prepare the characteristically shiny Barbados pitches which often reflected the players as in a mirror. For this they were paid a retainer, members frequently gave tips for their services, and they earned additional income from umpiring. It was a steady if hard life. Joe Benn and Tanny Archer, good enough players to be selected against touring teams, both died from tuberculosis.[75] With people like 'Chingham alias Fonix alias Phinx' it is difficult to sketch a background, but William Francis Jones and Oliver Layne are a little different.

Jones was born in Bridgetown during 1875 to Rosetta Jones of Constitution Road, the 17-year-old daughter of Elizabeth Jones from Codrington Hill.[76] In neither case is it possible to trace a father, but clearly either grandmother or mother, possibly both, had shifted to Bridgetown as part of the urban drift. William Jones was baptized in St Michael's Cathedral so it seems likely he lived close to the Bay ground where he was on the staff by at least 1895. Oliver Layne was born almost exactly a year after Jones. His father, Richard Layne, listed himself as a porter (a handcart operator) of Britton's Hill who had married Margaret Wharton in St Michael's Cathedral late in 1872. Like Jones, Layne was on the Wanderers staff by at least 1895, but by 1909 he was playing in Trinidad where more open attitudes provided Barbadian professionals with wider playing opportunities. Like Fitz Hinds, Layne then shifted to the United States where he played in the New York leagues before dying in the early 1930s. Archie Cumberbatch, among the earliest in a long string of famous West Indian fast bowlers, was another who left Barbados for Trinidad in the late 1890s and immediately attracted the attention of English touring players. Like Cumberbatch, Jones and Layne were excellent players, the latter taking 6 for 8 against a good Spartan side in 1900 and taking 57 wickets on the 1906 West Indies tour of England. By the turn of the century, opportunities for such men had broadened a little in Barbados because of the remarkable William Shepherd.

Building on his career at Spartan, Shepherd established a regular team of ground staff which was soon playing club teams in practices and providing matches for the Barbados team before inter-colonial tournaments. He expanded professional opportunities in 1900 by taking the team on tour to Trinidad, followed that with a British Guiana tour in 1904 then, during 1909, organized an inter-island team of professionals which he led through both Trinidad and British Guiana.[77] Shepherd was no ordinary net player, then, nor was his an ordinary skill. Against a Barbados XI in 1899 he took 8 for 45, and in 1900 against Pickwick made 54 runs out of 108 and then took 8 for 24. His playing and entrepreneurial skills helped professionals to be included in Barbados teams against touring sides from 1902 onwards. But even his efforts and the rapidly growing skills of his fellow professionals could not break the elite social strictures of the Barbados Cup competition – calls for the inclusion of professionals were consistently rejected on social rather than playing grounds, the argument being that club members and friends went to cricket to meet others of their rank and station.[78] This attitude meant Shepherd could enter his talented Fenwick team in what became known as the Frame Food competition but not in Cup fixtures.

When he was organizing Fenwick Shepherd informed at least one newspaper that a number of his players were *not* professional.[79] Some of those he mentioned were listed frequently as attached ground staff, which raises the distinct possibility that players referred to casually as 'professionals' may have been employed elsewhere. That is, they may have been working-class players improving their skills (and, incidentally, their incomes) by meeting Cup players in the nets. If that was even partly true, then there are at least two further interesting possibilities: the existence of a strong working-class cricket tradition in Barbados, and a growing rather than declining desire by the sugar and cricket elite to remain socially separate from such a tradition. Some scattered evidence supports these possibilities.

First, there was the immediate numerical strength of the Frame Food sponsored competition established in 1902 by Frederick Martinez, a man known throughout the Caribbean and Latin America as the 'prince of Commercial Travellers'.[80] Drawing its name from a milk-based food product popular with the working classes, the competition aimed at boosting cricket among those classes. Sponsored by a low-status commercial man and with little support from respectable quarters, the competition stood little chance of success. It collapsed within four seasons although its cup remained at stake for matches between working-class clubs until the 1920s.

Thirteen teams competed in the first year and included Police, Railways, West India Regiment (black troops), Volunteers, and Fenwick which won the first two competitions. Bankers entered a team later.[81] This was a clearly occupational and frequently artisan-based organization coming from earlier, sporadic holiday fixtures such as Printers versus Tailors.[82] Just as clearly, that number of teams and the administration required to organize them would not have developed instantaneously just because Martinez donated a trophy. This cricket must have been in existence for some time, its claims and growing strengths studiously ignored by the Barbados Cricket Committee on social rather than cricket criteria. For that reason, evidence relating to such cricket is rare, the bulk of cricket records being maintained by 'respectable' authorities with a sense of social mission. Then, the connection between this and Shepherd's apparently 'professional' team is provided by S.A. Merritt, a regular Fenwick player. He was appointed Secretary to the committee which ran the ambitious Frame Food competition. As he was in the company of an engineer, a company clerk and a freeholding wheelwright, he must surely have possessed skills other than those of a net bowler.[83] Fenwick, then, might have been as much the expression of frustrated working-class cricket as it was that of the frustrated professionals. But the Barbados Cricket Committee and the social system which it represented rejected both thrusts resolutely, though it did nominate William Bowring as its observer on the short-lived Frame Food Committee. For the most part, respectable society and cricket kept its distance seeing the 'excitement' caused by working-class matches as symptomatic of the social conditions it was trying to overcome.[84] But that was not the only alternative faced by organized cricket, for there remained the even more profane game played at large and in public thoroughfares.

In 1891 the 'stave bat and primitive ball of native manufacture' were taken for granted in a debate on public recreation facilities.[85] After the 1895 tour by an English team men and boys were said to be playing in every alley and field.[86] And in 1905 the English tourists were delighted by the fielding of the little boys who turned up to 'assist' them at the Bay ground.[87] Lower-class enthusiasm and elite concern for the game sometimes met in the courts, belying the view that in cricket all other inequalities were forgotten. Nathaniel Hutchinson must have tired of the 'primitive ball' because he received 14 days with hard labour 'for the larceny of a Cricket-ball' from Wanderers' pavilion, an illustrative meeting of very different cultures with quite separate cricketing and social objectives.[88] In 1899 a woman charged that two men playing cricket hit her first with the ball then with their fists; they counter-charged that she had detained the ball unlawfully! One was fined two shillings plus six shillings costs in lieu of seven days with hard labour, not at all the image sought by the promoters of organized cricket (it is too much to think that the Archie Matterson involved was the same man who played for a ground staff XI against an island team that year and who became treasurer to the Frame Food Committee!).[89]

However physically close to organized, respectable cricket this activity might have been, it was a vast social distance from the glitter of Wanderers at the Bay, confirming the rigid and complex social divisions which contradicted assertions that the whole society met in cricket and raising the question, naturally, of how successful the promoters of orthodox cricket ideology were in penetrating Barbadian culture and influencing the masses towards accepting their social standing. Like other writers, Stribling depicts Barbados as being more obsessed by the game and its Englishness than any other Caribbean community. But before 1914, at least, there were really three varying responses.

Outright acceptance of cricket and its English cultural provenance was demonstrated best by 'Britannia Bill', the Union Jack-carrying black who met the 1897 English team, watched their matches and followed them about praising their skills, character, country and monarch – 'Old England Forever' was his constant cry.[90] In 1905 a black spectator kissed the arm of an English bowling star.[91] Similar sentiments were expressed to most pre-1914 touring teams whose members were greeted warmly in their Bridgetown travels, especially 'Steady Stoddart' as he was dubbed, the most accomplished player to visit Barbados before the First World War.[92] There is the thought that some of this might have been directed against the local elite; a modified form of colonial resistance stemming from a natural warmth towards representatives of the Queen and country which had formally ended slavery. However, similar crowds turned out to watch the nearly all-white inter-colonial and the socially exclusive local club matches whose players received similarly approving treatment. An identification with the cause and philosophy of Barbadian cricket undoubtedly existed and 'the great unwashed' displayed a close knowledge of the game from very early on. Within half an hour of a 1900 Barbados victory being telegraphed from Trinidad, 'idle labourers' and others were discussing and celebrating it animatedly.[93]

Modified acceptance of the pure model was shown by the black who in 1895 was 'sanguine that we may yet propel our flag among the nations as the Colony which has humbled its Mother'.[94] The colonial elite could be happy with that, of course, because it demonstrated an identification with Barbadian interests. But it also indicated the beginnings of a local modification which did not meet with wholehearted acceptance from the authorities – crowd participation. If the crowds in the 'ring' (the cheapest sections of the grounds) were knowledgeable, they were also noisy and unhindered by the social reserve thought proper among cricket watchers reared on English precedent. Barbadian crowds offered a constant stream of advice to batsmen, bowlers, fielders and captains. One 1905 English player heard his bowlers urged to 'bowl him down' and the Barbados batsmen cautioned to 'watch dat man at square leg'.[95] And it was during this period that the ring developed its passion and encouragement for spectacular fast bowling. In 1900 larger crowds than normal followed the Wanderers team captained by E.A. Hinkson, lured by the *white* fast bowler M.L. Horne. They would applaud Horne as he arrived at the ground, then wait in the expectation that 'now Hinkson gwine tek he Horne an butt dem down'.[96]

24

Serious crowd demonstrations were rare (perhaps suggesting the strength of the behaviour code) but it was always with nervous self-assurance that good crowd temper was mentioned by the representatives of respectable society; and at club fixtures unrest was quelled immediately.[97] And there was always official embarrassment when visiting teams (the sensitive English particularly) had difficulty accepting local crowd performances.[98] Percy Goodman in 1909, for example, assured Trinidadians that a hissing incident over an umpiring decision had arisen in an unknowledgeable section of the crowd and was quite isolated and unusual (some thought it started in the elite pavilion!).[99] Such animated behaviour, however, had come to stay as perhaps the major local modification to imperial cricket ideology.

There are few explicit examples of direct rejection of or opposition to that cricket playing and behavioural code constructed by the Barbadian elite. A match at Lodge was interrupted by Federation rioters in 1876, but their objective was the adjoining Guinea estate rather than the players or their field.[100] It is also difficult to make out a case of premeditated colonial resistance by the two boys who in 1897 tore planks from the Pickwick pavilion, or by those who arrived at the Wanderers ground during an 1899 match to deride with a local form of taunt: 'Well played, Sop Biscuits.'[101] In each case, though, the culprits were dealt with promptly and severely for having brought disrepute to the game and its social mores.

The classic resistance weapon of rumour touched cricket occasionally. In 1897 relatives of T.W. Roberts were informed by 'bush telegraph' that he had broken his neck while playing for Barbados against the English tourists. It was incorrect, but the origins and purpose of the story remain intriguing.[102] An even more fascinating and direct act against cricket interests occurred during the 1895 English visit when an unknown hand turned on a tap and flooded the pitch on the eve of the first day. Local sources put it down to an 'inexplicable' bit of 'devilry' by a 'wicked urchin', while the visiting captain thought it the work of a 'native' (presumably lower-class) annoyed at having to pay an entrance fee for the first time.[103] He might well have reworked that as an expression of discontent at the exclusive nature of Barbadian cricket expressed in the size of the fee. That was an extremely tough year economically, and crowds of rioters later looted fields in Clermont, Boscobelle and elsewhere throughout the island while singing songs of Federation, invoking memories of the last major occasion on which the power of the sugar hierarchy had been challenged.[104]

There is little doubt that C.L.R. James was correct in identifying cricket as a major bulwark against social and political change in the English-speaking Caribbean. In Barbados and the other colonies, until 1914 at least, the colonial elites established a cultural primacy through cricket as much as through economic power and political position. As Gramsci suggests, these elites established and maintained their positions by determining that their values, traditions and standards be accepted by the populace at large as the cultural programme most appropriate to the community, even though the bulk of that community had no access to the institutions through which the programme was inculcated. One principal reason for the important place held by cricket was the significance of the game to the imperial power itself. Cricket and its associated moral code were regarded in two specific lights by the Caribbean elites: as a means of forging a close cultural bond with the imperial power, and as a means of establishing themselves as the arbiters and agents of that imperial philosophy within their own social and political environments. Consequently, agencies such as the church and the elite schools became as important in the Caribbean as they had been at home in fostering the skills and social traditions which carried in them the imperial messages of cricket. The consistent recruitment of religious and educational personnel from Great Britain was just the most obvious indicator of this cultural reproduction until the eve of the First World War.

For the most part, the colonial elites carried on this process unhindered, controlling those agencies of social reproduction identified by Pierre Bourdieu as being central in the creation of hegemonic cultural values. Cricketers outside the elite groups made little headway before 1914. A number of professionals emerged from the working classes, but they were the most bound to the ruling-class view of the game because their livelihood depended upon pleasing their masters. Men like William Shepherd were extremely careful lest their dress, demeanour and deportment should displease their superiors. Then, some non-elite competitions began before 1914, such as the Chinese and East Indian leagues in Trinidad and British Guiana as well as the Frame Food competition for lower-class blacks in Barbados. Most failed, with the provision of regular cricket for such social groups coming well after 1918. But before their failure, most of these non-elite competitions had demonstrated the power of the elite position by attempting to impose upon non-elite groups the moral and ethical codes derived from the imperial cricket model. Indeed, the failure of the alternative competitions was attributed as much to an inability to maintain these codes as to the antagonism of the controllers of elite cricket.

As for popular support, cricket was a positive mania in most areas of the British Caribbean by 1914, the feats of the cricketing and social elite cheered on by the masses who shared a belief in the social importance of the game if not the access to its playing arenas. The controllers of cricket were quick to point out that Caribbean crowds appreciated fine play (irrespective of teams), sportsmanship, dash, courage and temperament – the essential qualities of the imperial cricket ideology. Although the crowds were noisy and demonstrative, the elites interpreted this as only to be expected, coming as it did from the descendants of 'excitable' Africans and mixed-blood populations. Indeed, it was considered a testament to the social power of cricket that such crowds were not even more noisy and demonstrative. In all aspects of Caribbean cricket, then, the colonial elites' hold, organization and philosophy were deep-seated, with ramifications into political, commercial and cultural life, as C.L.R. James and others like him were to discover.

By 1914 cricket in the Caribbean, as exemplified by the Barbadian case, was not a monolithic social agency in which all classes and colour groups met uncaring of

26

the differences encountered in other sections of civic life. The game was played at all levels of society, clearly enough, but there were distinct and accepted areas of activity for them as potential reformers discovered. Within each level, too, a social coding system saw players, administrators and often spectators *by choice* move to their appropriate locations. Fitz Hinds proved the power of that. Immediately he entered Spartan the Barbados Cricket Committee enacted a new rule to ensure no repeat of the incident.[105] These elaborate social springs were situated far below the surface of Caribbean colonial life, their flavour determined by the specific local cultural mix of demographics, economy and patterns of prestige. Far from waning by 1914, this complex cultural power structure was still growing while other colonial bonds were showing signs of deterioration. This was demonstrated best in Barbados, appropriately enough, in the 1915 secession from Spartan which created the less socially prestigious Empire club, directed by the legendary Herman Griffith whose wonderful fast bowling and quicksilver temperament presented for the next generation a combined challenge to both cricket authority and the island culture which had produced it.[106]

NOTES

The research for this paper was made possible by a Professional Experience Programme leave from the Canberra College of Advanced Education, as well as by the kindness and encouragement of the History Department, University of the West Indies, Cave Hill, Bridgetown, Barbados which elected me an honorary Visiting Fellow for 1985. Thanks are due also to the staff of the Barbados Archives, to those who participated in the seminar on the original version of the paper, to Mrs Ida Kidney, and to Mr W.F. 'Ben' Hoyos. Particular thanks to Professor Woodville Marshall and Dr John Mayo.

Abbreviations

BCA *Barbados Cricketer's Annual,* published annually between 1894 and 1914, and compiled by J. Wynfred Gibbons.
BA Barbados Archives.

Note on newspapers

Where no page reference is cited, pagination was not employed in the original. For convenience I have dropped the word 'Barbados' from the *Barbados Agricultural Reporter, Barbados Bulletin, Barbados Globe, Barbados Advocate* and *Barbados Herald.*

1   T.S. Stribling, 'Cricket', in *Clues of the Caribbees: Being Certain Criminal Investigations of Henry Poggioli,* Ph.D. (New York, 1977 edn).
2   For the method: Michel Foucault: *Order of Things: Archaeology of the Human Sciences* (London, 1974). A good descriptive rather than analytical history of the island's cricket is Bruce Hamilton, *Cricket in Barbados* (Bridgetown, 1947). He shows the early and inordinate hold taken by cricket upon the population.

3   Pelham Warner, *Cricket in Many Climes* (London, 1900); Lord Hawke, *Recollections and Reminiscences* (London, 1924).
4   C. Wright Mills, *The Sociological Imagination* (Harmondsworth, 1973 edn), especially Ch. 8.
5   C.L.R. James, *Beyond a Boundary* (London, 1963).
6   H. Orlando Patterson, 'The Ritual of Cricket', *Jamaica Journal*, 3 (1969); Maurice St Pierre, 'West Indian Cricket – a Socio-Historical Appraisal', *Caribbean Quarterly*, 19, 2 and 3 (1973). Frank E. Manning's title 'Celebrating Cricket: the Symbolic Construction of Caribbean Politics', *American Ethnologist*, 8 (1981) is a little misleading here in that it deals with an area rather outside the Caribbean cricket culture proper. See also Vince Reid, 'Thoughts on England v. the West Indies, Edgbaston, 1973: or the People of the Caribbean Still Need to be Emancipated from One Type of Domination or Another', *New Community*, 2 (1973).
7   See the hopes of creating a West Indies touring team early in the 1890s, *Globe*, 20 February 1893. West Indians and British imperialists alike maintained the ideal of cricket and federation beyond the First World War; L.S. Smith (ed.), *West Indies Cricket History and Cricket Tours to England* (Port of Spain, 1922), pp. 6, 73, 127.
8   This section based on: *The British Guiana Directory and Almanack* (Georgetown, 1906); *The British Guiana Handbook* (Georgetown, 1922); T.B. Jackson (ed.), *The Book of Trinidad* (Port of Spain, 1904); *Trinidad and Tobago Yearbook* (Port of Spain, 1938); *Handbook of Jamaica* (Kingston, 1905). Smaller islands are not covered here, but most if not all played cricket; for example, J.H.D. Osborne, 'Cricket in St Lucia', *BCA*, 1901–2, 63 ff.
9   For example, J.I.M. Hewitt, 'West Indies in Big Cricket', *Silver Jubilee Magazine* (Bridgetown, 1935), 26; L.S. Smith (ed.), *West Indies Cricket History*, p. 7.
10   See, for example, the quarrel over the 1900 team involving W. Bowring: *BCA* 1899–1900, 136–7; *Agricultural Reporter*, 27 January 1900, 2–3.
11   *Queen's Park Cricket Club Diamond Jubilee* (Port of Spain, 1956), p. 91; W.A.S. Hardy (ed.), *They Live For Cricket* (London, 1950), pp. 12, 21.
12   *BCA*, 1895–6, 15.
13   Statistics from *Barbados Blue Book* (Bridgetown, 1900).
14   For the brief history of Barbados: F.A. Hoyos, *Barbados: a History from the Amerindians to Independence* (London, 1978); George Hunte, *Barbados* (London, 1974).
15   *Globe*, 16 October 1893. Also *West Indian*, 7 January 1876 and 19 January 1877.
16   A description of the working of the Act is in Governor to Secretary of State, 27 September 1881, Confidential, COL 2/1/26, BA. For an interpretation of post-emancipation industrial relations, B.M. Taylor, 'Black Labor and White Power in Post-Emancipation Barbados: a Study of Changing Relationships', *Current Bibliography on African Affairs*, 6 (1973).
17   See John Wickham, *Nation*, 10 March 1985, 4, for a discussion of the sugar culture.
18   For example, *Agricultural Reporter*, 4 September 1877, and 9 October 1877.
19   *BCA*, 1894–95, 16–28.
20   *Ibid.*, 1896–97, 171–2.
21   *Advocate*, 13 February 1905, 6–7.
22   *BCA*, 1897–8, 30 and 1908–9, 141–2.
23   *Bulletin*, 17 September 1897, 7–8. And, of course, 'What Is Death to Cricket Is Life to the Planting Interest', *Bulletin*, 10 September 1899, 9.

24 Paragraph based upon analysis of Voters Lists, BA, for the period 1880–1914.

25 For some indications on the economy: Governor to Secretary of State, 26 July 1884, Confidential, COL 211/28, BA; *Globe*, 21 September 1893; *West Indian Royal Commission: Barbados* (Bridgetown, 1877); Governor to Secretary of State, 15 January 1902, No. 12, COL 211/44, BA. On merchant loans and purchases see, for example: *Agricultural Reporter*, 17 February 1900, 1; 20 January 1900, 3; 10 March 1900, 3; *Globe*, 19 October 1893; *Advocate*, 14 January 1905, 5. Other 'rescue' legislation included the Plantations-in-Aid Act and the Sugar Industry Agricultural Bank: see Governor to Secretary of State, 20 August 1902, No. 177, COL 211/45, and Governor to Secretary of State, 4 March 1907, No. 30, COL 211/47, both BA.

26 *Advocate*, 11 January 1908, 6 and 4 January 1909, 6. The 1909 case concerned F.M. Alleyne who had owned Kensington estate from which Kensington Oval, home of Pickwick and Barbadian cricket had emerged; Hiralal T. Bajnath (compiler), *West Indies Test Cricketer* (Port of Spain, 1965), p. 88.

27 Unless specifically noted otherwise, biographical details for this paper have been accumulated from sources such as: Voters Lists; Gabriel Anciaux, *The Barbados Business and General Directory 1887* (Bridgetown, 1887); S.J. Fraser, *The Barbados Diamond Jubilee Directory and General West Indian Advertiser* (Bridgetown, 1898); *Barbados: Historical, Descriptive and Commercial* (Bridgetown, 1911); E. Goulbourn Sinckler, *The Barbados Handbook* (London, 1913); *Leverick's Directory of Barbados* (Bridgetown, 1921); *Barbados Yearbook and Who's Who* (Bridgetown, 1935); *BCA*, 1894–1914; newspapers.

28 For very different views on the origins, nature and purpose of the riots: James Pope-Hennessy, *Verandah: Some Episodes in the Crown Colonies, 1867–1889* (London, 1964), Book V; Bruce Hamilton, *Barbados and the Confederation Question, 1871–1885* (London, 1956); George A.V. Belle, 'A Study in the Political Economy of Barbados, 1876–1971' (Mona, 1972), and 'The Abortive Revolution of 1876 in Barbados' (Cave Hill, 1981).

29 For example, *West Indian*, 9 June 1876.

30 *Agricultural Reporter*, 2 March 1877; *West Indian*, 16 March 1877 and 27 March 1877; evidence in *Report of the Commission on Poor Relief, 1875–1877* (Bridgetown, 1878); *Times*, 12 April 1882; Anciaux, *The Barbados Business*, p. vi; *Agricultural Reporter*, 12 September 1893; *Globe*, 12 April 1894; J. Gardiner Austin evidence before *West Indian Royal Commission: Barbados*, p. 15; *Bulletin*, 21 September 1899, p. 8; *Agricultural Reporter*, 8 March 1900, pp. 2–3; *Advocate*, 6 March 1908, p. 5 and 22 March 1909, p. 5.

31 Paragraph based on: *Agricultural Reporter*, 10 August 1877; Governor to Secretary of State, 15 May 1880, No. 70, COL 2/1/26, BA; *Globe*, 22 December 1892; Governor to Secretary of State, 28 June 1899, No. 154, COL 2/1144, BA; *Agricultural Reporter*, 5 April 1900, p. 4; *Advocate*, 22 March 1909, p. 8.

32 The theory and practice for this general point lies with the field of cultural studies, especially the early work of the Centre for Contemporary Cultural Studies at Birmingham University. For some of the dimensions: Stuart Hall, 'Cultural Studies: Two Paradigms', *Media, Culture and Society*, 2 (1980); Raymond Williams, *Problems in Materialism and Culture* (London, 1980) and *Culture* (London, 1981).

33 *Wanderers Cricket Club Centenary, 1877–1977* (Bridgetown, 1977), p. 27; *West Indian*, 9 May 1876; *Agricultural Reporter*, 4 September 1877; Governor to Secretary of State, 9 September 1876, No. 200, COL 211/25, BA.

34 *Barbados: Historical, Descriptive and Commercial*, p. 53.

35 *Times*, 7 January 1882.

36 For an introduction to Gramsci see James Joll, *Gramsci* (London, 1977) and Joseph V. Femia, *Gramsci's Political Thought: Hegemony, Consciousness and the Revolutionary Process* (Oxford, 1981); for a sample of the work, Antonio Gramsci (translated by Louis Marks), *The Modern Prince and Other Writings* (New York, 1975).

37 Jackson, *The Book of Trinidad*, p. 148; *Handbook of Jamaica*.

38 For a flawed analytical version of the English story, see Christopher Brookes, *English Cricket: the Game and Its Players* (London, 1978), and for a comparative case of its colonial influence, Richard Cashman, *Patrons, Players and the Crowd: the Phenomenon of Indian Cricket* (Bombay, 1980).

39 See *Globe* for October 1894; *Bulletin*, 9 September 1897,12–13; *Advocate*, 13 February 1902, p. 7 and 16 January 1909, p. 7. In addition, the 'symbolical inscription of the great game' on the Inter-colonial Cup was said to depict Dr W.G. Grace, *Globe*, 28 December 1893.

40 See the editorial, *Herald,* 28 January 1895. This concern was widespread throughout the Empire; for example, W.F. Mandle, 'Cricket and the Rise of Australian Nationalism', *Journal of the Royal Australian Historical Society* (1973).

41 C.P. Bowen, *English Cricketers in the West Indies* (Bridgetown, 1895), p. 6; *Herald, 28 April* 1895.

42 *Agricultural Reporter,* 1 May 1899, 3–4.

43 *Belfast Telegraph*, 26 July 1923, Cricket Scrapbook 1923, BA. An even greater emphasis on the role of cricket in bringing English social life to the Caribbean was made in a 1932 speech by R.S. Grant who went on later to captain West Indies: *Sporting Chronicle Souvenir Annual* (Port of Spain, 1932), p. 41.

44 Section based on *Agricultural Reporter,* 11 September 1891.

45 E.C. Jackman, Letter to Editor, *Advocate,* 20 January 1909, 3.

46 *BCA*, 1904–5, 34 6; *Advocate*, 16 March 1905, 7.

47 For the English connections between sport and education through the period, J.A. Mangan, *Athleticism in the Victorian and Edwardian Public School; the Emergence and Consolidation of an Educational Ideology* (Cambridge, 1981). For the Barbadian 'education through cricket' philosophy, E.D. Laborde, 'Public School Cricket', *BCA*, 1910–11, 108–13.

48 *Barbados Blue Book*.

49 Lodge vicissitudes may be followed in the Governing Council Minutes, 1882–1914, BA.

50 A convenient reference for the background and growth of Harrison is *The Harrisonian: 250th Anniversary Commemorative Issue* (Bridgetown, 1983).

51 Somers Cocks is recalled in F.A. Hoyos, *Our Common Heritage* (Bridgetown, 1951).

52 For example, 'A very brilliant and treasured performance' saw Harrison's last-wicket partnership beat Spartan in 1895; the Lodge win over Wanderers in 1897 'caused a sensation for days', and the Harrison victory over Wanderers the same season was 'hailed with delight by the crowd'. *BCA,* 1894–5, 85 and *BCA,* 1897–8, 148 and 108.

53 The theory of cultural reproduction comes from Pierre Bourdieu. See his 'Cultural Reproduction and Social Reproduction', in Richard Brown (ed.), *Knowledge, Education and Cultural Change: Papers in the Sociology of Education* (London, 1973); with Jean-Claude Passeron, *Reproduction in Education, Society and Culture* (London, 1977), 'Sport and Social Class', *Social Science Information*, 17 (1978). For application to the educational area, Roger Dale *et al., Education and the State, II: Politics Patriarchy and Practice* (London, 1981).

54 Brian Stoddart, *Saturday Afternoon Fever: Sport in the Australian Culture* (Sydney, 1986).
55 Material drawn from *The British Guiana Directory and Almanack*.
56 J. Coleman Beecher, *Jamaica Cricket, 1863–1926* (Kingston, 1926); Herbert G. Macdonald, *History of the Kingston Cricket Club* (Kingston, 1938).
57 For a general view of the development of social divisions within Barbadian cricket, L. O'Brien Thompson, 'How Cricket Is West Indian Cricket?: Class, Racial and Colour Conflict', *Caribbean Review*, 12 (1983).
58 *BCA*, 1899–1900, 110.
59 The Hinkson-Deighton wedding was reported as a great society occasion and drew the largest crowd ever to that time at St Michael's Cathedral, *Globe*, 13 November 1893.
60 A description of Bancroft is in *Monthly Illustrator*, 15 (1897).
61 For the spirit, *BCA* 1902–3, 46 and 1903–4, 61; for the incident, *Agricultural Reporter*, 23 August 1895.
62 Personal information conveyed to the author.
63 Governor to Secretary of State, 3 February 1900, No. 32, COL 2/1/44, BA.
64 For mention of the crowds, 'clans' and excitement: *Agricultural Reporter*, 13 December 1895; *BCA*, 1898–99, 65–68; *Bulletin*, 4 December 1899, 8–10; Advocate, 5 January 1909, 2.
65 *BCA*, 1895–96, 132.
66 *Globe*, 20 August 1891.
67 For an account of him playing for a ground staff team in 1893: *Globe*, 28 August 1893.
68 Account based on *BCA*, 1899–1900, 31–3, and 129–32; *Bulletin*, all in 1899: 17 June, 8, 31 July, 8, 2 September, 16, 16 September, 12, 2 October 11; *Globe* 1899; 19 July, 31 July, 8 September.
69 Pickwick and Windward reactions seen conveniently in *Bulletin* 1899: 15 August, 8 and 9, 19 August, 8, 24 August, 9–10, 25 August, 8–9, 31 August, 8–10, 1 July, 10–11, 4 December, 10, 9 December, 14.
70 *Globe*, 4 August 1899.
71 *Agricultural Reporter*, 3 April 1900, 3.
72 *BCA*, 1912–13, 141–2.
73 *Queen's Park Cricket Club Diamond Jubilee*.
74 For ground strengths, *BCA*, 1895–6, 189, and 1901–1, 158. The 1893 match, *Globe*, 28 August 1893.
75 *BCA*, 1903–4, 157; *BCA*, 1913–14, 104.
76 Genealogical material drawn from Births, Deaths and Marriages, Parish Registers, BA.
77 *BCA*: 1899–1900, 170–1; 1900–1901, 72–4; 1904–5, 29; 1909–10, 27–34.
78 The best expression of this view is by 'Incognito' in *BCA*, 1899–1900, 129–32.
79 *Bulletin*, 18 August 1899, 8.
80 *BCA*, 1902–3, 186. For an idealized view of the Frame Food heritage, Clyde A. Walcott, 'The Home of the Heroes', *New World Quarterly*, 3 (1966–7).
81 *Advocate*, 4 January 1908, 5. There is the further point of an 1899 report claiming 600 members of island cricket clubs, *Globe*, 12 July 1899.
82 *Bulletin*, 11 October 1899, 8.
83 The membership of the original Committee appears in *BCA*, 1902–3, 186.
84 The report in *BCA*, 1904–5, 158, saw 'cause for fear that bats and wickets would be utilised for other purposes than negotiating the ball'.

85 *Agricultural Reporter*, 11 September 1891.
86 *Herald*, 25 April 1895.
87 *Advocate, 30* January 1905, 5.
88 *Agricultural Reporter*, 22 January 1895.
89 *Ibid.*, 7 February 1899, *3*.
90 Pelham Warner, *Cricket*, pp. 42–6; *Bulletin*, 3 December 1897, 4–5.
91 See the Hesketh-Prichard report, *Advocate*, 22 March 1905, 9–11.
92 Andrew Ernest Stoddart, England cricket and rugby union captain, 1897 tourist; *BCA*, 1896–97, 187.
93 *Agricultural Reporter*, 19 January 1900. For comparative Caribbean expressions of popular content with local victories: Sir Reginald St Johnston, *From a Colonial Governor's Notebook* (London, 1936), p. 152, and Lord Hawke, *Recollections and Reminiscenses*, p. 169.
94 Bowen, *English Cricketers*, p. 16.
95 *Advocate*, 22 March 1905, 9–11.
96 *BCA*, 1900–1901, 81–2.
97 *Globe*, 29 September 1899.
98 Such as the 'much merriment' expressed when bowler Clifford Goodman struck English batsman F.W. Bush in 1897, *Bulletin*, 14 January 1897, 9.
99 *BCA*, 1908–9, 46–7.
100 Sir John Hutson, *Memories of a Long Life* (Bridgetown, 1948), p. 23.
101 *Bulletin*, 29 September 1897, 9; *Globe*, 29 September 1899.
102 *Bulletin*, 14 January 1897, 8. My thoughts on colonial resistance have benefited from discussions with Ranajit Guha and from his book, *Elementary Aspects of Peasant Insurgency in Colonial India* (Delhi, 1984). Bowen, *English Cricketers*, pp. 2 and 14; *Agricultural Reporter*, 29 January 1895. For these and other disturbances that year: *West Indian Royal Commission*, p. 18; *Herald*, 1895: 4 April, 11 April, 12 April; *Agricultural Reporter*, 1895: 9 July and 16 July. *Bulletin*, 26 August 1899, 8; *BCA* 1903–4, 157.
103 Bowen, *English Cricketers*, pp. 2 and 14; *Agricultural Reporter*, 29 January 1895.
104 For these and other disturbances that year: *West Indian Royal Commission*, p. 18; *Herald*, 1895: 4 April, 11 April, 12 April; *Agricultural Reporter*, 1895: 9 July and 16 July.
105 *Bulletin*, 26 August 1899, 8; BCA, 1903–4, 157.
106 The Griffith story is told briefly in John Wickham, 'Herman', *West Indies Cricket Annual* (Bridgetown, 1980), pp. 12–14.

2

The origins and development of West Indies cricket culture in the nineteenth century: Jamaica and Barbados

Hilary McD. Beckles

I

Some time before Immanuel Wallerstein argued so persuasively that with the emergence of the modern world system organized culture began its career as a potent ideological weapon of the elite classes, West Indian 'plantation society' theorists had indicated the degree to which the 'liberated' progeny of enslaved blacks had systematically coopted the cultural activity and outlook of empowered Europeans.[1] This 'nativist' conceptual framework sought to illustrate the structures and parameters of nineteenth-century creole culture, and to establish the relative residual weight of its European and African derived value system. Unfortunately, cricket as a social institution with clearly defined value imperatives was not used to chart the evolution of creole culture. Black cultural resistance and tenacity was assumed, but subsumed nonetheless, within the contextual framework of hegemonic plantocratic cultural traditions.

Undoubtedly, the introduction of cricket within the nineteenth-century West Indian world is reflective of much of what was taking place within the British imperial sphere. The West Indian colonies constituted a specific territorial space that had been on the receiving end of transatlantic cultural inputs for over three centuries. The nature of this exchange was determined by the colonial nexus that placed European cultural expressions in a dominant relation to other forms. The Africanization of things European, however, was also a feature of the process known as West Indianization. The creole formation within which all nineteenth-century cultural institutions emerged and evolved, therefore, was determined by intense forces of cross-cultural and inter-cultural fertilization. In this sense, then, the social making of West Indies cricket is a history shaped by dialectical processes of conflict and co-option.

In addition, importance should be attached to the sense of spatial ordering and cultural movement intrinsic to the periphery/centre paradigm that informs world-system theory. If, however, such a construct can explain the presence of cricket within the culture zone of plantation West Indies, doubt must be raised about its further usefulness in assessing the specification of its internal logic and value system. The plantation society paradigm, on the other hand, departs from here and provides an incisive conceptual instrument in the search of sociological insights.

Distinguished cricket historians, such as the late C.L.R. James, Brian Stoddart and Keith Sandiford, have established that the imperial cricket culture arrived laden with coded philosophical messages conducive to the furtherance of empire building.[2] In addition, they have indicated that the nineteenth century witnessed the debut of mass sport as part of the leisure culture of the work-oriented plantation ethos. From these perspectives it is possible to argue that cricket was introduced into the West Indies and projected in particular ways because it represented the latest and principal form of imperial cultural technology. World-systems theory indicates that it was essentially an agent of Empire sent into the field as a politicized cultural protector of England's share of the spoils of global capitalism. From this perspective its mission was to consolidate the view that 'high' culture emanated only from the centre from whence the ideology of white supremacy came.

Given the contents of its mission statement the success of cricket over the duration of the century was remarkably swift. It penetrated first the insecure and dependent cultural world of the propertied white creole elite who embraced it as a celebration of the tight, unbroken bond between themselves and their metropolitan 'cousins.' For this elite it served all intended purposes; particularly, it assisted in the social elevation of its members above 'uncivilized' indigenes who lacked proper access to, or an informed appreciation of, things 'English.' By mid-century it was clear that cricket was at once an instrument of imperial cultural authority as well as a weapon of class and race domination within the plantation civilization that still clung to the fabric of a dying slavery ethos.

Within the context of Parsonian functionalism and Marxian mode of production analysis there is nothing particularly phenomenal about this sociological process. The white West Indian colonial community was a dependent one that looked towards the imperial centre as the source for all normative values and institutional edifices. From the seventeenth century it had been weaned upon an increasingly unconvincing cultural diet of imported 'Englishness' that required sanction by the colonial state in order to ensure its legitimacy. Cultural dependency, of course, came hand in hand with mercantile economic dependency which ultimately blunted the edge of the nascent eighteenth-century creole proto-nationalism that offered at best a token gesture of support to American political and cultural revolutionary independence.

Cricket, then, imported into most West Indian territories by the beginning of the nineteenth century, and carrying the 'made in England' hallmark, was marketed and consumed as a refined elite product in much the same way as was 'high Church' Anglicanism, which also explains in part the kinship-like bond that was forged between the two cultural forms. Within the recipient plantation world it reaffirmed the existing race/class division of labour while at the same time reassured supporters of empire that the central purpose of colonies in the industrial age was to consume with satisfaction things made at the centre. It was not relevant from the colonizers' viewpoint that such an unashamed level of mindless consumption would provide ideological evidence of colonial philistinism. Cricket, for them, fitted well into the existing scheme of things. Ships went out from the colonies carrying material product and vessels returned partly filled with cultural products, the value of which was such that Wallerstein need look no further for evidence of the unequal exchange endemic to the nineteenth century capitalist world system.

Within this framework the colonial elite moved swiftly to canonize organized cricket within its definition of what constituted civilized culture. The earliest pioneers of the game intimated that it was part of the cultural tradition of the English gentry, and that the corresponding colonial class merely inherited what was logically theirs by rights of ancestry. Cricket, by mid-century, had become part of the colonial elite's chest of 'customs' – the ultimate and most concrete status social cultural activity could acquire within a given formation.

In the promotion and legitimization of cricket as an institution of high culture for the civilized, and in the process integrating it within the wider system of hegemonic oppression, the colonial elite also succeeded in establishing a cultural sphere within which the anti-systemic resistance of disenfranchised blacks would be assured. The logical progression of this dialectical conflict created the circumstances within which the 'exclusive' activity of the elite was appropriated by subordinate social groups. The downward social mobility of cricket into the villages of blacks was guaranteed so long as the elite ascribed to it the normative values of respectability and honour, since the frantic search for betterment by this 'semi-free' population involved the attainment of these social goals. As the West Indian colonial elite basked unashamedly in imperial cultural mimicry, therefore, it also established a framework of oppositional behaviour for its subjected and dishonoured minions.

It was only a matter of time before the twin forces of culture/demographic creolization and black civil rights struggles coalesced to promote cricket as a popular transracial cultural expression. The desire of the coloured and black communities to play cricket their own way seemed to have grown in direct proportion to the white elite's determination to establish it as the exclusive sport of propertied, the educated, and the 'well-bred.' By the mid-century, versions of the game were being played and celebrated at all levels of colonial society. It is largely irrelevant to question whether the blacks and coloureds 'loved' it simply because the white elite did, or whether in the absence of other mass activity it captured their creative imagination and proved useful in their cultural and political struggles. The important point is that all sections of society valued its form and moral messages which is precisely why its growth was characterized by a dichotomous political history of intense racial contention and the search for an area of life in which a non-racial utopia could safely exist without producing any contaminating effects upon the general body politic.[3]

The body politic, of course, was no more than the ideological superstructure of the plantation-based establishment that kept firmly in sight the concepts of white supremacy, the power and privilege of private property, and the attendant fear of, if not hatred for, racial/social egalitarianism. The absorption of cricket in the 'psychic world' of the colonial structure, therefore, meant that major redefinitions of the game's values had to take place. If cricket was the finest gift of nineteenth-century English humanist culture, best played by persons of a particular moral attainment and social status, why then should it be influenced by the social consideration of keeping blacks in their 'place' within the plantation society? The answer of course is quite clear given our understanding of West Indian ideological history. In exactly the same way that whites defined a political system in which less than 10 per cent of the population was enfranchised as democratic, a place was found for blacks within the cricket culture that enhanced the divisions of labour insisted upon by plantations. Against this background are to be seen the peculiar features of early West Indian cricket culture, particularly its original elite origins, and subsequent social democratization.

Undoubtedly, this social and political history explores the institutional and ideological formation of plantation civilization. In explaining this history, the dependent mentality of the colonial elite is as important as their use of culture as a survival strategy. Indeed, the two ideological practices when placed together constitute but one side of the dialectic; the other being the cultural resistance and affirmation of non-white disenfranchised colonials who eventually claimed cricket as their own and repromoted it as a symbol of liberating, politicized mass culture. Power, here, as Humpty Dumpty suggests, being shown to be no more than one's right to define and to have one's definition accepted.

II

It is not surprising that Barbadian creole planter society seemed most determined to import and entrench metropolitan cricket culture. They had already defined their island home as 'Little England' and 'Bimshire', and held steadfast to the view that they were Englishmen in a far-flung 'shire' separated by a large sea and a few centuries. As far as they could see these divisive elements were insufficient to erode their cultural rights, and took great pride in defining themselves as the most loyal colonial subjects of the Crown; the worship of the cricket culture, then, was one way in which they expressed fidelity. But colonists in other territories had long captured a greater share of the London sugar market, dominated the executive of the West Indian Committee, two developments that forced Barbadian whites to accept a more pragmatic view of their relations with the metropole.

Throughout the nineteenth century, the printed media in the colonies were called upon to assist in the popularization of the cricket culture. Announcements of games were carried alongside references to the sale of slaves and the fluctuations of sugar markets. Such announcements spoke aggressively of a new and exciting leisure system within white elite society – all part of the overall cultural benefits of freedom and mastery. That these earliest references are specific to the endeavours of the garrisoned imperial military suggest that this largely 'English' group played the leading role in the pioneering of the cricket module. While at the end of the eighteenth century, these troops awaited instructions to put down rebellious blacks or keep out the acquisitionist Napoleon, they played cricket as a principal stress releasing activity – one that allowed them to 'play being at home' while being away from home.

What seems to be the earliest references to cricket within the West Indies press appeared in the *Barbados Mercury and Bridgetown Gazette* on Saturday 10 May 1806 and 17 January 1807.[4] The latter entry was an announcement by the treasurer of the St Ann's Garrison Cricket Club inviting members to a special dinner. Two years later the *Gazette* carried notice of a 'grand cricket match to be played between the Officers of the Royal West Indies Rangers and Officers of the Third West Indian Regiment for 55 guineas a side on the Grand Parade on Tuesday, September 19.' The match was arranged to start 'immediately after "gunfire" on the morning and continue until 8 o'clock a.m., then to resume at 4.30 p. m'. The royal Rangers were required to war 'flannel and blue facings' and the Third Regiment 'flannel and yellow facings'.[5]

St Anns Cricket Club, then, seemed to have been a pioneering West Indian social institution. Barbadian whites welcomed it, and appreciated the wider implications of its presence. The proprietor and editor of the *Barbadian*, Abel Clinckett, though admittedly consumed with reporting on the abolition of the Apprenticeship System, and the onset of 'full' legal freedom for blacks, found time in May 1838 to editorialize on the importance of this cricket club to the imperial mission. He wrote:

> We understand that to promote the gratification of the soldiers of St Anns Garrison, as well as the sake of their health, the Commander of the Forces has sanctioned their engaging in the truly British, and manly sport of cricket. A great match, we are informed, will be played on Monday next at 6 o'clock [a.m.] – the 78th Regiment against the Garrison.[6]

This was a single-innings game, and the next week it was reported in the same paper that the 78th Regiment had won the game having scored 91 runs to the Garrison's 53. An important issue to be noticed here is that the Garrison team was made up of lower ranking soldiers. This attracted the attention of Mr Clinckett when he stated that such social mixing of men of different classes showed 'the good feeling' entertained by officers for their soldiers.[7]

If the St Anns Club can claim to be the incubator of Barbadian/West Indian cricket culture it can also be justly proud of the rapidity with which the virus spread to neighbouring districts infecting elite communities with which it had close contact. Again, the *Barbadian* informs us in 1849 that 'gentlemen' in the parish of St Michael, in which the Garrison was located, had constituted themselves into two 'well organized cricket companies' – the 'City' and 'St Michael' Clubs. The editor described the first game between these clubs as an affair watched by 'highly respectable ladies and gentlemen' that 'evinced great spirit and extreme goodwill'.[8]

The game was played on a specially prepared field at Constant Plantation, owned by Mr Prettijohn, who also provided tents and refreshments for spectators.

It soon became the norm for cricket clubs to be patronized by Governors and other highly ranking administrative officials. Located among the sugar fields, these cricket grounds represented more than just entertainment for whites but the agency of a cultural renaissance that swept throughout the colonies. In 1857 the *Barbadian* claimed to have made a public appeal for the financial and social support of cricket among all sections of society. The Governor, meanwhile, had made it a matter of duty to attend the match between Codrington College and the Gallant 49th Regiment, bringing with him to the proceedings the full authority of colonial and imperial respectability. In the same year the Jamaicans, who had also been playing on their plantations, began the formal institutionalization of cricket when they established the St Jago, and the Vere and Clarendon Cricket Clubs. These organizations, like their Barbadian counterparts, were confined to the propertied elite classes, and both coloureds and blacks were excluded from membership.

In 1863, the Kingston Cricket Club was established in Jamaica – the first major urban-based organization – with the soon to be notorious Governor Eyre as patron. The significance of this development is twofold. First, that as was the case in Barbados, cricket could now claim to be an urban institution. Second, the 'heavy' official support the game received from the outset ensured its promotion as an activity that conferred or indicated social honour. The *Barbadian* was therefore not generating any scandal or controversy when it reported the following on the visit of Prince Alfred (Second son of Queen Victoria) to Barbados in 1861:

> Thursday, H.R.H. was supposed to rest from the fatigues of pleasure which had been inflicted on him; but instead of taking a siesta, he went to the Garrison to play cricket with the Officers, making his rest merely a change of amusement, and that a recreation requiring so much energy and activity as cricket does.[9]

West Indies cricket, then, was a game played by royalty, and on such occasions colonials (black, coloured and white) came out and celebrated, if not the gentler social side of Empire, the meteoric rise of a major cultural force within their midst.

The black community had been encouraged from the slavery period to use their 'free time' in full indulgence in the sort of cultural activity that did not in any way appear to whites as informed by a spirit of resistance. Any cultural expression that whites feared or considered rebellious was outlawed. By the end of slavery, then, a complex entertainment system was to be found within the plantation villages – and established tradition that was also characterised by the adoption and adaption of European forms to their own material and ontological condition.

African-derived performing and celebratory cultural practices absorbed the cricket missile – tamed and domesticated it as part of their culture complex. With their propensity to collectivize cultural ritual and to blend comic, heroic and tragic drama within the single form, blacks brought spectator theatre and participatory festiveness to bear upon the idealization of the physical and artistic elements of cricket performance.

Cricket, then, found a soft and safe resting place within the residual African ontology. Blacks needed only a little encouragement, and they received just this. The early records attest to this fact in the clearest manner. Take, for instance, the view of the Rev. Grenville John Chester whose literary sketches on the black poor of Barbados in the aftermath of slavery are frequently cited by social historians. He tells us in 1869:

> The labouring classes in Barbados are badly off for amusement. Tops and marbles seem almost the only sports of the school children, but when encouraged they take kindly to cricket. But it is hard to find places to play in, and parochial cricket clubs are either above or below the notice of the local clergy. Thus dancing is almost the only amusement, and the people dance well and gracefully.[10]

So here we have it. There was little assistance and no comfortable space within the early cricket culture for blacks at a time when plantations were creating room for the proliferation of whites only clubs and the established schools had placed cricket at the centre of the academic agenda for white children.

This racial division of space, however, did not prohibit black children from developing their skills and appetites for the game. The ways in which they adapted the technological instruments of the game to suit their environments points to the innovative consciousness that had long informed their survival strategies. If poverty is no enemy of ingenuity, then the cricket technology devised by blacks in the mid-nineteenth century constitutes supportive evidence. Algernon Aspinall, historian of the nineteenth-century British West Indies, describes the early cricket technology of Jamaican blacks:

> Black people are particularly enthusiastic about the game. It is quite common to see tiny black children innocent of clothing indulging in it with all the assurance of their elders, using, however, sugar canes for wickets, coconut palm leaf for a bat and whatever they can lay their hands on for a ball.[11]

What was true for mid-nineteenth-century Jamaica remained the case for most of the West Indies into the mid-twentieth century. The instruments of the poor remained unaltered for over a century while their capability consistently improved. With respect to early spectator practices, Aspinall states:

> The black spectators of cricket matches are very demonstrative, and it is not at all unusual to see many of them rush out on the ground and leap and roll about from sheer excitement when a wicket falls on the side which they do not favour, or when a brilliant catch is made.[12]

Aspinall also made reference to A.F. Somerset's observations of vociferous West Indies cricket crowds during the 1895 tour of an English team:

> A good ball dealt with brings a shout of 'played!' all around the ground, and to stop a 'yorker' evokes a yell that would not be given for a hit out of the ground in England.

> When that comes off a large part of the crowd spring on to the ground, throw their hats and umbrellas in the air, perform fantastic dances, and some of them are occasionally arrested by the police.[13]

In the Barbados match, he stated, the England captain was forced to use a whistle to get the attention of his fieldmen, so noisy and festive was the crowd.

The intensification of anti-black racial prejudice in the post-slavery period, in part a response of whites to the expressed socio–political and economic expectations of blacks, meant that cricket in its infancy was socialized by values of race hatred and conflict. While the blacks worked for whites in the cane fields whites refused to play with blacks on the cricket fields. They watched each other, but kept their distance.

As the century progressed, however, and the civil rights movement won some constitutional and moral battles, the pressure mounted to lower the racial barriers to the cricket world. By the end of the century, some middle-class coloureds played for white clubs or formed their own. In turn, they would engage black teams in 'friendly' games – but these teams were not generally invited to the club houses for refreshments during or after the game. It was within this ideological environment that the institutional formation of the cricket culture was well established. Barbadian teams competed for a Challenge Cup from 1892 and Jamaican teams did so from 1893. At first, the Challenge Cups allowed for the display of cricket skills only from the white clubs, but gradually coloured and black players and clubs performed their way into the competition.

Leading cricket clubs in Barbados and Jamaica, 1850–1900

Name	When established	Colony
St Jago	1857	Jamaica
Vere and Clarendon	1857	Jamaica
Lodge School	1850s	Barbados
Codrington College	1850s	Barbados
The Garrison	1850s	Barbados
Kingston	1863	Jamaica
Harrisons College	1877	Barbados
Wanderers	1877	Barbados
Kensington	1878	Jamaica
Pickwick	1882	Barbados
Leeward	1880s	Barbados
Windward	1880s	Barbados
Belleville	1890s	Barbados
Melbourne	1892	Jamaica
Spartan	1893	Barbados
Garrison Club (Up Park Camp)	1898	Jamaica
Lucas	1898	Jamaica
St Georges	1890s	Jamaica

The establishment of a network of cricket clubs had a great deal to do with the transformations taking place in West Indian social life at the end of the century. The convergence of an urban professional middle class of whites, coloureds and blacks challenged the dominance of the planter-merchant elite within the cricket culture. In Jamaica, for example, St Jago, and Vere and Clarendon Clubs were represented exclusively by the planter elite, while the Kingston Club catered for their wealthy urban mercantile allies. While the Kensington Club maintained a largely upper middle-class urban white membership, the Melbourne Club was the facility of the coloured professional classes who, from the slavery period, considered attractive the skin-lightening miscegenation approach to social mobility into elite white society.[14]

Not surprisingly, then, Melbourne Club harboured as many anti-black attitudes as the whites-only clubs – the colourism that separated the different shades of nonwhite society being as potent ideologically as the racism which divided blacks and whites. Not one black person, noted Soares, could be found among the 58 members of the club in 1894.[15] Whereas in Jamaica, Melbourne used the technicality of a complex fee structure to rationalize the absence of blacks from the club, in Barbados white officials categorized blacks as professionals not suited to participate in amateur competitions.

The plantation-based civilization of Barbados could claim an older history than that of Jamaica, Trinidad, Demerara or the Windwards. As a result its ruling inhabitants insisted upon the social projection of race/colour/class stratifications with greater precision and illiberalism. The formation of Wanderers Cricket Club in 1877 represented the planter elite's social need for an institutional agency to distinguish their cricket from subordinate 'others'. The Pickwick Club that followed in 1882 was the response of that collective of small planters, middling merchants, and professional whites on whom Wanderers had closed the membership list.

The Spartan Cricket Club, like Melbourne in Jamaica, was the institution of the racially oppressed but socially respectable coloured families. With a few whites and blacks admitted to its membership, Spartan's mission was to democratize Barbados cricket and discredit the long standing ideology of white superiority. Its first President was the distinguished Conrad Reeves, the mulatto Chief Justice, whose sense of racial pride was matched only by his loyalty to the political agenda of the white elite.

In both Jamaica and Barbados the black working class remained locked out from these institutionalized arrangements in spite of having established a reputation for producing very skilled professional players. The late nineteenth century 'Barbadian professionals', noted Ronnie Hughes, 'were groundsmen, young men employed as grounds bowlers, and occasionally helpers and hangers on, in other words, labouring class black Barbadians'.[16] These players, in spite of or probably because of, their ability were excluded from Challenge Cup competitions whether they played as 'guest' of established clubs or as a team. Whites would occasionally hire them a individuals or as teams to play in 'friendly' games as a means of providing exⁿ ment for spectators or to sharpen their own game. But there remained at thᵉ the century no respected institutional home for working-class players.

III

West Indies cricket, then, by the end of the nineteenth century had been trans-formed from a minority elite 'English' sport into the region's first expression of popular mass culture. By mid–century it had broken out of the mould represented by garrisoned English military men, and had spread into the plantations, villages and towns of the colonies. In so doing, cricket traversed a wide geographical space and slowly embraced all social classes and races in ways never before witnessed in the region. 'Every self-respecting colony,' at the end of the nineteenth, noted Aspinall, 'has one or more cricket clubs, and the keenest interest is taken in the game especially during the winter months in alternate years, when an Inter-colonial Cricket Cup is competed for by representative teams from Barbados, British Guiana and Trinidad'.[17] Initiating its social sojourn as an instrument of the imperial cultural mission, it soon became the leading leisure institution of a colonial elite in search of new methods of social differentiation. Seized by blacks and coloureds it became the focus around which an intensive civil rights war was waged as they sought the democratization of its culture as well as their organizational autonomy within.

At the beginning of the century, then, cricket was a pastime of a few resident Englishmen and at the end it was the region's premier cultural expression of the popular imagination. This process mirrored much of what was taking place within West Indian society as the socially liberating aspects of the emancipation event of 1838 began to impact upon social relations and structures. Bruce Hamilton, reflect-ing in his 1947 publication, *Cricket in Barbados*, captured with precision the West Indian cricket culture at the turn of the century when he concluded:

> If, as is often asserted, the game as played on the village green is the backbone of English cricket, an at least equally valuable contribution to West Indies cricket has been made by the contests fought out on a few square yards of pasture, with a quite well-prepared pitch on the only piece of level ground, but only one half-split ball and two old bats to go round, square leg out of sight in a gully, silly point standing on an outcrop of rock, and natural boundaries in the form of grazing goats and sheep. In Barbados at least the poorest black man has certainly no less love of the game than his white brother of rustic England, with a far deeper understanding of it and skill in playing it. Everyone who has practiced cricket in the island is aware that any bare foot boy hanging about the ground is likely, if he is tossed a ball, to bowl at least reasonably well with it . . . It is not a ques-tion of intelligence; it simply is that a love of cricket (as distinct from interest in any sporting activity that is given publicity) is confined to a small section of Englishmen, whereas in the West Indies it is implanted in the hearts of the entire people.[18]

This achievement, so aptly described here for Barbados was one hundred years in the making in the West Indies and is guarded today by a popular will that is 'old tes-tament' in its judgement. That Barbados won the Inter-colonial Cricket Cup six times in the first eleven contests after 1893 (Trinidad 4 and Demerara 1) is perhaps indicative of their early lead in the institutionalization of the cricket culture. But what is really important is that by 1900, a general distribution of cricket capability and enthusiasm was finally achieved in those territories where club formation had taken root.

NOTES

1 See Immanuel Wallerstein, *The Politics of the World-Economy* (Cambridge, Cambridge University Press, 1984), pp. 165–80. Also, 'The National and the Universal: Can There Be Such a Thing as World Culture', in Anthony D. Kind, *Culture, Globalization and the World Economy* (London, MacMillan, 1991) pp. 91–107. G. Beckford, 'The Dynamics of Growth and the Nature of Metropolitan Plantation Enterprise', *Social and Economic Studies, (SES)*, Vol. 19, No. 4, 1970. L. Best, 'Outlines of a Model of Pure Plantation Economy', *SES*, Vol. 17, No. 3, 1968.

2 See Stoddart, and Stoddart and Sandiford, in section one of the text. C.L.R. James, *Beyond a Boundary* (London, Hutchinson, 1969 edn).

3 See Maurice St Pierre, 'West Indies Cricket: a Cultural Contradiction?' in *Arena Review*. Vol. 14, No. 1, 1990, pp. 13–25.

4 *Barbados Mercury and Bridgetown Gazette*, 10 May, 1806, 17 January, 1807, Barbados Archives; see also Warren Alleyne, 'Cricket's Beginnings in Barbados', the *Sunday Sun*, Barbados, 17 March, 1991.

5 *Ibid.*

6 Cited in Bruce Hamilton, *Cricket in Barbados* (Bridgetown, Advocate Press, 1947) p. 7.

7 *Ibid.*

8 *Ibid.*

9 *Ibid*, p. 8.

10 Rev. Grenville John Chester, *Transatlantic Sketches, 1869* (Barbados Heritage Reprint Series, National Cultural Foundation, Bridgetown, 1990), p. 32.

11 Algernon E. Aspinall, *The British West Indies: their History, Resources and Progress* (London, Isaac Pitman, 1912), p. 153.

12 *Ibid.*, 153–4.

13 *Ibid.*, 154.

14 See Dave Soares, 'A History of the Melbourne Cricket Club, 1892–1962', unpublished MA thesis, History Department, University of the West Indies, Mona, Jamaica, 1987. H.G. McDonald, *The History of Kingston Cricket Club, 1863–1938* (Kingston, Gleaner Company, 1938); F.L. Pearce and T.L. Roxburgh, *The Jamaica Cricket Annual* (Kingston, DeSouza, 1897); Anon, 'The History of Melbourne Cricket Club', *The Sportsman*, Vol. 2, No. 1, 1929.

15 Soares, pp. 17–18.

16 Ronnie Hughes, 'Nineteenth Century Cricket Development in "Little England"', in *100 Years of Organized Cricket in Barbados, 1892–1992* (Barbados Cricket Association, 1992, Bridgetown), p. 2.

17 Aspinall, *The British West Indies*, p. 151.

18 Hamilton, *Cricket*, p. 62.

3

The elite schools and cricket in Barbados: a study in colonial continuity

Keith A.P. Sandiford and Brian Stoddart

Cricket has always been more than just another game in the Caribbean island of Barbados, possessing a rich symbolic importance and becoming the source of intense national pride.[1] Significantly, the 1966 independence celebrations to mark the end of over 300 years of formal possession by Great Britain centred upon a cricket match. Partisan spectators at Kensington Oval were genuinely surprised when their island representatives lost to a team made up of players drawn from the world's leading cricket nations.[2] After all, from the late nineteenth century onwards a remarkable number of regional and international stars had emerged from this 21 × 14 mile island which never numbered more than 250,000 people. Since winning the very first inter-colonial match against British Guiana in 1865 Barbados had dominated regional cricket, monopolizing the Shell Shield competition begun in 1966. When English county cricket was opened to foreign professionals in 1968, Barbadians immediately became an important force, with Hampshire alone having four of them on its staff as early as 1971.[3] That simply extended a Barbadian presence in English league cricket begun with George Francis in the 1920s. Consequently, Barbados has always contributed a disproportionately large number of players to West Indian Test and touring teams.

I

The single most important social condition underlying this cricket eminence (and one which stood apart from other colonial experiences in its contours) was the elaboration of what might be called the 'elite school' system in Barbados from the 1870s onwards, a system based quite consciously on the public and grammar school ideology of Victorian Britain. As Tony Mangan has observed, the majority of grammar and public schools in nineteenth-century Britain set considerable store on physical education. In an age dominated by muscular Christianity and Social Darwinism teachers and parents stressed the importance of games and recreation in the development of character.[4] Playing fields, gymnasia and swimming pools gradually

44

became as significant to educators as classrooms and curricula. As Bruce Haley has argued, the Victorians saw games not only as a means of strengthening the body but of teaching moral and spiritual values. They glorified and turned it into work largely because their Puritan ethics devalued relaxation. Recreation, to them, was not a matter of fun and games. It meant the constructive regeneration of mind and body.[5] As a result, soccer and cricket became vital features of the public school curriculum. The universities of Oxford and Cambridge also became involved in perpetuating this games ethic, their graduates disseminating muscular Christian ideas throughout the Empire.[6]

During the last quarter of the nineteenth century, when jingoistic imperialism peaked in Britain, cricket was considered an essential part of preparation for service in the Empire. The old boys of Eton and Harrow, Cambridge and Oxford, arrived in the colonies with cricket, classics and Christianity as the principal components in their intellectual, ideological and cultural baggage. Social groups in the colonies anxious for an accommodation with the imperial masters invariably took to cricket, imbibing the ruling beliefs in the game as a moral force.[7] Civil servants, soldiers, settlers, missionaries and traders carried cricket to all corners of the Empire, establishing complex social systems in which imperial model interacted with colonial adaptation. In the majority of cases, cricket became an important institution through which colonial conservatism was fostered, protected and preserved, often in the midst of substantial change to the wider social and political environment. Nowhere was this more clear than in the British West Indies where the development of cricket clubs was a principal feature in the evolution of class and colour divisions.[8] And as the Barbados case demonstrates, the role of the education system was central to that process.

II

The three elite schools were Harrison College, The Lodge and Combermere. All had lengthy histories but by the mid-nineteenth century had lost their way in the social, economic and political realignments which followed the abolition of slavery.[9] From the 1870s onwards, however, these schools became the major institutions in an education system revamped and shaped by the ruling minority of planters and merchants to ensure both its own primacy and the supply of the required skilled staff to service the sugar industry upon which the island's prosperity rested.[10] Lodge was primarily for the sons of the planting community at the ownership and managerial levels. Harrison catered largely for the white commercial community and the tiny emergent black professional and managerial groups. Combermere became oriented towards commercial education, its clientele drawn from both the black and white lower middle-class service groups. Until well into the twentieth century the numbers attending these institutions were small – the privileged few who passed beyond the primary schools which provided basic education for the school-age population. From their 1870s reformation onwards, the elite schools emphasized the importance of cricket in training future civic leaders for their economic and political roles. Moreover, the headmasters and teachers in the three schools became caught up in a self-perpetuating process which meant that ideas codified in the late nineteenth century lasted well into the twentieth.

The Lodge helped lay the foundations for cricket in Barbados before the establishment of regular clubs, playing frequently against teams from the military garrison and against more short-lived combinations such as St Michael's.[11] When club cricket was established by the formation of Wanderers in 1877 and Pickwick in 1882, many of the players had learned their craft at Lodge. Perhaps the best examples were the four Goodman brothers who came to Pickwick from a plantation management family. All four represented Barbados before 1900 with Percy touring England in one of the first West Indian teams, Sir Gerald (as he became) rising to the post of Chief Justice in the Straits Settlement, Clifford dying young and Evan migrating. But the supply of such players from Lodge dwindled during the 1890s as a succession of headmasters had little time to develop the traditions laid by Campbell Tracey who took up the position in 1882 after graduating with an MA from Oxford and spending time as an assistant master at Westminster School in London. A keen player and enthusiast, Tracey struggled to maintain cricket as a central feature of Lodge but financial pressures induced by a sugar market depression undercut his efforts. By the 1890s, then, the key role had passed to Harrison College, largely because of the work of Horace Deighton.

A mathematics graduate from Oxford, Deighton administered Harrison College from 1872 until 1905, setting the foundations for much of what was to follow. A firm believer in the value of games as a means of building character, he introduced many of the ideas then prevalent in English public schools and was the first Harrison College headmaster to appreciate the value of a regular school magazine. Under him, the *Harrisonian* was started in the 1870s and then revived in 1903 after a lapse of nine years.[12] Himself a fine cricketer, Deighton encouraged the boys to play, attended most of the matches with his immediate family, and inaugurated the annual Past versus Present in 1882.[13] He was also very active on the Barbados Cricket Committee from its inception in the early 1890s, and this public activity did much to gain acceptance for the social ideology of cricket among the ruling minority. The performances of the school cricket team were watched closely, their victories hailed by the public as a guarantee of the supply of future Barbadian civic leaders. It was appropriate, perhaps, that the end of Deighton's regime coincided with the emergence of perhaps the greatest cricketer ever produced by Harrison College, George Challenor, who was to become a partner in one of the island's largest commercial enterprises and be named by *Wisden's* as one of the top five players for 1923.

Deighton was followed by Dr Herbert Dalton, a grandson of the famous Bishop Blomfield. After graduating from Oxford in 1874, he served as headmaster of St Edward's School and taught at Winchester under Dr Fearon. Later, Dalton became headmaster of Felsted, where he fostered games after the manner of the leading public and grammar schools. Seeking a warmer climate because of his health, Dalton migrated to Barbados and took his muscular Christian ideas to Harrison College which he modelled on later Victorian Winchester. Under him, Harrison College prospered. It became known throughout the British Empire as one of the most famous secondary schools. Dalton introduced the Oxford and Cambridge certificates as well as the set and prefect systems. He encouraged every pupil to take part in sports and started the system whereby each boy paid a subscription to the Games Fund every term. He reorganized the library, introduced aquatic sports, and re-introduced the teaching of singing and drawing. When Dalton resigned in 1922, it was universally agreed that while Deighton had made Harrison College a good secondary school, it was Dalton who had made it comparable with the best public schools in England.[14]

In some respects, of course, the achievements of Deighton and Dalton were repeated elsewhere throughout the British Empire because the force and power of education were recognized everywhere by colonial rulers and aspirant leaders alike. But what was remarkable about Barbados was the universality of agreement about the social good of such elite education and of cricket. For many, many years, the products of the elite schools constituted the membership of island teams who played before admiring crowds made up largely from the lower orders whose access to such education and to cricket was severely limited. There was, that is, discrimination in access but agreed admiration for the colony's social structure in its major sporting form. Such a situation very rarely prevailed elsewhere in the imperial order because either elite education and elite cricket remained elite (as in India and, later Pakistan) or democratization set in at a much earlier point (as in Australia and New Zealand where state-sponsored education produced alternative forms of high-level access). Deighton and Dalton were therefore not alone in fostering this distinctive Barbadian condition.

The Lodge, meanwhile, had enjoyed a regeneration under the headship of Oliver deCourcy Emtage, widely known as 'Bill'.[15] From 1898 until 1931 he consciously set out to produce a replica of an English public school, introducing the prefect system and setting up a model boarding establishment. By far the most important headmaster of Lodge, he made it one of the most famous boarding schools in the British Empire, himself making vital contributions towards improving the school buildings and playing fields. He supervised games personally and encouraged senior boys to sit on the important Games Committee which he established.

An important feature of the Emtage story is that his career demonstrates the educational and cultural reproduction pattern which maintained the elite schools' ideological core of which cricket was such a substantial part. Born in Barbados in 1867, he studied under Deighton at Harrison College between 1879 and 1886, and won the blue ribbon Barbados Scholarship which took him to Worcester College, Oxford, where he performed well in mathematics and athletics. Returning to Barbados, he served as a Harrison College master under Deighton for eight years before his relocation to The Lodge. He never lost his interest in cricket or his belief

47

in its character-building powers.[16] For many years Emtage addressed the school through his 'Headmaster's Letter' which appeared in the *Lodge School Record*. On almost every occasion he alluded to the value of games, remarking in 1924, for instance, that a schoolboy 'is receiving by the practice of these arts very valuable training in obedience of the muscles to the eye, promptness in deciding and foresight in judging the motives of his opponents'.[17] In 1926, after lamenting some mediocre academic results he consoled himself and his boys that 'our lack of success in School is, however, to some extent made up for by a fairly successful year as far as games are concerned.[18] In 1927 his 'Letter' appealed for more assiduous practice at cricket, and in 1928 bemoaned the alarming frequency of unnecessary run-outs.[19] For Emtage, through games such as cricket came responsibility, teamwork and a set of moral precepts which would prepare boys for their adult lives. He was a direct product of both the Victorian system of faith in games and of its quite consciously adopted colonial derivative.

Over at Combermere, too, the clientele might have been different but the games education was not. At the time Deighton was remodelling Harrison College upon English public school lines, the Rev. T. Lyall Speed was performing an identical service for Combermere. An Old Harrisonian who had served briefly under Deighton in the early 1870s, Speed inevitably transported a number of Deighton's ideas to Combermere. A competent sportsman himself, he stressed cricket and the classics, order and discipline, and built up a solid reputation for the school. During the period of Speed's headship (1879–96) Combermere grew steadily in numbers and stature, becoming easily the most important of all the second-grade schools in the island.[20]

But it was really George Bishop Richardson Burton who consolidated Combermere upon muscular Christian ideas during his tenure as headmaster from 1897 until 1925. Like Emtage at Lodge, and Speed his predecessor, Burton was a Deighton product, having attended Harrison College in the mid-1870s. Winning an Island Scholarship allowed him to attend Codrington College where he took an external degree from Durham University. After service in local schools he took up his Combermere post and saw the school body rise from 102 to 250 by the time of his retirement.[21] The school performed very creditably in academic as well as extracurricular activities.[22] As the editor of the *Combermerian* once observed, Burton had not been 'much addicted to games himself but did his best to foster and encourage athletic talent at the school'.[23] He was largely responsible for the founding of the Combermere Cadet Corps in 1904 and the Combermere Scout Troop in 1912.[24] Like cricket, these were very important forms of colonial modelling. Again, the central influence of Deighton and the Victorian games cult was quite evident in the creation of a monolithic rather than dynamic educational culture.

By the mid-1920s, then, the cricket cult was well established within the three leading Barbadian schools. In terms of actual cricket results all three performed poorly. Harrison College won the club championship cup in 1927 and 1930 while Combermere had a solitary victory in 1940. Lodge never won the first division cup and its second division victories were to be as far apart as 1911 and 1956. But it was widely argued that the lessons learned on the field were more important than mere victories.[25] Schoolboy century-makers were looked to as the foundations for future Barbadian cricket teams and, because many of them came from the ruling minority, for civic life. Many Barbados Scholarship winners were scholar-cricketers, reflecting the emphasis placed upon the relationship between mind and body in the schools since the 1870s.[26] The widespread belief in the value of that nexus was as strong, perhaps even stronger than it had been in the late nineteenth century, the result of the long term work put in by men such as Deighton, Emtage and Burton. Their products dominated Barbadian life, while their successors were to hold firm to the ideals of athleticism during times of considerable social and political fragility. Unlike other colonial settings, then, it could be argued that the elite education structure in Barbados proved to be a vehicle for conservative adherence to nineteenth-century imperial ideas rather than for an explosion of twentieth-century colonial ones. The key here was that many of the successors to the Deighton era were either products of the schools or masters within them, sometimes both.

III

The socialization of masters into the dominant culture of public school ideology began very early, with Harrison College perhaps the most important site. Two exemplary figures in this regard were Arthur Somers Cocks and G.B.Y. 'Gussie' Cox. Somers Cocks was born in England, educated at Manchester Grammar School and Oriel College, Oxford, where he won blues for cricket and athletics. He joined the Harrison College staff in 1892, married one of Horace Deighton's daughters, and became one of the great all-rounders in West Indian cricket around the turn of the century.[27] There was considerable public discontent when he lost the headship to Dr Dalton upon Deighton's retirement, but Somers Cocks remained loyal to the school until his death in 1923 just after he succeeded Dalton. Gussie Cox was the son of a Barbadian dry goods store manager, and attended Harrison College as a pupil in the 1880s.[28] He won an island scholarship and was another man to take an external degree from Durham University through Codrington College. After a brief teaching stint in Antigua, Cox returned to Harrison College as a master just after Somers Cocks arrived. Like his colleague, Cox was a magnificent all-rounder and the two of them established a solid public school cricket code at Harrison. After 31 years at the college, Cox became headmaster at Combermere to replace Burton and, until his retirement in 1934, carried into his new school the devotion to cricket he had first learned under Deighton in the 1880s. These were the sort of men who inspired messages such as this:

> Never mind the Range [Ranji] glides or any gallery tricks, but let us strive to improve
> in Batting, Bowling and Fielding and to be keener, keeping alert and playing the game,
> for the sake of your game and your side.[29]

The sentiment might well have come directly from a nineteenth-century games manual.

By the 1930s it might have been expected that the rise of political associations led largely by the black middle classes, the organization of working-class movements and the appearance of more militant groups such as a Barbadian branch of Marcus Garvey's Universal Negro Improvement Association might have seen an attack on the Victorian ideology of the elite schools.[30] On the contrary, however, the period revealed the inroads made by the ideology into the local political culture. Most if not all of the new leaders were themselves products of the elite schools, and particularly of the cricketing social code.[31] Even radical leaders (and there were few of them) such as Charles Duncan O'Neal had learned their cricket and their social networks within the elite schools, and had carried those lessons into their club-playing days. Grantley Adams, who played once for Barbados and continued as a prominent club player well into the 1930s, was an especially fine example of cricket's ameliorating social influence – his participation in the game and its administration kept him in close and constant touch with the more reserved elements of Barbadian political culture. Black political leaders such as Adams found their ways on to the school boards and proved loath to change recruitment and appointment policies based upon the late nineteenth-century principles, so that even during the political turmoil of the 1930s, architects of the elite school's education and cricketing practices were direct replicas of those who had constructed the practices two generations earlier. This, perhaps, was the ultimate proof of the widespread public belief in the power of the island's educational philosophy

Harold Noad Haskell, who succeeded Somers Cocks at Harrison College, was an excellent example of this educational reproduction. Haskell was an able Oxford graduate in mathematics and was awarded his MA in 1920. At Merton College, he was also an ardent sportsman. He captained that college in cricket and represented it in rugby. He had first come to Harrison College in 1910 as one of Dalton's appointees.[32] As headmaster he spent the rest of his life trying deliberately to make that school the best and most famous in the world. To that end, he consistently tried to attract the most promising teachers from England and often complained that the Barbadian salary scales were not sufficiently competitive.[33] He applied for, and gained admission into, the celebrated Headmasters' Conference which then included such elite schools as Eton, Repton, Rugby, Marlborough, Charterhouse, King Edward's, Lancing, and Christ's Hospital (his own alma mater).[34]

During Haskell's tenure at Harrison College, academic results were outstandingly good and the school played consistently fine cricket. All of his Speech Day addresses were dominated by sporting news as he called unceasingly for more spacious playing fields until they were eventually provided in 1941. Thereafter, there was a marked improvement in the standard of athletics at Harrison College.[35] The majority of Haskell's appointees were fine scholar-athletes, and it is not accidental that when he needed three specialists in 1932 he promptly hired W.D. Isaac, a good classical scholar who had also done well at rugby and cricket at Trinity College,

Dublin; A. Milton, a Cambridge graduate, who was a keen participant in gymnastics, field hockey, and soccer; and E.C. Queree, an alumnus of King Charles I School and Jesus College, Cambridge, where he was renowned as a rower and rifleman.[36] When Haskell retired in 1948, under his direction Harrison College had won several athletic championships, two first division cricket cups, innumerable scholastic distinctions, and had grown to a population of over 500.[37] By the mid-twentieth century, significantly, it was an almost perfect Victorian school in which scholarship and athleticism were mutually interdependent.

Haskell was succeeded by an even more ardent supporter of the cult of athleticism. John Coleman Hammond was educated at Rossall and Cambridge and became headmaster of Sompting Abbotts School before accepting the Harrison College post. At Rossall, he had played rugby and also been cricket captain. At Harrison College, he immediately created more prefects to help in a new system of games supervision and coaching and, in his first Speech Day address in 1950, expressed a determination to make games 'compulsory in the near future'.[38]

Hammond never varied from this stance. He remained convinced that games were of inestimable value in the creation of worthy citizens. Towards the end of 1950 he invited Clyde Walcott, an old Harrisonian, to address the school on the triumphant West Indian cricket tour of England in which that great batsman/wicket-keeper had participated. Walcott strengthened Hammond's message by urging the boys to practise diligently.[39] In 1951, when Barbados and Trinidad were engaged in a two-game inter-colonial cricket series, Hammond ended the school day two hours earlier than usual to allow the boys to watch the matches at Kensington Oval. In his Speech Day address that year, he again called upon parents and boys for a balanced diet of work and play, insisting that it was his school's responsibility to produce healthy men as well as bright scholars.[40] Hammond's earliest appointments to the Harrison College staff included J.W. Rice, an Irish MA with a keen interest in cricket, and Sam Headley, the first black head boy of modern times at Lodge who had already built up a fine reputation as cricketer and footballer.[41] In praising his staff in 1955 for their help in extracurricular activities, Hammond once more argued that the time spent outdoors with scouts, cadets and games was just as important as the hours spent in the classroom and should be seen as an essential component of teaching.[42]

When Hammond retired in 1965, Albert Williams became the first non-white Barbadian native to be appointed headmaster of Harrison College. Williams was one of six brothers who had all been educated at Harrison College during Haskell's tenure. His family was especially keen on sports and one of his brothers, C.B. 'Boogles' Williams, played cricket with distinction for Barbados and toured with the West Indies. The Williams era and his devotion to games again revealed the powerful reproduction of the ideals taken up in the nineteenth century. Williams's Speech Day addresses, for example, might easily have come from Deighton, Haskell or Hammond with messages as much from the nineteenth century as for the twentieth. In 1975, for instance, he declared that 'Extra-curricular activities can do much

51

in this matter of character formation and the tradition that a teacher's work does not cease when he leaves the class room is one that we should foster.' Williams then proceeded to boast about the manifold sporting activities in which his pupils were taking part.[43] All this despite the massively altered social framework which had overtaken Barbados by then including political independence.

For more than a hundred years after its emergence as a first-grade secondary school, Harrison College was thus dominated by muscular Christians. Without exception, its headmasters were all keen on games. They encouraged the boys to play and quite often actively participated themselves in cricket and soccer. They invariably hired scholar-athletes to teach, and before independence many of these came from Britain. A classic example was Edward B. Knapp, a product of pre-war Clifton who spent 25 years (1913–38) with Harrison College promoting sports as the house master of set D. In his farewell address to the school he exhorted the boys to aim at becoming Christian gentlemen.[44] His conviction had always been that cricket was one of the most effective instruments for developing good Christians and that character was perhaps even more important than education in this regard.[45] The point, clearly, was that the long-lived belief in games sprang from particular views about social roles and responsibilities more than from a simple belief in the value of physical exercise.

The remarkable resilience of this ideology was also demonstrated at Lodge, especially by Bill Emtage's immediate successor who, as a clergyman as well as scholar and athlete, was almost the archetypal muscular Christian. Harry Beaujon Gooding grew up on plantations and went to school at Lodge before going to Harrison College during Deighton's last days. He won a Barbados Scholarship in 1906 and went to Oxford where he distinguished himself as one of the most brilliant classical scholars ever to attend that university. After serving for some years as the Principal of Wycliffe College he returned to Barbados for health reasons in 1926. He then taught classics at Harrison College for five years under Haskell before his appointment as headmaster of Lodge.[46]

As Emtage had done before him, Gooding combined scholarship with games as he regarded both equally vital to the development of human character. His philosophy was stated explicitly in his 'Headmaster's Letter' of 1940. He advised his pupils that a healthy body was just as important as a healthy mind, and urged them to participate actively in as many fields as possible for their own personal benefit as well as the honour and glory of Lodge. In his Speech Day address that year he appealed to parents 'to co-operate with us both by encouraging their sons to take the games and athletics of the School as seriously as possible and also to make it possible for them to do so'.[47] Insisting that games helped the boys to develop their abilities and to broaden their outlook while strengthening their characters, Gooding reorganized the house system to ensure healthy competition and rivalry by mixing the boarders and day boys as equally as possible. He introduced a third house, Emtage, to compete at games with the extant houses, Laborde and School. Under Gooding's direction Lodge flourished. Its numbers increased from 105 in 1932 to

178 in 1941, and it achieved outstanding results both in the classroom and on the playing fields.[48]

Gooding's successor, the Englishman T.L. Evans, was determined to make Lodge similar to Arnold's old Rugby and he revisited England in 1946 to study the major public schools there in the hope of utilizing their more effective methods. But he gave himself little opportunity to imprint his stamp indelibly on Lodge as he left Barbados shortly afterwards to take up an appointment in Nairobi. He did enough, however, to indicate that he was bent on following the tradition established by Emtage and Gooding.[49] No possible harm could have come to this tradition from the appointment which immediately followed.

Evans was succeeded by W.A. Farmer, who had enjoyed an almost unbroken connection with Lodge since he had first entered that school as a pupil in 1905. From Lodge, Farmer went on to Codrington College before teaching briefly at Harrison College. He returned to his alma mater in 1917 to teach under Emtage, his old mentor. Farmer, whose son and grandson were to play cricket for Barbados, had himself been an outstanding young athlete. From 1907 to 1911, in fact, Farmer was easily the most dominant force in Barbadian athletics. In the 1912 Lodge School sports he set an impressive long jump record of 21' 8½" which remained unbroken for more than 50 years. It was still standing triumphantly when Farmer himself died in 1957. He was also an able cricketer whose speciality was slow off-breaks, but (like his son Captain Wilfred) he is best remembered as a tremendously hard hitter of the ball.[50] It would have been most unusual had a headmaster with this background departed from the Emtage–Gooding policy. Farmer continued to stress the importance of games until ill-health forced him to resign in December 1953.[51] His whole career emphasizes yet again the strong socialization process inherent in the Barbadian elite educational culture.

IV

None of the recent headmasters of Lodge have moved away from the games ethic. Arthur Ralph Vernon Newsam, P. McD. Crichlow and C.E. Aurelius Smith have all been products of a similar system. Newsam, who succeeded Farmer in 1954, attended Harrison College during the period of Dalton's headship, studied at Durham and London Universities, then taught briefly at Cornwall College in Jamaica before joining the Lodge staff in 1931. He fell under Gooding's influence and even served as Games Master during 1931–32 and 1947–49. He, too, was a famous scholar-athlete who valued games as an integral feature of the school curriculum. He was an excellent all-round cricketer and good enough as a soccer player to represent Jamaica during his short stay there.[52]

Crichlow, who succeeded Newsam in 1965, was one of Haskell's prize pupils and won an Island Scholarship to Codrington College in 1931. He served Lodge almost continuously after his graduation in 1934 and his position with respect to games was the same as Newsam's.[53] The controversial Smith, who refused to be dismissed from his post by the Barbados Labour Party Government in 1985 after serving as head-master of Lodge for 13 years, was himself an excellent athlete at Harrison College in the 1940s and at the University College of the West Indies in the following decade.[54] His background and his training were markedly similar to those of Albert Williams, his contemporary at Harrison College.

The notion that cricket could somehow produce excellent scholars as well as loyal patriots was much encouraged at Lodge by such distinguished scholar-athletes as Val McComie, Leslie Arthur Walcott, and Graham Wilkes. Among this group, the most influential perhaps was 'Bessie' Walcott, an excellent all-rounder who repre-sented Barbados often during the inter-war years. He was almost 36 when selected to play in one Test match for the West Indies against England in 1929–30.[55] Walcott was a pupil at Harrison College during Dalton's tenure and won an Island Scholarship to Codrington College in 1913. After serving for many years as a most popular Games Master at Harrison College under Haskell, he accompanied Gooding to Lodge in 1932. There he became a legend, playing very good cricket for the school's second division until he was well past 50. As Games Master from 1932 to 1947 he began the system of awarding separate ties for athletics, cricket, football, and hockey and furnishing both cricket teams with caps. He kindled the boys' enthusiasm for all sports and left a profound impression on every student who attended Lodge from 1932 to 1953.[56]

As at Harrison College, then, the games tradition remained strong at Lodge as carefully selected appointees from outside Barbados combined with just as carefully selected Barbadians to consolidate an educational ideology which had its origins in later nineteenth-century Britain. The result was a strong strand of colonial conti-nuity down to 1966 and beyond into the post-colonial period. In all of this it is important to recall the wide-ranging and mutually reinforcing social cohort groups which proceeded from the schools with a firm belief in the 'cricket as life' model. Just as important as the consistently careful selection of teaching personnel was the outpouring of ideological converts from the school into Barbadian business, agri-cultural, financial, religious and cultural life. These converts helped the schools to perpetuate the beliefs in various ways, such as the captains of commerce who rou-tinely closed their shops and business houses for half-day holidays when important cricket matches were being played. These were the people who moved into posi-tions of responsibility in government, sporting and cultural circles, maintaining the role of the elite schools as the principal moulding influence for the support of cricket as a social as well as sporting institution.

Combermere differed little from the other schools in all this during its modern phase. The Rev. Arthur Evelyn Armstrong took over from 'Gussie' Cox in 1934, emphasizing the important part played by the clergy in propagating the Barbadian cricket gospel. An easy-going man, he seemed less committed to order and disci-pline than his Victorian predecessors but, like them, Armstrong was totally pre-pared to worship at the twin altars of classics and cricket. He, too, attended Harrison

College in Deighton's time and graduated from Codrington College in 1905 after winning an Island Scholarship in 1898. Earlier still he had attended Combermere during the period of Speed's headship. [57] A serious cricketer in his youth, Armstrong remained an enthusiast throughout his life. He captained St Ann's and played for Pickwick. He encouraged Combermerians to 'play the game' and enjoyed the tremendous thrill of seeing them win the first division cup in 1939–40. His boys also won the inter-school athletic sports competition for the fourth time in five years in 1940. [58] Combermere reached the peak of its athletic prowess during Armstrong's administration (1931–46) and the school's extra-curricular achievements featured prominently in all his Speech Day reports. [59]

This emphasis on manly recreation was encouraged by several members of Armstrong's staff, such as Frank Collymore, Stanton Gittens, Ralph Perkins, O.A. 'Graffie' Pilgrim, Derek Sealey, and V.B. 'Bull' Williams, who often played cricket and soccer for the school. It was Pilgrim, in fact, who was among the first to be impressed by the exceptional skills of the young Frank Worrell in the late 1930s. 'Graffie', an Emtage product at Lodge, had himself been an outstanding schoolboy athlete. In the 1911 inter-school sports, he established a high jump record of 5' 7½" which was destined to last for many years. [60] Pilgrim was also an excellent fast-medium bowler playing regularly for Spartan and Barbados from 1913 to 1926.

At one level, the differences between Armstrong and his immediate successor, Major Cecil Noott, were as striking as those which might be expected between a passive Barbadian priest and an energetic Welsh soldier. Beneath the surface, however, the belief in the consensual ideology was, if anything, even stronger. Noott set out to improve Combermere's image by making it more similar to the leading grammar schools in England and by closing the gap (as he perceived it) between Combermere and the first-grade schools in Barbados. To that end he reorganized the set and prefect systems, increasing the number of houses and extending the authority of senior boys. He introduced art, music and physical education, employing such specialists as Karl Broodhagen, the celebrated West Indian sculptor, James Millington the distinguished Barbadian violinist, and Bruce St John who was perhaps the first Barbadian to pursue a formal diploma in physical education. Noott not only built up the school library but he put G.R. Brathwaite, the scout master, in charge of a new book store which he established at the school for the benefit of the boys. He also instituted a sixth form in 1952 and had the satisfaction of seeing a handful of Combermerians achieve Advanced Level certificates for the first time in 1953. [61] All of this was designed to make Combermere fit the nineteenth-century ideological model more rather than less – again an unusual late-colonial experience.

Noott deliberately tried to redress the balance between work and play since he believed that the traditional focus on sports had not been accompanied by a sufficient concentration on studies. But he did not neglect games. He followed the extracurricular achievements of his pupils with a keen enthusiasm, encouraging young teachers like Deighton Maynard and Keith Sandiford to establish the Combermere hockey team as one of the strongest in the island. His interest in cricket was profound and abiding. Long after his retirement he could still be seen at Lord's and the Oval watching 'my boys' (as he affectionately termed the West Indians) play against England. His passion for the game was reflected in his habit of awarding expensive prizes to his pupils for outstanding performances on the cricket field. The West Indian fast bowler, Wesley Hall, for instance, recalled with pride that Noott presented him with a new pair of cricket boots for scoring 92 runs against Leeward in the early 1950s.[62] During that decade Combermere became a potent force in Barbadian cricket, thanks in large measure to the efforts of Ronnie Hughes, an old Lodge boy appointed cricket master by Noott. A large number of Combermerians whom Hughes coached eventually represented Barbados, and three of them – Rawle Brancker, Hall and Patrick Lashley – won selection to West Indian touring teams. Another West Indian Test player, Frank King, was also hired by Noott as cricket coach and groundsman in 1951. He was a fiery fast bowler whose presence guaranteed the Combermere XI a certain measure of respectability throughout most of the 1950s.

Noott had so thoroughly revitalized Combermere that, after his retirement in 1961, it was hardly possible for his successors to alter the course which he had steered. Under Stanton Gittens, C. de Vere Moore and Charles W. Pilgrim Combermere remained a highly competitive school in and out of the classroom. An old Harrisonian trained in the Haskell era, S.O'C. Gittens, emerged with a fine appreciation for the value of sports and was especially keen on cricket in which he had himself represented Barbados as a highly skilled wicket-keeper/batsman in the 1930s.[63] Moore and Pilgrim were not scholar-athletes in the Gittens mould but, like Gittens, they were both Haskell products and cricket fans who continued to aim at a fine balance between scholarship and recreation.

V

That such scholar-athletes could remain in the 1960s onwards points firmly to the uniqueness of the Barbadian condition. The long-lasting, pervasive influence of men such as Horace Deighton, Herbert Dalton and 'Bill' Emtage, the architects of the island's modem elite school system, was unmatched in most other British colonial settings where at least gradual change crept into the structure to reflect local social and cultural peculiarities. While it is certainly correct that other colonies also had elite schools, few if any of them held such dominance over the cultural production of cricket in their local environments as did those in Barbados until well into the post-colonial phase. While some of that dominance stemmed from a smallness of population which enabled a closer control over the evolving models of education and cricket, a good deal of it also sprang from the adaptation of the Victorian system with an undue emphasis on the merits of physical training. Deighton, Dalton and Emtage consciously chose to pattern their schools after nineteenth-century Eton, Harrow, Rugby and Winchester. They transplanted those Victorian models very effectively indeed. Hence, in twentieth-century Barbados, long after the leading public schools in England had abandoned the Victorian fetish for Latin and cricket, the elite schools were still clinging to outmoded gospels and practices. By the time of independence in 1966, education in Barbados was thus very similar to the English system as it had stood exactly 100 years before, a condition considerably removed from that in other imperial outposts.

This was an almost classical form of that process of cultural reproduction pointed to by Pierre Bourdieu and, as such, Barbados has retained a Victorian-like respect for cricket as the manliest form of recreation and one full of moral precepts along with symbolic and actual significance in the formation of social values.[64] The work of the elite schools lies at the heart of this process. Cricket had flourished in England during the nineteenth century largely because of its considerable appeal to the public schools and universities. It was the graduates from these institutions who did most to popularize the game, to encode its social values and to give it a degree of respectability and significance that it might otherwise have lacked.[65] They founded countless associations, leagues and cricket clubs, many of which are still in existence. This proved to be even truer of Barbados where all the major clubs and the Barbados Cricket Association itself were founded by men who had learned their cricket at the elite schools. Even the Barbados Cricket League, created in 1936 specifically to cater to the urban and rural poor, was the brain-child of old Combermerians such as Chrissy Brathwaite and J. Mitchie Hewitt.[66] Again, such a centralized source of cricket and social influence was unmatched elsewhere in the British Empire.

But perhaps the most remarkable and the most distinctive trait concerning the elite school influence over Barbadian cricket, and one which sets it quite apart from other colonial experiences, is that the game spread into mass appeal yet still followed the playing and moral codes established by the elites. In Samoa, Fiji and the Trobriand Islands, for example, love of the game certainly spread from the administrators, missionaries and educators who established it along with the imperial message, but the new converts soon subjected cricket to a quite radical reformulation so that it might better reflect the mass cultural customs.[67] This never happened in Barbados where Old Boys of the elite schools maintained strict control over the behaviour of their clubs and associations. While the game was taken up almost fanatically by the island's lower classes through such agencies as the Barbados Cricket League, the codes and standards to which they aspired were those established and maintained by the culturally dominant cricketing products of the elite schools. This was particularly important among the emergent black leaders who became steadily so Anglicized that they not only copied British political ideals but also mimicked Victorian attitudes and mores (including cricket) so successfully that Barbados became known throughout the Caribbean, somewhat derisively, as 'Little England'. The new elite followed the example of the old and deliberately preserved as much of the nineteenth-century culture as they could. The elite schools played the leading role in this process of cultural reproduction. In this respect, the

Barbadian experience was different from that of India, South-east Asia, the Pacific and Africa where local leaders, for the most part, resisted the British assault upon their conventions and their heritage. In Barbados, though, cricket became even more of a national obsession than it had ever been in Victorian Britain, the best single testament to the creation of a British mentality in a constructed colonial social order.[68]

Thus, the island's governing authorities thought it appropriate to declare 3 October 1950 a public holiday to allow all Barbadians to welcome home their heroes who had triumphed over England 'at home'.[69] Later, and even more remarkably, the Governor of Barbados, Sir Robert Arundell, advanced by several hours the 1 February 1954 ceremony to create ministerial government controlled by local political parties in order to avoid conflict with the third day's play involving the island side and the touring English team.[70] Perhaps best of all, these incidents help reveal the total Barbadian commitment to cricket, a condition due almost entirely to the importance placed upon the game by the producers and controllers of the Barbadian elite schools. To a man (and cricket *was* a major protagonist in the elaboration of a male-oriented society), Barbadian educators of the late nineteenth and twentieth centuries stressed the virtues of the great imperial game as the perfect medium for teaching invaluable lessons about morals, ethics and life itself.

NOTES

This article has been made possible by grants from the Research Board of the University of Manitoba and the Social Sciences and Humanities Research Council of Canada (to Keith Sandiford); and the Canberra College of Advanced Education and the University of the West Indies, Cave Hill Campus (to Brian Stoddart).

1 For an outline of the island's cricket story, see Bruce Hamilton, *Cricket in Barbados* (Bridgetown, 1947).
2 J.S. Barker, *In the Main: West Indies v. MCC 1968* (London, 1969), p. 10.
3 *Wisden Cricketers' Almanack*, 1972, p. 434. Keith A.P. Sandiford, 'Cricket and Barbados', *Cathedral End: the Journal of the Australian Cricket Society* (September 1984), 5, 1–3.
4 J.A. Mangan, *Athleticism in the Victorian and Edwardian Public School* (Cambridge, 1981), *passim;* and 'Grammar Schools and the Games Ethic in the Victorian and Edwardian Eras', *Albion*, 15 (Winter 1983), 313–35.
5 B.E. Haley, *The Healthy Body and Victorian Culture* (Harvard, 1978).
6 For example, see J.A. Mangan, 'Eton in India: the Imperial Diffusion of a Victorian Educational Ethic', *History of Education*, 7, 1 (1978).
7 Richard Cashman, *Patrons, Players and the Crowd: the Phenomenon of Indian Cricket* (New Delhi, 1980) demonstrates something of this process. Also J.A. Mangan, *The Games Ethic and Imperialism* (London, 1986).
8 C.L.R. James, *Beyond a Boundary* (London, 1963); Brian Stoddart, 'Cricket and Colonialism in the English-Speaking Caribbean to 1917: Steps Towards a Cultural Analysis' in J.A. Mangan (ed.), *Pleasure, Profit and Proselytism: British Culture and Sport at Home and Abroad, 1700–1914* (London, 1989), pp. 231–58.

9 On the evolution of Barbadian society: F.A. Hoyos, *Barbados: a History from the Amerindians to Independence* (London, 1978); George Hunte, *Barbados* (London, 1974); Hilary Beckles, *Black Rebellion in Barbados: the Struggle Against Slavery, 1627–1838* (Bridgetown, 1984); Louis Lynch, *The Barbados Book* (London, 1972 edn). There is still a good general history to be written.
10 For the histories of the schools: F.A. Hoyos, *Two Hundred Years: a History of the Lodge School* (Bridgetown. 1945); *The Harrisonian 250th Anniversary Issue* (Bridgetown 1983); *Tercentenary Christmas Number of the Barbados Advocate* 1627–1927 (Bridgetown, 1927).
11 Hamilton, pp. 18–22.
12 *Harrisonian* (December 1921), 7.
13 *Barbados Globe*, 20 November 1882.
14 *Harrisonian* (July 1922), 44–5, (July 1928), 2–3, (December 1948), 15–18.
15 F.A. Hoyos, *Some Eminent Contemporaries* (Bridgetown, 1944), pp. 112–14; *Harrisonian* (December 1942), 57–8.
16 For some theoretical insights into this pattern of cultural and educational reproduction, see: Pierre Bourdieu, 'Cultural Reproduction and Social Reproduction', in Richard Brown (ed.), *Knowledge, Education and Cultural Change: Papers in the Sociology of Education* (London, 1973); Roger Dale *et al.*, *Education and the State, II: Politics, Patriarchy and Practice* (London, 1981).
17 *Lodge School Record*, 1924, 4.
18 *Ibid.*, 1926, 6.
19 *Ibid.*, 1927, 3–4 and 1928, 3–4.
20 *Combermere School Magazine*, Third Term 1915–16, 2.
21 *Ibid.*
22 *Combermere School Magazine*, First Term 1925–26, 9–10.
23 *Combermerian*, 1934–35, 9.
24 *Combermere School Magazine*, June 1913, 6–7.
25 *Advocate*, 13 July 1937.
26 An outstanding example was Clifford de Lisle Inniss, a member of the Harrison College cup-winning team of 1927, Barbados Scholar in 1930, lawyer and later judge in Barbados and Africa, inter-colonial player in the 1930s and Barbados captain, knighted for his achievements.
27 *Harrisonian* (April 1923), 2–4, 12.
28 *Ibid.* (July 1934), 5–6.
29 *Harrisonian* (December 1924) 32.
30 For an introduction to this period, see F.A. Hoyos, *Grantley Adams and the Social Revolution* (London 1974).
31 *Ibid.*
32 *Harrisonian* (April 1949), 8–11.
33 *Ibid.* (April 1926), 31 and (April 1929), 21.
34 *Ibid.* (April 1926), 31 and (April 1929), 21.
35 *Ibid.* (April 1942), 31–5.
36 *Ibid.* (December 1932), 1–3
37 *Ibid.* (July 1948), 24.
38 *Ibid.* (July 1949), 4 and (July 1950), 26.
39 *Ibid.* (January 1951), 56.
40 *Ibid.* (July 1951), 63 and 84.

41 *Ibid.* (January 1951), 53–5.
42 *Ibid.* 1955, 6–7
43 *Ibid.* 1975, 7.
44 *Ibid.* (July 1938), 12–13, 16.
45 F.A Hoyos, *Contemporaries*, pp. 66–8.
46 *Harrisonian* (July 1941), 70–71; *Lodge School Record*, pp. 2–4.
47 *Lodge School Record*, 1940, 2 and 7.
48 *Ibid.* 1940, 7 and 1942, 4.
49 *Ibid.* 1943–44, 9, 1946–47, 20, 1948–49, 6.
50 *Ibid.* 1948–49, 6, 1954, 4.
51 See *Lodge School Record* (1948–54).
52 *Advocate Year Book and Who's Who 1951* (Bridgetown, 1951), p. 221. *Lodge School Record May 1947–June 1948*, 19.
53 *Lodge School Record*, 1964, 7.
54 *Ibid.* 1972, 1.
55 *Wisden Cricketers' Almanack*, 1985, p. 1203.
56 *Lodge School Record*, 1933, 1 and 1962, 66.
57 *Combermerian*, 1934–35, 11–12.
58 *Ibid.* 1940–41, 3, 18.
59 *Ibid.* 1934 to 1947.
60 *Lodge School Record*, 1912, 7.
61 This treatment of Combermere is based largely on a conversation with Ronnie Hughes, Earle Newton, Major Noott and Basil Sandiford on 10 March 1981. All the members of this group had been educated, or had taught, at Combermere.
62 Wesley Hall, *Pace Like Fire* (London, 1966), p. 20.
63 Hamilton, pp. 141, 154, 157.
64 Keith A.P. Sandiford, 'Cricket and the Barbadian Society', *Canadian Journal of History* (December 1986), 21, 353–70.
65 Keith A.P. Sandiford, 'Cricket and the Victorian Society', *Journal of Social History*, 17 (Winter 1983), 303–17.
66 L. Walcott, 'The Barbados Cricket League: Forty Years of Service', UWI undergraduate paper, Cave Hill, 1978, p. 26.
67 For an analysis of this process, see Brian Stoddart, 'Sport, Cultural Imperialism and Colonial Response in the British Empire: a Framework for Analysis', published in D. Benning (ed.), *Proceedings of the Fourth Annual Conference of the British Society for Sport History* (Stoke-on-Trent, 1986).
68 See Brian Stoddart, 'Cricket, Social Formation and Cultural Continuity in Barbados: a Preliminary Ethnohistory', *Journal of Sport History* (Winter, 1987).
69 The *Barbados Annual Review 1950*, pp. 167–70.
70 Alex Bannister, *Cricket Cauldron* (London, 1954), pp. 55–6.

4

Cricket, social formation and cultural continuity in Barbados: a preliminary ethnohistory

Brian Stoddart

Just 166 miles square and the most windward of the Caribbean islands, Barbados has long possessed a reputation for being culturally and economically dominated by the production of sugar, and for being a 'Little England'.[1] The two circumstances are inextricably connected. Barbados was a British colony from 1627 until the coming of political independence in 1966, and for all that time its level of prosperity was determined by fluctuations in the sugar industry. To some extent it still is, despite the encouragement of mass tourism since the 1960s. During the long colonial period the social organisation geared to produce the sugar wealth was based upon British concepts of economic ordering, political power and social distancing between elaborately defined caste categories. This social order was founded in the period from the 1650s until 1838, during which time Barbados derived its wealth from a slave-based economy organised in a plantation system. The owners were either British-based absentees or descended from British stock; the labour force was African or of African descent. Middle level management was largely white, as was the commercial trading sector, although in both a small mulatto element had appeared by the late eighteenth century. After the final emancipation of the slaves in 1838, the legal relationship between these groups might have altered but the social one did not – British law, British custom, British social conventions and British culture continued to direct the island's development. The results are intriguing. On an island with a population now exceeding 250,000 and a per square mile density of over 1,200, the 97 per cent of the community descended from African slaves are located in a cultural construct established by white arbiters whose descendants now comprise less than 3 per cent of the population.

The present legislative system, political parties, educational structure, Anglican religion and the English language itself (or, at least, a distinctive form of it) are all tangible products of this long British heritage as they are in a number of other non-white majority, post-colonial settings. But unlike those other settings, in Barbados it is cricket – that most English of games – which is the most striking and influential benchmark and cultural monument to the British social influence.[2] Barbados is renowned as the most prolific per capita producer of top flight players in the world

61

and Bajans, wherever found, are persistently and passionately devoted to the playing of and talking about cricket. This is quite unlike the situation elsewhere as in, say, India where only a tiny percentage of the population based in relatively few centres and concentrated in a restricted number of social communities displays a passionate devotion to cricket.[3] In Barbados cricket is not so much a game which inspires enthusiasm as a cultural institution, a way of life in itself.

This deep social reach may be illustrated briefly in a number of ways. From the late nineteenth century until well into the twentieth, and even now on special occasions, shops, offices and schools were closed while important matches were in progress. From at least the turn of the twentieth century, citizens would identify themselves by their playing or supporting connections with a cricket club, as in 'Spartan man', for example. When responsible government came to Barbados in 1954, the swearing-in ceremony had to be rescheduled so as to avoid a clash with an important match. Independence itself, in 1966, was celebrated with a special cricket game. Cricket is still a constant subject of conversation in rum shops, the workplace, the streets, homes, parties and on buses, while a match anywhere on the island will draw spectators from those passing by. Even visitors from other cricketing cultures, let alone those from non-playing areas such as North America, are overwhelmed at the extent of Barbadians' devotion to the game. Because of that deep attachment, then, an analysis of cricket's social dimensions and history necessarily becomes an investigation into the inner workings of Barbadian society as a whole.

This preliminary sketch of the relationship between cricket and its Barbadian social setting is based upon 1985 fieldwork which employed two main research strategies.[4] The first involved social history methods in investigating archival, institutional and private materials, surveying primary and secondary sources in both empirical and theoretical areas, as well as conducting extensive oral history sessions. The second strategy was ethnographic, principally through playing membership in a club participating in the major Barbadian domestic cricket competition. That membership (which according to one former Barbadian and West Indian cricketer meant 'living' rather than 'studying' the game) facilitated access to players, administrators, clubs and club life, cricket supporters, sports journalists, cricket folklore and the social practices of cricket in many different Barbadian contexts. The essay, then, analyses the centrality of cricket in Barbadian life in light of the game's history on the island, but begins with some necessary and fundamental observations about the cultural context in which the game developed there.

Debate concerning the precise nature of Barbadian social structure and 'culture' has swung largely upon whether or not its evolution has been influenced most by British, African or Creole emphases.[5] It is not an abstract debate because any positions adopted have a strong bearing upon prevailing attitudes towards class, colour and politics. One conventional wisdom, for example, has it that, since at least 1966, blacks have dominated political life in the island and whites the economy.[6] While this economic pattern and associated social patterns have begun to change recently, they still retain some validity. Such retentions have reinforced popular beliefs in the existence of separate, carefully delineated and vigorously defended social circles defined by colour, economic standing and status. Supporters of the Creolisation theory, however, have emphasised the steady emergence of a hybrid culture created jointly by blacks, whites and mulattos, thereby softening the idea of separate cultural circles. Important and interesting though these analyses are, they oversimplify or even ignore a more complex cultural condition in which cricket figures prominently.

It may be argued that two general and competing cultures have co-existed in Barbados until well into the twentieth century.[7] One was British-originated and identified historically with that white ruling class which dominated plantation ownership and commercial activity. From at least the beginning of the nineteenth century, if not earlier, these ruling whites gained considerable support from better-off, free blacks and mulattos who sought advancement, limited though it was, in the island's white-dominated social and economic hierarchy. As early as 1837, for example, many elementary schoolteachers were blacks who not only taught an English classical curriculum but also strongly upheld its attendant cultural values and behavioural attitudes.[8] Despite the small and steadily declining numbers of whites, then, their cultural practices from an early point gained considerable credibility as a result of its support by sections of the non-white community seeking an accommodation with the ruling order.

In distinction, and essentially in opposition to this, a folk culture persisted strongly within the black majority descended from African slaves. This folk culture was maintained through such practices as bush medicine, obeah (known more popularly and inaccurately as black magic), tuk band music (employing distinctly African rhythms and African-descended instruments such as drums and whistles), community dances and festivals.[9] These practices were essentially both a rejection of white culture and the defence of a black one, thereby establishing a considerable tension between the two.

The strengths of this folk culture, and the potential depth of the tension, were best revealed in the attacks made upon it by the ruling white order and its non-white supporters. For a considerable period after emancipation the police, the judiciary, the church and the educational system attempted to wipe out obeah and folk music in an effort to incorporate the black majority within the ruling culture.[10] These enforcing agencies were themselves part of a system of social coercion established by the plantocracy-controlled legislative bodies in order to replace the forms of authority held previously in the little political worlds of the individual plantations. A most important strand here was the 1840 master and servant legislation which turned chattel slaves into estate-tied wage slaves. But there also arose the police force, the militia and a range of incarceratory institutions (such as jails and asylums), designed to bring former slaves under direct state jurisdiction.[11] 'Undesirable' social elements became defined as vagrants, petty thieves, the insane and the poor, and were consequently subjected to an increasing range of thoroughgoing state controls. The creation of central markets for meat and vegetables, for example, was not simply about 'modernising' commodity supplies.[12] It also enhanced respect for property because by licensing dealers, state authorities sought to minimise praedial larceny (the stealing of food crops) which was directed largely against the major landholders, the former slave-masters.

While coercion certainly made substantial inroads into the folk culture, on its own it proved incapable of generating servility and acquiescence among the freed black majority. In the 1860s, food riots revealed possibilities for the rejection of constituted authority. The greatest challenge to that authority came during the so-called Federation Riots in 1876 when large crowds turned out against landholders, marching on plantations in support of an English governor who was apparently seeking to break planter power.[13] In 1895 rebellious bands again marched on food crop fields, invoking in song the memories and spirit of 1876.[14] Occasions such as these created fears within the elite about potential social dislocation and a breakdown in the dependent status of the black masses. It became clear, then, that the former slave-masters now required a new form of moral authority to augment, perhaps even to replace the coercive powers which in some senses had simply replaced one form of slavery with another.

As a result, such non-coercive and largely voluntary institutions as the education system and the church were utilised to instil in the population a set of values which produced the behaviour patterns desired by the powerbrokers whose traditional social, economic and political advantages would thus go untrammelled. This was achieved by such means as a careful construction of the school curriculum and by the teachings of the numerically powerful Church of England. This created the illusion of popular access to cultural agencies, yet, in reality, maintained the structural bases of discrimination and inequality. During the second half of the nineteenth century, for example, basic educational instruction was provided for most children, but the prominent education development lay in elite secondary schools such as Harrison College and The Lodge.[15] By 1900 there were 25,000 students under instruction, but only 205 of these were in the two elite colleges which serviced the plantation and commercial elite, grooming those who would inherit the relatively few positions available in the civil service and the professions.[16] The church, too, displayed internal divisions.[17] Throughout the island's eleven parishes, which were also local government bases controlled by rectors and church wardens, pew rents yielded positions of prestige and symbolic power to the local elites. From St Michael's Cathedral down, churches set aside specified areas for whites and blacks with the latter relegated to back rows or galleries.

Strong though these cultural institutions were in preserving the dominance of the white tradition over that of the folk while at the same time apparently accommodating a new, post-slavery social order, none were individually as powerful as cricket in creating *virtually without protest* a consensual Barbadian society. While the education system and the church might from time to time encounter criticisms for the reality of their discriminations as opposed to the illusion of their equality, cricket rarely if ever did, even though its practices were essentially more restrictive than those of the other agencies. While cricket apparently allowed the two cultures to meet in social unity, its organisational and participatory forms preserved the exclusiveness of those cultures more effectively and for longer than other institutions, and also maintained traditional hierarchies within the cultures. The consensual as opposed to the coercive manner in which this was achieved must be underlined because, as Ashis Nandy argues:

> Modern colonialism won its great victories not so much through its military and technological prowess as through its ability to create secular hierarchies incompatible with the traditional order. These hierarchies opened up new vistas for many, particularly for those exploited or cornered within the traditional order. To them the new order looked like – and here lay its psychological pull – the first step towards a more just and equal world.[18]

In Barbados, cricket constituted such a secular hierarchy as confirmed in two particular ways.

The first involves important theoretical literature which supports the significance of cricket as a Barbadian and Anglophone Caribbean cultural institution. In 1963 C.L.R. James emphasised the role of cricket and English literature in his personal development, arguing that the cultural code which they instilled made him quite different from his mainstream Marxist colleagues. Orlando Patterson later suggested that because of its connotations of a white colonial plantocracy and commercial domination, Caribbean people would never be 'free' until they rejected cricket. Subsequent commentators such as W.K. Marshall, St Pierre, T. Marshall and Thompson have developed aspects of this debate to explain the role of Caribbean cricket in the construction of colour relations, colonial class and postcolonial political evolution.[19] Throughout this writing runs the largely unstated themes of cultural domination, resistance and consensus. For that reason such analysis is further supported by the literature on social reproduction, cultural studies and social history derived largely from Gramsci. Briefly, work from analysts such as Gramsci, Bourdieu, Hall and Williams has confirmed the importance of cultural institutions in creating social consensus which often overrides the interests of the bulk of the community involved.[20] Cricket in Barbados was one such institution.

The second importance of cricket as a major influence in Barbadian cultural evolution centres upon the game's emergence in its modern form coinciding with the Barbadian ruling order's search for a moral authority. While the first recorded match occurred on the island early in the nineteenth century, regular games were being staged by the 1840s and Barbados played its first representative match, against British Guiana, in 1865. Given the particular needs of their political culture, the Barbadian ruling order then took up with enthusiasm that 'games revolution' which occurred in and was transported from Britain during the later nineteenth century.[21] Cricket gained a reputation as a game through which young people (men, mostly) might be trained for their social and occupational missions in life. Through games the middle and upper ruling classes learned respect for authority, loyalty, honesty, courage, persistence, teamwork and humility. The language of sport became a code, so that to 'play the game' meant not so much to be involved in simple physical activity as to subscribe to the social conventions and beliefs which sport symbolised. Manuals on all games were replete with advice on social etiquette and behaviour. Socialising institutions such as the public schools, universities and the established church embraced this sporting philosophy whose power underlay the life of Britain and its colonial empire by the last quarter of the nineteenth century.

It was this cultural modelling through cricket, specifically, which served as an important bridge between the two major Barbadian cultures where other institutions were not nearly so effective. Through cricket most Barbadians pledged their faith in a social system predicated upon British cultural values, British concepts of social progress, British morality codes, British behavioural standards and British attitudes towards social rankings. In so doing, Barbadians at large accepted the framework of social power elaborated by the dominant culture to replace that lost in 1838.[22] The transformation from slave-master to contract-master was acquiesced to by the former slaves become labour servants as were the social systems, cricket chief among them, which reproduced the patterns of inequality. For that reason, the structure of Barbadian cricket provides an important analytical starting point.

Given its small size and population, the island possesses an unusually elaborate cricket organisation strongly defined by its social heritage. The Barbados Cricket Association is the senior body, incorporated by a 1933 Act of Parliament as successor to the Barbados Cricket Committee which had been established in the early 1890s to organise local competition as well as control visiting teams.[23] Then there is the Barbados Cricket League, formed in 1936 to cater for the needs of the lower and working class black majority. Between them, these two associations now supervise in excess of 140 teams. In addition, however, there are modified cricket forms administered by such bodies as the Barbados National Softball Cricket Association and the Barbados Tapeball Cricket Association. Beyond these groups sectional bodies such as business houses, trade unions, local communities and groups of friends also organise matches on a regular competitive basis. At any given point in a competition season, there are probably in excess of 1,000 teams playing cricket on an island of 166 square miles where land is a scarce resource, a sure pointer to both the popularity and cultural importance of the game.

That popularity and importance is further revealed in the largely but not exclusively juvenile world of unstructured cricket found on beaches, waste lands, public parks and even on streets. This unstructured cricket has long provided the breeding ground for the island game and one interviewee recalled substantial sums of money resting upon the results of street matches played in one working-class village during the 1930s. That points to the necessity of qualifying the word 'unstructured' because such cricket, too, has had organised elements since the later nineteenth century as revealed in the persistence of 'firms' and 'marble' cricket.[24] In firms, a number of boys band together to control bat and ball at the expense of other players, thereby enhancing their opportunities to develop superior skills. Marble cricket is a miniature game designed to accommodate small playing areas with participants kneeling to bat, bowl and field. Beneath this elaborate, strong and deeply respected cricket structure lie the central concerns of a dominant culture which sought the widespread acceptance of its practices and objectives as a detailed analysis of that structure suggests.

The Barbados Cricket Committee was a self-appointed, self-constituted, self-selected and self-perpetuated group drawn from the most eminent sections of the late nineteenth century Barbadian elite. It was a cricketing extension of the economic and political oligarchy, and dominated particularly by wealthy merchants. As the plantations fell more and more into their hands from 1900 onwards, these merchants inherited the social mores of the plantocracy which had controlled the quest for moral authority and consensual cohesion to replace political coercion. The merchants on the Committee were joined in their beliefs by others of the elite whose fortunes, directly or indirectly, depended upon sugar: business executives, lawyers, accountants, medical practitioners, senior civil servants and elite school headmasters. A significant number of members remained with the BCC from its creation to its demise, a fact which emphasises the continuity of its cultural philosophy. Its colour remained as constant as its class – one or two mulattos appeared but it was otherwise overwhelmingly white.

By the early 1930s, however, the worldwide economic crisis had hit these sugar barons hard and many of them were unable to continue supporting cricket financially.[25] That led to the creation of a new administrative body, the Barbados Cricket Association, but not to new social attitudes because it has continued many Barbados Cricket Committee practices and traditions. Its Board of Management continues to be made up largely of business directors, company executives and managerial officers connected with trading conglomerates spawned from sugar industry concerns.[26] Service industry personnel such as lawyers and accountants are still prominent. There is still a high degree of personal continuity. In the more than 50 years since its foundation there have been just five Presidents, and one Secretary held his post from 1946 until well into the 1980s. Similarly, there have been just five Treasurers, and numerous examples of long committee service on the Board of Management. Besides their occupational backgrounds, the majority share an elite school and often post-secondary education, and high social status. This last point is complicated by being bound up in the changing colour structure of the Association.

Until at least 1966 the management was predominantly white, and only in recent years have blacks become numerous. In 1985, of the thirteen executive officers four were white including the President, Junior Vice-President and Secretary. This is a high proportion given the population balance between blacks and whites, emphasising both the continuity factor and the power of cricket as an agency of minority cultural dominance. While in the past the whites and non-whites would not have mixed outside Board circles, that is no longer entirely the case because non-white members are being drawn increasingly into the wider business managerial structure where they work along with and share many cultural values held by whites.[27] The colour composition of the Board might have changed, that is, but the inherent cultural attitudes continue to reflect those of the old Barbados Cricket Committee because the non-white members have consistently shared with the whites an occupational, educational and social background which has preserved many of the demarcations established between different social groups during the second half of the nineteenth century. The Association management, then, is a high status, homogeneous and largely static body in terms of its composition, even though it is theoretically subject to democratic processes within a general membership which now exceeds 1,100.

The Barbados Cricket League was founded in 1936, just after the Association, but enjoyed a far sketchier heritage than that provided by the old Barbados Cricket Committee. Some short-lived bodies organised cricket outside Committee auspices at various times beginning from 1902, but there was no continuous leadership or organisational structure.[28] The League's guiding principle was to provide regular competitive cricket for poor blacks whose colour and status ruled them socially ineligible for Association teams. As a result, the League is still perceived as the 'mass' cricket organisation in comparison with that of the 'elite' Association. That view is reinforced by most League teams (which far outnumber the 47 competing in the Association) having a strong country-village base unlike the Association whose teams are largely drawn from the Bridgetown city and suburban area. League administrators have come from more humble origins than their Association counterparts. J.M. (Mitchie) Hewitt, the founder, was a journalist come up from the ranks; a journalist colleague of similar background served as President, and artisans were prominent in management positions.[29] A recent change has seen the President come from a senior civil service position and a higher status educational background. The League shares continuity with the Association, however. Hewitt was Secretary from 1936 until his death in 1969, while his journalist colleague served a similarly long term. On the evidence of their management composition, then, the Association and the League have occupied quite different positions in the local status system and those differences have started to soften only recently.

From the cultural viewpoint, however, there has been a distinct similarity of objective between the two bodies: to have an increasing number of players accept the cricket code of behaviour and social ethics derived from Victorian England, first laid down by the Committee and later protected by the Association. Clearly, this acceptance involves the League not initiating its own code but inculcating its members into that promoted by the senior body. From its inception, the League has demonstrated a strong concern to match the playing and non-playing standards apparently reached in the Association. Individuals and teams have been consistently punished for breaches of discipline, violations of agreed ethical codes or 'unsportsmanlike' behaviour with the yardstick standards taken over from the Association.[30]

The objective has been to graduate players of lower status and caste ranking into the practices of a higher social order.

That point underlines the strong social ranking system which has dominated the evolution of Barbadian cricket, and emphasises that equality of participation has been based upon social recognition rather than playing attainments. League successes, such as having players selected for Barbados representative teams or having a League side accepted into the Association competition, have all been interpreted as evidence of social 'improvement' or acceptance rather than as recognition of simple playing ability.[31] But perhaps the strongest evidence for this social ranking and dominant cultural power within Barbadian cricket comes from the histories of its clubs.

Until 1939 there were four major long-term teams in the dominant Association competition: Wanderers, Pickwick, Spartan and Empire. Wanderers was founded in 1877 and until independence its members, playing and general, were drawn from plantation owners, major business house proprietors, very senior civil servants and people of otherwise high social status and independent wealth.[32] Until the late 1960s its playing membership was exclusively white, and it is still considerably white. Its general membership is still noticeably white leavened by mulattos and high status blacks, and it is now the main venue for the few white players seeking to play high class cricket. Pickwick was formed in 1882 and its membership has constantly differed from that of Wanderers, with the exception of its whiteness.[33] Business house wage staff, plantation and factory managerial or supervisorial personnel, commercial house employees such as insurance salesmen, and lower level civil servants have traditionally characterised the Pickwick membership. It was the mid-1970s before non-whites became a significant element in that membership, and the general perception of Pickwick still focuses upon its fiercely defended white heritage. One rival club supporter remarked acidly that a former Pickwick stalwart must be 'spinning in his grave' now that the first division side is largely made up of blacks.[34] Wanderers and Pickwick, then, were rival clubs within a numerically small white minority with the rivalry based on finely wrought class and status considerations. For example, one excellent Pickwick player of the inter-war period, a sugar factory manager, was once kept at work beyond the normal Saturday time by the owner of the factory who was a Wanderers supporter – the two normally had a good working relationship, but this was the occasion of a Wanderers versus Pickwick fixture.[35]

Spartan was formed in the early 1890s as the first non-white club and consisted mostly of lawyers, medical practitioners, elite schoolmasters, higher level civil servants and the few non-whites to have penetrated the managerial levels of the business, commercial and plantation worlds. Although not exclusively so, there was a significant mulatto element in Spartan.[36] Symbolically, its foundation President was a mulatto who became Barbados's first and only non-white Chief Justice until the second half of the twentieth century. Many Spartan members were involved in pre-1937 political life, and almost without exception were found in conservative rather than radical camps. Sir Grantley Adams, as he became, was a most interesting example.[37] Like C.L.R. James, Adams imbibed English cricket and culture from his schoolmaster father. He attended Harrison College and Oxford University, then became a lawyer, as well as a good enough cricketer to represent Barbados in 1924. During the 1920s he was a public critic of the fledgling radical movement, opposing its socialist tendencies. It was well into the 1930s before he moved towards a more mass-based political position, symbolised by the lending of his name to the low status Barbados Cricket League at its formation.[38] Adams became the first Chief Minister of Barbados, then Prime Minister of the short-lived West Indies Federation. He never lost his admiration for English cricket or English culture, or for Spartan and its membership which became increasingly influential in political, economic and social spheres.[39] Spartan maintained a jealous watch over that membership, a concern which led directly to the creation of Empire in 1914.

Herman Griffith, a lower middle class black player of outstanding ability was consistently denied membership in Spartan, some of whose members with minimum status (they included a minor businessman and a professional musician) subsequently seceded to form Empire in protest.[40] Griffith established an excellent inter-colonial and international career, and built around him at Empire a tightly knit group of similarly lower middle class players. It was said that Empire men were either sanitary inspectors or elementary schoolmasters, but self-employed businessmen, minor civil servants and shop clerks were also prevalent. Like Spartan, Empire has never had a white player and few if any amongst its general membership. While the lines of social demarcation between the two clubs have blurred somewhat, members of both date that from the mid-1970s at the earliest and even now there is a sense of Spartan being drawn more from the black managerial than from lower status groups.

Several points are worth making about the social ranking of these clubs and on their relationship with ruling cultural practices. Their strong and lengthy maintenance of exclusiveness is striking. The community at large was theoretically moving towards more open social interaction from the 1890s to the 1970s through the creation of popular political parties, a widening franchise, an extension of the education system, legislation against racial discrimination and reform in landholding patterns to name just some. But these cricket clubs have been instrumental in preserving conservative and dominant patterns of caste relationships consolidated during the second half of the nineteenth century until well into the second half of the twentieth century. This was achieved largely by a high continuity of membership type, as five-yearly profiles drawn up for the clubs suggest – by 1965 they retained essentially the same types of people as they had in the 1890s.[41] That continuity was itself maintained through an oversupply of players being constantly available for a restricted number of places. Even where they fielded teams in all three Association competitive levels following World War Two, these clubs catered for a very small percentage of the cricket-playing male population so that admission policies could maintain strict social criteria as well as playing ability. The most notable relaxation has been in the colour coding, not the least because of substantial alterations to white demographics since 1966 – total numbers have fallen steadily while the cricket-playing age brackets have been undermined further by either permanent or long-term temporary emigration for educational and/or occupational reasons.

Another important element in this exclusiveness was its self-imposed or, at least, non-contested nature. None of the clubs had any rules or constitutional provisions which specified the socially acceptable dimensions of their membership. [42] Former players recall that they 'knew' which club to join; it was a tacitly accepted conventional wisdom based upon rigid social categorisation.[43] Moreover, there was a recognised feeder system for these clubs. Whites and blacks might play together while at Harrison College, but upon leaving school they would 'find' themselves at Wanderers and Spartan respectively. Whites from The Lodge went to Pickwick more frequently than Wanderers, while blacks and whites from Combermere (with its commercial educational orientation) gravitated to Empire and Pickwick. Exceptions generally proved the rule. One player recalled that in the early 1930s he was among the first Harrison College products to join Empire, largely because he was a 'poor black boy' whose education resulted from a scholarship rather than from established family wealth or status. And the first black to join Wanderers in modern times (in the late 1960s) was an ex-Lodge man with an outstanding academic and athletic record as well as a respectable social background, and who went on to hold very high civil service positions. Clearly, the sociology of popular knowledge combined with careful club selection policies to maintain traditions of social differentiation until well into the post-independence period.

This rigid and persistent classification extended into all other clubs which joined the Barbados Cricket Association after 1914, and especially to the Barbados Cricket League whose membership from the outset ranged from agricultural labourers to skilled artisans and all the occupational categories between. The most obvious evidence of the low status accorded to these players concerns those who attempted to shift from League teams into the Association. Almost the only possible team available for such transfer was Empire and it guarded its ranks jealously. It might have been a black club with an underprivileged reputation but it was by no means 'poor black', so the working classes faced considerable difficulties in trying to enter Empire. One story has an Empire official altering an applicant's stated occupation from 'Ice Company employee' to 'ice vendor' – the status connotations in the change are both obvious and important. A League fast-bowling star of the World War Two period recalls that he attempted to join Empire in order to improve his cricket prospects, and was shattered to have his request denied on the grounds that he was a lowly 'messenger' for a small business and therefore socially unsuitable for the club.

Some very successful players did move from the League into the Association as early as the 1940s but they had to be exceptionally successful, show potential for adopting dominant cultural standards and be fortunate enough to strike the right circumstances. But it was really into the 1970s before such players began to move in numbers and with relative ease. That change coincided with the admission of whole League teams into the Association competition with one, St Catherine, now in First Division, and a number of others dominating lower grades. This is probably the beginning of a real change in the traditionally rigid status divisions but, even so, incoming clubs are vetted carefully for their off-field behaviour and their initial performances in that regard are monitored closely. Such clubs are still socially 'on trial' because they are perceived to differ substantially from those which have traditionally appeared in the Association. This attitude is firmly grounded in both a belief and an acceptance that quite complex social differences and venues exist within Barbados, facilitated by cultural institutions such as cricket clubs.

It is important to remember that from the immediate post-emancipation period onwards, these infinitely graded social divisions continued to be preserved in Barbados not so much by law as by social practice, as in the cricket case. From Schomburgk onwards, visitors to Barbados inevitably referred to the existence there of a greater degree of colour consciousness and discrimination than found elsewhere in the Anglophone Caribbean. Complex and closely defined social levels were codified and accepted upon the twin, intersecting indicators of class and colour. Trollope reported that non-whites were never met in Barbadian 'society', Chester thought Barbadian whites still maintained a 'strong feeling in favour of slavery'. McLellan confirmed the existence of numerous divisions based upon colour and class. Macmillan considered Barbados the most socially exclusive and conscious of the Caribbean territories. Fermor reported the existence of considerable colour prejudice. Swanton and Blackburne remarked similarly on the noticeable social distances observed in Barbados.[44] Local writers were not so prolific on the theme; many of them were more keen to accommodate the cultural elite. But the few who did comment were extremely critical as revealed in Bernard, Wickham and Harewood.[45] The consistency of these reports indicates the deep implantation in Barbadian life of ideas about social relations based upon the cultural precepts of the minority cultural elite, and mediated by institutions such as cricket.

In the century from 1870 these deepseated and rigid views were consolidated by the intersection of economic pressure and political conservatism through which the minority elite attempted to maintain its dominant position. The sugar industry experienced some 'highs' as in the World War One boom when European beet supplies were disrupted, in the early 1930s when British imperial preference systems boosted prices, and during the 1960s when world prices reached high levels.[46] For the most part, however, the industry faced depression as in the 1890s when a British Royal Commission was necessitated, during the 1920s when a world glut forced prices very low, and the 1970s when began a steady decline after a promising beginning.[47] In response to this pattern the Barbadian sugar aristocracy, from 1900 a coalition of the most successful and surviving members of the plantocracy together with the new businessmen planters, was moved reluctantly into changes in production systems, financing arrangements, labour relations and so-called peasant landholding patterns.[48] One major result was that living conditions for the black majority declined to such a point that by the outbreak of labour and political disturbances in 1937 they were among the worst in the region if not the Empire.[49] The long-term ruling elite held the ring through its control over the Legislative Assembly and the Executive Council, bodies whose power was untouched until the introduction of limited popular government in 1944, followed by the introduction of ministerial government in 1954, then independence in 1966.[50]

During this long period of economic and political change, cultural institutions such as formalised cricket vigorously maintained those patterns of social relationships, based upon class and colour considerations, which had been elaborated during the post-emancipation moral authority quest in order to maintain the social power of a cultural minority. As the cricket case demonstrates, cultural organisations maintained until well into the post-independence period quite elaborate systems of social discrimination which would have been unacceptable in government, civil service and commercial sectors. In 1900, for example, the Trinidad-born and Harrison-educated English cricket boss Pelham Warner argued that Caribbean cricket standards would not improve until non-whites participated without restriction. Yet as late as 1970 the Barbadian international player Charlie Griffith could still point to a high degree of colour and class prejudice in the organisation of Barbadian cricket.[51] During the intervening 70 years players and spectators alike had accepted the social parameters of cricket and few challenged them. It may be argued, then, that the process of social change generally was modified by the conservative construction of voluntary institutions such as cricket. As Herman Griffith is alleged to have remarked, 'if it had not been for cricket we would have been at each others' throats.[52]

While the sharpness of the divisions has now been blunted, the underlying attitudes are still extant. Wanderers members suggest that it took a long time to introduce non-whites to the club because of the need to preserve an atmosphere where 'talk' might be free and 'families' could be brought, so newcomers had to be vetted carefully.[53] At Kensington Oval in 1985 a match between two nonwhite teams, one representing Pickwick, saw players drift away quickly at the close of play so that in the bar just one or two non-whites mixed with perhaps thirty whites who were mostly Pickwick Club members. Changes have occurred but will take time to consolidate and some perceptions of the changes are guarded – one former international player believes that non-white players admitted to formerly all-white clubs have no voting rights.[54] There is some substance to his claim. Permeating this exclusivity and its modern residual remains is the widespread belief in all quarters that the other parties prefer it that way, whites with whites and blacks with blacks, itself a firm pointer to the power of the dual culture and of cricket as the carefully controlled bridge.

One guide to this fundamental but masked conflict lies in the history of traditional club rivalries. At first the highlight of any season was always Wanderers versus Pickwick, especially up until 1914 when Committee officials organising fixtures would pit those teams against each other on public holidays in order to give as many people as possible a chance to observe the great clash.[55] Early crowd data are unreliable but 8–10,000 spectators were not unusual, and many who attended wore appropriate colours to identify the team of their allegiance.[56] From these matches, Pickwick particularly gained a reputation for being relentless, determined opponents, and there was always a class-based edge to the clashes, the comfortable versus the non-quite-so-comfortable. Allegiance to a team was invariably for the entirety of a player's career because of that class consideration. Just before World War One it was reckoned a sensational moment when a former Wanderers player turned out for Pickwick against his old club.[57] It was not so much a desertion of a team as of a caste group. Although the championship significance of Wanderers versus Pickwick matches declined after 1920 and public interest declined as well, teams themselves still approached the fixtures as of old. During one match in the 1960s, for example, Pickwick players changed in their cars, refusing to enter the Wanderers' pavilion alleging that a female Wanderers supporter had spat upon a Pickwick player during the first day of the match.[58] With the increasing non-white composition of both teams the hard edge is disappearing rapidly but the spirit is remembered.

From 1915 onwards the great clash was always between Spartan and Empire, partly because of the controversial origins of Empire, partly because of the subtle colour shadings, partly because of perceived class differences and partly because of the marvellous players involved (at any point between the 1920s and the 1960s one of these matches might have seen two, three or even more international players on each of the teams). One Empire player of the early 1930s recalls the roar from his team's supporters when he went out to bat, and his silent prayer: 'Lord, let me not disappoint these people today'. Another Empire player who began early in the 1940s remembers being stopped in the streets weeks before a match against Spartan and being 'advised' by groups of well-wishers. Players of both clubs remember this spirit existing into the 1970s and even now, although club distinctions have blurred, there is still an 'atmosphere' to an Empire-Spartan match.[59]

Two points are important about this rivalry in relation to the creation of a shared culture via cricket which, in turn, had considerable significance for social relations on the island. First, the meeting of these clubs in the annual rituals of their matches helped create a general belief in the essential openness of the society; cricket, that is, provided an apparent avenue for the meeting of different colour and class groups. Pickwick, for example, had a tradition that visiting players always had their after-match drinks paid for by the club. Empire players of the inter-war years recall that at Wanderers they were always assigned to a home player after the match and looked after, even to the point of being driven home by the wealthier white players.[60] All this, of course, was a momentary suspension of the island's normal caste conditions, but one which was widely subscribed to as an indication of what people considered might be the normal Barbadian position. Second, the crowds at all these matches were overwhelmingly black, and blacks were the most avid supporters of Wanderers and Pickwick. By supporting these quite different class and colour groups, Bajans again were demonstrating support for the ideals of cricket and culture as established during the nineteenth century by the creators of the moral authority system.

This pattern has continued since the late 1960s in the form of a representative team from the Barbados Cricket League playing in the Barbados Cricket Association competition. The arrangement replaced an annual match instituted in the late 1940s between representative teams of the two competitions. Given the League's history it is not surprising that matches between its teams and those from the Association have had a fierce competitive spirit. One longtime League member recalls Mitchie Hewitt being criticised by a black Association member for attempting to give regular cricket to 'ill-behaved, ignorant working men'.[61] Matches against white teams were strongly contested, but those against the socially exclusive Spartan club were high points for the League and to a degree remain so. The rivalry, as with that between other major clubs is rooted very strongly in the evolution of the island's specific social relations system. League teams have a highly developed social image as having 'come from the people', and an equally developed sense of other teams having been drawn from more privileged sections of the society. It is from the history of such social rankings that emerge two other important aspects of Barbadian cricket.

One concerns the cricketer as popular hero, with the patterns of adulation charting the slow changes in Barbadian cricket. In early days the heroes were drawn from the elite white culture with the bulk of their support coming from the black majority. During the 1890s the Pickwick giant, Clifford Goodman, was idolised whether helping his club beat Wanderers or Barbados defeat visiting teams.[62] From before World War One until the 1930s George Challenor of Wanderers, Barbados and West Indies was feted as one of the best batsmen in the world.[63] Both Goodman and Challenor symbolised the power of the dominant cultural elite. Goodman came from a plantation managerial background and, of his famous cricketing brothers, P. A. Goodman became a secondary school headmaster renowned for discipline, and G.A. Goodman became Chief Justice in the Straits Settlement following a local political career. George Challenor came from a leading merchant family and, with his brother and fellow Barbados player, became a leading businessman planter. Challenor demonstrated this social position in classic English cricket cultural style. At practice he would place money on one of the three stumps and challenge net bowlers to claim it by bowling him. On the occasions when five dollars were put up, bowlers came from everywhere in the vicinity of the Wanderers ground.[64]

It is worth recalling that the very grounds themselves, such as Wanderers, reinforced the social hierarchies elaborated among the players, their spectators and the public at large. Playing areas were invariably donated by plantation owners and, in the League especially, this established a strong patron–client relationship between those owners and the cricketers, many of whom were often employed on the estates from which the grounds were carved. Even now, many of the smaller country grounds are overlooked by plantation houses. The strength of the subsequently created loyalties to team, plantation and patron were demonstrated graphically at

Wanderers and Pickwick. Their strongest black supporters came from the ten-antries of the old Bay and Kensington estates, respectively, and well into the 1940s those tenantries were among the worst slums in Barbados, underlining the ability of shared cultural values to override patently obvious social and economic inequal-ities.

Black cricket heroes began to emerge from the time of Herman Griffith whose Empire connections provided opportunities for a caste affiliation to parallel the loy-alties to localities developed within the ranks of common supporters. What the black heroes did in an important sense, however, was to justify the underlying social phi-losophy of cricket. By following its precepts they were thought to have 'improved' and 'succeeded', to have 'risen' from the mass. That is, they not so much symbol-ised a challenge to the dominant cultural elite as constituted a justification for that elite's ideology – many of the new stars were seen, significantly, not just as 'good' players but as 'good' blacks who had learned their social lessons. Many potential black stars failed to make the grade because of social rather than playing misde-meanours.[65] In this 'success' story pattern two of the most significant players have been Everton Weekes and Gary Sobers whose representative careers began in the early 1940s and early 1950s respectively.[66] Both came from poor, underprivileged backgrounds, Weekes from the New Orleans tenantry near Kensington Oval and Sobers from the Bay land adjoining the Wanderers ground. Both acquired their skills in 'gully', school and knockabout cricket, both frequented local Association club grounds where their talents were recognised by influential members. Both played for League clubs when very young, and both were 'drafted' into socially appropriate Association teams where places were made available: Weekes was helped to join the army which had an Association team for a short while; Sobers joined the Police as a band recruit. Only their exceptional talents made this Association entry possible, and both had patronage from influential Association men. Their very rise indicates just how rigidly prescribed the system was. By their cricket talents they then made their ways in the world as professional players, and cricket has continued to ensure their upward mobility.

It is difficult to convey adequately the awe in which these men have been held by the Barbadian public. Weekes retired in the mid-1960s, Sobers in the early 1970s, yet their stature grows rather than diminishes. Sobers received a knighthood from the Queen in 1975, an achievement interpreted as the ultimate sign of ability making all things possible in an 'open' society. Men in rum shops, at cricket grounds and other gathering places refer to 'Everton' and 'Gary' as if they were personal friends which, in one sense, they are. The Sobers story was thinly veiled in a mid-1970s fes-tival play, and he has been mentioned as a Barbadian cultural icon in a number of popular calypsos, a sure sign of social significance.[67] These men remain mass heroes even though the lifestyle and status of both is vastly removed from their humble origins. But despite the fierce pride in their achievements, their stories are consid-ered not so much a comment on the exclusivity barriers which they had to over-come, as an indication that through cricket in Barbados anything is possible provided the right lessons are learned. While they might recall how difficult things were, Weekes and Sobers are generally philosophical and harbour few if any grudges against a social structure which determined that, in the opinion of one of them, they had to be three times better than the average white player in order to be selected.

The widespread acceptance of this cultural consensus shows up best in the cases of players who did not conform, perhaps the best example being the late Sir Frank Worrell.[68] Born in Barbados he was a cricket prodigy playing for Combermere in senior competition at the age of twelve and attracting big crowds. Before he was twenty he had established world records and later became an international star; he was the first regular black captain of West Indies, and won a knighthood before his tragically premature death from leukemia. Although hailed, Worrell was never loved uncritically by Barbadians, largely because of his outspokenness about his dissatisfaction with cricket's social structuring and its relationship with the wider cultural pattern. He made no secret of his irritation with Barbadian exclusivity and prejudice and, after a stint in Trinidad, ended up in Jamaica. Shortly before his death he criticised Barbados for trying to demonstrate its regional superiority by organising the match against the Rest of the World XI, and his burial on the Cave Hill campus of the University of the West Indies in Barbados was not without controversy.[69] During 1985 one interviewee, a white woman, remarked acidly that Worrell should not have been buried on the island because he did not love it or accept its ways.[70] Hero status was, and to some extent still is, accorded only to those who accept without question the internal ranking scale which from the outset has marked Barbadian cricket and its consensus cultural context.

The second aspect, in addition to the role of heroes, which highlights the social depth and complexity of Barbadian cricket concerns crowd behaviour which is most instructively examined through its prominent personalities of whom three are especially important here: Britannia Bill, Flannigan and King Dyal. The three cover the history of organised cricket in the island. Brittania Bill became famous late in the nineteenth century as a black supporter of English touring teams who followed their players everywhere, carrying a Union Jack to pronounce his great loyalty.[71] His message was that England carried all before it, and that its cricket players were the epitome of civilized, gentlemanly demeanour and to whose monarch, Queen Victoria, he had pledged undying loyalty. Right up until World War One, visiting teams were astonished by the warmth of the welcome extended by the black majority, often to the point of being embarrassed by it.[72] While this loyalty was in line with a widespread allegiance to the monarchy and especially to Queen Victoria, in cricket it found its most popular expression. In particular, such allegiance sprang from a perceived shared bond with the Barbadian elite of the nineteenth century which established loyalty to both the monarchy and cricket after emancipation in 1838 (which symbolically, of course, matched Victoria's accession). The black Barbadian majority genuinely believed that obedience to the British cultural model, of which cricket was such a focal feature, was the means by which they would progress.

Fred Flannigan dominated the inter-war period and epitomised the idolising of white stars by black men.[73] Flannigan himself was a player of ability who earned a living, as did many lower class players, by providing practice to members of the Association clubs. In Flannigan's case it was Wanderers for whom he became an ardent supporter, and his idol was George Challenor. One of Flannigan's most famous remarks came during an inter-colonial match when a black fielder kneeled to tie a shoelace for Challenor who was batting. 'That's right', shouted Flannigan to the fielder, 'on your knees before the Lord thy God, George Challenor!'[74] It was a graphic and symbolic representation of Barbadian social relations. Challenor, in fact, paid a retainer to Flannigan who became a mascot for the Barbados team when it travelled, and Challenor was always hailed as the living symbol of what cricket and Barbados stood for. There was no equality in that cricket system, rather there was a very carefully defined sense of social ranking and distance recognised by all those who were part of it, both carried over from and reinforcing relationships in the community at large.

Dundonald Redvers Dyal, better known as the self-proclaimed 'King' Dyal, came of age in the Flannigan era and is a strong pointer to the role of cricket in linking the folk and dominant cultures.[75] The son of a master tailor, Dyal is a flamboyant character who dresses extravagantly in a society where clothing is generally conservative. During a 1985 test match he appeared in two suits within two hours, one bright lime green and the other bright red, both with matching accessories including appropriately coloured pipes and walking sticks. King Dyal's 'subjects', especially during major matches, are the patrons in the public stands drawn from the masses. But his decrees proceed from a dedication to English cricket culture and tradition, to the precepts laid down by the organisers of the Committee and their Association successors and drawn up upon the needs of the minority elite culture. King Dyal is fiercely loyal to the illusion of cricket as an apolitical social agency, thereby demonstrating its very power to mask the inequalities and prejudices which would be criticised if they appeared in any other social venue.

Britannia Bill, Flannigan and King Dyal represent more than just a passionate devotion to cricket as a game. Their allegiance is based upon an acceptance of the cultural context in which the Barbadian game evolved. Following the Victorian games model, cricket was 'emblematic', as older references have it, of life and social relations.[76] Any recognisable decline in cricket standards, therefore, has ramifications for wider social concerns. This concern is particularly noticeable in the contemporary 'hailers', the major supporters and constant followers of the important clubs. An excellent example occurred during 1985 after a team in a match-winning position failed to enforce victory. A younger player had batted for a long time, unable to adapt to the match circumstances. 'If you had known something about life,' advised the chief hailer in the clubhouse later, 'if you had some experience, you would have known what to do. Understand what I mean? You have to learn experience.' A few weeks earlier the same hailer observed that men who appeared in court with such folk culture nicknames as 'Tall Boy' and 'Roughhouse' were never found in cricket because cricketers knew how to behave.[77] This, too, is the direct cultural heritage of that public school cricket code adumbrated in late nineteenth-century Britain and transplanted so successfully in Barbados where its moral principles are shared by two quite different cultural traditions.

One logical extension to this ethical and behavioural code concerns discipline both on and off the field. During 1985 there was considerable public debate about the origins of a perceived decline in Barbadian cricket standards, and many critics returned to some central points: younger players were not learning discipline, especially in the schools, and club life had degenerated as a consequence.[78] Cricket clubs in Barbados are important male social centres (a further reminder of the social centrality of cricket) where at most times of the week may be found members playing cards, dominos, darts, backgammon or table tennis, discussing cricket, other sport or current affairs, drinking or organising social activities. This process has a long history and there is a concern in many quarters for a continued high standard of social conduct. Following one relatively insignificant after-match skirmish, two senior players of one club were suspended for the bulk of the 1985 season. They were allowed into the clubhouse but their suspension from playing was deliberately severe, according to some officials, in order to curb a decline in discipline: 'Fellows have to learn how to behave in public'.[79] Earlier in the season a promising young player was criticised severely for an open display of anger after being given out in a dubious umpiring decision. The decision might have been poor, said his critics, but as in life he must learn to take the hard knocks as well as to accept decisions made by those in authority.[80]

This deep, symbolic strain permeates Barbadian cricket crowds which are recognised as amongst the most knowledgeable in the world. That helps explain two of their most noticeable characteristics. The first is a pronounced social conservatism which has given the island a far better record of crowd behaviour than most of its Caribbean counterparts. This conservatism was displayed during a 1985 test match incident in which a New Zealand player on the field lowered his trousers to treat a leg injury. A now acceptable practice elsewhere in the cricket world, this act created an air of shock in Barbados. An off-duty police inspector in the members' stand seriously suggested that the player be charged with an indictable offence. The touring team's management was required to issue a public apology for what in Barbados was widely considered as a breach of the cricket/life morality code.[81]

The second important characteristic is the utter seriousness with which spectators approach the game, almost sharing in the action itself as they urge, encourage and almost will the players to better performances. At the heart of this activity is a desire to have observed and see performed the tacitly accepted conventions and traditions of play. Those players who do so are treated with respect, those who do not receive contempt. During the 1985 test match, for example, one spectator kept repeating to the New Zealand captain, 'Howarth, you can't bowl to Vivvy [Vivian Richards] without a sweeper'. When Richards proved the point by hitting yet another boundary the spectator held out his hands as if to say 'what more can I do?' and his neighbours all agreed.[82] The New Zealand captain had ignored a basic cricket concept and so was deemed unworthy of further assistance. In club matches it is not uncommon to see fielding captains adjusting their positionings in accordance with spectator advice such as 'give me a square leg'. When such adjustments are made, batsmen are then told to 'watch that man at square leg'. Spectators and players alike are involved in a joint process through which cricket and its attendant social symbolism proceed by way of a shared set of behavioural and moral principles which themselves have deep social significance more widely.

Cricket, then, has deeply influenced the shape and character of Barbadian life since the last quarter of the nineteenth century. Far from being a mirror image of community development, the game has been a major determinant of the unique cultural relationships established in Barbados between the descendants of a minority, dominant group and a mass, subordinate community whose potential for conflict has been considerable.[83] It is not simply that cricket has provided a 'safety valve'. Rather, in Barbados the game has provided on-going connections between two quite different cultural traditions through carefully regulated social meeting points, helping to reduce areas of potential conflict. At the same time, cricket has preserved well into the twentieth century a set of social relationships established during the mid-nineteenth century and which in other arenas of social life would be considered inappropriate. In cricket Barbados has one of its most conservative social and political institutions, a perfect example of the power of culture in the face of general social, economic and political change.

NOTES

The author wishes to thank the Canberra College of Advanced Education for making available the leave around which the research project was based, the University of the West Indies (Cave Hill) which elected him as Visiting Fellow in History for 1985, and all those people in Barbados who assisted the research.

1 For the Barbados story: R. H Schomburgk, *The History of Barbados* (London: Longman, 1847); Otis P. Starkey, *The Economic Geography of Barbados: a Study of the Relationships between Environmental and Economic Development* (New York: Columbia University Press, 1939); George Hunte, *Barbados* (London: Batsford, 1974), F.A. Hoyos, *Barbados: a History from the Amerindians to Independence* (London: Heinemann, 1978); Claude Levy, *Emancipation, Sugar and Federalism: Barbados and the West Indies, 1833–1876* (Gainesville: University of Florida Press, 1980); Hilary Beckles, *Black Rebellion in Barbados: the Struggle Against Slavery, 1627–1838* (Bridgetown: Antilles, 1984).

2 Bruce Hamilton, *Cricket in Barbados* (Bridgetown: Advocate 1947) describes the growth of cricket on the island. For an analysis of the early period, see Brian Stoddart, 'Cricket and Colonialism in the English-Speaking Caribbean before 1914: Towards a Cultural Analysis', in J.A. Mangan (ed.), *Pleasure, Profit and Proselytism: British Culture and Sport at Home and Abroad, 1750–1914* (London: Cass, 1987).

3 Richard Cashman, *Patrons, Players and the Crowd: the Phenomenon of Indian Cricket* (Bombay: Orient Longman, 1980).

4   The method here attempts to meet some of the points made by Bernard S. Cohn, 'History and Anthropology: the State of Play', *Comparative Studies in Society and History* 22 (April 1980): 198–221. Also Clifford Geertz, 'Blurred Genres' in his *Local Knowledge* (New York: Basic Books, 1983).

5   Richard Allsopp, *The Question of Barbadian Culture* (Bridgetown: Bajan, 1972); *Advocate*, 16 September 1985.

6   For an example, see the pamphlet *The High Cost of Living* (Bridgetown: National United Movement, 1981). A long-term view is in B.M. Taylor, 'Black Labor and White Power in Post-Emancipation Barbados: a Study of Changing Relationships', *Current Bibliography on African Affairs*, 6 (Spring 1973), 183–97.

7   For some general insights into the analytical possibilities here, see Peter J. Wilson, *Crab Antics: the Social Anthropology of English-Speaking Negro Societies of the Caribbean* (New Haven: Yale University Press, 1973); Paget Henry and Carl Stone (eds), *The Newer Caribbean: Decolonisation, Democracy and Development* (Philadelphia: Institute for the Study of Human Institutions, 1983); Audrey E. Burrowes, 'African Survivals: Aspects of African Continuity in Barbadian Culture' (Cave Hill: Caribbean Studies Papers, 1979). One very interesting view is that in Jack Berthelot and Martin Gaume, *Caribbean Popular Dwellings* (Guadeloup: Editions Perspectives Creoles, 1982), pp. 9–10.

8   Joseph Sturge and Thomas Harvey, *The West Indies in 1837* (London: Cass, 1968 edn), pp. 130–1.

9   Specifically, see J.E. Reece and G.G. Clark-Hunt (eds), *Barbados Diocesan History: in Commemoration of the First Centenary of the Diocese, 1825–1925* (London: West India Committee, 1925), ch. XIX; Jerome S. Handler and Arnold Sio, 'Barbados', in David W. Cohen and Jack P. Greene (eds), *Neither Slave Nor Free: the Freedmen of African Descent in the Slave Societies of the New World* (Baltimore: Johns Hopkins University Press, 1972), p. 253; Sir Harry Johnston, *The Negro in the New World* (1910; rep., New York: Johnson, 1969), p. 225. For the wider story, Hesketh J. Bell, *Obeah-Witchcraft in the West Indies* (1899; rep., Westport: Negro Universities Press, 1970). For an indication of the persistence of obeah, *Advocate*, 9 July 1935, p. 10.

10 For example, 'An Act for the Suppression and Punishment of Vagrancy', *Laws of Barbados*, No. 129, 7 January 1840.

11 For example, 'An Act to Establish a Police in Bridge-Town and the Parish of St Michael', *Laws of Barbados*, No. 78, 24 July 1834; 'An Act to Provide for the Building of Houses of Correction, and Police Establishments', *Laws of Barbados*, No. 87, 14 September 1835; 'An Act to Increase the Number and Efficiency of the Mounted Militia of This Island', *Laws of Barbados*, No. 105, 25 October 1837; 'An Act for the Better Care and Protection of Lunatics', *Laws of Barbados*, No. 522, 24 August 1872.

12 For example, 'An Act to Regulate the Trade and Business of Butchers, and to Check and Prevent As Much As Possible the Stealing of Stock', *Laws of Barbados*, No. 96, 23 November 1836; 'An Act to Consolidate and Amend the Several Laws of This Island Relating to the Market of Bridgetown', *Laws of Barbados*, No. 199, 20 November 1848; 'An Act to Provide a Summary Remedy for the Prevention of Persons Holding Markets in the City of Bridgetown', *Laws of Barbados*, No. 395, 11 September 1863.

13 Charles Pitcher Clarke, *The Constitutional Crisis of 1876 in Barbados* (Bridgetown: Herald, 1896); Bruce Hamilton, *Barbados and the Confederation Question, 1871–1885* (London: HMSO, 1956); George A.V. Belle, 'The Abortive Revolution of 1876 in Barbados', *Journal of Caribbean History* 18 (1984): 1, 34.

81

14 *Barbados Herald*, 4 and 11 April 1895; *Barbados Agricultural Reporter*, 12 April 1895, 9 and 16 July 1895.
15 The role of cricket in this area may be followed in Keith Sandiford and Brian Stoddart, 'Cricket and the Elite Schools in Barbados: a Case Study in Colonial Continuity', *International Journal of the History of Sport*, 4 (December 1987).
16 *Barbados Blue Book*, 1900 (Bridgetown: Government of Barbados, 1900), educational statistics.
17 The best guide here is Kortright Davis, *Cross and Crown in Barbados: Caribbean Political Religion in the Late Nineteenth Century* (Frankfurt: Lang, 1983). For a specific example, *Barbados Times*, 25 June 1870.
18 Ashis Nandy, *The Intimate Enemy: the Loss and Recovery of Self Under Colonialism* (Delhi: Oxford University Press, 1983), p. ix.
19 C.L.R. James, *Beyond a Boundary* (London: Hutchinson, 1963). For some thoughts, see Helen Tiffen, 'Cricket. Literature and the Politics of De-Colonisation: the Case of C.L.R. James', in R. Cashman and M. McKernan (eds), *Sport: Money, Morality and the Media* (Sydney: University of NSW Press, 1981); Orlando Patterson, 'The Ritual of Cricket', *Jamaica Journal*, 3 (March 1969), 23–5; W.K. Marshall, 'Gary Sobers and the Brisbane Revolution', *New World Quarterly*, 2 (1965): 35–42; Maurice St Pierre, 'West Indian Cricket', Parts I and 11, *Caribbean Quarterly*, 19 (June and September, 1973), 7–27 and 20–35; T. Marshall, 'Race, Class and Cricket in Barbadian Society, 1800–1970', *Manjak*, 11 November 1973: L. O'B. Thompson, 'How Cricket is West Indian Cricket?: Class, Racial and Colour Conflict', *Caribbean Review*, 12 (1983), 22–9.
20 Antonio Gramsci, *The Modern Prince and Other Writings*, trans. Louis Marks (New York: International, 1975); Joseph V. Femia, *Gramsci's Political Thought: Hegemony Consciousness and the Revolutionary Process* (Oxford: OUP, 1981); Pierre Bourdieu, 'Sport and Social Class', *Social Science Information*, 17 (1978): 819–40; Stuart Hall, 'Cultural Studies: Two Paradigms', *Media, Culture and Society*, 2 (January 1980), 52–72; Raymond Williams, *Problems in Materialism and Culture* (London: New Left Books, 1980). For some considerations, T.J. Jackson Lears, 'The Concept of Cultural Hegemony: Problems and Possibilities', *American Historical Review*, 90 (June 1985): 567–93; and M. Gottdiener, 'Hegemony and Mass Culture: a Semiotic Approach', *American Journal of Sociology*, 90 (March 1985), 979–1001. A stimulating view on sport is S.J. Parry, 'Hegemony and Sport', *Journal of the Philosophy of Sport*, 10 (1984), 71–83.
21 On this general point see J.A. Mangan, *Athleticism in the Victorian and Edwardian Public School: the Emergence and Consolidation of an Education Ideology* (Cambridge: Cambridge University Press, 1981) and also his *The Games Ethic and Imperialism* (London: Viking, 1986).
22 For the period, see Levy, *Emancipation, Sugar and Federalism*. For an interesting analysis of developments during that time, see Governor Robinson to Secretary of State for the Colonies, Confidential, 27 September 1881, COL 211126, Barbados Archives.
23 This section based on J. Wynfred Gibbons (ed.), *Barbados Cricketers' Annual* (Bridgetown: Globe), issues from 1894–95 to 1913–14; *Advocate*, 27 October 1925, p. 5 and 28 November 1931, p. 12; Act of Barbados, No. 12 of 1933, 22 December 1933.
24 For one account of 'firms' about the turn of the century see Frank Collymore's piece in *Combermerian*, 1973–4, p. 15.
25 For BCC economic difficulties, *Advocate*, 5 February 1929, p. 8 and 7 July 1932, p. 8.
26 Based on interview material.

27 See BCA, *Report and Statement of Accounts, 1 April 1984–31 March 1985* (Bridgetown: Letchworth, 1985) for the recent membership, analysis based on interview material.

28 See the foundation committee for the Frame Food Challenge Cup Series in *Barbados Cricketers' Annual* 1902–3 (Bridgetown: Globe, 1903), p. 186. For the extent of later Bank Holiday cricket, *Advocate*, 2 August 1932, p. 20. J.M. Hewitt, *The Annual Barbados League Cricketer* (Bridgetown: Cole's, 1952) indicates some of the early BCL activity. Louis Lynch, *The Barbados Book* (London: Andre Deutsch, 1972 edn), pp. 166–74 conveys the flavour of a 'country' match.

29 For Hewitt, see *Advocate*, 3 March 1969, p. 1; interview material.

30 In 1955, for example, one player was suspended for five years after removing the stumps in protest at an umpiring decision, *Advocate*, 12 November 1955, p. 10. Earlier, in 1946, the League had attempted to head off such behaviour by initiating a series of educational talks entitled, 'What the BCL Expects of You', *Advocate*, 26 July 1946, p. 4.

31 See, for example, comments which followed the selection of Gary Sobers in the 1953 West Indian touring team to India, *Advocate*, 27 January 1953 p. 10.

32 *Wanderers Cricket Club Centenary, 1877–1977* (Bridgetown: WCC, 1977). For a brief comparison of Wanderers and Pickwick, see David Lowenthal, *West Indian Societies* (London: Oxford University Press, 1972), pp. 82–3.

33 See Hamilton, *Cricket in Barbados;* interview material drawn from Pickwick personnel.

34 Interview material.

35 *Ibid.*

36 *Ibid.* Also, *Barbados Cricketers Annual* series.

37 F.A. Hoyos, *Grantley Adams and the Social Revolution* (London: Macmillan, 1974).

38 *Advocate*, 22 October 1936, p. 12 – he was appointed Vice President.

39 Interviewees invariably pointed to the fact that all post-independence Governors-General and Prime Ministers have been Spartan men, not to mention a preponderance of politicians and senior civil servants.

40 For an interesting outline, John Wickham, 'Herman', *West Indies Cricket Annual, 1980;* interview material.

41 These profiles were based upon *Voters' Lists* from the 1880s until the 1960s, supplemented by these biographical sources: S.J. Fraser, *The Barbados Diamond Jubilee Directory and General West Indian Advertiser* (Bridgetown: King, 1898); P.S. Leverick, *Leverick's Directory of Barbados* (Bridgetown: King, 1921); *Barbados Year Book and Who's Who* (Bridgetown: Advocate, 1934, 1951, 1964).

42 See, for example, *Rules of the Pickwick Cricket Club* (Bridgetown: Advocate, 1947).

43 Remainder of this paragraph and the next based upon interview material.

44 Anthony Trollope, *The West Indies and the Spanish Main* (London: Chapman & Hall, 1860), p. 215; Greville John Chester, *Transatlantic Sketches in the West Indies, South America, Canada and the United States* (London: Smith Elder, 1860), p. 99; George H.H. McLellan, *Some Phases of Barbados Life* (Demarara: Argosy, 1909), pp. 45–6, 54; W.M. Macmillan, *Warning from the West Indies: a Tract for the Empire* (Harmondsworth: Penguin, 1938), p. 49; Patrick Leigh Fermor, *The Traveller's Tree: a Journey through the Caribbean Islands* (London: Murray, 1950), p. 151; E.W. Swanton in *Advocate*, 27 July, 1960, p. 11; Kenneth Blackburne, *Lasting Legacy: a Story of British Colonialism* (London: Johnson, 1976), pp. 85–6.

45 George Bernard [Gordon Belle], *Wayside Sketches: Pen-Pictures of Barbadian Life* (Bridgetown: Advocate, 1934); Clennell W. Wickham, *Colour Question – Some Reflections*

on Barbados (no publishing details listed); Leroy Harewood, *Black Power Lessness in Barbados* (Bridgetown: Black Star, 1968).

46 See Starkey, *Economic Geography of Barbados*, Ch. 4 and Dawn I. Marshall, 'The Population/Environment System of Barbados in the 1930s' (Cave Hill: Institute of Social and Economic Research Paper, 1978); *Barbados Sugar Industry Review*, 15 (March 1973).

47 *Report of the West India Royal Commission* (London: HMSO, IS97); *Report of the West Indian Sugar Commission* (London: HMSO, 1930); *Sugar Confidential: a Visit to Jamaica and Barbados* (London: Cocoa, Chocolate and Confectionary Alliance, 1970); *The Economic and Social Development of Barbados: Characteristics, Policies and Perspectives* (Washington: OAS, 1976); *Nation*, 18 September 1985, p. 12.

48 Two accounts of this process may be seen in Ronald Parris, 'Race, Inequality and Underdevelopment in Barbados, 1627–1973' (Ph.D. dissertation, Yale University, 1974) and Cecilia Ann Karch, 'The Transformation and Consolidation of the Corporate Plantation Economy in Barbados, 1860–1977' (Ph.D. dissertation, Rutgers University, 1979).

49 For some indications: *Housing in Barbados: Report of a Committee* (Bridgetown: Advocate, 1943); *Report on a Preliminary Housing Survey of Two Blocks of Chapman's Lane Tenantry Bridgetown* (Bridgetown: Advocate, 1944); *Report on a Housing Survey of Eight Slum Tenantries in Bridgetown* (Bridgetown: Advocate, 1945). Later nineteenth-century conditions may be gauged from *Report of the Commission on Poor Relief 1875–1877* (Bridgetown: Government of Barbados, 1878). For the outline of political events, F.A. Hoyos, *Grantley Adams*.

50 For comments on the process of democratisation, J.M. Hewitt, *Ten Years of Constitutional Development in Barbados 1944–1954* (Bridgetown: Cole's, 1954) – this was the same Mitchie Hewitt who founded the BCL.

51 P.F. Warner, *Cricket In Many Climes* (London: Heinemann, 1900), West Indian section; Charlie Griffith, *Chucked Around* (London: Pelham, 1970), pp. 117–18.

52 Interview material; for a similar version, John Wickham, 'The First Hundred Years: a Salute to Wanderers Cricket Club', *Bajan (*1977), p. 45.

53 Interview material.

54 *Ibid.*

55 This practice began during the 1890s.

56 For example, *Barbados Cricketers' Annual 1895–6*, pp. 71–4.

57 *Barbados Cricketers' Annual 1909–10*, p. 47.

58 Interview material.

59 *Ibid.*

60 *Ibid.*

61 *Ibid.*

62 See the reception accorded Goodman for his outstanding performances against an English touring team in 1897. *Bulletin*, 15 January 1897, pp. 8–10.

63 After the 1923 West Indies tour of England, he was ranked among the top six batsman in the world, *Wisden 1924*, pp. 422–3.

64 Interview material.

65 Most cricket fans in Barbados have a list of players who, though good enough, were never selected for Barbados because they could not get a 'break', given their low social status. Interview material.

66 Based on interview material; see also Gary Sobers, *Cricket Crusader* (London: Pelham, 1966) and Trevor Bailey, *Sir Gary: a Biography* (London: Collins, 1976).

67 Flora Spencer and Geoffrey King, *Lost Ball – Six Runs* (Bridgetown: Barbados Festival Choir, 1973). Calypso examples are 'Hit It' and 'Miss Barbados', both by Gabby.

68 For an illuminating account of the Worrell experience, Ernest Eytle, *Frank Worrell* (London: Sportsmans Book Club, 1965) in which Worrell comments on each chapter.

69 Worrell thought the match displayed 'bigotry, vanity and insularity', *Advocate*, 2 October 1966, p. 14.

70 Interview material.

71 See Warner, *Cricket in Many Climes*, pp. 42–6: *Bulletin*, 31 December 1897, pp. 4–5.

72 See the account by the 1895 touring English captain in C.P. Bowen, *English Cricketers in the West Indies* (Bridgetown: Herald, 1895), p. 13.

73 For one account of Flannigan's style, see *Inter-colonial Cricket Tournament 1925* (Port of Spain: Chronicle, 1925), pp. 8, 85.

74 Interview material.

75 Following section based largely upon interview material. See also *Advocate*, 14 May 1966, p. 14; Alan Ross, *Through the Caribbean: England in the West Indies 1960* (London: Pavilion, 1985 reprint), pp. 27–8.

76 For example, *Bulletin*, 3 July 1899; *Advocate*, 12 January 1926, p. 9 and 4 January 1930, p. 12.

77 These points drawn from observation.

78 See the 'Cricket Crisis' series in *Sunday Sun*, 13, 20, 27 October and 3, 10, 17 November 1985.

79 Interview material.

80 Point drawn from observation.

81 *Ibid.*

82 *Ibid.*

83 For the 'reflective' approach, see Jack W. Berryman, 'Sport History as Social History', *Quest*, 30 (June 1973): 65–73; for a guide to a more structural and insightful approach, Clifford Geertz, 'Deep Play: Notes on the Balinese Cockfight', *Daedalus*, 101 (Winter 1972), 1–37.

Part II

Creolisation, ideology and popular culture

5

Cricket, carnival and street culture in the Caribbean

Richard D.E. Burton

Taking its inspiration from C.L.R. James's classic *Beyond A Boundary*, serious discussion of the relationship between cricket and society in the Caribbean has focused on three closely connected issues.[1] First, and most straightforwardly, it has dwelt on the way in which the changing racial and class composition of West Indian teams since 1900 (the year of the first West Indian tour to England) has mirrored with almost preternatural precision the evolution of West Indian society over the same period, as non-white cricketers came first to challenge and eventually to overthrow the almost complete domination of West Indian cricket by members of the white plantocracy that had obtained before 1914 and which, in a modified but still perceptible form, continued into the 1950s; in this perspective, the crucial event is the appointment, in 1960, of Frank Worrell as the first non-white captain of the West Indian Test team, thus consecrating the black cricketing supremacy that had existed *de facto* since the mid-1940s at exactly the same time that the West Indies were, painfully and with much uncertainty, attaining to political independence. Secondly, much attention has been devoted to the manner in which the West Indies' growing prowess in international cricket has not merely reflected but may actively have stimulated the rise of nationalist (and, to some extent, racial) self-consciousness in the British Caribbean. It was, some have argued, only when they saw their cricket team locked in combat with that of their English colonial masters that Jamaicans, Barbadians, Trinidadians and Guyanese came to see themselves as *West Indians* possessing a common historical, cultural and political identity transcending the insularity, isolation and inter-territorial competitiveness that many West Indians see as among the most baleful legacies of British colonialism in the Caribbean. In this view, the key date is without question 1950, the year that, to the accompaniment of steel bands, calypsos and mass enthusiasm among the newly installed West Indian migrant population, the West Indies defeated England in England for the first time, thanks to the formidable batting of the 'three Ws', Worrell, Weekes and Walcott, and to the scarcely credible bowling feats of 'those two little pals of mine/Ramadhin and Valentine',[2] thereby emerging as a world cricketing power on a par with England, Australia and South Africa. It was as though – to use an image that a number of West Indian writers have applied to the colonial context[3] – Prospero had taught Caliban the use of bat and ball only to find himself comprehensively 'outmagicked' by his upstart colonial pupil, thus betraying on the cricket field the vulnerability and fallibility that were becoming more and more evident in his governance of the West Indies as a whole: after 1950, it is argued, the 'mother country' would never be quite the same again in West Indian eyes. Finally, and more tentatively, West Indian cricket has been shown to present a dualistic structure corresponding to the dichotomous (or 'plural') character of West Indian society and culture as a whole,[4] a structure in which two traditions – that of the white elite and its coloured imitators, on the one hand, and that of the black masses on the other – have co-existed throughout the history of West Indian cricket, distinct in methods, aims and values, now clashing, now interacting creatively, but never wholly merging, with the 'Afrocentric' tradition of black cricket finally ousting and supplanting the 'Anglocentric' tradition of the white and coloured elite. An English game introduced into the Caribbean by Englishmen, West Indian cricket has, in this view, become progressively more and more 'African' in character, so that the 'blackwash' of English cricket in the summer of 1984 was accomplished not only by an overwhelmingly black team but, so to speak, by 'black' cricketing methods (notably the unrelenting use of bowling of exceptional pace and aggression) reinforced by and reflecting 'black' values and mores and giving rise to unforgettable displays of black triumphalism both on the field and off. West Indian cricket, in other words, has retained its English form while being injected with a new and specifically West Indian content and meaning. In the course of its transposition to the Caribbean, cricket, like so much else, has been comprehensively *creolized*.[5]

I

The present study – the provisional and tentative character of which I happily admit – takes as its starting-point these three related themes but seeks to go beyond them in its attempt to situate West Indian cricket within the broader contexts of West Indian culture as a whole. In particular, it dwells upon certain marked similarities – or so it seems to me – between the history, evolution and underlying meaning of West Indian cricket and the parallel development and significance of that other quintessentially Afro-Caribbean cultural phenomenon, carnival. In its turn, carnival will be shown to embody and crystallize in a particularly memorable form the intricate patterns of West Indian street culture, so that cricket, carnival and the street corner become overlapping expressions of a single underlying social, cultural and psychological complex. In everything that follows, players and spectators are seen as co-participants in an organic ritual, 'a social drama in which', as the Jamaican novelist and sociologist Orlando Patterson has written, 'almost all of the basic tensions and conflicts within the society are played out symbolically'.[6] Whereas in England it is not uncommon for players and officials to outnumber spectators at county matches, and even Test matches at Old Trafford, Edgbaston or Trent Bridge do not lose their meaning if they are watched by only a few hundred spectators, cricket in the West Indies is almost inconceivable – certainly at Test level – without massive and vociferous spectator involvement. What gives West Indian cricket its unique creole character is, precisely, the interplay of players, spectacle and crowd. The spectators are, in a very real sense, just as much participants as the players themselves, so that the frontier between players and spectators – the boundary-rope which, in England until a few years ago, represented a quasi-sacred *limes* (space) that no spectator would dare transgress – is, in the West Indies and in matches in this country in which West Indians are involved, continually being breached by members of the crowd to field the ball, to congratulate successful batsmen and bowlers and, in not a few instances, to express their disgust at umpires' decisions, the tactics of the opposition, and so on.[7] On occasions, as is well known, this disgust has ceased to be simply an empty gesture on the part of irate individuals to become a collective outburst of outrage and resentment on the part of whole sections of the crowd, culminating in the riots that have occurred from time to time on West Indian cricket grounds, not, I think, as regularly or as predictably as is sometimes claimed, but none the less with sufficient frequency for riots and rioting to be seen as an ever-present *potentiality* in West Indian cricket at its most intense and passionate; it is with a consideration of the circumstances and meaning of these riots that the present study concludes.

The constant and indispensable involvement of the crowd in West Indian cricket can be paralleled in many other Afro-Caribbean cultural institutions where there is no absolutely clear-cut separation between 'performers' and 'spectators': in cockfighting, for example, in all forms of Afro-Christian worship with its highly charged and passionate interplay between 'priests' and 'congregation' or, still more, in such African-derived possession cults as voodoo, pocomania or shango where again celebrants and congregation merge and co-participate in a manner foreign to most European religious practice.[8] Similarly, in carnival in Trinidad, the crowds that follow bands and masquerades are, in their way, just as much performers as the performers themselves so that, at its climax, Trinidad carnival becomes an immense, all-embracing festival acted out by the people for the people. It is, as I shall try to show, as just such a popular fiesta, a mass carnivalesque collective rite, that West Indian cricket can best be appreciated and understood.

In order to understand the place of cricket in contemporary West Indian society, it is necessary first to say something of the role of play, recreation and entertainment in the West Indies from the slave epoch onwards. We so associate slavery with manual labour of the most crushing and dehumanizing kind imaginable that we may fail to take fully into account the extraordinary variety and vitality of slave entertainments and pastimes whose function, it seems needless to add, was precisely to *rehumanize* the lives of men, women and children who were in other respects reduced to the level of animals, even of objects. There are numerous accounts in the literature of slavery of how slaves who, during the working day, appeared to be reduced to zombie-like insensibility and passivity would, when they returned to their own huts and yards at nightfall, suddenly become alive again and how music and dance, in particular, would almost magically revive and revitalize men and women who, in the fields, have moved above much like barely animate spooks.[9] Correctly identifying dance and music, especially drumming, as potential sources of slave resistance, slave-holders repeatedly tried to curb, even to repress completely, such activities, though always, it goes without saying, to no avail.[10] Many slave dances were, of course, of African origin, though others were clearly satirical imitations of the gavottes, pavanes and quadrilles that slaves would see their masters and mistresses performing in the Great House; mimicry and parody have long been recognized as one of the main sources of Afro-Caribbean culture, and it is not impossible that some such satirical intention lay behind the initial adoption of cricket by black West Indians in the early 1800s.

Interestingly, music, dancing and their associated ritual activities were often referred to as 'plays' or 'playing' by the slaves. In 1729, a certain A. Holt wrote that slaves in Barbados held gatherings on Sundays 'which they call their plays [. . .] in which, their various instruments of horrid music howling and dancing about the graves of the dead, they [give] victuals and strong liquor to the souls of the dead'; in 1788, again referring to slaves in Barbados, one Peter Marsden noted that 'every Saturday night many divert themselves with dancing and singing, which they style plays; and notwithstanding their week's labour, continue this violent exercise all night'. These 'plays' would reach their height at Christmas when, traditionally, rigid supervision was relaxed somewhat and slaves were for once free to move about from plantation to plantation. In 1790 the well-known Jamaican planter William Beckford wrote that

> some negroes will sing and dance, and some will be in a constant state of intoxication, during the whole period that their festival at Christmas shall continue; and what is more extraordinary, several of them will go ten or twelve miles to what is called a play and will sit up and drink all night; and yet return in time to the plantation for their work the ensuing morning.[11]

It is no accident, of course, that many of the most significant slave uprisings in the Caribbean took place, precisely at Christmas, most notably in Trinidad in 1805 when slaves organized resistance under the cover of drumming and dancing societies with quasi-military names like the Régiment Macaque, the Régiment Danois and the Couvri de Sans Peur;[12] still more significant was the largest single slave uprising in the British Caribbean, the so-called 'Baptist War' or 'Christmas Rebellion' that took place in Jamaica in December 1831 and January 1832 under the leadership of the celebrated black Baptist minister, Samuel 'Daddy' Sharpe.[13] A number of other examples could be given: let us merely retain the long-standing association between 'play' in the broad sense which slaves gave to the term – music, dancing, drinking, sociability – and latent, potential, symbolic or actual subversion of the established order of slave society.

II

The link between 'play' and resistance is still more marked in the case of carnival in Trinidad.[14] Before the abolition of slavery in 1834 it is clear that carnival in Trinidad was celebrated exclusively by the white elite, particularly the white French-speaking Roman Catholic elite, and some members of the coloured, again principally French-speaking and Catholic, middle class: blacks, free and unfree, were present, if at all, only as spectators. After abolition, however, carnival was swiftly taken over by the now free black population. The whites who had hitherto dominated the street processions henceforth celebrated carnival 'behind closed doors' in their own homes or in private ballrooms and theatres, leaving the streets to the mass of the population, and particularly to those members of the black lower classes known in nineteenth-century Trinidad as 'badjohns' or 'jamets', from the French *diamétre*, the 'other half', in other words the criminal or semi-criminal underworld.[15] There are, it seems to me, very definite parallels between this 'take-over' of carnival by lower-class blacks in nineteenth-century Trinidad and the similar, though more gradual, 'take-over' of cricket by black West Indians since 1900. As it was taken over by blacks, so carnival in Trinidad changed unmistakably in character. Before 1834, it appears to have been much the same kind of pre-Lenten festivity that it was in Roman Catholic societies throughout Europe and Latin America; after abolition, however, it clearly becomes a popular black festival of liberation with such rituals as the 'canboulay' (*cannes brûlées*) procession at midnight on the Sunday of carnival celebrating in a veiled, symbolic form the deliverance of the black population from the yoke of slavery.[16] Not surprisingly, carnival in Trinidad, especially in the capital Port of Spain, was often an occasion of confrontation between, on the one hand, black revellers and masqueraders and, on the other, the forces of law and order, local policemen and British soldiers alike. There were major clashes at carnival time in 1881 and 1883, leading to repeated attempts by the colonial government supported by the local elite to control the festivities and even to suppress them completely; a particular target of official ire was the 'tambour-bamboo' bands from which the modern steel band is ultimately derived.[17]

By the late nineteenth century, carnival had been to a large extent 'domesticated', and white and coloured Trinidadians who had shunned the street festivities for 60 years or more gradually began to venture out of their houses on the three days preceding Lent and tentatively and cautiously to mix once more with the black revellers on the streets. At one level – what we might call the ideal or mythical level – all racial, social and political hostilities in Trinidad are supposedly suppressed and forgotten for the duration of carnival; normally divided, even antagonistic, the whole population, says the myth, comes together as one. Yet very often, in bringing normally distinct and distant groups of the population together, carnival serves only to highlight the differences and hostilities between them; as recently as 1970, at the time of the so-called 'February Revolution', major political, social and, to some extent, racial confrontations occurred in Trinidad at carnival time.[18] In much the same way, an enthusiasm for cricket is, arguably, the *only* enthusiasm that truly cuts across social and racial dividing lines in the Caribbean. Cricket brings people together in the English-speaking West Indies as nothing else – religion, politics, or whatever – does, but precisely because it does so, it reveals the differences and hostilities between them. The dozen or so 'cricket riots' in the Caribbean are only the most extreme manifestation of West Indian cricket's unique capacity both to unite and to divide.

Other aspects of carnival have a direct bearing on the character of cricket in the West Indies, particularly the scope that it gives to forms of ritualized or stylized conflict that anthropologists have shown to be endemic in Afro-American culture in general.[19] Competition is at the very heart of carnival in Trinidad. There are, in the first place, organized competitions between calypsonians for the title of Calypso King in which there may be 200 or more contestants each singing two or three calypsos and each accompanied by bands of enthusiastic supporters;[20] there is, too, the nationwide competition for the title of Carnival Queen which always involves passionate and sometimes violent controversy, in part because of the importance commonly attached to the winner's ethnic identity and skin colour. On a less organized but no less formalistic or ritualistic level, there are the conventional confrontations, challenges and exchanges of abuse, derision and defiance between different bands of masqueraders who often represent different localities, different professional categories or different social and ethnic groups; all of these confrontations have the effect of externalizing and, at the same time, of channelling and sublimating tensions and hostilities between individuals and groups which, during the rest of the year, normally remain suppressed.

During the nineteenth and early twentieth centuries, a particular importance attached to the ritualistic and stylized conflicts between bands of so-called 'stick-fighters' who, armed with hardwood sticks variously known as *poui, gasparee, balata* or *anare*, would confront each other on the streets at carnival-time, hurl abuse and defiance at each other and then engage in mock – and sometimes not so mock – stick combat; introduced into Trinidad by slaves from the French speaking islands, stick-fighting, otherwise known as *calenda* or *calinda*, is clearly of African origin. In an island culture otherwise deprived of indigenous heroes and heroism, leading stick-fighters or *batonniers* such as the celebrated Mungo the Dentist – so called for his skill in 'fixing', the teeth of opponents![21] – reigned as virtual kings of the districts and peoples they represented; the reputation of a locality or street-gang became identified with the reputation of its *batonniers* who would both repel rivals from other areas and lead periodic sorties into enemy territory.

It is interesting that stick-fighting and the cult of the *batonnier* entered into decline at much the same time that black enthusiasm for cricket and the accompanying cult of black batsmen and black fast bowlers began to emerge, and it would be interesting, too, to know how far street sodalities such as the Jacketmen, the Hirondelles and Jockey Boys (from San Fernando), the Sweet Evening Bells and Tiepins (from Tunapuna) and Peau de Canelle, the Cerfs-Volants, the Bakers, Bois d'Inde and the s'Amandes (from Port of Spain) formed the nucleus of the black cricket clubs – themselves notoriously undisciplined and aggressive – that would emerge in the 1890s and early 1900s.[22] Whatever the answer, there are, it seems to me, possible continuities between the figure of the champion *batonnier* or 'kalinda king' and that of the champion black batsmen, and I was, to say the least, fascinated to come across the following description of how *batonniers* practised in nineteenth-century Trinidad:

> In practising, one of the best methods for quickening the eye, steadying the nerves and improving one's judgment was 'Breaking' [i.e. parrying a blow with your stick]. It con-sisted in having one or two fellows stand 15 or 20 yards off and hurl stones at you in rapid succession, and it was your business – and, of course, to your interest – to 'break' these stones successfully. A very proficient 'breaker' would often have three men hurling stones at him, and it was seldom, indeed, that he got hurt. (*Trinidad Guardian*, 2 March 1919)[23]

To my knowledge, not even the most diehard member of the 'Africa or bust' school of Afro-American anthropology has tried to trace back West Indian prowess at cricket to the people's African 'roots'. *Calenda*, though, could just con-stitute a link, and the possibility of *some* submerged continuity between the African past and the Afro-Caribbean present should not, perhaps be discounted in its entirety.

The world of carnival is, as many writers on the theme have stressed,[24] a negation or subversion of the structures, hierarchies and values that obtain in society during the rest of the year. Carnival is 'the world turned upside down', a make-believe counter-society over which the pauper or madman is king and the servant-girl queen, and it is noticeable in this respect how carnival societies in Trinidad – as, no doubt, elsewhere – have their own elaborate hierarchies of kings, queens, princes, princesses, dukes, captains and sergeants-at-arms, just as, one might further note, secret societies among slaves had their elected kings, queens, *dauphins* and *dauphines*.[25] Even today, Trinidadian calypsonians give themselves, or are given, mock-royal, mock-aristocratic or mock-heroic sobriquets such as Lord Kitchener, Mighty Sparrow, Lord Beginner, Black Stalin and Mighty Chalkdust (the *nom de carnival* of schoolteacher Hollis Liverpool)[26] as though to underline carnival's sym-bolic subversion of the structures of everyday life. The last shall be first, the first shall be last: during carnival, the popular imagination throws up its own hierarchies of prestige, achievement and charisma which, at every point, challenge and fictively negate the hierarchies and norms of established society.

And so it is, I tentatively suggest, with West Indian cricket. Often springing shaman-like from the lowest strata of black society, the Constantines, the Headleys, the Walcotts, the Soberses, the Richardses are the carnival kings and princes of the people, symbolic subverters and destroyers of a world where white is might and, as such, embodiments of a dream-world in which, by identification and projection, every black West Indian, be he never so poor, is monarch for the day:

We was *only* playin' de MCC, man;
M – C – C
who come all de way out from Inglan.

We was battin', you see;
score wasn't too bad, one
hurren an' ninety-

seven fuh three.
the openers out, Tae Worrell out,
Everton Weekes jus' glide two fuh fifty

an' jack, is de GIANT to come!
Feller name Wardle
was bowlin'; tossin' it up

sweet sweet slow-medium syrup.
Firs' ball . . .
'N..o..o'

back down de wicket to Wardle.
Second' ball . . .
'N..o..o'

back down de wicket to Wardle.
Third ball comin' up
an' we know wha' goin' happen to syrup:

Clyde back pun he back
foot an' *prax*!
is through extra cover an' four red runs all de way.

'You see dat show?' the people was shoutin';
'Jesus Chrise, man, wunna see dat shot?
All over de groun' fellers shaking hands wid each other

as if was *they* wheelin' de willow
as if was *them* had the power'

(Edward Kamau Brathwaite, *Rites*[27])

Carnival is a phenomenon of the street, and it is also to the street that, in the first instance, West Indian cricket belongs. If English boys learn to play cricket in back gardens, parks, playing fields and on village greens, it is on the street – or, in the smaller islands, on the beach – that West Indian boys develop their batting, bowling and fielding skills. As such, cricket in the Caribbean partakes of the immensely complex street culture of West Indian males, a culture whose main features we can, with the help of the writings of anthropologists such as Roger D. Abrahams[28] and Peter J. Wilson,[29] define, again very tentatively, as follows. According to Abrahams and Wilson, there is a marked contrast in West Indian cultures between the female-centred, female-dominated culture of the home or 'yard' and the male-centred, male-dominated culture of the street and its adjuncts, the rum-shop, betting-shop and barber's. The gynocentric world of the 'yard' stressed the values of family, community, solidarity and respectability, while the andocentric world of the street lays emphasis rather on the counter-values of individualism, competition and reputation; the yard is an enclosed enclave of seriousness while the street is an open, mobile world of play. Though there is a tension between the two worlds and their associated values, there is, according to Abrahams and Wilson, no necessary conflict between them: complementarity rather than antagonism is, in normal circumstances, the order of the day. The values and qualities most esteemed on the street are style, flair, 'cool', defiance, reputation and, in extreme instances, aggression, though both Abrahams and Wilson are at pains to stress that, again in normal circumstances, street hostilities between individuals and groups (or, to use Wilson's suggestive term, 'crews')[30] are commonly expressed in semi-ritualistic, sublimated forms; both writers, for example, attach great significance to the marked stylization and hyperbolization of verbal insult and defiance in the Caribbean and among Afro-Americans in general.[31] In the analysis proposed by Abrahams and Wilson, the values of the yard, based as they are on the concepts of order, respectability and seriousness, are closer to the established European-derived or European-influenced values of the dominant elite – closer, in other words, to the values traditionally embodied and enshrined in *English* cricket – whereas, says Abrahams, the play ethos of the street 'means not only switching styles to roles and behaviours regarded from household (and Euro-American) perspectives as "bad" or "improper"; in the Afro-American order of behaviours', he continues, '"play" is not distinguished from the "real" or "work" but from "respectable" behaviour [. . .]; playing then means playing *bad*, playing black, playing lower-class'.[32]

If Abrahams and Wilson are correct, I would suggest, again with great caution, that the values, mentalities and ways of behaving in evidence among West Indian cricket crowds are an extension – even a heightened, exaggerated and stylized form – of the already stylized values, mentalities and ways of behaving characteristic of West Indian male street culture in general: expansiveness, camaraderie, unruliness, jesting, joking – verbal and bodily bravado, clowning – in a word, *playing*. Not only this, but it would seem that the qualities that West Indians most prize in their cricketers are essentially 'street qualities': what counts is not the mere scoring of runs, but scoring with style, panache, flamboyance, an ostentatiously contemptuous defiance of the opposition.

Similarly, fast bowling must not simply *be* fast but *look* fast. West Indian fast bowling confronts batsman and spectators alike with an all-out exteriorization of the methods and signs of attack: a run-up of (usually) exaggerated length and speed, a momentous heave of arms, legs and torso at the instant of delivery, with the ball unleashed at colossal speed straight at batsman and/or stumps, either bouncing half-way or two-thirds down the pitch and rearing up to around the batsman's chest and face – the 'throat ball' as it is reputedly known in the contemporary West Indian dressing-room, firing into the batsman's block-hole (the 'yorker' at which Charlie

Griffith and Joel Garner have so excelled) or – a mode of attack apparently commonplace in black West Indian cricket in the 1920s and 1930s,[33] perfected (if that is the word) by Roy Gilchrist in the late 1950s, and now banned – 'beaming' on the full at the batsman's (until recently) unprotected head. No concealment or mystery here: just aggression projected in a pure and naked state, a total spectacle complete in itself and instantly understood, all to the accompaniment of a percussive crescendo of rattling beercans, clapping, hooters, whistles and shouts, as though the crowd not merely beholds but, through its active participation, actually *creates* this cathartic experience of controlled, directed violence.

West Indian men, it seems to me, watch and play cricket with minds, hearts, values and expectations shaped by the street culture of boyhood, adolescence and early manhood. Concerned as they are with the enhancing of individual and group reputation, those values are potentially – though rarely in fact – at odds with the values of respectability, seriousness, moderation and obedience associated with the home, the church and the ethos of the dominant white and coloured elites. So long as the course of the cricket match is such that street values and emotions can be expressed and released through a cathartic identification with the West Indian cricketers and their deeds, areas of potential conflict are avoided. But should something 'go wrong' in the symbolic drama being acted out – should, for example, one of the crowd's heroes be dismissed in a manner the crowd finds unacceptable – then, as Orlando Patterson has argued,[34] the conflict of values symbolized in the cricket match abruptly ceases to be symbolic and becomes *real*. The crowd's passions are no longer channelled and sublimated through identification with its heroes. The imaginative spell is broken and, no longer able harmlessly to project its feelings into the match and on to the players, the crowd now directs them towards and against those embodiments of law and order, the umpires, or against whatever representatives of the established order present themselves to its fury: administrators, selectors, the police, dignitaries in the pavilion or the main stand, though rarely, if ever, it should be stressed, the opposition team itself. Bottles, seat cushions and other missiles rain forth: a riot has begun.

III

Before I discuss some of the cases of riots at cricket matches in the West Indies, it will be necessary to say something of the physical conditions in which cricket is played and watched in the region. In the first instance, all of the Test match grounds are extremely small, built as they were in the late nineteenth and early twentieth centuries before cricket became a mass spectator sport in the Caribbean; the crowd is literally on top of the players at Sabina Park (Kingston), Kensington Oval (Bridgetown) and elsewhere, and almost always there are many more spectators than the grounds can possibly accommodate with comfort. People watch from surrounding buildings, from trees, lamp-posts and telegraph-poles; at Sabina Park, and probably at other grounds, smart operators make holes in the perimeter fence and actually charge others for the privilege of entering the ground via these improvised entrances. There are almost no facilities and refreshments available in those parts of the ground where poorer spectators congregate. A vast amount of beer and rum is consumed and in the cheap uncovered seats known in the Caribbean as 'bleachers', the heat, at around three or four in the afternoon, can be incredible; the crowd's already passionate feelings about the game are commonly heightened still further by the large amount of betting on batsmen's scores that is a regular feature at Test match grounds in the West Indies. In addition, as Patterson has neatly shown,[35] the lay-out of a ground like Sabina Park represents an exact microcosm of the structure of West Indian society: the pavilion for whites and the wealthiest coloureds, the main stand for other coloureds and the more affluent blacks, subsidiary stands for the black lower middle classes, the bleachers for the masses. The dichotomy of pavilion and main stand, on the one hand, and bleachers on the other comes over, in Patterson's description, as a modern equivalent of the dichotomy of Great House and barracoons on the slave plantation, an analogy that has been brought out still more in recent years by the presence at most Test matches in the West Indies of large numbers of police armed with nightsticks, riot shields, guns and tear-gas canisters. In such supercharged conditions, riot is an ever-present possibility, requiring only certain circumstances to actualize it.

In the last 30 years there have been four *major* instances of crowd disturbance at Test matches in the West Indies, plus a number of lesser incidents and four or five 'near misses', not least, I suspect, in England in 1976 when England captain Tony Greig – he of the Aryan good looks and unreconstructed South African accent – announced his intention not merely to defeat the West Indies but, in his singularly inept phrase, 'to make them grovel'.[36] Fortunately the West Indies overwhelmed England that year, and cricket-lovers will recall the endless chant of 'Grovel, Greig, grovel' that resounded across the Oval as Vivian Richards swept, drove and hooked his way to 291 and the West Indies reached 687 for eight declared in the fifth Test; to cap it all, the winning calypso at carnival in Richards's native Antigua the following February was entitled 'Who's Grovelling Now?' sung – or so I am told – to the tune of 'Who's Sorry Now?'!

The first major instance of crowd violence at a Test match in the West Indies occurred at Georgetown, British Guiana, during the unhappy MCC tour of the Caribbean in 1953–54. The Test match, it is relevant to note, took place against a background of political tension and crisis: just a few months previously, British troops had intervened directly in British Guiana to prevent the installation of an elected left-wing government under Cheddi Jagan, the constitution had been suspended and a number of local nationalist politicians interned.[37] The riot began when a partnership of 99 between McWatt and Holt of the West Indies ended with McWatt, a local hero, being given out, run out. There was, it seems, no doubt that the umpire's decision was correct, but it may be that the crowd was still upset by England's disputing of umpiring decisions during the previous match on the ground between MCC and British Guiana. A more likely cause is disappointment at the abrupt end of a partnership which seemed to be rescuing the West Indies from a calamitous first innings collapse; in addition, many members of the crowd are known to have placed bets on McWatt and Holt reaching a century partnership.[38] Whatever the cause, bottles and, according to *Wisden*, wooden packing cases were thrown on to the playing area, though there was no actual crowd 'invasion'. Despite urgent pleas from the President of the British Guiana Cricket Association, the England captain, Len Hutton, refused to lead his team off the field. Order was quickly restored, and England went on to win the match easily by nine wickets.

The second major incident again involved West Indies versus England, this time at Port of Spain in January–February 1960. Again a background of political tension *may* have had some bearing on events at Queen's Park Oval; though the links between politics and sport were far less clear-cut than in the earlier incident and in those that were to follow. It is more than likely, however, that the continuing controversy over the West Indian captaincy and its inevitable social and racial implications did have a considerable influence on events since the 1959–60 series was the last occasion on which the West Indies were led by a white captain, Gerry Alexander, who, in the eyes of Trinidadians, compounded the 'sin' of whiteness with being Jamaican as well. The immediate cause of the riot was, once more, a West Indian batting collapse: bottles were thrown on the third day when the home team had slumped to 98 for eight in its first innings. No controversial umpiring decision was involved, though both umpires had previously cautioned the West Indian fast bowlers, Hall and Watson, for excessive bowling of bouncers; significantly, perhaps, one of the umpires, Lee Kow, was of Chinese origin and, as such, a representative not merely of 'authority' and 'law and order' but also of probably the most strongly disliked ethnic group in West Indian society. Whereas the first disturbance in British Guiana had been but a brief affair, in Trinidad six years later play was abandoned for the day. The England players were escorted from the field by the police though once again no animosity was shown towards them; as in the earlier match, England went on to win convincingly by 256 runs and, in so doing, won a Test series in the West Indies for the first time.

In the third major incident – that which occurred during the West Indies versus England Test match at Sabina Park in February 1968 – we can discern a clear link between the crowd's reaction and the general social and political climate in Jamaica towards the end of the 1960s. By 1968 it was apparent that the 'honeymoon period' that followed the gaining of political independence in 1962 had finally ended. There was widespread hostility to the Jamaica Labour Party government led by Hugh Shearer and a growing feeling throughout society that independence had changed little either in the island's internal social, economic and racial structure or in its relationship of dependence towards the outside world. Political and criminal violence was on the increase – it was often impossible to tell one form of violence from the other – and there was a growing receptiveness among young black Jamaicans both towards Rastafarianism and towards the Black Power ideas and attitudes that were beginning to reach the island from the United States, from West Indians living in Canada as well as from elsewhere in the Caribbean. It was surely no accident that, seven or eight months after the rioting at Sabina Park, downtown Kingston was to witness a far more serious and violent upsurge of popular protest in the wake of the government's decision to refuse the Guyanese Black Power leader Walter Rodney permission to re-enter the country where he was working as a university lecturer.[39] In early 1968, the authorities in general, and the police in particular, were undeniably nervous, and, in retrospect, it is hardly surprising that, yet again, a seemingly trivial incident at a cricket match should have sparked off such considerable violence.

The riot began in mid-afternoon on the third day of the Test match when England appeared to be well on the way to victory. The West Indies had been forced to follow on 233 runs behind and had reached 204 for four when Basil Butcher of Guyana was given out caught at the wicket; the decision was, by all accounts, perfectly correct,[40] though once again it is relevant to note that the umpire concerned, Donald Sang Hue, generally thought to be the best umpire in the Caribbean at the time, was a Jamaican of Chinese origin. As he walked off, Butcher slapped bat against pad in annoyance at getting out, a gesture which the crowd appears to have interpreted, quite wrongly, as meaning that he disagreed with the decision; as the batsman entered the pavilion, bottles and stones began to be thrown on to the playing area from the bleachers. Over-reacting in a manner that was becoming increasingly common in Jamaica at the time, the policy duly released their tear-gas: unfortunately, the wind was in the wrong direction, and it was the players and the dignitaries (including the Governor-General and his wife) in the pavilion who suffered its effects! 'Order' was gradually restored, and after 75 minutes play was resumed though the England players, to say nothing of the hapless umpires, were clearly rattled. The West Indies recovered sufficiently to be able to declare at 391 for nine with Sobers making 113 not out, and by the end of the match England were struggling to survive at 68 for eight. The last innings, says *Wisden* with some understatement, 'was played in a feverish atmosphere, which seemed to unsettle the umpires'.

Later in the same series versus England there was another incident which, though not a riot, is again highly indicative of West Indian attitudes towards cricket. The fourth Test at Port of Spain seemed to be heading for a peaceful draw when Sobers, the West Indies captain, abruptly and without justification declared at 92 for two, leaving England to score 215 in 165 minutes, a target they achieved without undue difficulty. The fury among Trinidadians and West Indians in general at Sobers's suicidal declaration knew no bounds. There was, Clive Lloyd writes in his autobiography, 'an eerie silence when we walked off the ground', and that evening, in a classically carnivalesque gesture, an effigy of Sobers was hanged and burned in Independence Square in the centre of Port of Spain; 'it was then that I really came to realize what losing meant to West Indians', is Lloyd's comment, 'a lesson I have never forgotten'.[41] Sobers's reputation both among the West Indian players and among West Indian cricket followers collapsed literally overnight. Previously he had been an almost God-like figure for many West Indians, especially in his native Barbados; now his authority over his players vanished and in the next few years, the team disintegrated once more into a collection of highly gifted but disunited individuals, the West Indians underwent the leanest period in their recent cricketing history, losing not only to Australia but also to India, and managing only to draw with New Zealand.[42]

This violent swing of public favour away from the charismatic cricket-hero Sobers may be set beside the fate that has commonly befallen erstwhile or would-be charismatic political leaders in the Caribbean such as Eric Williams of Trinidad or Michael Manley of Jamaica. West Indian politicians are often projected less as leaders than as potential Messiahs, as Moses-figures or – to invoke the name widely given to Michael Manley in the early 1970s – as political Joshuas who will shortly lead 'their' people into the Land of Milk and Honey. So long as these Joshua-figures succeed, they can, it is claimed, count on total devotion from their followers, but should they fail or be seen to fail, as Williams, Manley and, in his own field, Sobers were seen to have failed, they will be rejected with that same passionate uncritical completeness that they were but a short while ago revered. Nursing an almost unbearable sense of betrayal, the theory goes, the erstwhile followers will seek scapegoats on whom to vent their frustration: the saviour-traitor himself and/or a variety of outside forces, groups and individuals. Whether or not this theory of the relationship between leaders and led in West Indian politics is correct, it is surely significant that the only clear instance in West Indian cricket of violence being directed at the opposition *players* occurred during and immediately after the self-inflicted *débâcle* at Port of Spain in 1968. The utterly blameless English captain Cowdrey was booed as he made the 71 that ensured England's victory and, after the final Test at Georgetown (a drawn match which gave England victory in that series), stones were thrown at the England team as it left the ground and poor Cowdrey was, it appears, virtually besieged in the pavilion until a police escort arrived to accompany him back to the team hotel.

The last 'incident' that I want to discuss, that which occurred on the final day of the Test match between the West Indies and Australia at Sabina Park in 1978, was in many ways the most serious, at least inasmuch as it led to the abandonment of a match which the West Indies were almost certain to lose. There can be no doubt that in 1978 the underlying cause of the riots lay in the widespread resentment throughout the West Indies concerning the organization of World Series Cricket by the Australian television magnate, Kerry Packer; characteristically, however, public resentment in the Caribbean was directed not at Packer himself, his organization or the players he had signed up – in the case of the West Indies, all the leading Test cricketers, minus Kallicharran – but above all against 'the authorities' as embodied in the West Indies Cricket Board of Control which, to a large extent, remained dominated by members of the old white and coloured West Indian elite.[43] After the West Indies had easily won the first two Tests with a team made up almost entirely of

'Packer players', a confrontation between the leading players and the Board was precipitated when three 'Packer players', Austin, Haynes and Deryck Murray, were dropped from the Test team. Clive Lloyd protested and resigned the captaincy, all the other 'Packer players' withdrew from the Test team, and the West Indies took the field for the third Test at Georgetown with an entirely new team composed of inexperienced but 'loyal' players captained by Kallicharran; not surprisingly, they lost by a considerable margin. Despite intense public feeling, there was, however, no crowd trouble either at Georgetown or during the fourth Test at Port of Spain compared with a normal Test attendance of 20,000 to 25,000 – and there was talk among cricket enthusiasts of boycotting the Tests completely until the Board· agreed to reinstate the 'rebel' players. By the time of the final Test in Kingston some kind of crowd disturbance was likely, particularly given, once again, the highly charged political and social climate in Jamaica at the time: a crippling economic and financial crisis, endemic gang warfare, a widespread belief that the left-wing or left-inclined Manley government was being 'destabilized' by the CIA, increasingly violent confrontations between the governing People's National Party and the opposition Jamaica Labour Party, and so on.[44] The origins and nature of the riots follow a familiar pattern: a probable West Indian defeat (when the riots began, the West Indies were 258 for nine with six overs to go) combined with a controversial umpiring decision when Vanburn Holder was given out caught at the wicket – not, for once, by a Chinese umpire! – and lingered at the crease, apparently disagreeing with the decision. Almost on cue, stones and bottles began to be thrown, followed by predictably severe police intervention and the abandonment of the match. 'So a series bedevilled by rancour and controversy ended unhappily', is *Wisden's* dry comment.

IV

What interpretation are we to put on such outbursts of rage and frustration which are now sufficiently commonplace to be regarded, as I say, as a permanent potentiality in West Indian cricket? It would, in the first instance, be simple minded and misleading to view them as straight-forward expressions of anti-English or anti-white hostility. With the one minor exception to which I have referred, the rioters' target – to the extent that they have identifiable targets – has been not the opposition team, whatever its colour, but the umpires or, more generally, 'the authorities' or, still more generally and, I suspect, most profoundly, 'the system'.

Orlando Patterson's explanation is more subtle. He argues that the West Indian attitude towards cricket is a deeply ambivalent one in which love and hate co-exist, but in which, contrary to appearances, it is actually the 'hate element' that predominates. Deep down, Patterson claims, West Indians hate cricket because it is the game of the colonizers and their local allies, the old white and coloured elites, and, to that extent, it embodies everything that the lower-class black West Indian is not; it functions as a constant reminder of his imposed economic, social, political, racial, cultural and personal inferiority. When black West Indians like himself triumph over the opposition – especially, obviously, when the opposition is white – his enthusiasm for the game knows no bounds. But should things go the other way, and the black heroes with whom he identifies be bested, or appear to be on the point of being bested, then his underlying hatred of the *game* – the game itself, not the players, the umpires or whatever – reasserts itself and in anger and frustration he destroys it with the most powerful and obvious, indeed the only, weapon at his disposal: violence.[45] Or, to use the cultural terms employed by Wilson and Abrahams, cricket, by dint of its English origins, embodies the established values of order and respectability from which the black West Indian male is alienated but, by dint of its subsequent creolization, has been, so to speak, turned against itself by black West Indians and made to embody the counter-values of aggression, reputation and individualism that govern street culture. All is well so long as the street ethic holds sway over the values of order and respectability but once order reasserts itself (that is, when the West Indies are defeated), the street culture of violence takes its revenge by stripping the whole affair of its symbolism and transforming it into an out-and-out physical confrontation of 'Us' and 'Them'.

This is all very well, but unfortunately for the theory there have been many occasions when West Indian crowds have peacefully and sportingly accepted the defeat of their team, even in such highly charged and dramatic circumstances as the fifth Test versus England at Port of Spain in 1974 when England won by 26 runs with an hour to spare with Tony Greig – an archetypal 'hate figure' if ever there was one – taking 13 wickets in the match. Patterson's theory also implies – and it is an implication which, one imagines, most West Indians would not accept – that the very success of West Indians at cricket is an expression not of achievement but of alienation and false consciousness. It could also be argued – and one can readily imagine certain Marxists taking this view – that cricket in the West Indies has the effect of neutralizing and defusing popular discontent and frustration by channelling them into an essentially harmless activity, an activity which, despite the violence it intermittently provokes, remains a play activity, a fiction, a lie. If this is so, then once again West Indian cricket closely resembles West Indian carnival whose long history, Michael Craton has written, 'shows how festival can actually be used as a safety valve or an anodyne by a ruling class, releasing harmlessly, or damping down, the energies of popular discontent so that actual revolution is averted or indefinitely postponed'.[46] Many questions remain: no doubt further research, less in libraries than at the Oval – Kennington or Kensington, it matters not – will help provide some answers.

NOTES

1 Among the mass of descriptive, historical and, above all, biographical and autobiographical material relating to West Indian cricket, three items, in addition to C.L.R. James's *Beyond a Boundary* (London, 1963) stand out. All have greatly contributed to the present study: Orlando Patterson, 'The Ritual of Cricket', *Jamaica Journal*, 3, No. 1 (1969), reproduced in Andrew Salkey (ed.), *Caribbean Essays: an Anthology* (London, 1973),

108–18; Maurice St Pierre, 'West Indian Cricket: a Socio-cultural Appraisal', *Caribbean Quarterly*, 19, No. 2 (1973), 7–27, and No. 3, 20–35; L. O'Brien Thompson, 'How Cricket is West Indian Cricket? Class, Racial and Color Conflict', *Caribbean Review*, 22, No. 2 (1983), 23–5 and 50–3.

2 The reference is, of course, to Lord Kitchener's celebrated calypso 'Cricket, Lovely Cricket'.

3 See, in particular, George Lamming, *The Pleasures of Exile* (London, 1960), especially pp. 15, 107 and 115.

4 For cultural pluralism in the Caribbean, see M.G Smith, *The Plural Society in the British West Indies* (Berkeley, 1965).

5 For the theory of creolization, see Edward Brathwaite, *The Development of Creole Society in Jamaica 1770–1820* (Oxford, 1971), especially pp. 307–9, and Sidney W. Mintz and Richard Price, *An Anthropological Approach to the Afro-American Past: a Caribbean Perspective* (Philadelphia, 1976).

6 Patterson, 'The Ritual', 109.

7 On the importance of the delimitation of space in play, see Johan Huizinga, *Homo Ludens, a Study of the Play Element in Culture* (London, 1970), pp. 28–9.

8 On religion in the Caribbean, see George Eaton Simpson, *Black Religions in the New World* (New York, 1978).

9 See, among many other examples, the remarkable entry for April 1790 in *Souvenirs du Baron de Wimpffen, Saint-Domingue a la Veille de la Révolution* (Paris, 1911), p. 147.

10 For the whole of this question, see Edward Brathwaite, *Folk Culture of the Slaves of Jamaica* (Port of Spain, 1970).

11 All quotations in Roger D. Abrahams, *The Man-of-words in the West Indies Performance and the Emergence of Creole Culture* (Baltimore, 1983), p. 52.

12 See Michael Craton, *Testing the Chains: Resistance to Slavery in the British West Indies* (Ithaca, 1982), pp. 235–6.

13 *Ibid.*, pp. 209–316.

14 The following account is based on Errol Hill, *The Trinidad Carnival: Mandate for a National Theatre* (Austin, 1972), and Bridget Brereton, *Race Relations in Colonial Trinidad 1870–1900* (Cambridge, 1979), especially Chapter 8, 'The Souls of Black Folk', pp. 152–75.

15 See Brereton, *Race Relations*, pp. 166–7.

16 Hill, *The Trinidad Carnival*, pp. 21–4.

17 Brereton, *Race Relations*, p. 162. On steel bands themselves, see Hill, *The Trinidad Carnival*, pp. 48–51.

18 For the 'February Revolution' in Trinidad, see Ivar Oxaal, *Race and Revolutionary Consciousness* (Cambridge, MA, 1971).

19 See especially Roger D. Abraham, *Talking Black* (Rowley, MA, 1976).

20 See Keith Warner, *The Trinidad Calypso* (London, 1983), pp. 11–20.

21 Hill, *The Trinidad Carnival*, pp. 24–7.

22 On jamet 'bands' in Trinidad, see Brereton, *Race Relations*, p. 167.

23 Quoted in Hill, *The Trinidad Carnival*, p. 26.

24 See above all Emmanuel Le Roy Ladurie, *Carnival in Romans: a People's Uprising at Romans 1579–1580*, translated by Mary Feeney (London, 1980), especially Chapter 12, 'The Winter Festival'.

25 Craton, *Testing the Chains*, p. 235.

26 Warner, *The Trinidad Carnival*, pp. 15–16.

27 Edward Kamau Brathwaite, *Islands* (London, 1969), pp. 40–6, reprinted here by kind permission of Oxford University Press. This magnificent poem is essential reading for all who would understand the elaborate psychodrama of West Indian cricket.

28 Abrahams, *The Man-of-words in the West Indies*, pp. xv–xxxi.

29 Peter J. Wilson, *Crab Antics: the Social Anthropology of English-speaking Negro Societies of the Caribbean* (New Haven, 1973), especially Chapters 7 and 8.

30 Wilson, *Crab Antics*, pp. 165–8.

31 See especially Abrahams, *The Man-of-words*, pp. 21–40.

32 *Ibid.*, pp. 51–4.

33 Referring to the MCC tour of the West Indies in 1934–35, the 1936 edition of *Wisden* states (p. 617) that 'while the West Indians never resorted to the "packed leg-side" and orthodox placing of the field was usual throughout the tour, some of the England players complained of occasional attempts at intimidation in the matter of short-pitched deliveries and full-tosses directed at the batsmen'.

34 Patterson, 'The Ritual', p. 117.

35 *Ibid.*, pp. 111–12.

36 The West Indians' reactions to Greig's 'grovel' remark is discussed in Trevor McDonald, *Viv Richards: the Authorised Biography* (London, 1984), pp. 10–11.

37 On the 1953 constitutional crisis in British Guiana, see Gordon K. Lewis, *The Growth of the Modern West Indies* (New York, 1969), pp. 170–5.

38 See the account of the match given by the West Indies' captain at the time, Jeffry Stollmeyer, in J. Stollmeyer, *Everything Under the Sun: My Life in West Indies Cricket* (London, 1983), p. 148.

39 On Jamaica in the 1960s, see Terry Lacey, *Violence and Politics in Jamaica 1960–1970* (Manchester, 1977).

40 I have been told that, as the English wicket-keeper, Parks, took the catch which dismissed Butcher, the back of his glove touched the ground. In the laws of cricket, so long as the *ball* does not touch the ground, this constitutes a perfectly legal catch, but my Jamaican interlocutor suggested that, according to the conventions of Jamaican street cricket, if the fielder's or wicket-keeper's *hand* touches the ground, as Parks's did, then the batsmen is 'not out'. If this is so and if I am right in attributing considerable importance to the formative influence of street cricket in the Caribbean, then the reactions of parts of the Sabina Park crowd become rather more comprehensible.

41 Clive Lloyd, *Living for Cricket* (London, 1983), pp. 45–6.

42 It is not always realized that between the third Test versus Australia in 1964–65 and the first Test versus England in 1973–74, the West Indies *failed to record a single Test match victory in front of their own crowds in the Caribbean*.

43 Many competing versions of the 'Packer intrusion' exist. The present account is based essentially on McDonald, *Viv Richards*, pp. 107–16 and Stollmeyer, *Everything under the Sun*, pp. 203–11.

44 For Jamaica in the 1970s, see Anthony J. Payne, 'Jamaica: the "democratic socialist" experiment of Michael Manley', in Anthony J. Payne and Paul K. Sutton (eds), *Dependency under Challenge: the Political Economy of the Commonwealth Caribbean* (Manchester, 1984), pp. 18–42.

45 Patterson, 'The Ritual', pp. 113–14. See also St Pierre, 'West Indian Cricket', No. 3, pp. 27–35.

46 Craton, *Testing the Chains*, p. 238.

6

West Indian cricket – Part I: a socio-historical appraisal

Maurice St Pierre

At a time when West Indians are in the throes of shedding the various vestiges of colonialism, one might be justified in asking why is it that the game of cricket, which is a manifestation, *par excellence*, of the colonial legacy, still features very prominently in the West Indian cultural and sporting scene. This chapter seeks to answer this question by firstly examining the historical underpinnings of West Indian cricket and secondly looking at the functional aspects of this game, as far as West Indians are concerned.

Cricket in the West Indies was forged and influenced by the same conditions which moulded other facets of West Indian social structure and culture. From the colonial experience, three such facets spring to mind: white supremacy; the degree of violence, both physical and mental, which has maimed the personalities of countless West Indians; and finally, the concept of divide and rule, which has so successfully kept West Indians of different ethnic and political persuasions at each other's throats. The first section of this article will therefore look at the impact of these three influences on West Indian cricket as well as the extent to which they have led West Indians to indulge in this form of cultural expression in a manner that is markedly dissimilar to that of other cricketing nations. At the same time this section will look at some of the factors generally advanced as being responsible for the current decline of West Indian cricket.

White domination in West Indian cricket

The first West Indian Cricket Team to go to England left in 1900, and in 1928 the West Indies were awarded full Test Match status. Table 6.1 shows that from then until 1957 every subsequent touring team to England was captained and managed by a white or 'near-white' West Indian. With the exception of 1957 when Walcott was Vice-captain under Goddard, the manager and vice-captains were also white. In the course of time there was a dramatic decrease in the proportion of white West Indians and a corresponding increase in the number of non-white West Indians

107

playing cricket for the region. However, although the numbers of white West Indian players declined, effective control and decision-making powers always resided in the hands of the whites.

Table 1 *Racial composition of West Indian touring teams to England, 1900–1957*

Year	Race[a]	
	White	Non-White
1900	10	5
1906	7	7
1923	8	8
1928	6	12
1933	6	10
1939	7	11
1950	7	11
1957	7	13

Note: [a] I am using the term in the sense of white West Indians, i.e., the extent to which an individual looks predominantly Caucasian.

The game of cricket, therefore, in a real sense mirrored life in general in West Indian society, where a similar dichotomy existed. Whites were represented in the top echelons of West Indian society, out of all proportion to their numbers in the population. They led, and non-white West Indians were expected to follow. Decisions with respect to who should play, on which grounds test matches in the West Indies should be played, amount of entrance fee for games and hence profits, continued to be made by the whites. Non-whites, as in other facets of West Indian life, laboured so that the white administrators might profit from their (non-white) labour. Thus when Denzil Batchelor[1] writes, in the manner not untypical of the white expatriate, that the West Indian 'picked up the lovely art of cricket as a child picks up a game, not as a factory worker picks up a trade', apart from the obvious reference to the 'childish nature of the West Indian', he may have been referring to this particular facet of West Indian life which has arrogated the power of control to white administrators and the role of hewers-of-wood and drawers-of-water to non-white West Indians.

We can see this in Barbados, where the caste-like stratification system, based on race/colour, allotted to black Barbadians – they were known as 'professionals' – the role of bowlers and fetchers of balls delivered during practice sessions in which whites batted and blacks only bowled. The emergence of the Barbados League, however, introduced club cricket in Barbados, and blacks were given the opportunity to bat as well as to bowl. This explains why, for years, the only Barbadian batsmen one heard of were white: Challenor, Tarilton, Hoad, Goddard, and the only bowlers one heard of were non-white: Griffith, Martindale, and E.A.V. Williams.

It is of some importance to note that it was the League's decision to have an annual match between a team from the League and one from the Barbados Cricket Association (which came into being before the League)[2]. This led to the weakening of the social barriers between the 'professionals' and the 'better-offs', by allowing Barbadians of disparate social positions to interact on the cricket field, presumably on an egalitarian basis.

It was also particularly as a result of the Thursday afternoon matches, sponsored by the League, that Weekes emerged before the last World War as a potential West Indian player. Not only did the number of clubs affiliated to the League increase from 26 in 1937 to 99 in 1966, but the effects of the weakening of social barriers by the expansion of cricket opportunities, thus provided the possibility for other poor but talented performers such as Hunte, Nurse and Sobers to achieve fame, as well as an enhanced economic position. The fragmentation of this role specialization produced with a vengeance a number of black Barbadian batsmen who, it seemed, were out to settle within a decade the social injustices of decades in the field of cricket.

In Guyana, the Georgetown Cricket Club (GCC), on whose ground, Bourda, all inter-colonial and international cricket was played, was a constant hindrance to the development of Guyanese cricket along serious lines. This was the club of the whites and the Portuguese, and it was no exaggeration to say that the colony team usually contained at least seven members from the Georgetown Cricket Club. Among the non-white, non-Portuguese element there was the opening pair (in the 1940s) Reece and Westmaas, the premier Guyanese batsman, Robert Christiani, a mercurial symbol of uncontained genius, McWatt the wicket-keeper, Gaskin the master of inswing bowling and sometimes Trim, a truly strong fast bowler, who played as a professional for the Georgetown Cricket Club.

These performed very creditably and for years Christiani and Gaskin were the best in their respective fields. But for years one watched, as a succession of light-skinned Georgetown Cricket Club Members and their sons, posing as cricketers, represented, or rather misrepresented Guyana. The team, of course, was always led by a white or a Portuguese member of the Georgetown Cricket Club and it took a black Barbadian, Clyde Walcott, himself a victim of the system, to help shift the basis of selection from one of colour to one of merit. This was achieved largely by his efforts (and to a certain extent those of Christiani) as a cricket coach and a welfare officer on Bookers' sugar estates. The rupturing of the ascriptive basis of selection produced batsmen of the calibre of Kanhai, Butcher and Solomon. This, it should be noted, was in the 1950s, when the drive for political independence was beginning to make irrevocable changes in the structure of Guyanese society.

In Jamaica the position was not dissimilar, though the interest taken by the sugar estates in cricket did help to provide the opportunity for the dispossessed to play the game with the more privileged. The most prestigious cricket club was Kingston Cricket Club whose policy of discrimination along colour lines managed to preserve the club as a bastion for the whites and near-whites in Jamaica.

In Trinidad we are assured by C.L.R. James in his book *Beyond a Boundary*[3] that life for the non-white cricketer was one of uncertainty, restricted upward mobility and discrimination along racial and colour lines. For example, one gets the impression that W. St Hill was left out of the 1923 West Indies Team to England for reasons other than cricketing ability or bad behaviour. Again, Learie Constantine, after a number of abortive attempts to play cricket and to keep his job in Trinidad at the same time, eventually gave up and went to England where he did both simultaneously. He played professional cricket. This problem obtained only for the non-white cricketer who, unless he was affiliated to a club as a groundsman or practice bowler, needed regular employment in order to be able to purchase cricket gear.

The position of the white cricketer was very much different because such a person usually had a better job, was more easily in a position to get time off to play cricket, and was generally in a better position to take advantage of the facilities in the society for those playing cricket.

Performance

There are some who would argue that those whites chosen to play for the West Indies were worthy of selection. To be sure, Tarilton, Challenor, Nunes, Goddard and Stollmeyer, to name some, were tall-scoring batsmen. (It has already been mentioned that bowling was primarily for non-whites.) However, the fact of the matter is that they only rarely demonstrated this abiliiy in Test cricket, at least not against England.

A look at table 6.2 reveals that the number of double centuries, centuries and fifties scored by non-white cricketers exceeded those scored by white cricketers against England on every occasion the West Indies played the latter during the period 1928 to 1959/60.

While West Indian batsmen scored no double centuries or centuries and on 25 occasions made 50 or more runs (but less than 100) their non-white counterparts scored 7 double centuries, 29 centuries and on 56 occasions made 50 or more runs during the period under discussion. While it is true that, as time went on, non-whites outnumbered whites on West Indian cricket teams, it is also true that since whites were not usually picked as bowlers (see table 6.3) and they did not perform as batsmen, then they must have been picked for some other reason.

In view of the foregoing, one can only conclude that they were picked as administrators and as leaders. Indeed, as mentioned before with the exception of the 1957 tour to England, when Walcott was vice-captain, every West Indian manager, captain with tenure, and vice-captain for the period 1928 to 1959/60 on tour to England was white. During the 1958/59 tour to India and Pakistan, the captain was near white (Alexander) and the manager was black (Gaskin), but that was cricket against non-whites, in front of non-white audiences and not against the 'mother country'.

Table 6.2 *West Indian batting performances in Test Matches against England by race at home and abroad, 1928 – 1959/60*

		White			Non-White		
Year	Venue	50+ Runs	100+ Runs	200+ Runs	50+ Runs	100+ Runs	200+ Runs
1928	England	–	–	–	3	–	–
1929/30	W. Indies	4	–	–	6	4	2
1933	England	–	–	–	4	2	–
1934/35	W. Indies	2	–	–	5	–	1
1939	England	3	–	–	3	3	–
1947	W. Indies	4	–	–	6	4	–
1950	England	5	–	–	5	5	1
1953/54	W. Indies	6	–	–	12	4	2
1957	England	1	–	–	5	3	–
1959/60	W. Indies	–	–	–	7	4	1
Total		25	–	–	56	29	7

Table 6.3 *West Indian bowling performances in Test Matches against England by race at home and abroad, 1928 – 1959/60*

	W. Indies	Whites 4 or more wickets per innings	Non-Whites 4 or more wickets per innings
Year	Venue	Times achieved	Times achieved
1928	England	–	3
1929/30	W. Indies	–	7
1933	England	–	3
1934/35	W. Indies	–	2
1939	England	–	-2
1947	W. Indies	1	-6
1950	England	1	-7
1953/54	W. Indies	–	-5
1957	England	–	-4
1959/60	W. Indies	–	-5
Total		2	44

Violence in West Indian Cricket

We have looked at the manner in which the structure of the West Indian society influenced cricket in the West Indies. But what effect did this have on the cultural framework of the islands? It created the framework for frustration.

Differentiation in West Indian society along lines of race, colour, class and power had a number of important consequences for the darker skinned members, nurtured as they inescapably were in a system characterized by violence – white master to slave.

At the same time the cultural emphasis in West Indian society upon things 'white' and de-emphasis on things 'non-white', buttressed the European slant of West Indian society by slavish emulation of whites by non-white West Indians. Such emulation was not, however, rewarded by upward mobility in West Indian society. The result was frustration which bespoke aggression and violence.

Non-whites set out to out-perform whites in all facets of European culture. There was the dress, the speech, the culinary habits – and there was cricket! The thirst for recognition produced non-white cricketers superior to white cricketers in every department of the game, but as in every other walk of West Indian life, these West Indians were denied entrance into the top echelons of West Indian cricket society.

Some exploded in anger and were destroyed, sometimes violently. There was, for example, the Jamaican, Hylton, who was hanged for the murder of his wife. There was Gilchrist, who was hounded out of West Indian cricket by allegations of ungentlemanly conduct (by European definitions, of course). Others like Walcott appeared to have retired from the game prematurely. However, Walcott's genius re-appeared in the form of other cricketers, as he coached others to greatness, and also helped to undermine the very system which had conspired to deny him his just rewards on grounds other than cricketing ability. But most sublimated their aggression into the only socially approved channel which allowed a form of violence with impunity, i.e., through the game of cricket itself.

Violence in cricket then must surely be an outgrowth of the inert violence which has characterized relationships between whites and non-whites. To my mind it produced a series of famous West Indian fast bowlers. When Learie Constantine almost immobilized the Honourable F.S.G. Calthorpe, captain of the 1926 MCC Touring Team, cricket captain of an English county and an English aristocrat, he was in a real sense striking out at the embodiment of his frustration (and that of the stratum of West Indian society of which he was a part) but in a socially acceptable manner – on the cricket field. Even so his colleagues had asked him to desist because it was felt that this would cause 'trouble'. He was told, 'do not bump that ball at that man . . . . The bowling is obviously too fast for him, and if you hit him and knock him down, there'll be a hell of a row, and we don't want to see you in any such mess. Stop it'.[4]

Of George John, the Trinidad and West Indian fast bowler, James, in the same book writes, "If he had been an Italian of the Middle Ages, he would have been called Furioso. He had an intimidating habit of following down after the delivery if the ball was played behind the wicket . . . . Almost every ball he was rolling up his sleeves like a man about to commit some long premeditated act of violence'.[5]

Wes Hall was in his heyday credited with being the fastest bowler in the world, and he took one of the longest run-ups in the history of the game. Roy Gilchrist, of whom mention was made, despite his slender build and relative lack of height for a fast bowler, was quoted as saying that when he runs up to bowl all he sees are pads standing in the way of the stumps which he aims to hit.

It is possible to argue that there are technical factors, namely the hardness of West Indian wickets and relative absence of heaviness in the atmosphere, which favour getting a batsman out by sheer pace. But Australia, too, has hard wickets, and though that country has produced Miller, Lindwall, Ron Archer, Davidson and Meckiff, none possessed either the pace of Hall or the ferocity of George John. Again one may argue that England produced Larwood, Voce, Tyson, Trueman[6] and Snow. But England cannot claim to have produced fast bowlers in such constant succession as have the West Indies. This is so in spite of the fact that the Trinidad wicket favours swing bowling early on the first day of the match.

With the cricket bat, violence is even more pronounced. The West Indies have produced such ferocious hitters of the ball as Learie Constantine, Headley, Weekes, Walcott, Sobers, Collie Smith, Kanhai and Lloyd. Constantine, although he was more famous as a bowler, hit especially the pace bowlers with tremendous power. Headley, despite his relatively small stature and the lack of support from other West Indian batsmen, was no mean hitter of the ball.

Weekes, though the shortest of the three Ws, was described after the 1950 tour of England, as having batted with a 'hammer'. One particular innings of his, of 94 against the MCC in the third test in Guyana during the 1953/54 tour, illustrates this point. Wardle the slow left-arm spinner bowled from the northern end to Weekes, who having very early spotted the delivery as being a trifle short, jumped around it seemed, so that his body was facing a westerly direction and drove (one can't say pull, though it really was a pull) the ball to the square leg boundary. The ball ricocheted off the railing, the impact removing pieces of whitewash. Even this removal may not be lacking in significance.

Walcott, who is much bigger than Weekes, was described after his 168 not out at Lords in 1950, as a batsman who makes a bat look like 'a teaspoon' and bowling like 'weak tea'. He had hit the ball with such force off the backfoot that it is said that on one occasion an English fieldsman ran alongside the ball for some time before attempting to pick it up. Though half of Walcott's size, it is perhaps not surprising that his protégé, Kanhai, should also hit the ball with such power. Indeed, his innings of 251 not out against Victoria during the 1960 tour to Australia was an explosion which hastened Meckiff's withdrawal from test cricket. Sobers and Lloyd are both left-handed batsmen with high backlifts which, in part, account for the force with which they hit the ball.

To be sure, Australia and England have produced tall-scoring and hard-hitting batsmen. The Australians have had Trumper, Woodfull, Ponsford, Bradman, Morris, Bill Brown, Harvey, Barnes, Miller and Benaud. None, however, not even Bradman, who once scored a century in 3-eight ball overs, nor Benaud who hit 8 sixes in a Festival Match at Scarborough, England, in 1957, could be described as possessing the murderous hitting power of Weekes, Walcott or Lloyd.

England has produced Grace, Woolley, Ranjitsinghji, Hammond, Compton, Graveney, Cowdrey, Dexter, May, Milburn and Boycott. However, with the possible exception of Dexter and Milburn (never a regular member of the England team) none matched the hitting power of the West Indies. Rather Woolley has been associated with 'grace'; Graveney's batting has been described as 'poetry in motion' and Cowdrey as an 'exquisite timer of the ball.'

The West Indies also produced batsmen of the calibre of Nunes, Grant, Tarilton, Challenor, Stollmeyer, Gomez, Goddard, Trestrail and Bayley who were white, but none was renowned for his hard hitting.

What can we infer from this record? In the first place it seems that the fastest bowlers and the hardest hitting batsmen all come from the West Indies. In the second place, it is obvious that these players are all non-white .

It is a well-known fact that race and colour were the principal means by which West Indian society was stratified. This meant that this caste-like stratification system, lacking as it did a powerful divine rationalization, such as religion in India, was bound to produce frustrations, which ultimately sought aggressive outlets. Because other outlets for channelling aggression were closed, either by cultural prescriptions (such as 'leh the white man rule') or structural constraints (such as white ownership and control of the means of production which supported their claim to make the rules of reward and punishment), non-white West Indian cricketers chose the game of cricket as the only available socially approved outlet. In the West Indies the racist ideology which asserted the supremacy of whites broke down as the transparency of this ideology was laid bare on the cricket field.

Performance before an audience of West Indians equally emphatic about violent and aggressive cricket, conspired to produce a change in this 'beautiful, difficult English game'. This change was essentially one of self-image, for not only has cricket been functional in this purely cathartic sense for West Indians, but it has facilitated a degree of upward mobility. Removal of frustration has been followed by a change in the stratification system away from a purely ascriptive one towards one based on achievement. The non-white cricketer is thereby putting himself not against the white player but against a 'super-star'.

Divide and rule in West Indian cricket

For a start, let us see how super-cricketer image compounded the divide-and-rule policy which has affected West Indian social structure. In the first instance a policy of divide and rule predisposed a spirit of competition among West Indians. In the second instance, this was compounded by a desire to emulate as much as possible whatever was defined as European.

Political independence was at this time merely wishful thinking and whites were still very much in control of the decision-making machinery at every level of West Indian society. For dark-skinned West Indians status was to be had by as complete an emulation as possible of the dominant European cultural apparatus. Behaviour on the cricket field was no exception.

The history of cricket in the West Indies, with the exception of the period of Worrell's captaincy suggests that the West Indian team has functioned primarily as a collection of brilliant individuals rather than as a team of brilliant cricketers working together for the achievement of a common aim.

In the early stages of Worrell's captaincy, the team was not selected on the basis of merit and ability alone. Race and colour were more important. Whatever commendations came to be showered on West Indian cricket during this period were due to the efforts of individual performers, such as Tarilton, Headley, Roach, Constantine, Martindale, John, Francis and Griffith.

In the field of cricket, as in other spheres of life, the above-mentioned factors were accompanied by the existence of a built-in feeling of insecurity and of urgency. Since the darker West Indian could not always count on merit to help him to make the team, then he was made to feel insecure because his selection sometimes hinged upon factors over which he had no control. In his desire to reduce this insecurity, the West Indian cricketer placed excessive emphasis on performance – individual performance that would bring him to the top. This meant primacy on intra-team competition and a consequent de-emphasis on team performance.

On the other hand, the sense of urgency inclined him to perform spectacularly so that the imprint of his performance could be indelibly placed on the minds of all, especially those who ran and controlled West Indian cricket – the whites. For this type of performance he found a willing band of supporters – the West Indian crowd.

The irony of the situation was that in his haste to perform spectacularly, the non-white West Indian cricketer often failed miserably. Many a non-white West Indian batsman needlessly gave away his wicket because of the urge to please. He failed to realize that 'bright cricket' is something that is preached by whites but not often practised by them.

The position of the West Indian cricketer was like the man in the ghetto. He is so accustomed to grovelling for an existence that when he gets a chance to get out, he climbs on top of his brother's shoulders in his haste to leave the ghetto. Such a situation cannot fail to breed individualism and to abort any sense of team spirit. It is very clearly up to the captain to infuse whatever *esprit de corps* is possible. This was not always possible where the captain was usually white and in many instances a less competent cricketer, not worthy of a position on the team, much less as a leader. In the period before Worrell's captaincy, therefore, leadership of the West Indian team was usually given to a white West Indian who it could be said was not always worthy of a place on the team, and selection on the team was not always made primarily by merit and ability.

The era of Worrell's captaincy started in earnest when he led the West Indian team in Australia during the 1960/61 tour and ended with his retirement in 1965. Worrell, it should be noted, had previously led West Indian cricket teams and

Commonwealth cricket teams, but these were on unofficial tours and not against 'the mother country'.

The period 1960–66 saw the rise of the West Indies to the premier cricketing position in the world. During this period the four major British West Indian territories attained political independence, and indeed, it was in no small measure due to the efforts of C.L.R. James that Worrell was given the captaincy. James, it should be noted, quite rightly viewed the refusal to give the West Indian cricket captaincy to the man best equipped for the job as symptomatic of a deeper underlying cause which had political implications at a national level. This is significant because it exemplifies an attempt by a major political figure to locate the game in the West Indian social-cultural matrix and to invite public scrutiny, and indeed, control in an area of West Indian endeavour which had long defied attempts to democratize it.

The status of West Indian cricket was due primarily to Worrell's astute captaincy, as well as his capacity to get the best out of team members, and more importantly, to weld a set of disparate units into a cohesive whole. Indeed, the performance of a former captain, Alexander with the bat, and behind the stumps during the 1960/61 Australian Tour was one example of Worrell's talents in the first direction. James (in his book) recalls that on speaking to Worrell after the tour, the West Indian captain spoke of players primarily in terms of their being or not being good team men – a clear indication of the importance Worrell attached to team spirit. Table 6.4 indicates that under Worrell's leadership, the West Indies played 15 Test Matches during the period 1960–63, of which 9 were won and 3 lost. This was the period when the West Indies were world cricket champions.

Table 6.4 *West Indian performances under Worrell 1960–1963*

Year	Country	Win	Lose	Draw	Tie	Matches Played
1960/61	Australia	1	2	1	1	5
1961/62	India	5	–	–	–	5
1963	England	3	1	1	–	5
Total		9	3	2	1	15

It is perhaps prudent to remember that during this period for the first time in the history of West Indian cricket, the leadership of the team was given to a man universally acknowledged to be the best man for the job – a black West Indian, Worrell. The members of the team enthused with the knowledge that at last merit and ability in the sphere of cricket had superseded ascriptive criteria for selection, such as race and colour, shrugged off their feeling of insecurity and played as they had never played before – as a team.

Again, under Worrell's competent leadership, and emphasis on team performance, anxiety receded and the West Indies became the best cricketing nation in the world. Finally, even in Australia during the 1960/61 tour, despite what was generally felt to have been undue assistance by Australian umpires to the Australian team, and though they did not win the series, the West Indian performance helped to transform the game from a dying sport into a viable one with increasing audience participation and gate receipts.

After Worrell's gentlemanly leadership, followed Sobers' brilliance; with Sobers leading the nucleus of the side which made the West Indians world cricket champions. Sobers has, however, been unable to match Worrell's success as a captain. The figures in table 6.5 show that in the last 39 last matches played under Sobers, the West Indies have won on 9 occasions, lost on 10 occasions and drawn on 20 occasions. It should also be noted that of the 9 matches won, 7 were won during the test series played 1965 to 66/67, i.e., the period immediately following Worrell's departure, and the West Indies have not won a Test Match since the 1968/69 tour to Australia.[7] India beat us for the first time in 28 test matches at Queen's Park Oval in 1971.

Table 6.5 *West Indian performances under Sobers 1965/72*

Year	Country	Win	Lose	Draw	Matches Played
1965	Australia	2	1	2	5
1965	England	3	1	1	5
1966/67	India	2	-	1	3
1968	England	-	1	4	5
1968/69	Australia	1	3	1	5
1968/69	New Zealand	1	1	1	3
1969	England	-	2	1	3
1971	India	-	1	4	5
1972/67	New Zealand	-	-	5	5
Total		9	10	20	39

By any standard this later performance makes dismal reading and much has been said about the inconsistent performance of West Indian cricketers, especially during the past two series against teams which at least on paper, were considered inferior to the West Indian team. On at least four occasions the West Indies had half of the opposing side out for 100 runs yet failed to get the whole team out for less than 300 runs. In the third Test Match against the New Zealanders in 1972 at least five catches were put down in one day, and so on.

The decline of West Indian cricket

The decline of West Indian cricket from 1968 onwards has been variously attributed to a number of factors of which the most important are poor individual performance; lack of team spirit; ineffective captaincy and short-sighted selectorial policy.

Individual performance in the field seen in terms of catches put down, poor batting, and evidenced by the number of dismissals due to casual strokes, and by getting run out, indicate an uninspired approach to the game. It suggests that some West Indian team members not only fail to regard themselves as part of a well organized integrated unit, but are not even motivated to perform creditably as individuals. It is almost as though some feel that the cause of West Indian cricket supremacy is a hopeless one.

The second main reason usually advanced for the decline of West Indian cricket is lack of team spirit in those incidents which, though they are not part of the game per se, are nevertheless crucial to the maintenance of group solidarity. When a West Indian batsman was given out against India and New Zealand, this was a signal for all the members of the team to hug and kiss each other, in addition to offering overt congratulations to the person or persons directly responsible for the batsman's dismissal. In other words, the dismissal of a batsman was used as a means of refurbishing group solidarity, and in so doing, reinforcing team spirit. No such comparable ritual accompanied West Indian successes on the field.

The West Indian captaincy

In recent times, much has been said about the suitability of Garfield Sobers as team captain and arguments have been advanced both for and against retaining him as the West Indian cricket captain for a further period. Those who argue in favour of his retention, do so on the grounds that his tremendous all-round skill and experience make him an automatic member of the team and provide him with the wherewithal to supply the sort of leadership which wins matches. Those who favour his removal from the captaincy argue that he is overworked and tired, seems to be more interested in things other than cricket, and most important, he has been a failure as a captain and is now beginning to fail as a player. For example, against New Zealand in 1972, he scored a total of 253 runs in 8 innings, was not out on one occasion with a highest score of 142 runs. In other words, in 7 innings he made a total of 111 runs which, with the one not out innings gave him an average of 18.50 runs for those 7 excursions to the crease. In the bowling department he took 10 wickets at an average of 33.20 runs per wicket.

Sobers, it is said, has failed to motivate team members to perform at their best. One notices the fall of a wicket of the opposing team is not accompanied by the same spontaneous fanfare of jumping, hugging and shouting that accompanies the fall of a West Indian wicket. Again West Indian on-the-field performances have not been characterized by the same dedication and application that opposing teams show. This was particularly true of the New Zealanders when they were fielding. Mention should also be made here of Congdon's determination which shone through a very shaky start and enabled him to score 166 in the first innings of the third Test in Trinidad, in 1971.

Again off the field, it has been said that Sobers spends less time discussing on-the-field performance than, for instance, Kanhai did whenever the latter had the opportunity to captain the team in state matches during the 1969 Australian tour. A man who made 70-odd runs and thinks he has done well might find that he is crit-icized by Kanhai for (a) the manner and mistakes made in compiling his runs and (b) for not having made a hundred. The immediate result of this type of off-the-field interest was an all-out on-the-field effort 'to please Rohan'. This manifested itself in brilliant fielding performances. The team spirit thus gained significant increments.

Last, but by no means least, it is possible that playing in the same team with Sobers, a man who has scored more than 7,000 Test runs (joining the select company of Walter Hammond and Cowdrey) including 26 Test centuries (only Bradman scored more) and who has taken over 215 Test wickets, must be an awe-inspiring experience. Often described as the greatest cricketer the game has known, it is not surprising that this manifestation of individual performance should have come from a West Indian cricketer. The social, cultural milieu which spawned him, emphasized individual performance in many instances to the detriment of team per-formance. Similarly, the Charlie Davis 'lapse of memory' which resulted in Lloyd's run out in the Guyana test against New Zealand in 1972 can be seen as a surrealis-tic act of individualism, where Davis unconsciously saw himself as performing alone. Both Sobers and Davis are products of the divide-and-rule system.

There are some, like Lloyd Best[8] who would argue that Sobers is primarily con-cerned with doing a job for money. Since we live in a world in which the cash nexus is a primary integrative force, Sobers is motivated solely by the mechanics of demand and supply. He subscribes to the motto – performance, proficiency, pro-fessionalism and pay. Such an argument, coming as it did from an economist, is perhaps understandable. However, cricket in the West Indies is a national pastime; it does not stop at the level of the individual in the game, but has wider societal implications. The reaction to Sobers's 'sporting' declaration against England in 1968, when England won after being given 165 runs to make in 215 minutes, and to his visit to Rhodesia early in 1971 bear this out quite clearly.

But the question of leadership in West Indian cricket ought not to be dismissed so easily. It is at the heart of the general question of leadership in the West Indies. Let us therefore look at it in some more detail. Frank Worrell, the first black captain of a West Indian cricket team, had attended a top secondary school in Barbados and eventually graduated from a British University. He was also reputed to be a cool tac-tician,[9] to be capable and aloof when necessary and possessed of the ability to deliver the goods, i.e., to win matches.

In sociological parlance Worrell took over the captaincy of West Indian cricket and by his role-making[10] changed the image of the game in the minds of West Indians and also the expectations of West Indians with respect to the performance of the captain, team spirit and the behaviour of the West Indian cricket hero. Worrell therefore by his behaviour had made himself acceptable to both those in the

Metropole and those of the Colony. He was the gentleman or as some may prefer to say the 'Afro-Saxon', and he had by his efforts, created in the minds of West Indians particularly high expectations with respect to the question of leadership in West Indian cricket. He was like the majority of West Indian politicians – a 'middle-class hero' leading a 'working-class crowd' with few traditional promulgated examples of heroism, where history had also predisposed them to accept uncritically a man with a background like Worrell in an era when only Jamaica and Trinidad had attained political independence (and only recently at that).

Now what of Garfield Sobers? An ex-policeman who made the West Indies team at the age of 18 years,[11] he neither attended a prestigious Barbados secondary school nor a university. His elevation to the position of West Indian captain was achieved at most solely on the basis of all-round excellence in the game. Therefore Sobers succeeded to a position which had been previously occupied by a relatively educated West Indian of middle-class background who had attained excellence at cricket, who by his re-making of the role had created a high level of expectation in the minds of West Indians with respect to the role performance as captain. What is more, Sobers was asked to perform during a time when West Indians,[12] some of whom had recently attained political independence while others were struggling for this status, were questioning old values and seeking to create new ones. It was a period of serious cultural re-evaluation.

Sobers was therefore being asked to do a job for which his main qualification was individual performance, but which required much more. It may be said, therefore, that he was under-qualified for the job and his employers were not sympathetic to his short-comings. So Sobers continued to use the tools in his possession to perform the job and his employers gradually became dissatisfied with his performance, until a number of them clamoured for his dismissal and received his resignation.

Selectorial policy

The final factor possibly accounting for the present state of West Indian cricket concerns the question of selectorial policy. While it is tempting when playing in the West Indies, to capitalize on the easy and relatively inexpensive accessibility of replacing players who are deemed to have failed, from match to match, many wonder at the wisdom of this policy. During the recent New Zealand tour, the West Indies tried no less than 18 players with only Davis, Fredericks, Findlay and Sobers playing in all the five Test Matches. Of these only Sobers played in all five Tests against the Indians. The tendency to place and replace is perhaps overdone, especially if it is hoped to build a future team around a nucleus of players, accustomed to playing together as a team.

The West Indies find themselves in this dilemma for two possible reasons. In the first place, there appears to be no set policy of replenishing the supply of West Indian cricket talent as each crop begins to fade out. To be sure, there is a yearly inter-territorial competition for youths as well as fully-fledged national players, but not much effort is made to scout around to look for talent to fill the gaps in the West Indian team. In other words, players can only make it if they come up through the formally designated ranks. The chances of discovering a Ramadhin, turning a coconut on a concrete pavement, are thus reduced.

Recently both Hall and Griffith made an attempt to give Jamaican fast bowler, Uton Dowe, a chance to fill one of the fast bowling slots in the West Indian team by giving him special coaching. Although this is admirable it should be encouraged at an earlier stage in the player's career, and it should be designed to fill particular needs in the West Indian cricketing body, where there are either no established players or where the established players are on the threshold of retirement.

Obviously this means taking the long-awaited step of 'nationalizing' West Indian cricket so that the game in all its aspects is open to any West Indian of ability. There should be no need for a West Indian Cricket Board of Control (the Board) which continues to allow particular individuals, belonging to particular clubs, to make large profits from the efforts of others by controlling match venues and admission prices.

At the present time, the Board has the power to invite and pay for the passages of cricketers whom it wishes to consider for selection on a West Indian team playing at home. It should be noted that usually other players are invited on the understanding that they pay their own passages, which would then be refunded if they are selected to play for the West Indies. Since this latter group of players is almost certain to play for their respective territories anyway, they are not usually out of pocket as their passages are then paid by the territories concerned, should they fail to make the West Indian team.

The Board also has the power to resolve itself into a selectorial sub-committee for the purpose of choosing the West Indian team and to decide, in conjunction with the territorial Cricket Board of Control, which club's grounds will be used as a venue for the Test Match. This ground is hired by the Board, which then also reserves the right to recruit concessionaires and to fix admission prices. The right to fix admission prices, by extension, carries with it the ability to determine profits, which I am told, are then divided among visiting team members, the West Indian team members and the various territorial Cricket Boards of Control. The money earned by the last named group is meant to be used for the improvement of cricket facilities in the respective territories.

This simple breakdown of the processes of decision making reveals the extent to which the power structure of this most popular West Indian sporting pastime is strikingly similar to other profit-making organizations in this part of the world. The Board which numbers eleven and which is elected for a period of two years, constitutes the ultimate policy-forming body in West Indian cricket. The members of the Board are equivalent to the managers of the firm, in terms of the power they wield, especially to hire and fire players and to determine the cost of the service produced by cricket.

Then come the players. These are the incumbents of middle-rung management positions. Their contribution is directly vital to the production of the service emanating from the cricket organization, but only indirectly to the determination of profits. They are equivalent to the foremen in the firm and their position of structural marginality exposes them to the same strains and conflicts as foremen, since they are required to please simultaneously both the upper-rung management and the lowest level of organizational participant – the spectators. The spectators are the largest in number and in practice possess the least power. In theory, however, they possess the most power in the organization, since without them there would be no serious cricketing atmosphere and *ipso facto* no players, no managers and no profits.

Two factors, however, conspire to reduce this potential power to a minimum. The first is that the spectators are not organized, or to continue in the vein of the industrial analogy, they are not unionized. Therefore, except when they spontaneously combine in protest as, for example, during riots and in noisy ridicule of players, spectators normally fail to influence the production of a service they help to generate. They may, therefore, be said to be lacking in consciousness.[13]

The second factor is that the advertising media, which emphasize the attractions of cricket and cricketers continually wed the spectator to the idea of the organization by underscoring continued participation in the latter. These two factors may also be said to indicate the spectators' lack of consciousness and further help to explain why they continue to watch cricket in the West Indies despite the poverty of facilities even in the premier cricketing grounds. One is left to wonder to what use are the profits of cricket being put, especially since it seems that much is not being spent on recruiting a second strong eleven to fill the vacancies created by the departure of more established players.

The second facet of selectorial policy concerns the allegation that players are not chosen so much on merit, but on the principle of specific numerical representation for each territory. Thus it has been said that Kallicharran's long-awaited entree into Test cricket was continually postponed by the Jamaicans' belief that they should have at least four players on the team. In fact the arrogance of the Jamaican position was probably borne out by the fact that a letter to the *Daily Gleaner* suggested during the last Indian tour that Jamaica should go it alone in the test arena, i.e., apply for Test Match status. Though the less said about that suggestion the better, it very clearly brings out the fact that some will stop at nothing to perpetuate the adverse effects or the divide-and-rule policy and weaken unnecessarily West Indian cricket and whatever regional co-operation exists.

The above-mentioned factors must, however, all be seen against the backdrop of West Indian social conditions which prevailed during the period of Sobers's captaincy. This period came soon after the failure of the West Indian Federation and soon after the attainment of political independence by Jamaica and Trinidad. It also saw the attainment of this goal by Guyana and Barbados. The period of Sobers's captaincy, i.e., from 1965 to 1972 thus coincided with a period when there was much change in the West Indian society.

West Indians began to experience the first set of post-political independence problems occasioned by new political constitutions and increased strain on the national purse. Increases in unemployment rates, transitional problems of change in personnel, especially in the civil service and some branch plants of foreign-owned multi-national corporations, failure to meet pre-political independence promises and the resultant disenchantment at the national level all contributed to a society which saw more rapid structural change than before.

This period also saw the beginnings of a cultural awareness in which the trappings of colonialism were being questioned in earnest for the first time. Matters of speech, dress, leisure pursuits, attitudes to West Indians in positions of authority, the need for West Indian heroes and a West Indian-oriented education system all became the focus of topical attention.

The combination of the structural and cultural changes produced a social atmosphere characterized by experimentation, trial and error, internal power struggles and a tendency toward intra-territorial autonomy. This atmosphere influenced the organization of cricket and the performance of managers, players and spectators.

Last, but not least, this period also saw the flight of West Indian cricketers, both established and potential, to play professional cricket in England and sometimes, Australia. Playing cricket throughout the English summer tended to tire out West Indian cricketers playing at home, thus reducing their capacity to perform to the best of their ability. However, perhaps more important, it enabled English players in particular to get accustomed to and know the secrets of West Indian players, thus reducing the capacity for surprise.

The point of the foregoing is to argue that in addition to a discussion of some of the problems at the level of the game, any serious assessment of the changing fortunes of West Indian cricket during the leadership of Sobers must also take into account the changing nature of West Indian society, coming in the wake of the quest for and the attainment of political independence by the four main territories which contribute to West Indian cricket.

So far in this article I have been content with pinpointing a number of features of West Indian cricket by relating them to specific factors of the colonial experience in the West Indies. Three such factors were dealt with, i.e., white supremacy, violence and divide-and-rule. It was argued that these three factors have conspired to produce a type of cricket played by West Indians which is markedly different from that played in England, despite the fact that the game was introduced to this part of the world at a time when British colonialism was in full sway.

In the second part of this article, I will attempt to answer, in much greater detail, the question: Why is cricket still so important, probably more so than ever now, to a nation of people who in various ways are showing a burgeoning tendency to shake off the trappings of British colonialism? The second part of the article will also deal with the contribution the game makes to West Indian society.

Notes

1 Denzil Batchelor, 'The Developing Game', in Learie Constantine and Denzil Batchelor (eds), *The Changing Face of Cricket*, London: Eyre and Spottiswoode, 1966, p. 62.
2 For a fuller discussion see Clyde A. Walcott, 'The Home of the Heroes', *New World*: Barbados Independence Issue, 1966, pp. 51–3.
3 C.L.R. James, *Beyond a Boundary*, London: Hutchinson, 1969.
4 *Ibid*, p. 112.
5 *Ibid*, p. 81.
6 Trueman, in particular was an interesting personality who, by his aggressive bowling and humorous antics on the field of play, was considered by some to be, at best 'not cricket' and at worst 'vulgar' – was certainly the most popular English cricketer when he toured the West Indies. He was, of course, a working-class Englishman.
7 This article was written before the 1973 West Indian tour of England, which restored West Indian cricket fortunes.
8 See Lloyd Best, 'Beyond the Boundary: Each Man for Himself', *Trinidad Sunday Guardian*, January 19, 1969.
9 It is said that he was capable of falling asleep while waiting his turn to bat.
10 Refers to the act of taking over a position and changing it in such a way that expectations of the role change accordingly.
11 Sobers was actually 17 years and 245 days and was the third youngest test cricketer in the history of the game.
12 Worrell's leadership during the early 1960s had come both before and during the period when the colonial experience had predisposed West Indians to accept as a fact of life leaders, who despite their indigenous origins were nevertheless close in orientation to the colonial masters. The period of Sobers's leadership from 1965–1972, coincided with the beginnings of the de-mystification of the aura of superiority of any one stratum in West Indian Society. It was during the period also that a greater awareness of the ability of men of humble origins to make it to the top began to surface.
13 The fact that the 5th Test Match between the West Indies and Australia in Trinidad was undersupported, a daily average of 500 spectators in attendance, now suggests that this may no longer be so.

124

7

West Indian cricket – Part II: an aspect of creolisation

Maurice St Pierre

Cricket and the West Indian cricketer

For the individual player in the West Indies, excellence at cricket promises now, as it has never done before, an education, upward social mobility, economic security and a chance to do 'his own t'ing'. However, it also reduces the player's anonymity considerably and excellence at cricket carries with it, its own congeries of disadvantages.

It is universally acknowledged that all learning does not come out of a book, one learns a considerable amount by just travelling. The West Indian test cricketer today gets the opportunity to visit every continent (for example, teams of West Indian cricketers have gone to Africa, India and the United States of America) and therefore gets the opportunity also to observe different cultures in different societies. Where he does not go as a member of an official test team he may go as a member of an unofficial test team or even as an individual player.

In days gone by, West Indian teams visited most often England. Before 1951, the only tour made to Australia was in 1931/32. Since then West Indian cricket teams have visited Australia and New Zealand on no less than three occasions. The first tour made to India was in 1948/49, and the first to Pakistan was in 1958/59. Thus, while the former West Indian players were restricted, both in terms of duration of tours, frequency of tours and variety of countries visited, no such problem exists for current West Indian cricketers.

Apart from the possibility of improving one's education and enriching one's experiences through travel, cricket serves to improve the economic condition of the players. C.L.R. James relates how Learie Constantine, Snr nearly missed the 1900 tour to England because of his financial position. We are also told how the son, Learie Constantine was forced to emigrate to England because he could not play cricket and keep his job at the same time. As I said before, the same was not necessarily true for white cricketers in the West Indies.

Today West Indian cricketers play cricket throughout the year and so are able to live by the activity at which they excel. An impressive number of West Indian cricketers have played and continue to play league cricket in England during the months May to September. An increasing number are playing county cricket in England;

and the earnings of Sobers, simply from playing cricket, are reported to be the highest of any cricketer in the world. I suspect, however, that South Africans Barry Richards and Mike Procter are not doing too badly.

Those who do not play for the West Indies, during what would be the winter months in England (December–March), may return to their jobs as coaches or like Sobers, Kanhai, Hall and now Lloyd, may find Australia a happy hunting ground financially. More and more efforts, however, are being made to keep West Indian test cricketers in the West Indies when they are not performing in England during the summer. It is reported that in one instance an expatriate firm in Guyana raised the salary of a Guyanese test cricketer who worked for them as a coach and welfare officer in order to dissuade him from leaving to play county cricket in England. Two factors here are of importance. In the first place, many West Indian test cricketers have been able to improve their status economically by playing test cricket, e.g. Butcher, Sobers, Kanhai, Ramadhin, the late Collie Smith, Valentine, Gilchrist, and so on.

Secondly, many West Indian test cricketers have used their widened horizons, not only to improve their economic position, but to maintain that improved status. Thus, Learie Constantine took the opportunity, while playing cricket in England, to become a lawyer and community leader there, which finally earned him a knighthood. Weekes became a coach and is now a hotel manager; Walcott moved from coach to welfare officer with Bookers in Guyana, and Valentine of Jamaica had similar fortune. Even where it is possible to argue that a cricketer may have improved his economic position considerably were it not for cricket, it would be nevertheless true to say that the pace and thrust of his mobility would not have been achieved so quickly had it not been for cricket. Thus Worrell, despite his mental ability, which incidentally was pressed into the service of cricket for several years, would hardly have reached his distinguished position in the fields of education and politics in the West Indies, if his mental ability and natural charm were not previously buttressed by a very outstanding cricketing career. By improving a player's economic position, cricket has improved his social standing and led to improvement in his status position (life-style, prestige, deference). It is a fact that cricket has provided an avenue for upward social mobility for non-white West Indian cricketers.

Naturally, it followed that amelioration of economic condition and improved education due to travel have enabled the West Indian cricketer not only to improve his life-style and to sophisticate his consumption patterns but to make provision to ensure the continuity of that life-style. This improvement in life-style has been accompanied by increasing prestige and recognition of a leadership role. The West Indian cricketer's prestige has been increased among other things, by the frequency with which he is being asked to accept lucrative coaching assignments. A request to coach, suggests, not only that one has mastered the game, but that one is in a position to impart one's mastery to a number of aspiring neophytes. A lucrative coaching assignment can, however, mean even more than that. It signifies a degree of social estimation of one's skill.

To the individual cricketer it means his society's acceptance of his skill per se and his possible contribution to the values of his society. This is an important development in West Indian society, where emphasis to the point of making it a creed, 'Work Not Play', has been the guide to young people choosing a means of livelihood. Many West Indian children were physically beaten for playing too much and paying too little attention to school work, despite the fact that such children consistently displayed no aptitude or interest in the formal education, and had both talent and interest in the game. The result was, of course, that they fell between the proverbial two stools, unable to earn a decent living at either 'play' or work.

Secondly, the new social assessment of cricketing skill must be seen against the backdrop of a society which has traditionally approved of a 'collar and tie' job, which certainly did not include cricket. It is interesting to note that the Jamaican musician, Byron Lee, in a radio interview in late 1972, made a similar point about musical talent. He recalled how hard he fought to get people to accept that 'musicians were people, too' and that playing music was an eminently honourable way to make a living. He, therefore, had to inform persons who hired his band in the earlier period that he and his band were not prepared to accept some food on a table outside in the garden. They were an integral part of the gathering, not to be relegated to the inferior status of hired servants.

Finally, a player whose economic position was gained by excellence at cricket, experiences a vastly increased amount of personal deference. Without getting into an argument as to whether deference is being paid to the man himself or to the man as a cricketer, let me merely say that the adoring glances and attentions of females and the adulation of the crowd, both on and off the field, do in a real sense fail to separate the man from the cricketer. Consequently, excellence at the game provides the player with possible satisfactions to a number of inner needs. A Freudian would probably argue that hitting a ball or bowling fast provides the actor with the satisfaction of a sexual need sublimated through the medium of cricket. There may be a lot in that on which I won't argue at this point.

However, I would argue that cricket does afford the player the opportunity to fully express his inner self. Anyone who has seen a vintage Worrell performance will understand what I mean. How else could one describe a stroke (or rather two strokes) in which he played forward and having realized that the ball was not up to the bat, lay back and late cut the ball out of the wicket-keeper's gloves to the third man boundary. The need to re-create the art of batting and simultaneously to raise himself from the prosaic level of mortality into the realm of immortality was all expressed in that stroke, or rather those two strokes.

The *Gleaner* cricket correspondent described Sobers's attainment of his second consecutive century against the 1971 Indian touring team thus: 'He got on his toes like a ballet dancer and with a flick of the wrist (characteristic of Sobers) put the ball down through a motionless field, to the deep leg boundary for four'.[1] No further comment I maintain is necessary, except to say that Sobers had asserted his authority. Finally, a few words about Rohan Kanhai in this context are also very necessary.

Kanhai is one of those batsmen whose performance at the wicket is capable of involving the spectator in the game – totally and painfully sometimes. I remember seeing a West Indian cricket fan, a noted West Indian writer and social commentator, spending his time, during Kanhai's innings at Lords in 1963 against the MCC, drinking at the tavern and only occasionally allowing himself the liberty of peeping out to see whether the batsman was still there. Like watching an Alfred Hitchcock movie, the viewer is anxious to know how the plot unfolds itself, but feels that he dare not watch the actual unfolding because it is too suspenseful. But the suspense pressures of not looking are equally centripetal; thus having been caught between the pressures imposed both by looking and not looking, he pretends to be asleep and only peeps when the suspense of not looking exceeds that of looking. The involvement thus is both total and painful.

Both Kanhai and Hitchcock qualify for the description of genius, but let me deal with the former. In the Guyana Independence Issue of the *New World* C.L.R. James, among other things, gives us a brief insight into the genius of Kanhai when he describes an innings played by the latter in a festival match at the end of the 1964 cricket season against England Elevens at Scarborough and Edgbaston. Kanhai had made a century in both matches.

At Scarborough one sensed that Kanhai was looking for something new. Not budging from his crease he lifted Trevor Bailey ten feet over mid on, wide of long on to the boundary 'he barely swung at the ball, yet as far as he was concerned it was predestined'.[2]

By the time he arrived at Edgbaston, on a wicket not unresponsive to spin and in an atmosphere not unresponsive to swing, he had found what he was looking for. I can do no better than to let James say it as it was:

Kanhai did not go crazy. Exactly the reverse. He discovered, created, a new dimension in batting. The only name I can give to it is cat-and-mouse. The bowler would bowl a length ball. Kanhai would play a defensive stroke preferably off the front foot, pushing the ball for one, quite often for two on the onside – a most difficult stroke on an uncertain pitch demanding precision footwork and clockwork timing. The bowler after seeing his best lengths exploited in this manner would shift whereupon he was unfailingly despatched to the boundary. After a time it began to look as if the whole sequence had been pre-arranged for the benefit of the spectators. Kanhai did not confine himself too rigidly to this pre-established harmony.

One bowler, to escape the remorseless billiard-like pushes, brought the ball untimely up. Kanhai hit him for six to long-on off the front foot. The bowler shortened a bit. Kanhai in the same over hit him for six in the same place, off the back foot this time. . . .He made over 170 in about three hours.[3]

Kanhai, it should be noted, is an East Indian Guyanese who had come from a none too prosperous region of Guyana and has been coached by Walcott and Christiani. His batting during the Edgbaston innings had combined the power of Walcott with the mercurial footwork of Christiani. But it did more. In the Oval test in 1963 against England, he had introduced to cricket what some have referred to as the 'falling pull', at Edgbaston he had used all his technical skill to play an innings which signalled to his audience his emergence as an individual – free to communicate his message in his own way, free to discover himself in his own way, free to liberate himself from the limitations imposed on him by the accident of birth. In short he had 'done his t'ing'.

However, while cricket has functioned to liberalize values in West Indian society, it has also created for the cricketer a new set of obligations and duties. Today, even more than before, the cricketer, who has been exalted to the status of a hero is required to behave in a manner commensurate with this status both on and off the field. Since bets are often placed on the anticipated performance of players, lapses of concentration on the field become unpardonable sins. The hero is also required to make himself available for photographs, shoulder rides (especially after an impressive performance on the field), offers to advertise products, such as the local rum; his preference for which product would not help either his performance on the field, nor ultimately his status as a hero.

Because of high visibility in small West Indian societies, distinctions between private and public life become merely academic. When a certain Guyanese test cricketer was married in Guyana, the entire city turned out to help him celebrate. Considering an invitation to be superfluous, spectator support had been transformed from on-stage to off-stage activity.

But apart from the personal obligations, the status of a hero now carries with it increasing expectations of political sophistication. Reaction to the visit of Sobers to Rhodesia in 1971 brought out a number of letters mostly criticising him for his disservice to the cause of non-white peoples. He was accused of lack of awareness of the struggle by blacks to unfetter themselves from the yoke of imperialism and racism – international sport being a most important area of desegregation.

In a real sense West Indian cricket fans were saying to Sobers that they who conferred on him the status of hero could therefore remove that status. In addition, they were saying that the hero role carries with it certain obligations, in this case not to betray the cause of non-white peoples – and if an action construed as constituting betrayal were perpetrated, then the traitor must be punished. The hero therefore becomes a villain. Finally the Rhodesian visit emphasizes the very close link West Indians are making between sport and politics, and by extension between cricket and nationhood.

If we look at the current political climate, the major territories in the West Indies have just obtained a form of political independence, which in effect has meant neither political, economic nor cultural independence. The colonial legacy has bequeathed to us West Indians, societies rife with all sorts of internal differences. This has meant that these societies are short of national heroes and bereft of a strong sense of nationhood.

The emergence of the West Indies, in the early 1960s, as world cricket champions has provided English speaking West Indians all over the world with a sense of togetherness and regional identity, such as no other event had done before. The participants in those notable contests in England and Australia in particular were taken for leaders and expected to do everything in their power to continue to keep that sense of nationhood alive. Instead the main hero stood accused of doing just the opposite.

In this short analysis of Sobers's Rhodesian visit, I have tried to look at the whole affair from the standpoint of a hero, who after having been revered for his contribution to society, then proceeds to behave in a manner incongruent with socially defined expectations of the status position. Viewed in a much wider context, it is possible to argue that the performance of West Indian cricketers is not only influenced by the colonial experience, but in a real sense by the ambivalence displayed towards them by West Indian society. The West Indian cricket crowd is swift both to praise and to blame. The ease with which a hero is vilified must inevitably cause West Indian cricketers further feelings of anxiety in addition to those originally generated by the colonial experience.[4]

Cricket and society

In addition to helping to promote a sense of 'nationalism' among West Indians, cricket has also sought to bridge the geographical gap (sometimes many miles of sea) between territories. By travelling to other territories and by receiving in turn visits from cricketers of other territories, cricket has sought to bring members of various territories somewhat closer together. Similarly by providing the opportunity to play together as one team, representing 'the West Indies', cricket has contrived to bring together representatives from various territories for the purpose of performing together as one united entity. However, as we have argued earlier on, the extent to which the West Indies team performs as a united entity, oblivious to territorial differences, leaves some room for doubt.

Cricket, as we have seen, operates as a leveller of differences in West Indian society. The game has succeeded in removing the ascriptive basis (e.g. on colour and race) for ranking individuals in society and for team selection and replacing it with an achievement oriented basis (e.g. merit and ability). The high esteem in which the late Collie Smith was held despite his humble origins[5] illustrates the influence cricket has had on the stratification of West Indian society. Similarly the decision of Sir Frank Worrell to play cricket for Boys' Town, on his return to Jamaica, is also indicative of the shift in West Indian values.

Cricket has also become an important national pastime in the West Indies. There are other sporting events such as football and horse riding and other localized events, such as the religious rituals of Pocomania and Revivalism and also political meetings, to which West Indians in general turn for recreation. But the game of cricket provides by far the longest period of recreation, since the fans indulge in giving a steady stream of advice to players on the field, gambling on results of a cricket match, have a ready opportunity to drink, to have a picnic and to engage in animated discussions on a wide range of topics. Cricket thereby provides its audience in the West Indies with the opportunity for emotional release as well as participation in a common pursuit.

The visitor to Sabina Park, Jamaica, cannot fail to see how the structural arrangement of seating accommodation reproduces a microcosm of the segmentation of Jamaican society.[6] But no amount of structural separation can prevent a West Indian audience from joint participation in paying homage to a 'heroic' performance. For example, a good innings may be rewarded by a standing ovation from those in the pavilion, which may later give way to a less impersonal demonstration of appreciation. However, the same performance will always be rewarded by a handshake, slaps on the back and shoulder high elevation by representatives of the masses. Despite various structural constraints on this particular kind of hero appreciation, the masses are always strategically placed in front of the elite section – the pavilion, perhaps for this very purpose. Cricket thus unites many from disparate social backgrounds, however temporarily, in this act of hero-worship.

Finally, I would add a comment on the contribution of cricket to the cultural apparatus in the West Indies. If one defines culture as a body of shared sentiments, beliefs, methods of communication, practices, myths, etc., then it is not hard to discern from previous discussion, the manner in which cricket has influenced West Indian culture – I however use the term 'culture' guardedly.

The untimely and tragic death of Collie Smith had served to underscore as never before the sentiments evoked by the loss of a sporting personality. Old timers talk of the agility of Learie Constantine and the legendary batting prowess of George Headley, Challenor and Tarilton. Places and streets are now being named after cricketing heroes, who are being honoured for their contribution to society. Imbedded in our language are many cricketing expressions. An acquaintance even used cricketing terminology in a eulogy of his late friend, viz:

> Ow! Boysie, [name of deceased] you had a good match. You cut, drove, hooked and pulled. You batted well for 78 runs, but you got out de las' ball, de las' over, de las' day. You also bowled well and even got 3 wickets for 14 runs.

Put in normal English, it would read:

> Ow Boysie, you have had a good life. You had a good time during your 78 years, with wine, women and song, but you died on the last day of the last month on Old Year's Day. Sexually you were productive and proved your manhood by fathering 14 children with 3 women.

Finally in a society desperately short of indigenous heroes, cricket provides young West Indian boys with the chance to grow up with a sense of national pride by identification with the exploits of West Indian cricket 'stars'. Whereas in the past it was generally acceptable to refer to George Headley as 'the black Bradman', future generations of West Indians will find it more appropriate and natural to compare foreign cricketers, by using West Indians as the point of reference – i.e. Bradman becomes 'the white Headley'. The desirability of developing this self respect augurs well for West Indian unity, pride and dignity.

Cricket and the crowd

On the subject of the crowd, we suggest that a match provides the crowd with the opportunity to act out many of their frustrated emotions originating in the social experience of a colonial people. Audience participation (which is akin to attendance at religious and political meetings) provides a sort of mass therapy for West Indians. But there have been at least three occasions in the West Indies when audience participation has transcended the mere verbal communication and has included bottle throwing on to the field of play. The rest of this article will be devoted to a short analysis of these manifestations of audience participation, disapproved by some, and misunderstood by many.

The first such incident occurred in February 1954 in Guyana, the second in January 1960 in Trinidad, and the third in February 1968 in Jamaica. Such occurrences are admittedly not peculiar to West Indian crowds, and although often considered the work of 'hooligans', let us note that 'hooligans' also exist in Australia, India, Pakistan and England.

During the 1878–9 MCC tour to Australia, spectators at Sydney rushed on to the pitch and assaulted Lord Harris, the Kent and England captain. In 1903 in Australia during a visit of the MCC a run-out decision against Hill, when he and Trumper were hitting Australia out of defeat, led the crowd to protest very violently. In Pakistan three years ago during the MCC tour, general unrest in that country forced a premature end to that tour during the third test match. In February 1971, spectators in Sydney, Australia, pelted bottles and beer cans at MCC's fast bowler, John Snow, after he had hit Australian tailender, Jenner, on the head with a delivery, thereby forcing the batsman to retire hurt.

In England 'hooligans', otherwise known as spectators in that country, regularly assault players and referees during football matches and destroy British Railway's property on the way home after the game. Let us, however, analyse the structural factors of the situations that precipitated these violent demonstrations by cricket crowds in the West Indies.

The Guyana incident

In Guyana, MCC batted first and scored 435 runs in one of the slowest scoring performances in test cricket. They had scored 153 for 2 in the first day, eclipsing their 128 in an entire day in the previous test in Barbados and scored 248 on the second day of the Guyana test. Hutton the captain had batted 460 minutes for 169 runs. One particularly more agonizing feature of the England innings, as far as the West

Indies was concerned, was Stollmeyer's missing Wardle at 6 off the easiest of catches. Wardle went on to make 38 and with Hutton added 79 runs for that wicket.

West Indies started their reply on the third day with Stollmeyer and Worrell, the latter opening in place of the injured Holt. In one of the most devastating spells of fast bowling ever seen at Bourda, Guyana, Statham, the MCC opening bowler, accounted for Worrell 0, Stollmeyer 2 and Walcott 4, before rain stopped play for the day with the home team 31 for 3, with Weekes and Christiani, the not-out batsmen, on 21 and 3 respectively.

Weekes, in particular, during that innings of 21 had shown a refreshing willingness not to be intimidated by the knowledge of Statham's fine performance. There was therefore hope in the midst of despair.

But on the fourth day, Christiani, after some spirited resistance against Statham, was given out, caught by Watson tumbling over. The batsman remained at the wicket for some time until the umpire gave his decision. The umpire was 'Badge' Menzies, for many years head groundsman at Georgetown Cricket Club at Bourda, and that time recently elevated to the status of test umpire.

Weekes, despite pulling a muscle, played a truly grand innings. One particular seemingly forward defensive shot off Statham had raced to the boundary as if by divine fiat – not a man moving. However, just when it looked as though his efforts would be crowned with a century, he played forward to one from Lock. The ball passed between bat and pad and chipped the off-bail. Weekes, it appears, hearing no sound, stayed his ground. There was an immediate appeal. Umpire Gillette at the bowler's end, apparently unsighted, gave no signal, whereupon an appeal was made to the square leg umpire, who gave Weekes out, fully 10 seconds after the ball had been delivered. Weekes had made 94. In the minds of the crowd it was worth 200.

The umpire was Badge Menzies and hope was fading.

With the score at 139 for 7, McWatt, a Guyanese and the injured Holt, with a runner, came together. Despite his handicap, Holt batted beautifully. McWatt also rose to the occasion and with a beautiful square drive off Statham for 4, sent the score past the 200 mark. Hope was returning. The West Indies now looked like avoiding the follow-on. With the score at 237, McWatt drove one, intending to take a couple that would have sent up the hundred partnership. Attempting the second run, he was adjudged run out for 54.

The umpire was Badge Menzies. Hope had died. The new batsman arrived to replace McWatt.

A section of the crowd in the North Stand demurred. Bottles were thrown on to the field. Play was held up for ten minutes. The West Indies were all out for 251, forced to follow on, and subsequently lost the match by 9 wickets. It was the first MCC test victory in the West Indies since 1935. England who had lost the previous two test matches drew the fourth and fifth, thus squaring the series.

In this summary so far, I have sought merely to recapture, not only some of the salient events of that test match, but also something of the tension-ridden atmosphere. There was for example England's slow batting, Statham's devastating spell and the manner in which Weekes, Christiani and McWatt (the latter last two were Guyana's only two representatives on the team) were given out – by a Guyanese umpire.

But this was most certainly not all. What of the situation at the societal level? The pre-1953 period in Guyana had seen an unprecedented mobilization of masses along political lines, culminating in a resounding victory for the People's Progressive Party (PPP) at the April 1953 elections, the first ever to be held under universal adult suffrage. By October of the same year, the PPP had been hounded out of office by what the political scientist, Gordon Lewis, describes as a piece of Churchillian gunboat diplomacy. British troops were sent to back up the suspension of the Constitution. There were many reported instances of these troops beating up Guyanese, who were overtly hostile to their presence. One of the deposed members of the PPP was facing sedition charges. Guyana was more politically aware than it had ever been, in particular, of the potential for collective action to make structural improvements which, as a means of protest, had been clearly exploited.

Finally, as C.L.R. James argues,[7] this MCC team had a bad reputation which no doubt, preceded their arrival in Guyana. It was against this background that the cricketing representatives of the country that had recently suspended Guyana's Constitution arrived to play cricket, as though nothing had happened. During that match then, not only was there despair then hope, and then despair, as well as tension at the societal level.

The irony of the situation, however, was that the crowd's ire, unlike the recent 1971 Australian example, was directed, not against the Englishmen (Hutton had kept his men on the field in 1954 – Illingworth had to lead his men off in Australia in 1971), but against the Guyanese umpire, Menzies.

Let us now look at the Trinidad incident.

The Trinidad disturbance

In the Trinidad disturbance, which occurred on the third day of the second test on January 30, 1960, England batted first and scored 382 after nearly 2 days' occupation of the wicket. At the close of the second day's play, West Indies were 22 for 0. Even at that stage a feature of the match was the number of bumpers bowled. Reporting in the *Trinidad Guardian*, on the previous day's play, Charles Bray, in an article captioned 'The Bumper War Is On' remarked thus of Trueman's bowling:

> There were three of the best in the first over with one in each of his next two overs and a couple of snorters in the last, one of which hit Solomon (the West Indian opener) in the ribs.[8]

The West Indies, he argued, had apparently started the 'bumper war'.

The end of play score of 22 for 0, however, had given the crowd some reasonable semblance of hope of a useful West Indian reply. After all, this same batting side had scored 563 for 8 declared in reply to England's first innings total of 482, in the previous test in Barbados. On the third day things began to happen. Before a record crowd of 32,000, Hunte played a fast ball from Statham on to his boot, the ball carrying to Trueman at leg slip who 'took a lazy one-handed catch' high in the air. Hunte was preparing to take guard again, when wicket-keeper, Swetman appealed, whereupon the batsman was given out by umpire Lloyd.

Ninety minutes later, the West Indies were 45 for 5, from which they moved to 98 for 8. At this stage, Ramadhin and Singh (both Trinidadians) were batting. The former was adopting a no-nonsense attitude to the bowling. He had hit three 4s. Singh was also shaping up with 'surprising confidence'. In attempting a run that was never there, he was given run out by Trinidadian umpire, Lee Kow.

The new batsman arrived on the scene, whereupon the crowd began to throw bottles. Press reports the next day claimed that 100 people were hurt and everyone, especially the Governor was 'bitterly ashamed'. The West Indies went on to score 112. England batted a second time and by scoring 230 for 9 declared, set the West Indies 500 runs to make. The latter scored 244 in the second venture and lost the match by 256 runs.

One spectator who claimed that he did not throw any bottles, nevertheless agreed with the crowd's reaction.

C.L.R. James has dealt quite adequately with many, but, in my opinion, not all of the important factors surrounding the crowd's behaviour he has cited the following:[9]

- There were too many people at the Queen's Park Club ground which meant too many people had to stand and were therefore made to feel uncomfortable.
- Charges for refreshments were too high, the high cost of concessions charged by QPC being passed on to the crowd.
- The management of QPC. represented the old regime to which the masses were hostile.

At the social level James instances the following:

- The public was disenchanted over the refusal of the West Indies Cricket Board, both to appoint a black man as captain, and to reinstate Gilchrist on the West Indies team.
- The public was dissatisfied with the seemingly non-impartiality of Trinidad umpires as far as Trinidadians and West Indians were concerned.

To the above points the following can be added. The match itself was one during which hope and despair alternated. At 22 for 0 there was hope, then there was despair as the West Indies collapsed. Finally as James put it, though not a soul in the ground expected Ramadhin to make 20, nevertheless some flicker of hope remained until this was extinguished by Singh's run out. Secondly, the crowd was perplexed by Hunte's dismissal, and for a long time the manipulators of the scoreboard were unable to determine whether he had been given out lbw or caught. No doubt many were also angry at the circumstances surrounding his dismissal. Thirdly, the 'bumper war' was an ongoing concern and no doubt the spectators felt that this in some way contributed to the poor showing of the West Indies. There was, therefore, anger and frustration.

At the societal level, it must be remembered that January 1960 found Trinidad in somewhat of a political turmoil. Elections were to be held the following year, there was talk of political independence which came in 1962 and the People's National Movement was in the thick of a struggle to get back the Chaguaramas base from the Americans. The highlight of this struggle, the march in the rain to the American Embassy, led by Dr Williams, on 22 April 1960, was to take place less than three months after the bottle throwing incident. Trinidadians, it may be argued, were at the time in a struggle against another white imperialist nation, the Americans, who were beginning to make their presence felt in the Caribbean.

The Jamaica disturbance

The disturbance occurred on 12 February, 1968 during the fourth day's play of the second test match against the MCC. England batted first and scored 376 runs. The West Indies on what was generally accepted an atrocious wicket were bowled out for 143 runs, the MCC fast bowler Snow taking 7 for 49. As in Guyana and Trinidad, the West Indies had opening batsmen problems. At the end of the third day's play, the West Indies, having been asked to follow on, were 81 for 0. There was at this stage definitely hope that the West Indies would improve considerably on the first innings' performance which had been the cause of so much despair.

On the fourth day, after an opening partnership of 102 runs, the West Indies were 204, just 29 runs being needed to make England bat again with Butcher and Sobers batting. Butcher, who had been caught behind the wicket in the first innings for 21, after hitting two 4s off Jones and Snow, both described as 'thrilling strokes, all of them that gave the jam-packed crowds a long delayed chance to cheer',[10] was now on 25. Sobers, after a shaky start, seemed to be settling down to a big score, which he eventually got – 113 not out.

It was at this score (204) that Butcher, it was generally agreed, was brilliantly caught on the leg side by the wicket-keeper Parks. Once more there was despair and frustration.

Nothing happened until Holford got to the crease, then bottles and beer cans began to be thrown on the field. E.W. Swanton, writing in *The Daily Gleaner* on the following day, had this to say about the incident: 'the ignorant venom of a few betrayed the sportsmanship of many. . . . Sobers cried out to the turbulent section, "Butcher was out" but those bent on mischief were past hearing'.[11] The crowd as they invaded the pitch in an effort to avoid tear gas fumes were heard to chant, 'Sang Hue no more'. Sang Hue is a Jamaican test umpire, who was on duty during the match. Apart from Swanton's misunderstanding of the underpinnings of crowd behaviour, this excerpt shows that the crowd's ire was being directed not against Sobers or the visiting team, but against the Jamaican umpire, Sang Hue.

It must also be remembered that as Orlando Patterson argues, in an article on cricket,[12] perhaps more than in any other territory, the Sabina Park audience presented a microcosm of Jamaican society with its obdurate class-colour divisions. In addition, Jamaica was just beginning to manifest the first serious indicators of black awareness and black dignity. In 1967 there was, for example, open disagreement with the manner in which the 'Miss Jamaica' beauty contest was run. The implication was that it was biased against black Jamaicans. Also later, in 1968, saw the expulsion of a Guyanese university lecturer as an undesirable resident or visitor. As a result of ensuing demonstrations, one man was killed and a number of others injured.

Analysis and comment

There are similarities in all these three disturbances at cricket in the West Indies. On all occasions the home team was playing against England, whose opportunity to bat first was well used, and left the visitors poised for victory. By comparison the West Indies batted poorly and were asked to follow on. But despite a poor first innings, there was still hope that the West Indies would save the game – in Guyana and Trinidad in the first innings, in Jamaica in the second innings. In fact, however, the West Indies had problems with their opening batsmen, and faced hostile fast bowling by English (Statham in Guyana, Trueman in Trinidad, Snow in Jamaica). In Jamaica the wicket was blamed; batsmen had to dig out shooters. These technical factors added to uncertainty about the manner in which key (No. 1) batsmen were given out, did little to relax the large crowds in attendance, and for whom inadequate facilities were provided.

In fact, the crowds were doubtful of the impartiality of the dismissal of their local batsman in favour of the visitors. To the spectator, if not to the umpire, a catch in the outfield or clean bowled is much less doubtful than a run-out or caught behind the wicket.

The anger of the crowd seemed to be directed most specifically at the umpires – Menzies in Guyana, Lee Kow in Trinidad and Sang Hue in Jamaica, light skinned nationals in their home territory, and not against the England team of white players. The disturbance occurred upon the arrival of the new batsman at the wicket.

Lastly, the social and political climate in each of the territories was one of a growing militant nationalism.

A test series lasts for over a month and a test match for five days, thus even more than a religious or political meeting, a cricket match provides opportunity for a collective response of some fervour. Besides victory over an English touring team is sweeter, since the master is beaten at his own game. Collective behavioural response is assisted by the size of the crowd and the easy communication of any grievance, or emotional reaction, despair, hope or frustration. The precipitating factor is the arrival of the new batsman at the wicket.

Now it is very noticeable that the anger of the crowd was directed towards one of its own, albeit a light skinned one – the umpire. This is the typical result of a colonial process which has predisposed West Indians to seek for the enemy among themselves. It may well be that when the course of nationalism has been further advanced, future demonstrations may not be directed against the umpire, but against members of the opposing team, as in 1971 in Australia. Since a cricket match does not take place in a vacuum, but in a given society, then political and other tensions producing strains for members of society will inevitably be exported into the context of the game, thus compounding any tensions and frustrations currently in existence in the game itself. Here political tensions and uncertainties at a national level and similar tensions at test matches, primarily occasioned by large crowds uncomfortably accommodated, and poor West Indian performance, constitute the basic ingredients for a demonstration. In addition, if the crowd believe that local umpires are a contributing factor to the poor performance of the West Indies, then a precipitating factor, such as a run-out or a police indiscretion, could quite conceivably spark off a disturbance.

The analysis of these three events also shows that cricket enables West Indian audiences to come together in large numbers to enjoy a highly rated pastime, and in so doing, West Indians refurbish group solidarity. By their ready and continuous participation in the game, West Indian spectators take part (albeit at a low level) in the government of cricket as well as act out some of the frustrated emotions which spring from the social experience. A cricket match thus performs a cleansing function, especially when circumstances provide the opportunities for demonstrations.

Summary and conclusions

In this two-part article I was primarily concerned with the problem of why in the midst of various decolonizing efforts on the part of West Indian governments, the game of cricket still ranks high in the cultural apparatus of many West Indians.[13] To this end, an analysis was made of the socio-historical condition that produced and influenced West Indian cricket, by looking at the contribution cricket makes to West Indian society.

The creolized nature of West Indian cricket was perhaps particularly borne out by crowd reaction and participation in the game, where West Indians have a chance to act out some of the frustrations occasioned by the weakness of the economic situation characteristic of ex-colonial territories.

It is obvious the game has been re-shaped in sympathy with the experiences of its exponents whose dominant cultural apparatus reflects the combination of the European and non-European cultural variations. This deviation from the way the game is played in England, not only tends to belie the meaningfulness of the saying 'it's not cricket', as far as West Indians are concerned, but also suggests the extent to which cricket, like other facets of the West Indian situation, reflects the impact of this duality of cultural influences. I refer here to other facets, such as the existence of many female-headed households among lower-class West Indians of African descent, the syncretic nature of lower-class religions, such as Shango, Pocomania and Revivalism and the continued belief in the complementary therapeutic value of obeah to scientific medical practices.

Disturbances in the cricket arena, such as those dealt with could be seen as spontaneous eruptions of a dispossessed people in what is still very much a colonial situation. This explains why West Indians tend to attack their own umpires. Though such disturbances become more a gesture of despair, than any attempt to hurt anyone specifically, such disturbances indicate the existence of possible ingredients for revolutionary activity. We recall Frantz Fanon: 'The colonised man will first manifest this aggressiveness which has been deposited in his bones against his own people'.[14]

> Where individuals are concerned a positive negation of commonsense is evident. While the settler policeman has the right the livelong day to strike the native, to insult him and to make him crawl to them, you will see the native reaching for his knife at the slightest hostile or aggressive glance cast on him by another native; for the last resort of the native is to defend his personality vis-a-vis his brother.[15]

Fanon's view may also help to explain a number of other behavioural manifestations attributed to West Indians. In addition to the contribution of needs at the level of the crowd, cricket also provides fulfilment for the individual cricketer and the wider society. Significantly, however, ambivalences at the wider societal level also find expression among the audience and on the cricket field. In concluding, I suggest that because of the socio-cultural aspect of cricket in West Indian society, the game will continue to form an integral part of West Indian cultural expression, though it will probably further be moulded to suit the environment.

NOTES

1 *The Daily Gleaner*, 29 March 1971, p. 14.
2 James, C.L.R. 'Kanhai: a Study in Confidence', *New World*, Guyana Independence Issue, (eds) G. Lamming and M. Carter, 1966.
3 *Ibid*, p. 15.
4 *Caribbean Quarterly*, June 1973, Vol. 19, 2.
5 The late Collie Smilh played for Boys Town, a team which represented an underprivileged section of the Jamaican community.
6 For a fuller discussion of this, see Orlando Patterson, 'The Ritual of Cricket', *Jamaica Journal*, Vol. 3, No. 1, March 1969, pp. 22–5.
7 C.L.R. James, *Beyond a Boundary*, London: Hutchinson, 1969.
8 See *Trinidad Guardian*, January 30, 1960, p. 14.

9 James, *Beyond a Boundary*, p. 237.
10 *The Daily Gleaner*, 13 February 1968.
11 *Ibid.*, p. 12.
12 Orlando Patterson, in James, *Beyond a Boundary*.
13 It seems to me that any activity in which spectators spend six hours for three to five days in boiling hot sun must be of significance to the social scientist.
14 Fanon, Frantz, *The Wretched Of the Earth*, New York: Grove Press Inc., 1963
15 Constantine, Learie and Denzil Batchelor, *The Changing Face Of Cricket*, London: Eyre and Spottiswoode, 1966.

1   Sunday afternoon, beach cricket played with a tennis ball. Courtesy of Nation Library

2   Boys and girls in the back yards of their homes; playing cricket is their principal cultural activity. Courtesy of Nation Library

3   Kids at a coaching clinic: Desmond Haynes is the instructor

4   Schoolkids giving the 'highfive'

5 Street cricket: respect, commitment and love of methodical technique are found among kids who are playing to pass the time. Courtesy of Nation Library

6   Going to cricket with a drum at Kensington Oval, 1991

7 Sir Gary Sobers showing the kids at a coaching clinic, 1991

8 Oldster showing West Indies batsman what is wrong with his technique

9 West Indies Women's Cricket Team, 1979

10   Girl playing 'softball cricket'

8

The ritual of cricket

Orlando Patterson

In the 1953–54 test series between Britain and the West Indies a riot broke out on the Bourda Ground in Georgetown, British Guiana. Britain went on to win the match by nine wickets.

In the 1959–60 series between the same two sides another riot erupted at Queens Park Oval, Port of Spain, Trinidad. England won the match – and as a result, the series – by 56 runs.

On Monday 12 February 1968 a riot broke out on the third day of the second test match being played at Sabina Park, Kingston.

In accounting for these riots (the article will be concerned primarily with the incidents in Jamaica) one must go beyond the superficial explanations offered by socially unsophisticated sports commentators – the weather, the fact that the home side was losing, just plain lack of discipline, and so on. These simply beg the question. Why should a home team become so terribly involved in a game that the dismissal of one batsman sparks off a full-scale riot? If, as a few of the English sports writers claimed, the West Indian masses are so ill-disciplined and barbaric, why have they not revolted long ago against conditions that are infinitely more frustrating than the simple dismissal of a batsman?

A closer look at the record of these riots poses further interesting issues. For one thing, although we have had Australian, Indian and Pakistani touring teams which, in the case of the Aussies, have routed the home side before large audiences, it is only against the English teams that riots have taken place.

A second interesting fact is that cricket, outside of test matches, is rapidly losing ground both as a participant and spectator sport in the West Indies, the one exception being Barbados. In the three areas where riots have broken out first class matches are generally dismal affairs.

We must begin to answer the questions posed above by first observing that in the West Indies the test match is not so much a game as a collective ritual – a social drama in which almost all of the basic tensions and conflicts within the society are played out symbolically. Furthermore, that at certain moments the symbolic content of this ritual acquires a special quality – what I shall call transubstantive –

141

which not only reinforces its potency, but in so doing creates a situation that can only be resolved in violence. Finally, that in a society remarkably devoid of social dramas of this kind, cricket, precisely because it is the only such ritual, becomes extremely important for the expression and channelling of certain deeply rooted grievances and tensions within the society. It is, in short, the only institution (with the possible exception of lower-class religious cults) performing certain basic cleansing functions.

What is it then about West Indian society which transforms cricket, a normally staid and complicated game which at first sight would seem peculiarly devoid of any deep cleansing value, into such an intense ritual? Almost everything, one is tempted to answer, but space permits us to make only three basic points about the society.

First there is the cultural dualism peculiar to all WI societies. If we take the case of Jamaica, we find not one cultural core shared by all members of the society with regional and class variations in life-style, but really a dominant culture and another more fragile and subordinate quasi-culture, partly conflicting in their value-systems, partly supplementary. On the one hand, there is the culture of the elite group, essentially British in orientation, the creolized version of the culture of the former colonial masters. On the other hand there is the culture of the masses, which, in its traditional form, is a tenuous syncretism of the fragments of African culture which survive slavery and the local adjustments to the demands of the plantation system.

As one would expect, the relationship between these two cultures is one of sub-ordination and superordination. The British colonial master defined his culture, his values, as superior and such was his economic and political power that what was originally only ideologically defined soon became socially real. The slaves and their descendants had little real choice in the matter. They lived their way of life only by default. The 'superior' culture of the white master was accepted with all its impli-cations of lowly conception of things black and Afro-Jamaican. The way one looked, the way one spoke, the way one behaved were all negatively evaluated. The black lower-class Jamaican accepted this and despised himself for having to accept it. While accepting the superiority of British culture the Jamaican also hated it for what it had made of his own culture and of him. It was in short, a deep-seated love-hate relationship.

The second important feature of the society is its rigid class division. A recent report indicates that, of countries with available data, Jamaica has one of the most unequal distributions of income in the world. Much has been said – although little done – about the increasing gulf between the haves and the have-nots in this society and there is little need to elaborate here.

Colour, although of decreasing significance as an active determinant of status (i.e. there has been a marked decline in job discrimination on the basis of colour) still largely coincides with class. While colour discrimination has decreased however, colour prejudice is still rife. To the black, lower-class Jamaican however, all this, understandably, appears to be simply splitting hairs. The combined effect of the persistence of colour prejudice and the correlation of light shade with high status simply reinforces his own prejudice that racial discrimination is still rampant (a prejudice, incidentally, which also serves the added psychological function of excusing his own low status). For these reasons then, the society has not benefited in terms of racial stability as much as it should have done from the significant reduction in racial discrimination in recent years. Indeed urbanization, improved educational facilities and generally rising expectations have led to a growing sense of racial exploitation.

The final feature of the society we must take note of is partly implied in what has been said above – that is, the fact that there is little shared behaviour among the different groups that make up the society. The Jamaican rarely experiences any sense of social solidarity either with the total society or with any sizeable groups within the wider context of the nation state. It would be no exaggeration to say that the society is literally bursting at the seams with conflict. Cultural, colour and class conflicts we have already mentioned, but there are other sources of conflict within the system – conflicting political allegiances, rural–urban conflicts, sexual conflicts – all fraught with a degree of animosity unheard of in more stable social orders. The masses then are as much in conflict with themselves as they are with the elite. It would be the height of left-wing romanticism to imagine that the great gulf separating the elite from the masses has led to any kind of group consciousness or sense of solidarity among the latter. In the daily struggle to survive it is every man for himself.

Consider now, the situation at Sabina Park on that dramatic Monday afternoon several months ago. Both the setting and the game constituted a microcosm of Jamaican society. The differing qualities of the spectators in the various stands reflected to an almost absurd degree the differences within the society. It is difficult to resist the temptation to pun on the German word 'stand' (meaning, 'status group') by remarking that the stands were literally 'stands'. To the western end of the grounds was the pavilion, its members over 90 per cent white or very light in colour, rich and upper class. The sprinkling of browns and blacks were typical of those who had made it in this group: the Governor-General – black, resplendently attired; his wife a little way down amidst a group of patronizing white ladies – cheerful, chubby and well dressed, looking for all the world like a black version of the British Queen Mother. There were a few Ministers of Government, the odd uppity civil servant, the occasional black businessman. Five to ten per cent. More than that and the Sabina Park pavilion would not be the place it used to be.

Opposite the pavilion, at the eastern end of the grounds were the bleachers – the hard wooden benches beneath the hot sun, every inch of which exploded with people. Here were the masses, securely fenced off from the rest of the grounds with chicken wire. Their faces were nearly all black. If one scanned diligently enough the odd white or high brown face may have been spotted but these, as often as not, belonged to some too earnest resident of Mona.

Then to the northern end of the grounds were the covered stands with concrete seats. The spectators here were better clad, their colour, on average, a cooler shade of black. There were fences here too. But not as high as the ones in front of the bleachers. Here it was possible to move about more freely. With the naked eye one could just about scan the (social) cream on the pavilion.

Finally, there were the southern and grand stands: clean, shaded, comfortable, the view excellent, the spectators orderly and well dressed. These shared with the pavilion the privilege of having no fences. Occasionally there was an exchange of greetings between a spectator from the grand stand with one from the pavilion – always polite, always cordial but somehow not without a lingering flavour of awkwardness, if not embarrassment.

And now the game. Its meaning. Its ritual significance. Need one spell it out? Cricket is the Englishman's game par excellence. The very term 'cricket' has become a byword for all that is most English in the British way of life. The vocabulary of cricket is a standard pool of stock images for Tory statesmen. No better symbol of English culture could be found. Yet, this is the game which West Indians have usurped, have come to master. What the former colonial subject has done is to literally beat the master at his own game. But, more important, he has beaten him symbolically. Here all the ambivalence of the black lower-class West Indian towards English culture can be played out. Cricket is the game we love for it is the only game we can play well, the only activity which gives us some international prestige. But it is the game, deep down, which we must hate – the game of the master. Hence it becomes on the symbolic level the English culture we have been forced to love, for it is the only real one we have, but the culture we must despise for what it has done to us, for what it has made of the hopeless cultural shambles, the incoherent social patchwork, that we have called Afro-Jamaican culture. How better to express our pent up rage, our agonizing self-contradiction than to acquire and master this culture, then use it to beat the group that forced us into acquiring it? This is precisely what cricket has done for the West Indian. This is why victory – victory against the Englishman – is a matter of such great moment.

But the game does more than this. It resolves internal conflicts in that it functions symbolically in expressing strong class hostility. Hence it is not only the means by which the ex-colonial gets back at the culture of his former master but a means whereby the masses express their rage against their present 'betters', the current carriers of the dominant English culture in the local society. Hence it is significant that the present West Indian team is almost entirely dark brown or black and of lower-class origins. Further, it is no accident that during the bad old days when the team was dominated by whites no riots ever took place. It is also significant that the really popular members of the team are not Sobers and Kanhai but Hall and Griffith. Sobers for example, is respected, revered, awed: as one spectator was heard to say when he once again saved the team from defeat, 'Im not no cricketer – 'Im is God!'" But it is in the nature of deities that they are removed from the immediate obsessions and problems of mortal men. Not so the response of the crowd to Hall and Griffith. The feeling here comes straight from the gut. One reason perhaps is that, as pace-men, they perform the most aggressive roles on the team. No one who has seen Hall making his long, muscular run-up to the wicket can fail to be impressed by the beautiful, sweet violence of the act – the slow, menacing beginning, the gathering pace, the sudden climactic explosion of energy on delivery, the dashing follow-through, the plight of the lonely batsman at the other end. In this cathartic moment of truth, it is 'us' versus 'them'. 'Us' constitutes the black masses. 'Them' is everything else – the privileged, the oppressor, the alien, dominant culture.

This brings us to the third symbolic function of cricket. The test match is one of the few occasions on which the lower classes experience any kind of group solidarity. The self-destructive atomism created by poverty, conflicting values, deprivation and charismatic politics loses its disintegrative power in the presence of the game. Here at last, via the media of genuine heroes – the only heroes in a land barren of heroes or a heroic tradition – the masses respond as one, share a common experience, bite their nails in a common war of nerves against a common enemy – 'them'.

But if cricket demystifies there is a sense in which it also enhances mystification in that it facilitates not only proletarian solidarity but bourgeois nationalism. As such, it fully evokes the ambivalence of the masses towards the elite. For 'them' over there also claim to be against the British touring team. On the one hand 'we' would like to deny 'them' the right to feel that they are allies with 'us' against the common foe, but on the other hand, it is difficult not to succumb to the temptations of bourgeois nationalist sentimentality. The elite, after all, are paying homage to 'our' heroes too. 'We' hate the bastards but 'we' must admit a little feeling of pleasure at their submission. As long as the game follows its natural course and as long as the home team, the heroes, are winning we are prepared to be generous: 'We' shall allow 'them' to share some of the glory with 'us'.

Is this perhaps a collective projection? Do 'we' somehow in this moment of triumph fool 'ourselves' into thinking that it is possible to share some little of their particular glory with them? It is a fool's paradise. But a beautiful one while it lasts. Tomorrow the sports commentators will say how proud 'we' all are, how well 'we' played.

However the demystifying function of cricket is only possible when the game is going the right way. It is a different matter when the heroes are losing, when they are being humiliated by the English team before the very eyes of the masses, as they were on that fateful Monday.

And it is at this point that the symbolism acquires a new dimension, one far more telling. Let us look briefly at the series of incidents sparking off this symbolic escalation.

The test began on Thursday 8 February. Cowdrey won the toss and from the first ball it was clear that this would be no ordinary test match. The West Indian bowlers toiled all day with little reward. The crowd left disappointed, worried. The next day the innings continued. Already the wicket had begun to crack up. England were all out in the late afternoon for 376 runs. By now the wicket was like a jig-saw puzzle with several enormous chasms, one of the worst ever witnessed in the history of test

145

matches. As the West Indian batsmen came in the tension rose. It was in no way relieved by the surprise of seeing Murray, the young wicket-keeper and normally the No. 7 batsman, opening. Clearly, even the great Sobers was worried. It was a gamble which did not come off, for before the end of play that day, disaster struck twice, as the opening pair was dismissed with the total number of runs too humiliating to mention. The next day, Saturday, the West Indian side was routed for a miserable 143. The follow-on was forced and it was during the fightback on the following Monday that Basil Butcher was brilliantly caught by Parks behind the wicket off the bowling of Basil D'Olivera. Sang Hue, the Jamaican Chinese umpire, had no hesitation in giving him out.

But the crowd could not believe it. Did not wish to believe it. As Holford came in to join Sobers the bottles began to pop over the fence separating the bleachers from the field. Slowly at first, then as Cowdrey, the President of the Jamaica Cricket Association and later Sobers appealed to them, the bottles poured down even more profusely. The police then came on the scene. It was a classic display of police mismanagement. After failing to make any impact by shouting at the crowd from the playing field side of the fence, the riot squad was called in. This had precisely the opposite effect of that intended. Dressed in gas masks and carrying tear-gas guns they appeared somehow both frightening and absurd. There was something quite unreal about them for, hidden behind their masks, they appeared more like actors in a Pirandello drama of tyranny than real policemen. The police unwittingly placed themselves in the role of playing themselves. As such they became simply an extension of the drama that was already being played out.

The crowd paused for a moment and watched them. This new scene. These new actors. These strange messengers of terror. Then the actors acted. They began to throw the tear-gas bombs into the crowd. Suddenly the ritual took a new crucial turn. As the vile fumes burned the eyes and turned over the stomachs of the masses, the drama became real. Everything was transformed – the actors lived their roles, the symbol became the thing symbolized. This was no longer a game, no longer a vivid metaphor. This was Jamaican society in all its stark, brutal reality. Now it seemed as vulnerable, its brutality so transparent. The opportunity had to be seized. It must be destroyed. And so the masses rioted.

So far we have largely attempted to explain how the ritual of cricket functions as a symbolic expression of certain basic conflicts in West Indian society. We have yet to explain the reasons for the riot itself. Indeed what we have said would seem more to indicate why a riot should not take place rather than why it should. An understanding of why the riot occurs requires an appreciation of two things. One concerns the nature of cricket itself. The other relates to the nature of symbolism.

[The most striking thing about cricket, as a game, is its emphasis on order.] All games, it is true, involve some acceptance of rules and cease to exist when such rules are neglected. But[cricket is exceptional both for its complexity and its almost consciously articulated ideology of obedience and authority, the latter being symbolized in the person of the umpire. Nor is it an accident that cricket is one of the few games which requires two umpires.

[It is because of this internal quality, this emphasis on obeying the rules, of unquestioning acceptance of the decision of the umpire, that cricket is able to perform another vital, if negative, symbolic function. Namely, that of disobeying the rule, of refusing to accept the decision of the umpire which in terms of its symbolic identity with the society which I have outlined above, amounts to a denial, a threat to the very existence of the society.]

The ritual of cricket then belongs to that category of symbols that is potentially self-destructive in that it is most potent where it denies its reality as symbol and in the act of so doing becomes qualitatively transformed. I have called this category of symbols transubstantive. A substantive symbol must by definition, remain a sign, i.e. an object or act which mediates the meaning of some referent to a subject or group of people. However in the case of a transubstantive symbol there is an inherent tension derived from the impulse to acquire the substance of the meaning which originally the symbol was meant only to mediate. The symbol, in short, ceases to be something meaningless in itself, ceases to be simply a mediator and becomes inherently meaningful, becomes the thing being mediated. It no longer stands for something else. It *is* the something else.

A further point worth noting is the fact that a transubstantive symbol rarely if ever, exists as an independent type. Instead, it remains vested in ordinary substantive symbols as a latent or postponed possibility – a possibility which certain rare moments of deep involvement with the ritual is realized by the subject.

Cricket as an ordinary substantive symbol, mediates and symbolically resolves certain basic conflicts within Jamaican society. It is also, however, a transubstantive symbol and acquires the quality when it ceases to mediate and canalize social conflicts and instead becomes identified with such conflicts. Such an identification is likely to occur at moments when the believers' (the spectators of the game) devotion and identity with their heroes are in a state of crisis. And just such a moment was the point in the game when Butcher was dismissed. Like certain devout Christians for whom the ritual of communion is one in which the wine and the bread are actually the blood and flesh of Jesus, so to the Jamaican lower-class spectator in that moment, the game became the society, symbolized partly in the entire game, but more concretely in the person of the umpire who in this case was Chinese (as in the case of the Guyanese riot) a racial type inevitably associated with the dominant capitalist class in the West Indies. And when the society literally enter the drama through the medium of the fearsome police who then proceeded to play themselves, [the experience could only be consummated by the expression of the most basic wish of the lower-class spectators. The wish to destroy the society, the system which is the source of their poverty, their humiliation, and their oppression.]

If my interpretation is correct the wonder is not that so many riots have taken place in test matches between England and the West Indies but that so few have occurred.

9

The political ideology of West Indies cricket culture

Hilary McD. Beckles

Chris Searle, in a splendid essay which examines the relations between the spread of cricket throughout the British Empire during the nineteenth century, and the consolidation of white supremacy ideologies within these subjugated territories, defines West Indian cricket, in contrast to that found in other areas, as a 'game of resistance'.[1] Its inner logic, symbols, moments of transformation, and connections to popular struggles, he tells us, punctuates and flavours the political history of modern Caribbean peoples.

Searle insists, furthermore, that cricket, at an early stage, became an area of revolt; the heroic figures that occupy the crease being made from the same politicized materials as revolutionary writers such as C.L.R. James, George Lamming and Edward Brathwaite. For him, cricketers and artists alike contributed to the 'same anti-imperialist cultural momentum' that resides at the centre of the West Indian radical tradition. For this reason, therefore, he concluded that 'cricket could never be a mere past time or weekend affectation for the black player of the Caribbean. It was a means of struggle and achievement through it a powerful expression of Caribbean progress and nationhood'.[2]

Undoubtedly, Searle's approach to the study of West Indies cricket culture is informed by a number of critical assumptions about the nature of the region's political history and how such a history has facilitated the structuring of social experience and ideological consciousness. Furthermore, it is informed by the methodological employment of post-Hegelian dialectical analysis, particularly the Marxian concept of hegemony and counter-hegemonic struggle within the superstructure. These analytical tools and concepts allow Searle to hold steady 150 years of West Indian cricket history for an internal pathological analysis which, in turn, is placed within the specific context of conflict and co-option within the British Empire and the wider modern world system.

The late C.L.R. James, to whom Searle's essay is dedicated, pointed us in this general direction with his early political and philosophical writings. His ideas concerning the ideological character of West Indian civilization, clearly articulated in his 1938 analysis of Toussaint L'Ouverture and the Haitian Revolution, are also to be found within the political and intellectual infrastructure of his pioneer 1963 text on West Indies cricket culture.[3] With James, as with so many other writers who prioritize the role of cultural struggle within social change, one feels the intensity of his analytical search for a dialectical solution to the mechanistic formula which showed that in the West Indies history made cricket, and cricket made history. Points of origin and beginnings had to be identified in order to grasp the ideological meaning over time of this basic truth. In other words, the formula, simply stated, said little, but internally examined, it says everything.

A concept of West Indian history, then, seems the appropriate place to begin a search for the internal motion and ideological meaning of the cricket culture. Here we assert, with reference to a notion of what is the 'essence', that no matter how many times and how many ways we toss the coin of West Indian history, more often than not it comes down on the side of resistance rather than accommodation. The implication of this view is clear, certainly with respect to the issue of popular consciousness and political action. It says, principally, that though the experiences of West Indian people have been shaped by the need to come to terms with powerful hegemonic, colonial and imperialist structures and ideas, their essential response has been one of anti-systemic resistances.

Whether it was during the period of the Amerindian–European encounter, or the subsequent slavery epoch, the majority of West Indian inhabitants have sought to define their own existence in terms of an appropriation of space that could be autonomously manipulated in the building of discrete realities of freedom. Cricket, then, became enmeshed in all these considerations, and represented an ideological and cultural terrain on which this very intensive battle was fought. This is precisely why James was able to argue that the cricket history of the region is but a mirror within which its modern social undertakings can be examined and assessed. It is also expressive of the manner in which black West Indians took the plough share of Empire and turned it into a sword which they later placed at the throats of the imperial order.

As far as the late nineteenth-century English sponsor of cricket in the Empire was concerned, 'cricket was an essential and symbolic part of the imperial order and manners'.[4] Could they have envisioned that West Indian recipients in the late twentieth century would promote cricket as an agent in the dismantlement of the imperial order and a symbol of liberation? Perhaps not, but it is necessary to be clear on what is made of the present state of affairs, as 'confessed' by Searle, an English middle-class radical intellectual:

> There is no doubt that for some English and Australian cricket 'experts', sunk into the conservative traditions of the sport, the prospect of an exceptionally fast Caribbean man with a cricket ball carries the same threat as a rebellious, anti-imperial black man with a gun. They want him suppressed, disarmed – he fits nowhere into their rules and ways of the game and only challenges them.[5]

For anyone who seeks nothing but 'a simple game of cricket', none of this can be understood. Indeed, it is outright disturbing of the senses. But if Englishmen and

149

West Indians find themselves thinking that what lies 'beyond the boundary' are important to, if not determining the nature of, the contest then the question of what we do about concepts of guns and warfare must be answered, and there is no better way to do this than with a presentation of the relevant historical facts of the case.

The politics of West Indies cricket, and the history of West Indies politics in the century after Emancipation in 1838, were driven by the same basic consideration. This, according to Learie Constantine was: 'how to keep the black man in his place' and maintain white institutional hegemony.[6] There is nothing particularly contentious about this assertion. The apartheid policy that survived the slavery period remained in place, with minor constitutional adjustments that had varying sociopolitical impact across the region, well into the twentieth century. Cricket entered the Caribbean vein in much the same way that the concept of representative government did. Both were considered by the importing white elites as their private cultural property, with the ideological effect of disqualifying black participation in cricket in colonial competitions. The politics of the ancient plantation system, then, had determined the ideological foundations on which West Indies cricket rest. The struggle for the political franchise by blacks would follow the same course as the efforts to break down the boundary that separated the cricket cultures of whites, browns and blacks. Cricket was, therefore, a highly politicized business, riddled with the expressed ideological concerns of the time. The desire of blacks to penetrate the formal structures, and then to dominate them by sheer weight of numbers and quality of performance, determined the evolution of both cultures – politics and cricket. It is in this sense, then, that the most sensitive observers of West Indies cricket during the nineteenth and twentieth centuries have commented on the importance and potency of political activity beyond the boundary.

During the nineteenth century, when West Indians had developed their game to the regional level, the global cricket culture was understood to be another area of life in which whites engaged in gentlemanly competition devoid of overt political rancour. White elites in the West Indians, Australians, Canadians, Americans, and Southern Africans played each other as often as they could, and clamoured for exchange arrangements with England – the perceived centre of cricketing philosophy and methodologies. The political exclusion of non-whites, and the reasons offered to rationalize the consequences, meant that blacks confronted cricket at the outset as an activity associated with racial elitism, respectability and ideological authority. Their response to it was one of ambivalence, and indication of the pressure of historical circumstances that evokes from the colonized both admiration and hostility for the culture of the oppressor.

It is interesting to note that creole white West Indians, unlike their counterparts in Canada, the United States and Australia, did not develop the ideological position that a cricket defeat by England, in particular, constituted a severe blow to their rising national consciousness and sensibility. Cricket had survived the revolutionary independence process in the USA, but not the civil war a century later. By then, American political leadership was bent on subduing English cultural influences, and sought to 'create' their own nation-games, language, political institutions and social values. Cricket disappeared along with several things English, and was replaced by football and baseball, symbols of a new nation.

The Canadians were tugged along by American influences, while Aussie nationalism embraced cricket as a politicized weapon in their anti-colonial and independence struggles, which explained in part the bloody trench war fought between the two teams in the 'bodyline' series in 1932/33. Never before had international cricket contests assumed such militancy, and by the time it was over all involved were clear that its motivating forces came, not only from within the internal process of the game, but as a result of ideological infiltrations from beyond the boundary. West Indian whites, who by this time were still the dominant representatives of West Indies cricket, shuddered at the idea of West Indian independence, and their continued subservience in political life shaped the ideological profile and posture of West Indies cricket.

While Australian nationalists were flexing their muscles in the 1932/33 bodyline series, and sending serious political messages to Westminister, black West Indians were taking note. The Garvey movement, insisting on black political and economic enfranchisement, had integrated the masses in ways hitherto done only by the sugar plantations on which they 'slaved'. Black nationalism became the cutting-edge ideological force throughout the West Indies, and by 1938 the masses had confronted local whites and the imperial state in a series of rebellions during which they demanded the political franchise, social reform, and access to economic resources. It was a revolutionary decade for the West Indies, and cricket, the people's primary cultural form, became infused by this ideological temperature.

As is always the case radical struggles are fought on the ideological as well as the organizational level. The simultaneous nature of these actions ensures that political directions are guided by the contents of consciousness. The question of black racial oppression in West Indies cricket, especially after 1928 when test status was achieved, was placed on the front burners of West Indies politics. This issue occupied the popular imagination in much the way that the struggle for legal trade unionism did. Only concerted political organization was required. The ideological point was won. The West Indies team, captained and managed by 'whitemen of dubious cricketing ability', had become politically problematic. Blacks were being told on no uncertain terms that they were invitees of the establishment which was 'composed of plantocrats, professionals, and merchants, to a man white or a generous part of white', who were 'a class fearful of successful black endeavour'.[7]

During the 1930s, according to Cummings, the presence of George Headley and Learie Constantine, superlative black West Indies players from Jamaica and Trinidad respectively, laid the foundation for the political struggle. Michael Manley saw very clearly the relationship between the 1937/38 workers' rebellion and the black struggle within West Indies cricket.[8] Searle noted that the display of genius by Headley within the context of the workers' uprising 'meant that cricket became a black man's game and the challenge was against white interests who con-trolled it'.[9]

The challenge came at two levels; references to both of which are to be found in the writing of Learie Constantine. First, the ideological position of white cricketers and administrators that contest with England was essentially a non-political event in which 'cousins' exchanged mutual admiration which had to be defeated and rejected. Black West Indians did not share the outlook of their white team mates, and this divided and weakened West Indies cricket. The division was political, and had to be removed by political means. Constantine wrote:

> Of all Test playing combinations the West Indies team alone is composed of men of dif-ferent race. And there lies a difficulty which I believe few of the West Indian selectors themselves realise. As I shall have occasion to point out more emphatically in a moment, Test Match cricket to-day is no sort of game. It is a battle. And to win you need not only the strenuous effort of individual players: the work of each player must be backed by a sense of solidarity, of all the others supporting him, not only actually but, so to speak, in the spirit. The lack of this is the chief weakness of the West Indies team in big cricket. We have not been able to get together in the sort of spirit which says 'Look here, we are going out to-day against those fellows and it is war to the knife!' It is difficult for us, but not by any means impossible. I have played on West Indian sides which had that spirit and I have played on sides which had not. Until all members of a West Indies side realise that every consideration must give way before the necessity of uniting in spirit and in truth to win through a series of Test Matches the West Indians will not play the cricket that I know they can play. Much depends on the players, much more depends on the leadership, which must itself be above pettiness, sympathetic, and yet be strong and command respect from all in the team.[10]

Constantine had doubts as to whether white West Indian cricketers could feel the same intensity of purpose as blacks, especially with regard to contests against England. He did not doubt their ability as players. In fact, he had the highest regard for the genius of H.B.G. Austin and George Challenor, in particular. For this reason, he moved to the second position, which was that black leadership of the West Indies team was necessary in order to infuse it with those aggressive ideological and psy-chological considerations and feelings found beyond the boundary. If cricket resides at the heart of the West Indian social view, he said, then their exploits on the field should reflect all those emotional concerns that inform their vision.

The linkage of these two issues within Constantine's analysis suggests that West Indies cricket was hamstrung by very serious political concerns. Cricket, he said, is the 'most obvious, and some would say the most glaring, example of the black man being kept "in his place", and this is the first thing that is going to be changed'.[11] The 1933 West Indies team which contained black stars such as E. Martindale, B. Sealy and George Headley was captained by G.C. Grant, the Trinidadian Cambridge Blue, who supported the view that England was the motherland that deserved loyalty and respect from its colonists in all areas of life. The leadership of the West Indies team by persons of this political ilk, Constantine intimated, had 'rotted the heart out of our cricket'. I only hope before I die, he surmised, 'to see a West Indies team, chosen on its merits alone, captained by a black player, win a ribbon against England'.[12]

The attainment of black leadership dreamt of by Constantine would not be easy. As far as the establishment was concerned too much was at stake; the political implications would be severe and long lasting. It would be a battle fought on many fronts, and determined by that party beyond the boundary – the West Indies public, for whom it had become a religious sort of activity. They, of course, knew the historical background. Communities throughout the region could speak with passion and conviction about this or that player whose ambitions died on the vine on account of white domination of the game. They knew also that whites had taken the view that cricket was 'their' game and that blacks should accept subordinate roles.

There was, of course, only one West Indies team. But the culture beyond the boundary indicated that there were many social demarcations. For whites, the issue was a simple political one. They controlled political and economic power throughout the region, and it was only logical that representation at the international level should remain their portfolio. Black radicals, then, who understood these ideological dimensions, realized that only the highest political campaign, rooted within the wider anti-colonial, black nationalist movement could secure their objective.

C.L.R. James, by the 1940s a seasoned anti-colonial activist in the West Indies, and veteran Pan-Africanist revolutionary, came forth and made this struggle as a top regional priority. He possessed all the relevant skills to lead this campaign. He knew the issues, saw their relevance to West Indies liberation, and was an activist by political nature. In his typical literary style, he described the 1958 political movement for black leadership under Frank Worrell as follows:

> Once in a blue moon, i.e. once in a lifetime, a writer is handed on a plate a gift from heaven. I was handed mine in 1958. I had just completed a draft of this book up to the end of the previous chapter when I returned to the West Indies in April 1958, after twenty-six years of absence. I intended to stay three months, I stayed four years. I became the editor of a political paper, the *Nation*, the official organ of the People's National Movement of Trinidad, and the secretary of the West Indian Federal Labour Party. Both these parties governed, the one Trinidad, the other the Federation of the West Indies. These were temporary assignments, as I made clear from the start. Immediately I was immersed up to the eyes in 'The Case for West Indian Self-Government'; and a little later, in the most furious cricket campaign I have ever known, to break the discrimination of sixty years and have a black man, in this case Frank Worrell, appointed captain of a West Indies team. I saw the beginning, the middle, but I am not at all sure that I have seen the end of violent intervention of a West Indian crowd into the actual play of a Test match. The intimate connection between cricket and West Indian social and political life was established so that all except the wilfully perverse could see. It seemed as if I were just taking up again what I had occupied myself with in the months before I left in 1932, except that what was then idea and aspiration was now in the open and public property.[13]

153

The *Nation* became a Caribbean forum in which intellectuals and workers, politicians and lawyers, teachers and students participated in or followed the heated debate in which three issues were linked: (a) the politics of black nationalist decolonization; (b) movement towards Nation State (singular or federated Independence); (c) black leadership of West Indies test cricket. This was undoubtedly the most historically significant movement of the century, and the politics of cricket were at the heart of the matter. Black leadership of West Indies cricket, political independence, and nationhood were all symbols of one historic process – the liberation of blacks from colonial bondage, and the cricket struggle was in the vanguard.[14]

It was, of course, much more than just the replacement of white leadership by black leadership. It was about the question of merit, democracy, and social justice. It was clear to all informed cricket observers in 1958/59 that Worrell was the obvious man for the job on the basis of merit. He did not qualify under existing social criteria. He was neither planter nor merchant, and had no intimate social relations with these communities. In fact, he had been a thorn in their flesh for some time for insisting that proper wages be paid to professional cricketers. But his cricket genius was obvious and the future of democracy in the West Indies required the populace to stand up on principle and reject blatant racial injustice.[15]

Public indignation, noted Michael Manley, 'swept the cricketing world', as West Indians stood up and demanded that merit should not give way to mediocrity. C.L.R. James led them into an ideological crusade that signalled the end of the *ancien regime*. Cricket was now in the hands of the masses who had given breath to it at critical life and death moments. Worrell was appointed captain in 1959 for the upcoming tour of Australia. He was the first black man to be appointed captain of the West Indies cricket team. Blacks had captained in the occasional match when the official captain was indisposed, but this appointment was the grand historic moment, and it took a regional high profile political movement to accomplish it.[16]

White West Indians, Barbadians in particular, took the decision of the West Indies Board very badly. They knew it was the end of the line for white domination. Adult suffrage in Barbados in 1950 led to the clinical removal of whites from the Assembly in 1951. They knew Worrell as a man who did not buckle under the pressure of racism on the island. He spoke his mind, told them what he knew they did not want to hear, and adopted Jamaica as his home. As far as they were concerned, they ran Worrell out of Barbados. He could not get work in the economy which they controlled, and they called him a racist for criticizing their racial bigotry. Worrell was a political rebel with a cause, and white West Indian society moved against him.

It was not Worrell that white West Indians feared. It was the entire political process that had thrust him into the leadership position by discrediting mediocrity from their ranks. In most territories, whites rallied against labour unions, the formation of the University of the West Indies, adult suffrage, and most importantly, independence. These institutions, they believed, were adding fuel to the flame raging in black hearts, while independence would leave them stranded in black states without the protective armour of the 'motherland'. Whites, then, took a grand political stand against the tide of democracy and freedom, which in turn meant that they could no longer support the West Indies cricket team against a white team. Race first was their dominant ideology, and in 1960 and 1963 they withdrew full support from the West Indies in their series against Australia and England respectively. In Barbados this was particularly obvious, though it was also evident in other places.

There is evidence to show, however, that the process of white withdrawal of support for the West Indies team had started from the time that blacks had attained numerical superiority with the team. Len Hutton, for example, the England captain of the West Indies tour in 1953/4, stated that while in Jamaica native whites persistently impressed upon him at social functions how important it was to them that the blacks did not win the series. Also, Keith Miller, the Australian all rounder, reported similar experiences in Barbados where he found that black and white team mates did not visit each other's homes on account of the intensity of anti-black racial prejudice on the island. Miller noted that during the test against the West Indies in Barbados in May 1955, white players did not invite the three Ws to their homes when cocktails were prepared for the Australians, which was a source of embarrassment for the visitors.

The issue of anti-black racism in West Indies cricket was not only an affront to the Australians, but also to members of the English touring team in the 1958/59 test series. E.W. Swanton, the distinguished English cricket scholar, who accompanied the English touring party had much to say about his own personal experiences in his 'memoirs' of the series. White members of the West Indies team, in addition to white natives who attended tests, clearly offended Swanton in their expression of negrophobic attitudes. In summarising the report on the tour he wrote:

> This is a cricket book, not a treatise on West Indian problems, but there was one aspect of current life in the islands which one noticed more this time, in relation to the cricket, than on previous visits, and I must therefore mention it though, I hope, with due diffidence. I mean the matter of colour prejudice – in both directions – and what had been dubbed 'shade distinction'.

> Cricket in the West Indies was planted like the sugar, the citrus and the cocoanuts, by white colonists. They gave the lead, and when the coloured West Indians followed it with such gusto and skill it became a bond between them, as games should always be a bond between creeds and classes. The first West Indian teams to England before the first war contained some four or five coloured men, the rest white. By 1939, when R.S. Grant's team had to hustle back home ahead of the German submarines, the balance had been almost exactly reversed. Now it happens that the Test team is likely most times to be almost wholly coloured, though it by no means follows that men who have done so much for West Indian cricket, such as John Goddard, Jeffrey Stollmeyer and Gerry Gomez, may not have their successors among the teams of the 'sixties.

> All this is an inevitable evolution, the racial proportions being what they are. But the situation makes it the more surprising that one finds people apparently insisting on a certain line of policy, or the selection of a certain man, on grounds of colour, disguised or thinly veiled though their arguments may be.[17]

Swanton's call was for the removal of race politics from the game, and celebrated the selection of Worrell as Captain since it was not possible to find within the team a 'better example' of leadership. West Indian whites, he intimates, should let go of old, bankrupt ideologies and support 'their' team irrespective of the opposition.

In much the same way that West Indian people rose up against apartheid in West Indies cricket and assured Frank Worrell the captaincy, they swiftly moved Captain Sobers in 1970 when he visited apartheid Rhodesia for two days and participated in a double wicket tournament with South African Ali Bacher. It had taken black West Indians a century of intense struggle against racism to place their cricket leadership in the hands of a working-class player. They did not take too kindly to Sobers's trip which was conceived as offering support and legitimacy to a racist regime – especially since he met with Ian Smith and was reported to have said that the leader of the racist regime was 'not so bad after all'.[18]

Throughout the West Indies public opinion called for Sobers's neck. How could the leader of the only popular West Indian institution – the cricket team – not recognize that since the 1920s the region's cricket culture had been highly politicized and ideologically charged to resist racial injustice? Frank Walcott, leader of the Barbados Workers Union, condemned Sobers, and called for his resignation. In Antigua, the *Workers Voice* described Sobers as a 'white black man' and stated that he had 'abdicated his loyalty to Africans everywhere.' The Guyana *Chronicle* was clear that if 'Sobers does not appreciate what being a leader is, then he should not be entrusted with leadership'. Guyana's President, Forbes Burnham, demanded an apology from Sobers for 'his foolish and ill-advised stand', while Michael Manley in Jamaica stated that unless the apology was offered 'Sobers may not be welcomed anywhere by people who believe that justice is bigger than even sport'.[19]

Sobers, unlike Worrell, his predecessor, was not attuned to the historical and ideological nature of his location within West Indies cricket. No one doubted his genius as a player, but the question was asked: how could he have inherited the finest gifts of a grand cricketing tradition without acquiring at the same time an understanding of its sociological and political characteristics? All along, Sobers's view was that he was a cricketer and not a politician, and that he hoped his action would assist in the promotion of multi-racial sport. Two contradictions are evident here. First, as a result of high-level political action the role of captaincy was placed within his grasp and therefore his situation was intrinsically politicized. Second, his desire to assist the promotion of non-racial democracy in a country where bloody armed struggle was taking place in order to remove apartheid meant that the cricket game in which he participated was obviously a major political intervention. Trevor Bailey, former English test captain, and a Sobers's biographer, completely misunderstood the nature of West Indies cricket when he stated that Sobers was 'appointed to captain a cricket team . . . and not to lead an ideological crusade'.[20] The weight of the evidence suggests, however, that Sobers was an integral part of an ideological crusade which had begun some 150 years earlier and had only began to bear fruit in his own lifetime.

If these matters were not clear to Sobers in 1970 they certainly were to Viv Richards a generation later. Like Sobers, Richards was the world's greatest batsman in his time, and assuming West Indies captaincy, found himself compelled to represent the ideological tradition established by Constantine, Headley and Worrell. He was clear on where he stood ideologically, and on the nature of his time. 'The whole issue [of race/apartheid] is quite central to me', he wrote, 'coming as I do from the West Indies at the very end of colonialism'. 'I believe very strongly', he said, 'in the black man asserting himself in this world and over the years I have leaned towards many movements that followed this basic cause. It was perfectly natural for me to identify, for example, with the Black Power movement in America and, to a certain extent, with Rastafarians'.[21]

Richards, therefore, took into cricket much of what cricket had given to him. His cricket and his politics fused into an ideological force that shaped his genius and determined the principled positions adopted with respect to apartheid and the South African cricket culture. While Sobers adopted and maintained the rather simple position that politics should not be involved in sports, Richards emphasized that 'you cannot evade the point that playing cricket is in itself a political action'.[22] From this position, he could not follow Sobers into Southern Africa. He says:

> Once I was offered one million Eastern Caribbean dollars [1 US $ = 2.60 EC $], and there have been all kinds of similar proposals [to play cricket in South Africa]. They all carried a political burden and in each case it was a very simple decision for me. I just could not go. As long as the black majority in South Africa remains suppressed by the apartheid system, I could never come to terms with playing cricket there. I would be letting down my own people back in Antigua and it would destroy my self-esteem.[23]

Many other players, of course, succumbed to the financial temptations and found themselves categorized as 'honorary whites' in order to play cricket in South Africa. Political consciousness, like cricketing ability, varies from player to player, but for Richards cricket allowed for his self-expression 'in a way that is totally pure'.[24]

The Sobers–Richards experience, then, is illustrative of the dialectical process of accommodation and resistance that resides at the core of Caribbean history. Within this dialectic the forces of resistance are invariably the greater, which is why 12,000 Barbadians had great problems with the 1992 'test' between South Africa and the West Indies at Bridgetown.[25] A massive boycott of the historic single test was planned before the South Africans arrived in Barbados. Eventually no more than 3,000 people attended the opening days when test matches usually attract upwards of 12,000 per day.

Before the test started on Saturday 18 April, the Pan-African movement of Barbados was referring to the West Indies Board of Control as 'traitors' who, in league with West Indian governments, had 'reneged on the duty which they owe to the exploited, suffering and struggling black people of South Africa'.[26] The movement called for the boycott of the test in a press release which said:

Virtually the only practical and effective way in which the Caribbean nations can contribute to the international isolation of South Africa and to the cause of the black South Africans is in the field of sport in general and cricket in particular. It is therefore utterly shameful that the Governments and cricket administrators of the region could so casually throw away the 'cricket weapon' and join the members of a privileged racial elite to frolic and make sport in the Caribbean sun. . . . It is now left to the Barbados people to demonstrate that at least one island population is serious about their responsibility to the black struggle by boycotting the test match and sending a stern message to the international community and the racist Government of South Africa.[27]

Richards, recently retired from test cricket, took the view that no test should be played against white South Africa until democratic systems were put in place, in spite of the fact that Nelson Mandela had urged West Indian governments and the West Indies Cricket Board of Control to support the test. Sobers, on the other hand, was a prime mover in the arrangement and was photographed at the Barbados airport hugging and kissing South African officials – led by the same Ali Bacher who had participated in luring him into Rhodesia in 1970. While large sections of public opinion felt that the very successful boycott was due to the exclusion of Barbadian pacer, Andy Cummins, from the West Indies team, it remains inescapable that the mood of the country was that West Indies cricket should not freely interface with 'white' South Africa cricket within the context of their domestic apartheid policy. Once again, West Indies cricket found itself in the vanguard of the political movement, dividing those who saw it as an activity to combat racism and those who considered that it could serve to a greater degree the interests of racists.

Given this ideological character and political history, it should not be surprising that cricket has been called upon to perform the task of healing the wounds and building the bridges of a fragmented nationalism that has been established in the wake of the passing colonial order. Bound historically by the sugar plantations regime and now by the cricket culture, West Indians are aware, according to David Lowenthal, that 'outside the world of cricket the West Indies is not a nation and does not act as one'.[28] The political weight being carried, and the mission expected of West Indies cricket, then, are really quite extraordinary.

These matters were not lost on the 'West Indies Commission' who in 1989 were mandated by CARICOM governments to prepare a report in order to guide West Indian nations into the next century with a revitalized commitment to a sense of collective independence, sovereignty and nationhood. In the 1992 official report, a blueprint for change for the next generation, commissions, led by Sir Shridath Ramphal and Sir Alister McIntyre, Vice Chancellor of the University of the West Indies, were very explicit in their reflection of information received from citizens about the political role function of cricket. It stated:

When we lost a particularly vital World Cup match, a commentator tried to get a dismal, undedicated performance by the West Indies cricket team into what he thought might be the right perspective by saying: 'after all, it is just another game'. He made a fundamental mistake. To us it was not, it is not, 'just a game'.

No West Indian believer can afford to underestimate or neglect this game. It is an element in our heritage which binds us close and is seen as such both by ourselves and the outside world. When first Frank Worrell in that famous tour of Australia in 1960 and then later Clive Lloyd, followed by Viv Richards in the 1970s and 1980s, led the West Indies to a dominant position in world cricket, it built our stature as a people both in our own eyes and in the eyes of others. When we stood as one in the cricket boycott of South African apartheid it really mattered. And when we failed as a team in crucial games in the World Cup throughout the Region we felt ourselves indefinably but definitely diminished as a nation in those performances.

The performance of the West Indian team in their miracle win in the historic Test match against South Africa revalidated the supremacy of cricket in the West Indian psyche as an enduring source of inspiration and as demonstration of the fact that we do it better when we do it together.

It may be instructive that it was in a presentation made to the Commission on the sources of West Indian success in building a great cricket team in the late 1970s and 1980s that we heard what we thought was perhaps the most succinct recipe for success in all the endeavours we pursue as a community of nations acting together.[29]

As a result, the Commission in making recommendations to governments with respect to the promotion of a federated nationhood, made 12 distinct proposals for the furtherance of cricket's contribution to the deepening of the regional integration movement.

But democratic, multi-racial cricket and the political movement for integration and nationhood in the West Indies grew up together, oftentimes, under the same parentage. They are therefore 'family', bonded and torn by emotional concerns that are found only in domestic conditions. V.S. Naipaul gives us an insight into this world when he eavesdrops on a discussion among West Indians at the Oval test between England and the West Indies in 1963:

'What, they have politics in Grenada?' Laughter.
'Boy, I had to leave Grenada because politics were making it too hot for me.'
'What, they have politics in Grenada?' Laughter.
'You are lucky to see me here today, let me tell you. The only thing in which I remain West Indian is cricket. Only thing'. . . .
'I hear the economic situation not too good in Trinidad these days.' 'All these damn strikes. You know our West Indian labour . . .'
'But the cricket ever returns . . .'
'My dear girl, I didn't know you followed cricket.'
'Man, how you could help it at home? In Barbados. And with all my brothers.'[30]

It is for reasons so described that Richards was to discover within the context of the international game that cricket is 'not some irrelevant, eccentric sport played by a handful of countries, but a game that gets right to the root of the societies involved'.[31]

Modern West Indies cricket, then, is a mass supportive festival culture in which nationalistic, liberationist ideologies are expressed. From inception it has been an effective instrument that indicated ideological forces with society, and at the same time functioned as a field on which the process of conflict and co-option was played out. Like every social fact, West Indies cricket is a perpetual creation of the men who practise and organize it, and who are, in turn, transformed by their very creation. Its political ideology is embedded not only in its moral codes, but within the historical struggle against colonial oppression and its social legacies. Furthermore, its ideological effects are witnessed daily within West Indian life, with the result that for most persons cricket is about life as 'lived' rather than endured.

NOTES

1 Chris Searle, 'Race before Cricket: Cricket, Empire, and the White Rose', *Race and Class*, Vol. 31, January/March, 1990, No. 3, pp. 343–5. See also, Christine Cummings, 'The Ideology of West Indies Cricket', *Arena Review*, Vol. 14, No. 1, May 1990, pp. 25–33; Hilary Beckles, 'Barbados Cricket and the Crisis of Social Culture', in *100 Years of Organised Cricket in Barbados* (Bridgetown, Barbados Cricket Association, 1992) pp. 50–1.
2 Searle, 'Race before Cricket', p. 37.
3 C.L.R. James, *The Black Jacobins: Toussaint L'Ouverture and the San Domingo Revolution* (1938) (Vintage Books, 1963 edn); *Beyond a Boundary* (London: Hutchinson, 1963); 'The Black Scholar Interviews C.L.R. James', *Black Scholar*, Vol. 2, No. 1, September 1970, pp. 35–43.
4 Searle, 'Race before Cricket', p. 31.
5 *Ibid.*, p. 38.
6 *Ibid.*, p. 35.
7 *Ibid.*, p. 34.
8 Cummings, 'The Ideology'; See Michael Manley, *A History of West Indies Cricket* (London, Andre Deutsch, 1988), pp. 55–66. Manley states: 'The 1920s, which produced Marcus Garvey and George Headley, can be seen as a time of ferment . . . awakening of mass consciousness and the first stirrings of racial self-assertion', p. 55.
9 *Searle*, 'Race before Cricket', p. 35.
10 Learie Constantine, *Cricket and I* (London, Allan, 1933), p. 172.
11 Searle, 'Race before Cricket', p. 35.
12 Learie Constantine, *Cricket in the Sun* (London, Allan, 1947); Searle, 'Race before Cricket', p. 34.
13 James, *Beyond a Boundary*, p. 217.
14 C.L.R. James, *The Case for West Indian Self-Government* (London, Hogarth, 1933); 'The Caribbean Confrontation begins, *Race Today*, Vol. 2, 1970, pp. 311–14.
15 Manley, *A History*, p. 146.
16 *Ibid.*, p. 148.
17 E.W. Stanton, *West Indies Revisited: the M.C.C Tour of 1959/60* (London, Heinemann, 1960), pp. 279–80.
18 Trevor Bailey, *Sir Gary* (Glasgow, Fontana/Collins, 1976), p. 137.
19 *Ibid.*, pp. 39–40.
20 *Ibid.*, p. 140.
21 Viv Richards, *Hitting Across the Line* (London, Headline Books, 1991), p. 188.
22 *Ibid.*, p. 186.

23 *Ibid.*, p. 187.
24 *Ibid.*, p. 186.
25 *Sunday Advocate*, Barbados, 19 April 1992.
26 *Weekend Nation* (Barbados), Friday, 17 April 1992.
27 *Ibid.*
28 David Lowenthal, *West Indian Societies* (Oxford, Oxford University Press, 1972), p. 229.
29 *Time for Action: Report of the West Indies Commission* (Black Rock, Barbados, 1992), p. 328.
30 V.S. Naipaul, 'England v. West Indies, 1963', in Michael Davie and Simon Davie, *Cricket* (London, Faber, 1987), p. 184.
31 Richards, *Hitting across the Line*, p. 76.

Part III

Ethnicity, social ideology and politics

10

How cricket is West Indian cricket?
Class, racial, and color conflict

L. O'Brien Thompson

Enthusiasts of international sports are perhaps aware of the passionate interest in the game of cricket in the Commonwealth Caribbean. From the inception of international competition in the nineteenth century until the 1950s, England and her former colony, Australia, vied with each other for supremacy. Since the 1950s, however, an outsider, the West Indies, threatened and eventually became the dominant force in the game.

West Indian cricket is best understood by analyzing its relationship to social structure. The penetration of European powers into the Caribbean was responsible for bringing together people of diverse racial and ethnic backgrounds. Colonialism compounded these differences and led to a history of racial, color, and class conflict. These are the ingredients which give substance and meaning to the West Indian tradition in cricket. The contribution of the Afro-West Indian has been so prominent as to obscure the impact of the other racial and ethnic groups on this art form. Since transplanted Africans learned the game from transplanted Englishmen, it is appropriate to start with an examination of the game in the place of its origin.

The roots of cricket

The game of cricket was conceived in the latter part of the eighteenth century. By the early nineteenth century, with social and financial support coming from the upper class, aristocrat, peasant, and proletarian combined to make it the refined art form we know today. Cricket became an English institution for all intents and purposes in 1827, when Oxford and Cambridge first played the "University Match." It has been an annual event of much social significance ever since. By the 1850s, influenced greatly by the headmaster of Rugby College, Matthew Arnold, the game came to be perceived as a molder of character. Accordingly, participation was strongly encouraged at the great Public Schools – Eton, and Harrow, for example. The masses were not far behind in cultivating enthusiasm for a game which was soon elevated to the status of a national pastime. Despite its overall appeal, cricket,

165

nevertheless, became identified with the British aristocracy. The pursuit of leisure is typically associated with this class. For them cricket became an important social and recreational outlet. One would be hard pressed to find a game which matches cricket as a reflection of the traditional ethos of the aristocracy.

Cricket is a team sport played from 11.30 in the morning to 6.30 in the evening. Although it can be tiring, it is not as physical as American football or basketball. As if to consciously minimize the effects of possible exhaustion, the organizers of the game have included periods of respite. Fun and relaxation seem to be the maxim. There are breaks for lunch (40 minutes) and tea (20 minutes). While on the field of play, drinks are served. Selection depends on the vagaries of the weather. It is not unknown for some cricketers to order brandy on wintry days in the notorious English weather.

The emphasis on decorum and etiquette as reflected in the culture of the aristocracy are hallmarks of the traditional game. Good behavior and deportment are stressed. Chatter commonly found in baseball, football, and basketball has no place. Courtesy dictates that distractions likely to impair the concentration of players are forbidden. When a captain has to say something to a player, the whisper is the rule. By the same token, players who "appeal" to the umpire for a decision are expected to abide by his ruling without question, even though his judgement is obviously bad. The unhappy player finds himself accepting the inevitable with a stiff upper lip. And batsmen who know that they are out should not be disposed to await the umpire's decision but anticipate it and walk. It is as if a baseball batter anticipates that he has struck out and elects to walk without checking with the umpire.

The attire worn by cricketers is formal, given the circumstances: long-sleeve shirts, conservatively tailored cream flannels, and white boots. In chilly conditions, cricketers may augment their attire with long or short sleeve sweaters of standard design. When the monarch pays the annual visit to "Lords," the famous cricket ground and headquarters of the game, blazers become part of the ritual attire. This social event is the "Ascot" of the cricket season.

Once the upper class gained control of the game, class distinctions became a characteristic feature. Those who played in championship matches for love rather than money became known as "gentlemen." Those who could not afford this luxury were dubbed "players." At cricket grounds "gentlemen" and "players" used different dressing rooms and entered separate gates onto and from grounds. Each year the best of the "gentlemen" competed against the best of the "players." These distinctions were abandoned in the 1950s and the annual contest has accordingly been discontinued.

What has been described represents the culture of a game which accompanied British colonizers as they accumulated a vast empire from the seventeenth century right through the nineteenth century. The game took root in Australia, New Zealand, India, and the West Indies.

If Englishmen played cricket in the latter part of the eighteenth century, it is assumed that the role performed by slaves must have been marginal. The arduous task of preparing pitches and fields was doubtless their responsibility. Maybe a few favorite slaves were allowed on the field to retrieve balls or even bowl. This situation must have prevailed up to emancipation in the nineteenth century. What spare time slaves earned must have been spent learning the rudiments of the game, among other things.

There is reason to believe that this situation took a change for the better after emancipation in 1834. Since this historic event coincided with a refinement of the technical aspects of the game in England, a few years must have elapsed before this development was introduced to the colonies. In turn, the freed slave would have been the last sector of the society to be exposed to the refinement of this complex art form.

At this early stage the Afro-West Indian would not have been able to purchase the equipment required for formal games. His social and economic plight necessitated improvisation. Given the traditions that have endured in "bat and ball," the Afro-West Indian was not lacking in ingenuity. Too poor to buy a "willow," the Afro-West Indian invented the bat made out of the branch of a clammy-cherry or a coconut tree. A young breadfruit or a knitted ball took the place of the well stitched leather ball. A variety of objects were used for stumps – "tin-can," "rocks," or even a piece of cardboard. Any available piece of land was appropriated for a playing field. Ingenuity extended to rule making and procedure. Take firms as an example. Two or three players may enter a pact which local custom referred to as a firm. If a member of a firm takes a catch, it is the turn of his firm to bat. He may give the ball or he may bowl it in such a manner as to minimize the chances of the member of his firm getting out. The key to this cooperative adaptation is for the firm to dominate the "crease" rather than engage in the more arduous pursuits of bowling and fielding. For those not batting, possession of the ball is important since it is one way of gaining control of the bat. In this milieu a premium is placed on solid batting, aggressive bowling, and fielding. Firms have many variations.

Knee cricket is another improvisation. One knee is placed on the ground and a miniature bat takes the place of a standard bat. Similarly a marble is substituted for the usual ball. When a bowler underhands the marble and the batsman strikes it, he gets off his knee and runs to the bowler's end. Should the marble pass the bat, however, and the wicket-keeper breaks the wicket before the bat touches the ground the batsman is out. Very often play is held up as participants argue back and forward about whether the batsman is out or not.

Beach cricket should not go unmentioned as another interesting innovation. A pitch is chosen on that part of the beach where the waves encroach, therefore leaving a relatively firm surface. A used tennis ball is substituted for the obvious reason that it bounces on this surface. Fielders take positions on the beach and in the water. In this game, in addition to being declared out when a fielder catches the ball right off the bat, one may lose one's wicket when the fielder catches the ball after one bounce. The ability to hit hard over a fielder's head or to stroke the ball along the ground becomes important in this adaptation. Once again the game may take several forms depending on the whim of the participants.

The settings and adaptations only begin to give us a glimpse of the uniqueness of the West Indian tradition in cricket as it emerged over the decades. At an early age quickness of eye and nimbleness of foot are cultivated. In the absence of formal coaching and with a disposition to get on with the game, unorthodoxy of technique prevails. The approach to the game is uninhibited and aggressive rather than stifled and defensive. There is zest and spirit whether bowling, batting or fielding. In this milieu, fun, camaraderie, and enjoyment supersede the will to win. It is not an exaggeration to claim that "bat and ball" came to represent a way of life for the West Indian masses.

The West Indian game

The West Indian cricketer is depicted as moving with "feline grace," being "lithe," "panther-like," "tigerish," and "loose-muscled." A correlation between his movements and the flair he brings to this trade is implied. Thus the West Indian is known for his attacking game, his relish of playing with "abandon," and his spontaneity. We are told that when the flow of the game is in his favor, he is "devastating." In the midst of adversity, however, he is said to lack resiliency, the will to discipline himself and grind the situation out.

There is no doubt that the impression has been left that the manner in which the West Indian plays the game is due to "native characteristics" or "instinct." However, when one examines the formation and development of the West Indian personality, a different picture may be drawn. Slave-masters and European travellers almost to a man described the slave as a "noble savage." Recent research provides an alternative interpretation of the life the slave carved out for himself in a hostile environment. In spite of the attempt to deracinate and deculturate the African slave in the West Indies, he is said to have successfully resisted cultural assimilation. While manipulating his environment, the slave developed distinctive patterns of speech, song, dance, humor, religion, spirit, movement, and expression.

Enough has been said about movement. Expression, on the other hand, calls for more analysis, especially since West Indian spectators are "notorious" for their lively and active engagement in the proceedings on and off the field of play. Indeed their participation in this regard often influences the tempo of the game. The contrast of expression with the colonizer should therefore enhance our understanding. The West Indian is predisposed to be more boisterous than the Englishman. He gesticulates more, is more of an exhibitionist, and more gregarious. Often characterized as "easy-going," the West Indian is nonetheless depicted as aggressive and volatile. The elan and effervescence of the West Indian cricketer is thus inextricably tied to his social nature rather than instinct.

The post-1834 period is important in helping us grasp the dynamics of the growth of cricket among the non-white masses. There was a need for providing the emancipated slaves with an education if they were to be absorbed into a changing economy. Since racism predominated, it was felt that a rudimentary education was sufficient, it did not take long for the plantocracy to come to the conclusion that it was to their advantage to broaden the educational opportunities of the more fortunate non-white. Accordingly, he was permitted limited access to secondary schools. The impact of the non-white on the game is directly linked to this development.

Cricket is an expensive game. In order to play formal matches, it is necessary to gain access to a field, maintain it, and get personal and team equipment. Catering and transportation have to be added to basic costs. The pittance paid to peasants during the nineteenth and first half of the twentieth century precluded the playing of the game in a formal setting. "Bat and ball" was the alternative. However, as increasing numbers of non-whites attended and graduated from "colleges" and obtained public-sector jobs, a material base for elevating themselves to formal competition was laid.

Following the tradition set by the great English public schools, those responsible for secondary education made cricket an integral part of school activity. The English notion that cricket and scholarship combine to mold the personality of a gentleman filtered into the educational system in the colonies. C.L.R. James, in *Beyond a Boundary*, explains:

> our masters, our curriculum, our code of morals, *everything*, began on the basis that Britain was the source of all light and leading, and our business was to admire, wonder, imitate, learn: our criterion of success was to have succeeded in approaching that distant ideal – to attain it was, of course, impossible. Both masters and boys accepted it as in the very nature of things. The masters could not be offensive about it because they thought it was their function to do this, if they thought about it at all: and, for me, it was the beacon that beckoned me on.

In like manner the culture of the great English game was transmitted to those non-whites who attended secondary schools in the colonial West Indies. They learned to obey the umpire's decision without question even though his judgement might have been obviously questionable. They were taught to be magnanimous to their opponents in defeat. They were socialized to be modest and play down their victories. They cultivated the habit of presenting a stiff upper lip in the face of adversity. They learned all about *esprit de corps*. Whereas the great English public schools had coaches on their staff, this was not the case in the West Indies. The style cultivated on backyards, beaches, streets, and any available piece of land tended to dominate on the playgrounds of secondary schools. To recap, it was aggressive, zestful, and unorthodox. A master or groundsman would pass on a few tips here or there but nothing was suggested which was likely to alter the player's style radically. The combination of a passionate love of the game, regular practice, and formal competition blended to produce outstanding talent. The "college boy" tradition was ready to stamp itself on the regional and international scene given the opportunity.

International recognition was, however, slow in coming. Unlike their English counterparts who continued the marriage of sports and scholarship at universities, few talented scholar-cricketers in the colonies could afford a university education. To begin with there was no regional university until 1948 when the University College of the West Indies was opened. And during the period, 1834–1900, there were very few scholarships for colonials to attend metropolitan universities. The intellectually ambitious son of the plantocrats, of course, had no such constraints. As a result, on graduation from secondary school, non-whites either entered the civil service or the teaching profession. In these halcyon days of colonialism, non-whites were rarely appointed to the highest positions in secondary schools and the civil service. Racial exclusion reigned in the established white clubs. There was no other alternative for non-whites who wanted to play the game consistently in a formal setting, but to form their own clubs. As indicated, the growth in number of graduates facilitated this move. Given the inordinate stress on color and other status differences in colonial society, it was not surprising that club affiliation duplicated the line of stratification.

We have seen that as a result of colonization the West Indian population was made up of people of African, European, and Asian stock. Miscegenation between Africans and Indians was insignificant when compared to what took place between Africans and Europeans. The different shades and colors produced by the latter combination have plagued West Indian society. Suffice to say that the more Africanesque one's appearance, the closer one was to the pit of the stratification system.

No West Indian island matched Barbados in the enduring emphasis on social distinctions based on color. As the major secondary boy schools of this island – Harrison College, Lodge, and Combermere – increased the pool of non-white graduates during the first half of the twentieth century, a number of cricket clubs were founded predicated on class and color distinctions. Thus, in addition to Wanderers and Pickwick, established clubs which catered to patrician and middle-class whites respectively, Carlton and the Young Men's Progressive Club attracted other whites and browns, and Spartan and Empire sponsored blacks. These clubs competed against each other every Saturday during the cricket season under the auspices of the Barbados Cricket Association (BCA). It is fair to say that cricket was in the forefront of the attack on social exclusivism. At this stage, however, it was benign as a political force.

Analogous cricket clubs emerged in other West Indian territories. Since most of the members came out of the "college boy" cricketing convention, decorum and conduct were in the classic tradition. Style and expression were rooted in native custom. During what may be called the golden era of inter-colonial cricket, the 1940s, this tradition was arrayed in all its glory. One of the famous products of this era, Frank Worrell, captures its styles and spirit: "This period cricket-wise could be called the roaring forties. This was the swashbuckling era of the West Indies cricket when in each inter-colonial match none could see a combination of flash, style, solidarity in technique and a high degree of camaraderie between players of both teams."

It is not surprising that an observer of international cricket for many a year was able to appreciate and give us an insight into the heart of the uniqueness of the West Indian tradition in cricket. In a tribute to the former Trinidad and West Indian cricketer, Lord Constantine, the Englishman, Neville Cardus wrote: "His cricket was a prophesy which has gloriously come to pass, for it forecast, by its mingled skill, daring, absolutely un-English trust to instinct and by its dazzling flashes of physical energy, the coming one day of Weekes, Worrell, of Headley, of Walcott, of Kanhai, of Sobers. All of these cricketers remain, for all their acquired culture and ordered technique, descendants of Learie, cricketers in Learie's Lineage."

The decade of the 1940s heralded the dominance of non-whites in West Indian cricket. A unique tradition in style, flair, and approach to the game was firmly established. The cake of custom with respect to control of the game at the highest levels – administration and captaincy – had to wait further social and political developments. Since the "college boy" tradition monopolized the playing scene and plebians were noticeably under-represented, class and race still remained major stumbling blocks to the ideal of equal opportunity in cricket.

Social change

The entry of plebians into the mainstream of West Indian cricket was facilitated by an unprecedented series of disturbances in the late 1930s. The masses "revolted" against an oppressive colonial system which denied them a stable economic life and exclusion from the franchise. The politically conscious middle-class non-white supported this uprising. Although many of this class qualified to vote, they were excluded from political power. Almost overnight organizations dedicated to bringing about social, political, and economic changes sprung up. In some quarters it was felt that political parties were the best force for change. The stark reality was that union leadership held greater promise. In Barbados, for example, both the Progressive League and the Congress Party antedated their labor unions. In both cases the moving spirits were educated middle-class men of color who saw the colony's problems in political terms but found out that the masses were more concerned with their economic plight. This was the social context in which a cricket association for the Barbadian masses was founded.

Joseph Mitchinson Hewitt saw the need for an association which could cater to the aspiring cricketer "whose chances to bring his talent to the forefront in cricket did not depend on the school he attended and his social class." The Friendly Cricket Association saw the light of day in 1937. Grantley Adams, who emerged from the 1937 disturbances as the most influential labor leader and politician in Barbados, was the first president of the association. As the organization thrived its name was changed to the Barbados Cricket League (BCL).

171

Youth and adults whose cricketing experiences were limited to matches between "streets," "alleys," and "parishes" on any available piece of land revelled in the improved conditions. Headmasters made what playing fields they possessed available to the organization. The plantocracy chipped in; they rented and gave land to the people of their district for playing fields.

The conduct and decorum of the game in this setting frequently deviated from the norm found in the more prestigious BCA. This should be expected given their social origins. Agricultural workers and the "urban" proletariat made up the bulk of BCL players. Acute subordination characterized their relationships with white Barbadians. Nor was their interaction with the colored middle class any more respectful. The first half of the twentieth century was one in which the typical educated non-white West Indian remained alienated from the masses. Indeed many of the pejorative terms used liberally by whites to refer to the disposition of blacks found ready acceptance among this category. No wonder that their behavior on the field often bordered on the irreverent.

It was not unheard of for matches to be abandoned in the BCL due to disorderly conduct. There were fights between players and players, players and umpires, and players and spectators. This conduct was more prevalent among teams from the "country" than from the "town." Deviance extended to illegal deliveries – pitching or throwing the ball rather than bowling it with a straight arm. The beamer – a delivery aimed at the batman's head – eschewed in the BCA, found an outlet in this environment. Similarly the convention proscribing the use of "bouncers" against tailenders – players listed low in the batting order because of limited skills – was often violated. In polite society this type of conduct was dismissed as "not being cricket," as hooliganism.

And yet to overlook its source, as was common practice, is to misunderstand the message behind the act. To demand that BCL players conduct themselves on the field in the manner befitting BCA players is nothing less than ethnocentric. Whites and the educated men of color, "college boys," are products of a different type of socialization. Whatever problems exist at home or on the job can be left behind on Saturday afternoons. The "college boy" tradition mandates that a competitive spirit prevail while having fun, entertainment, and relaxation. The occasional dubious decision by an umpire can be shrugged off lightly as "hard luck." As James put it: "when you enter the sporting arena you left behind you the sordid compromises of everyday existence." Not so with the typical BCL player.

Poor, treated as social pariahs, unemployed or given a subsistence wage, cricket matches on Saturday afternoons provide for these players a temporary escape from the miseries of everyday life. Frustration and repression are given free reign on the playing field. All too often aggression is not only meted out to the ball but on players of opposing teams. The umpire too comes under fire. The poor fellow has aggression displaced on him, a symbol of authority. Misbehavior in this milieu has underlying political overtones: it is an unwitting rebellion against the status quo. As a cultural phenomenon, cricket in the West Indies should be viewed as a reflection and expression of class, racial, and color conflict.

The circumstances, conduct, and behavior found in the BCL were so dissimilar from that found in the BCA as to deserve distinctive treatment. The "plebian" tradition seems an appropriate designation. Pitches and playing fields did not match those in the senior league. Umpires were less qualified. Very often there were no tables, benches, or drinks for lunch. When water was needed and a "standpipe" was within distance, players would get their respite. Frequently players could not afford to wear boots and sometimes shared a pair of pads instead of wearing both.

Impoverished means did not, however, dampen the style and approach to the game cultivated on the beaches and yards. The technique of the typical BCL player was not as sound as that found in the BCA. On the other hand there was more spirit, zest, and enthusiasm. It made for smaller scores and excitement. Whether batting, bowling or fielding, there seemed to be more abandon. The culture dictated that batsmen get into an attacking mode and endeavor to dispatch as many balls as possible to the boundary. For the fast bowler, less attention was given to out-foxing the batsman; the impulse to shatter the stumps with most deliveries prevailed. And in fielding there was the irresistible urge to make every catch and stop spectacular. Solidarity of technique took a back seat to showmanship and exhibitionism. The game in this milieu was theater at its best.

The batmanship of Everton Weekes epitomized the spirit and flair of the plebian tradition in cricket. As he graduated to the more competitive international arena, he was forced to discipline himself. Frank Worrell, a member of the famous "W" partnership, saw it this way: "[Weekes] improved his technique as the years went on. His years in the League [English] provided him with the opportunity of tightening up his defense which in 1948 was vulnerable." The aggressive flair characterizing his pre-international days never deserted him, however. A close observer notes that "Weekes remained a real tigerish batsman who dictated to bowlers once he got going."

Coalescence of traditions

By 1950 the "college boy" tradition in cricket was well established on the regional and international scenes. Players from a plebian background had also penetrated the exclusive social circle. The cricketing world was to witness these two traditions coalesce into a unique spectacle. What better place to show off this extraordinary talent but England! The 1950 tour of this country proved historic in that it was the first time that the colonized trounced their masters in their backyard. This event had significant psychic and political ramifications. Euphoria was short lived. In the following year the West Indies challenged Australia for the "championship" and was soundly defeated. This defeat was an ominous one in that the seeds for an attack on racial and class privilege in the highest realms of West Indian cricket were sewn.

173

Frank Worrell, later knighted for his contribution to cricket and sportsmanship and a member of the 1950 and 1951 West Indian cricket teams, questioned the leadership capacity of the captain, John Goddard, the son of a wealthy Barbadian white family: "Having not assimilated sufficient cricketing knowledge uptil 1952 . . . he floundered and the team with him." In justifying his criticism, Worrell noted that Goddard had learned his cricket in the 1930s and the 1940s when "there wasn't the same science in the game . . . as there seems to be now. The field placing was unimaginative." At the same time, one may infer from Worrell's logic that had Goddard been a serious student of the game, his experience in club, inter-colonial, and international cricket should have been enough.

The Australian disaster was a clear signal that new and effective leadership was needed regardless of race and class. The cricket authorities felt otherwise; they stuck with tradition, summoned an aging and unfit Goddard out of retirement to lead the regional team to England in 1957. Although all of the blame for the poor showing should not rest with the captain, there is little doubt that he was a part of the problem. However, the changing social and political climate contributed to pushing the West Indian cricket authorities in a direction they had hithertofore strenuously resisted.

We have already seen that the unrest of the 1930s acted as a catalyst for the founding of BCL. By the 1950s middle-class people of color were less apt to disassociate themselves from the masses and their West Indian heritage. More people were being drawn to the towns and the urban–rural dichotomy was breaking down. The University College of the West Indies was increasing its numbers and graduates, thanks to policies enacted by newly self-governing colonies. Positions in teaching, the civil service, and even the private sector, formerly the exclusive preserves of whites or near whites, were opening up for blacks. These developments ushered in a period of change in the cricketing arena.

In Barbados, the black middle-class political leadership was responsible for building publicly owned social centers and playing fields where the masses could ply their art in more congenial and adequate settings. More teams joined the BCL. The coming of age of the BCL was celebrated with the initiation of an annual competition between the BCA and the League – shades of the Gentlemen vs. Players contests. Social progress likewise penetrated the BCA. Spartan and Empire, for example, relaxed the qualification for entry. And more and more dark skinned Barbadians found their way into YMPC and Carlton. Notwithstanding these developments, it took a political crusade to expedite the hiring of a black as captain of the West Indies as a routine matter.

The force of the crusade resided in an objective assessment of the facts. One could not help but notice that the political leadership of the time, Norman Manley, Eric Williams, Grantley Adams, and Forbes Burnham, was technically superior to that which superseded it. These men of color had graduated with honors from elite British universities where they imbibed such qualities as achievement, expertise, competence, professionalism, and universalism. Their predecessors, colonial whites, fostered charlatanism, amateurism, and particularism. A residue of these characteristics could be found among members of the West Indian Cricket Board of Control. The obvious question needed to be posed for public discussion: If Prime Ministers and Chief Ministers are non-white, what's wrong with a non-white captain?

In the midst of constitutional changes and social progress, C.L.R. James was brought to the West Indies to assist in organizing a new political party in preparation for the historical federal elections. More than anyone else he politicized the issue. His case was made more convincing because of the presence of a number of black candidates with impeccable qualifications. James's choice, Frank Worrell, was a great cricketer, a professional who had mastered the technical and tactical aspects of the game. He also served successfully as captain of a Commonwealth team to India. It did not hurt his cause that he was likeable, socially respectable, and well educated.

Worrell was appointed to lead the West Indies team to Australia in 1960. The team was a hit both on and off the field. On the field the West Indian tradition was seen at its best – dashing, zestful but competitive cricket. Worrell's captaincy was especially lauded: "He was firm with them [players], yet gentle. . . . On the field he was never demonstrative. He remained calm . . . in all crises the team faced."

It is largely as a consequence of Worrell's impact that within four years he handed over the captaincy to Garfield Sobers, who, like Worrell before him, was knighted for his contribution to sportsmanship and the game. Unlike Worrell, Sobers did not have a grammar school education. His nursery was the plebian tradition. No one was more pleased than Sir Frank Worrell that the democratic tradition had now fully permeated West Indian cricket. Before his death he stated: "A lot of capital is made of the fact that in the West Indies team now there is a preponderance of coloured players over whites as opposed to the old days when the reverse obtained. But nowadays selection is a matter of ability. This is the determining factor. Formerly a chap might win selection because he came from the correct drawer of society. Nowadays your social standing doesn't carry much weight."

The international game

In turning to trends in the international game, once again it is best to view them from the standpoint of their social base. The particular issue for analysis is the changing character of the conduct and decorum of players and spectator behavior.

In 1954 an England team toured the West Indies under the captaincy of Leonard Hutton, who was later knighted. His team was one of the most unpopular ever to visit the region. A dour and defensive professional batsman, he sought to mold his team after his image. Needless to say the play was uninspiring. It is speculated that the will to win at the price of spectator enjoyment was partly related to Hutton's personality and partly a response to pressures of the white community in the West

Indies who were finding it difficult to accommodate to social change. Whatever the reason, Hutton's tour coincided with the introduction of bottle throwing on the West Indian cricket scene.

Not only did Hutton's approach to the game run counter to the West Indian tradition, the contrast between spectator behavior in Britain and that in the West Indies compounded the situation. West Indian spectators tend to be active participants of the game. Running commentaries are the norm. If one is not accustomed to constant chatter by spectators during play, it can be disturbing. Players can expect unsolicited advice. Should they fail to comply and come "unstuck," jeering is the usual response. By the same token, appreciation of an excellent piece of bowling, batting or fielding is expressed noisily and enthusiastically. In short, the cricket scene is a dramatic scene, an interplay of players and spectators.

Fun and entertainment during the breaks sustain the drama. The consumption of spirits adds levity to the proceedings. Excesses are to be found primarily in the "bleachers" where the masses are located. This part of the ground is separated from the area where the more "respectable" watch the game. In fact, during test matches the seating pattern of spectators follow along the lines of social stratification: whites enjoy the game from one corner and browns and blacks, depending on social class, take their places elsewhere as if prescribed by law. Bottle throwing incidents usually originate in the "bleachers."

In an era of growing political awareness and social change, test matches between England and the West Indies provided the setting for the disaffected to vent their frustrations. These important social occasions possess the elements capable of precipitating social disorder: class, racial, and international conflict.

International conflict is included since national honor is perceived by many to be at stake in these contests. This is especially true of matches in which England is involved because of the legacies of colonialism and the efforts of Labor and Conservative governments to restrict colored immigration to Britain. Nor has it gone unnoticed that the initial decision to ban South Africa from the Commonwealth Cricket Conference was urged by the "colored Commonwealth" on their reluctant peers. And so, in a community of states bifurcated along conflicts such as white/colored, rich/poor, underdeveloped/developed, is it surprising that the traditional game was touched by these social forces?

The emphasis on results in modern societies helps to fill in the backdrop for an understanding of the decline in conduct and decorum in the international game. The values of utility and success, primarily material success, are pre-eminent in bourgeois culture. Ruthless competition in pursuit of personal, corporate, political, and national goals has become an everyday feature of social life. Some observers maintain that the prevalence of the use of illegitimate and illegal means to achieve goals has become a way of life for many. In America, the distinction between pre- and post-Watergate morality reinforced this perception. The dishonesty and hypocrisy of public officials in authority perhaps fed tendencies to buck authority which were already present in the system. These tendencies, in the era of satellite communication, were diffused around the globe and provide background for an understanding of boorish behavior on the international cricket scene.

International cricket began to boom as never before after cessation of hostilities in 1945. By 1960, in Britain, changes had taken place in the game. The abolition of the distinction between "gentlemen" and "players" is especially germane since the status of amateur all but disappeared. Once the emphasis of playing for a livelihood became exclusive, the compulsion to do well and win at all costs became paramount. This development helped to make it fanciful for some to bend the rules to achieve their goals; increasing consciousness of the use of "illegal" deliveries underscores this point. No one country held monopoly on this form of cheating. England had her Loaders and Locks; Australia her Meckiffs and Slaters; and the West Indies had her Griffiths and Gilchrists. In a similar vein rule changes were suggested and made to stymie the assets of opponents. Rules relating to "leg before wicket" and "cutting and crease" come to mind. Some home teams were known to "doctor" pitches to suit their needs and so tip the outcome of matches.

Enough has been said to render an understanding of the growing tendency of violence and intimidation in the international game. Given the climate and the acceptance of the new ethic, if it takes the infliction of an injury to a batsman to shake his confidence or dislodge him, so be it. Deadly offensive weapons such as super-fast bowlers are therefore prized. And since for every action there is a reaction, why not invent helmets and protective clothing. Cricket matches, therefore, ceased being contests in "friendly strife" and are now outright battles. The old English game has become Americanized in more ways than one.

More and more, then, the attitude of playing the game for fun – "for its own sake" – has given way to the spirit of winning at all costs. An occurrence in a limited-over match between Australia and New Zealand best illustrates this point. With the last ball to be bowled, a New Zealand batsman had an outside chance of giving his team a victory if he could score six runs. To prevent this outcome, the Australian captain ordered his bowler to deliver the ball underhand so that it would roll along the pitch. The desired end was achieved and Australia won the match.

Two other incidents are worthy of mention. During a tour of New Zealand in 1980, the West Indian fast bowler, Michael Holding, reacted to what he considered a bad and biased decision by kicking down the stumps. He was not restrained by the "college boy" code of responding with a stiff upper lip. Nor was this the case with the Australian bowler, Dennis Lillee, when he kicked the Pakistani captain during a test match at Perth in 1981.

The reaction to these occurrences was predictable: "it is not cricket." Administrators rushed to include clauses in touring players' contracts to cover public displays of temper and flouting of authority. In the old days the code was sufficient to keep boorish behavior in check. Those who failed to abide by the rules had to get out of the game. Today severe penalties could well lead to a player boycott.

These trends have led many to the conclusion that cricket is no longer the sporting spectacle it used to be. Players are creatures of their times. The businesslike approach to the game will continue. Players will be very methodical. Those whose instincts favor attack, dash, and flair will remain in the limelight as long as they are consistently successful. The reward system will force the average player to choose defense over attack. The element of risk and uncertainty will be reduced. In treating the game as a business and thus ignoring traditional loyalties and practices, the Australian entrepreneur, Packer, merely capitalized on tendencies already inherent in the game. To blame him for destroying its spirit is myopic.

A unique tradition emerged in the nineteenth century and blossomed in the twentieth century. Its character was derived from the African and English experiences. In terms of code of conduct and behavior, the earliest discernible strain, the "college boy" tradition, was classically English. From an inauspicious beginning at the local level, by 1950, it gained international acclaim. As social and political development proceeded under predominant non-white leadership, the "plebian" strain began to flourish locally. The behavior of this tradition was in keeping with the class situation of the participants. In terms of style, both strains cultivated an aggressive approach, replete with flair and abandon.

By the mid-1950s, there was a boom in international cricket. In a generation of turmoil and change, certain social and cultural tendencies in the advanced democracies seeped into the international game. Increasing professionalization also had an impact on the approach, style, and behavior of cricketers. The spirit of friendly strife gave way to an attitude of grim struggle where no quarter is asked and none given.

In responding to a comment which the respected English cricket journalist, E. W. Swanton, made about the relationship between the cricket ethic and social life in the West Indies, C.L.R. James asserted: "There is a whole generation of us, and perhaps two generations, who have been formed by it not only in social attitudes but in the most intimate personal lives, there more than anything else." And yet, one would have expected the cricket scene to be more in evidence as background material for short stories and novels than it has. Indeed, the cricket scene in the West Indies, involving the interaction of players and players, players and spectators, and spectators and spectators, is fraught with humor, pathos, irony, tragedy, and excitement. Cricket is the focal point of discussion under street lights, on the beaches, in the barber and rum shops, at parties, and in drawing rooms. Here then is a challenge to West Indian self-understanding.

11

African and Indian consciousness at play: a study in West Indies cricket and nationalism

Hubert Devonish

Introduction

Nationalism has two ultimate objectives. One is to secure a state for those who consider themselves to share a common identity. The other is to promote the interests of that state over all others. Every other identity, whether within the national group or outside it, is a competitor. A competing identity either has to be made to submit to the overarching dominance of the national identity or be deemed anti-national and treated accordingly. Ethnic cleansers, their gas chambers and killing fields, are the constant companions of nationalism.

In the cricket playing Caribbean, imperial nationalism stamped a British identity on all its subjects. No other identity was allowed. As an act of resistance, the nationalists of the various anti-colonial movements proceeded to create images of alternative national identities. These new images were equally monochrome, simply black where they were previously white. The nationalist struggle aimed at changing the relationship between the colours within a totally European view of the nation and the state. The colour palette borrowed from the European original did not allow the shades of competing identities to blur the new vision which was taking shape. This was true of the individual national identities created in each emerging newly independent state and of the larger and more diffuse West Indian identity of which the West Indies cricket team is a symbol.

Communities are organised into overlapping units made up of people sharing common identities. Any single individual is a composite of a multiplicity of identities. These may involve gender, age group, language group(s), community of origin, occupation and religious persuasion to name but a few. Social life for a person is, therefore, a game or drama in which the players constantly switch roles. When, in the name of nationalism, however defined, people are prevented from playing out any of their identities, their social rights are violated. West Indian nationalism created in the image of its European counterparts, is as prone as any other to having such censorship imposed in its name.

The cricket field is a screen against which the drama of West Indian society is

179

often starkly projected. The cricketers do not simply play with a ball. Whether or not they are aware of it and do so willingly, they play roles which are assigned them by the spectators. These roles reflect the various identities which spectators have to take on in the course of everyday life. In Guyana and Trinidad, Indian people in the Caribbean make up a significant portion of the spectators at cricket matches. The way in which they interpret the acts performed by the players on the field provide an important insight into the way they interpret their own roles outside the ground. Equally important is how other members of the community respond to the Indian Caribbean interpretation of play. This provides a good guide to their responses to identities assumed by Indian Caribbean people as these are played out away from the cricket field.

Play seen through Indian Caribbean eyes

Indian Caribbean people and their relationship to a West Indian national identity and cricket first became a public issue in 1953. This was the year the Indian cricket team first toured the West Indies. Shiwcharan (1988: 54) relates an incident told to him by his grandfather who had made his first trip to Georgetown in that year. The trip was to see the Indian team play the West Indies at Bourda. 'An ebullient Hindu priest of considerable repute, unleashed a string of popular Hindi curse words, punched the air, uncoiled his sacred turban, turned to the crowd and waved it triumphantly. . . . All this, because the Indian bowler, Ramchand, had bowled Bruce Pairaudeau, the West Indies opening batsman, a white Guyanese from Georgetown'.

Note the identities highlighted in the anecdote, i.e. that the bowler, Ramchand, was Indian, that the batsman was playing for the West Indies, was white, was Guyanese, and was from Georgetown. The Hindu priest was Indian as was the grandfather relating the incident. There is a good chance that both of them would have been born in India though they would have spent the bulk of their lives in Guyana. Most certainly his grandfather and probably the Hindu priest were from rural Guyana. They are likely to have both worked in the ranks of the rural proletariat on the sugar plantations. Almost the only thing they shared in common with the batsman was country of residence. Given the role of Europeans as owners, managers and overseers on the Guyana sugar plantations, the class rift was wide enough to rule out any desire by these two men to identify with him. They chose instead to emphasise the common core of an Indian identity which they shared with the bowler. The bowler was playing the role of the warrior from the motherland avenging the wrongs heaped upon the heads of her children exiled in Guyana.

Shiwcharan (1988: 54) indicates that the Indian Guyanese community was thrilled by the fielding of the Indian tourists and the quality bowling of the leg-spinner, Subhash Gupte. The fact that the Indian team drew four tests with the West Indies, losing only one, was a matter of great pride. There was enormous support for the Indian team amongst the Indian Guyanese community. Like Shiwcharan's grandfather, Indian Guyanese travelled long distances just to see the Indian cricket team. That the visitors were from India was as important as the fact that they were accomplished cricketers. Oral tradition has it that one Indian man arrived at the cricket ground having journeyed the whole of the previous day. When the Indian team took the field, he asked a spectator to identify by name the players on the Indian team, Ramchand, Mankad, Subhash Gupte, etc. This done, he nodded in satisfaction and left the ground heading for the train station to begin his journey back home.

The attitude of African Guyanese to this outpouring of support for the Indian team was one of tolerant amusement. The year 1953 was the one in which the mass of Guyanese, Africans and Indians, rallied behind the non-sectarian anti-colonial movement headed by the People's Progressive Party (PPP) led by Cheddi Jagan and Forbes Burnham. In that year the PPP was voted into power. In the space of a few months, however, the British had suspended the constitution and jailed many of the PPP leaders. Notions of nationalism whether at the level of Guyana and the wider West Indies, had yet to gel. Like their Indian Guyanese counterparts, the claims of African Guyanese to either Guyanese or West Indian identity were circumscribed by European power both outside the field of play and within it. The accession by an African Caribbean cricketer to the permanent captaincy of the West Indies team was some seven years in the future. It was the general feeling that African cricketers within the West Indies team were discriminated against by a European dominated West Indian cricket hierarchy. In relation to the anecdote related by Shiwcharan, African Guyanese cricket fans would hardly have been upset by the dismissal of a European Guyanese by a bowler in the Indian team nor the attendant celebration by the Hindu priest. In fact, some African Guyanese may well have been inclined to have joined in the celebration.

A second reason for African Guyanese tolerance was their awareness of the ambivalent position which the Indian Guyanese found themselves in when dealing with Indians from India. Shiwcharan (1988: 63) refers to the experiences which returning migrants to India suffered. They were often discriminated against on grounds that they had lost caste through the act of having crossed the ocean. As a result, many of these had remigrated to Guyana bringing with them accounts of their unpleasant experiences in India. In addition, according to stories circulating within the African Guyanese population at the time, Indian Guyanese fans had been trying to use what they considered to be Hindi to talk to the visitors. Unfortunately, however, communication was difficult. This is, however, not surprising. The vast majority of Indian immigrants to the Caribbean came from north-east India, mainly from around the area outside the Hindi heartland and in which Bhojpuri, a related but quite distinct language, is spoken. The use of Guyanese Bhojpuri to speakers of Hindi, therefore, was bound to cause a great deal of communication problems.

A third reason for the tolerant African Guyanese response was the fact that up to this point the Indian Guyanese population was not perceived to be making a serious bid for political and economic power. It was to be two years later in 1955, that the last ship sailed from Guyana for Calcutta taking repatriated former indentured servants back to India. This may have signalled an important change in the way the Indian Guyanese population saw itself and was seen by others. Now the mother country had been severed, a new identity began to gel. Indian Guyanese as a group were no longer a marginal immigrant group. They had clearly now become full competitors in the local arena.

With this divergence between the identities of Indian Guyanese and Indians from the sub-continent, the former needed their own champions. The conditions for this were being laid since 1950. Shiwcharan (1988: 52–5) neatly sums these up. Firstly, there were the conditions external to the Indian community. In 1948, malaria which had been endemic to Guyana was eradicated. This was achieved through the work of the malariologist, George Giglioli, who had been employed by the Sugar Producers' Association. In 1950, Jock Campbell, a Fabian socialist, was appointed to the chairmanship of Bookers, the British sugar company which dominated the sugar industry in the country. His appointment seemed to have triggered a number of social reforms on the sugar estates. Health centres, community centres and sports facilities were constructed and maintained on the sugar estates. One feature of the sporting facilities provided were excellent cricket grounds. Robert Christiani, a Guyanese batsman in the West Indies team, was sent to Port Mourant estate as a cricket coach. In 1954, Clyde Walcott, the Barbadian batsman on the West Indies team, was employed by the Sugar Producer's Association as a sports organiser.

There were also conditions internal to the community. In 1955, the African-Indian anti-colonial alliance broke apart into Jaganite and Burnhamite factions of the PPP. The split was originally ideological but, in due course, African support rallied behind the Burnhamite-PPP eventually renamed the People's National Congress (PNC). Indian mass support swung solidly behind the Jaganite-PPP. Even though Jagan as a good socialist never presented himself in this light, the Indian community had found in him its political champion. The Indian Guyanese community had begun to see itself and be seen as a serious challenger for political and economic power in the society.

At the same time, the talent spotting and coaching of Clyde Walcott had begun to bear fruit. A string of four players were about to make their way first into the Berbice, the British Guiana and the West Indies teams. They were all from the sugar estate of Port Mourant in Berbice, the same estate from which Cheddi Jagan had come. The first and greatest of these was Rohan Kanhai who entered the West Indies team for the 1957 tour of England. This was also the year in which the PPP under Jagan won the general elections, defeating the PNC led by Burnham. Kanhai and to a lesser extent the other two Indian players from Port Mourant, Joe Solomon and Ivan Madray, had very difficult roles to play. They had to act as symbols of the newly emerging Indian Caribbean identity.

Shiwcharan (1988: 59) refers to the insecurity within the Indian Guyanese community. My comment would be that this was coming from three different sources.

There was, of course, the feeling of inferiority in the face of the Europeans and European Caribbean people who dominated the society. There was also a sense of inferiority when dealing with Indians from the sub-continent. Finally, there was the feeling of inferiority brought on by the scant respect paid them by the African Guyanese population alongside whom they lived. The goal was to grab for the community the attention, respect and acceptance from these three groups. Shiwcharan (1988: 59–60) suggests that the Indian Guyanese community felt that one way to achieve this was to produce a truly great Indian Guyanese cricketer.

Kanhai was chosen for this role, to parallel the success of Jagan in politics. At first Kanhai failed to live up to expectations. In the test series of the 1957 tour of England, the West Indies lost 3–nil. Kanhai's performances were barely better, totalling 206 runs at an average of 22.88. The interests of the Indian Guyanese community and those of the West Indies team coincided. Cricket is a team game. It would, therefore, have been difficult for their champion to excel in the midst of the total disaster which his team faced. The mood amongst Indian Guyanese was gloomy as they listened to the radio commentary on the test series. 'The victory of Cheddi Jagan in the elections of August 1957 transported us out of the blankness of the summer' (Shiwcharan 1988: 58).

During the 1958 Pakistan tour of the West Indies, Kanhai's performance improved with a batting average of 37.37. Shiwcharan (1988: 59) again presents the Indian Guyanese perspective when he states, 'This was slight in the midst of the Olympian effort of Gary Sobers whose average was 137.33'. Kanhai's performance could not impress African Caribbean people when viewed alongside that of the equally young and promising African Barbadian, Sobers.

The 1958–9 West Indies tour of India was a special occasion. Two Indian Guyanese, Kanhai and Joe Solomon, were travelling to the land of their foreparents for the first time, and were doing so as players on the West Indies cricket team. In the meantime, Ivan Madray, another player from Port Mourant had played for the West Indies in two tests against Pakistan in 1958. One must add to this the consistent presence of Sonny Ramadhin, the Indian Trinidadian off-spinner on the side over the previous several years. It was becoming clear to Indian Caribbean people that membership of the cast of the West Indies cricket team was opening to them. The West Indian test cricket was, therefore, becoming an arena in which they could have issues concerning their own emerging identities played out for them. This was becoming equally clear to non-Indians who saw these new identities as challenging theirs. In the second test match between the West Indies and Pakistan in Trinidad, a country with a sizeable Indian population, Ivan Madray was playing his first test match. He reports fielding at deep third-man and someone shouting from the crowd, 'We don't want more coolie in this side'. This was followed up with a cigarette end flicked on to his back and a bottle thrown at him (Madray 1988: 118).

The Indian team was no longer perceived as playing the role of champions of the Indian Guyanese population. Subhash Gupte, the same leg-spinner on the Indian team who was their hero in 1953 had been transformed into their arch-enemy. In the first two test matches, Gupte seemed able to capture the wicket of Kanhai at will. For the Indian Guyanese population, 'with Kanhai seemingly a possession of Gupte, to us this now inspired shame, a reassertion of patriarchal authority, snuffing out tentative autonomy' (Shiwcharan 1988: 61). In the third test at Calcutta, Kanhai proceeded to demolish the Indian bowling attack including that of Gupte. Kanhai made a score of 256 in what was the first test innings in which he scored a century. Joe Solomon made 69 not out. Basil Butcher, an African Guyanese also from Port Mourant, made 103. This conquest of the Indian bowling was filled with symbolism for the Indian Guyanese community. Shiwcharan (1988: 63) suggests that Kanhai's performance was revenge for Indian returnees from the Caribbean humiliated through loss of caste. This was particularly satisfying since Calcutta was the port from which the vast majority of the Indian immigrants to the Caribbean sailed and to which the returnees were repatriated.

The involvement of Butcher in the triumph introduces an additional dimension. The success of Kanhai, Butcher and Solomon was seen as a triumph for rural Guyanese over their urban counterparts. The county of Berbice and in particular the Corentyne coast and Port Mourant had prevailed over the county of Demerara and the capital, Georgetown. According to Ivan Madray (1988: 108), John Trim, an African fast bowler from Port Mourant who played for the West Indies in the late 1940s, was viewed by Indians of Berbice as one of their own. He blazed the trail for the string of West Indian test players, Kanhai, Butcher, Solomon, Madray, Alvin Kallicharran, and Roy Fredericks all coming out of the Berbice sugar estate cricket system.

The excitement of the Hindu priest during the 1953 test match was partly because Pairaudeau was a symbol of urban dominance over the the rural population. The image of a rural identity which transcended the African–Indian divide was not confined to the minds of those who watched cricket or listened to it on the radio. This was also how the players saw the situation. Shiwcharan (1988: 55) quotes Butcher as crediting Clyde Walcott with 'advancing their [those of Butcher and fellow Port Mourant players] claims to the czars in Georgetown'.

The rural, regional and Caribbean identities played out in Kanhai's brilliant performances as a batsman tended to be overlooked by African Guyanese. The Indian identity as expressed in his play was the image which usually overshadowed all others in their minds. The PPP won another electoral victory in 1961. Between 1962 and 1964, the government was challenged strongly by the local African community and big business, aided and abetted by the colonial authorities and the Central Intelligence Agency (CIA) of the USA. This took the form of civil disobedience, industrial action, riots and inter-communal terrorism. Against this background, Shiwcharan (1988: 70) suggests that 'the fact that Kanhai's work was infused with a profoundly Westindian spirit the character of his art recognized and appropriated by all Westindians, save we suspected by most Afro-Guyanese fired by a black messianism, made it possible for us to carry our massive racial burdens'. The suspicions of Shiwcharan and the Indian community were correct. The first name 'Rohan' is

fairly common amongst African Jamaicans born during or after Kanhai's international cricket career. Amongst African Guyanese, the name occurring with equivalent frequency is 'Gary' after Garfield Sobers. 'Rohan' is so rare amongst African
Guyanese that one is tempted to speculate that it is never used.

In the midst of the destabilisation of the PPP government under Jagan, the
February 1964 match between Guyana and Barbados took place in Bridgetown. The
game meant one thing for most African Guyanese, many of them descended
from African Barbadians. For them, the game would play out the assertion of
the African Guyanese identity vis-a-vis that of African Barbadians. In the eyes
of the former, the latter were seen as immigrants with strange speech habits
who had come in to Guyana over the years to weaken the bargaining power of
local labour. For Indian Guyanese, a totally different plot was unfolding.
Remarkably, the feared Barbadian fast bowling pair of Wesley Hall and Charlie
Griffith were being assigned the part of African Guyanese terrorists. Guyana are
down 13 for three. Kanhai and Solomon come to the rescue. Kanhai scores 108,
Solomon 63. 'And through the three hours that he (Kanhai) ruled, in our nervous
jubilation, we saw each boundary hit as a blow against Burnhamite terror'.
(Shiwcharan 1988: 71)

The British impose a change in the electoral system in Guyana. Fresh general
elections are held in Guyana in 1964 and the PNC under Burnham in alliance with
a small party supported by the business class, manages to snatch political power
from the PPP. The Indian Guyanese community is devastated and haunted by a
sense of defeat. In the test match at Bourda a few months later in April 1965, Kanhai
receives massive support from the Indian Guyanese crowd as he scores 85 in the
first innings. His role was, as the expression goes, 'to take shame out of their eyes'.
Cheered lustily to the wicket in the second innings, he scored 0. He was booed back
to the pavilion by people 'haunted and shamed by Cheddi's fall . . . we were booing
ourselves to pre-empt the blacks from booing us' (Shiwcharan 1988: 73).

The new game in town

After the change of government, the new game in town was consolidating with the
aid of state power an African Guyanese community imbued with a sense of its right
to rule. In 1968, two years after the country received political independence from
Britain, this right to rule became institutionalised. During that year, the first of a
series of brazenly rigged general elections took place. Rigging elections became an
amusement for the PNC and the African elite who dominated it. National elections,
while made to look like a game which either side could win, became a play which,
with minor script variations, was enacted every five years or so. The ending of the
play was always the same, of course. African Guyanese as a group either played
active parts in the farce, applauded it or looked the other way and pretended it was
not happening. This was to continue until the 1992 elections when the presence of

neutral umpires in the form of international observers helped restore the process to that of an electoral game played according to established rules.

State power was, however, only a means to an end. The power and influence which the Indian Guyanese community had accumulated had to be destroyed. Race was not an acceptable basis for publicly rationalising and justifying moves by the Guyana government. Therefore, measures had to be adopted which were not explicitly directed at Indians. The strategy was to target those sectors of the society and economy in which Indians were dominant. Since the rural agricultural population was predominantly Indian, this sector was singled out for special attention. Resources would be transferred from a rural agricultural sector composed mainly of Indians to a state dominated by Africans.

Though comparable tactics were employed in the rice industry, we will focus on the sugar industry, the area of agriculture which had the most relevance for cricket. In 1974, the PNC government slapped a sugar levy on the profits of the sugar industry. This was done on the pretext that the earnings from sugar should be used to benefit the entire nation rather than just sugar workers (Debiprashad and Budram 1987: 152). Then there was the master stroke. The sugar industry is nationalised in 1976, placing it and its work force directly at the mercy of the state. The African dominated state ran down the industry through lack of investment and while transferring surpluses to itself. All of this reduced the share of the revenue available to sugar workers either directly through profit sharing or indirectly through estate expenditure on health, housing, and social amenities.

The sporting facilities developed by the sugar industry from the beginning of the 1950s were poorly maintained after nationalisation. Many of the estate cricket grounds were allowed to revert to pasture. By 1976, Alvin Kallicharan and Roy Fredericks, the last of the products of the sugar estate cricket programme to appear with any frequency for the West Indies, were already in the team. Since the late 1970s, the only new Guyanese entrants to the West Indies test team have been Roger Harper and Carl Hooper, both urban Africans. No Guyanese Indians have played on the West Indies team for over a decade. The mission has been accomplished. This has, however, been at the expense of Africans on or near the sugar estates who, like their Indian counterparts, have also been denied access to cricket playing opportunities.

We have so far examined moves which were made to limit the ability of Indian Guyanese to use local and West Indies cricket to act out roles which express and strengthen their group identity. There was as well a programme to have the symbols of African Guyanese, PNC and Burnhamite dominance projected into the arena of West Indies cricket. This took the form of seeking to have African Guyanese players promoted to positions of power and influence in the West Indies team. The major power play by the PNC regime was the efforts it made to ensure that African Guyanese Clive Lloyd became captain of the West Indies team.

Ever since the struggle to have Frank Worrell appointed as the captain of the West Indies team, the captaincy has acquired an enormous symbolic importance. In 1973,

Gary Sobers distinguished the captaincy of the West Indies team. The candidate of the Burnham government in Guyana for the post was Clive Lloyd. The problem was that, due to poor batting performances, Clive Lloyd had not even been named to the original squad to play against the Australians during their Caribbean tour of that year. In fact, it was Kanhai who was appointed as Sobers's successor. Given the kind of symbolic role which Kanhai played for the Guyanese population, this was not as bad news for Burnham and the PNC as it might at first seem. Kanhai was almost at the end of his career as an international cricketer. He was therefore merely warming the seat for a successor. Burnham was determined that Lloyd would be that successor.

When the West Indies cricket board realised that Gary Sobers might be unable to play during the series because of injury, it cabled Lloyd requesting that he put himself on standby. According to McDonald (1985: 58), at this point Prime Minister Forbes Burnham intervened personally 'by asking his friend, the Australian Prime Minister, Gough Whitlam, to make sure that there would be no problem getting Lloyd's release from his commitment to club cricket in Australia'. In Manchester in the UK where Lloyd resided, he was informed through the Guyanese High Commission in London that the Guyana government was paying his fare back to the Caribbean. Burnham preferred that he wait on standby in the Caribbean. Lloyd's response was that, '"The point was that my Prime Minister made a request that I come back home and I found it impossible to refuse and certainly, I wanted to be near the action"' (McDonald 1985: 58).

Lloyd distinguished himself in the match between Australia and the Guyana team. As a result, he forced himself back into the West Indies team, scoring 178 on the first day of the fourth test. McDonald (1985: 60) cites Cozier's description of Burnham as 'basking in reflected glory'. Lloyd went on to secure his place in the team and eventually the captaincy. The image which Indians saw within West Indies cricket of a Caribbean identity in which they had no presence became even more sharply defined with the 1990 a statement by Lloyd's successor as captain, Vivian Richards. In an interview with the *Outlet* newspaper in Antigua, he is reported to have stated that 'the West Indies cricket team . . . is the only sporting team of African descent that has been able to win repeatedly against all international opposition, bringing joy and recognition to our people' (West Indies Cricket Annual 1990: 33). Subsequent efforts by Richards to 'clarify' would have done little to change the original impression.

This is the background against which one needs to understand the evolution in the behaviour of Indian cricket spectators in Guyana. They know instinctively that the absence of any Indians from Guyana on the West Indies team is probably not a matter of chance. The captaining of the team by Clive Lloyd, otherwise known as 'Burnham Magic' made the entire team a symbol of everything hated by the oppressed Indian majority in the country. The team in its conquest of the cricketing world for over a decade, was for Indian Guyanese an acting out of the trampling of their rights by the African dominated state.

From the visit of the first Indian touring team to the Caribbean in 1953, there has been a tendency for Indian Trinidadians and Indian Guyanese to support visiting Indian and Pakistani teams. As was pointed out earlier, however, this support became rather ambivalent at least amongst Guyanese Indians, as long as there were prominent Guyanese Indian players such as Kanhai in the West Indian team. In spite of these nuances, however, Africans have become increasingly hostile to expressions of support for visiting teams from the Indian sub-continent. In Guyana, when such behaviour occurred during the 1980s, articles and letters appeared in the PNC controlled government press accusing those involved of being disloyal and unpatriotic. The typical response in the *Mirror* newspaper of the opposition PPP was that Indian Guyanese at cricket matches were paying patrons and had the right to cheer for who they please.

African Trinidadians and Guyanese who see themselves as being besieged by an expanding and increasingly self-confident Indian community stubbornly refuse to recognise this right, however. One typical example of this attitude occurred during the 1976 Indian tour of the Caribbean. The support of Indian Trinidadians for the Indian team in the test matches played in Trinidad was overwhelming. Africans in the crowd regularly threw orange skins at groups of Indians cheering for the visitors.

To add insult to injury, India won the third test at Queen's Park in Trinidad by scoring 406 in the final innings. The celebrating Indian Trinidadians in the ground on the final day of the match serenaded each boundary hit by the Indian batsmen with the carnival road march tune for that year, 'La La' by Nelson. One African Trinidadian remarked that what hurt him most of all is that they chose this tune rather than some much more appropriate properly Indian melody. Interestingly enough, here again we see the tendency to assume that symbols of collective identity such as the calypso belong to Africans and them alone.

Up to at least the end of the 1970s in Guyana, it was the norm for Indian Guyanese to support the West Indies against any team except those from the sub-continent. The principle of multiple identities was at play here. Depending on which was the opposing team, their Indianness or West Indianness would be the one which receives particular emphasis. With the increased alienation of Indian Guyanese from the political process and West Indian cricket, they swung to a position of supporting any team against the West Indies. In 1990, many of them turned out to support the MCC in the one day matches against the West Indies played at Bourda. In the 1991 test match against Australia at Bourda, the Indian section of the crowd is reported to have strongly supported Australia and booed members of the West Indies team. In the light of his description of the West Indies team as a sporting team of African descent, the captain, Vivian Richards, was singled out for special treatment. The then Prime Minister, Hamilton Green, quickly apologised to the West Indies team for the behaviour of the crowd. This indicates the extent to which support for the West Indies had become a matter of state policy rather than an expression of individual personal preference.

With the entrenchment of rigging within the electoral process of Guyana, Indian Guyanese along with many other of their countrymen, despaired of being able to change their government by the casting of a ballot. The very word 'ballot' owes its origin to the casting of votes or lots using balls. The electoral game had been turned into a farce, in effect into 'lots of balls'. The early 1980s was a period during which pressure built up for electoral reform. Indian Guyanese therefore chose symbolically to cast their lots in another ball game, that of cricket. Here at least, rules were still followed, umpiring still impartial and the outcome not prescribed by an already written script.

At the beginning of the 1990s, the nationalised sugar industry was in poor shape. The sugar conglomerate, Booker Tate of the UK, was brought in on a management contract to run the sugar industry. The new British chief executive of the industry, Neville Hilary, announced significant increases in wages for sugar workers. Steps were also taken to improve the various facilities provided to workers by the industry. Sport and cricket in particular was to benefit by the reappearance of this welfare oriented approach to managing the industry. In 1992, it was announced that Joe Solomon, himself a product of an earlier period of investment in cricket on the sugar estates, had been contracted to train sugar estate cricket coaches and to develop young talent on the sugar estates (Razak 1992b: 14). All of this was taking place amidst the build up of the campaign for free and fair elections and eventually the defeat of the PNC in the October 1992 elections.

This situation has created a surge of public expectation concerning sport on the Guyana sugar estates. This is clearly expressed in a series of articles on sport on the sugar estates published in the PPP organ, the *Mirror*, in the course of which Razak (1992a: 12) states, 'With the present re-organising of the sugar estate community centres by Guysuco [the Guyana Sugar Corporation], hopes run high for a return of the glory days that this estate [Port Mourant] once enjoyed'.

On the pitfalls of nationalism: the cricket test

The arrogance of African West Indians in trying to dictate to their Indian compatriots who they should support at a cricket match, clearly shows up the pitfalls of nationalism. Nationalism requires the suppression of all other identities in favour of that defined as national by those with the power to make such a definition. When large crowds of people of West Indian origin throng the cricket grounds in England to support the West Indies against the land of their residence and very often citizenship, their right to do so is firmly supported by African West Indians. African West Indian public opinion was very loud in its condemnations of the British Conservative member of parliament and cabinet minister, Norman Tebbit, who proposed the application of the cricket test. According to this test, when England played the West Indies or India in England, a test of loyalty should be applied to the spectators. Those who supported the opposing team against England would be deemed to have failed the test. They would therefore be deported from England to their countries of origin.

The test has been applied in the Caribbean to people other than Indian West Indians. It was the 1975 Shell Shield match between Trinidad and Tobago and the Combined Islands. Large numbers of people from the Leeward and Windward Islands residing in Trinidad turned out to cheer the visitors on to their first ever victory over Trinidad and Tobago. This was immortalised in the Paul Keens Douglas short story 'Tantie Merle at the Oval'. Trinidad public opinion was scandalised. These 'small island people', enjoying milk and honey purchased with Trinidadian oil, had bitten the hand which fed them. The only appropriate measure was to banish them back to the barren little rocks from whence they came. That this was more than mere rhetoric can be seen by a subsequent incident. The mid-1980s represented the peak of the Guyanese migration, both legal and illegal, to Trinidad. A crowd of Guyanese turned out to support the visiting Guyana team in a Shell Shield match. Immigration officers surrounded the stand occupied by Guyanese supporters. Some fled. Others were arrested and presumably subsequently deported as illegal immigrants. This was certainly not cricket. It was nationalism pure and simple.

Ethnic cleansing, the constant companion of nationalism, may take the form of the application of the cricket test in relation to Leeward islanders, Windward islanders, or Guyanese resident in Trinidad and Tobago. It may be applied to people of Caribbean origin in the UK or Indian Caribbean people in Guyana and Trinidad and Tobago. If it can be justified in one case, it can be in any other.

Nationalism and all with which it is associated are the natural enemies of any notion of genuine unity amongst people, either within individual Caribbean states or across these states. The view that any group of people could be made to express themselves by way of a single common identity is both contrary to good sense and the experience of everyday life in the Caribbean. Such a scenario is essentially Afro-Saxon in nature. This is true whether its players are of conservative demeanour and bear the title of knights, in the style of the West Indian cricket captains of the 1960s and early 1970s, or are of more radical comportment and wear the red, green and gold symbols of the Rastafari as did the captain who retired in 1991. More importantly, the scenario represents a violation of the social rights of Caribbean people. The challenge, both within and beyond the boundary, is to create an atmosphere which tolerates and encourages the inter-play between the multiple identities which exist within Caribbean societies.

References

Debiprashad, S. and D. Budram, 1987, 'Participation of East Indians in the transformation of Guyanese society 1869–1978', in D. Dabydeen, and B. Samaroo (eds), 1987, *India in the Caribbean*, Hansib Publishing Ltd, London, pp. 145–72.

Madray, I. in conversation with C. Shiwcharan, 1988, '"Da coolie ga mek abi hunt ledda"', in Birbalsingh, F. and C. Shiwcharan (eds), 1988, *Indo-Westindian Cricketers*, Hansib Publishing Ltd, London, pp. 89–128.

McDonald, T., 1985, *Clive Lloyd*, Granada Publishing Ltd, London.

Razak, S., 1992a, 'Port Mourant – Home of Outstanding Sportsmen', *Mirror*, 29 November, 1992, p. 7, p. 12.

Razak, S., 1992b, 'Clyde Walcott's Contribution to Cricket in Guyana', *Mirror*, 6 December, 1992, p. 12, p. 14.

Shiwcharan, C., 1988, 'The Tiger of Port Mourant – R. B. Kanhai', in F. Birbalsingh, and C. Shiwcharan (eds), 1988, *Indo-Westindian Cricketers*, Hansib Publishing Ltd, London, pp. 41–88.

West Indies Cricket Annual 1990, 'How the Media Dominated the Controversy', p. 33.

12

The making of the first 'West Indian' teams, 1886–1906

Hilary McD. Beckles

The origins and development of the concept of a West Indian cricket team have mid-nineteenth century roots. Though it is now common knowledge that 'the' West Indies cricket team became a leading edge international organization in the last quarter of the twentieth century, the initial formative sociological process involved in this 'becoming' has not been systematically outlined.

It is instructive to note that use of the term 'West Indies' in reference to a given territorial space is imperial in origins, and preceded the popular use of the term 'West Indian' (an indicator of consciousness and identity) by at least two centuries. Though records suggest that the imperial description of persons resident and born in these territories as West Indians was commonplace in the seventeenth century, it was only in the late eighteenth century that their 'creole' voice is clearly heard and confidently used within metropolitan socio-cultural, political and economic spheres.

Determining the organizational history of West Indian cricket is the fact that the sugar plantation culture and its supportive imperial structures had integrated and considerably homogenized the social world and life experiences of West Indians during and after slavery. Sugar economy, mercantilist trade theory, the ideology of white supremacy, and black resistance determined the framework of everyday life in the Indies, and shaped the meaning of what social anthropologists describe as West Indianness as a social fact.

The regional planter-merchant communities had moved away from the earlier practice of cut throat competition among themselves for the largest share of the London sugar market, and had adopted a policy of cooperation which was coordinated by their London-based lobby, the West India Committee. Though suggestions of political integration did not find favour with territorial legislatures, this social elite had recognized by the end of slavery that economic cooperation via the West India Committee should be supported by socio-cultural interaction in the furtherance of its collective West Indian interests.

The development of West Indies cricket organizations, then, was determined by the evolution of the socio-political consciousness outlook within and across white colonial societies. By the late nineteenth century, the game had emerged as the principal social mechanism of interaction for the transcolonial elites who now visited each other on a regular basis, not as farmers and merchants but as cricketers. West Indianization as a socially experienced cultural process within ruling class society, therefore, first took form within the ambit of the cricketing world.

Before a 'West Indian' team could be assembled, however, it was necessary to intensify and widen the base of the cricket culture within individual territories. It was also essential that these territories play each other on a regular basis and in the process allow for the establishment of a regional knowledge base about particular players, and specific local conditions that would influence performances. Players and organizational supporters, also, needed to be assured that the economic basis of the cricket culture could support inter-colonial activity. Since, of course, the early years were exclusively those of the amateur, the financial matter was critical as players were required to finance their own games and the travel involved in regional contests.

In all of this, the year 1865 is important. Though the best West Indian school kids would tell you that this was when land hungry Jamaica blacks rose up at Morant Bay in search of secure access to land, and were massacred by local and imperial military forces, they may not know that it was also the first time that representative teams from two West Indian colonies played each other in cricket. On this occasion the teams were from Demerara and Barbados and the two innings game was played on February 15 and 16 at the Garrison ground in Barbados. The home team won by 138 runs in spite of low scores made on both sides.[1]

It was, of course, a historic moment surrounded by celebratory extravaganza. Bridgetown merchants gave workers the afternoon off to attend the match and to participate in the festivities. In September the same year a Barbados team visited Demerara for the return match, again the home team won in a closely fought contest. Six years later, in 1871, two teams from these colonies clashed once again in Barbados. Again, the home team won after being given a winning target of 59 runs which they scored for the loss of two wickets.[2]

The pioneering contest between teams from Barbados and Demerara opened the way for a range of other inter-colonial contact across the West Indies. In 1879, for example, a team of masters and students from Harrison College in Barbados toured St Kitts and Antigua where they won all games against the Leeward Islanders whom they considered neophytes. In September, 1883, Demerara sent another team to Barbados where they played a two day game against a side made up largely of players from the Wanderers Cricket Club that was formed in 1877. The match was described as the 'scene of bustle, confusion and jollity, for there a thirsty aristocracy did congregate'.[3]

During the early 1890s Trinidad was finally integrated into the touring cricket fold. After being unable to accept several earlier invitations from Demerara and Barbados, Trinidad agreed to participate in a triangular 'cricket festival' in Barbados with these other two colonies. On this occasion, commercial interests in

Barbados showed their commitment to the game when no fewer than 'eighty Bridgetown firms' agreed to close for the afternoon 'on all four days when Barbados was playing the visiting colonies'. With strong home support, and excellent bowling from the young (soon to be legendary) Clifford Goodman, the Barbadian team won the tournament.[4]

In 1891, Jamaica was integrated into the West Indies touring network when a team from the Garrison Club in Barbados visited Kingston. An all-Jamaican team, drawn largely from the Kingston Club, competed with the Barbados-based soldiers. With Jamaica now in the ranks inter-West Indies cricket contests now included most major sugar producing territories.

In 1893, an Antiguan team visited Barbados, and Trinidad played host to a visiting colonial side for the first time, the circumstance under which Queens Park Cricket Club sprung into prominence. In 1896, teams from Barbados and St Vincent exchanged visits, and a Barbadian team visited St Lucia. Also, in that year, Jamaica was able to send a team on a debut West Indian tour. On this occasion the Jamaicans played against teams in Barbados and Demerara. During the Barbados match a toast was raised to the health of C.W.K. Chandler of the Jamaica side, a Barbadian who had a decade earlier distinguished himself as a bowler for Harrisons College.

Inter-regional cricket, then, as a social and organizational experience, was entrenched by the end of the nineteenth century. This regional structure, however, was built upon the competitive cricket culture that had developed in particular territories. In 1892, the Barbadians had put in place a competition among clubs for a Challenge Cup, and Jamaica did likewise the following year. It was also in 1892 that a well organized tournament between Barbados, Trinidad, and Demerara for the Inter-colonial Challenge Cup was launched. There was, therefore, by the mid-1890s, both colonial and inter-colonial Challenge Cups around which white elite cricket flourished.

It is important to note, however, that by this time the concept of a representative West Indies team was already quite popular in cricketing circles. It was commonplace to see references within the regional media to a West Indies team, though it was recognized by all concerned that the exclusion of black players from such selections would ultimately bring into question the relations that arose between race, colour and class ideologies on the one hand, and the power of merit within the gradually democratizing political order on the other. The issue, of course, was one that centred around the manner in which planter-merchant hegemony determined the projection and political actualization of West Indianness. Though occasionally in the 1880s some colonial teams did include an exceptionally talented coloured or black player, the core concept of a West Indian team was formulated exclusively by the sugar interests.

The year 1886 was the first occasion that a 'West Indian' team was selected to play in an extra-territorial match. On this historic occasion the all-white team went on a tour of Canada and the United States where the cricket culture could claim a longer pedigree than in the West Indies. As early as 1844 Canada and the United States had clashed in their first international – thirty years before the much acclaimed England-Australia contest.[5] English teams toured Canada and the United States in the summer of 1859 by which time the Canadians had declared cricket 'the national' sport.[6] English teams also toured the United States in 1868 and in 1872; on the latter occasion none other than the legendary Dr W.G. Grace took part, scoring an expected and impressive 142 against a Toronto side. Australia toured Canada for the first time in 1878, so that when the West Indies team arrived eight years later, the Canadian public was long accustomed to periodic 'international' cricket.

The 1886 West Indies tour of North America was the brainchild of George Wyatt of the Georgetown Cricket Club in Demerara. As expected, the team was drawn from the 'Big Four', though eventually Trinidad could not send its selected players probably on account of the cost involved – $350 per player. The touring team eventually consisted of six Jamaicans, two Barbadians and four Guyanese. It was captained by Wyatt, and the appointed Vice-Captain was L.K. Fyfe of Jamaica. In all, thirteen matches were played. The West Indies team won 6, lost 5, and 2 were drawn; on the whole it was a fairly mixed sort of tour from the point of view of results.[7]

The following year the Americans returned the visit, but played against territorial sides rather than a West Indies team. It was a weak team and was defeated by Trinidad, Demerara, Jamaica and Barbados. The Barbados and Jamaica matches were billed as 'America vs Barbados' and 'Gentlemen of America vs All-Jamaica' respectively, but the evidence was now clear that the civil war had ravaged the American cricket culture leaving it a poor third to baseball and football.

By this time, West Indians were looking toward England as the direction to go in the consolidation and internationalization of their cricket. England, of course, was recognized as the premier cricketing nation on account of its claim as the 'inventor' of this now globalized cultural activity. It was also undeniably a case of white West Indian colonials seeking approval and recognition of their achievements from their 'motherland' in this cultural arena. By the early 1890s, they seemed frantic (similar to the Australians two decades earlier) in the quest for approval from the MCC. They badly wanted a contest with England, but England was slow in responding.

Both Wyatt of Demerara and Fyfe of Jamaica, Captain and Vice-Captain respectively of the first 'West Indies' team, sought separately to arrange West Indies tours of England in 1888 and 1889. Their efforts were not successful, and it seemed then that the region's first encounter with England would take place under the circumstance of a touring English team playing against individual colonies. This occasion finally came when Slade Lucas assembled an English eleven which arrived in the region in January 1895.

Implicit within this first encounter was some measure of English contempt for white West Indian cricket standards. The touring team was made up of low-level amateurs with one, maybe two, recognized players – hardly a first class eleven. Yet, thousands of West Indians came out to greet them with great fanfare wherever they went. The perception of West Indian standard was confirmed by the tour results. The English teams won 10 of the 16 matches and lost only 4. In front of a crowd in excess of 6,000 at Kensington Oval, Bridgetown, the Barbados team was beaten. St Vincent, not considered a cricket power, however, succeeded in defeating the Englishmen.

Reports in the West Indies indicate that colonials, in spite of getting a sound thrashing by the English team, were overcome with excitement by the experience. References suggest that colonial sport writers expressed in no uncertain terms the sense of low self-esteem seemingly evident among West Indians with respect to the English. In their losing game, Barbados scored 517 in the second innings, a West Indies record at the time, and an achievement that presented an opportunity for the local press to unilaterally claim their 'arrival' and to indicate in a self-denying sort of way, reverence for standards supposedly established by their opponents. *The Times* of February 9, 1895 reported:

> Englishmen at home and abroad must have learnt with mixed feelings the news wired on Tuesday evening announcing to the world pre-eminent achievements that Barbados batted the whole day and had, at the call of time on Tuesday evening, still 3 wickets to fall with the score standing at the magnificent total of 359. Three centuries and a half would have been as fine a cricketing feat for a Colonial team that could possibly be accomplished in the presence of English batsmen and bowlers of renown, that would cause any Colonial combination to be inordinately proud of. But when it comes to be thought of that a team of cricketers in this little England beyond the seas could put in the field capable of greater things, though having for their opponents stalwarts hailing from the home of cricket, it seems to us to suggest a something not dreamt of in our cricketing philosophy. A West Indian batting-record has been established in the cricket annals of these parts, and whatever the pride and elation we feel in knowing that it has been given to Barbadians to chronicle that fact in their history, cannot but be pardonable. That Barbados possessed the ability to compile 517 runs in a single innings was what the most judicious observers of our boys' play or even the most sanguine spirits among us would have described as belonging more to the region of exuberant imagination than to be within the bounds of possibilities'.[8]

Immediately following the departure of the Lucas team, West Indians rejoiced on hearing the news that arrangements were being made in England for other touring teams to test the 'colonial cricket steel'. In 1896, two English teams, one led by A. Priestly (later Sir) and the other by Lord Hawke arrived in the West Indies. Popular opinion was that both these teams were stronger than the Lucas eleven, though all were still considered amateurs.

The family linkages of Empire being what they were, Priestly's team contained Dr Gilbert Elliot, a Barbadian, who refused to play in the Barbados match on the grounds that he could not compete against his own country. The Hawke team also included a West Indian: Pelham Warner, the distinguished Trinidadian. Both teams did well against colonial sides. Jamaica and Demerara received humiliating defeats, while Trinidad won two matches against each side. The Barbadian team won 2–1 in three games against the Priestly side, and lost 1–0 in two games against the Hawke side.

The impressive record of the Trinidadian team, which had hitherto been considered the weakest of the 'Big Four', drew particular attention for one special reason. Pelham Warner, star batsman of Hawke's side, who scored a hundred against the Barbados team, studied the matter closely and concluded that Trinidad's victories were due to the inclusion of two black professional bowlers, Woods and Cumberbatch.[9] This was a new and critical development in West Indies cricket, and signalled the beginning of the non-racial democratizing process in selection policy.

Black professionals had long been excluded from colonial teams for the Intercolonial Challenge Cup, though a few were included in 'all-island' teams for 'friendly' games. Without black players, it was recognized, the Trinidadian team was no match for Barbados and Demerara. Warner considered this development of great importance to West Indies cricket. He concluded that only the integration of blacks into colonial and West Indies teams could raise the standard, increase competitiveness, and liberate the culture for the quantum leap into global recognition.

It was the 'illiberalism' of the racist mentality in Barbados and Demerara especially, Warner argued, that continued to insist upon the suffocating all-white race policy. Furthermore, he said, the talent of black players was necessary to 'make the game more popular locally,' and could assist in assuring 'great and universal enthusiasm amongst all classes of the people'. The first West Indian team selected for a proposed tour to England, he insisted, should include 'four or five' black players, since this would be the only way to prevent embarrassments against county teams.[10]

The late 1890s, then, witnessed calls for the introduction of blacks into intercolonial cup competitions and West Indies touring teams. With a 'voice' as distinguished as Pelham Warner, West Indian cricket elites felt compelled to listen and rethink selection policies. There had been no opposition in England to the presence of blacks in competitive cricket. By this time, such crude expressions of racial ideologies were confined to the colonials who found it particularly difficult to consider blacks as equals in any sphere of social activity. During the 1890s, Barbados had stated its refusal to play against Trinidad in the Challenge Cup if they included black players. In the 1897 competition the truth of Warner's argument was accepted when Trinidad arrived in Barbados without its black bowling stars and was massively beaten by an innings and 235 runs; centuries were scored for Barbados by H.B.G. Austin (129) and Gussy Cox (161). If Trinidad had not learnt their lesson by this time, White Barbadians had received the message when in 1899 Spartan, the coloured middle-class team, won the island's Challenge Cup, defeating traditional whites-only teams, and undermining their ideology of white supremacy in social culture. The rise to dominance of Spartan within Barbados cricket indicated to all that racism in West Indies cricket was a major inhibiting factor and an embarrassment to the ideals of cricket culture. The Trinidadians had initiated the policy of selection on merit, and now, at the end of the century, the word was out that ammunition for the future growth of West Indies cricket was to be found in large quantities within the black communities.

The recognition of this fact raised a number of questions concerning the sociology of West Indies cricket. Would whites accept blacks as equals within the boundary, and in the social activities beyond it? Were facilities available to blacks to acquire the 'personality' required of colonial representation? Would whites allow blacks access to leadership in this vital area of West Indian life? These questions generated controversy throughout the region, while the English cricket world listened with a mixture of amusement and horror.

Responding to the debate over the relative quality of black and white cricketers in Barbados a leader writer for the *Reporter* argued that 'there is absolutely no provision of playgrounds attached to primary and elementary schools' attended by black children, and yet their fidelity to the methods and values of the game was well inculcated. Blacks, it was understood, had established their own cricket culture about the 'gullies' of plantation villages and urban ghettos.[11] Their game was learnt at the community level rather than formally within the school system. For them, cricket had become as instinctively cultural as religion and the performing arts. Behind Spartan's success in 1899, could be found a spring of black talent waiting to be liberated. Professional black teams, such as the Fenwicks and Carrington Cricket Clubs, both working-class organizations, represented this plank within Barbados cricket. It was known that these teams did defeat established Challenge Cup sides, but were excluded from formal competition on the basis that they were professionals, though it was also known that racial prejudice was the sole reason.

By 1899, then, blacks were poised to force their way *en masse* into first-class colonial cricket and therefore to secure selection for West Indies teams. Everything was in place to attain these ends. When in 1899, therefore, it was announced that Lord Hawke had invited a West Indian team to tour England in the summer of 1900 the time for the grand 'international' debut of multi-racial West Indies cricket had arrived.

P.F. Warner's brother, R.S. Warner, was appointed to Captain the West Indies side. A Selection Committee, representing all the West Indian cricket territories, met in Trinidad in January 1900 with the mandate to choose a representative team. Shortly thereafter the news came: at least five blacks were selected to the touring party of 15. These players were Fitz Hinds (Barbados), W.J. Burton (Demerara), C.A. Ollivierre (St Vincent), and S. Woods and G.L. Constantine (Trinidad). Pelham Warner wrote:

> It has been decided to include black men in the coming team, and there is little doubt that a fairly strong side can be got together. Without these black men it would have been quite absurd to attempt to play first-class counties, and no possible benefit would have been derived from playing those of the second class only.
>
> The fielding will certainly be of a high class. The black men will, I fear, suffer from the weather if the summer turns out cold and damp, as their strength lies in the fact

that their muscles are extremely loose, owing to the warm weather to which they are accustomed. Woods takes only two steps and bowls as fast as Mold!

Englishmen will be very much struck with the throwing powers of these black men, nearly all of them being able to throw well over a hundred yards. On the whole, I feel pretty confident that the team will attract favourable attention all round, and my view is, I know, shared by many sound judges of the game. The visit of any new team to England is always an experiment, attended with more or less possibilities of failure; but that they will be a failure I do not for a moment think, and in any case West Indian cricket will be greatly improved.[12]

The tour was not given first-class status as there seemed to have been considerable belief among English officials that the West Indians were not ready for 'serious' 'international' cricket. Wisden described the tour as an 'experiment', but P.F. Warner had no doubt that by its end the West Indians would be ready for first-class status.

The English press both welcomed the 'second-class' West Indians and criticized heavily their 'slipshod and lazy' attitudes. The *Boys Own Paper* (BOP), however, was particularly concerned to inform its readers about the 'great novelty of the presence of coloured men playing on a cricket field in England', and indicated that before the tour began there had been much comment that the blacks would go on to the field 'without boots and in a very sparse attire'. W.L.A. Coleman, surveying the socio-logical contours of the tour wrote in *The Cricketer:*

> Apparently the coloured members of the team were much impressed with England and they indicated that in the West Indies the question was being asked as to whether white and coloured cricketers should play together in the same team. It had been the form to allow only white cricketers to play in cup and Inter-Colonial matches in the West Indies and the BOP Editor ventured to suggest that 'on the return home, many of the islands must have found themselves in a very awkward position over the matter. If, for instance, any of the coloured players are good enough to represent the team in an international match, it is difficult to see how they can be refused opportunities of playing at home'. This throws interesting light on the prevailing attitudes in the West Indies and how at that time their cricket was dominated by the whites. The manager indicated that the coloured players had apparently 'very quickly fallen into English ways' and that 'they gave no trouble whatever during the tour. Indeed, they lived in the same hotels and were treated exactly like the white members'. Woods is purported to have said 'what a lot of white people they have got in this country', when playing at Crystal Palace.[13]

The performance of the team was not particularly impressive. It suffered consecu-tive defeats in its first four county matches, and was slaughtered in the sixth game against Gloucestershire whose first innings total of 619 included three centuries and a partnership of 201 made in an hour. In one over, Jessop who scored 157, struck six 4s, during which the blacks on the team, according to Warner, 'sat down on the ground and shouted with laughter at the unfortunate bowler's discomforture'.[14] In this game they were defeated by an innings and 216 runs. Its best performance was against Surrey whom they defeated by an innings and 34 runs with Woods returning figures of 7 for 48 and 5 for 68, and Cox and Olliviere putting on an opening partnership score of 208 runs. The tour was, however, a major historic occasion for black players, and more importantly, the beginning of modern non-racial West Indies 'international' cricket. All that was left was to consolidate the achievements of this start.

In December/January 1904–5, an English team arranged by Lord Brackley, toured the West Indies capturing the spirit of a return bout. While in the region Lord Brackley was clearly impressed with the improvement in the West Indies game since 1900, and made arrangements for a second West Indies team to tour England during the following summer. He also insisted that the tour be designated first-class – with a few second-class fixtures to satisfy reluctant commentators.

The 1906 Inter-colonial Challenge Cup competition was held in Trinidad, and immediately after its completion a selection committee comprising Messrs Gail and Belgrave (Demerara), P.A. Goodman and H.A. Cole (Barbados), and A.E. Harragin and G.C. Learmond (Trinidad) met at Queens Park Cricket Club to select the West Indies team for the tour. The 14 member team chosen was considered an improvement upon the 1900 team, more balanced and stronger in each department. This time the blacks were in the majority.

Composition of the West Indies touring team to England, 1906

Name	Country	Race
H.B.G. Austin (Captain)	Barbados	White
G.C. Learmond	Trinidad	White
W.J. Burton	Demerara	Black
L.S. Constantine	Demerara	Black
J.J. Cameron	Jamaica	Black
R.C. Olliviere	St Vincent	Black
O.H.. Layne	Barbados	Black
J.E. Parker	Demerara	Black
C.P. Cumberbatch	Trinidad	Black
C.K. Bancroft	Barbados	White
G. Challenor	Barbados	White
P.A. Goodman	Barbados	White
S.G. Smith	Trinidad	White
A.E. Harragin	Trinidad	White

The English cricket press welcomed the team on arrival at Southampton on Monday, June 4, and remained divided throughout the tour on its designation as a first-class outfit. The first West Indian first-class 'integration' team – still not test standard (that came in 1928) – was described by the English press as follows:

1   H.B.G. Austin (Barbados), Captain. A graceful bat with an especially good drive. He uses his weight to advantage, and although not too good a starter, he ought to make a lot of runs. 1904–5 batting average, 33.40.

2   C.K. Bancroft (Barbados). He is in residence at Cambridge as the team arrives in England. A wicket-keeper who is said to be very alert with the gloves. He kept well against Lord Brackley's Xl and is also a steady bat. 1904–5 batting average, 9.00; 3 caught and 2 stumped.

3   G. Challenor (Barbados). A member of a famous cricketing family who should score a fine average. He is an attractive bat who combines brilliant hitting with sound defence. He is young but most promising.

4   P.A. Goodman (Barbados). A 1900 tourist, who, with four centuries, was regarded by some as the best bat in the side. He has a good defence and can hit hard. He makes a pretty cut and uses his wrist well. He can bowl medium pace right hand with a break from leg. A capital slip. 1900 batting average, 28.15; 1904–5, 45.00. 1900 bowling, 5 wickets at 54.00; 1904–5, 7 wickets at 14.42.

5   O.H. Layne (Barbados). A professional and fast right hand bowler who can make the ball bump and is none too pleasant to play on a bad wicket. He is a fine long field with a dashing return and is a sound careful bat. 1904–5 batting average, 23.66, bowling 12 wickets at 28.50.

6   G.C. Learmond (Trinidad). A 1900 tourist, he has in turn been identified with Barbados, Demerara and Trinidad. A splendid bat, who having to keep wicket, failed to do himself justice on the previous tour. He has now cultivated cutting, is a useful slow change bowler and a capital field in the slips. 1900 batting average, 9.10; 1904–5, 18.00.

7   L.S. Constantine (Trinidad). A 1900 tourist, another of the old brigade who proved himself very strong on the left side and can bat with power. He fields in the slips and can bowl right hand medium pace if required. He was consistently good with the willow against Lord Brackley's Xl, being second in the averages. 1900 batting average, 30.50; 1904–5, 36.80.

8   J.J. Cameron (Jamaica). A student at Edinburgh University and a fine field at cover point; a useful change bowler and sound bat.

9   A.E. Harragin (Trinidad). A player who can punish all types of bowling. He captained the Trinidad team this season and had fared particularly well in the intercolonial matches. A brilliant man in the country, fast and a sure thrower. 1904–5 batting average, 17.87.

10 S.G. Smith (Trinidad). He is regarded as the crack bowler of the side, a left hander with easy delivery who can make the ball break either way, and who sends down a deceptive fast ball. He can hit with vigour and precision and cuts well. He is a good field in the slips. 1904–5 batting average, 12.55, bowling 20 wickets at 13.95.

11 C.P. Cumberbatch (Trinidad). A professional who may be looked on as the mainstay of the attack. He bowls fast right arm, with an off break, the balls rising very sharply from the pitch. He has a good defence and is a safe field. 1904–5 batting average, 12.00, bowling, 24 wickets at 11.45.

12 J.E. Parker (Demerara). A slow bowler of the Armstrong type, with a field placed on the on-side; a fair defensive batsman and excellent slip.

13 W.J. Burton (Demerara). A professional who is a fine right hand medium pace bowler with plenty of break and a deceptive flight. He secured a fine record on the 1900 tour and hit well on several occasions. He is a sure field. 1900 batting average, 11.64; 1904–5, 9.60. 1900 bowling, 78 wickets at 21.55; 1904–5, 20 wickets at 16.90.

14 R.C. Ollivierre (St Vincent). He is one of the famous brotherhood and a hard hitter. He is quite the Jessop of the Indies, but combines the penchant of A.N. Hornby for short runs. Being the reserve wicket-keeper and a capital fast bowler, he is a good all round exponent. 1904–5 batting average, 26.50; bowling 21 wickets at 12.57.[15]

The insightful assessment of the tour given by Gerry Wolstenholme leaves no doubt that for most English spectators and officials the tour revealed the two faces of Empire and Imperial ideology.[16] On the one hand it was necessary to encourage the colonials in a paternal sort of way even if to put them in their subordinate place by example of defeat. On the other hand, given the racial ideology endemic to Empire, and the fact that the West Indies team had now for the first time acquired the image as a black force in spite of white leadership, elements of the press considered it necessary to cast the contest within a racial paradigm.

The team, on arrival, was invited to dinner by their sponsors, the West Indian Club, at the seemingly appropriate Imperial Restaurant. The official scaffold of imperial hospitality in place, Sir Cavendish Boyle, Chairman of the evening's proceedings, toasted the team with language that removed any doubt about the perception that West Indies cricketers in England were part of a wider scheme of Empire consolidation and promotion. The West Indian guests were admonished:

'You are to show of what good stuff the children of Britain living in the beautiful climes known as the West Indies are possessed'. And in conclusion, he added 'I hope you pull together, train together, bowl together, bat together, field together for the honour of our sunny homes and add another link in the chain of oneness and wholeheartedness which binds the sons of Great Britain with the children of the greater Britain in that undefeated, age undaunted, whole – our British Empire.'[17]

In reply to Sir Cavendish Boyle, the West Indies Captain indicated, particularly to the press, that his team was a revolutionary exercise in resource organization as it was drawn from five colonies 'thousands of miles apart' and had never played before as one.[18]

The performance of the team, like its 1900 predecessor, started poorly but showed marked improvement as the tour progressed. The first game was against the W.G. Grace Xl, on 11 June, at Crystal Palace – the same date and venue as the first match in 1900. The West Indies was trashed by 247 runs. In the second match against Essex they lost by 111 runs, and the third against Lord Brackley's Xl, a second-class game, they lost by two wickets.

Following their first defeat, the press went to work promoting the argument that the blacks from the West Indies were not a first-class lot, and that the decision to offer them this status was premature. One reporter stated: 'The West Indians gave a poor display of fielding. They dropped no less than seven catches (a rather kind estimate); they did not seem to be able to catch anything except the train to take them home'.[19] After the game against Brackley's Xl, one cricket reporter complained that 'All their bowlers are as mild as the weather itself'. Caricatures such as the one beneath showing the West Indian team as represented by a monkey-like black child being spanked by W.G. Grace, appeared in the press. On the whole, the world of Kipling – black primitives and sub-humanoids – was unleashed, in spite of Jeremiah Coleman's (Chairman of Surrey) claim that the 'visit tended to create Imperial good fellowship'.[20]

The match against the MCC at Lords on 16 July, the tenth of the tour, provided another opportunity for the press to harangue the West Indians. They were defeated by 6 wickets after giving the home team 87 runs to win. In an article by cricket journalist E.H.D. Sewell, under the caption, 'What is the Matter with the West Indian Team?,' readers were informed:

> Once again the West Indies have failed to do themselves justice – as a side . . . It is a most extraordinary thing that the side, as a side, cannot get going in cricketer's phraseology. Is it just all the difference between first and second class, I wonder – I was chatting with one of the Kent XI and he wondered why they did not get more runs. He said their field was badly placed and *only the coloured men are good catchers*. They are certainly a mysterious side – and I cannot help thinking they may one day do something surprising.[21]

Following this tour, however, the concept of a first-class multi-racial West Indies team was well established. Finally, they were elevated to test status for the 1928 tour of England in which three official test matches were played. By this time West Indies cricket had moved a long way from the planter-merchant culture in which it was incubated, though the management and other economic relations remained firmly in the hands of this group.

Blacks, however, had brought their cricket from the gullies of their villages to the international stage and had impressed wherever they went as excellent representatives of the modern game. In so doing they had broken the barriers of institutionalized racism and forged the way towards a new democratic ethos. As in all liberation struggles, determination and commitment to an ideal was necessary. Cricketers, then, led the way in many respects, and have demonstrated that in the West Indies cultural resources cannot be divided on ideological terms if maximum efficiency is to be attained with their use.

West Indies in England, 1906 – tour results[22]

Opposition	Dates/venue	Results
W.G. Grace XI	June 11–12, Crystal Palace	Lost by 247 runs
Essex	June 14–16, Leyton	Lost by 111 runs
Lord Brackley's XI	June 18–20, Lords	Lost by 2 wickets
Minor Counties	June 21–23, Ealing	Won by 215 runs
Surrey	June 25–26, The Oval	Lost by 10 wickets
Wiltshire	June 29–30, Swindon	Lost by 86 runs
Hampshire	July 2–4, Southampton	Lost by 6 wickets
South Wales	July 9–10, Cardiff	Won by 278 runs
Kent	July 12–13, Catford	Lost by an innings and 14 runs
MCC	July 16–17, Lords	Lost by 6 wickets

tour results[22] *(contd)*

Opposition	Dates/venue	Results
Derbyshire	July 23–25, Derby	Lost by 6 wickets
Scotland	July 23–25, Edinburgh	Won by 4 wickets
An England Xl	July 26–28, Blackpool	Drawn
Durham/Northumberland	July 30–Aug 1, Sunderland	Won by 145 runs
Yorkshire	Aug 2–4, Harrogate	Won by 262 runs
Leicestershire	Aug 6–8, Leicester	Lost by 24 runs
Norfolk	Aug 10–11, Norwich	Won by an innings and 118 runs
Nottinghamshire	Aug 13–15, Nottingham	Drawn
Northamptonshire	Aug 16–18, Northampton	Won by 115 runs

Overall results: lost: 10 games; won: 7 games; drawn: 2 games.

NOTES

1 Bruce Hamilton, *Cricket in Barbados* (Bridgetown, Advocate Press, 1947), p. 25.
2 *Ibid.*
3 *Ibid.*, p. 30.
4 *Ibid.*,,, p. 39.
5 George Plumtree and E.W. Swanton (eds), *Barclays World of Cricket: the Game from A–Z* (London, Willow Books, 1986 edn), p. 78.
6 *Ibid.*, pp. 127–8.
7 Hamilton, *Cricket*, pp. 32–4; Dave Anthony Soares, 'A History of the Melbourne Cricket Club, 1892–1962'; unpublished MA thesis, Department of History, University of the West Indies, Mona, Jamaica, 1987.
8 *The Times*, 9 February, 1895, Barbados Archives.
9 Hamilton, *Cricket*, p. 53.
10 *Ibid.*, p. 56.
11 *Ibid.*, p. 63.
12 Cited in Michael Davie and Simon Davie, *The Faber Book of Cricket* (London, Faber & Faber, 1987), p. 37.
13 W.L.A. Coleman, 'The First West Indians', in *The Cricketer*, ed. Christopher Martin-Jenkins, June, 1988.
14 *Ibid.*
15 Gerry Wolstenholme, *The West Indies Tour of England, 1906* (London, Nelson, 1992), pp. 7–8.
16 *Ibid.*
17 *Ibid.*, p. 9.
18 *Ibid.*
19 *Ibid.*, p. 13.
20 *Ibid.*, p. 15.
21 *Ibid.*, pp. 20–1.
22 *Ibid.*, pp. 35–7.

Ethnicity 'not out': the Indian cricket tour of the West Indies and the 1976 elections in Trinidad and Tobago

Kevin A. Yelvington

Cricket has always been more than a game in Trinidad. In a society which demanded no skills and offered no rewards to merit, cricket was the only activity which permitted a man to grow to his full stature and to be measured against international standards. Alone on a field, beyond obscuring intrigue, the cricketer's true worth could be seen by all. His race, education, wealth did not matter. We had no scientists, engineers, explorers, soldiers or poets. The cricketer was our only hero-figure. . . . The individual performance was what mattered. That was what we went to applaud; and unless the cricketer had heroic qualities we did not want to see him, however valuable he might be . . .

V.S. Naipaul, *The Middle Passage*

Introduction

One particular "moment," charged with potent symbolism, over the course of an electoral campaign often stands out when viewed retrospectively. In these "moments" the electorate is galvanized when deep-seated emotions are laid bare as embedded social symbols coalesce around historical events. These examples of the conjunction of affect and instrumentality often occur in the idiom of popular culture. When the context becomes one of resource competition and "contested terrain," seemingly innocuous and spontaneous instances such as sporting events take on new and powerful meaning.

Few sports assume the symbolic burden that West Indian cricket does. Caribbean cricket is rooted in the colonial past, and cricket matches in the modern era between England, the former masters, and the West Indies, the former slaves, have taken overt and covert themes of ethnic and national redemption. The only time inter- (and intra-) island rivalries are put aside and their peoples show solidarity, it has been said, is when the West Indies cricket side is playing.

But do all individuals in these competitive societies experience feelings of communitas and draw together in the face of a common foe? And are matches between the West Indies and opponents other than England characterized by the same issues of redemption and resistance?

When India toured the Caribbean in a test match series in 1976, Trinidad and Tobago was on the verge of holding national elections. Trinidad and Tobago's politics were ethnic politics, typified by a rivalry between those of African descent and East Indians, the descendants of indentured sugar workers brought from India, and this rivalry saw the formation of political parties along ethnic lines. Although each group comprised more than 40 percent of the population, the state, colonial and post-colonial, since 1956 had been dominated by a political party identified with those of African descent. The mid-1970s, though, saw a challenge to this hegemony. But the reaction of East Indians and blacks to events on the cricket field served to fuel old prejudices and to further entrench the ethnic politics game – a game in which the country could only lose by playing.

Cricket's place in West Indian society

Responding to the notion that the cricket ethic has shaped West Indian social life, the Trinidadian writer C.L.R. James says:

> It is an understatement. There is a whole generation of us, and perhaps two genera-
> tions, who have been formed by it not only in social attitudes but in our most intimate
> personal lives, in fact there more than anywhere else. The social attitudes we could to
> some degree alter if we wished. For the inner self the die was cast. (1983 [1963], p. 49)

The catch phrase "It's not cricket," meaning "It's not fair," took on the same significance as it did in England.

Throughout his classic *Beyond a Boundary*, James weaves his cricketing experiences and the experiences of others into a discussion of Trinidad's colonial social structure and the central role of ethnic and class prejudice in it. Following James, sociological analyses of cricket's place in West Indian society (e.g., Patterson 1969; St Pierre 1973a, 1973b; Manning 1981; Burton 1985; Birbalsingh 1987) have shown how the changing class and ethnic composition of the West Indian cricket side has "mirrored with almost preternatural precision the evolution of West Indian society" (Burton 1985, p. 179). This evolution entailed the gradual supplanting of whites by blacks on the field and in society from the year 1900 on – the year of the first West Indian tour to England. However, this process was not a coherent, linear one and it was not without difficulty and hardship that it came about.

Cricket was introduced to the Caribbean by British military officers. It has been suggested that the slaves initially picked up the game to satirize "massa's" ways. Slaves and their descendants were also incorporated into games with whites, but they performed restrictive roles. At first, they were "allowed" to prepare pitches and fields and a few were "allowed" only to bowl and retrieve batted balls during practice sessions. When the apprenticeship period that followed the abolition of slavery finally ended in 1838, blacks did not have access to the financial or social wherewithal to participate in organized cricket, which was the province of elite sporting and social clubs. In a colonial society which placed a philistine value on "whiteness" and what was defined as "European" culture, most blacks did not have the "symbolic capital," or economic capital for that matter, deemed necessary for entry. On this score, East Indians – brought to the Caribbean from 1838 to 1917 and who now comprise almost half of Trinidad's and more than half of Guyana's populations – had even less symbolic capital as their non-Western ways were considered "heathen." Blacks and East Indians, who had far less leisure time than whites, were relegated to playing cricket with makeshift equipment and in makeshift settings: in a pasture, on the road, on a beach.

Eventually, "browns" (mulattos), blacks, East Indians, and other groups in Trinidad formed their own clubs based on ethnicity, class, and prestige (cf. James 1975, pp. 14–16) and competed with other clubs on parallel, but not equal, terms. In Barbados, there was even a bifurcation of organized cricket into two leagues, one more prestigious and "respectable," and the other "plebeian" (cf. Thompson 1983, pp. 25, 50). The 1900 West Indian team that toured England was dominated by members of the plantocracy. However, from this point on the numerical superiority of whites on the field gave way to blacks, who not only began to appear in greater numbers in West Indian sides but also quickly began to dominate in terms of performance. Despite brief periods of decline, the West Indies have been the dominant side in test cricket in the last 20 years and this success has been built on the accomplishments during the first two-thirds of the century of such legendary figures as George John, Learie (later Lord) Constantine, George Headley, Collie Smith, Garfield (later Sir Garfield) Sobers, Wes Hall, Roy Gilchrist, and "the Three Ws," Weekes, Worrell, and Walcott.

Yet, it was not until 1960 that a black man, Frank (later Sir Frank) Worrell, was named captain of the West Indies side. And this was so despite the largely mediocre performance of white cricketers in test matches from 1928, when the West Indies was accorded full test match status, until 1960 (St Pierre 1973a, pp. 10–12). It is significant that the Barbadian Worrell was middle-class, educated, and "respectable." It is also significant that the West Indies played nine test series from 1928 to 1950 before an East Indian – Trinidad's Sonny Ramadhin – was included (Birbalsingh 1987, p. 265). Since Ramadhin, East Indian stars for the West Indies have included Rohan Kanhai, Joe Solomon, and Alvin Kallicharran of Guyana. The reason why whites were accorded the position of captain, which is symbolically important in the West Indies because of a cultural emphasis on personable leadership, was that they still controlled the institutional means of team selection, which was organized through the club system. In Trinidad, the dominant club was the Queen's Park Cricket Club, which also owned the test cricket ground in Port of Spain (Martindale 1980, pp. 208–10).

The merging of social structural and cultural factors is evident in the way the game is played in the West Indies. The Jamaican sociologist Patterson observes that

> in the West Indies the test match is not so much a game as a collective ritual – a social
> drama in which almost all of the basic tensions and conflicts within the society are
> played out symbolically. (1969, p. 23)

He goes on to show how society's divisions are played out spatially too, as if *de jure*,
at Kingston, Jamaica's Sabina Park. There, in the covered pavilion sit the upper
class, most of whom are white or "high brown," while opposite are the uncovered,
sun-baked bleachers, whose black occupants are separated from the field by a tall
fence. In the covered northern stand sit middle-class blacks and in the southern end
sit the upwardly mobile "brown" fans.

Burton (1985, pp. 180–9) situates West Indian cricket in the context of "street
culture," the Carnival tradition, and Afro-American culture in general. He argues
that West Indian cricket is a collective rite which, like Afro-Christian forms of
worship and Carnival itself, involves the indispensable and crucial interplay
between the players and the spectators. More importantly, Burton argues, all of
these elements of popular culture embody the link between play and *resistance* and
the spirit of *competition*. If the essence of Carnival represented a way to rehumanize a dreadful existence by "turning the world upside down," it is true that competition and hierarchy – symbolic and real – are at the heart of Carnival and "street
culture." Perhaps this is why *West Indians themselves* see their cricket as played with
aggressive "style," "flair," and a "vengeance" pertaining to Afro-Caribbean culture
and to societal violence – symbolic and real. "The result," writes St Pierre, "was
frustration which bespoke aggression and violence" (1973a, p. 12). Often, cricket
was the only outlet to express this frustration and to advance in the society:

> Performance before an audience of West Indians equally emphatic about violent and
> aggressive cricket, conspired to produce a change in this 'beautiful, difficult English
> game'. This change was essentially one of self-image, for not only has cricket been
> functional in this purely cathartic sense for West Indians, but it has facilitated a degree
> of upward mobility. (St Pierre 1973a, p. 15)

Burton, invoking an image used by writers to describe the colonial situation, likens
the psychological processes attached to cricket to the Prospero–Caliban relationship. While this literary duality has been criticized by Baker (1986) for eliding
Caliban's voice, in the cricket sense the critical date for the giving of more than voice
to Caliban was 1950. That was the year the West Indies defeated England in
England for the first time, behind the batting of "the Three Ws" and the bowling
of the spin twins immortalized in Lord Kitchener's calypso, "Cricket, Lovely
Cricket," "those two little pals of mine/Ramadhin and Valentine." The "mother
country" would never be the same in the eyes of all West Indians after the 1950
series. "It was as though," writes Burton, "Prospero had taught Caliban the use of
bat and ball only to find himself comprehensively 'out-magicked' by his upstart
colonial pupil" (1985, p. 179). By implication, though, cricket means something different to East Indians, who have been incorporated into Caribbean society on different terms than those of African descent.

Nevertheless, what is clear is that success in cricket combat versus the colonizer has fundamentally changed the nature of Afro-West Indian ethnic identity where a positive self-image emerges. However, it could also be that, upon self-reflection, black West Indians associate the prowess of their cricketers and the success of their world-beating side with "natural" attributes of those of African descent (East Indians have always been few in number on test sides and have been virtually absent in the 1980s). This could be partially due to the incipient Americanization of the region as this stance is associated with the pernicious ideology that the "blackening" of American sports is due to the putative "natural" athletic and physical qualities of Afro-Americans rather than socio-economic factors. Psychological emancipation, then, is far from complete.

Still, it is possible to disagree with Patterson who argues that, even though West Indians love cricket because they excel at it and it accords them international prestige, deep down it is a game they must hate because

> it becomes on the symbolic level the English culture we have been forced to love, for it is the only real one we have, but the culture we must despise for what it has done to us, for what it has made of the hopeless cultural shambles, the incoherent social patchwork, that we have called Afro-[Caribbean] culture. (1969, p. 24)

However, besides denying cultural inventiveness, this view does not give West Indians credit with seeing things too. West Indians associate cricket with the English aristocracy and the English warfare prowess "is-traced-to-the-playing-fields-of-Eton-and-Harrow" ethic as much as any academic. This is why beating England is of such great importance and why cricket is cherished precisely because it allows West Indians the continued possibility.

Based on his anthropological studies of Bermudian politics, Manning (1981, p. 617) suggests that cricket "dramatizes a fundamental, racially oriented conflict" in the society. The conjunction of identity, politics, and spectator involvement congealed in a number of major disturbances and riots during matches versus English teams in the West Indies (see, for example, Burton 1985, p. 189–94 and St Pierre 1973b, pp. 27–34). The three most famous incidents occurred when events on the cricket field sparked off pent-up political frustrations. In British Guiana in 1954, bottles were thrown after an umpire's unpopular decision. The match came only months after the colony's constitution had been suspended and British troops brought in the aftermath of an election, the first under universal adult suffrage, which saw the election of a left-wing government under Cheddi Jagan. In Trinidad in 1960, bottles were thrown and the match abandoned for the day in response to poor West Indian batting. Trinidadians in 1960 were taking the last troublesome steps to independence, there was a struggle to get the Chaguaramas military base back from the Americans, and, perhaps more immediately, the pleas for a black West Indian captain had reached their apogee. And in Jamaica in 1968, bottles were thrown onto the field as the result of a controversial umpiring decision and the police sprayed tear gas into the crowd, causing the crowd to riot in reaction. Jamaica during the late 1960s was rife with political violence as the population grew more disappointed with the "benefits" of independence and a few months after this incident were the "Rodney Riots" and the start of the Black Power movement in the Caribbean (cf. Payne 1983).

In all these situations, the West Indies side was losing or about to lose and in all three cases hostility was heaped not upon the opposing team but upon local umpires who were from hated economic and ethnic groups – light-skinned in the case of British Guiana and Chinese in the Trinidad and Jamaica cases. The crowd was reacting to what it perceived as a symbol of authority and a local representative of colonial and neo-colonial power (see James 1975, pp. 117–18 for a slightly different take on the umpire's dilemma). As Thompson writes: "Misbehavior in this milieu has underlying political overtones: it is an unwitting rebellion of the status quo. As a cultural phenomenon, cricket in the West Indies should be viewed as a reflection and expression of class, racial, and color conflict" (1983, p. 50).

In Trinidad, the coming to an end of British rule and the advent of the nationalist movement coincided with James' politicization of the issue that Worrell should become captain of the West Indies side. "The intimate connection," writes James, "between cricket and West Indian political and social life was established so that all except the willfully perverse could see" (1983 [1963], p. 217). Following this, cricket has been used in the Caribbean in the fight against apartheid in South Africa by helping to censure that country from international cricket and by sanctioning players who play there. So Naipaul's arguments in this article's epigraph seem ironic indeed: In Trinidad an individual's "race, education, wealth" *did* matter – in cricket as in everything else.

Ethnic politics in Trinidad and Tobago

Electoral politics in Trinidad and Tobago have been characterized by voting along ethnic lines, as a number of studies have shown (e.g., Bahadoorsingh 1968; Oxaal 1968; Malik 1971; Ryan 1972; Yelvington 1987). From the time of the first election under universal adult suffrage in 1946, politicians have made overt appeals to ethnicity in seeking support from the black and East Indian masses, who, in any case, were split along occupational and geographical lines: urban-dwelling blacks were in professional and skilled employment, in many cases with the government, while rural East Indians were primarily agricultural workers and in most cases poorer than blacks.

The arrival of party politics saw an intensification of this trend. In 1955, Dr Eric Williams, an Oxford-educated historian, and a group of middle-class blacks and "browns" formed the People's National Movement (PNM) to contest the 1956 elections. The party soon received fervent support from working-class urban blacks who rallied around "the Doctor." As Oxaal describes him, Williams was seen as a "racial messiah" who "had come to lead the black children into the Promised Land" (1968, p. 100).

210

The PNM's main opposition was the People's Democratic Party (PDP), led by Bhadase Sagan Maraj, who was also the leader of the largest sugar workers union (whose members were almost all East Indians) and the main Hindu religious organization. Although it featured a few East Indians and other minorities in top positions, and thus could claim it was a multi-ethnic party, the PNM became identified with blacks, and the PDP became for all intents and purposes the "Indian" party. The PNM defeated the PDP in the 1956 elections.

For the 1958 Federal elections, the PDP combined with another group to form the Democratic Labour Party (DLP). The DLP won 6 out of 10 Federal seats and, even though seven of its candidates were non-Indian, in a bitter post-election speech Williams alluded to the East Indians as a "recalcitrant and hostile minority."

The 1961 elections would determine the party that would lead the country to independence in 1962. By this time, the leadership of the DLP had passed to Dr Rudranath Capildeo, a mathematics lecturer and barrister, whom East Indians began to identify with as blacks did with Williams. Ethnic violence during the campaign between blacks and East Indians led to the declaration of states of emergency in rural areas, which is where East Indians were predominant. During the campaign, Williams, no doubt capitalizing on feelings that surfaced in the test match violence a year before, chastised the white elite and told the populace "massa day done." Ethnic tensions became further exaggerated after the election when the victorious Williams and the PNM refused the DLP opposition any say in the writing of the new constitution. Widespread violence was averted when Williams finally compromised.

Symbolic identification with the PNM was backed up with material benefits. Craig (1974) has shown how the PNM's patronage system operated at the local level, a system that was designed to favor blacks at the expense of East Indians. The DLP only controlled seats in "Indian" areas for a decade, and PNM dominance remained unchallenged until the Black Power demonstrations of 1970 (cf. Nicholls 1971; Oxaal 1971; Sutton 1983). Using symbols largely borrowed from North America, and tending to exclude East Indians, local blacks complained that political independence had not improved their lot, citing foreign multinational and local white domination of the economy. These feelings had a basis in fact. Harewood and Henry show that society-wide income distribution in 1971 was worse than in 1958, two years after the PNM took over. They also show that in 1972, the average monthly income by ethnicity was: TT$240. for East Indians; $279. for blacks; and $442. for the "other" group, which included Syrian/Lebanese, Chinese, whites, and mixed individuals. However, this distribution improved somewhat when the oil money began to flow and, by 1975, East Indians' incomes actually exceeded blacks' by an insignificant amount (Harewood and Henry 1985, p. 65).

For the 1971 elections, the DLP merged with a Tobago-based party led by former PNM deputy prime minister A.N.R. Robinson. But Robinson surprised many, including those in his own party, by boycotting the elections a short time before they were to be held. Against virtually no opposition, the PNM's candidates won in all

36 constituencies with the support from only 28 percent of the electorate. The country remained in a political and profound economic crisis and Williams indicated he would resign as prime minister in 1973. Cynics point out that he only changed his mind when it became apparent that the country would benefit greatly from the oil boom. Indeed, the oil boom allowed the PNM to bestow patronage on even greater levels and, although it was targeted primarily at blacks, East Indians were to benefit directly as well.

By 1975, Basdeo Panday, a charismatic Hindu barrister, had gained control of the largest sugar union. Calling for working-class unity, he led the merging of two predominantly East Indian unions with two predominantly black unions that combined to form the United Labour Front (ULF). The black union leaders did not contest seats and, with Panday as leader, the party seemed to be a case of the old DLP all over again. However, this time things were somewhat more complicated.

The society's ruling groups were concerned with the prospect of black–East Indian working-class solidarity. The run-up to the election saw the establishment make virulent attacks on the ULF, calling its leaders "communists" who wanted to take away private property. The ULF leaders refuted these allegations, saying that the ULF was a "party of the working class preaching the doctrine of the working class" (quoted in Ryan 1979, p. 8). There were also attempts to isolate the ULF from the increasingly significant number of upwardly-mobile East Indians – individuals who had advanced in the professions and, especially, by entrepreneurial activity – by warning them that the ULF threatened their hard-won status. Other East Indians were warned by the new incarnations of the DLP that Panday was being manipulated by "Black Power elements" in the ULF.

In March, 1976, the ULF released a letter purportedly coming from the US Embassy, addressed to Prime Minister Williams. The letter warned that victory for the ULF would represent a threat to the friendly relations between the countries and it urged that the prime minister prohibit the state-owned media from giving exposure to the ULF candidates. It said the ULF represented a threat to US businesses operating in the country and, ultimately, a ULF victory would mean the termination of immigration to the US, thus exacerbating the unemployment problem (Ryan 1979, pp. 5–6, f.n. 2. Ryan accepts that the letter was genuine.). It also should be remembered that US forces stood at the ready to help Williams when he was confronted with a military mutiny as part of the Black Power disturbances a few years earlier.

Shortly after the letter was released, the National Broadcasting Corporation banned the voices of Panday and other leaders of the party on the grounds that they were preaching subversion. And the corporation's chairman openly warned of a situation when East Indians controlled most of the property and the government, urging "sensible people" to "make a conscious effort to counter any undesirable consequences that could develop from such a possible situation" (*Trinidad Guardian*, April 25, 1976, cited in Ryan 1979, p. 12, f.n. 18). At the same time, the powerful daily newspaper *Trinidad Guardian* began to write a series of anti-ULF editorials, and Williams embarked on a subtle campaign to denigrate socialism. Panday fought back by ordering his sugar workers to go on a 24–hour strike.

In order to try to escape from the "communist" and "Indian party" labels, the ULF tried to form an alliance with Robinson's new party, the Democratic Action Congress (DAC), which would appeal to blacks and ostensibly to middle-class East Indians. Yet there was bitter public haggling between representatives of the two sides and, ultimately, no merger was formed. It was in this emotionally charged atmosphere – and when international news from South Africa, Rhodesia and the frontline states was prominent, and when Trinidad was rocked by a series of strikes and demonstrations – that the Indian test side arrived in March, 1976.

Drama at the Queen's Park Oval

Trinidadians have perhaps as much emotional investment in a test series versus India as in one versus England, albeit of quite a different order. India and the West Indies first met in 1948–49 when the West Indians toured the subcontinent. When India arrived in Trinidad as part of their 1952–53 tour,

> people [i.e., East Indians] who had never before made the journey to the capital, Port of Spain, left their paddy fields and sugar plantations for the day to see the representatives of their mother country, India, play in the test match at the Queen's Park Oval. Much to the annoyance of some West Indian cricket supporters, the East Indians were vociferous in their support of V.J. [sic] Hazare's Indian test side (McDonald 1984, pp. 68–9). (For similar experiences in subsequent visits to Guyana, see *ibid.*, pp. 68, and Martindale 1980, p. 108–9.)

In 1971, much the same happened when India toured with conspicuous success in the wake of the Black Power revolution. India won 1 test and 4 were drawn with Sunil Gavaskar, playing in his first test series, scoring 774 runs, including 116 in the test at Georgetown, Guyana, and 124 and 220 in the Port-of-Spain test. "The Little Master" was soon immortalized in Lord Relator's calypso of the same name.

India's 1976 tour was one to be remembered. It was, as McDonald writes, "one of the more controversial of all time" (1984, p. 83). Before the start of the tour, the *Trinidad Guardian* issued an editorial which included – perhaps unintentional – understatement and wry irony. It read, in part,

> cricket is a most unpredictable enterprise.
> Because of historical circumstances visits of the Indians will always have an appeal even greater than its quality of mere entertainment alone can offer. Such visits bring together in entrancing communion peoples who have undergone much of similar social affliction but have grown to assimilate from their former rulers cultural elements that will long direct them – sportsmanship, ardent affection for cricket and a certain political ethic. (*Trinidad Guardian*, March 3, 1976, p. 6)

The West Indies had beaten India in the first test by an innings and 97 runs in

Bridgetown, Barbados. The Port of Spain test, the second of the series, started March 24, 1976. Rain prevented play on the first day, much to the disappointment of the crowd of 18,000 that gathered at the Oval. When the play finally got going the next day, India made a dramatic start. On the second ball of the morning's opening over, Roy Fredericks was bowled out. The newspaper report read: "In a dramatic opening, Fredericks was bowled neck and crop for nought. And before the cheers had died down from the 18,000 crowd, Mohinder Amarnath also scattered Lawrence Rowe's stumps" (*Trinidad Guardian*, March 26, 1976, p. 18).

However, the West Indies recovered, thanks to the remarkable batting of Vivian Richards. Richards also had some remarkable luck. Needing 17 to get his hundred, Richards found himself scrambling to make his ground after an accurate throw left him stranded. The Indian wicket-keeper caught the ball, but inexplicably did not complete the stumping. As McDonald writes: "India paid dearly for that mistake. Richards went on the rampage to celebrate his good fortune. When he was eventually out he had scored 130, including 21 boundaries. The entire Oval crowd rose to acclaim the hero of West Indian batting" (1984, p. 85). The crowd reacted long and loud for the Antiguan Richards and extolled his abilities. But their hero-in-the-making would soon be involved in controversy.

When India batted, Gavaskar responded well in front of a capacity crowd of 25,000. Gavaskar ended up with 156, his seventh century in 22 test matches, his fifth against the West Indies, and his third consecutive at the Oval, going back to 1971. India was captained by Bishen Singh Bedi, who wore a colorful *patna*, a kind of lightweight turban, while he played. He wore a different one every day and sometimes changed during the match.

While India was batting, Richards pulled a thigh muscle and had to receive a pain-killing injection before playing on the final day. But Richards injured himself again while batting on the final day when the West Indies were fighting back for a draw. Play was held up for 10 minutes while the captains and umpires discussed the issue while Richards hobbled around in pain. Bedi refused to allow Richards to retire, which West Indies captain Clive Lloyd said was "bad sportsmanship." Bedi told Lloyd that Richards would be allowed to resume his innings as last man.

The rule about retiring states that a batsman may retire at any time, but may not resume his innings without the consent of the opposing captain, and then only on the fall of a wicket. Richards resumed his innings at the fall of the fourth wicket. Bedi said afterwards that he changed his mind and allowed Richards to come to bat instead of being last man. Richards then made 20 before being run out, a decision which the crowd objected to wildly, booing umpire Ralph Gosein for the rest of the match, which ended in a draw.

The treatment meted out to Gosein is significant and it relates to previous crowd reactions. It is important to note that Gosein is a Trinidadian East Indian and the crowd's reaction came on the heels of "improper" treatment of their hero: not only was Richards not allowed to retire hurt, but he was given out by an East Indian umpire who the crowd perhaps thought was in cahoots with the Indian side.

Incidentally, Gosein's umpiring partner that day was Douglas Sang Hue, the umpire in the controversial 1968 West Indies–England test in Kingston.

A letter to the editor by "A Concerned Observer" in Tunapuna exemplified the "It's not cricket" ethic which James has written about (Tunapuna, incidentally, is James's home town):

> yesterday I was utterly lost for words to describe the bitterness I felt at the rank barbarity displayed by a faction of the crowd at the Oval . . . . After a decision of 'run out' against Richards, the crowd booed umpire Gosein for the rest of the day; and even though the decision may have been a controversial one a mature crowd should have the sense to see that good and bad decisions will always be made and should be accepted. (It should be noted that after the humiliation of booing and snide comments Mr Gosein had to be escorted off the pitch by four armed guards.) . . . This debased action of the crowd, compounded in its misery by ignorance, dishonour, disrespect and shame, left distrust and regret with all those who witnessed it. (*Trinidad Guardian*, April 3, 1976, p. 6)

The two sides moved on to Georgetown for the third test. There, the Mahatma Gandhi Organization requested that the days of the test be changed because some were to fall on the anniversary of Lord Rama's birth, one of Hinduism's holiest days which should be spent in fasting and prayers. In any event, heavy rains and flooding forced the test to be shifted back to Port of Spain. At one point, water was 18 inches deep at the Bourda Oval. Twice previously on an Indian tour a test match had to be shifted from Guyana: in 1953 because of rain and in 1962 because of race riots.

The third test in Port of Spain proved historic. And in its midst, James returned to Trinidad from England. Asked the purpose of his visit, James said only "I am on contract with the BBC." A BBC producer later said James and a film crew were in Trinidad to make a documentary version of *Beyond a Boundary*. Rumors, possibly originating in government circles, about the *real* reason for James' visit began to circulate. After he broke with the PNM, the Marxist James once returned to Trinidad in the early 1960s to cover a cricket tour as a journalist when he was placed under house arrest, ostensibly to prevent his involvement in "subversive activities." In 1976, it seems, the PNM used James as part of its anti-"communist" strategy, and the BBC was denied production cooperation by the state-owned television station. Williams spoke out in parliament, though, protesting that the government in no way sought to muzzle James.

India's spin bowlers started the match by wreaking havoc on West Indian batters, with Bhagwat Chandrasekhar even getting Kallicharran for a duck. However, the brilliant Richards (again) led the recovery. The West Indies ended the day with 320 for five, with Richards undefeated on 151, which included 2 6s and 19 4s. Following India's respectable reply, the West Indies batted again. Their score of 271 meant that India would have to score over 400 runs to win, something thought to be impossible to accomplish.

Behind another century by Gavaskar, a 112 by Gundappa Vishwanath, and an 85 by Amarnath, India stormed back, cheered loudly by Trinidadian East Indians. Brijesh Patel was one short of 50 and undefeated when he dramatically struck the winning run as India won by six wickets. India's "fans" invaded the grounds to congratulate the victors. Bedi became only the second man to captain a team to score over 400 runs in a fourth innings (Don Bradman was the only other when Australia beat England at Leeds in 1958).

West Indian fans, while stunned, did not question Lloyd's decision. As one opinion writer said,

> It was a good declaration which left India to score 403 runs for victory in 535 minutes, taking into consideration how tricky the Oval turf plays most of the time. Lloyd's gamble just backfired. (*Trinidad Guardian*, April 15, 1976, p. 14)

However, "Our fans," said Richards, "weren't very happy" (McDonald 1984, p. 86). Indeed, they were incensed not only because the West Indies lost when they really should have won, but because the East Indians vociferously supported the winning side. A front-page picture in the *Trinidad Guardian* under the headline "Indian Supporters Storm Oval" showed East Indian fans mobbing Patel and Madan Lal, the other batsman (*Trinidad Guardian*, April 13, 1976).

And the cricket result was not without a political implication. Again, cricket was the site for a challenge to the dominant order and it spoke to the divisions within the society and the political process. As Ryan writes,

> The question of race and voting [came] alive following the visit of the Indian cricket team to Trinidad. A majority of Indians appeared to support the Indian team against the West Indian cricketers and there were some ugly incidents between Africans and Indians whose behaviour was described as being treasonable. The feeling on the part of some political commentators was that these incidents gave a clue to what would happen on election day. (1979, p. 10)

The reaction

Tensions were still high when news of the Kingston test reached Trinidad. Throughout the series the Indian manager Polly Umrigar had complained about what he saw as intimidating bowling by the West Indians, especially by the superfast Michael Holding. At Sabina Park, a number of Indian batsmen were injured when struck by the ball. The normally mild-mannered Bedi was furious at the West Indian bowlers and at the umpires for refusing to do anything about it. On 97 for five, India was just 12 runs ahead of the West Indies when, to make his protest, Bedi declared India's second innings closed. At first it was thought Bedi had declared India's innings closed on an unlikely score, but to make his protest against the bowling stronger, he said he wished it to be recorded that India's innings had ended 97 for five. "The match," writes McDonald, "had therefore been virtually conceded to the West Indies and the series ended on a thoroughly bad-tempered note" (1984,

p. 89). Thus, the West Indies took the series with their first test win at Sabina since a 1965 victory over Australia.

In Trinidad, the events surrounding the two tests at the Oval confronted the society with facts about itself. The newspapers were filled with commentary from editorial writers, politicians, and from the population at large who reasoned why Trinidad's East Indians supported India, when the West Indian side featured not only Kallicharran, but Trinidadian East Indians Raphick Jumadeen and Imtiaz Ali. There were those who defended the actions of the East Indians, arguing that, given the society's composition, power relations and history, this was to be expected because of the East Indians' subordinate position. On the other hand, feelings were expressed that the East Indians were traitorous. This view was usually accompanied by feelings of shock and dismay because there was, after all, no need for the East Indians to feel marginalized because Trinidad was a racial democracy. This conformed to the official view of the PNM, which promulgated and purveyed the "All ah we is one" motto, revealing an ideology that, among other things, regarded East Indians and anyone else as "racial" for refusing to accommodate change. The implication is that there is danger when such a group "takes over" the country. Still other commentators denied any conflict, saying that good cricket was what the Oval fans were applauding.

Predictably, politicians were among the first to chime in. In an interview with columnist Therese Mills, Panday lamented the tradition of ethnic politics, saying that ethnicity colors every decision that is made in the society. The part of the interview which appeared under the headline "Panday Explains Reaction of Trinidad Indians at the Oval" is of importance here:

Q: Last week's response by Indians to the Test victory of the visiting Indian team has raised in many minds . . . the old bogey of race. By openly supporting the Indian cricket team against the West Indies, did not the East Indians in Trinidad show that race is still a big thing with them?

Mr Panday: This is a genuine observation. The Indian in this country, because he has always been in political opposition, and because he has not participated in political power and because he has not been in the political mainstream of the country has never really developed a loyalty to the country . . . he has always been left out of the mainstream and I think this is what causes reactions such as were seen at the Oval, and I agree that it is not the kind of reaction that helps to weld people together.

Q: Do you agree, that it is this sort of behaviour on the part of Trinidad Indians which make others feel that once an Indian-based party takes over, heaven help the non-Indians?

Mr Panday: People who think this are not looking at the society as a whole. They are not examining the objective positions in the society. In fact what has really happened, is not that one race has got along and the other not. In fact it is a class of people and the class includes a lot of Indians. . . . You see those who control our affairs today are not Africans, Indians, Buddhists or Sikhs. It is a class of people, made up of both races. Once this is made clear to the people the fear of race will die.
(*Trinidad Guardian*, April 18, 1976, p. 13)

Here, of course, Panday is saying different things to different people. He is assuring East Indians that he has their interests at heart, while trying to assure blacks that he is analyzing the society's problems in class terms. One letter to the editor, from "Ram" in Penal, summed up creole society's reactions to the events at the Oval and to Panday's remarks:

> The touring Indian cricket team played better and deserved to win the Third Test which they did so convincingly. I have no quarrel with that, after all it's cricket.
>
> But, despite the explanation offered by Mr Basdeo Panday . . . the reaction of the Trinidadians of East Indian descent was revolting to say the least.
>
> That was not cricket! (*Trinidad Guardian*, April 25, 1976, p. 12)

Mills later interviewed PNM general secretary and senator Nicholas Simonette. Mills questioned whether, given the persistence of ethnic voting after 20 years of PNM rule, did this not indicate a failure of PNM policies? Simonette countered by saying that the PNM had been able to maintain "good racial harmony." Mills asked, alluding to the events at the Oval, if it were not true that Trinidad East Indians identified with India because they were shut out of national life:

> *Senator Simonette*: This is a false view. If there is a residue of this feeling one could understand it. But there has been no keeping out of East Indians from the mainstream of national life. One has only to look at the institutions of this country to recognise this.
>
> If there was a marked difference between the position of Indians and non-Indians prior to 1961 or 1966 one can point today to a considerable reduction in any situation like that.
>
> There is equal opportunity for everyone and this has been embraced by people of all ethnic origin, including those of East Indians [sic]. Remarks like the one referred to by Mr. Panday are just calculated to encourage people to believe that they have been deprived and left out. (*Trinidad Guardian*, April 25, 1976, p. 20)

One letter to the editor, from "Cricket Lover" is ignoring religious divisions among East Indians. The majority of Trinidad East Indians are Hindus and many would have identified with India on these grounds alone. But the symbol of India would have been more alluring, and its representatives seen as "pure" in contrast to local "creolized" East Indians. Ryan understands this when he writes "In a vicarious sense, it meant that 'they' had 'defeated' creole society which had not conceded them their rightful place" (*Trinidad Express*, April 11, 1976, cited in Ryan 1979, p. 10, f.n. 16).

One letter-writer, himself East Indian, took issue with the way the media was treating Panday as the "Indian spokesman" and offered a rather sophisticated analysis of the country's ethnic politics:

> The fact is that Mr. Panday is no more qualified than Rampartap in Penal to offer any authoritative explanation for Indian support of India at the Oval. And I am quite sure than Mr. Panday with his obsession for a seat in Parliament and his desire to appease negroes would be the first to admit this . . . . Mr. Panday, however, was not far wrong in his opinion of why Indians supported India during the Third Test. His contention

[is] that Indians have not participated in the mainstream of political life for so long that they have not developed a sense of loyalty towards the country.

This is putting it euphemistically. Indians have been deliberately kept out of political life. Let us not forget these hallowed words of the 1950s – 'The Indians are a hostile and recalcitrant minority'.

The writer went on to complain about what he saw as the inequality of opportunity in government-sponsored projects, the "cultural imperialism" that obtains in the promotion of a "national" culture, and he wondered why the government chose to express solidarity with Angola and why $100,000 worth of taxpayers' money went to buy medical supplies for Mozambique when, after the Bangladesh War, no such assistance was offered. He also wondered there was no official condemnation of Idi Amin for kicking Indians out of Uganda and why, to the contrary, a Ugandan envoy was welcomed in the country a few weeks later, "to ask the Indians to ignore all of this and still be loyal to the country," he continued, "is to ask them to display a quality not possessed by humans at all." He concluded:

> Basically, the situation in 1976 is the same as it was in 1956 as far as racial unity goes. What exists now is not racial unity but Indian acquiescence in Negro domination. Such a situation does not augur well for the future for there will come a time when the problem will not be able to fit anymore under the carpet. (*Trinidad Guardian*, April 25, 1976, pp. 21–2)

In any event, such discourse continued up until the elections, which were held in September. Although it was not completely able to shirk its "Indian party" image, it seemed to some that, despite the failed merger with the ADAC, Panday and the ULF had gained some support from black workers in the industrial East–West Corridor, an urban sprawl which stretches from Port of Spain to Arima. Then, on the eve of the elections, another event of similar significance to the cricket matches occurred. The ULF organized a motorcade as a show of strength, which moved out of central Trinidad, where East Indians are more numerous, and into the creole areas of Port of Spain and the western suburbs, as far as Carenage and Diego Martin. This jolted the residents of those areas and played on their old fears and anxieties. An eyewitness gave this account:

> It was about three miles long. The front cars had big green and red flags and there were mini-buses full of tassa drummers. They had a loudspeaker system so powerful you could hear it a mile away.
>
> The whole motorcade is Indians. And they driving down the Eastern Main Road chanting "don't vote PNM" and Indians on the pavement waving to them. [And blacks saying] "Is PNM or them." (*Tapia*, Sept. 19, 1976, p. 3)

The PNM won the election handily, with the ULF capturing a mere 10 seats, all in East Indian areas, the DAC winning only the 2 Tobago seats, and a number of minor parties winning none (a full description is found in Ryan 1979). The electorate was clearly dismayed with the nature of the country's politics: to wit, voter participation went from 88 percent in 1961 to 66 percent in 1966 to 54 percent in 1976.

The election results may have indeed been very similar had the events at the Oval – which involved a complex web of cultural traditions – or the motorcade – which had the proximate effect of providing a warning to blacks of the dangers of splitting the "black vote" – not in fact occurred. However, the event of the Indian cricket tour to Trinidad at such a historical juncture provides cultural historians now, as it provided Trinidadians then, with an insight into the symbolic and cultural construction of identity, emotion, and politics in a post-colonial society. Cricket was the idiom through which creativity and resilience flourished in the face of colonial oppression. In 1976, it became the idiom through which another subjugated people resisted their subjugators.

Conclusion

In his rich study of cricket and politics in Bermuda, Manning (1981) calls on Geertz's (1973 [1972]) analysis of the Balinese cockfight. Geertz argues that the cockfight is a "metasocial commentary" on Balinese society and a way its members learn about their culture. However, this case study suggests that cricket symbolism is not merely a commentary about wider social relationships but an example of how those relationships are ordered. Cricket is not divorced from the social structure, so it cannot be analyzed as if it were. It is reductionist to suggest that cricket and the cockfight can tell us all about the society: Cricket in Trinidad is a *site* of intersocietal conflict and the convergence of social relations, with their attendant symbolic, structural, and cultural aspects.

Roseberry makes a similar point when criticizing Geertz's treatment of the cockfight, writing that for Geertz,

> Culture as text is removed from the material process of its creation; it is therefore removed from the historical process that shapes it and that it in turn shapes . . . [Geertz's] image implies separation, a removal of culture from the wellings-up of action, interaction, power, and praxis. (1982, p. 1027)

Yet, surely, the second point, that cricket (and the cockfight) is one way in which members of the society learn about the society, is borne out by this study. Manning (1981, p. 617) rightly suggests that the study of cricket – and I would go so far as to include other forms of popular culture – "can provide a unique understanding of the conceptual parameters in which political awareness is developed and expressed."

References

Bahadoorsingh, Krishna. 1968. *Trinidad Electoral Politics: the Persistence of the Race Factor.* New York: Oxford University Press.

Baker, Houston A., Jr. 1986. "Caliban's Triple Play," *Critical Inquiry*, 13(1): 182–96.

Birbalsingh, Frank. 1987. "Indo-Caribbean Test Cricketers." pp. 265–77 in *India in the*

Caribbean, edited by David Dabydeen and Brinsley Samaroo. London: Hansib, Centre for Caribbean Studies, University of Warwick and Macmillan.

Burton, Richard D.E. 1985. "Cricket, Carnival and Street Culture in the Caribbean," *British Journal of Sports History* 2(2): 179–97.

Craig, Susan E. 1974. "Community Development in Trinidad and Tobago 1943–1973: from Welfare to Patronage," *Working Paper No. 4*, Mona, Jamaica: Institute of Social and Economic Research, University of the West Indies.

Geertz, Clifford. 1973 [1972]. "Deep Play: Notes on the Balinese Cockfight," pp. 412–53, in *The Interpretation of Cultures*. New York: Basic Books.

Harewood, Jack and Henry, Ralph. 1985. *Inequality in a Post-Colonial Society: Trinidad and Tobago 1956–1981*. St Augustine, Trinidad: Institute of Social and Economic Research, University of the West Indies.

James, C.L.R. 1975. "Cricket," pp. 112–26, in *David Frost Introduces Trinidad and Tobago*, edited by Michael Anthony and Andrew Carr. London: Andrew Deutsch.

—. 1983 [1963]. *Beyond a Boundary*. New York: Pantheon.

Malik, Yogendra K. 1971. *East Indians in Trinidad: a Study in Minority Politics*. New York: Oxford University Press.

Manning, Frank E. 1981. "Celebrating Cricket: the Symbolic Construction of Caribbean Politics," *American Ethnologist*, 8(3): 616–32.

Martindale, Colin A. 1980. "The Role of Sport in Nation Building: a Comparative Analysis of Four Newly Developing Nations in the Commonwealth Caribbean," Unpublished Ph.D. dissertation, City University of New York.

McDonald, Trevor. 1984. *Viv Richards: the Authorised Biography*. London: Pelham Books.

Naipaul, V.S. 1962. *The Middle Passage*. London: Andre Deutsch.

Nicholls, David G. 1971. "East Indians and Black Power in Trinidad," *Race*, 12(4): 283–326.

Oxaal, Ivar. 1968. *Black Intellectuals Come to Power*. Cambridge, MA: Schenkman.

—. 1971. *Race and Revolutionary Consciousness*. Cambridge, MA: Schenkman.

Patterson, Orlando. 1969. "The Ritual of Cricket," *Jamaica Journal*, 3(1): 22–5.

Payne, Antony. 1983. "The Rodney Riots in Jamaica: the Background and Significance of the Events of October 1968," *Journal of Commonwealth and Comparative Politics*, 21(2): 158–74.

Roseberry, William. 1982. "Balinese Cockfights and the Seduction of Anthropology," *Social Research*, 49(4): 1013–28.

Ryan, Selwyn D. 1972. *Race and Nationalism in Trinidad and Tobago*. Toronto: University of Toronto Press.

—. 1979. "Trinidad and Tobago: the General Elections of 1976," *Caribbean Studies*, 19(1–2): 5–32.

St Pierre, Maurice. 1973a. "West Indian Cricket Part I: a Socio-Historical Appraisal," *Caribbean Quarterly*, 19(2): 7–27.

—. 1973b. "West Indian Cricket Part II: an Aspect of Creolization," *Caribbean Quarterly*, 19(2): 20–35.

Sutton, Paul. 1983. "Black Power in Trinidad and Tobago: the 'Crisis' of 1970," *Journal of Commonwealth and Comparative Politics*, 21(2): 115–32.

Thompson, L. O'Brien. 1983. "How Cricket is West Indian Cricket?" *Caribbean Review*, 12(2): 23–5, 50–3.

Yelvington, Kevin A. 1987. "Vote Dem Out: the Demise of the PNM in Trinidad and Tobago," *Caribbean Review*, 15(4): 8–12, 29–33.

14

A purely natural extension: women's cricket in West Indies cricket culture

Hilary McD. Beckles

Viv Richards, West Indian cricket megastar and legend within the global sports culture, in his recently published autobiography described West Indies women's cricket as a 'purely natural extension' of the men's game. Rachel Heyhoe, captain of the 1970 England touring team to the West Indies, identified with this conceptualisation by stating that Jamaican women cricketers, such as Vivalyn Latty-Scott and Dorothy Hobson have the 'same inborn quality of being natural game players as their male counterparts'. Richards, however, recognised that this 'natural' phenomenon has not found popular acceptance within contemporary West Indian nor English ideological conditions. As a result, he called for the removal of discriminatory attitudes and practices against women's cricket by means of the adoption of innovative strategies and non-sexist values.[1]

Such emphasis upon the alleged 'natural' ability of women cricketers and their 'natural' relation to the dominant male cricket culture provides a valuable instance within which the social consequences and ideological effects of patriarchy within West Indian society can be examined. Certainly, women cricketers in the West Indies have long been popularly received as most 'unnatural' persons. They have evoked responses at different levels of communities that suggest their reception as being exotic and spectacular, raising questions concerning their sexual ideologies and proclivities. The popular imagination has not been 'respectful' of their organised activities, which continue to raise eyebrows rather than sponsors and spectators.

These attitudes have contributed to the suppression, textual trivialisation, and gendered distortion of information concerning women's cricket in the region. While being stereotyped as cricket fanatics, West Indian male 'sportists', for example, whose encyclopaedic grasp of cricket matters is well known, are generally 'empty' on the basic and rudimentary information concerning the women's game. While information relevant to the hegemonic men's game has transcended the sports sections of the regional media, competing favourably for prime time and space with corporate and political issues, women's cricket continues to fight for minimal, non-sexist coverage.

While these circumstances provide yet another arena within which the gender consciousness of empowered West Indian males can be explored, they also indicate the degree to which the marginalisation of women in society has been effected through the ideological environment of popular institutions.[2] Since the nineteenth century, West Indian males have seen cricket as an exclusive manifestation of their activated world view. The social consumption and reproduction of its practice is guarded by gendered ideological boundaries that indicate the limits and nature of female involvement. In spite of significant encouragement in recent years by corporate sponsors, women cricketers throughout the region continue to share emotional experiences not dissimilar to those of black male players in the early decades of the century. Treated as 'girls' playing a man's game, women cricketers are, at best, 'tolerated' in their protest against marginalisation by officialdom, which is generally seen as the correct 'political' approach in an increasingly gender sensitive social culture.

So settled within contemporary West Indian male consciousness is the view which says that the social possession of cricket is maintained by their gender enterprise that discourse in relation to ownership patterns have centred exclusively around race and class issues. While black men and white men jostle for position in relation to the historic rights of ownership, women have remained silent with respect to their rights after several decades of participation. For example, a letter entitled 'Away with Cricket' published in the *Dominica Star*, 17 May 1969, stated that black power leaders have urged West Indians to 'throw off the white Imperialist culture and adopt Black African ways', and made reference to the disgrace involved in 'young men who ape their white masters by playing cricket – a truly *whiteman's* game'. The question which followed is even more indicative of the gendered West Indian view: 'Isn't there a good African game our young men could play in the Botanical Gardens on Sundays?' The voice of women with respect to this discourse is not heard though by this time their cricket activity was an established part of popular culture.[3]

The postmodernist discourse within which the colonised 'other' has had new conceptual images of itself thrust upon it, emphasises the superordinate degree to which colonial cultural formations have reflected the liberated consciousness of the European male. The subordination of the white female to the male perception and general objectives of the colonising mission, and the allocation of specific supportive roles to her within the imperium, suggest her overall powerlessness with respect to defining and participating autonomously in the social process of institutional formation.[4]

In the realm of organised cricket leisure, the white woman's role was defined within patriarchal ideology as that of facilitating the building of a family approach to participation which would ensure its popular legitimacy. Cricket was the game of her husband, father, and sons; she was expected to support the moral claims and virtues of the activity, accept her roles as domestic organiser and passive consumer. Furthermore, she was required to surround the game with an aura of respectability that represented a barricade designed to exclude men of other races whose 'hidden' claim to participation was understood by white males as directed at her sexuality. The location of the woman, then, within the early ideological formation of cricket, was understood to be well 'beyond the boundary.'

The domestication of cricket within the socio-political context of the nineteenth-century plantation society, however, provided a politicised arena within which coloured and black men could challenge within the limits of civic society the monopolistic authority of a white planter-merchant oligarchy. The struggle for the democratisation of this elite institution within the undoubtedly superordinate patriarchical colonial West Indian world, therefore, was socially understood as characterised by rivalry between men – the politically enfranchised of European descent and the dispossessed of African descent.

Those who observed the nineteenth century formation understood this competitive encounter, furthermore, as one between men of varying socio-economic standing and ideological interests, and conceived it as consistent with and supportive of, the uncompromising maleness of the plantation mode of production. In addition to all its supposedly moral expressions, cricket embraced the ideological construct of 'manliness' as central to its very essence and meaning. It tolerated, however, with great difficulty and pain, those males who were socially constructed as less than 'men', since it symbolised within the colonial mind the refinement and sophistication of male power and consciousness. Giving support to these ideological forms were concepts of muscular beauty, gentlemanly pride and honour, and most critically, notions of civic duty and social respectability.[5]

Nineteenth-century West Indian cricket, then, by virtue of its location within the matured, creole, plantation culture was a formidable gendered creation. Like other activities in which empowered white males invested considerable social revenue, such as political leadership, corporate management, and intellectual creativity, competitive cricket was promoted as unsuited to women. West Indian men, furthermore, more than other men within the nineteenth-century cricket world, were able to enforce their monopoly of the cricket culture, and in so doing they mirrored the ideological circumstances of the plantation system in which they were bound together as owners, managers, and agents.

It should not be considered phenomenal, then, that white women in the nineteenth-century West Indies did not establish a cricketing culture of their own. While they were often described as colourful spectators at cricket matches, no evidence exists so far to indicate that they ever did play among themselves in an organised fashion. Their English 'cousins', however, were active in this regard since the late eighteenth century. Certainly, the evidence shows that by the 1830s matches were played frequently between 'single' women and 'married' women, and in 1840 the 'Original English Lady Cricketers', two professional teams, the Reds and Blues, toured the country playing exhibition matches.

In spite of some exposure to cricket within the curricula of some West Indian elite schools, white women of propertied families, unlike their male counterparts, did not emulate the cricketing culture of their 'English' cousins. Nothing had changed in the West Indies up to the 1930s, despite major developments in women's cricket throughout the Empire. In 1886, for example, New Zealand women were playing organised matches in the Nelson province, and in 1931 the well developed Australian women's cricket culture witnessed the foundation of the Australian Women's Cricket Council. New Zealand followed with the establishment of their Cricket Council in 1934.[6]

The year 1934 was an eventful one in other respects. Dutch women, long involved in the fledgling cricket culture of continental Europe, moved to establish the All Holland Women's Cricket Association (Nederlandse Dames-Cricket Bond). Their 'sistren' in the West Indies did not follow, and the Dutch colonies of Aruba, Curacao and Surinam experienced no organised women's cricket. Also, in 1934 the first English women's team toured Australia, captained by Betty Archdale, and the first ever Women's Test Match, Australia v. England, was played at Brisbane. In 1935, England toured New Zealand, and in 1937 an Australian touring team visited Holland. In 1952, white women in South Africa and Rhodesia also established Cricket Associations, leaving West Indies women very much an unaccounted element with the imperial cricket culture.

By the 1940s, West Indies white male cricket, after a century of dominance, was on the retreat. Blacks had become the main numerical force in both the inter-colonial contests and the West Indies team. The shifting demographics of West Indies men's cricket undoubtedly had a dampening effect upon whatever initiatives white women would have wished for, and certainly by the end of the war it was clear that the further expansion of West Indies cricket required the social democratisation of its culture. It was at this historical juncture that black and coloured women began to discuss plans for the autonomous organisation of their cricket.

Organised women's cricket in the West Indies, then, awaited the transformative years of the post-war era when the black nationalist and socialist movements finally broke the constitutional power of the ancient imperialism, seized political office, and established the social ethos necessary for a democratising political culture. It was during this period that blacks finally attained leadership of the West Indies men's cricket team – an achievement that required a high profile regional political campaign that insisted upon selection based upon merit rather than criteria of race and class.

It was also a period in which official efforts were made to legitimise and institutionalise the popular culture of the masses. The 'living' culture of the oppressed working people was appropriated and refashioned into something called 'the national identity' – the possession of which was a requirement of all new nation-states. Alongside the dance, song, story telling, and street drama of the communities, in town and country, cricket as a social practice among women was caught in the upsurge of 'recognition' politics. It was now politically right for women's cricket to enter the field.

Though black women's cricket had been visible throughout the West Indies at an earlier period, it was not until 1966 that Jamaican women, who had already established a reputation as leaders in the regional anti-colonial and nationalist movements, took the initiative and established a Women's Cricket Association. This was a critical movement in the social history of West Indies cricket culture. No longer was women's cricket confined to the leisurely pass time within rural villages and urban slums, or seen exclusively as a diversion for middle class women on the grounds of private clubs. It had now moved to secure for itself a reputation of competitive organisation and professionalism.

The specific circumstances that informed the Jamaican case have not been fully documented, but some important things are known. By 1965 there were about thirty to forty women who displayed interest in the game as a profession and a series of friendly matches were arranged on a fairly regular basis. The popularity of these games became so evident that the suggestion was put to Johnny Wong Sam, cricketer-coach-umpire, to facilitate the formation of an association. The result of the meeting was the establishment of the Jamaica Women's Cricket Association (JWCA) on 26 January 1966. The objects of the Association were outlined clearly in the constitution:

(a) To preserve, foster and promulgate the game of Ladies Cricket throughout the Island of Jamaica and to improve the standard of Ladies Cricket in the Island of Jamaica;
(b) To promote and conduct Ladies Cricket in and over the Island of Jamaica;
(c) To prescribe rules of eligibility of participation in games under its own auspices;
(d) To consider and pass upon reports of dishonest, unethical or improper conduct of participants in games and to bar or suspend persons guilty of such conduct from further participation;
(e) To conduct such other activities as may be in keeping with its principal objectives.[7]

First president of the JWCA was Mrs Monica Taylor, an established player, and a prominent upper-class 'coloured' businesswoman. Taylor was an aggressive and determined campaigner who immediately went about the task of putting in place a national infrastructure for women's cricket. In addition, she saw the need for regional organisation and established contacts with women's groups in Trinidad and Tobago, and Barbados. At the end of the 1967 national season, Taylor had secured arrangements for a Jamaica tour to Trinidad, which took place between 4 and 21 February, 1967. Three 'test', and three second-class matches, were played over the 17-day tour. The 'test' series resulted in a draw.

Meanwhile, still in Jamaica, through the efforts of Sally Kennedy, the Diamond Mineral Water Company and the Canada Dry Bottling Company donated trophies – the Ferdie Yap Sam Trophy for the league competition and the Canada Dry Trophy for the knock out competition. These trophies were competed for in 1968 by teams that took the names of their corporate sponsors.[8] Five teams entered the League competition: Kilowatts, Waterwell, Kingston and St Andrew Council (KSAC), Canada Dry, and Diamonds. It was the first showing for the country team Waterwell, which nonetheless gave the more experienced Kingston teams a hard fight, and were in fact the only team to beat Canada Dry, the trophy winners. Immediately after the league competition the five teams competed for the Canada Dry Knock Out Cup and this time the Diamond Team was able to take revenge for their defeat in the league by knocking out both Canada Dry and Waterwell. Bowling and batting averages for the season were dominated by V. Latty and S. Kennedy respectively (see tables 14.1 and 14.2).

Table 14.1 *Averages for 1968 JWCA season, batting*

Names	Team	No. innings	Times not out	Total runs	Highest score	Ave
S. Kennedy	Diamond	8	3	180	45*	36.0
A. Brown	Canada Dry	7	3	116	34	29.0
Z. Plummer	Waterwell	6	1	125	40*	25.0
M. Powell	Canada Dry	5	1	95	52	23.5
A. Innis	Canada Dry	6	1	90	54*	18.0
M. Taylor	Kilowatts	7	1	105	32*	17.5
I. Morgan	Diamond	3	–	48	25	16.0
J. Cadogan	Diamond	7	2	83	30*	16.6
B. Williams	Canada Dry	6	–	84	25	14.0
V. Latty	Canada Dry	7	1	85	33	14.8

Note: *denotes 'not out'.
Source: The West Indian Sportsman, December–January 1969/70.

Table 14.2 *Averages for 1968 JWCA season, bowling*

Names	Team	Overs	Runs	Wickets	Ave
V. Latty	Canada Dry	67.4	96	29	3.3
B. Alexander	Canada Dry	12	44	8	5.5
M. Diah	Diamond	100.5	141	24	5.8
L. Noble	Waterwell	95	143	22	6.5
M. Laurence	Diamond	63	150	21	7.1
Y. McLean	Canada Dry	42.2	76	10	7.6
N. Wright	Waterwell	35	48	6	8.0
E. Boyle	Kilowatts	23	63	7	9.0
M. McCalla	Waterwell	43	103	11	9.4
A. Brown	Canada Dry	53.1	125	13	9.6

Source: The West Indian Sportsman, December–January 1969/70.

Jamaica, furthermore, under the leadership of Taylor, led West Indies Women's Cricket into another era – that of the extra-regional and international game. By 1970, while women in Barbados, Grenada, St Vincent, Guyana, and St Lucia were making efforts to put their own game on a similar organisational standard to Jamaica, and Trinidad and Tobago, the JWCA had already finalised plans for an inaugural 'test' series against England in Jamaica. The English team, led by Rachel Heyhoe, and managed by Derief Taylor, a Jamaican who coached youth players at Warwickshire, arrived in Jamaica on 15 January, 1970 to play in three two-day 'test' matches. Arrangements were also made for the visitors to play one-day games against established League teams at 'country' venues.[9]

The first 'test' at Sabina Park was attended by some 6,000 spectators on the second day. Among these was the legendary West Indies star of the inter-war era, George Headley, who told the *Sunday Gleaner* that 'if women's cricket continues in the same trend then there is every indication that not only the West Indies but Jamaica will have people who love cricket flocking the cricket grounds of the world'.[10] 'Strebor', the sports columnists for the *Sunday Gleaner* reported:

> Some of the catching I have seen by the women of both sides should be an object lesson for the butter-fingered male cricketers. Another lesson for the men was the use of the feet in getting to the pitch of the ball. It was nice to watch the women as they danced down the wicket to make their shots.[11]

Rachel Heyhoe, the England Captain (who arrived with an experience of 15 tests) describing the tour, commented:

> It was such a delight to play in front of such fanatical crowds. At test matches in England we often struggle to get 1,000 spectators to the series. I can honestly say that I have never played in front of such a large crowd as the 6,000 fans who greeted us all at Sabina Park. It was marvelous to be accepted as an international cricket team rather than a team of peculiar women playing cricket, which is so often the reaction of the public in the other countries, which I have toured.[12]

Heyhoe, however, would have recognised that both teams did attract a different set of responses 'beyond the boundary'. On Saturday, 17 January, for example, the teams paid a courtesy visit to a KSAC Public Health Department. A sports reporter for the *Saturday Star* described the experience in the following terms:

> Male attention was distracted when the girls . . . walked into the Council Chambers. The girls showed that their shapely legs were not only to be seen on the cricket field but even in ordinary clothes. Their mini and near micro-mini skirts were to be thanked for this. Councillor Rose Leon, perhaps sensing that her male counterparts were too tongue-tied and spellbound *to say* anything, welcomed the cricketers'.[13]

Councillor Leon expressed her admiration for the women in 'taking up the difficult task of cricket' and indicated her respect for their 'courage' in doing so. Though England were the clear favourites to win the series all three test matches were drawn. The Jamaican team, however, seemed ready for further 'test' status contests.

The next opportunity for a 'test' encounter came the following year with another visit from the English team. This time the English won the three-match series 1–0, taking the Pearl and Dean trophy. On this tour the English team also visited Bermuda and the Bahamas before moving on to Trinidad (with the Jamaica team) to take part in a triangular tournament for the Jack Hayward trophy. This contest was won by Trinidad. In May, 1973, the Australian team, on its way to England for the first Women's World Cup championship, in which Jamaica was also a participant, stopped off in Jamaica to play a three-match series with the national team. Both teams used the opportunity to get into shape for this pioneering international event. Playing for the World Cup, which started on 20 June, were teams drawn from Jamaica, Australia, Trinidad and Tobago, New Zealand, England and an Invitation team that consisted of two players from each of the competing countries. In addition to the 'A' team of England, a 'Young England' eleven also contested. The declared favourites to enter the finals of the World Cup were England and Australia. This perception proved correct, and England succeeded in defeating the Aussies in the final at Edgbaston. The two teams from the West Indies were not very highly rated.

1973 World Cup results of matches played by Jamaica, and Trinidad and Tobago

23.6.73	Jamaica v. New Zealand	No play – rain	Hove
23.6.73	Trinidad & Tobago v. New Zealand	New Zealand won by 136 runs	St Albans
30.6.73	Jamaica v. Young England	Jamaica won by 23 runs	Sittingbourne
30.6.73	Trinidad & Tobago v. Australia	Australia won by 7 wickets	Tring
4.7.73	Trinidad & Tobago v. Jamaica	Jamaica won by 2 wickets	Ealing
7.7.73	Jamaica v. England	England won by 63 runs	Bradford
11.7.73	Jamaica v. Australia	Australia won by 77 runs	York
14.7.73	Jamaica v. International XI	International XI won by 5 wickets	Leicester
14.7.73	Trinidad & Tobago v. Young England	Trinidad & Tobago won by 5 wickets	Cambridge
18.7.73	Trinidad & Tobago v. International XI	International XI won by 7 wickets	Liverpool
20.7.73	Trinidad & Tobago v. England	England won by 8 wickets	Wolverhampton

Source: England Women's Cricket Association; World Cup Competition 1973: Official Report.

Of more importance, however, for the spread of women's cricket throughout the region, was the first ever Caribbean double-wicket competition which was played in November 1973 at the Kensington Oval and Carlton Cricket Club in Barbados. These contests were part of the country's 7th Independence Anniversary Celebration.[14] Five countries, Jamaica, Guyana, St Lucia, Trinidad (excluding Tobago) and Barbados, guests of the Barbados Women's Cricket Association, met to compete in the historic contest. Two teams from Barbados were declared and the 'A' team won the championship from the 'B' team in a four-over play-off final after both teams tied at the top of the points chart with eight points at the end of the fifth and final round. Jamaica finished in third place with six points, while Guyana collected four. Trinidad and St Lucia failed to score any points.

Participants in the 1973 Double-wicket Contest (Barbados)

Country		Players
Barbados	A-team	Angela Harris
		Pat Whittaker
	B-team	Janet Selman
		Janet Mitchell
Jamaica		Vivalyn Latty-Scott
		Evelyn Boyle
Guyana		Fay Cadogan
		Daphne Batson
Trinidad		Florence Woods
		Menota Tekah
St Lucia		Francisca Didier
		Priscilla Phillip

With Jamaica, and Trinidad and Tobago, operating at the international level as separate teams, West Indies cricket was unable to impose its authority on the playing field. Opinion in the region, as a result, moved in favour of a united West Indies team as a remedial measure. Before such an institution could be established, however, it was necessary to put in place a vibrant regional competition in order to expand the catchment and make meaningful selections.

Jamaica, and Trinidad and Tobago became members of the International Women's Cricket Council (IWCC) in 1973 in order to participate in the World Cup that year, but as the game grew in popularity so did the cost of hosting tours and sending teams abroad. Against this background a meeting was held in St Lucia on 25 May, 1973, with representatives from Barbados, Grenada, Jamaica, St Lucia, and Trinidad and Tobago, in order to establish a regional framework for women's cricket. In 1975 the Caribbean Women's Cricket Federation (CWCF) was formed as the vehicle on which women's cricket would travel into the future.[15]

At the 1973 meeting, the opinions and visions of veterans and newcomers alike were discussed. From Jamaica, the now legendary Monica Taylor, and the distinguished Vivalyn Latty-Scott and Dorothy Hobson, were prime-movers in this organisational development. The objectives of the CWCF were specified; to make tours more affordable, by sharing costs; to develop a West Indies Team; and to promote more interesting cricket.

It was a meeting of historical significance. Delegates decided that the body would become affiliated to the IWCC as a group, host regional competitions between countries every two years, and select a West Indies team, based on the results of each competition. Monica Taylor was elected President and served until 1982. It was also agreed to have tournaments at the following venues: 1975 Barbados, Grenada, and Trinidad and Tobago; 1977 Grenada; 1980 Guyana; 1982 Jamaica; and 1988 Trinidad and Tobago. Barbados won the first encounter, and held proud the Monica Taylor Trophy. Trinidad and Tobago won the four subsequent encounters.[16]

The leadership of the CWCF showed both vision and determination. At the Second Conference of Delegates held in Port-of-Spain on 12 July, 1975, involving member countries Barbados, Jamaica, Trinidad and Tobago, and Grenada, the decision was taken to select the first West Indies woman's cricket team for international competition in 1976. The final selection was made on 27 October, 1975, after the Jamaica v. Barbados match at Kensington Oval.

First selected West Indies Women's Cricket Team (1976)

Name	Country	Description
Beverley Broan	Trinidad & Tobago	Middle order bat, medium pacer
Dorothy Hobson	Jamaica	Leg spinner, middle order bat
Gloria Gill	Barbados	Opening bat, reserve keeper
Louise Brown* (captain)	Trinidad & Tobago	Opening bat
Sherill Bayley	Barbados	Front line bat, leg spinner
Jasmine Sammy	Trinidad & Tobago	Opening bat
Grace Williams	Jamaica	Pace bowler, middle order bat
Janet Mitchell	Barbados	All rounder
Peggy Fairweather	Jamaica	Pace bowler
Angela Harris	Barbados	Right arm medium pacer, left hand bat
Nora St. Rose	Trinidad & Tobago	Pace bowler
Vivalyn Latty-Scott	Jamaica	All rounder
Pat Whittaker (Vice-captain)	Barbados	Pace bowler, good bat
Yolande Hall	Jamaica	Wicket-keeper/bat
Joan Alexander	Grenada	Wicket-keeper/bat
Menota Tekah	Trinidad & Tobago	All rounder

The Executive of the Federation knew of Australia's intention to visit England during 1976 to participate in England's women's cricket Jubilee Celebrations, and immediately extended an invitation to them, to travel to England by way of the Caribbean, and engage the West Indies Team in three two-day 'tests.' It was agreed that the series would take place in Jamaica during April in order to facilitate the travel plans of the Australian visitors. In a keenly contested series, all three matches were drawn – again largely on account of insufficient time.

By 1976, then, the organisational infrastructure had reached a level of sophistication, and presented players and spectators alike with opportunities to promote the culture of women's cricket. 'West Indies Cricket Ladies Team', playing under the auspices of the CWCF, was now in place. Tours were arranged to India at the end of 1976, and to England in 1979. An earlier series which was scheduled against England was cancelled because of the participation of some of the English players in South Africa. They drew the 1976 six-test series against India 1-1, and lost the 1979 three-test tour against England 1–0. Since then the West Indies women's team has become a regional institution, though not reaching anywhere near the popularity or international standing as its male counterpart.

The considerable achievements of women's cricket administrators and players have not brought them into a close working relationship with their counterparts in the men's game. They have never sat in session with the West Indies Cricket Board of Control (WICBC) to discuss matters of common interest. Neither has the WICBC expressed a policy position with regard to the active promotion of women's cricket. In individual territories, officials of men's cricket have expressed irritation over adjustment in competition schedules resulting from women's request for the use of first-class grounds and other facilities.

Women cricketers, in addition, have good reason to see the WICBC as a bastion of unsupportive male power within the region's cricket culture, a perception that has not elicited any significant comments from executive officers. Indeed, when, a few years ago, the WICBC advertised a vacancy in the regional press for a public relations administrator the wording of the job description was made explicitly male centred. This raised some critical comments from a woman's action group in Trinidad, but the WICBC saw no need to explain an already clear position. In addition, since the 1970s women players throughout the region have protested the practice of not inviting females to the prestigious annual dinner function of the WICBC.

The institutional discrimination against women cricketers, furthermore, is deeply ingrained within the culture of club cricket. For some players, it has been accepted as a way of life rather than an area of social exchange desperately in need of political struggle and social redress. This can be identified at both the level of the village club and the international test venues In Jamaica, for instance, the Kingston Cricket Club that manages Sabina Park, the well-known cricket venue, has maintained the century-old policy of not allowing women to use as equals the facilities of the members' pavilion. The members' bar, for instance, is considered off limits to women – even though they may be West Indies players. The same is true also for Queens Park Cricket Club in Trinidad. Indeed, it was only in the 1980s that this policy, or custom, was fully removed from the Pickwick Cricket Club that manages the members' facilities at Kensington Oval in Barbados.

Though many former West Indies men players, such as Allan Rae, Jackie Hendricks, Michael Holding, Viv Richards and Gordon Greenidge have taken time out to support and encourage women's cricket, and thereby seeking to gain greater official and governmental support for it, the evidence continues to indicate general male disinterest. When, for example, in 1989 Barbados lost the charismatic energy of cricketing star Angela Harris, the national game sunk into disrepair, and has not recovered sufficiently to supply players to recent West Indies teams. The Barbados government, well known for its generous contribution to men's cricket, has made no significant investments towards its revival. It is not seen, according to a government official, as a priority area within the promotion of sport; more media and resource attention being given to golf, surfing, tennis, motor racing, and soccer.

Starved of adequate financial resources and denied easy access to first-class institutional facilities, West Indies women cricketers are asked, nonetheless, to perform within the international arena at the level now expected of their male counterparts. That West Indies men cricketers have dominated the international game since the 1970s has therefore placed considerable pressure upon the women's team. Dorothy Hobson, manager of the West Indies team during the 1993 World Cup Championship in England, indicated that spectators, particularly West Indians, found it difficult to accept their defeats in matches against England and Australia. Their attitudes, she surmised, were informed from experiences and observations derived from the men's game. Indeed, she stated, the media and English cricket officials expected the West Indies women to be a team of superstars by virtue of their being 'West Indian'. It is noteworthy, furthermore, that as West Indies women suffered a series of defeats they became the 'darlings' of the section of the same British press that has long questioned the professional ethics of West Indies male stars and teams.

West Indies female stars, while cognisant of the inadequacy of professional relations with their male counterparts, have had no difficulty in admitting that their role models are more male than female. They speak more passionately of the exploits of male players than their own, indicative of the effect of popular culture upon subjective consciousness. Grace Williams, the legendary Jamaican/West Indies fast bowler of the 1970s, for example, admits that as a young girl she was 'hypnotised' by the fast bowling skills of West Indies stars – Wes Hall and Charlie Griffith. She sought to model her style upon Griffith, and even 'part' her hair in the middle to 'resemble' him. He was her hero, and fast bowling became her love on account of the artistic beauty of the physical explosion involved.[17] She admits to learning her cricket within the social context of the male game, and as a result identification with its heroes seemed inevitable – the ultimate ideological success of male hegemony.

To some extent, the resource insufficiency and press indifference that contribute towards the suppression of West Indies woman's cricket have to do with its class characteristics. Whereas the administration of West Indies men's cricket has remained within the hands of the propertied white and 'near' white coloured elites – which constitutes a marked contrast to the working-class nature of the team – women cricketers and administrators (since the pioneering years of Monica Taylor) have been drawn predominantly from the black working class and lower middle class. Women's cricket, therefore, represents a more democratic and egalitarian institutional culture, and is not haunted by the class and race considerations that continue to feature so prominently in the ideological discourse and social practices of men's cricket. These sociological processes within women's cricket culture have problematised easy access to large-scale corporate funding, state resources, and supportive media attention. It is particularly striking in small West Indian societies the manner in which access to institutional power and media support vary in direct proportion to relation and proximity to elite groups.

The overtly gendered responses of men, particularly sports journalists, have also had a telling effect upon the emotional and professional attitudes of women cricketers. C.L.R. James, the distinguished doyen of West Indies cricket scholarship, who chronicled in several dozen treatises the ideological evolution of its social culture, offered no opinions and concepts of women's intervention and contribution essentially because his vision was 'seduced' by the intellectual attractiveness of early Victorian cricket philosophy. The social elements within this scholarship are the curricula of elite boys grammar schools, English literature within which the gentleman-scholar-sportsman concept was constructed, the impact of the Adamite image of W.G. Grace, and the politics of the struggle to liberate the black male player from a bankrupt planter-merchant managerial authority. Tony Becca, for example, a leading regional sports writer, while reporting the performance of Trinidad and Tobago's Shirley Bonaparte (in a Championship game against Jamaica) described her as 'a confident player who bats with the skill of many men'. The 1973 Women's World Cup brochure which was produced in England carried an advertisement by Kendall Travel Services with a picture of little boys (not girls) playing cricket, under the caption: *'Another Gary Sobers/Given Time He Could Well Be – We All Have to Start at the Bottom before We Can Get to the Top'.*

The bottom, for women, historically, has been those 'special' places where social services are rendered with little or no social honour and financial remuneration. Not surprisingly, the 'bottom' within the cricket culture has been disproportionately inhabited by women. The tea ladies, the nut sellers, the honorary treasurer/secretaries, scorers, commentators, and more recently, second-class match umpires are now established icons within the cricket world. Often times the view is expressed that club members should elect/select female secretary/treasurers on the basis that they are less likely than men to raid and disappear with club revenues. On the other hand, the view is seldom expressed that women should be elected presidents and managers of these institutions. The number of women's roles, then, have increased considerably, but their general locations remain the same.

In addition to these popular social consequences of patriarchal consciousness, the ideological effects within the public media have been overtly hostile to women's search for institutional respectability. The definition and categorisation of women's discourse as devoid of vigour, ideological clarity, and internal intellectual integrity, present the context for the denigration of its sub-text. In 1973, for example, on the eve of Jamaica's departure to this World Cup, difficulties erupted within the executive of the Women's Cricket Association. Board discussions over the resolution of these difficulties were reported in the *Daily Gleaner* by Buz Freckleton under a headline 'Women's Cricket Cas Cas'. Here, Freckleton referred to the debate as 'cas cas' and 'su su', which in national parlance means gossip, malicious slander, loud invective and quarrelling – all supportive evidence, he states, that 'Hell hath no fury like a woman's scorn'.

West Indies cricket, then, originated and matured within the context of a white-male dominated plantation society. In this ideological world women – white, coloured, and black were socially ostracised from autonomous involvement in civic institutions through which the values of elitism, public authority and respectability were transmitted and represented. Cricket was conceived by propertied elite males as a principal instrument of their dominance within the sphere of leisure/social recreation.

West Indian white women, unlike those elsewhere in the Empire, did not, or could not, challenge the right of white males to monopolise such a universally respected institution. Organised women's cricket, then, emerged within the West Indies as a social expression of the black community during the post-war years. Black men had challenged white men to democratise the structures of the organised game since the late nineteenth century, creating the context within which the community as a whole could embrace and promote it as popular culture. In spite of their own struggle for participation, black men came to consider cricket as a principal index of their own achievements, and have enforced gender values and attitudes designed to marginalise the autonomous women's game. Women, then, are involved in a struggle to legitimise their activity within a male-centred social world that sees them as competitors.

NOTES

1 Viv Richards, *Hitting Across the Line* (London, Headline Books, 1992), p. 198; 'Magical Mystery Cricket Tour', by Rachel Heyhoe, in *the West Indian Sportsman*, March–April, 1970.
2 See Stephanie L. Twin, 'Women in Sport', in Donald Spivey (ed.), *Sport in America: New Historical Perspectives* (New York, Greenwood Press, 1985), pp. 193–219. Jack Scott, 'A Radical Ethic for Sports', *Intellectual Digest*, 2, No. 11, July 1992, pp. 49–50; Darlene Kelly, 'Women in Sports', *Women: a Journal of Liberation*, Vol. 3, No. 2, p. 16.
3 *Dominica Star*, 17 May, 1969.
4. See Bill Ashcroft (*et al.*) eds, *The Empire Writes Back: Theory and Practice in Post-Colonial Literatures* (London, Routledge, 1989), pp. 2–15; Richard Holt, *Sport and the British: a Modern History* (Oxford, Clarendon Press, 1989), pp. 204–23.
5 See Jennifer Hargreaves, 'Where's the Virtue? Where Is the Grace? A Discussion of the Social Production of Gender through Sport', *Theory, Culture and Society*, Vol. 3, No. 1, 1986; J.A. Mangan, 'Gentlemen Galore', *Immigrants and Minorities*, July 1982, pp. 154–5; K.A Sandiford, 'Cricket and the Barbadian Society', *Canadian Journal of History*, December 1986, pp. 367–8; K. Moore, 'Sport, Politics and Imperialism', in Proceedings of the Fourth Annual Conference of the British Society of Sport History, 1986, pp. 46–57. C.L.R. James, *Beyond a Boundary* (London, Hutchinson, 1963).
6 See K.E. McCrone, "Play Up! Play Up! and Play the Game! Sport at the Late Victorian Girl's Public School', *Journal of British Studies*, Vol. 23, Spring 1984; K.E. McCrone,

'The "Lady Blue": Sport at the Oxbridge Women's Colleges from their Foundation to 1914', *British Journal of Sport History (BJSH)*, Vol. 3, September 1986; Jennifer Hargreaves, 'Playing like Gentlemen While Behaving like Ladies: Contradictory Features of the Formative Years of Women's Sport', *BJSH*, Vol. 2, May 1985.

7 'History of Women's Cricket in Jamaica' in the official brochure, *Jamaica v. Australia*; *Women's Cricket Series*, 29 May–5 June 1973.

8 'History of Women's Cricket in Jamaica', in *Inaugural International Womens Cricket Series: Souvenir Programme, January 1970*; '1968 Women's Cricket: Ferdie Yap Sam Trophy', *The West Indian Sportsman*, December–January 1969-70.

9 *The Daily Gleaner* (Jamaica), January 16, 1970; see also, *The West Indian Sportsman*, March–April, 1970.

10 *Gleaner*, 18 January 1970.

11 *Ibid.*

12 *The West Indian Sportsman*, March–April, 1970.

13 *Star*, 17 January 1970.

14 *Advocate News* (Barbados), 30 November, 1973.

15 'Caribbean Women's Cricket Federation', in *Caribbean Women's Cricket Federation: Inaugural Test Series, West Indies vs. Australia*, May 1–17, 1976 (official brochure).

16 'Background on the Jamaica Women's Cricket Association/CWCF', in brochure, Caribbean Women's Cricket Competition (1989).

17 'Grace Williams', in Carribean Women's Cricket Competition; brochure, 1989.

Part IV

Nationalism and liberation

15

Caribbean cricket: the role of sport in emerging small-nation politics

Brian Stoddart

On 29 June 1950 a team of cricketers playing as the 'West Indies' beat England in a test match for the first time since their accession to international status in 1928. The victory was all the more historic for being recorded at Lord's, the London ground dubbed the Cathedral of Cricket.[1] As the last English wicket fell to produce the win, those at the ground witnessed a 'rush of West Indian supporters, one armed with an instrument of the guitar family'.[2] That was Lord Kitchener, the famous calypsonian from Trinidad whose words and music led the celebrations in honour of a new cricket power, for West Indies went on to win two more tests and so the series that summer. For the cricket world it was the moment when the name West Indies began to evoke images of rum, calypso, and exciting play. But there was another dimension, too, missed by many outsiders: the rich political vein within Caribbean cricket which was both an inheritance of empire and a prophecy for independence.

This chapter sketches some of the political richness inherent in Caribbean cricket, and it is important to note that it is really a discussion of the game's political culture. While in recent years there has been an increase in the number of works devoted to what is loosely described as 'sport and politics', little of that material has proceeded from a base in political theory.[3] It has been overwhelmingly descriptive, seizing upon sport as an interesting political sidelight or political issue. That has been most noticeable in political coverage of the Olympic Games, for example – it is as if the 'politics' come around only every fourth year.[4] Much of the writing on sports politics, then, might fairly be described as incident based, providing little in the way of continuing momentum or accumulating knowledge. There are exceptions, of course, but they generally serve to demonstrate the rule. This Caribbean case study suggests, however, that it is more fruitful to approach sport as a constant and complex political factor inextricably bound up with the cultural evolution of the society within which it is located. That is, it is not so much the facts of political history which determine the political nature of sport (development of constitutions, suffrage, parties, and so on) as the cultural history of which it is part.

The composition of that victorious West Indies team, to begin with, symbolized the Caribbean colonial inheritance. There were three players from Jamaica, now just over an hour's flying time from Miami and less from Havana (to highlight the regional political variety). One came from British Guiana, the only British possession on the South American continent and surrounded by Venezuela, Dutch Guiana (now Suriname), and Brazil. Jamaica and BG, as it was known, were well over 1,000 miles apart so that these 'West Indian' players very rarely saw each other except for a limited number of inter-colonial encounters and the even more limited number of overseas tours. Another six players came from Barbados, a tiny 21 by 14 mile island out on the Atlantic side of the Caribbean island chain and the second oldest British possession in the world. The remaining six cricketers came from Trinidad, one of the truly multicultural countries in the world, which lies to the south west of Barbados.

That distribution points immediately to the need to qualify the use of the term 'Caribbean cricket'. The game was clearly restricted to the English-speaking sections of the Caribbean and was dominated for a long time by its major population centres. And while the passion for cricket was prominent in all centres, it was more highly developed in some than in others. As a longtime British dependency it was (and remains) appropriate that Barbados constituted *the* great cricket centre with the game spread all over the island. In Jamaica, however, partly because of a more difficult geography and partly because of a more mixed historical evolution, the game was more centralized in Kingston.[5] 'Caribbean cricket' is a useful generic term, then, but should be used in the knowledge of the quite distinct patterns within the region.

Team photographs of 1950 reveal men of very different skin colours whose names reflected the diverse cultural backgrounds from whence they came and which were the products of colonialism: Gomez, Pierre, Christiani, and Ramadhin (the first man of East Indian descent to play for West Indies), to name a few. The captain was John Goddard, a white Barbadian whose family rose from obscure origins to become one of the island's major trading houses. His vice-captain was Jeff Stollmeyer, another white man of German and English descent whose family became business and political leaders in Trinidad.[6] The great stars of the team were the 'three Ws': Worrell, Weekes, and Walcott, darker coloured men from Barbados with the first two of humble origins and the last from a lower middle-class family.[7] These backgrounds are important because they indicate the only real common reference shared by all these men in cricket: the political economy of slavery and sugar and its postcolonial consequences. From the middle of the seventeenth century these British Caribbean territories produced sugar for the world's metropolitan markets aided by the labour of black slaves taken from Africa. By the early nineteenth century a minority of whites controlled commercial and political life while the majority black populations maintained the production.[8]

Relatively few alterations occurred in that economic relationship after the abolition of the slave trade in the British territories in 1807 and the final freeing of all slaves in 1838. There were some significant cultural shifts, however, in a region where British, French, Dutch, Spanish, and Portuguese influences had all been felt at some stage. During the middle of the nineteenth century, for example, indentured labourers from India and China were engaged to replace the lost black slaves, especially in British Guiana and Trinidad, and this would serve in time to render even more complex the search for a Caribbean identity.[9] (One of Trinidad's best-loved cricketers of the 1940s and 1950s was Rupert Tang Choon of Chinese and black extraction.) The rise of cricket in the second half of the nineteenth century, then, coincided with the crucial post-emancipation period which was marked by significant social realignments within the individual colonies themselves and by a new awareness of the necessity for an elaborated regional outlook. Inevitably, a significant institution like cricket became a political consideration in and of itself within this shifting cultural environment.

By the turn of the twentieth century cricket had become an obsession throughout the British West Indies and has largely remained so.[10] Early English touring sides were astonished by the interest their visits aroused, inter-colonial matches were occasions for public holidays, the game was a major topic of conversation and public discussion, cricketers were pre-eminent public figures, and when the 1950 side returned to the Caribbean it landed first in Barbados where yet another public holiday was declared. In 1954 the timing of the ceremony to grant ministerial government in Barbados would be altered so as not to interfere with a major match, and on the same island independence itself in 1966 was marked by a cricket match.[11] In the Caribbean today politicians of all persuasions have an interest in cricket with at least two of them, Wesley Hall in Barbados and Roy Fredericks in Guyana, being former prominent test players while Michael Manley, former prime minister of Jamaica, has now written a history of Caribbean cricket.[12] In Barbados it is said that if you want to see every politician and public servant at the one time, go to the members' stand at Kensington Oval during an international match.

The root of this passion was a conjunction of circumstances which guaranteed that cricket in the English-speaking islands would become more than a game. For one thing, cricket was synonymous throughout the British empire with the concept of fair play.[13] The English language itself reflected this: 'it's not cricket' described something unfair, 'caught out' meant to be discovered in a transgression, and 'playing by the rules' meant to observe social etiquette and rules of behaviour. Given that late nineteenth-century Caribbean society was preoccupied with community-building and social ordering (and what Norbert Elias would later term the 'civilizing process'), such a game was a powerful instrument in the hands of those directing such realignments.[14]

Conversely, of course, to excel at cricket became an objective for those people in the lower orders who sought an accommodation with the ruling elite. That led directly to the creation of clubs organized on the basis of social ranking rather than playing ability with colour, education, and wealth being the intertwined determinants of membership.[15] Where Chinese and Indians were numerous, separate leagues were even established,[16] while in Barbados lower-class blacks eventually had to establish a competition of their own – their class position excluded them from the regular cricket culture. Even the very construction of cricket teams and competitions, then, developed from the political conditions left by slavery and emancipation.

What gave the game commonality was its emergence from the British athletic revolution of the late nineteenth century, allied with the ease of its being played in the Caribbean.[17] Because cricket was considered such a benchmark of English culture and civilized behaviour, the Caribbean communities naturally turned to it in their search for cultural distinction. And it did not demand the use of sophisticated equipment to learn its basics. Many stars learned their skills with a rough piece of wood and either a breadfruit or rolled-up rags.[18]

From the first appearance of the game in the islands, its local devotees harboured the ambition of beating the mother country to demonstrate colonial progress. Of course, that attitude varied from group to group within the regional cricket hierarchy. The early bosses were whites from the plantation and commercial elite whose families had been among the founders and early developers of the West Indian colonies and whose objectives were to reproduce English society and culture in what were seen as the outposts of empire. These were anglophiles like Sir Harold Austin, considered the 'father' of West Indian cricket and a prominent political-commercial figure in Barbados until his death in 1943.[19] By contrast, among the early stars were men like Herman Griffith, the Barbadian and West Indian fast bowler of the inter-war years whose experience of whites (and blacks) in authority gave him a fierce desire to beat them overwhelmingly at cricket.[20] This pattern was strongly political, emanating as it did from a system of social ordering and the shaping of social relations in which cricket played a principal role. It was inevitable that the politicization of West Indian cricket should spill over into the realms of nationalism, ideology, party politics, and international relations.

The first important manifestation of this process came with the rise to prominence of Learie (later Sir and finally Lord) Constantine who played for West Indies in the first official test match of 1928 and who continued to play with distinction until 1939.[21] His great-grandparents on both sides had been among the last African slaves shipped to Trinidad before abolition and his father, a cocoa plantation worker, toured England with the first West Indian team to go there in 1900. Constantine left school for a law office and became an outstanding cricketer, being selected in 1923 to tour England where some critics thought him already a great player, a reputation enhanced by a further tour five years later. His turning point came with an appointment as a professional cricketer with the Nelson club in the Lancashire League, one of the first of many West Indians who have joined sub-county competition in England. While Constantine's time in Nelson was largely happy, it was also there that he learned about illusion and reality in the social side of cricket. While he was accepted as a fine player, that did not mean he was immediately accepted as a social equal. To be blunt, he discovered that there was as much discrimination in English cricket as there was in Trinidad, and that colour was the common cause. The discovery heightened his political consciousness, and he began to campaign for social and political change in the West Indies. He was assisted in his work by C.L.R. James who joined Constantine in England during 1932.

James is a remarkable figure not only in the West Indian literature but also in that of sport and politics generally.[22] In his 1963 autobiography, *Beyond A Boundary*, he laid out a powerful analysis of the relationship between sport and political culture, an analysis moulded by his personal history as a Marxist. Since the 1920s his cricket writings have been shaped by political experience, and it has been to the detriment of many working in the field of sport and politics that they have discovered him so late or, even worse, have yet to do so.[23] Born in Trinidad in 1901 he was a lower middle-class, brown-skinned scholarship winner to the island's premier educational institution. A very fine player close to inter-colonial standard, his love of English cricket was complicated by his desire for political independence from Britain. By the time he joined Constantine, James's position on the left had been fully delineated.

The importance of the activity undertaken by Constantine and James was that the late 1920s and early 1930s marked the beginnings of organized political movements in the English-speaking Caribbean and of concomitant demands for political reform involving increased popular responsibility.[24] It was best symbolized, perhaps, in the work of Marcus Garvey whose United Negro Improvement Association had a major influence not only in the Caribbean but also in the United States. Additionally, though, more localized figures and movements started questioning the social order which had developed during the previous one hundred years. By the later 1930s the new sentiments were being expressed through labour union disturbances and political agitation in Barbados, Trinidad, St Lucia, Jamaica, and other centres. While local power elites were reluctant to relinquish much of their authority, Labour party pressure in Britain helped prompt official and unofficial inquiries into West Indian affairs.[25] These reviews created a growing recognition that political dependence, a weakening economic position, and often quite appalling social conditions were a potential source of major disturbance.

Constantine, unlike his friend and collaborator James, never advocated radical or revolutionary activity and in that represented visibly in Britain the mainstream of what constituted nationalist sentiment within West Indian politics. A good example of such moderate opinion was Sir Grantley Adams in Barbados.[26] A lawyer, Adams played one inter-colonial match as a wicket-keeper and was a long-standing member of the Spartan club which served the cricket and social needs of the rising black middle class from the 1890s onwards. Throughout his career as chief minister in Barbados and then as prime minister of the ill-fated West Indian federation, Adams constantly followed a moderate line as the widening franchise gave political voice to a larger cross-section of the public. By the time John Goddard's men won that 1950 series, politicians such as Adams had begun taking the Caribbean colonies towards independence, but they were facing competition from increasingly radical politicians. While the moderates saw the victory as proof of increased standards and social progress, the more radical saw it as confirmation that the West Indian polities were ready for immediate change.

Against that dual background it is useful to review the common claim that cricket has been a force for integration within the West Indian geopolitical region, the one social institution in which all classes and colours could meet to promote a common cause and identity.[27] At one level that is a valid view, but at another it is quite misleading. From the beginning the very composition of representative teams was highly charged, with each colony claiming that its players were being discriminated against. For a long time the criteria for selection included not only ability but also colonial origin: there must never be too many Guyanese or Jamaicans or whomever else. And for a similarly long time the politics of colour were particularly delicate. There were a considerable number of hesitations and resentments at work within the successful Goddard team, for example, even though the popular vision was of a strongly united team. Goddard himself had a reputation for anti-black sentiments, and the Barbadian black stars had bitter memories of some of his actions as leader of the island team.[28] The whites constituted the authority bloc within the 1950 team, a condition resented by someone like Frank Worrell who was recognized around the world not only as a very fine player but as the possessor of a highly astute cricket mind. The West Indian team, then, had the capacity to be the most internally divided of any international team, and that to a large degree paralleled the status of West Indian political development by the early 1950s.

While an extreme case in some respects, developments in British Guiana provide a good indication of the tensions.[29] The colony received its first elected parliamentary majority in 1943 and by 1952 had universal adult suffrage along with a constitution allowing for popular elections. It also had the People's Progressive Party (PPP) which won the first elections in 1953 led by the two men who were to dominate political life in Guyana for the next thirty years: Dr Cheddi Jagan and Forbes Burnham. Within a few months the constitution had been suspended, British troops were in residence, and considerable political tension was evident which resulted in Jagan seceding from the PPP to form a party comprised largely of Indians, leaving Burnham with a predominantly black one. Similar battles were proceeding in Jamaica where Alexander Bustamante and his cousin, Norman Manley, ended up leading separate labour parties with Bustamante adopting a strong anti-communist stance.[30] Violence was not uncommon in these political contests, Bustamante openly admitting to carrying a gun. Given the state of the domestic political climate, the social significance of cricket and the importance attached to it by the public as well as these leaders and others, it was probably inevitable that the 1953–4 English tour of the Caribbean would become highly controversial.

Because West Indies had beaten England in 1950 and England had defeated Australia in 1953, cricket fans in the Caribbean and elsewhere pointed to the 1953–4 tour as the decider for an unofficial 'world championship'.[31] That was given some credence by English authorities who chose the strongest possible team. Leonard Hutton became England's first-ever professional captain (another dimension of sport in politics) so that he was particularly concerned to come away without losing, yet another source of tension as dour play was and remains unpopular with West Indian crowds. In cricket terms the result was two wins apiece and one draw (England staging a remarkable comeback from 2–0 down), but in public relations and political terms the tour was a disaster. Dubious umpiring decisions incensed some English players who showed open dissent, smashing the West Indian image of England as the home and arbiter of cricket and fair play. But two particular incidents revealed the depths of the all-pervading political sensitivity.

The first occurred during the third test match of the series played in Georgetown, Guyana, where an umpiring decision sparked off a major crowd disturbance. Late on the fourth day West Indies were fighting hard to save the match when a batsman (Clifford McWatt from Guyana itself, significantly) was given out, much to the chagrin of the crowd. As bottles, tins, and boxes showered onto the field from several directions for at least ten minutes, the English team huddled in the middle of the field with the police apparently powerless to curb the disturbance. The game eventually proceeded, but under strained circumstances and a suspicion that the demonstration had been politically inspired. After all, this was at the end of February 1954, just a few weeks after the constitution had been suspended by Britain – an action highly criticized by Jagan and Burnham – and the deployment of British troops in the city had aggravated sensitivities. Then, word about the transgressions of the English team both on and off the field had preceded it to Georgetown so that whatever politically ambassadorial role the tour might have had in the Caribbean context was already well and truly undermined in such a highly charged environment.

A second and similarly damaging occurrence came during the fifth and final test in Kingston, Jamaica. The English captain was playing a long and crucial innings and, with his score on 205 after having batted for almost nine hours, Hutton returned to the pavilion for one of the meal breaks. On hand to congratulate him was Chief Minister Alexander Bustamante, a cricket enthusiast like his fellow leading West Indian politicians. Tired and not concentrating on who was in the crowd, Hutton walked past Bustamante's outstretched hand and was soon abused by a Jamaican official for having snubbed the politician. Although Bustamante himself was not upset, local officials were, several garbled newspaper stories appeared, and an official English apology was not published in full. Tempers ran high on both sides.

Underlying both incidents was the touchy issue of interracial relations fanned by local political aspirations and strongly nationalistic tendencies.[32] One of the most famous calypsos of the period, for example, was Attila's 'Britain, Why Don't You Give Up the West Indies'. Some of the English behaviour was the customary cultural aloofness, particularly on Hutton's part, but much of it was interpreted by blacks as condescension. Worse, many Caribbean white residents aggravated the situation by urging the English visitors to defeat West Indies in order to uphold British tradition, not to say political authority. Cricket had become a test of white

supremacy at the very time political responsibility was being increasingly transferred to representatives of the black majority.

The racial division within the West Indies was underlined by one glaring practice in West Indian cricket, the habitual selection of a white as captain. With the
political climate moving inexorably towards independence, it was clear that if non-
whites were considered fit to run governments then they ought to be able to captain
cricket teams, especially given the presence of such talented players as Frank
Worrell. Because of cricket's symbolic power in the region, the captaincy issue
became the subject of widespread and politically charged discussion. It was in many
ways the forerunner of several battles over which social group would control which
sections of the culture. The catalyst for change would be C.L.R. James whose return
to Trinidad in 1958 after a lengthy spell in the United States coincided with the rise
of Dr Eric Williams and the People's National Movement (PNM) on the island.

The connections between cricket, culture, and politics in the West Indies are
evident in any discussion of Williams and the PNM.[33] The Trinidadian-born
Williams was a brilliant historian whose Oxford doctoral dissertation led to
Capitalism and Slavery, the book which redirected the debate about the nature and
consequences of Caribbean slave society. After teaching at the black Howard
University in the United States, Williams joined the Caribbean Commission as its
research leader and produced vital works on economics, culture, and constitutional
development. Given his background, his People's National Movement which won
the 1956 elections was likely to give a good deal of attention to the role of culture in
the creation of national identity. Williams firmly believed that cricket was important in that respect, as he demonstrated on two occasions. One was in 1964 when
Gary Sobers was appointed to succeed Frank Worrell as captain of West Indies.
Sobers was under contract to the South Australian Cricket Association at the time
and Williams wrote to the Australian prime minister, Sir Robert Menzies, seeking
assistance in obtaining a release.[34] Williams based his case entirely upon the importance of Sobers and cricket in the shaping of an emergent society. Sobers was
released. But an even more important intervention had come during the events
which brought Worrell the captaincy in the first place.

Quite simply, the cricket captaincy had long been regarded and preserved as the
fief of the dominant white elite, a symbol of its control of matters West Indian. In
1928 the honour had fallen to Sir Harold Austin, the legislator-businessman from
Barbados. He was followed by the brothers Grant, G.C. and R.S., who came from
a Trinidadian trading family. For the 1930–1 tour of Australia, G.C. was chosen to
lead West Indies even though he had been absent at Cambridge University for some
time, and he first met many of his players when he joined the team in Australia.[35]
Goddard was the next major figure and after relinquishing the leadership to
Stollmeyer in 1953–4, he returned for a disastrous English tour in 1957 when West
Indies lost the series 3–0. That loss rankled in the Caribbean, not the least for its
coming on the eve of federation.

The concept of a federated West Indies had a long history in British colonial thought, but its modern elaboration began early in 1945 when the Secretary of State for the colonies announced that West Indians themselves would decide the issue of closer regional relations. A series of conferences over the next ten years tested the way, culminating in the London conference of 1956 which resolved upon a federation of twelve islands with the headquarters in Trinidad. In 1958 the idea came to fruition, but by 1962 the federation was dead, an impossible dream which evaporated for many of the same reasons that made West Indian cricket such a politically fragile institution: a centralized and artificial authority attempting to meet the psychological doubts and economic jealousies of numerous territories feeling their way towards national identities.

During those difficult years, West Indies' fortunes as a cricket power had fluctuated: a series win at home over Pakistan (which began its international cricket programme with a series against India in 1952–3, just five years after the Hindu–Muslim butchery which accompanied the partition of the subcontinent), a win against India then a loss to Pakistan in away fixtures, losses in England then Australia, then wins at home over India and England. It was a disappointing record for a region which invested so much emotional capital in its international cricket showing, especially as federation was so clearly failing. And if the one highlight was Gary Sobers's 365 not out against Pakistan at Kingston in 1958 (which stood as the highest score by an individual in a test match until broken in 1994 by Brian Lara who scored 375 against England at the St John's ground in Antigua), then the low point was undoubtedly the Port of Spain riot during the 1959–60 series against England.[36] In response to a run-out decision against a West Indies player, bottles poured onto the field followed by thousands of the people who had thrown them. The English players stayed on the field, hoping the crowd might disperse, but even appeals by Premier Eric Williams and Learie Constantine himself failed to take effect. Only after almost an hour of action involving the use of firehoses, mounted troopers, and riot police did the disturbances subside. For many analysts it was just another demonstration against umpires (one of them a Chinese), but C.L.R. James saw it differently, placing the matter at the heart of West Indian political economy in the context of a federation whose capital was, of course, Port of Spain. It all emerged, he argued, from a fear amongst the people that anti-nationalist sentiments were gaining strength as independence grew nearer and that the symbol of this lay in the machinations of the power elite (mostly white) over the appointment of white cricket captains.[37]

By the late 1950s the black Barbadians, Worrell, Weekes, and Walcott, were highly experienced, the white John Goddard was at the end of his career, and there was no obvious white successor. The selectors, however, opted for inexperienced leaders (if good players) such as Denis Atkinson and Gerry Alexander, much to the chagrin of the West Indian cricket public. Then, at the beginning of the English tour in 1959–60, James, as editor of the *Nation* newspaper in Trinidad, initiated a campaign to have Frank Worrell installed as captain. (The *Nation* was the official voice of the PNM.) His purpose was succinct: for the public which had no national tradition because of its tragically decultured past, black cricketers helped 'fill a huge gap in their consciousness and in their needs'.[38] Just after the riot James published an article calling for Worrell to replace Alexander, and the matter was supported by Eric Williams in his address to the PNM conference. Cricket and politics were clearly closely related, and Frank Worrell was eventually chosen to lead the tour to Australia in 1960.

James and others were right in ascribing deeper causes than cricket itself to what are, in fact, the remarkably few riots which have occurred at West Indian grounds. Although far better than they were, those grounds are still tiny, cramped, short on facilities, long on excitement, and fuelled by rum.[39] With the political strain added, these venues provide highly charged atmospheres at the best of times. In Kingston in 1978, for example, the Australian team experienced a serious demonstration set off by an umpiring decision but caused by a deeper political condition.[40] Police in riot gear and some armed with automatic rifles ringed the ground while the outbreak raged, even to the point where a fire was lit in one of the stands. Broken bricks thrown from the top decks of the stands suggested premeditation. The game had begun in a tense atmosphere following the exclusion from the West Indies team of those players who had signed with a breakaway international group known as World Series Cricket.[41] That exclusion was protested by trade union groups, and the Kingston chapter of the Pan-African Secretariat was refused permission to parade placards at the ground. Kingston was in a state of high political tension at this time.[42] The forthcoming 1980 elections were to end the eight year rule of Michael Manley's People's National Party and put into office Edward Seaga's Jamaican Labour Party. Manley was a brown-skinned democratic socialist, Seaga a white conservative pledged to support Reaganite policies in the Caribbean. And at the heart of this continuing ideological battle lay two particular issues: living standards, and the degree to which political intervention by outside agencies such as the government of the United States and the International Monetary Fund would be tolerated. During 1979 the struggle engendered widespread violence and hundreds of deaths, particularly in Kingston. Given the significance of cricket, it was clear that Sabina Park would become a natural venue for potential political demonstrations. As James had pointed out almost a decade earlier, the resentment was at outside interference. There was as much antipathy towards international cricket authorities for their hard line on World Series Cricket (and the consequent banning of Caribbean stars by the West Indies Cricket Board of Control) as there was towards the United States for its quite open hostility to Michael Manley.

All that lay ahead, of course, as Frank Worrell led the West Indies team to Australia late in 1960. He was in a delicate position, carrying the deeper-than-cricket hopes of the Caribbean people and symbolizing a new era even as federation was crumbling fast. That Australia was still dominated by a white Australian policy, which meant that few of his players would have qualified as immigrants had they wanted to do so, provided a further complication. Worrell was a marvellous success socially in Australia, and the sparkling play of his team makes it the most affectionately remembered of all sides to have visited the country.[43] Indeed, if it was not for cricket most Australians (and probably a number of other nations as well) would know little if anything of the West Indies. While it is true that West Indies achieved other sporting glory, most notably in the late 1940s and early 1950s through a quartet of magnificent Jamaican sprinters, Arthur Wint, George Rhoden, Leslie Laing, and Herb McKenley,[44] the sustained advertising of the West Indies through sport concerned cricket. When Worrell relinquished the hardwon captaincy, he handed over to his successor, Gary Sobers, the makings of one of the world's great teams from which the West Indies drew great pride.

In many ways Sobers was the real break with the past.[45] Worrell won the captaincy only after having spent a long time in England, taken a university degree, and become acceptable within establishment circles in the Caribbean. Before his early death he went on to become an important figure within the University of the West Indies. Sobers was a brilliant player whose skills and charm took him well beyond his poor beginnings, but he remained essentially a people's man. He was far less concerned with the wider social issues than Worrell and that led to some awkward moments. During the fourth test against England in Port of Spain in the 1967–8 series, West Indies compiled a huge score, dismissed England for a reasonable total, and the match seemed headed for a draw. But Sobers, astonishingly, declared his team's second innings closed, left England a reachable target, and West Indies went one down in the series which they eventually lost. The crowd and the West Indian public was outraged at such a gift to the former colonial masters. In Port of Spain an effigy of Sobers was hung in a public square.[46]

A far more serious issue overtook Sobers towards the end of his test career when in 1970 he accepted an invitation to play in Rhodesia. At a time when the anti-apartheid movement in sport was gaining strength this was ill considered, at best. But when it is recalled that West Indian cricket authorities had for some time taken a consistently strong line against racism in South Africa, his action seemed inconceivable. South Africa, while in world cricket, never played West Indies for the very obvious reason that it would have meant black players appearing in that country or white South Africans having to meet blacks in the West Indies. For a region so keen to establish an independent identity and international respect as the West Indies, that South African attitude was anathema, especially when the background of Caribbean slavery was so easily equated with what was happening in South Africa. Rhodesia was considered in similar light. Sobers was criticized severely for losing sight of the political symbolism inherent in the Caribbean game.[47]

It is in this matter of cricket and racism that perhaps the most notable connection between West Indian cricket and politics has been found in recent years. From the mid-1970s until the late 1980s West Indies has been the undisputed world cricket champions and as such has greatly influenced world cricket opinion, especially among non-white participants including India, Pakistan, and Sri Lanka. Throughout that period, in order to meet an increasingly hard-line West Indian attitude towards South Africa, international cricket authorities have moved very cautiously in their relations with South Africa, no matter how willing they might have been to interact otherwise.[48] Even if the objective of the International Cricket Conference (the world ruling body) was to prevent a split between the white and non-white cricketing nations rather than simply to appease the West Indies, the fact remains that on this crucial issue the Caribbean has found its greatest influence and presence in the world political arena. That the West Indian authorities were prepared to move quickly and strongly was obvious. During 1982 several West Indian players (the so-called Rand rebels) played in South Africa, attracted by the lucrative financial offers from authorities (political and cricketing) anxious to revive flagging cricket and related political fortunes. West Indian authorities banned the rebels from international competition for life.[49]

This growing intransigence had been signalled the year before when England toured the Caribbean. A late replacement in the team was Robin Jackman who had prominent South African connections. The Burnham government in Guyana refused him entry, the test scheduled for Georgetown was cancelled following England's refusal to play, and the tour itself was very nearly called off. This revealed that Caribbean governments had begun to realize the political potency of cricket and the leverage it provided. A similar incident occurred during the next English visit of 1986. The English culprit this time was Graham Gooch who was quite unrepentant about his South African ties. Lester Bird, deputy prime minister of Antigua (and son of Prime Minister Vere Bird), was prominent among the politicians who called for action against the visitors, but the tour proceeded without undue incident amidst a good deal of careful manoeuvring.[50]

While the West Indian attitude towards South Africa has been radical, in some eyes at least, it would be misleading to imagine that the game in its contemporary phase has broken completely free of the colonial past in all of its social aspects. Indeed, the radical exceptions prove the rule. A leading radio commentator of cricket, Antigua's Tim Hector, is also leader of the Antigua Caribbean Liberation Movement which is really more social democratic than revolutionary. Throughout the 1980s Hector was indicted by the Bird government for his political activities, but it is notable that his cricket affiliations won him little support in the wider political context.[51] That is particularly significant in that Antigua boasted the then West Indian captain (Vivian Richards) and a leading batsman (Richie Richardson). The Jamesian view about the essential conservatism of cricket, dictated by its social roots, is most apt here.

The cricket establishment has also been suspicious of new social movements, such as Rastafarianism. With its mixture of Old Testament beliefs, mysticism, and revivalism, along with its telling extension into reggae music and the associated drug culture, the movement has spread quickly and deeply throughout the Caribbean (and elsewhere – there are now Rasta cults amongst the New Zealand Maoris and among political activists in some Pacific island nations such as Fiji).[52] But cricket has treated it with great suspicion. There was wide concern expressed when Vivian Richards was observed wearing wristbands which bore the Rasta colours, and a number of regional cricket associations have banned Rastas from their competitions. The Rasta trade mark is long, ringleted hair. But when Everton Mattis walked out to face the English bowlers for the first time as a West Indies player in 1981, his dreadlocks had been cut. According to the English journalist, Frank Keating, there was 'a whiff of discrimination in the air'.[53]

In part, such action may be a rearguard attempt to maintain the dimensions of cricket as set in the colonial past but, if that is so, it seems likely to fail. Local politicians still turn up to watch a club match, an indication of the game's continuing electoral significance. Yet it is interesting to note that the smaller islands, such as Antigua and St Vincent, are now producing a greater number of international players. Some observers put that down to social change in the larger islands where cricket is beginning to lose its cachet. And some fear that the increase in 'tourist' cricket (playing host to lower-grade cricketers, especially from England, out on tourist packages) is somehow devaluing the game. Still others fear that widespread emigration will eventually erode the cricket base. While all that is yet to be proved, Caribbean cricket *is* undergoing changes which have political significance both within and without the West Indies.[54]

The migration issue, for example, has introduced a new dimension to the politics of Caribbean sport in general and cricket in particular.[55] From the late 1940s onwards there was a substantial Caribbean migration to Great Britain, and by the 1970s the presence of those migrants had become a major political issue in classical terms: racism fanned by economic discontent. It is incontestable that most of the West Indian population in Britain was kept within the lower socio-economic ranks. As they sought a way out through participation in professional sports such as soccer, rugby league, and boxing, racist sentiments became more apparent. It took them longer to penetrate county cricket ranks where middle- and upper-class sentiments are still predominant, even though most of the teams had hired contract staff direct from the West Indies since the county clubs opened their doors to foreign players in the late 1960s. The situation became complex. It was ironic that one England player on the 1981 tour was Roland Butcher, a black born in Barbados but raised in England, while playing for West Indies was Gordon Greenidge, born in Barbados but resident in England.

As the racial situation in England became more difficult, Caribbean sentiment and sensitivity stiffened. This was borne out very clearly in 1984 when West Indies executed a historic massacre of England in England (5–0 in five matches, with the dose repeated at home in the Caribbean in 1986). West Indian supporters were there in their thousands, just as Lord Kitchener and friends had been thirty-five years earlier. But this time it was an all-black team with a black captain, the incomparable Clive Lloyd, a leader in the cricketing and social style of Worrell.[56] The rout was labelled by these supporters as a 'blackwash' (as opposed to a whitewash), and it was very clear that they were celebrating not just a cricket victory but a far wider one in the wake of the Notting Hill and Brixton riots, inquiries into which revealed the full social and political plight of West Indian communities in Britain.

As West Indians look back now upon sixty years of international cricket competition and at least 120 years of regional play, it will be clear to them as it should be clear to others that the game is not just a sporting code but a political institution as well. That has come about because cricket was introduced by the imperial authorities for reasons other than recreation, because the colonial elites took it up for reasons other than exercise, and because the modern players have seen in cricket lessons other than purely sporting ones. And those of us attempting to understand the real wellsprings of the connection between politics and sport would do well to remember the words of C.L.R. James: 'What do they know of cricket who only cricket know?'[57]

Notes

1   See National Library of Australia, Menzies Papers, 1950s correspondence between Sir Robert Menzies, prime minister of Australia, and Sir Pelham Warner, English cricket administrator.

2   *Times*, 30 June 1950, 4.

3   See: Benjamin Lowe, D.B. Kanin, and A. Strenk, eds, *Sport and International Relations* (Champaign IL: Stipes 1978); Maaret Ilmarinen, ed., *Sport and International Understanding* (Berlin: Springer Verlag 1984); Lincoln Allison, ed., *The Politics of Sport* (Manchester: Manchester University Press, 1986). All these works are of interest, but produce little in the way of an integrated view on the sports politics phenomenon. John M. Hobermann, *Sport and Political Ideology* (Austin: University of Texas Press 1984) attempts a pioneering view.

4   Richard T. Espy, *The Politics of the Olympic Games* (Berkeley: University of California Press, 1979); David B. Kanin, *A Political History of the Olympic Games* (Boulder CO: Westview, 1981); Alan Tomlinson and Garry Whannel, eds, *Five Ring Circus: Money, Power and Politics at the Olympic Games* (London: Pluto, 1984). Again Hobermann attempts a different analysis – *The Olympic Crisis: Sport, Politics and the Moral Order* (New York: Caratzas, 1986).

5   For Barbadian cricket, Brian Stoddart, 'Cricket, Social Formation and Cultural Continuity in Barbados: a Preliminary Ethnohistory', *Journal of Sport History*, 14 (Winter 1987). A quite different cricket is described in Frank Manning, 'Celebrating Cricket: the Symbolic Construction of Caribbean Politics', *American Ethnologist*, 8 (August 1981) – it is about Bermuda, an island not generally considered part of the Caribbean cricket culture.

6   Jeff Stollmeyer, *Everything under the Sun: My Life in West Indies Cricket* (London: Stanley Paul, 1983).

7   These three players figure prominently in any history of the game, be it about the West Indies or the world.

8   There is a vast literature concerning Caribbean slavery, emancipation, and economic development. For some stimulating views in this area, Sidney W. Mintz, *Sweetness and*

Power (Harmondsworth: Penguin, 1986). A case study is in Ronald Parris, 'Race, Inequality and Underdevelopment in Barbados, 1627–1973', doctoral dissertation, Yale University, 1974.

9 See *Caribbean Quarterly*, 22 (March 1976), for a special edition of the Caribbean Indian community, and 32 (September and December 1986) for a subsequent examination of the same community.

10 For the history of West Indian cricket: Christopher Nicole, *West Indian Cricket* (London: Phoenix 1957), 158; Tony Cozier, *The West Indies: Fifty Years of Test Cricket* (London: Angus and Robertson, 1978); Clayton Goodwin, *Caribbean Cricketers: from the Pioneers to Packer* (London: Harrap, 1980); and *West Indians at the Wicket* (London: Macmillan, 1986).

11 Keith A.P. Sandiford and Brian Stoddart, 'The Elite Schools and Cricket in Barbados: a Study in Colonial Continuity', *International Journal of the History of Sport*, 4 (December 1987).

12 Michael Manley, *The History of West Indian Cricket* (London: Deutsch, 1988).

13 For a description, Keith A.P. Sandiford, 'Cricket and the Victorian society', *Journal of Sport History*, 17 (Winter 1983).

14 For the Eliasian approach to sport in society, Norbert Elias and Eric Dunning, *Quest for Excitement: Sport and Leisure in the Civilizing Process* (Oxford: Blackwell, 1986).

15 The first real examination of this process came in C.L.R. James, *Beyond a Boundary* (London: Hutchinson, 1963), chap. 4.

16 The *Barbados Bulletin* of 2 December 1897 reported that some Chinese youths had begun playing cricket on land provided by the colonial government in British Guiana.

17 For the British background, J.A. Mangan, *Athleticism in the Victorian and Edwardian Public School: the Emergence and Consolidation of an Educational Ideology* (Cambridge: Cambridge University Press, 1981).

18 Conrad Hunte, *Playing to Win* (London: Hodder & Stoughton, 1971).

19 The Austin heritage is outlined in Dora P. Burslem and Audrey D. Manning, 'An Old Colonial Family, 1685–1900' (ms held by the Barbados Historical Society Library).

20 John Wickham, 'Herman', *West Indies Cricket Annual* (Bridgetown: WICA, 1980).

21 See the excellent biography by Gerald Howat, *Learie Constantine* (London: Allen & Unwin, 1975). Constantine's own writings are important. See, for example, *Colour Bar* (London: Stanley Paul, 1954), *Cricketers' Cricket* (London: Eyre & Spottiswoode, 1949), and *Cricketers' Carnival* (London: Stanley Paul, 1948).

22 For some of James's other works, see: *Cricket* (edited by Anne Grimshaw) (London: Allison & Busby, 1986) and *The Black Jacobins: Toussaint L'Ouverture and the San Domingo Revolution* (London: Allison & Busby, 1980).

23 For one such late discovery and the thoughts so generated, Alan Metcalfe, 'C.L.R. James' Contributions to the History of Sport', *Canadian Journal of History of Sport*, 18 (December 1987).

24 A convenient background work is Gordon K. Lewis, *The Growth of the Modern West Indies* (New York: Monthly Review Press, 1968). Franklin W. Knight, *The Caribbean: Genesis of a Fragmented Nationalism* (New York: Oxford University Press, 1978) provides a briefer history.

25 See *West India Royal Commission Report* (London: HMSO, 1945); W.M. Macmillan, *Warning from the West Indies* (Harmondsworth: Penguin 1938); John La Guerre, 'The Moyne Commission and the West Indian Intelligentsia, 1938–9', *Journal of*

Commonwealth Political Studies, 9 (1971); G. St J. Orde Browne, *Labour Conditions in the West Indies* (London: HMSO, 1939).

26 F.A. Hoyos, *Grantley Adams and the Social Revolution* (London: Macmillan, 1974).

27 The former West Indies captain, Clive Lloyd, is one who has promoted this view recently (*Barbados Advocate*, 11 April 1985), again revealing the generally close links between Caribbean cricket and politics. A fictional view is in Edgar Mittelhozer, *A Morning at the Office* (London: Heinemann, 1974), 128–9.

28 Interview material. In 1939 the deputy mayor of Kingston called a protest meeting on the grounds that too few Jamaicans were chosen for the English tour that year: *Barbados Advocate*, 10 February 1939, 1.

29 For an account, Lewis, *Modern West Indies*, chap. 10.

30 One outline is in Michael Manley, *Jamaica: Struggle in the Periphery* (London: Third World Media, 1983).

31 For the 1953–54 events: E.W. Swanton, *West Indian Adventure: with Hutton's MCC Team, 1953–54* (London: Museum Press, 1954) and Alex Bannister, *Cricket Cauldron: with Hutton in the Caribbean* (London: Stanley Paul 1954). For Hutton's account of the Jamaica incident and the tour: Len Hutton, *Fifty Years in Cricket* (London: Stanley Paul, 1984), chap. 6; also see Fred Trueman, *Ball of Fire* (London: Granada, 1977), 45–9, and Denis Compton, *End of an Innings* (London: SBC, 1959), chap 9.

32 For some important discussions in this area: David Lowenthal and Lambros Comitas, eds, *Consequences of Class and Colour: West Indian Perspectives* (New York: Anchor, 1973); M.G. Smith, *The Plural Society in the West Indies* (Berkeley: University of California Press, 1965); Peter J. Wilson, *Crab Antics: the Social Anthropology of English-speaking Negro Societies of the Caribbean* (New Haven: Yale University Press, 1973).

33 See Lewis, *Modern West Indies*, chap. 8.

34 Menzies Papers, Eric Williams to Sir Robert Menzies, 13 July 1964.

35 Cozier, *West Indies: Fifty Years of Test Cricket*, 80.

36 An extensive account may be found in Ray Robinson, *The Wildest Tests* (Sydney: Cassell, 1979), chap. 6.

37 James, *Beyond a Boundary*, chap. 18, details the story and the campaign.

38 *Ibid.*, 225.

39 Orlando Patterson, 'The Ritual of Cricket', *Jamaica Journal*, 3 (March 1969); Maurice St Pierre, 'West Indian Cricket', parts I and II, *Caribbean Quarterly*, 19 (June and September 1973); L.O'B. Thompson, 'How Cricket is West Indian Cricket?: Class, Racial and Colour Conflict', *Caribbean Review*, 12 (1983).

40 Robinson, *The Wildest Tests*, chap. 20.

41 The World Series Cricket story is outlined in Christopher Forsyth, *The Great Cricket Hijack* (Melbourne: Widescope, 1978).

42 For some explanations, Tom Barry *et al.*, *The Other Side of Paradise: Foreign Control in the Caribbean* (New York: Grove, 1984), 341–51. For the deeper background, Diane J. Austin, *Urban Life in Kingston, Jamaica: The Culture and Class Ideology of Two Neighborhoods* (New York: Gordon & Breach, 1984). For recent Caribbean political trends, Paget Henry and Carl Stone, eds, *The Newer Caribbean: Decolonization, Democracy and Development* (Philadelphia: ISHI, 1983).

43 A.G. Moyes, *With the West Indies in Australia, 1960–61: a Critical Story of the Tour* (London: Heinemann, 1961). For Worrell himself, see: Ernest Eytle, *Frank Worrell*

(London: SBC, 1966). Ivo Tennant, *Frank Worrell: a Biography* (London: Lutterworth, 1987), reveals a very thin grasp of the cultural complexity of Caribbean cricket.

44 In the Helsinki Olympics of 1952 they won the 4×400-metre relay while Wint and McKenley finished 1–2 in the individual 400-metre event in both the 1948 and 1952 Olympics, and McKenley won silver in the 100 metres in 1952. See David Wallechinsky, *The Complete Book of the Olympics* (New York: Penguin, 1984), 19–20 and 66.

45 There is an excellent social analysis of Sobers in W.K. Marshall, 'Gary Sobers and the Brisbane revolution', *New World Quarterly*, 2 (1965).

46 Cozier, *West Indies: Fifty Years of Test Cricket*, 52.

47 Interview material; daily issues of the *Barbados Advocate* for September and October 1970. For the South African situation, Robert Archer and Antoine Bouillon, *The South African Game: Sport and Racism* (London: Zed 1982).

48 This was borne out very clearly in the 1987 International Cricket conference compromise over a hard-line West Indian proposal relating to players with South African connections.

49 Goodwin, *West Indians at the Wicket*, chap. 17.

50 For the 1981 tour, Frank Keating, *Another Bloody Day in Paradise!* (London: Deutsch, 1981). For the 1986 tour, Frances Edmonds, *Another Bloody Tour: England in the West Indies, 1986* (London: Heinemann, 1986). Also, Manley, *History of West Indian Cricket*, 292–4.

51 Interview material.

52 *Caribbean Quarterly* 26 (December 1980), special issue on Rastasfari; Horace Campbell, *Rasta and Resistance: From Marcus Garvey to Walter Rodney* (London: Hansib, 1986); Leonard E. Barrett, *Rastafarians: the Dreadlocks of Jamaica* (London: Heinemann, 1977).

53 For the Richards case, Trevor Macdonald, *Viv Richards: the Authorised Biography* (London: Sphere, 1985). For one case arising from the banning of dreadlocks by the Leeward Islands Cricket Association, see *Barbados Advocate*, 21 August 1985. Keating, *Another Bloody Day in Paradise!*, 37.

54 Interview material. For 'festival cricket', Goodwin, *West Indians at the Wicket*, chap. 14.

55 Ernest Cashmore, *Black Sportsmen* (London: Routledge & Kegan Paul 1982). For some earlier general thoughts, John Figueroa, 'British West Indian immigration to Great Britain', *Caribbean Quarterly*, 5 (February 1958).

56 Clive Lloyd, *Living for Cricket* (London: Stanley Paul, 1980).

57 James, preface to *Beyond a Boundary*. For some information on Caribbean sport in this respect, Colin A. Martindale, 'The Role of Sport in Nation-building: a Comparative Analysis of Four Newly Developing Nations in the Commonwealth Caribbean', doctoral dissertation, City University of New York, 1980.

16

Cricket and the politics of West Indies integration

June Soomer

Conceptualization of a model for West Indies integration has been dominated by concerns deemed important from the colonial period. Undoubtedly, these concerns with integration and the concept of a West Indies have evolved around sugar and slavery. For, despite the fact that early administration of the colonies was done on an individual basis, the one body which epitomized the region at the time was the powerful British West India Interest. A powerful lobby group in the British Parliament, this body represented the sugar and slavery interests of all the British West Indian colonies. No legislation affecting these colonies could be passed without the assent of the West India Interest during the centuries of colonization. Therefore, deeply entrenched within the concept of a West Indies was the dominance of the sugar interest.

The decline of sugar and the subsequent weakening of the West India Interest in the late eighteenth and early nineteenth centuries created an administrative dilemma for the imperial government. No longer could the less prosperous colonies be administered on an individual basis. This preoccupation with profitability provided the impetus for the evolution of the concept of integration. The emerging imperial concept was based on the premise that efficient administration of the sugar colonies would result in economy; consequently more profits would be accrued by those who controlled and administered those colonies. For this reason, centralization of administrations was pursued imperturbably throughout the entire colonial period, despite only marginal success in the Leeward islands.

This concept of integration was also influenced by the domination of a very large black population which resisted subjugation. Before emancipation in 1838, the enslaved blacks had already began envisaging the region as a whole. This can be justified by examining the efforts of liberated blacks in maroon societies and later in Haiti to export revolution to other territories. Consequently, the labour uprisings which intensified throughout the region, at a time when sugar prosperity was declining, was a manifestation of the ideology that all black people in the region had to be liberated.[1]

It was this ideology that the imperial model of integration tried to counteract.

The first step was the granting of emancipation; but this was the only concession to be made to black labour as subsequently every effort was made to maintain the control of sugar over labour. It was envisaged that a strong central administration would be better able to control labour in the Leewards and Windwards where sugar profits were rapidly declining. Although efforts were made to amalgamate the administrations of Barbados and Windwards in 1876, it was not pursued because of planter resistance.[2] In Trinidad, Guyana and Jamaica planters would regain control through massive importation of labour from China and India.

Despite these efforts in the post-emancipation period black workers continued to envisage the region as a whole. By becoming mobile they were able to take advantage of higher wages and to acquire land in islands where these were available. Another noticeable phenomenon was the fact that they did not limit themselves to the British colonies but exploited conditions in Cuba, Santo Domingo, Martinique and Guadeloupe. Thus each black West Indian community managed to form a niche in islands where conditions permitted.

Clearly, two concepts of West Indies integration were evolving simultaneously. The imperial concept which focused on the domination of sugar, functional co-operation, administrative centralization and government control; and the concept evolving around the mobility of black labour to overcome cultural, political, social and economic barriers by becoming integrated into their new societies. However, the former concept would take precedence with no consideration given to the adaptability of the latter. This is the model which would survive into the twentieth century – this model which emanated from Englishmen not West Indians.

By 1922 the more impressive title of 'West Indies Federation' was concocted. It is not surprising that it was the chairman of one of the frequent royal commissions of sugar, Lord Halifax, who assured that the imperial government would recommend the formation of a West Indies, but this did not materialize.[3] A subsequent sugar royal commission in 1930 suggested the amalgamation of the Windward and Leewards for more efficient running of the sugar industries in these islands. Clearly, these integration attempts still focused on sugar and its administration. But the planter governments resisted the centralization of administrations because it would mean the minimizing of their political power in individual islands.

This desire to control individual islands was strong enough to resist subsequent attempts at integration. Unfortunately when the black nationalist movement with its traditional loyalty to the imperial government and its uncertainty about the best means of achieving political autonomy, agreed to accept the imperial model of integration as the best development path for the region, it also inherited all the inherent inter-island differences which colonialism had created.

During the post-World War II period plans towards the establishment of a West Indies federal government continued to be pursued. This process which started in 1945 saw the eventual establishment of a weak, colonial central administration in 1958. This British West Indies Federation established by the imperial government and the governments of the unit territories was achieved without participation by the West Indian public. Unfortunately, this government was not able to overcome the problems which it inherited and was therefore dismantled in 1962.[4]

The present focus on West Indies integration continues to be centred around attempts at unification at the political, economic and administrative levels. This of course is the manifestation of the class ideology in the region, where upper and middle class images of integration takes precedence over those of the lower-class, consequently the integration which has been fostered from the bottom up has been ignored. It is rather unfortunate that it is only because of the successive failure of these ventures to address societal imbalances in the region, that attention has shifted to the social and cultural aspects of integration; aspects which lower class West Indians have been building into popular culture. Ignorance of the intricate intertwining of social and cultural integration with those facets deemed as imperatives for unification has ensured the inadequacy and subsequent failure of integration models implemented in the region. This has also accounted for the lack of enthusiasm for the regional integration movement by the majority of West Indians, who view it as a political device best left to the political elite and idealists.

Yet, to dub integration within the region as a complete failure, would be to undervalue the less recognized dynamics of social and cultural integration which are epitomized by the West Indies cricket team and the University of the West Indies. Although these two institutions demonstrate the success of integration in the region cricket has managed to become part of the popular culture in a way that the UWI can only hope to project itself in the future. The institutionalization of cricket in the region has become a phenomenon many in the more visible political and economic spheres undoubtedly envy. However, the imbalanced focus on integration has prevented West Indies cricket from being thoroughly examined in order to determine, how an institution confronted with problems similar to those which plague the regional integration movement, has spanned an entire century and remains poised for survival into the twenty-first century.

The evolution of cricket into part of the popular culture could not have been predicted during the late nineteenth and early twentieth centuries. This was because of the fact that cricket teams derived their importance from the success of the sugar economies. Barbados, the most prosperous sugar colony was in the forefront of emerging cricket teams, with its numerous planter clubs and organized competitions for white players. The other three major sugar producers, Jamaica, Trinidad and Guyana were the other recognized cricketing nations in the region. The Leewards and Windwards, the least prosperous sugar societies, with a dwindling planter class were grouped together for inter-colonial matches. It is clear then that the early cricket in the region was an integral part of the imperial model of regional integration; both had the survival of the sugar plantations at their focal point.

Unfortunately, the evolution of cricket from the imperial model of integration has ensured the entrenchment of many historical inter-island rivalries. The less prosperous sugar colonies envied the Barbadian position not only in terms of sugar but also in relation to cricket. It was always their aim to overcome 'Little England' in a game at which they excelled. This rivalry was perpetuated by the fact that the majority of the early West Indies team were dominated by Barbadian planters. The other three major sugar producers also made vital contributions as the team evolved; while the Windward and Leeward players were not considered for selection and in fact were marginalized. This image of the 'big four' as the better cricketers continued to be perpetuated right up to the 1970s much to the chagrin of the 'small' islands. Thus inter-island rivalries with strong historical bases came to be entrenched not only in the more recognized political and economic aspects of integration but also within cricket. Yet, this has not hampered the success of the West Indies teams since the 1960s. The success of West Indies cricket to serve as a model for integration of the region is explored below.

Many writers have alluded to the potential of cricket as a unifying force in West Indian society. Clive Lloyd, former West Indies captain, in his introduction in Michael Manley's *A History of West Indian Cricket*, writes:

All our experiments in Caribbean integration either failed or have maintained a dubious survivability; but cricket remains the instrument of Caribbean cohesion – the remover of arid insularity and nationalistic prejudice.[5]

He attributes this internal cohesion to the recognition and dignity which cricket has brought internationally. Embedded within this thought is the concept of gaining internal strength through contention with external forces. Which raises the question, did the West Indies cricket team survive because of external factors? Undoubtedly, West Indies cricket first had to break through racial, insular, nationalistic boundaries to attain regional acceptance before the impact of international factors could be felt. Perhaps these external factors have subsequently given it sustenance, but the cohesion necessary for the development of cricket in the region had to come from internal forces.

Long before Lloyd had penned these words, C.R. James had thrown out the challenge to West Indians to visualize cricket as a unifying force. Writing in the *Port of Spain Gazette* in June, 1933 he predicted

The day West Indians White, Brown and Black learn to be West Indians, to see nothing in front to right or left but West Indian success and the means to it, that day they begin to grow up. [6]

This article was written during the 1933 England versus West Indies test match in Port of Spain, at a time when the English press was questioning the fairness of using fast bowlers like Constantine on a fast pitch. It was an appeal to overcome the adversity of the negative press by focusing on success and the development of their unique talents. These were the two areas which endeared the game to all West Indians – the almost assembly line perfection of specialist fast bowlers, all-rounders and batsmen, spinners and fielders, who have been able to dominate and influence international cricket.

Perhaps one of the primary reasons for the survival of West Indies cricket as an institution was its metamorphosis from being a white elite dominated game of the late nineteenth and early twentieth century, to one which reflected the West Indian personality and sense of community. The pre-1938 teams were dominated and administered by whites and had not achieved public appeal. In fact, to call these teams West Indies cricket teams would be fallacious as they were not representative of the social or racial structure and certainly held no wide appeal for the majority of West Indians. But talented individuals of non-European origin had already started making inroads into this sport at which they were not expected to excel. The image perpetuated by the English was that of innately good cricketers who did not take the game seriously and who inherently, did not have the ability to concentrate long enough to become successful. Despite the success of West Indies cricket this myth has not been dispelled on the international scene and perhaps is responsible for the recent rulings on over rates and short pitched deliveries – the logic being, that emasculation of West Indian fast bowlers would once again see the revival of white batsmen, who are able to concentrate for long hours, therefore reinforcing the view that they are the better cricketers.

The failure to recognize that the success of West Indian cricket goes beyond the ability of batsmen and bowlers has prevented any of these strategies from impacting negatively on the West Indies cricket team for a prolonged period. John Figueroa, writing on post-war West Indies tours to England states that,

> when a group appear to be playing in a certain way, or to excel at a certain game, it is likely to have something to do with their genetic inheritance, but more to do with their cultural experience, and more to do with the circumstances under which they commonly play.[7]

These circumstances for the West Indies cricket team have entailed overcoming domination by a political and economic system which envisaged cricket simply as a means of rest and relaxation on weekends after its weekly exploits. However, West Indies cricket has mirrored the evolution of West Indian society; with more democratization in the region; with the passing of the captaincy to a black West Indian; with the acquisition of independence; and with continuous cricketing success over previous colonial masters.

Essentially the experiences of black lower class and white upper and middle classes with the term 'West Indies' has been different. For the latter, the West Indies represented a place to live at certain times of the year; where economic and political control formed the basis of the attachment. Thus, fundamentally the relationship was one based on exploitation and domination. It is not surprising therefore that before and after the 1960s and the captaincy of Worrell when white cricket teams visited the West Indies the majority of white West Indians would support them over the West Indies cricket team. This phenomenon was recorded by Keith Miller writing on the Australian tour of the West Indies in 1955. Despite the successes of the West Indies teams they will never be considered as better than the

England or Australia teams simply because of their skin colour. It is no surprise that George Headley continues to be called the black Don Bradman instead of vice versa.

In spite of contentions over who should be part of the West Indies team, black West Indians know exactly which team they support. Perhaps, identification with the West Indies as their home and as a society where they have created their own cultural institutions despite years of oppression, accounts for the differences in attitude. They recognize that as a transplanted people it was necessary to create their own unique culture. This awareness also accounts for the survival and popularization of cultural institutions as opposed to the more artificially imposed political and economic institutions. It is therefore no wonder that black people were becoming more West Indian at a time in the 1960s when the administrative and political structure of the British West Indies Federation was collapsing.

From the onset West Indian cricket teams with their array of fast bowlers and fine stroke players have creolized cricket and made it something with which they can identify. C.L.R. James, in his address to the 1963 West Indies team in the Tavern at Lords noted,

> The West Indies have reached where they are because certain of them have had the opportunity to absorb to a large degree and to adapt to their own uses, a certain definite tradition. But they bring something of their own now to the life they have to live, and I believe in the cricket they have . . . found something of their own.[8]

It was through this creolization that the sense of 'West Indianness' emerged and support for the game grew. Creolization, at least in this aspect of West Indian life has managed a decolonization process that has been hindered in other colonial structures imposed on the region.

Cricket is perhaps the one area of life in the West Indies where black lower-class men have been afforded the opportunity of making an enduring input into the society. Centuries of struggles to deconstruct the ideology of white superiority have been endured and it is through the 'West Indianization' of cricket that the most remarkable strides have been made. The injustices encountered in the political and economic spheres and reinforced in the social sector were being settled 'man to man', on weekends, on the cricket pitches everywhere in the West Indies.

Throughout the region the creolization of cricket contended with race, class and ethnic conflicts at the national level before West Indies cricket could emerge with solidarity. G.K. Lewis advocates that cricket created an opportunity for social manoeuvrability, especially in islands like Barbados with its rigid social structure. The ability of men like Sobers, Worrell, Weekes and a host of notable Barbadian cricketers managed to break the colour barriers of the long established clubs thereby challenging the status quo. Lewis believes then, that, the possession of an individual skill became transformed . . . into the championship of the game as a carrier of national culture'.[9]

Two important questions still need to be answered here. Firstly, when did the national barrier lower enough to accommodate the idea of something West Indian;

and secondly, were these national barriers overcome? For, despite its successes, like the various regional political and economic institutions, West Indies cricket is plagued by insularity and parochialism.

Advocates of the oneness of West Indies cricket, credit the captaincy of Frank Worrell with removing insularity from the team. All previous West Indies teams had been captained by white men and the granting of the captaincy to Worrell over Gerry Alexander was acknowledgement of his leadership skills and set the foundation for the outstanding leadership by the black captains who were to follow. Clive Lloyd writes that before Worrell's captaincy,

> There was insularity, the call for arithmetical representation from each territory, there was prejudice, and there was a lack of confidence that the general and particular methods of selection guaranteed that the best talent emerged.[10]

As the first black captain of the West Indies cricket team, Worrell encouraged the best from his players and endeared the team to the West Indies public. He left a legacy of leadership that subsequent captains have had difficulty emulating and undoubtedly made inroads into the parochial problems facing the team. Worrell has also been credited with the prophetic statement, 'The nucleus of West Indian teams in the future, . . . would be provided by the islands of the Leewards and Windwards.'[11]

Recently, the players from the Leewards have made a niche for themselves on the team and the inclusion of a wicket-keeper from Grenada was heralded throughout the region. Yet despite the West Indian outlook of Worrell these problems with insularity continue to re-surface especially when the team experiences lean seasons or when new players have to be selected.

Problems with insularity are encountered because of what has been considered unfair selection practices. The islands of the Windwards and Leewards have often protested against apparent and sometimes blatant discrimination. As early as the first meeting of the West Indies Cricket Board of Control, held in June 1927 in Trinidad the decision was taken to arrange for matches between touring teams and the Windwards and Leewards to be played in Barbados or Trinidad. Further, these teams would have to cover their costs and would be repaid by gate receipts on the discretion of the Barbados or Trinidad authorities.

Winston Lloyd writes that following this decision,

> no such matches were played as English teams come and went in the 1930s and 1940s. Nor were any Islanders chosen for West Indian teams, either at home or abroad.[12]

This institutionalized discrimination remained until 1954 when an MCC team played three day games in the Windwards and Leewards. The islands would have to wait another two years before a Vincentian could enter the West Indies team. It was not until 1977, with a touring Pakistan team, that these islands saw the introduction of four-day matches, on their cricket grounds.

In lamenting this situation, Tim Hector in an article entitled 'The Roots of Islands' Cricket: Acceptance at Last after Years of Frustration', noted,

The Leeward and Windward Islands were often considered obscure cricketing entities, relegated to the cellar and deemed incapable of really producing anyone of Test Match calibre.[13]

This article which examines the various Windward and Leeward Islands players who were never selected to the West Indies team, because they were not from the 'larger' islands, highlights the feelings of the people from these islands, who despite these views still continue to support West Indies teams. Further, they continued to struggle to ensure a place in the team. Hector assured that,

When all is said and done, the struggle to break into West Indies Cricket was far more satisfying, in spite of, or because of, the frustrations and tragedies along the way . . .[14]

Seemingly, the honour of selection to the team has placated or at least temporarily halted the calls for more representation by the 'smaller' islands. The issue however never dissipated and Vivian Richards in *Hitting across the Line* wrote,

I am not saying that there has been a conspiracy to keep down players from the smaller islands. It is just that the system has never favoured the smaller island players.[15]

He blamed the early WICBC for this institutionalized favouritism through its lack of encouragement of talented players. Further, he pointed out that this problem also existed within the groupings for the Shell Shield, now Red Stripe, tournament. Antiguans believe that they 'do not get a fair deal in the Leeward Islands set up'.[16] Similarly, St Lucians or any island in the Windwards complain about their under-representation. Yet whenever any of these amalgamated teams play a match they have the support of everyone from their sub-grouping. The wrangling over selection is soon forgotten especially if the team is successful, that is, until the next cricket season.

The Windward and Leeward Islands have also felt marginalized because of the fact that all the presidents of the WICBC have always come from the 'big four'. Therefore, these islands have not been able to affect the administration of cricket. This is one of the main reason behind the call for a separate Antiguan team. This island has dominated Leeward Islands cricket for more than ten years and has contributed famous cricketers like Vivian Richards, Andy Roberts, Richie Richardson and Curtley Ambrose to the West Indies team. It therefore feels that it has earned a place with the 'big four'; second-class status will no longer be accepted. Unfortunately, unless the WICBC sets established criteria for team selection, individual territories which see cricket as their last hope to influence regionalism, will continue to feel marginalized.

This persistent quarrel over selection of teams has revived the call for some form of quota system. Unfortunately, such a measure would only serve to weaken the various teams both locally and internationally. Critics of the present selection system are constantly silenced with success of teams only to resurface in the face of defeat. Yet, no one calls for an end to West Indies cricket. Neither have these problems affected relations within the teams as players unite against the opposition. The game has emerged as greater than its various components.

Recently, the problems of selection have taken on new dimensions. The influx of Leeward Islands cricketers into the West Indies team in the last decade has caused the traditional suppliers to suspect a conspiracy. The selection of Richie Richardson as captain of the team and the overlooking of Desmond Haynes has caused an up-roar in Barbados. This issue was accentuated by the scant respect with which the WICBC treated Malcolm Marshall and Gordon Greenidge, who recently retired. To add fuel to the flame, the decision to omit Anderson Cummins from the team which played against South Africa, caused Barbadians to call for a boycott of the Kensington Oval test match. The success of this boycott revived the traditional anti-Barbadian sentiment throughout the region.[17] Yet, despite what was seen as an extreme act of insularity, a situation when a player took precedence over the team, once again the calls were for renewed support of the team in its attempts at rebuild-ing. These situations point to the depth of involvement of West Indians in the game. Everyone is a cricketer, a commentator, a critic, a captain, a selector, an umpire and a supporter. The alienation from other facets of West Indian life has created an inte-gration where the people can assert themselves even when they do not make the final decisions.

This insularity and parochialism, sharply emphasized with the treatment of Richie Richardson during the one-day match, West Indies versus South Africa, at Sabina Park, Jamaica, has in some ways served to weaken West Indies cricket.[18] Theoretically, the selection of the 'best' team based on ability and performance does not occur because the issue of representation takes precedence. Such problems surface with the selection of administrative staff during the 1958 British West Indies Federation. This 'territorial division of labour' served to affect the functioning of the federal administration as the need to appease each territory took precedence over ability. Logically, if all the most capable players come from one or two islands then they should be the ones selected. However, such a suggestion would lead to chaos and suggestions of partiality would prevail.

Ironically, one of the reasons for this insularity is the success of the team. The desire to be part of a team with such notoriety is the wish of every young West Indian cricketer. Joel Garner views it as a means of bettering oneself and a chance for social recognition. Further, it is a way of earning a living while participating in something fulfilling. But it goes beyond the desire for success or monetary gain, rather, it centres around wanting to make a genuine contribution to something which sym-bolizes West Indian achievement. Therefore, every cricketer believes that he could be a formidable asset and every island rallies around that one player who they believe is the 'best' and calls for his selection echo, even when there are better players elsewhere.

Many question whether the WICBC has any definite selection policy especially as certain precedents with the selection of players and captains have recently been ignored. In the past more experienced players who had served as vice captains were certain to become the next captain. This was the case when Kanhai was chosen as captain over David Holford. However, this did not seem to be the policy with the selection of Richie Richardson over Desmond Haynes; and this breaking of tradition has angered many and increased insularity. It will be an uphill task for Richardson to gain acceptance from the Barbadian cricketing public, only with perpetual success could this criticism be quelled.

West Indies cricket has been affected by many international issues and pressures which have also encouraged division. The issue of financing which was highlighted during the Kerry Packer series (1977) also showed the division within the WICBC. Jeffrey Stollmeyer, then president of the Board expressed the view that he had no objection to players trying to earn as much money as possible during their limited careers. Other members like Allan Rae and Berkeley Gaskin questioned the loyalty of those players. The players on the other hand did not see the 1978 Parker series as clashing with their commitment to West Indies cricket. This questioning of loyalty of men who had to overcome economic and social barriers locally and internationally to make able contributions created a rift between the Board and the players which has seemingly widened. In the end, this division could not withstand the pressure by the ICC to ban 'rebel' players. This incident also highlighted the lack of a common political initiative by West Indian governments on the issue of South Africa and pointed to the lack of foresight in relation to international politics and its impact on sports in the region.

The attempts by the WICBC to placate the ICC and international critics is yet another hurdle with which West Indies cricket has had to contend. The result has been public criticism of the Board by players who view their conservatism as unprogressive. This open conflict has in some ways affected the morale of the players and the decision by Malcolm Marshall and Vivian Richards to retire from the game with such negativity can attest to that fact.

West Indian cricket continues to demonstrate resilience and endurance in the face of such adversity. This ability to survive has endeared each succeeding generation of West Indians to the game. Continued success symbolizes a mastering not simply of cricket but of the social, economic and political inequalities both regionally and internationally. Occasional failure demonstrates that the struggle is not over and that change and improvement are still needed.

The support for the West Indies cricket team demonstrates that the seeds for regional integration are firmly planted within the psyche of the disposed majority in the region. Further, it is evident that this socially deprived majority recognized the necessity to decolonize a colonial institution and reinforming it with creole values before giving it legitimacy. This is a powerful lesson for those intent on remaining informed by colonial structures and ideologies within the regional integration movement. This movement can never gain legitimacy among West Indians unless it is demonstrated that democratization can occur, giving them a stake in the development and outcome of the entire process.

Entrenched within the support for West Indies cricket is the notion that integration must be people centred. The much written about effervescent West Indian cricket crowd and its active participation further demonstrates that integration does not occur in a vacuum, there must be societal input. According to Maurice St Pierre, 'cricket enables West Indian audiences to come together in large numbers to enjoy a highly rated pastime, and in so doing, West Indians refurbish group solidarity.' He elaborates by stating that this participation must be continuous, a feature lacking in the political and economic spheres of West Indian society. Clearly, despite the structural differences of the seating arrangements at the various cricketing grounds and the economic and social connotations of these arrangements, West Indies cricket has served as a levelling force in the region.

There are numerous insights in relation to regional integration which can be gained from West Indies cricket. The decolonization of the game achieved through its creolization can only serve as a beacon to those who continue to uphold colonial theories of integration as the only means by which unity can be achieved. Further, it shows that integration must be all encompassing, instead of continuing to focus on economic and political unification; social and cultural integration must be the core of the movement. The parochialism and insularity which continue to surface shows that if channelled properly strength can be drawn from disunity especially when the people of the region rationalize the importance of the greater good. This rationalization can only come through legitimization and democratization of the integration process.

Notes

1 The ideology of black liberation is fully explored in *Black Rebellion in Barbados. The Struggle against Slavery, 1627–1838* by Hilary Beckles (Bridgetown, Antilles: 1984) 1–8. Here the actions of the enslaved to achieve certain socio-political rights are examined in relation to their contribution to a state of freedom.

2 The Barbadian planters did not want to be burdened with the weak economies of the Windward Islands. Further, amalgamation would have meant loss of control over labour as much land was available in the Windwards. Finally, it was a rejection of the attempt by the imperial government to implement Crown Colony Government in an island where planters had always controlled the Assembly.

3 This attempt was resisted by the planters in the larger islands who envisaged the notion of a 'West Indies' as encroaching on their individual political power.

4 The British West Indies Federation collapsed in 1962. Much has been written about the reasons for this event and most writers have blamed insularity and separation by water. New trends in the literature point to an institution which was so colonial in nature that it never had the support of West Indians. In fact its dismantling seemed inevitable as it stood in the way of independence and the establishment of black nation states.

5 Clive Lloyd in Michael Manley's *A History of West Indian Cricket*. (London: Andre Deutsch Ltd, 1988), v.

6 C.L.R. James, 'Port of Spain Gazette', June, 1933 in *Cricket* (London: Allison and Busby Ltd, 1986) 34–8.

7 John Figueroa, *West Indies in England: the Post-War Tours* (London: Kingswood Press, 1991), 123.

8 C.L.R. James, 'Journal of the Cricket Society', Spring, *Cricket*. 134–47.

9 G.K. Lewis, *The Growth of the Modern West Indies* (New York: Modern Reader Paperbacks, 1968), 86.

10 Lloyd, in *A History of West Indian Cricket*, v.

11 Winston Lloyd, 'The Game in the Leewards and Windwards' in *The West Indies Cricket Annual*, 1977 edn, 15.

12 Winston Lloyd, 'The Game in the Leewards and Windwards', 15.

13 Tim Hector, 'The Roots of Islands' Cricket: Acceptance at Last after Years of Frustration', *The West Indies Cricket Annual*, 1977, pp. 13–14.

14 Hector, 'The Roots of Islands' Cricket'. 13.

15 V. Richards, *Hitting across the Line* (London: Headline Book Publishing, 1991), 184.

16 M. St Pierre, 'West Indian Cricket, Part II – an Aspect of Creolization,' *Caribbean Quarterly*, Vol. 19, No. 3, September.

17 This anti-Barbadian sentiment stems from the attitude of Barbadians that they are the best West Indian cricketers. This sentiment grew with the success of the white planter teams who had money to spend on cricket because of the success of sugar in that island. It has been perpetuated by the success of the island in the Shell Shield and Red Stripe tournaments. The other islands have a less established club tournament than Barbados and have always seen the defeat of a Barbadian team as the ultimate achievement.

18 The Jamaican crowd at this game were most likely more angry with the WICBC for not selecting noted Jamaican wicket-keeper Jeffrey Dujon for the World Cup. Richie Richardson was appointed captain for that tour and therefore unfortunately received the brunt of the anger. With his recent successes as captain against Australia and Pakistan his popularity in Jamaica and Barbados has increased. Acceptance by crowds in these two islands is an indication of respect earned and beyond parochial boundaries.

Bibliography

1 Axline, A.W., *Caribbean Integration: the Politics of Regionalism*. London: Nichols Publishing Co. Ltd, *c.* 1979.

2 Burton, Richard D.E. 'Cricket, Carnival and Street Culture in the Caribbean', London: Institute of Commonwealth Studies, 1986.

3 Figueroa, John, *West Indies in England: the Post-War Tours*, London: Kingwood Press, 1991.

4 Garner, J., *'Big Bird': Flying High*, London: Weidenfeld & Nicolson Ltd, *c.* 1988.

5 Hector, T., 'The Roots of Island's Cricket: Acceptance at last after years of Frustration', *The West Indies Cricket Annual*, 1977, pp. 13–14.

6 James, C.L.R., *Beyond a Boundary*, London: Stanley Paul & Co. Ltd, *c.* 1976.

7 James, C.L.R., *Cricket*, London: Allison & Busby Ltd, *c.* 1986.

8 Lewis, G.K., *The Growth of the Modern West Indies*, New York: Modern Reader Paperbacks, *c.* 1968.

9 Lloyd, W., 'The Game in the Leewards and Windwards', *The West Indies Cricket Annual*, 1977, p. 15.

10 Manley, M., *A History of West Indian Cricket*, London: Andre Deutsch Ltd, *c.* 1988.

11 Richards, V., *Hitting across the Line*, London: Headline Book Publishing, *c.* 1991.

12 St Pierre, M., 'West Indian Cricket: a Socio-historical Appraisal', Part I, *Caribbean Quarterly*, Vol. 19, No. 2; June 1973, pp. 7–27.

13 St Pierre, M., 'West Indian Cricket, Part II – an Aspect of Creolization', *Caribbean Quarterly*, Vol. 19, No. 3; September. 1973, pp. 20–35.

14 Thompson, L. O'Brien, 'How Cricket is West Indian Cricket?', *Caribbean Review*, Vol. 12, No. 2, 1983, p. 22.

15 Whitington, R.S., *Fouus Galore*, Victoria: Cassell Australia Ltd, 1969.

11   Gordon Greenidge and Curtly Ambrose singing a duet, 1989

12   Mac Fingall inspires the West Indies team with his musical melodies. Courtesy of Nation Library

13   King Dyal, a famous Barbados character, staunch supporter of England and relentless critic of West Indies, dresses for cricket at the Kensington Oval. Courtesy of Advocate Co. Ltd.

14   Ina Howard, a well known West Indian supporter

15 Clyde 'Oney', a well recognized West Indian (Barbados) groundsman

16 Cricketers and calypsonians feting at a fundraising by the West Indies Players Association, l–r Lord Kitchener, Viv Richards, 1989

17 Richie Richardson, the West Indies captain, about to lecture to university students on 'Leadership and West Indies cricket' in Barbados, 1992

18 Professor Hilary Beckles, 4th from left, with his first group of students studying the 'History of West Indies Cricket since 1820' course at the University of the West Indies in Barbados

19   Empty seats: the 'Cummings Affair', the boycott of the West Indies vs. South Africa test in Barbados, 1992

20 l–r: The cricketer Anderson Cummins, Professor Hilary Beckles, and David Holford, the chairman of the West Indies selectors, at the University campus after the boycott, 1992

17

Celebrating cricket:
the symbolic construction of
Caribbean politics

Frank E. Manning

> Cricket has suffered, but not only cricket. The aestheticians have scorned to take notice
> of popular sports and games – to their own detriment. The aridity and confusion of
> which they so mournfully complain will continue until they include organized games
> *and the people who watch them* as an integral part of their data.
>
> C.L.R. James 1963: 191–2; emphasis in original

The failure of art critics to appreciate the aesthetics of popular sport has been no
less myopic than the failure of anthropologists to grasp its social importance.
Although folklorists and protoethnologists of the previous century showed an interest in games – much of it inspired by E.B. Tylor's evolutionary and diffusionist
speculations – the anthropology of play did not advance appreciably until the late
1950s (Schwartzman 1978: 5). A great deal of the recent attention, however, has
been directed at either children's play or at relatively small-scale games – a corpus
pioneered by the early collaborative studies of Roberts and Sutton-Smith (1962,
1966). A significant literature on mass ludic spectacles such as popular sports events
and public celebrations is only now emerging, much of it inspired by the interest of
Gluckman and Turner in "secular ritual" (Moore and Myerhoff 1977) and by
Geertz's (1972) paper on the Balinese cockfight.

The seminal work of these latter figures converges on a conceptual approach to
the relationship between symbolic and social phenomena. For Turner (1977), "lim-
inoid" performative genres such as festivals and carnivals are "proto-" or "meta-
structural," generating cultural comprehension by abstracting and recombining –
often in novel, metaphorical ways – a social structure's basic principles. For
Gluckman (see Gluckman and Gluckman 1977), whose views were articulated in
the last article published before his death, symbolic events such as sports attractions
and theatrical productions differ from traditional religious rites in being an imaginative "presentation" of society rather than a "re-presentation" or copy of it. For
Geertz (1972), the cockfight is a fictive story about its social context, a "metasocial
commentary" in it that is analogous to a literary text in using the devices of aesthetic
license to disarrange conventional semantic contexts and rearrange them in

unconventional ways. Geertz also underscores a point that is less forcefully made by Gluckman and Turner: that symbolic forms are not only a reflexive interpretation of social life, but also a means through which people discover and learn their culture. The lesson for anthropology is that symbolic inquiry, besides laying bare a social system, can also tell us a great deal about the epistemological processes whereby that system is revealed to those whose lives it shapes.

Drawing from these positions, as well as other perspectives that have thrown light on public play and mass performance, this paper examines Bermudian cricket festivals. I focus on the social history of these festivals, on the manner in which they are celebrated, and on a highly significant side activity, gambling. My contention is that the total genre dramatizes a fundamental, racially oriented conflict between cultural identity and economic interest – a conflict that is generalizable to the Caribbean (and perhaps other decolonizing areas) and that underlies the region's political situation. Consistent with Cohen's (1979: 87) observation that anthropology's chief contribution to the study of politics has been the analysis of nonpolitical symbols that have political implications and functions, I propose that celebration can provide a unique understanding of the conceptual parameters in which political awareness is developed and expressed.

Blacks in whites

In the West Indies the game of cricket is played with elegant skill, studied with scholarly intensity, argued with passionate conviction, and revered with patriotic pride. Young boys with makeshift bats and balls play spiritedly in yards, fields, and beaches, learning the skills that in the past century have made West Indians among the world's outstanding cricketers. Organized competition begins in school and continues – often through middle age – in amateur sports clubs. Island-wide teams drawn from the clubs provide the Caribbean's premier sports attraction when they play annually in a touring series known as the Shell Shield. There is also a pan-West Indian team that represents the region in "test" (international) matches and that has been the outstanding exception to a catalog of failed attempts at West Indian unification.

One gleans the historical significance of the game in *Beyond A Boundary*, C.L.R. James's (1963) autobiography cum cricket analysis. A Trinidadian journalist, teacher, historian, political critic, and, above all, cricket devotee, James contends that in the West Indies cricket was traditionally seen as embodying the qualities of the classic British character ideal: fair play, restraint, perseverance, responsibility, and the moral inflections of Victorian Puritanism. Paradoxically, Afro-West Indians were taught to esteem those standards but were denied the means of achieving and demonstrating them. Cricket organizations – clubs, leagues, selection committees, governing bodies – conformed to the wider system of color-class stratification, and when the races occasionally played together, it was customary for whites to bat and blacks to bowl (St Pierre 1973: 7–12).

The phrase "put on your whites" is instructive. Literally, it means to don the several items – white or cream-colored – that make up a cricket uniform: shoes, pants, shirt, sweater, protective gloves, knee pads. Figuratively, it is a metonym of the black struggle in cricket, itself a metonym as well as an instrument of the more general black struggle under British colonialism. In cricket there were a succession of black goals: to get to bat, to gain places on island-wide teams and regional tours, and, as recently as the 1960s, to be named vice-captains and captains of test teams, positions reserved for whites even after racial criteria had been virtually eliminated from selection procedures. Cricket successes brought recognition to Afro–West Indians both internationally and, more begrudgingly, in the upper strata of local society, gradually transforming the sport into a powerful symbol of black ability, achievement, and aspiration.

Bermudian cricket is a variation on these themes, but one that, like Bermuda itself, caricatures and often strikingly illuminates the Caribbean pattern. Lying a thousand miles and a climatic zone north of the West Indies, Bermuda has a five-month summer cricket season and therefore does not participate in most major West Indian tournaments, which are held during the winter. Nor do Bermudians take the game as seriously or as professionally as West Indians do. In the Caribbean, for example, festival games – occasions when a cricket match takes place in a setting of festive sociability – are relatively informal, localized, and of little general interest (James 1963: 20–1).[1] In Bermuda, however, festival games are both the highlights of the cricket season and, aside from Christmas, the calendar's most significant holidays. Bermudian festival cricket is the counterpart of Caribbean carnivals, but it enriches the spirit of celebration with the drama of a popular sporting classic.

The racial division of Bermudian cricket was shaped by an apartheid-like form of segregation, rather than by the West Indian system of color-class stratification. Introduced by British military personnel in the nineteenth century, the game was originally played in white sporting clubs. Blacks responded by forming neighborhood cricket clubs that have since evolved into the country's major centers of sport, entertainment, and sociability (Manning 1973). Through the clubs, blacks gained unquestioned superiority in cricket; when racial integration was nominally introduced in the 1960s, whites virtually withdrew from the game.

Two of the oldest black clubs, Somerset and St George's, were begun primarily to promote an informal cricket contest held each August 1st in commemoration of the 1834 emancipation of slaves in British territories – an occasion marked by varied festivities throughout the Commonwealth Caribbean. Under club sponsorship the event developed into Cup Match, the oldest and most prominent cricket festival. Now held on the Thursday and Friday closest to August 1st, the game's historical identification with blacks is maintained by the white practice of observing the first day of Cup Match as Somers's Day, named after the British Admiral Sir George Somers who discovered Bermuda in 1609.

Besides Cup Match there are the Eastern, Western, and Central County Games, each involving four clubs in a series of three matches staggered between June and

271

September. As these series progress there is a buildup of festivity and sporting interest, so that the final games – in effect, sequels to Cup Match – are like Cup Match as occasions of mass celebration. In white society the County Games are paralleled by summer yachting competitions, notably the renowned Newport-Bermuda race. Nowhere in the Caribbean is there a more striking example of the pluralistic segmentation that Smith (1965) attributed to British West Indian societies.

While Cup Match commemorates emancipation from slavery, the County Games celebrate diffuse aspects of the black tradition and life-style. The Eastern and Western series, the two most popular, reflect variants in the black situation that figure in the deeper level meaning of festival cricket. Begun in 1904, the Eastern Games involve clubs that draw from old, demographically stable neighborhoods. In each neighborhood there is a core of black extended families, typically small property owners deriving modest incomes from family stores, trades, service jobs, and, in earlier generations more than now, part-time farming and fishing. The principle of family-neighborhood integrity is the basis of Eastern County selection rules. Eligibility is based on having been born in the club's neighborhood – the usual and preferred criterion – or having been a resident of it for at least two years. Although in a number of cases current players have moved away from their ancestral neighborhoods and play for other clubs in league games, their return for the County Games makes each club roster a roll call of familiar surnames, re-creating the networks and reviving the sentiments of traditional social organization.

The Western County Games, begun in 1962, are a product of newer social influences. The Western parishes have grown appreciably since the time when the series started, as new luxury hotels have created employment and as the demand for housing among blacks short of middle age has been met by the conversion of large estates into fashionable residential subdivisions (Newman 1972: 3). Reflecting these trends, the Western Games are touted not as neighborhood rivalries, but as slick, highly competitive all-star games. Clubs vie intensely for Bermuda's best cricketers, offering lucrative incentives that lure players from outside the Western parishes and that encourage opportunistic switching between clubs from one year to the next. The clubs have even extended recruitment into the Caribbean, scouting the region for prospects and arranging their immigration. In the mid-1970s, the final game of the Western series was extended from one day to two, a move aimed at raising the caliber of play, generating wider public interest, and boosting gate receipts. The emphasis on aggressive commercialism is also seen in other areas of club activity, notably entertainment. Two of the clubs involved in the series (as well as other clubs in the Western parishes) have built elegant lounges which remain open as late as 5 a.m., offering formidable competition to the area's hotels.

Underlying the varying inflections of the Eastern and Western County Games are changes in the terms of clientage, the basis of the black Bermudian socioeconomic condition. Traditionally, Bermuda was run by a white aristocracy whose relations to blacks were paternal in both a biological and social sense. Descendants of the original seventeenth-century British settlers, the aristocracy were seafarers until the 1870s, agricultural exporters from then until the 1920s, and more recently an interlocking establishment of merchants, bankers, and corporate lawyers. Functioning as a ruling class in an almost feudal sense (Lewis 1968: 323), they used the instruments of patronage – jobs, loans, credit, mortgages, charity – to maintain the allegiance and even the endearment of blacks, who make up three-fifths of the population, as well as a white underclass consisting of old "poor cousin" families, newer immigrants from Commonwealth countries, and Azorean Portuguese imported as indentured agricultural laborers. Patron-client relations were typically transacted within neighborhoods and parishes and between extended families, reinforcing residential identity and producing alliances between black and white kin groups that crosscut the system of institutionalized racial segregation. The common Caribbean metaphor of island society as a single large family (Wilson 1973:47) was powerfully resonant in Bermuda, yielding a meaningful context in which patronage took the social form of a relationship between benevolent, although demanding, white patriarchs and filial black dependents.

Since the early 1960s, however, the power and prestige of the aristocracy have been substantially eroded. The tourist boom has made foreign-owned hotels the major employers and, along with the development of an offshore corporate business sector, brought to Bermuda a class of expatriate managers who wield an appreciable influence in local affairs. In addition, the buoyancy and expansion of the economy has allowed the aggressive rise of underclass whites, notably Bermuda-born Portuguese, and a handful of black professionals and entrepreneurs. Tellingly, many of the aristocracy's merchant houses on Front Street, the commercial frontispiece of Hamilton, are now dominated by whites whose rise to economic prominence has come about within the past two decades.

What these changes have done to the patronage system is alter its character and style while maintaining, and perhaps strengthening, its grip on the overwhelming majority of blacks. The benevolent paternalism of the aristocracy has been replaced by the bureaucratic orientation of the new elite, and largess has been escalated to include company directorships, investment opportunities; business partnerships, and well-paid managerial positions. Blacks enjoy the life-style provided by an affluent economy, but at the cost of remaining in a position of clientage and subordination.

"We black Bermudians," an old man cautioned, "can easily fool you. We're laughing on the outside, but crying on the inside." This commonplace statement derives its impact from oxymoron, the figure of speech that combines conceptual and emotional antitheses. Viewed as a collectively enacted "text," festival cricket is also built on oxymoron. Overtly and purposefully, these games articulate the meaning of freedom, family, community, club, and, above all, cricket itself – symbols that manifest to blacks their identity, their solidarity, their survival. But the games also reflect, implicitly but no less significantly, the field of socioeconomic relations in which blacks are dependent on a white power structure that has lost its traditional

273

character but preserved its oppressive force. In this juxtaposition – this dramatic oxymoron – lies the basis of both the political system and the political imagination.

Food, liquor, clothing, and money

Soliciting a description of festival cricket early in my first Bermudian fieldwork, I was told it was the time "when we eat everything in Bermuda, drink everything in Bermuda, wear everything in Bermuda, and spend everything in Bermuda." Although popular interest in the game runs unusually high, festival cricket is an occasion of participation, not spectatorship. The festival ethos is one of hedonistic indulgence, gregarious sociability, histrionic exhibitionism, lavish hospitality, conspicuous consumption – behaviors that epitomize and celebrate the black Bermudian self-image. In Singer's (1955) terms, festival cricket is a cultural performance, a dramatic spectacle in which a people proclaim and demonstrate their sense of who they are.

Like Carnival, festival cricket involves a period of preparation that is considered nearly as much fun as the event itself. For weeks before Cup Match there is intense speculation about the selection of teams. Pundits offer their personal choices in letters to the editor, and the subject is heatedly discussed in bars, in buses, and on street corners. The principal centers of activity are the black clubs, where people go, in the words of one informant, "just to hear the arguments." The arguments peak a week before the game, when the club selection committees announce their picks to the membership at a meeting in which dramatic suspense, flamboyant and often fiery oratory, and uproarious entertainment combine ritualistically to induct chosen players into the club tradition. In the final days before the game there is a general buildup of festive sociability, a flurry of shopping activity for food, liquor, and clothing, and extended expressions of team loyalty through the display of club colors on cars and items of apparel. For County Games the scenario is similar, but on a smaller scale.

Game days begin early, as fans laden with coolers, umbrellas, collapsible chairs, and briefcase-sized portable radios arrive at the grounds several hours before the first ball is bowled at 10 a.m. Locations around the periphery of the field are carefully staked out, mostly by groups of friends who have made arrangements to contribute to a common supply of food and liquor. A more enviable location is in makeshift pavilions erected at the edge of the field or on surrounding hillsides. Wooden frames covered with canvas or thatch, the pavilions bear colorful names such as "Honey Bee Lounge" and often fly flags made of liquor banners or team insignia. Organized by club-based peer groups, the pavilions accommodate 10–20 couples who pay a set fee – as much as $100[2] for the two days of Cup Match – for food, liquor, and other amenities. Most pavilions are wired to the clubhouse, enabling the use of lights, appliances, and stereos that typically have auditorium-sized electronic speakers.

In all groups there is emphasis on extravagance, sophistication, ostentation. Bottles of brand-name liquor ranging from the 40-ounce to the 1-gallon size are set out on coolers and tables, flanked by cherries, lemons, limes, angostura bitters, and more specialized garnishes and liqueurs for concoctions that gain popularity during a particular festival season (Scotch, milk, and grenadine was the favorite one year). Food is plentiful and of two kinds: the cherished "soul" dishes built around chicken, fish, and "hoppin' john" (black-eyed peas and rice); and festive specialties, notably cassava pie and a chicken and pork filling baked pastry made from shredded cassava). At the Eastern County Games one is also likely to see a number of festive seafood dishes, including mussel pie, conch stew, and hash shark. For those without enough food or liquor, there are at least 2 bars in the clubhouse and 2 or more bar concessions, along with 20 or more food concessions, on the grounds.

Liquor is a basis of hospitality patterns that link individuals and groups with the larger audience. People generously offer drinks to passing friends, whose visit is enlivened by joking, teasing, insult swapping, and other forms of verbal performance characteristic of Afro-Caribbean and Afro-American culture (Abrahams 1970; Kochman 1970). The visitor invariably extends an offer of reciprocal hospitality, creating an opportunity, and something of a social obligation, for the hosts to return the visit later in the day. In the pavilions persons are allowed to entertain two guests at a time, an informal rule that balances the importance of hospitality with a check against overcrowding.

The continuous traffic around the field is known as the "fashion show." Celebrants sport outfits acquired for the festival cricket season, occasionally hand-made but more often purchased during the advertising campaigns that retail merchants mount in the weeks before the Cup Match. Drawn from black American and West Indian trends, styles are valued for combining smartness with sexuality. A decade ago, for example, the style known in Bermuda as "black mod" was dominant. Women paraded in arousing "hot pants" outfits, suggestive two-piece ensembles, bell-bottom and two-tone slacks, close-fitting pants suits, wool knit skirts and jerseys, low-slung chain belts, bubble blouses, leather collars, suede fringed handbags, large round earrings, ostentatious bracelets and necklaces, pink and yellow tinted sunglasses, and "natural" coiffures. In the same period, men wore jump suits, silk shirts slit open to expose the chest, two-tone and wide-cuffed flair pants, bolero and ruffled shirts with dog-ear collars, and suede vests over the bare skin. More recent styles have been varied, ranging from "black disco" to "unisex chic." Women have adopted pleated balloon pants, terry cloth outfits, and "cornrow" coiffures elaborated with beads and braids – a style that can cost upwards of $100 in Bermudian hairdressing salons. Men have taken to West Indian styles, notably shirt-jacs, kareba suits, and among youth, Rastafarian dreadlocks. The jewelry portfolios of both sexes center on a half-dozen necklaces of various sizes and designs. Designer jean outfits are in vogue, as are athletic shorts that are worn by women with halter tops, by men with athletic shirts, and by both sexes with inscribed T-shirts.

The popularity of T-shirts warrants special comment. The leading black dealer in the field estimates selling 1,000 to 1,500 shirts for Cup Match alone, many of them at the cricket grounds in a concession stand that he equips with his printing and dyeing machines. His most popular line is what he calls his "black" shirts – motifs about festival cricket, pan-African identity, racial solidarity, and black entertainment genres. Next in popularity, and sometimes combined with racial motifs, are sexual themes, most of them using slang double entendres for genitalia and copulation in conjunction with humorous inscriptions of invitation, challenge, and braggadocio. The manufacture of T-shirts at the game epitomizes the rapid popularization of new styles and the ready satisfaction of customer demand for them, central values in black Bermudian fashion culture.

Performative and provocative, the fashion show is closely observed by radio commentators, who mix accounts of the cricket game with animated descriptions of fashion plates. Indeed, one of the major reasons fans bring radios to the game is to hear these accounts of themselves and their fellow celebrants. Like liquor, fashion is a medium of exchange that integrates an aggregate audience into a cultural community. It is also, again like liquor, what Sapir (1934) termed a symbol of condensation: it exemplifies what it signifies, namely an ethos of affluence, hedonism, sophistication, and display. An observable result of this symbolism is that fashion evokes the black conversational mode known as "rapping," a lewd and lively exchange between men and women aimed both at entertainment and at the initiation or enhancement of sexual partnerships. Like Carnival, festival cricket has a rich lore as a period of license and sexual hyperactivity.

Other modes of performance compete with fashion for public attention. Steel, brass, and rock bands play on the sidelines, stimulating impromptu dancing. Also present are Combey Dancers, masked mummers who render a Bermudian version of the John Canoe dance to the rhythm of drums, fifes, snares, and whistles. High on surrounding hillsides are groups of Rastafarians, who smoke *ganja* (marijuana), translate the festival ambience into poetry, and orate philosophically about a black millennium. A profane version of that millennium is enacted on adjacent waterways, where "boojee" (black bourgeois) yachtsmen display their boats and hold swank deck parties.

The cricket match concludes at 6:30 p.m., but festivities continue well into the night. The clubhouse is jammed with revellers who fraternize with the cricketers, replay and comically argue every detail of the game, and get very drunk as the evening wears on. Other fans extend their merriment onto the field and may remain there all night. Several clubs run evening events ranging from dances and parties to outdoor concerts featuring black American and Caribbean performers.

A final ancillary activity warrants separate discussion for both ethnographic and analytic purposes. That activity is gambling, which takes place during the cricket game on the periphery of the field in a large tent known as the "stock market." As festival cricket amplifies a mode of behavior that is manifest in less spectacular ways on a day-to-day basis, stock market gambling caricatures a general style of acquisition premised on calculated opportunism (Manning 1973: 87–114), as well as a particular fondness for gambling that has put soccer pool agencies and off-track betting parlors among Bermuda's lucrative businesses and has, within the club milieu, given rise to regular bingo nights, organized card games, raffles, lotteries, and so on. The significance of gambling here is twofold: first, it explicitly symbolizes a relationship between culture and money that is represented more implicitly in other phases and spheres of festival cricket; second, at a deeper level, it dramatizes the culture-money relationship in a manner that qualifies and questions the meaningful thrust of the total festival. Juxtaposed to its own context, gambling illustrates the tension that pervades black political life.

The stock market

Framed with wood or tubular steel and covered with canvas or sheet plastic, the stock market is a makeshift casino for a dice game known as "crown and anchor." Played on boards set atop wooden horses, the game involves betting on one or more of six choices: the four suits of cards, a red crown, or a black anchor. Three dice are rolled, their sides corresponding to the choices on the board. Winners are paid the amount of their bet times the number of dice on which it is shown, while losers have their money taken by the board. If a croupier rolls a crown and two spades, for example, he collects the money on the four losing choices, pays those who bet on the crown, and pays double those who bet on the spade.

Like cricket, crown and anchor is a game of British origin that has gained immense popularity in the Caribbean, particularly at festivals. I have personally watched it being played by Antiguans at Carnival and by Jamaican Maroons at the celebration of Captain Cudjoe's birthday in the remote mountain village of Accompong.[3] In Bermuda the game is distinguished by the amount of money that is displayed and bet. Croupiers hold thousands of dollars in their hands, and players are likely to hold several hundred. The minimum bet is one dollar, but only novices and casual players, mostly women, bet that little. Regular players tend to bet between $10 and $50 each time, although much higher bets are common. Some boards place a ceiling of $100 on bets, but the larger boards – i.e., those with bigger cash floats – generally have no ceiling. An informant lighted on the ostentatious display of cash as the chief difference between festival cricket and Christmas, the calendar's two major holidays. At Christmas, he observed, money is spent; at festival cricket, it is both spent and shown.

Crown and anchor is marked by a peculiar paradox. Although the odds marginally favor the board, regular players say that an effective strategy is to bet on choices that have not come up for two or three rolls of the dice and are therefore "due" simply by the laws of probability. A more defensive tactic, and one that is easily combined with the above, is simply to double bets on the same item until it eventually comes up and all losses, as well as the initial bet, are recouped. The only limitation is lack of ready cash, but this is minimized by the substantial sums that players carry and by the ready willingness of the boards to accept personal checks and even to loan money.

In practice, however, players tend to bet erratically and lose, often substantially. In the parlance of the stock market, they succumb to "greed" and "lose their heads" in a futile attempt to "break the board." What is potentially a game of strategy – the type associated with mastering the environment – is in effect a game of chance – the type associated with divining an uncontrollable environment (Roberts *et al.* 1959). The following example from my field notes is representative of a pattern evidenced by the stock market's "high rollers":

> Placing $10 and $20 bets unsystematically, a man lost his own money – about $60 – as well as $50 that he borrowed from the board. He then borrowed another $50 and increased it to about $85 by winning a few small bets. He next bet $70 on the club, which came up on three dice to add $210 to his money. But although he owed the board $100, he kept playing rather than pay back the debt and quit with a net winning. Within a half hour he had lost all his money, as well as a third loan of $50. As he left the board he quietly told the croupier: "I owe you $150. I'll see you Monday morning."

The familiar experience of losing is offset by the claim that gambling money is expendable. As one man put it after losing $100, "If I have money to spend, I spend it. If I lose it, I don't give a fuck. I'll go back to work next week and get some more."

Although the overwhelming majority of bettors are black, the running of boards – the profitable side of the stock market – has been dominated by the Portuguese. In the 1930s, Manuel de Souza (a pseudonym), the teenage son of an Azorean-born farm laborer, watched crown and anchor being played in the segregated white section of the racetrack. Surmising the game's appeal to blacks, he started going to festival cricket matches with a dice cup, a small table, and a tarpaulin that he stretched between some trees to make a crude tent. De Souza's winnings put him on the road to acquiring a modest complex of businesses: a fleet of taxi cabs, several small farms, and a restaurant. "You can say that I owe what I have to crown and anchor," he acknowledged. "It gave me my start in life."

As de Souza's business and gambling profits grew, he began running more boards in partnership with other Portuguese. In the 1960s he was challenged by the clubs, which successfully pressed the claim that the stock market should be under their control. De Souza countered with patronage, supporting club building projects and occasionally contributing a share of his winnings. In return he was given first option on buying the entire gambling concession, an arrangement that gave the clubs a substantial cash flow to stock their bars for festivals and that made de Souza something of a "czar" or, better perhaps, "godfather," of the stock market. With his partners he ran a half-dozen tables and reports that his share of their net profits averaged $30,000 per season. He made a further profit by selling the remainder of the space in the stock market, chiefly to a growing group of Portuguese who had acquired gambling reputations in private house parties.

Although de Souza and other Portuguese board operators were generally astute enough to hire black assistants, black gamblers gradually pushed the clubs for a bigger stake in the stock market, and ultimately for control of it. Their efforts have been partially successful; for several years the concession of Cup Match and the Western County Games has been sold to a syndicate of black businessmen, while in the Eastern County series one club continues to favor de Souza and the others run the stock market themselves. The change has resulted in more blacks and fewer Portuguese, although the new concession holders sell choice space (near the outside and sheltered from the afternoon sun) to the remaining Portuguese, including de Souza, who are respected in gambling circles and known to attract heavy bettors.

Yet the racial change in the stock market is less radical than it may appear. Many of the black-run boards, and a clear majority of those which have no ceiling on bets, are backed financially by whites, including Portuguese, or by racially mixed investment syndicates. The backers provide the cash float – as much as $15,000 at some boards – in return for a 40 to 60 percent share of the winnings. The parallel between the stock market and the wider economic system is frequently observed: blacks are in visible positions and appear to be making money, but whites are behind them and in control. Reflecting on the situation, one black gambler observed: "You know, come to think of it, I don't know a single black person in this country who has made money without having a white sponsor."

Another parallel between the stock market and the broader Bermudian situation is observed in connection with mid-1970s legislation requiring the host club to pay $500 for a one-day gambling permit and preventing the boards from taking bets later than one hour after the scheduled end of the cricket game. The cost of the permit has been passed on to the concession holders and, in turn, to individual board operators, while the time regulation has stopped boards from staying open to increase winnings, recoup earlier losses, or simply capitalize on late betting action – a restriction that has hurt mainly the smaller, black-run boards, which are on the inside and therefore wait longer for bettors. For blacks, these new statutes typify a pattern of reaction against black economic gain. As one black board operator put it, "When the stock market was run by the Portuguese, it was wide open. As soon as we boys started to get a little piece of the action, Government stepped in. That's the general trend in Bermuda."

Whatever the economic position of blacks in the stock market, their cultural presence there is highly visible and clearly dominant over whites – another correspondence, of course, to the larger society. The Portuguese play quietly and dress plainly, almost dourly. Their boards are about six feet long and staffed by two, or at most three, croupiers. They keep a supply of cold beer but do not offer it until a player has begun betting. They rarely socialise with bettors or other operators, viewing the gambling relationship as an exclusively economic transaction. As de Souza explained, "People don't play at my board because they like me. They play because they want to break me." The Portuguese leave unobtrusively after the game and abstain from the evening festivities. I once went looking for de Souza after an

Eastern County Game and found him working soberly in his restaurant. He said that he cleared $1,800 from his three tables – "a day's pay" – but volunteered that his lack of emotion made it impossible for most people to tell whether he had won or lost.

The image of black gamblers, by contrast, is an ideal type of the highly performative, black-oriented expressive style that Wilson (1973: 227–8) terms "reputation" – the ethos that pervades the entire festival. Croupiers dress and behave flamboyantly, standing on platforms to increase their visibility, spreading their bills like a fan, throwing their dice cups high in the air, handing out one dollar bills to passersby to engage them in the game, and barking stock invitations to bet: "Get some money for your honey . . . . Come in here on a bike, go home in a Rolls Royce . . . . Take your hands out of your pocket and put your money on the table . . . . Wall Street slumps, but this stock market pays double." The black tables average eight to ten feet, with sets of betting squares on each end and often with added decorations such as the signs of the zodiac. At the larger tables there may be a staff of six, typically a "house man" who shakes the dice and holds the $50 bills, two or three assistants who collect and pay the bets, and one or two others who serve as bartenders and greeters. Both liquor and beer are freely offered to onlookers as well as bettors, and when a person's drink is half empty it will be wantonly thrown on the ground and replaced with a fresh drink.

Black gamblers extend and exploit the festival's sexual license. At least two black operators have reportedly imported prostitutes, a commodity virtually absent from Bermuda, from the United States. The more common practice is to give gambling money to well-endowed women in return for their appearing at the board in plunging necklines, loosely crocheted blouses, diaphanous T-shirts, tight shorts, and similar fashions aimed at attracting – and distracting – male gamblers. As a sequel to this gimmick, a few black operators have begun hiring female croupiers and even forming gambling partnerships with women. Conversely, women have increasingly become regular and sometimes heavy bettors, a trend that is particularly noticeable in the western parishes where a good number of well-paid hotel positions are held by women. The effort to attract – and hold – women bettors enlivens the barking calls with colorful exchanges.

> A middle-aged woman was about to bet on heart, but withdrew the money. The operator countered: "Don't blame me if three hearts come up, lady. Cause you and I – I've been looking at you for a long time – I figure our hearts could get together. We don't need no crown and anchor, honey. Our hearts could really do something."

> A woman was betting, and winning, on the black choices (spades, clubs, the anchor), which are all on the bottom of the board. The operator tried to persuade her to diversify her betting: "You gotta go topside. No woman in the world is satisfied on the bottom side".

> A woman in her early thirties had been breaking even on small bets and drinking heavily. Towards the end of the day she put a double entendre to the operator: "All I

want is a piece of you." He took up the challenge and carried on a series of lewd but playful insults that drew raucous laughter from those at the table. But she got the last word: "Knobby, you wouldn't know what to do if you tripped and fell on top of me."

Black operators indicate that their gambling success depends on establishing their reputations within a broader context of public sociability. One prominent operator spends several hours per day outside the bar that he owns in partnership with another black and two whites, engaging passersby in brief conversation, waving at pedestrians on the other side of the street, and shouting at passing cars. This strategy, he explains, provides the exposure that is needed to attract people to his crown and anchor board (as well as to his bar and to a nightclub that he owns with his partners).

A modern Bermudian proverb is at this point appropriate: "Black is black and white is white, but money is green." Culturally different and socially divided, the races nonetheless come together for a common goal: the acquisition of money. There is no better illustration of this proverb than stock market gambling, which magnifies the unique black cultural identity that is celebrated in festival cricket at the same time that it brings the races together in a staged encounter aimed at fast and easy wealth. That scenario is a dramatic rendition of what Bermudian politics, at bottom, is all about.

Racial inversion underlies the dramatic form of festival cricket. Blacks dress up in "whites" to play a white game that they have transformed into a celebration of black culture. Blacks take a white gambling game and make it the setting for a hyperbolic performance of their social personality. Whites enter a black milieu and baldly demonstrate their superordinate position. Such inversion exemplifies the carnivalesque, a genre in which the characteristic multiplexity of symbolic expression is extended by the tendency for symbols to be used playfully and for primarily aesthetic effect. This tendency creates what Babcock (1973) calls a "surplus of signifiers," a Rabelaisian profusion of images and condensed metaphors framed in a mode of liminality.

While the range of significance is vast, fragmented, and often highly individualized, the exegete can take clues from recurrent and centrally placed symbols. A major, meaningful thrust of festival cricket, manifest in the tradition and style of celebration, is the relation of a reflexive version of black identity to hedonism, high style, and money. Turner's (1964: 29–31) contention, that dominant clusters of symbols interchange social and sensory material themes, is appropriate. Like similar symbolic formulations in the club milieu, festival cricket contributes to the multifaceted process whereby black Bermudians are rejecting a stance of social inferiority in favor of a positive and assertive sense of self-awareness (Manning 1973: 149–83).

There is also an antithetical thrust of meaning, reminding blacks of their economic subordination and dependency on whites. The reminder is implicit in the overall emphasis on fashion and indulgence, for Bermudian blacks are acutely aware, even in festival, that consumerism keeps them in clientage. In the stock market, however, the message is explicit: big money and effective power are still in white hands. Blacks can commemorate their traditions and exhibit their ethos, but they must also deal with whites, who have the odds – mathematical and psychological – in their favor. If festival cricket is viewed as a dramatic form, the black gamblers are both heroes and clowns. In the former role they glamorize a social vision of black culture, while in the latter they enact an economic relationship in which the vision is transparently irrelevant. Like the ludic inversion of racial categories, this sense of juxtaposition and self-parody is characteristic of the carnivalesque.

As a formative feature of the black Bermudian experience, the culture–economics interplay has a variety of demonstrable references. The most clear and currently paramount, however, is the system of party politics. An arena of intense interest and extraordinarily high participation, Bermudian politics bears both a striking conceptual similarity and an uncanny ethnographic correspondence to festival cricket. Let us briefly consider this double relationship.

Party politics came to Bermuda in 1963 with the formation of the Progressive Labour Party (PLP) by black groups who had previously been active in the successful universal suffrage movement.[4] In the election of that year, the party contested 9 of 36 parliamentary seats, winning 6 of them and clearly demonstrating the practical benefits of party organization. The aristocracy responded to the challenge a year later by forming the United Bermuda Party (UBP), which was initially joined by 24 of the 30 independents in the House of Assembly, all but 1 of them white. For the remainder of the decade the UBP sought to coopt the issues pressed by the PLP, espousing, at least nominally, constitutional reform and the bread-and-butter issues of universal free education, health and welfare benefits, and the Bermudianization of the labor force. The UBP's trump card, however, was the promise of a thoroughgoing "partnership" – the term used in campaign slogans – between blacks and whites in the running of Bermuda. The partnership was demonstrated politically by strenuous efforts to recruit black candidates in the 1968 and subsequent elections, a general tactic of putting blacks in highly visible positions in both the party organization and the Cabinet; the naming of a black premier between 1971 and 1975; the appeasement of a black-dominated parliamentary "reform" group which forced the resignation of that premier's white successor in 1977; and, from the late 1970s onward, the gradual implementation of demands put forth by an internal black caucus seeking greater leverage in both the party and the national economy.

Rhetorically, the UBP presents the partnership as a guarantee of security as well as an opportunity for gain. Only through the visible demonstration of racial integration, it is claimed, can Bermuda continue to attract tourists and international companies, the sources of prosperity. The UBP couples this appeal with an emphasis on its traditional role as manager of the economy. In the 1980 election campaign, for example, Premier David Gibbons, a white who also holds the finance portfolio and whose family controls Bermuda's largest conglomerate, told an audience:

> This election is not about personalities. It is about the conditions of people's lives. Day in and day out. People's jobs, income, housing. And, above all, the strength and stability of our economy, upon which all else depends.

> Look to the United Bermuda Party's management of our economy. At a time when so many nations in the west are struggling and losing ground, Bermuda maintains one of the highest rates of per capita income in the world . . . . Stability, security. These are facts. And they've come to pass because of experience and prudent, efficient management.

The UBP gave its economic theme a dimension of grave urgency in a full-page newspaper advertisement published on polling day:

> Today is the day when you vote . . . either to maintain Bermuda's economic growth and your own financial security and stability or . . . take a chance on the PLP. Think carefully and vote UBP.

The UBP's accommodations to black interests and its emphasis on economic security have given it an unbroken winning record at the polls, albeit by successively reduced majorities. The PLP's reaction, moderated in tone as its political position has improved, has been to emphasize its "true" blackness and therefore its legitimate and logical claim to black voter support. For the first decade of its existence, the PLP projected a posture of militant racial chauvinism, articulated through American and Caribbean "Black Power" rhetoric. In the middle 1970s, the PLP embraced the idiom of revivalist religion, a move aimed at making inroads among black church groups and, more generally, at appealing to racial consciousness implicitly rather than explicitly by stirring the powerful and pregnant association between revivalism and black culture. In the 1980 campaign, the PLP balanced the emphasis on religion with a more secular appeal to racial identity. The campaign slogan was "Xpress yourself', ' a black Bermudian colloquialism borrowed jointly from American soul music and Jamaican reggae lyrics and combining an allusion to the marking of a ballot paper with a slang encouragement for self-assertion. One television commercial showed a group of blacks, dancing funky style, while a singer chanted "express yourself" and an announcer extolled the merits of the PLP.

Whatever their stated differences on issues – and these have converged considerably in recent years as both parties have sought a center ground – the essential partisan distinction is racial. Recent surveys indicate that whites vote almost unanimously for the UBP, and that four-fifths of the black votes go to the PLP – a division that crosscuts and overrides class, age, sex, ideological disposition, and other pertinent social factors (Manning 1978a: 199–209). The choice for blacks remains what it has always been: cultural attachment or economic security, loyalty and commitment to blacks, or strategic alignment with whites.

The distinction between the parties is manifest ethnographically in the festival setting. Hodgson (1967: 311), a black Bermudian historian and PLP polemicist, describes Cup Match as "the one and only true symbol and celebration of the black man's emancipation." Her enthusiasm, however, is offset by a skepticism that blacks will forsake such symbols in order to participate in white festivities that have now dropped the color barrier. This concern, while lacking empirical foundation, has prompted PLP politicians to present a high profile at cricket festivals, making the general environment one in which PLP supporters are familiar and welcome and UBP supporters are somewhat isolated and uncomfortable. The festival's partisan association is extended by the PLP's considerable efforts to court the club constituency (Manning 1973: 210–49), a tactic exemplified by party leader Lois Browne-Evans's speech at a club dinner in 1978.

> Your long and illustrious history . . . needs to be told. Essays ought to be held for your children to write what they think Daddy's club is all about . . . .
>
> Let not economic strangulation be the cause of your enslavement. For I am convinced that you have a part to play in the Bermuda of the future, just as your forbears played a vital role in the Bermuda of the past.
>
> You must continue working until your country is free from paternalism and patronage, free from all the shackles that we know. Do not remove one form of chains for another. You must avoid the tendency to be dependent.

The stock market, however, presents a striking contrast to the overall festival milieu. The black table operators, like their Portuguese counterparts and white backers, are primarily UBP supporters. The coterie is informally led by a black UBP member of the House of Assembly, who is also renowned, on a few occasions scandalously, for the organization of invitational crown and anchor parties in private homes. At least two prominent backers also hold UBP seats in Parliament, and it is widely known that several black board operators are being groomed as future UBP candidates. Talking to me on the street, one of the blacks who operates a table on which there is no betting limit explained his support for the UBP as follows: "There is not one black person in Bermuda with any money who is PLP. Not one . . . . If the [white] man looks after you, then you've got to protect him." When a PLP member within earshot began to challenge him, the gambler yelled: "Shut the fuck up. It's niggers like you that are holding back motherfuckers like me."

PLP activists, on the other hand, tend to eschew the stock market, or at most to congregate outside or walk through without betting. Observing the action at a crown and anchor board, one PLP politician told me with a wink: "I only watch the stock market. I never invest." This avoidance is encouraged by the PLP's oft-stated position that gambling is functionally supportive of the status quo and by its general desire to adhere, publicly at least, to the strong moral condemnation of gambling made by the black churches.

Festival cricket, then, is a metapolitical commentary. It is a carnivalesque rendition of the semantic context in which Bermudian politics is conceived, institutionalized, and transacted. Through celebration, black Bermudians dramatize – and, indeed, define and discover – a fundamental aspect of their social position and its relationship, conceptual and ethnographic, to their political options. (Logically, of course, the argument is reversible; politics could be construed as a concordance for festival cricket. From a Bermudian standpoint, however, it is politics, not festival, that requires comprehension, choice, and commitment. Festival is merely for enjoyment, and perhaps profit.)

It is here that the relationship of symbolic to social phenomena, of festival to politics, is crucial, and that the convergent positions of Turner (1977), Gluckman and Gluckman 1977), and Geertz (1972), attributing creative autonomy to ludic symbolic forms, are useful. Although festival cricket evidences myriad correspondences to the political system, it is no more a mere reflection of politics than it is a functional appendage of it. The festival version of black culture is not the ideological and instrumental type of racial awareness propounded by the PLP, but a comical caricature of the black life-style and a joyous fantasy that links racial identity to the material wealth and glamor promised by a white-dominated, consumer-oriented economy. Likewise, the festival version of biracial partnership is not the liberal and pragmatic plea for partnership advanced by the UBP, but naked dramatization of white control that lays bare both the crass acquisitiveness of blacks and their continuing subordination to whites, and that further plays on these meanings in a burlesque of the whole patronage system that transforms money from an object of need to one of show.

In Durkheimian terms – which are the ancestry of much symbolic theory – festival cricket is a "transfiguration" of Bermudian political society (cf. Nisbet 1965: 74). The semantic essence of festival cricket is that it throws the realm of politics into relief by disassembling its parts and reordering them in patterns consistent with the aesthetics of celebration, fun, and performance. Festival cricket reveals politics in the way that only an extended metaphor can – by creatively connecting disparate realms of experience in a manner that highlights the definitive features (in this case, the interplay of cultural identity and economic interest) on which the connection is predicated. To borrow Bateson's (1972: 177–93) classic model of cognition, festival cricket is a map for the territory of politics – not a literal, drawn-to-scale map that merely replicates its referent, but a metaphorical map, an interpretive guide, that figuratively situates its referent and conveys social knowledge about it. It is this knowledge that makes Bermudian politics a comprehensible phenomenon.

Conclusion

Like any venture into the analysis of symbolic forms as texts, the interpretation offered here rests ultimately on the anthropologist, who "strains to read over the shoulders of those to whom they [the texts] properly belong" (Geertz 1972: 29). In part, the validity and value of such an interpretation depends on whether it can be generalized, as a theoretical construct and heuristic device, to other cultures. Limitations of space and scope make it impractical to address that consideration here, but a few condensed examples from the West Indies may suggest the basis of a comparative approach.

The major festival genre of the eastern Caribbean is Carnival, which evolved in Trinidad but has diffused throughout the Windward and Leeward islands with minor changes in format.[5] Like Bermuda's Cup Match, the historical referent of Carnival, for blacks, is emancipation from slavery. The festival's major performative symbols – from the canboulay parade, ritualized stick-fighting, and gang warfare in earlier times, to calypso and steel bands in recent generations – make it unequivocally black. Naipaul (1973: 364), one of the Caribbean's leading literary figures, describes Carnival as "a version of the lunacy that kept the slave alive . . . the original dream of black power, style, and prettiness . . . a vision of the black millennium." Calypsonians put it more simply, toasting Carnival as the "Creole bacchanal ."

But the blackness of the Carnival ethos is confronted by a strong nonblack influence in the festival's economic organization. East Indian, Chinese, and Lebanese bandleaders predominate, as do white and mulatto choreographers, and, of course, the government-controlled Carnival Development Committee – all of these groups striving, rather successfully in recent years, to make the event an international tourist attraction. Celebrants are exposed to the poignant contrast between the revelry of "jump-up" on the streets and the ribaldry of the calypso tent, on the one hand, and a variety of scenarios that demonstrate the racially based socioeconomic class system, on the other hand: the judges' stand, the paid grandstand, the commercial nightclub scene, the maze of bureaucratic rules imposed by organizers and censors, and the presence of local elites, and even metropolitan tourists, in the privileged sections of masquerade bands.

Jamaica lacks a Carnival tradition but has the entertainment idiom of reggae music, a symbol system replete with religious and political significance (Barrett 1977; de Albuquerque 1979). One of the best indigenous artistic commentaries on the reggae milieu is Perry Henzell's (1973) film *The Harder They Come*. Its protagonist is a country boy who comes to Kingston to learn the fast side of Jamaican life. The voyage of discovery is twofold. He becomes a reggae star and a "rudie" (rude boy), mastering expressive styles that are quintessentially black, often in a militant, even revolutionary sense. But he also learns that the music industry is controlled by Chinese, mulattos, and other groups deemed white from the black cultural viewpoint, and that the authorities – police, government, and international economic interests – are geared to crushing the challenge that he represents. Ultimately, he is shot down by their guns.

Are such symbolic forms a metacommentary on West Indian politics? Correspondences are harder to draw than in the Bermudian case, partly because, in the Caribbean, race is a figurative more than a phenotypical category. Virtually all local political actors are generically black, and whiteness is associated less with a visible local elite than with the abstractions of foreign ownership and imperial influence. In short, a racial analysis is a more complex and problematic task in the West Indies than it is in Bermuda.

Still, it is notable that, ever since the "Black Power" wave of the early 1970s, the most dynamic and ideologically intense political conflict in most of the West Indies has come from the challenge made to established political parties by radical movements, most of them extraparliamentary. These radical movements revive indigenous linguistic terms (Morris 1973), stress cultural affinity and social solidarity with Africa, and associate themselves with Afro-Caribbean religions, notably Rastafarianism, which has spread from Jamaica throughout the Caribbean and has become a cultural rallying ground and pervasive symbol for revolutionary politics (de Albuquerque 1980). Contrastingly, established politicians are vilified as "Afro-Saxons" (Lowenthal 1972: 278), imitators of white values who court foreign investment, sell out to multinational corporations, embrace the image promoted by mass tourism, and compact unholy alliances with metropolitan countries.

A litany of citations from academic, popular, and polemical literature could be introduced here, most of them familiar (and indeed, redundant), to scholars of the Caribbean. For present purposes, however, it is better to make two broad and general assertions. First, economic interest and cultural identity are often perceived in the West Indies as conflicting concerns. Second, the conflict is focused in racial symbolism, dramatized in festivity and other artistic productions, and current to political discourse. If these assertions are granted, they suggest an agenda aimed at integrating symbolic and political analyses of Caribbean societies, and perhaps of other areas that have undergone comparable historical experiences. The discussion of Bermudian cricket festivals offered here shows one direction in which such an agenda can proceed.

Notes

Acknowledgments

I am grateful to the late Max Gluckman, cricket aficionado and analyst par excellence, whose conversations with me were an inspiration to develop this paper, Jeanne Cannizzo and Jim Freedman offered helpful comments on a draft. For fieldwork support I am grateful to the National Science Foundation (GS-2549) and to the Institute of Social and Economic Research, Memorial University of Newfoundland; grants from these bodies enabled me to witness the Cup Match in 1970, 1976, and 1978, and to see 20–odd County Games since 1969. Earlier versions of this paper were presented to the Canadian Ethnology Society, in 1979, and to the Association for the Anthropological Study of Play, in 1980. Part of the present version was delivered as a guest lecture at the University of Michigan, in 1980.

1 I know of no other written sources on West Indian festival cricket, but am informed by a Jamaican student that "bush cricket" in Jamaica has the same general characteristics as James's example from Trinidad.
2 The Bermuda dollar is at parity with the US dollar.
3 I am told by Leanne Cannizzo (1979: personal communication) that a version of crown and anchor is played at festivals in Sierra Leone. I have also seen it played at a number of

287

fairs and amusement exhibitions in Canada, usually in booths where a wheel is spun, rather than dice thrown, to determine winning bets.

4 For a fuller discussion of Bermuda's recent political history, see Hodgson (1967), Manning (1973, 1978a), and Ryan (1973).

5 The most accessible general overviews of the Trinidad Carnival are those of Hill (1972) and Pearse (1956). Literature on other Caribbean Carnivals includes Abrahams (1970) on Tobago, Abrahams and Bauman (1978) on St Vincent, Crowley (1956) on St Lucia, and Manning (1978b) on Antigua.

References

Abrahams, Roger (1970) "Patterns of Performance in the British West Indies", in *Afro-American Anthropology: Contemporary Perspectives*, Norman E. Whitten, Jr. and John Szwed, eds, pp. 163–79. New York: Free Press.

Abrahams, Roger, and Richard Bauman (1978) Ranges of Festival Behavior, in *The Reversible World: Symbolic Inversion in Art and Society*, Barbara Babcock, ed., pp. 193–208. Ithaca: Cornell University Press.

Babcock, Barbara (1973) "The Carnivalisation of the Novel and the High Spirituality of Dressing Up," Paper presented at Burg Wartenstein Symposium No. S9, Ritual: Reconciliation in Change, Gloggnitz, Austria.

Barrett, Leonard (1977) *The Rastafarians - Sounds of Cultural Dissonance*, Boston: Beacon Press.

Bateson, Gregory (1972) *Steps to an Ecology of Mind*, New York: Ballantine.

Cohen, Abner (1979) "Political Symbolism," *Annual Review of Anthropology*, 8: 87–113.

Crowley, Daniel (1956) "Festivals of the Calendar in St Lucia," *Caribbean Quarterly* 4: 99–121.

de Albuquerque, Klaus (1979) "The Future of the Rastafarian Movement," *Caribbean Review* 8(4): 22–5, 44–6.

—(1980) "Rastafarianism and Cultural Identity in the Caribbean," Paper presented at the Caribbean Studies Association meeting, Willemstad, Curacao.

Geertz, Clifford (1972) "Deep Play: Notes on the Balinese Cockfight," *Daedalus* 101(1): 1–38.

Gluckman, Max, and Mary Gluckman (1977) "On Drama, and Games, and Athletic Contests," in *Secular Ritual*, Sally F. Moore and Barbara Myerhoff, eds, pp. 227–43, Assen/Amsterdam: Van Gorcum.

Henzell, Perry (1973) *The Harder They Come*, Kingston, Jamaica: New World Films.

Hill, Errol (1972) *The Trinidad Carnival: Mandate for a National Theatre*, Austin: University of Texas Press.

Hodgson, Eva (1967) *Second-Class Citizens, First-Class Men*, Hamilton, Bermuda: Published by the author.

James, C. L. R. (1963) *Beyond a Boundary*, London: Hutchinson.

Kochman, Thomas (1970) "Toward an Ethnography of Black American Speech Behavior," in *Afro-American Anthropology. Contemporary Perspectives*, Norman E. Whitten, Jr and John Szwed, eds, pp. 145–62, New York: Free Press.

Lewis, Gordon (1968) *The Growth of the Modern West Indies*, New York: Monthly Review Press.

Lowenthal, David (1972) *West Indian Societies*, New York: Oxford University Press.
Manning, Frank (1973) *Black Clubs in Bermuda: Ethnography of a Play World*, Ithaca: Cornell University Press.
—(1978a) *Bermudian Politics in Transition: Race, Voting, and Public Opinion*, Hamilton, Bermuda: Island Press.
—(1978b) "Carnival in Antigua: an Indigenous Festival in a Tourist Economy," *Anthropos*, 73: 191–204.
Moore, Sally F., and Barbara Myerhoff (1977) *Secular Ritual*, Assen/Amsterdam: Van Gorcum.
Morris, Desmond (1973) "On Afro-West Indian Thinking," in *The Aftermath of Sovereignty: West Indian Perspectives*, David Lowenthal and Lambros Comitas, eds, pp. 277–82, Garden City, NY: Doubleday Anchor.
Naipaul, V. S. (1973) "Power to the Caribbean People," in *The Aftermath of Sovereignty: West Indian Perspectives*, David Lowenthal and Lambros Comitas, eds, pp. 363–71, Garden City, NY: Doubleday Anchor.
Newman, Dorothy (1972) *The Population Dynamics of Bermuda*, Hamilton, Bermuda: Bermuda Government, Department of Statistics.
Nisbet, Robert (1965) *Emile Durkheim*, Englewood Cliffs, NJ: Prentice-Hall.
Pearse, Andrew (1956) "Carnival in Nineteenth Century Trinidad," *Caribbean Quarterly*, 4: 176–93.
Roberts, John, Malcolm Arth, and Robert Bush (1959) "Games in Culture", *American Anthropologist*, 61: 597–605.
Roberts, John, and Brian Sutton-Smith (1962) "Child Training and Game Involvement," *Ethnology*, 2: 166–85.
—(1966) "Cross-Cultural Correlates of Games of Chance," *Behavior Science Notes*, 1: 131–44.
Ryan, Selwyn (1973) "Politics in an Artificial Society: the Case of Bermuda," in *Ethnicity in the Americas*, Frances Henry, ed., pp. 159–92, The Hague: Mouton.
St Pierre, Maurice (1973) "West Indian Cricket: a Sociohistorical Appraisal," *Caribbean Quarterly*, 19: 7–27.
Sapir, Edward (1934) "Symbolism," *Encyclopaedia of the Social Sciences*, 14: 492–5.
Schwartzman, Helen (1978) *Transformations: the Anthropology of Children's Play*, New York: Plenum Press.
Singer, Milton (1955) "The Cultural Pattern of Indian Civilization," *Far Eastern Quarterly*, 15: 23–36.
Smith, Michael G. (1965) *The Plural Society in the British West Indies*, Berkeley: University of California Press.
Turner, Victor (1964) "Symbols in Ndembu Ritual," in *Closed Systems and Open Minds: the Limits of Naivety in Social Anthropology*, Max Gluckman, ed., pp. 20–51, Chicago: Aldine.
—(1977) "Variations on a Theme of Liminality," in *Secular Ritual*, Sally F. Moore and Barbara Myerhoff, eds, pp. 36–52, Assen/Amsterdam: Van Gorcum.
Wilson, Peter (1973) *Crab Antics. The Social Anthropology of English-Speaking Negro Societies of the Caribbean*, New Haven: Yale University Press.

18

The proof of the pudding

C.L.R. James

Once in a blue moon, i.e. once in a lifetime, a writer is handed on a plate a gift from heaven. I was handed mine in 1958. I had just completed a draft of this book [*Beyond a Boundary*] up to the end of the previous chapter when I returned to the West Indies in April 1958, after twenty-six years of absence. I intended to stay three months, I stayed four years. I became the editor of a political paper, the *Nation*, official organ of the People's National Movement of Trinidad, and the secretary of the West Indian Federal Labour Party. Both these parties governed, the one Trinidad, the other the Federation of the West Indies. These were temporary assignments, as I made clear from the start.

Immediately I was immersed up to the eyes in 'The Case for West Indian Self-Government'; and a little later, in the most furious cricket campaign I have ever known, to break the discrimination of sixty years and have a black man, in this case Frank Worrell, appointed captain of a West Indies team. I saw the beginning, the middle, but I am not at all sure that I have seen the end of violent intervention of a West Indian crowd into the actual play of a Test match. The intimate connection between cricket and West Indian social and political life was established so that all except the wilfully perverse could see. It seemed as if I were just taking up again what I had occupied myself with in the months before I left in 1932, except that what was then idea and aspiration was now out in the open and public property.

On 30 January 1960, there crowded into the Queen's Park Oval at Port of Spain over 30,000 people, this out of a total population of some 800,000. They had come to see a cricket match and I for one loved them for it. They have been slandered, vilified and at best grievously misunderstood. I can't say that I understand them, I wouldn't make such a claim, but at least I have always paid attention to them and their reactions to politics as well as to cricket. I have something to say on their behalf.

Particularly that day they had come to sun themselves in West Indies batting, 22 for none on the previous evening. Alas, the West Indies batsmen collapsed and were 98 for eight! At that stage Singh was given run out. The crowd exploded in anger, bottles began to fly; soon they flew so thickly that the game could not be continued.

The Governor; the Premier, Dr Eric Williams; Learie Constantine, apologized to MCC in England and to the MCC team. The majority placed the blame on a few hooligans. Some few hinted at political tensions. Others talked vaguely about betting. There is not a little truth here and a little truth there which can all add up to something. There is not a glimmer of truth in all this. And if anything annoyed the Trinidad public it was to be lectured about the umpire being the sole judge. They continue to say that they know this and in fact on innumerable occasions have shown that they do.

First, to get out of the way what was not the cause of the explosion. In Melbourne in 1903 there took place a demonstration famous in cricket history. Its cause has never been in doubt. Australia had begun their second innings against England 292 behind. Trumper and Hill made a stand for the fourth wicket and by brilliant and courageous batting were putting Australia back in the game. Playing such cricket as from all accounts no one on the ground had ever seen before, not even from him, Trumper hit Braund for 3 4s in an over and forced the last ball past mid-off. The batsmen ran 3, took another for a bad throw and tried for a fifth. Hill was given run out and both pavilion members and the crowd around the ropes protested so violently and so long that the protests re-echo in the pages of the history books to this day.

There is no problem here. The Australians had been losing, they had seen a chance of winning and winning by play grand and gallant. Hill as a popular idol was second only to Trumper. Hill went back to the wicket to continue batting, which showed that he thought he was in. This was enough to unloose the pent-up emotions.

Nothing of the kind has ever taken place in the West Indies.

When the bottle-throwing in Trinidad began the score was 98 for 8, nearly 300 behind. Not a soul on the ground believed that Ramadhin could make 20. They would have cheered Singh as a hero if he had made 10. The fate of the match was not at stake.

It was not too different in British Guiana in 1954. England had made 435. From seven for 139 the score had been taken to 238 when a run-out precipitated the disturbance. Ram and Val were the remaining batsmen. All witnesses agree that the decision had been given, the batsman given out had reached the pavilion, the incoming batsman came in and took guard. It was only then that the bottle throwing began.

In Jamaica in 1953 the umpire was threatened when Holt was given lbw at 94. Stollmeyer was threatened when he refused to ask the England team to follow on. None of these faintly resembles the situation in Melbourne in 1903. Again: none of these was a political demonstration against an imperialist Britain. The 1953–4 MCC team was actively disliked. This was not due merely to unsportsmanlike behaviour by individuals. There is evidence to show that the team had given the impression that it was not merely playing cricket but was out to establish the prestige of Britain and, by that, of the local whites. On account of the bad reputation of the 1953–4 MCC team many feared for the 1959 team. Such fears proved needless. Before long the 1959 team was so popular that when May in Jamaica committed the blunder of refusing Kanhai a runner, although the match was at stake, nobody bothered very much. If the crowd was given to losing its temper when a game was being lost there could have been an awful row then. There were a few boos, that was all. May is a certain type and when genuine it still commands respect in the West Indies. He had forced a point and played on in Barbados to give Barbados the chance of a win. Robins spoke his mind freely about any question that was asked him and altogether created a feeling that he was meeting the local people as a man who felt at home. He was an outstanding success. Cowdrey is genial in appearance, almost bucolic and yet shrewd. Trueman, who had had a bad time on the previous tour, bowled so well and clowned with such success that the past was forgotten. It must be quite clear that such politics as there were in the outburst, and it was drenched in politics, did not in any way involve either Britain or the MCC. My belief is that consideration for the MCC moderated it both at the time and afterwards.

What then caused the 1960 and other outbursts? It was the conviction that here, as usual, local anti-nationalist people were doing their best to help the Englishmen defeat and disgrace the local players. That is the temper which caused these explosions and as long as that temper remains it will find a way to express itself. This particular political attitude is not declining. It is increasing, and will increase until a new social and political regime is firmly established and is accepted by all.

The history of this in the West Indies is as old as the West Indies itself. No imperialist expatriates can rule an alien population alone. The British therefore incorporated the local whites into their ranks. Later, as the pressure from the people grew, the light-skinned were given privileges. Universal suffrage and the nationalist passions and gains of the last fifteen years have driven many of the former privileged classes to side openly with the British, with Americans, with all or any who for one reason or another find themselves in conflict with or hostile to the nationalist movement. There is the seat of disturbance. It is particularly true of Trinidad. Against Britain as such there is surprisingly little hostility. And despite the passions aroused over the desire for the return of Chaguaramas,[1] where there is an American naval base, and recurrent spasms of anger at racial persecution in the United States, America and Americans are not unpopular.

But those suspected of anti-nationalism are usually rich whites and their retainers. Local politicians, editors, officials, policemen, selectors, umpires, are under scrutiny whenever they have to act on behalf of or on the side of what the people consider a nationalist cause. People feel that in the past some have served the foreigners against the local people and that many of them are still doing it. The nearer the people get to independence, the greater is the suspicion that the enemies of independence and nationalism are scheming against them. You will find this conflict running through every aspect of life in Trinidad, where political development has been late and is all the more explosive. This type of suspicion is embedded deep in the minds of the majority of the people. In the chapter [in *Beyond a Boundary*] on Wilton St Hill I have shown how deeply my friends and I (no hooligans) were affected by the failure of the selectors to include him in the 1923 team and I believe I have dealt fairly with the case. We did not throw bottles, but we would have understood the feelings of those who had.

Now for some details closer to the event.

It is still confidently affirmed that in 1947–8 Jamaica refused to play against England at all if George Headley, a black man, was not made the captain as he had every right to be.[2] There were all sorts of manoeuvres and in the end Headley played in only one game. You cannot bluff a public about a captaincy, and the scandal was discussed in every island.

The year 1950 brought another scandal. Many Jamaicans thought Headley should have been in the team to England and should have captained the side. Headley was offered the captaincy of the Jamaica side in the trial games. There was a complicated row over status and finances. (I have in my possession a detailed account of the whole affair written by Headley himself and I have told him that in my opinion he acted unwisely.) George didn't play in the trials, he didn't go to England. But the people did not forget. George played league cricket in England and scored so heavily that the Jamaican public felt that it would be unjust for him not to re-enter big cricket. They raised £1,000 by public subscription to bring him home so that he would be sure to play in the trials. When public feeling is running that high anything can happen. Obviously the public, or certain sections of it, distrusted the officialdom. From there the transition to the explosion over Holt is easy to understand. Holt, like Headley, is a black man, his father was the W.G. of Jamaica. If the batsman given out at 94 had been Headley the explosion would have been even easier to understand. But it is a dangerous blindness which does not see that this is not a question of ignorant or malicious disagreement with an umpire's decision.

It is a historical commonplace that social explosions take place when most of the fundamental causes of dissatisfaction have been removed and only a few remain. This is the result of a feeling of power. In West Indies cricket today selection is honest and straightforward and sometimes brilliant. Anyone, whatever his colour, can become captain of an island team. That is all the more reason why it is the captaincy of the West Indies side on which attention centres.

Clyde Walcott cannot by any stretch of fact or imagination be called a cricket Bolshevik, a term applied to Worrell in the past. Yet Clyde in his *Island Cricketers* had made several pointed references.

Before the Australians arrived the West Indies Board did something which at first seemed strange in announcing the names of captain and vice-captain for our tour of New Zealand which was to take place almost a year later. The names were Denis Atkinson and Bruce Pairaudeau. Only after this announcement had sunk in – and had caused a good deal of controversy – did the Board announce that Jeff Stollmeyer and Denis Atkinson would be captain and vice-captain respectively for the Australian series about to start. Although it was hard to see why the announcement of the officials for

293

New Zealand had to be made so far in advance the apparent discrepancy in selection was more easily explained.

West Indies had no delusions, nor false politeness, about the strength of New Zealand cricket, and they had decided to send a young side, omitting all but a few of our established Test players. The choice of Atkinson as captain and – to gain experience – as vice-captain against Australia was in line with this policy. The public were not slow to ask why the 'three W's' had been left out of the reckoning, particularly after Frank Worrell had been vice-captain against MCC during the 1953–4 series. The public feeling seemed to be that the West Indies Board did not relish the prospect of having a coloured captain, but I do not think this was, in fact, the case. Much more likely, it seemed to me, was that West Indies were following the old-fashioned precedent of standing out against the professional captain: a precedent which, despite Len Hutton's reign as captain, still has its roots deeply laid in England . . . .

Shortly before the First Test Jeff Stollmeyer hurt a finger in practice, so had to withdraw from the side. Automatically his vice-captain, Denis Atkinson, succeeded him, but the Press and the public took this as an excellent opportunity to renew their plea that Worrell should be given the captaincy. They rightly made the point that he was the more experienced player and captain, but they overlooked the fact that the thing had been decided in the selection room some time before and was unlikely to be changed now.

Atkinson's experience was, in fact, very slight. Until his selection to captain the side to visit New Zealand he had not normally led his colony, Barbados. But after the announcement John Goddard, the usual Barbados captain, handed over to Atkinson, presumably to help the younger man gain experience. And so, lacking experience and the full confidence of West Indies cricket followers, Denis had a difficult task which was not eased when he had the misfortune to lose the toss.

Have cricket enthusiasts in any country had to endure a state of affairs as is expressed in *Wisden* for 1956?

> Injuries to Stollmeyer could not have helped the West Indies. Stollmeyer, who captained the side against England in the previous season, hurt a finger while practising before the First Test and the inexperienced Atkinson took over the leadership. Stollmeyer returned to the captaincy for the next two Tests, but damaged a collarbone while fielding in the third, so that Atkinson was again appointed for the fourth and final representative game.

When you turn to the First Test you see on the West Indies side E. D. Weekes, C. L. Walcott and F. M. Worrell being led by 'the inexperienced' Atkinson. After fifty years of it, to this day I still am unable to understand how people can do these things.

The exclusion of black men from the captaincy becomes all the more pointed when the Prime Minister of the West Indies and Chief Ministers all over the islands are black men. Clyde himself may never speak to me again for writing what I shall now write. I can only plead that the cause must stand higher than the man.

Walcott should have played for the West Indies in Australia in 1960–1. All critics agree that his sixty-odd on a turning wicket in the last Test against Pakistan in 1958 was batting at the peak. I had a good look at him in England, both at the nets and in matches. I saw him bat in a practice game in British Guiana in 1958. For defence and power in putting away the length ball this is one of the greatest of all batsmen. Only Bradman can be mentioned in the same breath for commanding hooking of fast bowlers. His physique is still one of the most powerful in cricket. I begged him to come back, in person, through friends, by overseas telephone. He finally played in one or two matches against the Englishmen, but at the height of his powers Clyde had put big cricket behind him. Why? I would say a general feeling that he was tired of intrigues and manoeuvres which were not based on cricket ability.

One evening in British Guiana we were talking about captaincy. Suddenly Clyde, who is always circumspect in his speech, blurted out: 'You know who will be captain in England in 1963? You see that Barbados boy, Bynoe, who went to India? He only has to make fifty in one innings and he will be the captain'.

Bynoe is white.

Walcott was not claiming the captaincy for himself or for anybody in particular. I repeat: he is not that kind of person at all. His chief complaint, as I have gathered it over the years, is: if you are the captain, then captain, carry out your ideas; don't come bothering me about them.

An individual easily gets over the fact that he is disappointed in his desire to be captain. It is the constant, vigilant, bold and shameless manipulation of players to exclude black captains that has so demoralized West Indian teams and exasperated the people – a people, it is to be remembered, in the full tide of the transition from colonialism to independence.

I knew all this. I now heard it and saw it at first hand. The discrimination against black men was now an international scandal. After the 1953–4 tour Trevor Bailey had written about it guardedly in his book on cricket. Now Keith Miller, in his *Cricket from the Grandstand,* had put the issue with a refreshing if brutal frankness. He had written:

> . . . Another problem in West Indies cricket is that the captain has usually been chosen from among the European stock. Just think of the most famous West Indies cricketers . . . Learie Constantine, George Headley, Frank Worrell, Everton Weekes, Clyde Walcott . . . all are coloured, but none has led his country. Yet Worrell was often skipper of Commonwealth tours in India, and he did a fine job.

Miller has also written:

> Politics interfere with cricket more in the West Indies than in most places. There is a terrific bias in each of the various islands in favour of their own players . . . .

From what I saw in the West Indies that was no longer true.

I was editor of a newspaper. I was primed for action and made up my mind to clean up this captaincy mess once and for all. When the MCC tour drew near I gave notice in the *Nation* that I proposed to wage an all-out campaign for Worrell to replace Alexander as captain. My argument was simply this: there was not the slightest shadow of justification for Alexander to be captain of a side in which Frank Worrell was playing.

Worrell had been offered the captaincy after the 1957 season in England, but owing to his studies at Manchester University he had had to refuse. That offer didn't matter very much to some of us who were watching. Worrell as captain at home or in India was bad enough, but that could be swallowed by the manipulators. What was at stake was the captaincy in Australia and still more in England. Their whole point was to continue to send to populations of white people, black or brown men under a white captain. The more brilliantly the black men played, the more it would emphasize to millions of English people: 'Yes, they are fine players, but, funny, isn't it, they cannot be responsible for themselves – they must always have a white man to lead them'.

The populace in the West Indies are not fools. They knew what was going on and, if not altogether sure of all the implications, they were quite sure that these, whatever they might be, were directed against them. I was told of an expatriate who arrived in Trinidad to take up an important post which the people thought should be filled by a local candidate. Such a storm arose that the expatriate had to be sent away. In 1959 British Guiana was thrown into turmoil and strikes over a similar issue and the Governor had to retreat. In cricket these sentiments are at their most acute because everyone can see and can judge.

What do they know of cricket who only cricket know? West Indians crowding to Tests bring with them the whole past history and future hopes of the islands. English people, for example, have a conception of themselves breathed from birth. Drake and mighty Nelson, Shakespeare, Waterloo, the Charge of the Light Brigade, the few who did so much for so many, the success of parliamentary democracy, those and such as those constitute a national tradition. Underdeveloped countries have to go back centuries to rebuild one. We of the West Indies have none at all none that we know of. To such people the three Ws, Ram and Val wrecking English batting, help to fill a huge gap in their consciousness and in their needs. In one of the sheds on the Port of Spain wharf is a painted sign: 365 Garfield Sobers. If the old Maple–Shannon–Queen's Park type of rivalry was now insignificant, a nationalist jealousy had taken its place.

All this was as clear to me as day. I tried to warn the authorities that there was danger in the air. Many of them, I am sure of this, were unable even to understand what I was saying. Our argument centred around the case of Gilchrist.

Gilchrist had been sent home from India and had been censured by the Board. The terms of its censure had been so couched as to imply that Gilchrist was banned for ever from Test cricket. Members of the Board denied this and there is no reason to disbelieve the denial. In any case, the denial was never officially made.

Gilchrist was not merely another West Indian cricketer. He was one of the plebs and to them a hero – he was their boy. They would not judge him by ordinary standards. Let me try to illustrate by a remote example.

Some years ago Mr Azikiwe, then Premier of Eastern Nigeria, was accused of improper transactions in relation to a bank he had founded in Nigeria. We need not go into the charges. An official inquiry found that they were justified, but made it quite clear that Mr Azikiwe had in its opinion been guilty only of political impropriety, he had not personally profited in any way. Mr Azikiwe resigned, ran for election and was re-elected. Nigerians have told me of popular reaction. 'We had no bank here. All the money used to go to England. Zik made a bank for us. *If even Zik took a little for himself, that is OK with us*'.

In dealing with a nationalist agitation you have to reckon with such sentiments or you go badly astray.

I was very much interested in Gilchrist. Following the West Indies team around in 1957, I saw Gilchrist against Kent at Canterbury. I got the impression that he resented not being given the new ball by Walcott, acting captain, in the second innings, and didn't care who knew. If it was so, I strongly disapproved.

In the next match against an England XI at Hastings we saw Gilchrist driven for 5 4s in an over by Cowdrey. Later I learnt the reason.

Frank Worrell was the captain and he had told Gilchrist that this was a festival game and in festival games you didn't bowl bumpers. Gilchrist, determined to oblige, preferred to bowl half-volleys and be driven for 4 after 4 rather than run the risk of appearing to disobey Frank. Gilchrist worships Frank Worrell (and among West Indian Test players, past and present, is not alone in so doing). They lived about twenty miles apart in England, and when Gilchrist wanted to buy a shirt he drove over to consult Frank.

On a visit to Jamaica I sought out people who knew Gilchrist. I was sent to his employer and patron. He told me how he had first met Gilchrist in a rural area, how he had brought him to Kingston, given him a job, sponsored him. He most certainly did not think Gilchrist a paragon of virtue, but 'Gilchrist', he said, 'will do anything I tell him to do and would never do anything which he thought would offend me'. I made all this public.

The Board could not understand Gilchrist. The Board could not or would not understand what was the attitude of the public to Gilchrist. They were misled by pontificating articles in the biased Press, preaching that the game was greater than the player and similar irrelevancies. What I soon discovered was that very few people paid the slightest attention to the extremely grave charges which, it was freely rumoured, had been made and substantiated against Gilchrist. Not only the ordinary man in the street but middle-class people were indifferent: a surprising number of people said: 'What is all this about "It isn't cricket"? Who are they to talk? They have been cheating about the captaincy for years'. Most people thought that there was a clash between black plebeian Gilchrist and the light-skinned Cambridge graduate Alexander.

I called up Gerry Gomez and told him what I thought should be done. The Board had taken a firm stand and would have been very wrong not to do so. Now, however, it should go further. Gilchrist was a young man of obscure origin suddenly hurled into the world Press as the fastest of living bowlers. He had made grave mistakes, but it was to be presumed that with time he would mature. I suggested that the Board get in touch with Frank Worrell and ask him to talk to Gilchrist (I had in mind also that some English friend of West Indian cricket should go with Frank, preferably E.W. Swanton, who alone had written about Gilchrist with a touch of sympathy.)

The Board simply could not understand its responsibility for Gilchrist. It thought it could just excommunicate him and adopt the pharisaical attitude that we were no longer responsible for what he did. They are terribly – and may well be catastrophically – wrong. Gilchrist, we were reliably informed, was bowling bumpers and beamers at league batsmen, an altogether reprehensible and, what was more, dangerous business. He was a West Indian Test cricketer. Unless the Board discovered a way of scrubbing him white he would be considered one of us, whatever decrees the Board might issue. I was convinced that the Board should use Frank Worrell to bring Gilchrist back into the fold. The West Indian populace would be vastly pleased and grateful, and this surely would be the most powerful of influences to make Gilchrist conform to accepted standards.

Gilchrist should be helped to write a substantial apology, both to the Board and to individuals. This would be published, and, with Frank to sponsor him, he could be brought back. If Gilchrist proved obdurate then this too would be published and public unrest would be pacified. Gerry's reply was that West Indian cricketers had gained a great reputation for sportsmanship everywhere and no one should be allowed to spoil it. I simply could not accept that West Indians' reputation at cricket could be spoiled by anything one individual could do, especially if the Board was known to have acted in a firm and yet paternal manner.

The cricket reputation of the West Indies could be spoilt in many ways. I wrote in the *Nation* asking the Board to reconsider: in vain. The Board received another clear warning. Some of Gilchrist's plebeian admirers in Trinidad printed posters calling upon the public to boycott the Trinidad Tests if Gilchrist did not play. One of their leaders came to me and asked me: what next? *I* told him to take it easy. Even before the situation had become acute Frank Worrell had been broadcasting from England to the West Indies giving discreet but clear hints to the Board that some attempt should be made to bring Gilchrist back. The Board continued to emphasize what Gilchrist had done.

This was not the first time that I had had doubts of the inability of the Board to understand the age in which it was living. First there had been the readiness of McLean and Waite, the South Africans, to go to the West Indies with E.W. Swanton's team. From the start I took the position that if at all possible they should have been welcomed. *They were ready to break the barrier.* We should have been ready to accept. I wrote to the West Indies to that effect. I understood finally that the Board was afraid that there might be incidents either from the public or a section of the Press. I think I know the West Indian crowd better than they do. All that was needed was that responsible political figures should have been asked to give their approval publicly, and West Indians would have welcomed them. It would have been different if one of the visitors had been a fast bowler given to bumpers. Instead, one hook off his face by McLean would have made him a favourite of the crowd.

Later there was another rather sharp dispute over the proposal of the 'cricket Bolshevik' Worrell to take a team of coloured West Indians to play against Africans in South Africa. Canon Collins and others protested against this as accepting apartheid. Constantine was with them. I took an opposite view. The team, I thought, should go. Apartheid sought the isolation of the Africans not only from whites but from free blacks. The tour would have had world-wide publicity. The African cricketers and the African crowds would have made contact with world-famous cricketers who had played in England and in Australia. There might have been incidents? So much the better. A pitiless light would have been thrown on the irrationality and stupidity of apartheid. African cricketers would have benefited, and, it was to be hoped, one or two African cricketers might have emerged and become widely known as naturals for an All South African team. From the beginning I was certain that, whatever the South African Government might say, it did not want this tour. Racialists do not ever want the eyes of the world on their crimes. Constantine and I differed openly on this issue in the *Nation*. The public discussion was wide and acute. It is the sort of problem that the ordinary West Indian pays close attention to. I would say that at the beginning he was against. But I found that he listened attentively to my arguments. He knew me as a life-long opponent of racialism and an established supporter of African nationalism. He knew that whatever opinions I might express *I was on his side*. All this was stirring in the people just before the MCC tour. The conduct of West Indian crowds, like everything else West Indian, is open for judgement. But those who judge should remember that there are no more devoted lovers of the game anywhere. That prejudices me in their favour. And secondly, before you judge, find out what they are thinking and why.

I firmly believe that if the Board had taken the steps I suggested, whatever had been Gilchrist's response, there would have been no outburst in Trinidad. The people would have felt that the Board was on their side, was with them and the whole temper would have been different. If Gilchrist had shown himself obstinate I would certainly have upheld the Board and strongly condemned him. Things being as they were, I was pretty certain that there was an even chance of a violent explosion in the coming series, though I and others expected it in Jamaica over Gilchrist, and this also I made clear in the paper. But with crowds you never can tell exactly what will set off an underlying tension. In this case it was the umpiring, nor was this strange.

Trinidad inter-colonial cricketers have a slogan about local umpiring. 'They do not do such things in England and in Barbados'. It is a tradition that Trinidad umpires are severe with Trinidad players. Let me give an example.

In 1946 in Port of Spain, Trinidad, the home team faced a total of 671 in the fourth innings with plenty of time left for play. Trestrail, who made 151, and Ganteaume, who made 85, put up over 200 runs for the first wicket, when Ganteaume was given run out by a Trinidad umpire, a very close decision. The umpire, V. Guillen, is an old inter-colonial cricketer, a friend of mine for many years, with whom I have played and talked a lot of cricket. I sat and listened to him and

Andy Ganteaume discuss the decision in the most amicable manner. Whether Ganteaume was out or not did not and does not interest me in the slightest. What I was interested in was popular opinion that in England or Barbados a local umpire would not have given a local player out at such a time in a decision which was admittedly a matter of inches.

I remain convinced of my own views because I at any rate was paying close attention and I have not yet met or heard of anybody who was.[3]

In the matches against the Englishmen three decisions had caused comment. The boy Davis, batting well, had been given run out, a decision which displeased the crowd. An English batsman had been given out but remained at the crease, presumably unaware of the decision. When the bowler appealed again the umpire changed his mind and gave the batsman not out. This he was perfectly entitled to do. In that situation it was an additional stick of dynamite. The islands are small – during big cricket people talk fanatically about nothing else. Every street corner is a seething cauldron of cricket experiences, cricket memories, fears, suspicions, hopes, aspirations. On that very 30 January Hunte had been given out, and for a long time even those manipulating the scoreboard had been unable to say how he was out, whether lbw or caught by Trueman on the leg-side. The crowd had watched the collapse of the West Indian batting, that same batting which had made 563 in the Barbados Test. When Ramadhin hit a boundary or two and showed that he was not going to give in the crowd woke up. This had nothing whatever to do with winning or losing the match. They sensed the opportunity for some fun and rejoicing and took it gladly. If after their excitement Singh had been bowled for nought they would have laughed uproariously as at a good joke against themselves. It was the abrupt termination of their quite facetious gaiety which brought decades of dissatisfaction to a head. There is no question in my mind or in the minds of many that Singh was out. The three decisions I have mentioned gave far more ground, as decisions, for popular protest. But no one can tell how and when these outbursts will take place. Revolutions, someone has said, come like a thief in the night. The apparent causes are nearly always trivial and to the superficial eye unjustified.

The theory of a few hooligans is not only dangerous but without sense. I know of no instance where a few hooligans have disrupted a major public function, unless they knew or sensed that public opinion was either on their side or at least neutral. I have made systematic enquiries both at the time and since and a secret poll would to this day show a majority for the view: 'Wrong, yes, but the people had to do something'. A recurrent defiance was the following: 'The bottles should have been thrown into the pavilion'. Not a word was ever said against the English players.

Who doubts the validity of the above has to reckon with what now followed. I had been waiting to get a sight of Alexander as captain and before the Test was over I launched an attack against his captaincy: Alexander must go. I based it on Worrell's superior experience and status and Alexander's errors of judgement. I refused to make it a question of race, though I made it clear that if the rejection of Worrell was continued I would reluctantly have to raise the racial issue. To have raised it would have switched the discussion away from cricket and involved all sorts of other issues. The anti-nationalists, with their usual brazenness, would have countered with 'Race introduced into sport'. And in any case everybody in the West Indies understood what I was leaving out even better than what I was actually writing.

The effect was beyond all expectation. The *Nation* was an official organ and a highly political paper. (Some even queried whether such a paper should express an opinion on cricket captaincy at all.) They were wrong. This was politics and very serious politics. The 'Alexander Must Go' issue was sold out by the day following publication. People who had read or heard of the article rushed around looking for copies to buy. The man in the street expressed deep feelings. 'Thank God for the *Nation*'. 'Someone to speak for us at last'. He was not speaking about the explosion. The *Nation* had been as uncompromising as any in condemning it.

Week after week I carried on unsparingly, putting everything that I had into it. Here, for the sake of the records, is one example of many.[4]

Frank Worrell is at the peak of his reputation not only as a cricketer but as a master of the game. Respect for him has never been higher in all his long and brilliant career . . . .

His bearing on the field, all grace and dignity, evoked general admiration [in England in 1957]. In every sphere, and others beside myself know this, the opinion was that he should have been the captain . . . .

In India, owing to his many tours with Commonwealth sides, during one of which he took over the captaincy with great success, he is remembered as one of the greatest cricketers of the age . . . .

But, more important than this: *Australia Wants Him As Captain.*

This is the authentic fact. When Australian critics talk of Trumper, Kippax and the few half-dozen batsmen who have batted as if they were born to it they include Worrell. As a man he made a tremendous impression in Australia. Thousands will come out on every ground to see an old friend leading the West Indies. In fact, I am able to say that if Worrell were captain and Constantine or George Headley manager or co-manager, the coming tour would be one of the greatest ever.

It was hard on Alexander. He was not a good captain and in any case he was keeping wicket, which is no place for a captain. But it was hard on me also. Alexander is a fine soccer player, he kept wicket magnificently, he is a good defensive bat and is a hard fighter. I put my scruples aside and I think that for the first, and I hope the last, time in reporting cricket I was not fair. But I was determined to rub in the faces of everybody that Frank Worrell, the last of the three W's, was being discriminated against. Charles Bray of the *Daily Herald*, no mean campaigner himself, told me that he wondered how I was able to keep it up. I would have been able to keep it up for fifty weeks, for there was fifty years' knowledge of discrimination behind it and corresponding anger. When I confessed I was angry, even sympathizers balked at this. According to the code, anger should not intrude into cricket. I understood them well, I had been as foolish in my time. According to the colonial version of the code, you were to show yourself a 'true sport' by not making a fuss about the most barefaced discrimination because it wasn't cricket. Not me any longer. To that I had said, was saying, my final good-bye[5]; and no one knew better than I how much dangerous trouble was ahead if that sort of thing continued. Worrell was finally appointed and then, strange but not unusual, there was universal jubilation. All classes approved. It is often so. Even those who had been led astray to give silent support to their extremists seemed genuinely relieved that the whole mess was over and they could participate with their fellow men in the general rejoicing. H.B.G. Austin was the natural captain of the West Indies as long as he chose to play. You took that for granted. But I don't believe that any cricket appointment in the West Indies was ever so universally and warmly approved as that of Frank Worrell as captain of our team to Australia. I have kept the politics out of it, but great cheers rang from the audience as the Premier, Dr Eric Williams, in his address to the Fourth National Convention of his party, said:

> ... If C. L. R. James took it upon his individual self to wage a campaign for Worrell as captain of the West Indies, and in so doing to give expression not only to the needs of the game but also to the sentiments of the people, we know as well as he that it is the *Nation* and the P.N.M. to whom the people will give the praise.

Those words were the literal truth. The 'Case for West Indian Self-Government' and 'It isn't cricket' had come together at last and together had won a signal victory.

I didn't like the look of things after the bottle throwing, I didn't like it at all. So on 12 February 1960, I summed up the whole, all the past, the present and hopes for the future, in an open letter to the Queen's Park Club. Here it is:

The Queen's Park Cricket Club

Gentlemen:

You are exercising a public responsibility, the importance of which seems to have exceeded your comprehension. It is for this reason that I address you this letter. The letter has to be an open letter because the matters it deals with are now wide open, not only to the public in this territory and in the West Indies but to the whole world.

You are in charge of the organization and management of cricket tours at home and abroad. Recent events should have shown you that among us today, this is one of the most responsible tasks that is being performed by a non-governmental body. What has happened to Carnival should teach us all a great deal. The people of Trinidad and Tobago are devoted to their Carnival. It is possible that they would be better employed studying Shakespeare, listening to classical music or taking physical culture in order to improve the health of the community. They don't. They play Carnival, spend time and money on it. That is what they want to do. With the jump that all our affairs are taking, Carnival expanded until the old organizers had to be cast aside.

It is equally clear, to a degree of which I had no conception, that cricket has made mighty strides among our people. International cricket matters to them. They are passionately interested in it. That from a small island like this you can get well over 30,000 people to see a Test match, much the same number that you get at Lord's or the Oval in a London of ten million people, that is a circumstance which, as far as I know, is unprecedented in its scope and implications. It confers tremendous credit upon the game of cricket and upon the people of Trinidad and Tobago. It also confers great credit upon you as the local representatives of the West Indian Board of Control. I am not only aware of this, I am anxious to point it out.

In this letter I shall have to say some hard and unpleasant things. For this reason I wish to make my own position in regard to you as a club and as organizers of international cricket quite clear from the start. There have long been murmurings, and now they are very strong, that the management of international cricket which has grown to such remarkable proportions should no longer be in the hands of what is a private club. Such a responsibility, runs the argument, should be held by a democratically elected body representing the cricket clubs and associations of the country; the Football Association is run that way and very efficiently and satisfactorily run. It would doubtless surprise you to know that, though not an opponent of that view, I am not at present an advocate of it. We in the West Indies have very little historical background to which we are able to look. It is over sixty years that the Queen's Park Club has been organizing international tours. It has helped more than any other organization to build the game of cricket here. It has produced some great players and still produces them. The Queen's Park Oval is a magnificent cricket ground, one of the most beautiful in the world. There are even some with experience abroad who give it pride of place.

Looking over the booklet produced by the Club to celebrate its Diamond Jubilee, I saw the following in the message from the Governor, Sir Edward Beetham.

'In this year in which the Queen's Park Cricket Club celebrates the Diamond Jubilee of its occupancy of the Oval, the club can look back on a proud record of achievement.

'In its sixty years of occupancy the club has taken the lead in promoting and financing inter-colonial and international cricket tournaments, and the Oval has become a focal point of first-class cricket in Trinidad and the West Indies. The club's unremitting initiative for more than half a century in relation to first-class cricket, and the encouragement which it has given to other forms of sport, represents a signal service to sport generally in the Caribbean. It also represents a public service to the sportloving people of Trinidad and Tobago who, through the club, have been enabled to see the world's leading cricketers in action at the Oval. That the club has been recognized as the Cricket Authority for Trinidad is fitting tribute to the service it has rendered to West Indies cricket for so many years.'

That I think is a just statement of a fine record.

There is also the example of M.C.C. Here is a private club which runs big cricket on a truly international scale. No theory of democracy can overcome the fact that Australia, South Africa, the West Indies, New Zealand, India and Pakistan, cricketers the world over, give their ungrudging allegiance to M.C.C. Furthermore, as a general rule, I am always in favour of public affairs being carried on by organizations of citizens who are not in any way connected with the government (except to get some money out of them every now and then). The inherent strength of the older countries owes much to the fact that they have had time and opportunities to develop such bodies. Some of them are very old and very reactionary. Nevertheless some can be transformed, as Oxford and Cambridge have been transformed so that today 80 per cent of the students are not the sons of the aristocracy and the wealthy but are winners of scholarships. If things can be so developed that the Queen's Park Club continues to manage or to exercise an assured position in the organization and management of international cricket in the West Indies and in Trinidad and Tobago, I see nothing against that and

I see much to be said for it. But that requires a vivid and active sense of public obligation on your part. Unfortunately at the present time what you are heading for is a clamour to the Government that the projected stadium be begun immediately, and that the Board of Control in Trinidad be represented by a body elected from top to bottom.

That is what you are heading for. It is possible that this is inevitable. Meanwhile, however, we are faced with an immediate and present situation. I had hoped that things would stay more or less as they are until the tour is over; we do not want any unnecessary agitation while our visitors are in the West Indies. But the public mind is unsettled and as a responsible public body you have to take that into consideration and you have to act.

The *Nation* has suggested that a public enquiry be instituted into the events that took place on January 30th. Nothing else will ever be able to give an authoritative account of what happened and why and what to do to prevent it happening again. It is possible that the Government may in the end institute such an enquiry: it can well come within the province of the Ministry of Home Affairs, or the Ministry of Education and Culture, or the Police. The West Indies Board of Control may order an enquiry. The incident took place on your ground. A public enquiry can very well be instituted by you. The Queen's Park Club not only has every right to appoint a commission of enquiry. It is its duty to do so. But let me give you a warning. Such a commission of enquiry should not be appointed to whitewash the club. Its business should be to give the public the confidence that what is being done is in the public interest. It would not be at all difficult to select a body of men and women, not necessarily all members of the club, whose very names would inspire confidence.

Why is this so necessary? It is necessary because although public sentiment, as far as I have been able to discover, realizes that what took place was wrong, nevertheless, too many continue to think that the people were justified. What is still more alarming, many people who have never thrown and would never throw a bottle remain obdurate in their opinion that what was done, however wrong, was necessary, being the only way in which attention could be drawn to grave grievances.

A commission of enquiry would have to bear in mind the following:

1 The Oval on Saturday, January 30th, was over-sold. There were too many people in the ground.
2 Too many people have to stand. No one should be asked to stand at a Test when he may enter the ground at half past nine, have to stay there till five o'clock, and do this for six days.
3 Charges for refreshments such as are bought by the ordinary folk are too high, and it is believed that the reason for this is the high price of concessions.
4 The public is profoundly irritated by its conviction that the captaincy of the West Indies team for years has been manipulated in such a manner as deliberately to exclude black men.
5 The public is convinced that the Board has mismanaged the Gilchrist affair and that Gilchrist should be playing in the West Indies side.
6 The public is not satisfied that the umpires appointed in Trinidad carry out their duty with the impartiality that they should. They have felt this for years.
7 There is a widespread rumour that the bottle-throwing was not begun by the crowd but was a retaliation for a bottle thrown at it.

8 Finally there is the conviction now deep-seated that the Queen's Park Club represents the old regime in Trinidad and that it is indifferent and even hostile to what the masses of the people think.

Gentlemen, I ask you to believe me when I say that the above is a mild statement of public sentiment. Merely to list them is not to accept them. To take No. 1, the overcrowding. When Secretary Botha Tench says that he would gladly have given back all the money if what happened could have been avoided I quite believe him. I have stood outside Lord's for hours only to be shut out in the end, and along with others used all our powers of persuasion to try to get ourselves in. (Finally I had to pay £5 to a scoundrel who had bought some tickets for just such an emergency.)

I do not bring prejudice to any of the charges. In the campaign I am carrying on against Alexander instead of Worrell as captain I shall exhaust every argument before I touch the racial aspect of it. Public sentiments, however, are as I have stated them. You are a body exercising a public function. You cannot be indifferent to what the public thinks. This cannot be answered by saying: hooligans. If to have the kind of doubts and suspicions that the people have is to be a hooligan, then I have been a hooligan for fifty years and my brother and sister hooligans include some of the most highly placed and responsible people in the country.

If the Queen's Park Club is indifferent or shows indifference to these public sentiments then it is totally unfit to control or manage big cricket in the island any longer. The only way that it can show that it is not indifferent and that it recognizes the responsibility that it holds is to take steps along the lines that I have outlined here. Whenever there are disturbances anywhere the British Government does not hesitate to appoint a commission of enquiry consisting for the most part of trusted public figures who at any rate make the facts known and draw their own independent conclusions.

The Queen's Park Club, like the M.C.C., is a private club. Obviously members of the club and their families enjoy certain advantages in regard to seats at important events, etc. As with the M.C.C., there are continued complaints and criticisms of the exclusiveness and privileges enjoyed by members of such a club. M.C.C. has taken pains to see to it that all cricketers of a certain standing and number of years of service to the game should become members. For the rest the membership of a private club which is exercising a public function is always likely to cause dissatisfaction. I pay little attention to it because if the feelings and needs of the general public are taken into consideration the public will not be particularly concerned as to the privileges exercised by a few individuals. The public does not think in those terms.

If, gentlemen, you are unable to understand, or if you understand but for one reason or another you refuse to take action along the lines I have indicated, then events will take their course. I shall tell you some of them.

1 There is certain to arise a clamour which in the end will be irresistible for the stadium as a means of removing your club entirely, except on the same basis as other clubs, from the management and organization of international tours.
2 The *Nation* printed the other day some extracts from the book of Clyde Walcott on cricket. No one should mistake the moderation of the tone and the obvious desire not to give offence and thereby believe that the three W's do not bitterly feel the injustice and humiliation to which they have been subjected by the attitude of the Board towards them and the captaincy of the West Indies. This is not lost on the

younger players. And before very long we shall see some of our finest cricketers abandoning League cricket and taking up county cricket as Marshall has done and Ramadhin tried to do. They will have a beautiful ground to play on if they are batsmen, they will play cricket to their hearts' content, and after some years they will be granted a benefit which may well give them eight or ten thousand pounds about the time when their powers are beginning to wane. That is not clear on the horizon today. It will be clearer tomorrow. Who will blame them for thus letting West Indies cricket see after itself? You who could have done so much for them have not only done very little. You stand accused of having deliberately contrived to deprive some of them of honours which in any other country under the sun would have been theirs.

This which I shall now say is the most important of all. I have heard repeatedly that the bottles should have been thrown not on to the ground but into the pavilion. I state freely for all to know that in the middle of my work and sometimes awakening suddenly in the middle of the night I have some terrible moments thinking of how easily this might have happened and the awful consequence for all of us which would have ensued.

I repeat: when the disturbances broke out in 1937 in the West Indies the British Government did not say: hooligans. It sent to find out what had happened and why and to seek recommendations to cure the ills. You, gentlemen, should not feel yourselves above doing that. It will be a sign of strength, not of weakness. It will make for peace and not for a continued cold war. I talked to Denis Atkinson in England in Hastings in 1957 and he told me that he was a member of the old club of H.B.G. Austin and the Challenor brothers and I told him I was glad to hear that: I hoped the time would never come when a member of that club, the originator of the great tradition of Barbados batting, would not represent the West Indies. Here as everywhere else I am primarily concerned with the building of a truly national community, incorporating all of the past that is still viable.

Among you is the head of a West Indian family that for three generations has distinguished itself in religion, education, commerce, sport, politics and social work. Two world-famous cricketers are now active in your councils and were yesterday active on the field. They know a great deal more about cricket than I do. I want to assure them, first that I know much more about crowds than they do, and, secondly, that they do not exceed me in love for the game, respect for its traditions and a desire that these should flourish in the West Indies to a degree inferior to no other part of the world. If this letter, which draws to their attention and to the attention of their fellow members the true state of affairs in Trinidad and Tobago and what to do about it, if this letter meets with no response, then here, as elsewhere, the general prospect for harmonious development and adjustment is bleak indeed. It would have been very simple for the *Nation* to have gathered up enough of the mass of information floating around and launched a ferocious and sustained attack against the Queen's Park Club. Vast sections of the public would have greeted it with deep satisfaction. But if the problem is urgent it is not urgent in the way that the removal of Alexander as captain is urgent. On that we are giving no quarter at all. But on this far larger question we have preferred a more friendly and more cautious approach. If, however, there has to be a fight to cure our society of a dangerous abscess which has now burst, then fight there will be. Foremost in the desire for a peaceful solution, the *Nation* likewise, if nothing else suffices, will lead the attack: it will be strategic, comprehensive and final.

Yours, gentlemen,
I assure you, very sincerely,
C.L.R. James

Once more the general public read with deep satisfaction. It saw in print what it wanted expressed. I believe that, in Trinidad at least, a great deal of tension, dating back many years, has been eased. The selection committee made a brilliant selection for Australia. Gerry Gomez was appointed manager, a good choice. Gerry is popular at home among all classes and in Australia, knowledgeable and tough. The *Nation*'s approval was freely expressed and generously approved. Despite the public request of Frank Worrell, the new captain, the Board refused to reinstate Gilchrist. I thought it was a mistake, but I let it pass. I have said that explosions can occur again. They most certainly can, but only if an atavistic idiocy persists in outmoded and discredited foolishness.

I must say that after it was all over my regard for cricket and my interest in it were greater than ever before. During all this time the *Nation* was vigorously supporting the Premier in political campaigns against the Colonial Office and the State Department, campaigns in which it was made clear that in pursuit of what he considered legitimate and inalienable rights the Premier was ready to take Trinidad and Tobago out of the Federation and out of the Commonwealth if need be. He was confident of the support of the people. All that is now over. Yet considered opinion is that the campaign for Worrell was the most popular and the most effective of all the *Nation* campaigns. The people simply saw it as a part of the whole movement. There might be arguments, and considerations to be taken into account in regard to the other issues – this one they understood and accepted completely. All art, science, philosophy, are modes of apprehending the world, history and society. As one of these, cricket in the West Indies at least could hold its own. A professor of political science publicly bewailed that a man of my known political interests should believe that cricket had ethical and social values. I had no wish to answer. I was just sorry for the guy.

It is easy to misunderstand and overdraw conclusions from the above campaign, sharp as it was. West Indian society isn't easy for outsiders to understand. Our Maple–Shannon–Queen's Park rivalries, keen as they were, never, or very rarely, exceeded the bounds. So it is today, despite the apparently irreconcilable antagonisms. The secretary of Queen's Park, Botha Tench, is an old and favourite pupil (I had refereed or umpired countless matches in which he and Victor Stollmeyer, boys in short trousers, played). He complained to me that I had certain facts wrong. I offered him the paper to correct them, but he didn't accept the offer. Yet when we spoke about it I hadn't seen him since I had come home and our greetings were warm and cordial.

The two cricketers referred to in the open letter are, of course, Gerry Gomez and

Jeffrey Stollmeyer. Soon after I came home I tried to find outstanding sportsmen who were popular with all classes and could play a mediating social role in the acute political tensions. Two names were given to me: Gerry Gomez and Lindsay Grant. When Gerry was appointed manager for Australia I wrote in the *Nation* quite plainly what are his opportunities and responsibilities in the building of a national community. He did not take it amiss.

The other cricketer is Jeffrey Stollmeyer. Looking for someone to write capably for the paper about a visiting English soccer team his name was mentioned to me. (He and Gerry starred in inter-colonial soccer as well as in international cricket.) I called him up and asked him to write. He said he was very sorry but it was just about the time the matches were played that he had to deal with his workers. I regretted this. I had found his judgement on West Indian players to be as sound and more balanced than all I had heard with the exception of Andy Ganteaume's. He would have been quite willing to write and surprised me by not merely giving me condolences about my father's death but spoke about him in a way that showed he had some idea of my father's work and personality. Cyril Merry must have talked to him. Jeffrey and Gerry are, of course, and have been for many years, the embodiment of Queen's Park. Michael Gibbes, the assistant secretary of the Queen's Park Club and an able journalist, wrote regularly on cricket for the *Nation.*

The other person referred to, Lindsay Grant, is head of the Grant family and the Grant business firm, brother of two West Indian captains, umpire in Tests and a Queen's Park stalwart. When there was a financial problem about my staying in the West Indies Lindsay subscribed substantially, though he knows my political views. Premier Williams wanted Jack Grant to come home and be the Chief Officer in the Education Department. But Jack will not leave his missionary work in Africa. One day an African in transit who had been President of the African National Congress of South Africa paid me a visit. I asked him if by any chance he knew Jack. Most surprisingly, he said yes: once when attending a conference of the Congress he had stayed incognito at Jack's house. I called Lindsay and they had a long conversation. Whenever I want information which Lindsay may have I call him or drop in at the office and am always welcome. We both won exhibitions the same year and came up the school side by side.

The most pointed reference of all in the open letter is to the organization of football. The secretary of the West Indian Football Association is my brother Eric. He had managed two teams to England, had brought one to the West Indies and was bringing another. He had been the secretary of the Government committee in charge of the projected stadium. About the cricket controversies he was noncommittal, but everyone knew that the Football Associations which he was responsible for were run on strictly democratic lines, all clubs and all classes represented, and were supported by the entire community. The football organization interested me enormously, owing to the perfect integration of all elements in the community. That it is so is no accident, and nationalist politics are not confined to speeches and laws. My brother has made it that way and kept it that way, though he will recoil with horror at the mere thought of being called a politician. He has had his troubles, and speaks of the unswerving support he has had, among others, from Courtenay Rooks, a white man who was at school with me, and from George Rochford, at one time head of Gordon, Grant & Co., perhaps the biggest firm in the island. The most curious fact to the stranger who would read my open letter is that some of the staunchest supporters of the Football Association and members of its committees have been and are active members of Queen's Park. In fact it is precisely because of the above that I could write so freely. Under different circumstances the open letter would have been tantamount to a declaration of war. Staunch Queen's Park members told me, 'A little harsh in places but not so bad'.

So there we are, all tangled up together, the old barriers breaking down and the new ones not yet established, a time of transition, always and inescapably turbulent. In the inevitable integration into a national community, one of the most urgent needs, sport, and particularly cricket, has played and will play a great role. There is no one in the West Indies who will not subscribe to the aphorism: what do they know of cricket who only cricket know? But what is most strange is that what I have written here and in the early chapters [in *Beyond a Boundary*] on Maple-Shannon-Queen's Park has been known to everyone in the West Indies for the last fifty years. Yet it had been allowed to fester under the surface, a source of corruption and hypocrisy. From now on that is over.

Notes

1   That agitation is for the time being deadened – C.L.R.J.
2   From my knowledge of him, and I am fortified by Constantine's opinion, Headley is a master strategist and tactician.
3   Three or four years ago I could have had a lot to say about English crowds at cricket, and twenty-five years ago I was quite familiar with Lancashire League crowds. But you have to keep in close touch.
4   The *Nation*, 4 March 1960.
5   Certain critics, not only West Indian, deplored the tone of my advocacy and doubted if the high-minded Worrell would approve of it. If any of these delicate souls had shown me models of advocating one of the three Ws as a West Indies captain I might have benefited from their instruction. Unfortunately, none of them offered any model, reproved not selectors but me. Hence my untutored vulgarity.

Part V

Philosophy, art and literature

19

C.L.R. James' materialist aesthetic of cricket

Kenneth Surin

In his quasi-autobiographical work *Beyond a Boundary*, C.L.R. James complains that '[the] aestheticians have scorned to take notice of popular sports and games'.[1] *Beyond a Boundary*, a unique historical study of cricket as a social and cultural form, is in part a sustained attempt to repair this neglect.

James had Neville Cardus, arguably the greatest of all cricket writers, specifically in mind when he made his criticism of 'the aestheticians', but his strictures have a wider applicability. For in the historical-cultural world associated with the growth and dissemination of cricket as a national and then an international institution, a world of English culture that has held its place roughly since the time of the Industrial Revolution, certain dominant axes of power have effectively excluded that which is thought to be 'popular' from the domain of 'the *(properly)* aesthetic'. Within this domain powerful and selective pressures tend to promote a seemingly automatic conflation of 'the popular' with 'the mass', and hence with 'the vulgar' (and by extension with 'the undesirable' and 'the invalid').[2] James's criticism is also applicable to historians and cultural theorists, and this, perhaps, surprisingly, includes those who profess to work from a Marxist or neo-Marxist perspective. Even Raymond Williams, who studied the many components and dimensions of culture with a seriousness and penetration unsurpassed by any British writer in this century, published (to my knowledge) only one short essay on a topic connected with sport.[3] Likewise, T.W. Adorno, whose writings on cultural themes extend from analyses of American television comedy to disquisitions on the 'regression to magic under late capitalism' typified by the horoscope columns of Los Angeles newspapers, confined his reflections on sport (as opposed to 'play') to a few remarks about its permeation by the 'culture industry' of late-capitalist societies.[4] The omissions of Williams and Adorno testify to the magnitude of James's achievement in recognizing the centrality of cricket and sport in general as an active cultural force (a centrality whose principle and spirit students of culture like Williams are seemingly unable fully to acknowledge); and in seeing that *(pace* Adorno) this kind of cultural valence does not necessarily preclude cricket (and sport) from being a vehicle for the aspirations and struggles of subordinated groups and nations. While many commentators on his writings have acknowledged the profound significance of cricket and its *mores* for James, few or none have analysed his accounts of the game in any depth or detail.[5] I hope at least to provide a more substantial treatment of the convergence, at once theoretical and practical, of Marxism and cricket in the life of this exemplary 'post-colonial' intellectual.[6]

A cultural history of cricket

Two guiding principles are discernible in James's history of cricket. The first is his profound sense of the intricate connections existing between a *knowledge* and a *place*. The second, and related, principle is his (avowedly) Marxist and (unavowedly) Weberian application of an 'algebra', to be found in Hegel's *Science of Logic,* which according to James could be 'used in any analysis of constitution and development in nature or in society'.[7] This 'algebra' makes possible the dialectical relationship between two movements which are determinative for a Hegelian philosophy of history namely, the movement of thought and the movement of history (which James the Marxist, in his *Notes on Dialectics* explicitly identifies with the history of labour).

In his always evident sense of the indissoluble connection of knowledge and place, James has an affinity with Raymond Williams, who, it may be recalled, begins his essay 'Culture is Ordinary' with an account of a bus journey from Hereford Cathedral (where he had been viewing the Mappa Mundi) to his home village in Wales.[8] As the journey begins, Williams notices the streets of the city, and when the bus traverses the surrounding countryside, he takes note of the fields, the nearby Black Mountains, the small villages and their white houses, and then the industrial valleys, with their mills, pitheads, gasworks and terraced houses. This is followed by a depiction of family and village life – life in a place, a community, that forms the sub-text of the characterization of culture that follows.

James displays a similar power of evocation, a similar grasp of the 'materiality' of places, particularly in the section in *Beyond a Boundary* devoted to his childhood and youth.[9] Like the story of his own life, James's cultural history of cricket is propelled by a series of rich descriptions – an 'imaginative geography' (to borrow a phrase from Edward Said) – of certain spaces and their specific characters, spaces in which are located the decisive events and processes that constitute the sub-text of this historical narrative. Thus, the great all-rounder Learie Constantine is 'placed' in both Trinidad and Nelson (Lancashire); the batsmen Walcott, Weekes, Worrell and Sobers (who was of course remarkable for being able to bowl in several styles at Test Match level) in Barbados; Kanhai, the mercurial batsman of Indian origins, in British Guiana (now Guyana); and so on. James's early conspectus of West Indies cricket, published in 1933, does not get to its advertised subject until the reader has been through a geographical, historical, and sociological account of the islands.[10]

Implicit in James's connection of historical knowledge with place is the assumption that the places where human beings are born and formed are the *loci* of deep currents of thought and feeling, currents which generate the 'unstated assumptions' we are 'often not aware of' and which are 'usually the mainspring of [our] thought'.[11] These 'unstated assumptions', which mediate between place and knowledge, belong to imaginative structures that enable agents to 'reproduce' their social and cultural positions in their practical activities (in James's case this would clearly include the game of cricket).[12] The concept of an 'imaginative structure', when given a properly 'materialist' specification, substantiates James's claim that a player's style and thinking is the outcome of the *zeitgeist* of cricket, and that these can be changed only when there is 'a change in society'.[13]

Numerous examples can be given of the instantiation in James's writings on cricket of what has here been referred to as an 'imaginative structure'. One of his 'strongest early impressions of personality in society' was provided by his boyhood encounter with the local ne'er-do-well, Matthew Bondman, who was also James's 'first acquaintance with that *genus Britannicus,* a fine batsman'.[14] James registers clearly the discrepancy between Bondman's genius as a batsman and his shiftless way of life. Yet while no doubt is left in the reader's mind about the connection which James does not even trouble to state – between Bondman's self-destructive behaviour and his inability to sustain his career as a cricketer, James says that after 1953 he 'discovered that I had not arbitrarily or by accident worshipped at the shrine of W.G. Grace and Matthew Bondman' (page 29). Now this is a wholly unlikely association, because James regards W.G. Grace as the one cricketer who comes nearest to being a world-historical individual (understanding this term in its full Hegelian sense, albeit as filtered, for James, through Marx), and Matthew Bondman is evidently anything but such an individual. To understand the coupling of the great Grace and (but for James's non-forgetting) the very much unnoticed Bondman, it is necessary to mention one of the principal convictions expressed in James's writings on West Indian cricket, namely, that until the islands severed their formal colonial ties with Britain in the 1960s, the 'social passions' of non-white West Indians were 'suppressed politically', and could therefore 'find vigorous if diluted expression' only on the cricket field.[15] The freedom and competence which Bondman displayed (only) in his batting were thus the manifestation of personal and collective powers which could not be given expression in a wider public sphere regimented by the system of colonial administration.

Cricket is so integral a part of British and colonial (and neo-colonial) culture that for James even the implements of the game could not be mere 'material' objects. This is evident in James's characterization of W.G. Grace, a description in which the bat used by the first of the great modern cricketers is accorded a metonymic function: the doctor used his bat to build 'as much of that old [pre-Victorian] world into the new . . . .'[16] Bondman, the *de classé'* Bondman, was not situated in a historical conjuncture, and hence in the appropriate imaginative structure, in which he could build a world in this way. He and other black West Indians were not then allowed to build any such worlds. Bondman, however, could testify *with his bat* to the absence, in the prevailing social and political realms, of that world which would come to exist once West Indian self-government became a reality. More importantly, he and other West Indian cricketers could begin, there and then, to create and to anticipate that not yet realized world of freedom by the way in which they wielded bat and ball.

Bat and ball, especially when used by players from the subaltern classes, also possess for James an irreducible political meaning. This conviction is explicitly stated with regard to the Test-player Wilton St Hill, of whom James says:

> I know that to tens of thousands of coloured Trinidadians the unquestioned glory of St Hill's batting conveyed the sensation that here was one of us, performing *in excelsis* in a sphere where competition was open. It was a demonstration that atoned for a pervading humiliation, and nourished pride and hope.[17]

St Hill could not have 'conveyed the sensation' described by James had he been formed in, say, the very different imaginative structure which shaped St Hill's gifted white West Indian contemporaries Challenor and Tarilton. Had he been formed in that alternative imaginative structure, St Hill would not have 'reproduced' (even as he 'defined'), in his batting, a certain social and cultural position. St Hill did not simply bat, he batted *as one of the oppressed*. He was able to decompose, in his batting (if not in anything else), the culture of subordination in which black West Indians were immured.[18] Given the appropriate historical conjuncture, and the requisite *habitus*, it was possible for cricketers like St Hill to articulate, through the game, a new horizon of possibility for the ruled classes in the colonial West Indies. Placed as he is, and placed as they are, the batting of St Hill gives West Indians a 'new' knowledge, namely, that the superiority of their colonial masters is not a fated superiority. It is a superiority that could be, and indeed was already being, challenged on the cricket field. This generated, slowly and unevenly, the realization that the paramountcy of the colonial rulers was also challangeable in other domains, in particular the area of administration and government. In the batting and bowling of cricketers like St Hill and Constantine an ideological and political groundshift was thus manifesting itself.[19]

The position so far ascribed to James asserts that cricket's capacity to express social and political impulses is determined, at least in part, by the positions occupied by its players and spectators in a particular social and political 'space'. James, however, wants to say much more than this. As he sees it, cricket is able to bear this weight of 'social response' only because it is also 'a game of high and difficult technique'.[20] In other words, there is something inherent in the game itself which makes it possible for cricket to have played so significant a part in the anti-colonial struggles of the West Indian people. This is why James's cricketing writings effortlessly blend discussion of cricketing technique and strategy with consideration of economic, political, and socio–cultural themes. Rarely is the one mentioned in isolation from the other. It is widely accepted in cricketing circles that some of James's pieces on technique are among the best ever written: his article on S.F. Barnes, the Lancashire and England bowler, drew the attention of Neville Cardus, and led to James's becoming a cricket correspondent for the *Manchester Guardian*.[21] Even in his mid-eighties James produced cameos in which he analysed with a sharp technical eye the hitting of Botham and the problems on and off the field which have impeded the career of the talented David Gower.[22]

While James indicates clearly that in the West Indies cricket carried this 'load of social response' precisely by being a vehicle for the expression of emancipatory and democratic impulses in a colonial setting, he is, noticeably, less concerned to analyse the part that cricket also played in reducing the force of the social and political pressures fed by these impulses. James does of course state frankly that while cricket expressed the West Indian passion for autarchy, this expression, for all its 'vigour', remained one that was 'diluted'.[23] He also says of Trinidad club cricket that while 'the class and racial rivalries were . . . intense . . . they could be fought out without violence or much lost except pride and honour'.[24] There can therefore be little doubt that West Indian cricket in the period of British rule, as a cultural formation, belonged to a culture which merged elements of both a 'culture of consolation' *and* a culture which actively resisted the colonial apparatus of coercion and exploitation. However, James, while certainly acknowledging the fact, seemingly never really sought to understand fully the cricketing ingredient in this 'culture of consolation'.[25]

This is strange, because James's perceptive analysis of the causes which led to the breakdown of the West Indian Federation got to the heart of the problem, namely, that the West Indies still had 'its centre – intellectual, financial and economic – in London, so that the lines of communication ran from Port of Spain to London, from Kingston to London, from Georgetown to London and from Bridgetown to London', whereas 'federation demanded that the lines of communication should run from island to island, not from island to the control body in Britain'.[26] If London constituted (and still constitutes?) the metropolitan centre from which the economic and political life of the West Indies was (and is?) generated, then it is likely that the capital of the Empire also served as a vital productive centre for the descriptions, and their attendant self-understandings, that non-white West Indian cricketers gave of themselves. The demise of the Empire may not have changed things all that much: the international governing body of the sport continues to have its headquarters in London, as of 1989 the constitution of this body – the International Cricket Conference – even decrees that its chairman will be 'the President of the Marylebone Cricket Club or his nominee', and it is rare for a gifted West Indian cricketer not to pursue a career in English county cricket or in one of the northern professional leagues. Cricket, on this account, is part of a hegemonic project, a project of cultural assimilation, which uses cricket as a field for *producing* an image of the 'ideal' Englishman, an image which bespeaks the subordination of those who are invited to become the native versions of this image.[27] *Beyond a Boundary* itself testifies that cricket was imbricated in 'the old

317

Colonial System' (and thus the 'new' neo-colonial system?) just as much as any other area of West Indian life cited by James, and this inevitably had, and maybe even still has, the effect of transmuting and blunting, while still expressing and embodying, some of the radical social and political passions associated by James with his beloved game. Certainly more work needs to be done by cultural historians on the ambivalent functions served by West Indian cricket in the colonial and neo-colonial dispensations.

James's stress on the intrinsic connection between knowledge and place, despite the illuminating and productive use to which it is put in his history of cricket, is nevertheless not without its problematic aspects. Some of the claims he makes in the course of applying this principle are difficult to sustain. For example, the contention, made in a fine essay on Garfield Sobers, that 'there is embodied in [Sobers] the whole history of the British West Indies', has credence for James only because of his deep attachment to a version of the Hegelian notion of 'the world-historical individual'.[28] This is not the place in which to demonstrate precisely how Hegel, and therefore James, is vulnerable to the well-known charge that a troublingly idealistic conception of individual and collective praxis attends the concept of 'the world-historical individual'. But if one assumes that a myriad forces and experiences constitute West Indian history, then it is hard to see how a single individual, even one so significant for West Indian culture as Gary Sobers, can 'express' even a fraction of these many impulses and dispositions.

The claim that cricket is 'a means of national expression' is just as untenable, especially in the last two decades or so, when capitalism has moved into a globally integrated phase.[29] Cricket, as a commercial sport, has had to respond to this transformation as a condition of its financial survival. This shift is especially evident in the way in which the modern (one might as well say 'post-modern') West Indian professional cricketer now earns a living, namely, by playing several 'seasons' in the course of a single year: the domestic West Indian season, an English summer of county cricket, a winter tour abroad, and if this can be squeezed in, maybe a spell playing for a state team during the Australian summer.[30] Cricketing styles are homogenized in consequence of this 'internationalization' of the game, and even the 'subjectivities' of cricketers become fungible. Hence the great Indian batsman Sunil Gavaskar is frequently likened to his English counterpart Geoffrey Boycott, who in turn is said to have been stylistically indistinguishable from the Australian Bill Lawry; the Pakistani Imran Khan, the New Zealander Richard Hadlee, the Australian Dennis Lillee, and the West Indians Roberts, Holding, Garner and Marshall have acquired virtually identical Test Match records by each bowling with similar effect on just about any cricket ground in the world; and so forth. About a hundred of the world's top cricketers play each other repeatedly in twenty or so major international cricketing venues (The Oval, Sabina Park, Melbourne Cricket Ground, the Feroz Shah Kotla Ground, etc.) year after year, and with the unrelenting 'internationalization' of commercial cricket, they no more express a 'national' spirit or identity than do tennis players domiciled in Monte Carlo but who continue to represent their 'home countries' in the Davis Cup. It has also become common for leading players to entrust the management of their careers to business agents, and these agents often sign up players belonging to several international teams: Michael Manley, in his history of West Indies cricket, records that in 1977 an Australian agent, David Lord, managed Zaheer Abbas of Pakistan and Viv Richards and Alvin Kallicharran of the West Indies (though the latter is now a British citizen and threw his lot in with the 'unofficial' West Indian team that toured South Africa in 1983), so that it is now not uncommon for a Test Match player to take the field and to find himself confronted by an opponent and a business partner in the same person.[31]

Towards the end of his life James did register these irresistible processes of standardization so characteristic of present-day international cricket, but he did not really know how to analyse them. This is indicated by his lukewarm praise for the phenomenally successful West Indian team of the 1970s and 1980s led by Clive Lloyd. In his 1984 essay 'West Indies vs England' James maintained that this team – the most successful ever in the history of international cricket – contained only one truly great player in Viv Richards, and attributed its success to the fact that Australia and England, the principal rivals of the West Indies, were in a time of cricketing decline during that period.[32] Rather than seeking to account for the success of Lloyd's team by identifying its 'great players' (and finding only one), James should have looked at what some usually far less perceptive British and Australian cricketing writers were groping towards when they commented on, or rather complained about, the unprecedented 'professionalism' of Lloyd's team. This team had, among other things, hired an Australian trainer to develop its fitness and other *non-cricketing* skills, so that just as much time was devoted in practice to exercise programmes as was given over to playing the game itself. Cricket correspondents noted how the West Indian team continued to practise as if everything were at stake even after it had trounced its opposition in a Test Match series. Of all the international teams, the West Indies had a body of players who now perhaps most resembled Max Weber's *ordnungmenschen*, men whose cricketing lives were in many crucial respects based on the principles of a purely instrumental rationality (in this case applied to sport). In a new kind of globally integrated game, cricketers with 'genius' had come to be rivalled, or even supplanted, by players who, in a Weberian sense, had successfully 'organized' themselves into having winning *careers*. No wonder James could not account for the success of a team that, in his eyes, lacked the 'historic players' of previous West Indian teams that were relatively much less successful than the one led by Lloyd.

It would be foolish to pretend that the success of Clive Lloyd's team was due solely to its ability to turn cricket into a kind of technology. No other team has come near to matching the winning record of the West Indies, despite having tried in more than one case to organize itself on the basis of the same 'technological' principles (the implementation of 'squad' systems, appointing a full-time trainer, allowing the remuneration of players to be determined by 'market forces', and so on). Other economic and cultural factors have undoubtedly been significant in making the West Indies a so-far unsurpassably successful team. But James, having saddled himself with Hegelian ideas of 'representative' and 'world-historical individuals', and in the process having also underwritten a Marxist rendition of Hegel's problematic theory of an 'expressive causality', was unable to account for what has been for cricket a new historical conjuncture. This failure on James's part is perhaps indicative of a deeper problem in his analysis of cricket, one having to do with his adherence to another, more architectonic, principle – a principle which curiously blends his Hegelian Marxism with a Weberian understanding of historical development. James, early in *Notes on Dialectics*, gives a statement of the Hegelian 'algebra' which provides the organizing principle for his history of cricket. Determinative for James's application of this 'algebra' is 'the knowledge of the labour movement beginning in 1789 and continuing to our day' (page 8). This knowledge, which for James necessarily includes knowledge of the economic realities of colonialism and neo-colonialism, is said by him to make possible a Marxist understanding of the movement of thought delineated by Hegel in his *Logic:* 'when we worked on the *Logic* we were able to understand its movement by testing this movement against the history of the labour movement and, conversely, the movement of the Logic enabled us to understand and develop for contemporary and future needs the history of the labour movement' (page 8).

Very much the same procedure is followed in James's history of cricket. Cricket – the game and its *mores* – is permeated by the productive relationships of capital, and for James is to this extent an inextricable part of 'the history of the labour movement'. Any putatively Marxist account of the game, such as the one provided in *Beyond a Boundary* (that is, 'a movement of thought'), must therefore be tested against 'the history of the labour movement' (that is, cricket as an element in the productive relationships of capital); and, equally, any such account of the game must itself furnish an understanding of the 'contemporary and future needs' produced by 'the history of the labour movement'. Only in this way can 'truth' be made available. 'Truth' in turn is identified by James with 'the total emancipation of labour', which 'can only be achieved when it contains and overcomes its complete penetration by its inherent antagonism, the capital relation' (page 10).[33]

Although there are a few passages in his writings, especially in a more theoretical work such as *Notes on Dialectics*, when James seems almost close to promoting something akin to a 'deterministic' Marxism, this superficial impression must be resisted. James is resolutely Hegelian in many of his theoretical formulations, but he is emphatic in his rejection of the theodicy which drives Hegel's philosophy of history. James, like Gramsci, refuses to dress the Hegelian theodicy in Marxist clothes. Socialism is inevitable, he says, but this is not because a secularized providence is 'working' to make it so. Marxists have a warrant for saying that socialism is inevitable only because the working class is actively working to bring about its realization. For James, therefore, the assertion that socialism is inevitable can be made only because of the practical activity of the working classes to transform the material world. Despite James's repudiation of any kind of historical determinism, he persisted in his conviction that history possessed a 'logic' (one which however was not the 'inner logic' of a theodicy) that could be deciphered by recourse to Marxist principles. As long as capitalism prevails, the 'logic' of the historical process would be the ceaseless dialectic of the 'logic' of capital and the 'counter-logic' supplied by capital's adversary, the working classes. The 'counter-logic' of socialism – which has as one of its projects the analysis of capital and its 'logic' from the standpoint of the consciousness and practice of the working classes – affirms the inevitability of socialism not as an inexorable 'law' underpinning history, but as precisely the 'truth content' of the *experience* of these classes, a situation-specific experience which makes it unavoidable for members of these classes to see and to know the world except in a way which 'posits' the final abolition of capitalism.[34]

Acknowledging the force of this principle of Marx's, which James would never have dreamt of relinquishing, raises the important question of the specific relationship this 'logic' of history had to the game of cricket.

James therefore perceived what no one else had articulated before, namely, that the narrative of cricket's history has everything to do with the singular narrative Marxists are drawn to provide about capitalism. What can be questioned, however, is the plausibility of the specific narrative furnished by James when he articulates his realization that, in those countries where cricket is played and watched, the story of cricket and the story of capitalism have to be elaborated as parts of a single extended story. By itself, the recognition that these two ostensibly disparate stories are nevertheless parts of one comprehensive story is not something that is problematic. But what James does, in creating a narrative of the always material intertwining of cricket and particular economic and socio-cultural realities, is, very surprisingly, to tell a story which, while it is still Marxist, is at the same time more recognizably Weberian than anything else. In his account of the historical development of cricket, James presents a schema which shows cricket to be not merely the enactment, in material terms, of certain forms of cultural protest and resistance. Nor is cricket simply claimed to be the means by which certain impulses and energies, denied expression in other areas of social and political life, can come to manifest themselves.

Cricket, whether directly or indirectly, does all these things, of course, but what is really interesting and significant for the cultural historian is James's insistence that the techniques and the socio-cultural meanings constitutive of the game pass through recognizable stages of historical *development*. Cricket for James is situated inescapably within a historical trajectory which can be understood by us in terms of Max Weber's threefold schema of charismatic inauguration, traditionalization, and routinization. James never mentions Weber, but that his account of the history of cricket is just as much Weberian as it is Marxist is hard to doubt. The point at which *Beyond a Boundary* becomes Weberian resides in its author's brilliant account of W.G. Grace, who is regarded by James as the founder of modern cricket:

[W.G. Grace] seems to have been one of those men in whom the characteristics of life as lived by many generations seemed to meet for the last, in a complete and perfectly blended whole. His personality was sufficiently wide and firm to include a strong Victorian streak without being inhibited . . . . My contention is that no crusader was more suited to his time than was W.G. to his own; none rendered more service to his world. No other age that I know of would have been able to give him the opportunities the Victorian Age gave him. No other Age would have been able to profit so much by him. He had enriched the depleted lives of two generations and millions yet to be born, He had extended our conception of human capacity and in doing all this he had done no harm to anyone.[35]

The Weberian schema, already in place with James's depiction of W.G. Grace as the charismatic inaugural figure, is extended in an essay on Frank Worrell. In this essay, published in 1970, James asserts that '[the] twentieth century has seen three captains who have expressed a certain stage of cricket and of society. Without some grasp of what they represent, cricket is just a lot of men hitting a ball and running about in flannels. The three men are Pelham Warner, Don Bradman and Frank Worrell'.[36] James wants to say that, as individuals and great captains, Warner, Bradman and Worrell stand in a homologous relationship with certain stages of historical and social development.

The story that James wants to tell about our three representative captains is even more resolutely Weberian. According to this story, in *fin de siècle* England, and up to the First World War and just after, the modern game of cricket, which had been 'invented' virtually single-handedly by W.G. Grace, was taken all over the world, thereby 'making it clear that there were other things in British civilization besides the Union Jack and preparation for world power' (page 256).

Warner, who had been born in the West Indies, was captain of the 1903–4 English team which toured Australia, and is taken by James to represent a particular stage of development both in the game (that associated with its 'Golden Age' of technical virtuosity) and in British history (that period when Britain's imperial 'greatness' was perceived to be at its remorseless zenith). With Warner as a representative figure, the game has now attained to its next historical stage, namely, that of its traditionalization. Bradman, the 'next great captain' and an Australian, is characterized by James as the

the cricketer symbolical of the age which can be called the age of J.M. Keynes . . . . Like Keynes, Bradman systematically and scientifically used all that there was, carried it to an extreme . . . . Despite the fact that some gifted individuals continued to express their personality, cricket followed the lines that had been laid down by Bradman. The systematic refusal to take risks, and to concentrate on what could be reasonably safe dominated cricket for years'. (page 256)

With Bradman as a representative figure, cricket now reaches the next and (for a Weberian at any rate) the final stage of development, namely, that of its routinization. For James, however, the story continues because it is also a story of renewal, of the arrival of new resources of charisma from the newly independent West Indies.

Thus for James, Frank Worrell, the great West Indian captain of the 1960s, is the representative figure who more than any other stands for the repudiation of the legacy of Bradman and his routinized times:

> It is not too much to say that in the world at large, today and in recent years, we have seen a massive instinctual rejection by people everywhere of the kind of systematized social organization which began with the organization of the economy by J.M. Keynes. This I know is somewhat difficult to accept in regard to a game like cricket, but I cannot think of it otherwise and that is the significance of Frank Worrell as a cricket captain'. (page 256)

Worrell, the first black man to captain the West Indies, made West Indian self-government a reality on the cricket field by turning what had previously often been an assorted collection of gifted players – who alas lost frequently to English and Australian opponents – into a unit that managed to win and to play marvellously attractive cricket at the same time.

This narrative is so far persuasive, but unfortunately for the reader, James in his last years did not provide a sustained analysis, along these lines, of Clive Lloyd's West Indian team, a team that acquired an unparalleled winning record in international cricket by, if anything, perfecting the methods James associates with Bradman and the deplorable 'Age of Keynes'. In a period which has ostensibly seen the demise of the Keynesian and the Bradmanian *ethos*, Lloyd and his team-mates scorned to take cricketing risks, primarily by relying in each match on a roster of four very fast bowlers (Roberts, Holding, Garner, Marshall, Patterson, Walsh, Benjamin, Ambrose, Bishop, Davis, Gray, *inter alia*) who would be ceaselessly rotated to wear down – 'psychologically' as much as anything else – opposing batsmen; and by preferring cautious and unspectacular batsmen – for example, Haynes, Gomes, and Murray (who was also an unobtrusively safe wicket-keeper) – to more aggressive, but perhaps unreliable, players. James never expressed much enthusiasm for this team, but he did not tell us why Lloyd's team would, in so striking a reversal, bear the mark of Bradman and not Worrell. Why would the most successful team, not only of the 'post-modern' 1970s and 1980s but of all time, be one that has ostensibly espoused a playing philosophy hardly different from the one which James identifies with the brutal and stagnant 1920s and 1930s? Why would this team come, not from a metropolitan country (as was the case with the equally successful, dominant English and Australian teams in Bradman's time), but from the peripheries of the Wallersteinian world economic system?[37] What causes these apparent aporias in James's historical scheme?

If James were purely and simply a Weberian, there would be no real problem in dealing with the phenomenon of Clive Lloyd's team: what we have with this team, James could say, is simply a new routinization (one which therefore bypasses or moves very rapidly a highly abbreviated stage of traditionalization) of the 'charismatic' West Indian team of the 1960s. The difficulty here, of course, is that someone who takes up James's position can be a Weberian only in a highly qualified sense: staunch Marxist that he is, James must relate any transitions made by the game from one stage of historical development to another to actual changes in the material configurations of the societies in which cricket is played and watched. A Marxist cannot remain content with Weber's claim that the stages of development represented by his tripartite schema – charismatic inauguration, traditionalization and routinization – are merely 'theoretical' or 'ideal-typical' constructions because for the Weberian there can be no 'objective' laws of cultural development.[38] That is to say, a Marxist cannot confine himself to doing what Weber does when he purports to identify a transition from one stage of development to another, namely, to register, by using what amounts to a social phenomenology, changes in the 'subjective' responses, the 'value-oriented' actions, of the kinds of historical agents involved in the making of that transition. The resolutely Marxist James could not plausibly track down the 'historical' changes that took place when the 'charismatic' West Indian team of the 1960s became the 'routinized' teams of subsequent decades purely and simply by trying, *à la* Weber, to account for changes in the respective kinds of 'spirit' displayed by the teams in question. A self-avowed Marxist could not seriously contemplate halting here with Weber: to do so would be to immure oneself in the idealism always lurking in his delineations of the 'spirit' of capitalism, the 'spirit' of the Indian caste system, and so forth.[39] James, good Hegelian that he also is, would moreover not share Weber's neo-Kantian misgivings over any historical scheme which invoked even the most attenuated notions of teleological development – James does say explicitly that if a succeeding age has a 'spirit' different from that of its predecessor this is precisely because it is able, in the figures of its representative individuals, to 'organize' and 'sublate' the age it supersedes.[40] There is no way that the staunchly anti-Hegelian Weber could countenance such a proposition (one which happens of course to be significant for any putatively Marxist, and hence neo-Hegelian, historiography).[41]

It is my conviction, regarding this aporia, that James started to travel down the wrong road as soon as he began to tell the story of cricket as a (Weberian) story of a decisive modern inauguration (W.G. Grace), a Golden Age (the period from 1895–1914 associated with C.B. Fry, Ranjitsinhji, Jessop and Trumper), a stasis or relative decline (the inter-war period associated with Ponsford, Bradman, Hutton, Jardine and Larwood), and a 'post-colonial' renaissance (the 1960s of the first world-beating West Indian team). The problem with this historiography, I have been contending, is that it is premised on a series of 'ideal-typical' constructions which, while they may pose no problem for the unreconstructed Weberian, are the source of much difficulty for anyone who espouses a 'materialist' understanding of culture (and this holds true for James even if he does not recognize this pitfall). Theories which invoke models of cultural decline, stasis or resurgence are notoriously difficult to evaluate, simply because they inevitably imply that there is some clear and decisive standard of authenticity, power or excellence, a standard which happens also to be trans-epochal and supra-contextual in respect of its various applications. Such theories may however say more about the imaginary terms in which the game's history is appropriated by particular historians of cricket than they do about the genuineness and superiority (or otherwise) of any specific way of playing or appreciating cricket.[42] James, it would seem, did not have the 'imaginary' (in the non-pejorative sense deployed in semiotic theory) needed to theorize the forms taken by cricket in the new historical conjuncture represented by the integrated world-capitalism of the 1970s and 1980s. His recourse to a flawed Weberian developmental scheme confirms this suspicion.

In the last decade or so it has become clear that not just the West Indies, but also India and Pakistan (and even New Zealand) have the beating of the traditionally dominant England and Australia. It has also become evident these days (that is, the 1980s and 1990s as opposed to, say, the 1960s) that 'what goes on', in cricketing terms, when anyone of these teams is on a cricket field bears a less direct relationship to 'what goes on' in the nation from which that team hails. As I suggested earlier, present-day international cricket approximates to a well organized, global travelling circus. Teams are therefore not as likely to reflect particular national or cultural identities as they were in the past. Gone are the days when a major West Indian Test-cricketer would live most of the year in, say, Barbados or Antigua and play nearly all his cricket there. 'Home' for such a player is now probably only a place for a 'holiday' during the off-season. Indeed, after a cricketing career spent in other lands, 'home' can become the country where that career was based: for example, Garfield Sobers now lives in Australia, and Sonny Ramadhin, Clairmonte Depeiza, Alvin Kallicharran and Clive Lloyd (to pick out a few names randomly) are domiciled in Britain. Lloyd, having become a British citizen, even joined the English cricketers Gatting and Emburey in the Conservative Party's 'celebrity' campaign during the 1987 General Election. (Learie Constantine, the first great West Indian all-rounder and James's life-long friend, had been appointed to the House of Lords in 1969, but from all accounts would never have dreamt of campaigning for the Conservative Party.) The *leading* players from outside England and Australia, particularly those from the West Indies, tend to play professional cricket in these two countries; are remunerated on the same scale as their English or Australian counterparts; often have the same lucrative British or Australian sponsorship arrangements as their team-mates; and so forth. The days when, say, a public subscription had to be hastily organized in Trinidad to enable L.S. Constantine (the father of Learie) to tour England with the 1900 West Indian side are now, as they say, 'just history'.[43] It would of course be foolish to claim that the system which subserves this cricketing elite is entirely self-maintaining: this system is necessarily complemented, in the West Indies especially, by an integrated organizational structure which, among other things, continually replenishes the elite echelon of players by giving virtually a whole society, including children of primary school age, relatively easy access to the game in its most competitive and disciplined forms.[44] On the whole, however, players of international class today find themselves in a playing environment less directly exposed to a specifically West Indian politics of race (as James points out, the business of having a black man captain the West

Indian team was no longer an issue the moment Worrell came to be internationally recognized as a great and remarkable captain); to the politics of inter-island rivalry (a 'professionalized' selection system and air travel put an end to this where cricket was concerned); to the struggle for self-government (this was achieved during the 1960s); to the every-day realities of poverty and deprivation in the islands (the best players spend most of their time outside the West Indies and are themselves often extremely wealthy by West Indian standards).

The relationship a top-class cricketer has to his West Indian 'base' has thus been quite radically transformed in the course of two decades. On top of this, the very nature of the sport itself has changed throughout the world in that time: the economic base of international cricket has been progressively detached from the national economies of individual nation-states. These changes, which were never acknowledged by James, have been extensive and profound enough to render problematic any *uncomplicated* notions of cricket being a vehicle for the expression of impulses and experiences whose character is determined not only by the contingencies of place and time, but also in the end by the 'stage' of historical development – emergence, stasis, decline or resurgence – a particular nation or culture happens to be in at the time.[45]

To make this criticism is not however to dismiss James. All subsequent social and cultural historians of cricket, whether they profess themselves to be Marxists or not, will have to engage with his analyses and proposals. We will have to work through James, not circumvent him. Besides, he was right, deeply right, most of the time. But what exactly did he get right? What kind of space needs to be opened so that his formulations can be made *productive* for the theorist of cricket endeavouring to follow in his footsteps?

In the suggestive article on Lukacs's classic *History and Class Consciousness* referred to above, Fredric Jameson says that the 'most original feature' of Lukacs's essay 'Reification and the Consciousness of the Proletariat' is his stress on 'group experience'.[46] Jameson credits Lukacs with making a 'unique conceptual move' in this essay, a move which Jameson, following Lukacs's usage, calls 'standpoint theory'. This theory rests on the presupposition that

> owing to its structural situation in the social order and to the specific forms of oppression and exploitation unique to that situation, each group lives in the world in a phenomenologically specific way that allows it to see, or better still, that makes it unavoidable for that to see and know, features of the world that remain obscure, invisible, or merely occasional and secondary for other groups.[47]

'Standpoint theory', employing as it does the concept of the 'conditions of possibility' of the kinds of thinking inherent in a particular class position, makes possible both the analysis of the obstacles and limits to knowledge (what Jameson calls 'the variable structures of "constraint"') and the theorization of any new modes of knowledge (seen here as a process) available at *that* position. The great advantage of 'standpoint theory' for someone seeking to pursue and consolidate James's insights is that it enables us to retain his crucial Marxist principle that each group within social and political 'space' will generate its own specific viewpoints, its own distinctive claims to truth, without requiring us at the same time to retain James's implausible historical scheme. In fact it enables us to identify the point at which James backed himself into the Weberian cul-de-sac. Instead of deploying such slippery and malleable categories as those of 'a stagnant civilization' and 'western civilization' (to mention just two examples), James would have been better served if he had talked instead of the many and complex relationships which exist between the different social groups who play and watch cricket, and capitalism in its different modes and phases (capitalism has after all to be the central object of any putatively Marxist analysis). James's somewhat haphazard excursions into the characteristics ostensibly possessed by the 'Age of Keynes', and so on, make him lose sight of the centrality which the particular narrative concerning capitalism has for his wider historical narrative. In particular, he is somewhat at a loss when it comes to forming an estimation of the extraordinary achievements of Clive Lloyd's team precisely because he seems to have no really 'productive' way of talking about capitalism *beyond* the point at which the European powers gave up the struggle to retain their colonies. He is thus not able, in his cricketing writings at any rate, to register the full force of the new conjuncture which is integrated world-capitalism. He does not really see that Clive Lloyd (undeniably great West Indian cricketer, subsequent British citizen and 'celebrity' supporter of Mrs Thatcher) is precisely the product of this new conjuncture and the West Indian/British component of its attendant 'cultural logic'. 'Standpoint theory' enables us to account for, or at least it makes unsurprising, the apparent homology between Bradman (belonging to the now supplanted 'Age of Keynes') and Clive Lloyd (who in James's account obviously belongs to a 'post-Keynesian' dispensation). James astutely recognizes the palpable connection between the 'bodyline' bowling of the 1930s and the rise of fascism – 'bodyline' bowling, he avers, was 'the violence and ferocity of our age expressing itself in cricket'.[48] However, as we have seen, his historical scheme requires him to say that the epoch of violence and sterility associated with fascism, Jardine, Ponsford and Bradman (and Keynesianism) was overtaken and overturned by a new 'post-colonial' age – an age which saw a remarkable efflorescence in art and sport, reflected in the West Indies by the writings of George Lamming and Wilson Harris and in cricket by Worrell and the incomparable Sobers. James is therefore unable to conceive that once the energies released by this 'new age' were stabilized or transmuted by a succeeding phase of capitalism, it would actually become possible for West Indian cricket, 'after' Worrell and Sobers, to 'complete' something that Bradman and the players of the 1930s were only just in the process of realizing, namely, that cricket could become a kind of engineering (in precisely the way that Keynesianism, according to James O'Connor, presented itself as 'economic engineering'[49]).

Adorno has perceived with brilliance in *Minima Moralia* that an 'engineering' which involved the apotheosizing of *techne* into a metaphysical principle was

possibly the decisive characteristic of fascism, and that this principle was fundamentally 'unstrategic', since (in war) it took the form of 'the accumulation of overwhelming forces at particular points, the crude frontal breakthrough, the
mechanical encirclement of the enemy stranded by armoured spearheads'. Adorno
goes on to say of this principle that it is 'wholly quantitative, positivistic, without
surprises, thus everywhere "public" and merging with publicity'.[50] Present-day
international cricket operates on the same principle: the most successful batsmen
in the 1970s and 1980s with few exceptions (Greg Chapell, David Gower, Ian
Botham and Viv Richards) have all been unspectacular and largely 'patient' accu-
mulators of runs: Gavaskar, Boycott, Border and Miandad (respectively the largest
Indian, English, Australian and Pakistani Test Match run-scorers of all time), were
commonly referred to as 'batting machines' in the cricketing press. The slowest
Test Match century and double-century ever were scored in this period, and they
were scored not by an Englishman or Australian but by a Pakistani (Mudassar
Nazar) and a Sri Lankan (Brendan Kuruppu) respectively. Clive Lloyd handled the
most formidable bowling side in the history of the game 'without surprises': where
successful captains of past times had at least sought to give the appearance of changing their bowlers according to a strategy, he merely changed them according to a
routine (or so it seemed).

The upshot is that today no one country enjoys an uncontested monopoly (except
perhaps in terms of winning) when it comes to playing cricket in this truly contemporary way, that is, a way that has relativized or abolished any cricketing distinction between 'art' and 'engineering'. In these times when cricket (like
capitalism) is in a integrated global phase it is not only a Bradman or a Hutton who
can bat like an automaton: today a Hanif Mohammad (the Pakistani who holds the
world record for the highest score in first-class cricket) or a Graeme Hick (the white
Zimbabwean who in 1988 scored the first quadruple-century in English first-class
cricket since 1895) are likely to bat as unrelentingly as any of the great Australian or
English batsmen did in the 1930s.[51] The same mode of cricketing 'production' can
thus be found in such economically and culturally disparate nations as, say, England
and Sri Lanka, and this is only to be expected in 'late capitalism', a new conjuncture associated in part with a socio-economic shift which Toni Negri calls 'the subsumption of society by capitalist development'.[52] In a time of 'a new international
unification of work', it makes less and less sense to talk in an unqualified way, as
James does, of cricket being homologous with, and 'expressive' of, particular social
and cultural formations. What cricket does more and more is simply to 'express' its
own situation as a commodity produced and consumed within a unitary and stan-
dardized flow of production and consumption which now straddles the world (and
thus the entire cricketing world).

Before making a proposal regarding how James's cultural history of cricket
should best be viewed, given the fairly substantial misgivings I have expressed about
some of his claims and formulations, it is necessary to look at his very important aesthetics of the game.

An aesthetics of cricket

James is to my knowledge the first and only writer on cricket to have produced an aesthetics of the game. For this reason alone this aesthetics, which as one would expect is undeniably 'materialist' in its premises and approach, is deserving of close attention: we cannot think of cricket in the 'old', 'idealist' ways, with their banalities about the 'stylishness' of Woolley, Graveney, Vengsarkar, *et al.*, now that James has so amply demonstrated that any attempt to characterize cricketing 'style' must analyse the constitutive rhythms of the game, and that this analysis must necessarily take the form of an engagement with the history of a wider political economy and culture.[53]

James rightly emphasizes the centrality of the pre-Victorian origins of cricket for any understanding of its characteristic rhythms, something often overlooked by the less discerning student of the game, for whom cricket is archetypically a product of the Victorian age. A quite marvellous paragraph in *Beyond a Boundary* summarizes the history of the game, and portrays its pre-Victorian origins:

> In all essentials the modern game was formed and shaped between 1778 . . . and 1830 . . . . It was created by the yeoman farmer, the gamekeeper, the potter, the tinker, the Nottingham coal-miner, the Yorkshire factory hand. These artisans made it, men of hand and eye. Rich and idle young noblemen and some substantial city people contributed money, organization and prestige. Between them, by 1837 they had evolved a highly complicated game with all the typical characteristics of a genuinely national art form: founded on elements long present in the nation, profoundly popular in origin, yet attracting to it disinterested elements of the leisured and educated classes. Confined to areas and numbers that were relatively small, it contained all the premises of rapid growth. There was nothing in the slightest degree Victorian about it. At their matches cricketers ate and drank with the gusto of the time, sang songs and played for large sums of money. Bookies sat before the pavilion at Lord's openly taking bets. The unscrupulous nobleman and the poor but dishonest commoner alike bought and sold matches . . . . Cricket took its start from the age in which it was born, both the good and the bad. That the good could predominate was a testimony to the simple men who made it and the life they lived. (*Beyond a Boundary*, pages 158–9)

The Victorian bourgeois appropriation of cricket would come later, when the moral outlook of this class would pervade all areas of British life, thereby also 'colonizing' the 'life-world' of cricket (to appropriate a Habermassian phrase). Two features stand out in regard to this historical development.

The first is that this 'moment' of cricket is inescapably conjunctural, in that we have taking place here the coalescence of the sporting interests of a declining aristocracy, the moral outlook of an ascendant bourgeoisie, and the decisive contribution of an 'actively' residual artisan and rural class in creating the forms and techniques that constitute the modern game. This, as James points out, made the game an inextricable constituent of English culture, and helped give the game an element of universality which made it easier for it to be taken beyond the place of its origin.[54]

The second feature arises from the game's provenance in the activities of a rural and artisan class not bound by the daily work-cycle and rhythms of an emergent industrial order. Conforming as it did from the beginning to the rhythms and daily patterns of a largely pre-industrial way of life, cricket would require its practitioners to play matches that normally lasted from morning to evening, often extending over several days. Its ethos, soon to be transposed into the grinding routines of daily life in the industrialized cities of Victorian England, would thus always be resolutely 'anti-work'. This, even for those who may not be lovers of cricket, is surely testimony to the deep and abiding sanity of the masses of ordinary human beings who played and watched the game as they were beginning to be dragooned into the factories and over-crowded tenements of England's manufacturing towns and cities.

James also points out that the long hours of the game – an aspect of it 'which so irritates those who crave continuous excitement' – give its players enough time in which to express their subjectivities, to allow their characters to be registered with its spectators. A batsman playing a five- or six-hour innings, a bowler who performs uninterrupted for two or three hours, a fielding side that is on the field for nearly two days, are in a position to create a kind of narrative with their performances, a narrative whose 'object' is not just the game itself, but also complex dimensions of personality and a larger practice of life which extends beyond its specific confines.[55]

When it comes to discussing the game itself as an aesthetic object, James again shows himself to be deeply Hegelian. He observes that cricket is 'a dramatic spectacle', and then notes that

> it is so organized that at all times it is compelled to reproduce the central action which characterizes all good drama from the days of the Greeks to our own: two individuals are pitted against each other in a conflict that is strictly personal but no less strictly representative of a social group. One individual batsman faces one individual bowler . . . . The batsman facing the ball does not merely represent his side. For the moment, to all intents and purposes, he is his side.[56]

This is simply too essentialistic a view of drama, and it takes no account of the very many kinds of drama which simply do not 'pit' representative individuals against each other. Thus, even in the case of tragic drama – the form perhaps most likely to depict human action in ways that accord with James's account of what he regards as the 'central action' in drama – there are many kinds (of tragic drama) which clearly do not manifest this 'central action' in any way. Examples would be tragedies which explore conflicting motives within the same person, which depict how individuals bring destruction on themselves by their own actions, which depict the sheer failures of connection between family members, and so forth. Raymond Williams's reminder on tragedy is therefore salutary for anyone tempted to find an 'essence' of tragedy (and, by implication, of drama): 'Tragedy is . . . not a single and permanent kind of fact, but a series of experiences and conventions and institutions'.[57] But why make the claim, on which nothing important seems really to hang, that in cricket the batsman ('the individual') is his side ('the social') in a way not found in any other sort? The answer is given by James himself: 'This fundamental relation of the One and the Many, Individual and Social, Individual and Universal, leader and followers, representative and ranks, the part and the whole, is structurally imposed on the players of cricket'. Cricket is superior because '[what] other sports . . . have to aim at, the players are given to start with . . . . Thus the game is founded upon a dramatic, a human, relation which is universally recognized as the most objectively pervasive and psychologically stimulating in life and therefore in that artificial representation of it which is drama'.[58]

There are a number of thoroughly implausible assertions about sport and 'psychology' in this declaration of James's which I do not propose to examine since they are of not much interest to cultural historians and philosophers. What is really interesting, however, is the presence in this declaration of a powerfully Hegelian view of art. According to this view, the universal in human beings can come to consciousness of itself only when individuals engage in a co-operative project which overcomes the conflicts that exist between individual self-consciousness. From this engagement in a shared project emerges a common ethos. When this happens, says Hegel, the individuality given expression in the 'work' of the whole community becomes the explicit embodiment of the universal. Hegel therefore regards artistic activity as the vehicle for this eminently social attainment to absolute spirit: 'Art . . . [is] the [mode] in which the Absolute Spirit is present for non-philosophical people'.[59] In artistic activity, the object, as a 'sensuous' or 'natural immediacy', displays the Idea in the world of appearance precisely as 'beauty'.[60]

'Appearance', though a particularization of absolute spirit, nevertheless leads to it by manifesting, socially, the truth of the reconciliation of subject and object. The artwork for Hegel thus provides the universal basis of community and individuality, of what Josef Chytry calls 'the aesthetic state'.[61] The aesthetic state, typified for Hegel by the classical Athenian *polis*, was none the less a failure inasmuch as it did not succeed in integrating all individuals within the spiritual community that was the State. The institution of slavery was maintained by the Athenian *polis* with destructive effects for any project of reconciliation, a problem acknowledged by Hegel to persist to his day, when modern capitalism, by systematically pauperizing whole classes of people, negates even more decisively the aesthetic state's project of reconciliation. This reconciliation in Hegel's philosophy of world history therefore cannot but be what it is – a (mere) *philosophy* of reconciliation – and art cannot but be what it is in Hegel's philosophy, to wit, a (mere) *philosophy* of art. Hegel's account of the place of art in human life is thus exactly what Terry Eagleton has called it: an 'ideology of the aesthetic'.[62] What Hegel's aesthetics needs is a 'return to life' of the kind proposed by Marx in the *Economic and Philosophical Manuscripts*, that is, a 'return' to the material circumstances which stand in the way of a *real* reconciliation between human beings.[63]

It is now not difficult to see that what James takes to be a condition 'structurally imposed on the players of cricket' – the resolution of the dialectic between the one and the many, the individual and the social, and so forth – is only an abstract, an

331

ideal, resolution. As such, it too needs to be 'returned to life'. We have thus to ask what happens to James's aesthetics of cricket when the batsman 'who is his side' happens to be Mike Gatting, the Englishman who has had no compunction about playing cricket in South Africa. And when the side in question is an 'unofficial' English touring team visiting South Africa in defiance of the international ban on sporting contacts with that country. What takes place when, during this team's visit to South Africa, someone watches Gatting batting in a match in Pretoria, say, and having read *Beyond a Boundary* (if it were not then already on the government's list of banned books), affirms *this* event – Gatting facing up to a bowler in Pretoria – to be a structurally guaranteed 'resolution' of the dialectic between the individual and the social? What kind of 'objectively pervasive psychological stimulation' is being afforded to *these* particular spectators? Would this not perhaps indicate that James is somewhere along the road which leads inexorably to a Hegelian 'ideology of the aesthetic'? James's mistake (and in saying this I readily admit I may have misread him) is – and here my remarks have necessarily to be confined to his aesthetics of cricket – that he fails to realize that this 'reconciliation', far from being 'structurally guaranteed' anywhere, is still very much an 'unfinished project'. After all, Hegel himself not only saw 'reconciliation' as an 'unfinished project', but, in the *Philosophy of Right*, also conceded it to be fundamentally 'unfinishable' in a society which consigns countless men, women, and children to poverty in order to 'facili-tate the concentration of disproportionate wealth in a few hands'.[64] Hegel could see no way out of this impasse in the civil society of his time, and since the present eco-nomic order that is integrated world-capitalism is simply an intensification, albeit on an immense scale, of the one which prevailed in Hegel's time, any 'dialectic' between the individual and the social, the particular and the universal, and so on, must necessarily await a resolution that will come only when an economic order predicated on the 'necessary' pauperization of whole classes of human beings gives way to an order in which no-one is *required* to be poor any more. Only when no-one has to be poor any more will cricket be a truly beautiful game: cricket can never pro-claim its beauty in any system which kills and impoverishes in so many ways count-less human beings. What James or anyone else discerns, aesthetically, in cricket must therefore come to be seen as part of a wider 'project' of liberation that is await-ing the moment of its completion.

Conclusion: the history of cricket as an 'unfinished project'

I have tried to suggest that cricket today is imbricated in a new conjuncture, that of an integrated world-capitalism. I have also tried to indicate that James has by no means given us a final position on the place of cricket within that ceaselessly dynamic *process* which is capitalism. His great achievement is to have been the first writer on cricket to have told us something that was there in front of our eyes, but which we (that is, those of us who profess to be lovers of the game like James) were unable to recognize, namely, that cricket is inextricably bound up with this thing, capitalism, and that we cannot therefore narrate the history of this game in isolation from the history of capitalism itself. His even greater achievement is to have theorized this relationship between cricket and capitalism from a standpoint which, for all its problems (for example, the unsustainable Jamesian appropriation of a 'Weberian' or 'quasi-Weberian' historical scheme, the problematic 'expressive causality', and so on) is nevertheless remarkable for the judgement it delivered on previous phases of capitalist and cricketing development, to wit, the ones which prevailed up to the 1960s. In his claims that capitalism was no longer the 'same' once the European colonies in Africa, Asia and the Caribbean became self-governing nations, that cricket really became a different game when Frank Worrell and Garfield Sobers played it, James was pointing to a development which he, writing nearly thirty years ago *(Beyond a Boundary* was written in the late 1950s and early 1960s), could not really hope then to chart fully and adequately. He was registering the first movements of a restructuring of capitalism and the material import of this irreversible change for cricket; he was indicating the emergence of a new terrain of struggle, but understandably he could not at that time accomplish much more than this. What James had a glimpse of all those years ago, I believe, is what Tony Negri and others have been describing to us in considerable detail in recent years: that the epoch of 'planned capitalism' (which Negri, like James, associates with Keynesianism) had by the 1960s been supplanted by a new configuration of capitalist development which, among other things, saw the creation of a global market, a new international unification of work (the same job, which invariably takes only a couple of hours to learn, can now be done by a worker in, say, Venezuela and Indonesia alike), a 'socialization' of what had previously been the 'mass' worker (car manufacturers now divide their work-force into 'islands of production' which have the 'freedom' to decide how they want to execute a particular task), and so forth.[65]

James, I have been arguing, saw as clearly as anyone that the anticolonial struggle was just as much a *response* to a crisis of 'planned' capitalism as it was a repudiation of the imperial and colonial politics sanctioned by that particular mode of capitalism. But he seemed unable to theorize, properly, the next phase taken by capitalism, which saw the generation of juxtapositions that would in many cases have been completely incongruous in previous phases of capitalist development. This is a time in which, for instance, the poorer nations enjoy self-government while having at the same time to submit to the disciplinary power of organizations like the International Monetary Fund; in which impoverished countries are often administered 'development aid' in ways which compel them to become even poorer and more 'dependent' on the economies of donor countries (the phenomenon of 'compulsory underdevelopment'); in which cricketers who sport 'Rasta' sweat-bands and who spend most of their leisure time listening to Bob Marley records can nevertheless play cricket in a way that, *purely* as cricket, would surely have secured the approval of the 1930s English captain Douglas Jardine (who as one of its foremost cricketing representatives was anything but a critic of the British imperial order); in which the most successful West Indian captain of all time can become a British citizen and a supporter of Mrs Thatcher and still write the Foreword to a history of cricket written by a socialist Prime Minister of Jamaica; and so forth.

The reader of James's cricketing writings in the 1980s sensed a certain puzzlement on his part regarding such developments, but by this time James was evidently more concerned to remind his now much younger friends of what they had never seen: the peerless batting of George Headley, the astonishing cover-point fielding of Learie Constantine, the still dangerous bowling of Barnes when he was sixty. James was going to imprint these figures on our short and truncated memories. Now we could no longer say that we had never been told. James, like Walter Benjamin, was always, but even more so towards the end of his life, engaged in the work of an unrelenting, loving, anamnesis: he was going to summon for us the overlooked (but for James the still unforgotten) Matthew Bondman, Wilton St Hill, George John; the monumentalized and therefore (until recuperated by James) lifeless W.G. Grace; the ordinary and nameless club cricketers in Trinidad and their counterparts in the Lancashire league; and many others. The historical project of liberation is still 'unfinished'. It continues to engage us, to state itself to us. It does this, differently of course, in our different places, and as it claims us it comes to us, again differently, from different historical times and from always particular places. (Here I have tried to take into account the 'post-modern' reconstruction of space and its concomitant 'simulation' of sporting places: we are talking now of a 'cultural logic' which in the manner of Disneyland 'makes' India for us when we watch Bishen Bedi bowling in his 'exotic' turban, or is evocative of 'oriental wizzardry' when Abdul Qadir bowls his leg-spinners and googlies for Pakistan.[66]) Places and times inhabited and shaped by, among others, those cricketing figures recollected by James. This is not a recollection both out of nostalgia. What these people were and did can be used for the future. James uses them in this way. Hence, W.G. Grace, Ranjitsinhji, Learie Constantine, Frank Worrell, the sublime cut stroke of Arthur Jones, all lie ahead of us even as they are behind us. Their time, and our time, says James, is the time of a freedom and justice still to come: for what else did Bondman and Grace, Headley and Sobers. do, but bat, bowl and field in a glorious and material prefiguration of that new and wonderful time?[67] We have to put C.L.R. James in their company, because he of course lived and wrote, irreducibly, for just that time.

Acknowledgements

An abridged version of this chapter was printed in the *New Left Review*, Volume 190. The author is grateful to the editor of *New Left Review* for permission to publish an expanded version in this volume.

Notes

1 C.L.R. James, *Beyond a Boundary* (London, Stanley Paul, 1963), pp. 191–2. (Hereinafter referred to as *Boundary.*) News of James's death came when the penultimate draft of this chapter was being prepared.

2 Sylvia Wynter, in her informed study of James's cricketing aesthetic, invokes Mikhail Bakhtin's study of Rabelais to give weight to the proposition that the 'canons of bourgeois aesthetics' promoted the separation of the so-called 'fine arts' from the 'popular arts' and thus systematically devalued the latter. See her 'In Quest of Matthew Bondman: some cultural notes on the Jamesian journey', *Urgent Tasks*, 12 (1977), pp. 54–79.

Important here too is the work of Pierre Bourdieu and Raymond Williams. See especially Bourdieu, *Distinction: a Social Critique of the Judgement of Taste*, trans. Richard Nice (London, Routledge & Kegan Paul, 1984); and Williams, *Culture and Society* (Harmondsworth, Penguin, 1963). On page 248 Williams credits a tradition that extends from Leavis to Burke (and which proceeds via Arnold and Coleridge) with developing the notion of *culture* as 'a positive body of achievements and habits, precisely to express a mode of living superior to that being brought about by the "progress of civilization."' See also Morag Shiach, *Discourse on Popular Culture: class, gender and history in cultural analysis, 1730 to the Present* (Cambridge, Polity 1989).

3 This essay, 'What Happened at Munich', dealt with the massacre of Israeli athletes by the Black September movement at the 1972 Olympic Games, and was published in the *Listener*, 14 September 1972. It is reprinted in Alan O'Connor (ed.), *Raymond Williams on Television: Selected Writings* (London, Routledge & Kegan Paul, 1989), pp. 21–4.

4 In *Prisms*, Adomo said that 'if one were to summarize the most important trends of present-day culture, one could hardly find a more pregnant category than that of sports'. See *Prisms*, trans. Samuel and Shierry Weber (Cambridge, Massachusetts, Harvard University Press, 1981), p. 56. But in the course of endorsing Veblen's characterization of sport as an archaic regression, Adorno says: 'Modern sports . . . seek to restore to the body some of the functions of which the machine has deprived it. But they do so only in order to train men all the more inexorably to serve the machine. Hence sports belong to the realm of unfreedom, *no matter where they are organized'* (p. 81). (My emphasis.) Adorno was less negative in his estimation of the emancipatory potential of 'play', but it is clear from his description of 'play', that few or none of its distinctive features are carried over into modern 'competitive' sport. For his description of 'play', see Adorno, *Aesthetic Theory*, trans. C. Lenhardt (London, Routledge & Kegan Paul, 1984), pp. 43, 57, 74, 148, 200, 281–4, 314, 315, 354, and 437–40.

5 No full-length treatments of James's writings on cricket are listed in the bibliography of studies on his work to be found in his *At the Rendezvous of Victory: Selected Writings, Volume 3* (London, Allison & Busby, 1984), pp. 291–9. Paul Buhle's fine study, *C.L.R. James: the Artist as Revolutionary* (London, Verso, 1988), does not meet this lack, which is understandable: the (mere) juxtaposition of interests brought about by James's being both a Marxist and an authority on cricket would have been unusual enough, but he of course went further in maintaining a rigorously dialectical relationship between cricket and his Marxism, and few commentators can be expected to absorb so much from such disparate fields of theory and practice.

6 The phrase 'post-colonial intellectual' is taken from Edward Said, 'Intellectuals in the Post-Colonial World', *Salmagundi*, No. 70–1 (1986), pp. 44–64. James is mentioned by Said as one such intellectual.

7 On this 'algebra', see *Notes on Dialectics: Hegel, Marx, Lenin* (Westport, Connecticut, Lawrence Hill, 1980), p. 8.

8 Raymond Williams, 'Culture is Ordinary', in *Resources of Hope: Culture, Democracy, Socialism* (London, Verso, 1989), pp. 3–18.

9 *Boundary*, pp. 13–54. This section is titled 'A Window to the World'.

10 'West Indies Cricket', in James's *Cricket*, ed. Ana Grimshaw (London, Allison & Busby, 1986), hereinafter referred to as *Cricket*, pp. 12–33.

11 The quoted phrases are taken from *Boundary*, p. 63. James thus says of George John and Wilton St Hill, who belonged to the first generation of great black West Indian cricketers, that '[everything] they were came into cricket with them' (p. 83).

12 I borrow the term 'imaginative structures' from Michael Sprinker, *Imaginary Relations: Aesthetics and Ideology in the Theory of Historical Materialism* (London and New York, Verso, 1987), p. 33. In my view James is referring to something like an 'imaginative structure' when he maintains, in *Notes on Dialectics*, that an analysis of society requires notice of 'certain mass impulses, instinctive actions, spontaneous movements, the emergence of personalities, the incalculable activities which constitute a society' (p. 9). It is precisely the function of an 'imaginative structure' to generate these elements of 'impulse', 'instinct', 'spontaneity', 'personality' and 'incalculable activity', and to give them their specific and active characters. I was tempted at one point to ascribe these functions to what Pierre Bourdieu calls the *habitus*, that is, the shared subconscious internalized scheme of dispositions which underlies agency, but decided that Bourdieu's own elaboration of this notion was in the end too deterministic to do justice to James's understanding of society and social forces. The notion of an 'imaginative structure' allows agents to 'define', and not *(pace* Bourdieu) merely to 'express', the social realities which are productive of their agencies. Here I rehearse the criticism of Bourdieu to be found in Michel de Certeau, *The Practice of Everyday Life*, trans. Steven F. Rendall (Berkeley, University of California Press, 1984), pp. 45–60.

13 *Boundary*, p. 45.

14 *Ibid.*, pp. 13–14.

15 'Cricket in West Indian Culture', *Cricket*, p. 121. James goes on to say that 'individual players of the lower class, most often black men, became popular national heroes in whom the masses took great pride' (p. 122).

16 *Boundary*, p. 176.

17 *Ibid.*, p. 98. Several pages of *Beyond a Boundary* are devoted to a discussion of St Hill's omission from the 1923 West Indies team to tour England. James was convinced that this was because the (white) selectors did not want too many black batsmen in the team. See *Boundary*, p. 100. The idea that cricketers can express, in their play, as yet unrecognized social powers is clearly stated in James's 1975 essay 'Cricket and Race': 'I believed and still believe that the generations of Grace, Trumper, Ranjitsinhji, of Worrell and his men, all were expressing powers inherent in a section of society but hitherto dormant'. See *Cricket*, p. 279.

18 *Beyond a Boundary* vividly describes the way in which this culture of subordination was instituted in the education that James and his non-white fellow pupils received at the Queen's Royal College, Trinidad. See especially pp. 38–9.

19 Cricket was not of course the only area of West Indian colonial life in which this fundamental ideological and political change was taking place. James says that in World War 1
   . . . [the] West Indian soldiers . . . demonstrated . . . that in the very serious business of
   modern war, the ordinary West Indian soldier, despite lack of experience, could hold his
   own with British, Australian, Egyptian and Turkish soldiers. After that experience . . . no
   kind of freedom or democracy was beyond the capacities of the West Indian people'. See
   Party Politics in the West Indies, Trinidad (1962), p. 2.
20 *Boundary*, p. 43.
21 C.L.R. James, 'The Greatest of All Bowlers: An Impressionist Sketch of S.F. Barnes's,
   Cricket, pp. 7–10. An extensive bibliography of James's writings on cricket is to be found
   in *ibid.*, pp. 305–12.
22 See 'Botham Hitting Sixes', *Cricket*, pp. 303–4; and 'The Captain and His Team: an
   Injustice to Gower', *Cricket*, pp. 287–90, and 'West Indies vs England', *Cricket*,
   pp. 298–301.
23 See 'Cricket in West Indian Culture', *Cricket*, p. 121.
24 *Boundary*, p. 72.
25 The phrase 'culture of consolation' has been made well known by Gareth Stedman Jones,
   who uses it to describe British working-class culture between 1870 and 1900, as opposed
   to the more oppositional culture which existed during the period of the 'making' of this
   class (1790–1830). See Stedman Jones, 'Working-class Culture and Working-class
   Politics in London, 1870–1900: Notes on the Remaking of a working class', in *Languages
   of Class: Studies in English Working-class History 1832–1982* (Cambridge, Cambridge
   University Press, 1983), pp. 179–238. Buhle mentions this ambivalent function of cricket
   when he says that cricket '. . . "proved" to the colonizer . . . that "civilizing" had been a
   successful mission; and to the colonized that civilization was by no means the monopoly
   of the mother country but a larger game that anyone could play' (p. 18). Buhle does not
   indicate whether he believes James to have taken enough note of this ambivalence.
26 'A National Purpose for Caribbean Peoples', in James, *At the Rendezvous of Victory:
   selected writings volume 3*, p. 155. James calls this reliance on the former British overlord
   'the Old Colonial System' *(ibid.)*.
27 An excellent account of how this image of the 'ideal' Englishman was produced in British
   India is to be found in Gaun Viswanathan, 'Currying Favor: The Politics of British
   Educational and Cultural Policy in India, 1813–1854', *Social Text* No. 19/20 (1988),
   pp. 85–104.
28 For James's statement about Sobers, see 'Garfield Sobers', *Cricket*, p. 219.
29 For the claim that cricket is 'a means of national expression', see James, 'Kanhai: a study
   in confidence', *Cricket*, p. 171.
30 Michael Manley notes in his *A History of West Indian Cricket* (London, Deutsch 1988),
   pp. 372ff., that domestic competitive cricket in the West Indies was 'increasingly affected
   by the heavy programme of international cricket' during the 1980s. So much so that Shell,
   who sponsored this competition from 1966 to 1987, dropped their sponsorship for it, and
   had their place taken by a Jamaican brewery.
31 See Michael Manley, *A History of West Indian Cricket*, p. 259.
32 James, 'West Indies vs England', *Cricket*, pp. 298–301.
33 *Notes on Dialectics* was first published in 1948. James, to my knowledge, never subsequently modified his view that 'history' was governed by an inexorable emancipatory
   dialectic. In an essay published in 1962 he praised Raymond Williams for being 'a gifted

and devoted theorist of socialism', but severely criticized Williams for not accepting in his book *Culture and Society* that 'Marx's inevitability of socialism was a philosophical, a theoretical postulate, a necessity of thought, based on his conviction that capitalism would inevitably end as it is ending'. See James, 'Marxism and the Intellectuals', in *Spheres of Existence: Selected Writings Volume 2* (London, Allison & Busby, 1980), pp. 113–30. See especially p. 118. Buhle correctly maintains that James's earlier works about the crises of advanced capitalism are not easy to reconcile with the desiderations of a current politics. See Buhle, p. 154. On p. 150 Buhle also plausibly points out that James tended to underestimate the recuperative capacities of capitalism.

34 Here I am trying to formulate James's insights when he says: 'Marx's inevitability of socialism was a philosophical, a theoretical postulate, a necessity of thought, based on his conviction that capitalism would inevitably end as it is ending. With this postulate you approach every political, every social, every economic problem or set of circumstances; you look for those forces, movements, objective or subjective, which advance the cause of socialism and hasten the destruction of capitalism'. See 'Marxism and the Intellectuals', p. 118. In trying to understand James in this way, I have borrowed the formulations of Fredric Jameson, in his 'History and Class Consciousness as an 'Unfinished Project', *Rethinking Marxism*, 1 (1988), pp. 48–72.

35 *Boundary*, pp. 175–9.

36 'Sir Frank Worrell', *Cricket*, p. 255. Subsequent references to this essay will be given in the text.

37 James clearly identifies cricketing superiority with a nation's ability to sustain or to resist a cultural and political hegemony when he says: 'The English had a great period of cricket, from 1895–1914. That was also the last stage of the domination of Western civilization by Britain, and the preparation for the new stage of the British struggle for their place in the sun: . . . 1914 was the end and since that time, and more than ever since the end of World War II, Britain is on the defensive'. See his 'Two Cricketing Societies – Glorious Windies and the Defensive English', *Cricket*, p. 189. Equally, James relates the success of the 1960s West Indian team to the successful struggle for self-government waged off the cricket field by the people of the West Indies. See, for example, his 'Sir Frank Worrell: the man whose leadership made history', *Cricket* pp. 202–5.

38 See Max Weber, *Economy and Society* (translation of *Wirtschaft* und *Gesellschaft*), ed. Guenther Roth and Claus Wittich (Berkeley, University of California Press, 1978), p. 882. Weber's theory of socio-cultural development is usefully discussed in Guenther Roth, 'Rationalization in Max Weber's Developmental History', in Sam Whimster and Scott Lash (eds), *Max Weber, Rationality and Modernity* (London, Allen & Unwin. 1987), pp. 75–91.

39 Karl Lowith, in his classic study of Weber and Marx, puts the matter succinctly: 'Marx proposes a therapy, while Weber has only a "diagnosis" to offer'. See his *Max Weber and Karl Marx*, trans. Hans Fantel (London, Allen & Unwin, 1982), p. 25. For an overview of this Marxist criticism of Weber, see Johannes Weiss, 'On the Marxist Reception and Critique of Max Weber in Eastern Europe', in Robert J. Antonio and Ronald M. Glassman (eds), *A Weber–Marx Dialogue* (Kansas, University of Kansas, 1985), pp. 117–31.

40 For this claim, made with regard to W.G. Grace, see *Boundary*, p. 176.

41 Weber, for example, maintains that Marx's analysis of capitalism has a purely 'heuristic' significance because all his analytical constructs are no more than 'ideal-types'. See his

'Objectivity in Social Science and Social Policy', in Max Weber, *The Methodology of the Social Sciences*, ed. and trans. Edward A. Shils and Henry A. Finch (New York, Harper, 1949), p. 103. At the same time several commentators have noted the complexity and ambivalence which characterize Weber's attitude to Marx. See, for example, Jurgen Kocka, 'The Social Sciences between Dogmatism and Decisionism: a Comparison of Karl Marx and Max Weber', in Antonio and Glassman (eds), A *Weber–Marx Dialogue*, pp. 134–66; and Stephen P. Turner 'Explaining Capitalism: Weber on and against Marx', *A Weber–Marx–Dialogue*, pp. 167–88.

42 This point is well made about cultural history in general by Morag Shiach in *Discourse on Popular Culture* (1989), p. 12.

43 For James's account of the Constantine episode, see *Boundary*, p. 106. On p. 110 James notes that E.A. McDonald, the great Australian fast bowler of the 1920s, had to leave Australia because he could not get a job there.

44 For this, see Michael Manley, *A History of West Indian Cricket* (London, Deutsch, 1988), pp. 377ff. In *Beyond a Boundary* James shows that Trinidad club cricket was already highly organized during his boyhood. This book however makes no mention of the presence of organized competitive cricket at the schoolboy level. The turning-point in the fortunes of the professional cricketer came with the forming of the Cricketers' Association in 1968. The definitive study of the modern British professional cricketer is Ric Sissons, *The Players: a Social History of the Professional Cricketer* (London, Pluto Press, 1988).

45 For an excellent conspectus of the place of the Caribbean economies in this world capitalist economy, see Carl Stone, 'The Caribbean and the World Economy: Patterns of Insertion and Contemporary Options', in Jorge Heine and Leslie Manigat (eds), *The Caribbean and World Politics: Cross Currents and Cleavages* (New York, Free Press, 1988), pp. 75–93. The cultural implications for the Caribbean of this mode of insertion in the world capitalist system are delineated in Paget Henry, 'Decolonization and Cultural Underdevelopment in the Commonwealth Caribbean', in Henry and Carl Stone (eds), *The Newer Caribbean: Decolonization, Democracy, and Development* (Philadelphia, Institute for the Study of Human Issues, 1983), pp. 95–120. James was aware of the phenomenon of 'cultural under-development', but he never seemed to have appreciated the force of its impact on cricket.

46 Fredric Jameson, 'History and Class Consciousness' (1988), p. 64.

47 *Ibid.*, p. 65. Here it seems to me that Jameson places a stress on 'experience' perhaps not found so explicitly in his previous work; a stress which resonates somewhat with the viewpoint of Raymond Williams.

48 *Boundary*, p. 186.

49 James O'Connor, *Accumulation Crisis* (Oxford, Oxford University Press, 1984), p. 201.

50 Theodor Adorno, *Minirna Moralia: Reflections on Damaged Life*, trans. E.F.N. Jephcott (London, NLB 1974), p. 107. Adorno says that Hitler's opponents had themselves to employ this principle in defeating the Nazis. Paul Virilio has provided an illuminating study of this (military) 'logistics of perception' in his *War and Peace: the Logistics of Perception*, trans. Patrick Camiller (London, Verso 1989). On p. 4 he says: 'In a technicians' version of an all-seeing Divinity, ever ruling out accident and surprise, the drive is for a general system of illumination that will allow everything to be seen and known, at every moment and in every place'.

51 It could be argued that today an Australian or Englishman may even be less likely to play a long, slow innings than his West Indian counterparts. Thus Michael Manley ascribes

the strength of West Indian cricket in part to the prevalence there of the multi–day cricket match (even at club level). See Michael Manley, *A History of West Indian Cricket*, pp. 393ff. In England and Australia, by contrast, the one–day game has been highly promoted in recent years for largely commercial reasons.

52 Toni Negri, 'Interview', *Copyright*, 1, 1987, p. 83. Negri talks about this phenomenon in relation to Brazil, which 'has every kind of production imaginable, from the tribal production of the Indians to computer technology so advanced that it competes with the United States. It is a country that is mediated to an extraordinary degree: even precapitalist forms of cooperation have been integrated into the social mechanism of production' (p. 83). Negri does not discuss 'the subsumption of society by capitalist development' in my sense, namely, the presence of, say, computer technology in such disparate societies as the United States and Malaysia, or the presence of the same mode of cricketing 'production' in, say, Australia and India. But these are all part of the same development, which Negri calls 'a new international unification of work' *(ibid.)*. My claim that the same mode of production can be found both at the centre and the peripheries of the world capitalist economy needs of course to be qualified: as A. Sivanandan has pointed out, there exist in this economy clearly demarcated hierarchies of production which function to ensure that the most advanced productive modes remain at its core. See his 'New Circuits of Imperialism', *Race and Class*, 30 (1989), pp. 1–19. See also Saskia Sassen, *The Mobility of Capital and Labor: a Study in International Investment and Labor Flow* (Cambridge, Cambridge University Press, 1988), pp. 151–68, on the redeployment of 'downgraded manufacturing' to South-East Asia, the Caribbean Basin and Mexico. For an excellent summary discussion of the literature on this subject, see Herman M. Schwartz, *In the Dominions of Debt: Historical Perspectives on Dependent Development* (Ithaca, Cornell University Press, 1989), pp. 9–29.

53 There were times towards the end of his life when James forsook the analysis of political economy and the politics of culture for unabashed nostalgia. In one of the last published pieces he wrote on cricket, he reproduces E.W. Swanton's description of R.H. Spooner's batting, and says he makes 'that quotation with regret', because 'I too belong to that generation and I used to see what we no longer see. I used to revel in what we no longer see'. See James, Cricket Notes, *Race Today*, 15 (1984), p. 20.

54 *Boundary*, p. 164.

55 *Ibid.*, p. 193.

56 *Ibid.*, pp. 192–3. At this juncture James wants to say that no other team sport rivals cricket in requiring its players to be 'the sole representatives of their sides' for so long and on such a scale – even in baseball the batter who makes a fine hit finds himself standing on a base, which makes him dependent on the batters to come'. (See p. 194.)

57 Raymond Williams, *Modern Tragedy* (London, Chatto & Windus, 1979), pp. 45–6.

58 *Boundary*, p. 193.

59 G.W.F. Hegel, *Introduction to the Lectures on the History of Philosophy*, trans. T.M. Knox and A.V. Miller (Oxford, Oxford University Press, 1985), p. 28. See also Hegel, *Lectures on the History of Philosophy*, trans. Elizabeth S. Haldane and Frances H. Simson (London, Cambridge University Press, 1896), Vol. 3, p. 540; and *Lectures on the Philosophy of World History*, trans. H.B. Nisbet (Cambridge, Cambridge University Press, 1975), p. 101.

60 See *Hegel's Philosophy of Mind (Part Three of the Encyclopaedia of the Philosophical Sciences 1830)*, trans. William Wallace and A.V. Miller (Oxford, Oxford University Press, 1971), p. 293.

61 1 am deeply indebted to Chytry's massive study *The Aesthetic State: a Quest in Modern German Thought* (Berkeley, University of California Press, 1989), and have borrowed several of his formulations. See especially pp. 178–219.

62 Terry Eagleton, 'The Ideology of the Aesthetic', in Paul Hemadi (ed.), *The Rhetoric of Interpretation and the Interpretation of Rhetoric* (Durham, North Carolina, Duke University Press, 1989), pp. 75–86. According to Eagleton, this 'ideology' allows bourgeois society to 'produce' in the aesthetic realm the reconciliation and harmony which is effectively banished from its social and economic orders.

63 Jean Hyppolite echoes Marx when he says that the 'negation which remains speculative does not lead to any real transformation of the object. Hegel's *Philosophy of Right* is consequently an *acceptance* and even a *justification* of the political world and the contemporary state'. See his *Studies on Marx and Hegel*, trans. John O'Neill (London, Heinemann, 1969), p. 134.

64 G.W.F. Hegel, *The Philosophy of Right*, trans. T.M. Knox, p. 150. For a helpful discussion of Hegel's account of poverty, see Shlomo Avineri, *Hegel's Theory of the Modern State*, (Cambridge, Cambridge University Press, 1972), pp. 147–54.

65 See Negri, 'Interview'; and *Marx beyond Marx: Lessons on the Grundrisse*, trans. Harry Cleaver, Michael Ryan and Maurizio Viano (South Hadley, Massachusetts, 1984). See especially pp. 105–25 where Negri describes the processes whereby capital posits itself as 'sociality'. For other discussions of this phase of capitalist development, see Claus Ofte, *Disorganized Capitalism: Contemporary Transformations of Work and Politics*, trans. John Keane *et al.* (Cambridge, Polity, 1985); and Scott Lash and John Urry, *The End of Organized Capitalism* (Madison, University of Wisconsin, 1987).

66 On this 'cultural logic', see especially Fredric Jameson, 'Postmodernism, or The Cultural Logic of Late Capitalism', *New Left Review*, No. 146 (1984), pp. 53–92; and Jameson's interview with Anders Stephenson titled 'Regarding Postmodernism', in *Social Text*, 17 (1987), pp. 29–54.

67 Here I follow the hermeneutics of Fredric Jameson, who says that such works as Lukacs's *History and Class Consciousness* (and *The Communist Manifesto*) lie ahead of us 'because we are called on to achieve them through the slow and intricate resistances of historical time'. See his 'History and Class Consciousness' (1988), p. 72. It seems to me that *Beyond a Boundary* and the objects of James's anamnesis can be similarly viewed.

20

Cricket and national culture in the writings of C.L.R. James

Neil Lazarus

To begin an essay, intended for publication in the United States on the subject of C.L.R. James and cricket is inevitably to feel oneself under the shadow of an objection. The problem is that although James is unthinkable without cricket, cricket is unintelligible to most Americans. Within the United States, cricket is popularly represented as an alien game, aimless, quaintly decadent, and, as a sport, unassimilable. Yet it is not only James's ideas about sport but also his ideas about history, politics, and ideology that bear the decisive imprint of his encounter and lifelong fascination with this game. The conclusion that James is likely to remain a dead letter where American readers are concerned seems inescapable. Thus the celebrated British Marxist historian E.P. Thompson, writes that "I'm afraid that American theorists will not understand this but the clue to everything [in James] lies in his proper appreciation of the game of cricket."[1] External facts would seem to support this conclusion: when James's classic autobiography *Beyond a Boundary* (1963) was issued in an American edition in 1986, for instance, it failed miserably despite the positive reviews that attended its publication. American readers were evidently unable or unwilling to appreciate a book that, in its author's own words, "is neither cricket reminiscences nor autobiography [but] . . . poses the question *What do they know of cricket who only cricket know?*"[2]

This problem of access to James's thought is doubtless a substantial one. It would be regrettable, however, were it to be viewed as grounds for American readers not to grapple with James's work. The claims that one would like to make for James are not modest. Hazel Carby has written that *Beyond a Boundary* is "one of the most outstanding works of cultural studies ever produced."[3] In this chapter I would like to build upon this proposition. It will be my argument that in his writings about cricket, James reveals himself to be one of the truly decisive Marxist cultural theorists of our century. To neglect these writings would therefore be to neglect a body of work of the stature of those of Georg Lukács, Mikhail Bakhtin, or Stuart Hall.

One's first encounter with James's writing about cricket is likely to induce a sense of shock or displacement. It is not that one will not have come across such prose before; rather, it is that one will not have seen it deployed with reference to sport.

Consider the following passages for instance – chosen not, of course, at random, but representing nevertheless only three of literally hundreds of passages that might have been cited:

> There is nothing of the panther in the batting of Sobers. He is the most orthodox of great batsmen. The only stroke he makes in a manner peculiar to himself is the hook. Where George Headley used to face the ball square and hit across it, Denis Compton placed himself well outside it on the off-side, and Walcott compromised by stepping backwards but not fully across and hitting, usually well in front of and not behind square leg, Sobers seems to stand where he is and depend upon wrist and eyesight to swish the short fast ball square to the boundary. Apart from that, his method, his technique is carried to an extreme where it is indistinguishable from nature.[4]

> A great West Indies cricketer in his play should embody some essence of that crowded vagueness which passes for the history of the West Indies. If, like Kanhai, he is one of the most remarkable and individual of contemporary batsmen, then that should not make him less but more West Indian. You see what you are looking for, and in Kanhai's batting what I have found is a unique pointer of the West Indian quest for identity, for ways of expressing our potential bursting at every seam.[5]

> I haven't the slightest doubt that the clash of race, caste and class did not retard but stimulated West Indian cricket. I am equally certain that in those years social and political passions, denied normal outlets, expressed themselves so fiercely in cricket (and other games) precisely because they were games. Here began my personal calvary. The British tradition soaked deep into me was that when you entered the sporting arena you left behind you the sordid compromises of everyday existence. Yet for us to do that we would have had to divest ourselves of our skins. From the moment I had to decide which club I would join the contrast between the ideal and the real fascinated me and tore at my insides. Nor could the local population see it otherwise. The class and racial rivalries were too intense. They could be fought out without violence or much lost except pride and honour. Thus the cricket field was a stage on which selected individuals played representative roles which were charged with social significance. (*B.B.*, 72)

In the third passage, James identifies cricket as a privileged site for the playing out and imaginary resolution of social antagonisms in the colonial and post-colonial West Indies. In the second passage, he suggests that only a sociopoetics of cricket will be able to do justice to its complexity and ideological resonance. Cricket, he writes in *Beyond a Boundary*, "is a game of high and difficult technique. If it were not it could not carry the load of social response and implications which it carries" (43). We will return to these formulations in due course. First, however, it is necessary to reflect on the first of the passages cited above. In this passage, crafted in the rhetoric of esthetics and taking as its object the question of form – of cricketing *style* – James situates cricket unambiguously and unhesitatingly as art. The register of his descriptions of Garfield Sobers at bat, or of the technique of fast bowler Wesley Hall, derives unmistakably from the universe of high cultural criticism. What James writes about a glorious drive past point by Learie Constantine, off the bowling of Walter Hammond in 1926 – that the stroke had never been seen before, but that, having been made, it instantly entered cricket history as defining of the square drive – is reminiscent of, and strictly comparable with, Walter Benjamin's observation that "all great works of literature found a genre or dissolve one."[6]

Nor is this gesture on James's part remotely an accident. Cricket is in his view not an instance of "light" art, which he happens to find stimulating nor an instance of "popular" culture although it is certainly popular. On the contrary, James insists that cricket is a form of art to exactly the same degree as drama, opera, or lyric poetry. Attempting to specify the conditions of cricket's estheticism thus, he points first to the extraordinary balance within the game between structure and agency. Each cricket match consists of an indefinite number of discrete events, each with its own resolution, whose objective meaning can only be read at the level of the match as a whole. Yet the logic of the game is such that each and any one of these discrete events bears within itself the potential to shatter the objective pattern of the match as it has unfolded (often over the course of several days) to that point. To win a cricket match, a team needs first to place itself in a position from which victory is possible. Time is involved, and also application; advantages must be consolidated, opportunities seized, mistakes systematically capitalized upon. Yet a cricket match balances upon a hair trigger. A single ball can change its direction and outcome; a single stroke, in anger or defiance or disdain, can shatter and reconstitute the meaning of all that has preceded it. "The total spectacle," James writes,

> consists and must consist of a series of individual, isolated episodes, each in itself completely self-contained. Each has its beginning, the ball bowled; its middle, the stroke played; its end, runs, no runs, dismissal. Within the fluctuating interest of the rise or fall of the game as a whole, there is this unending series of events, each single one fraught with immense possibilities of expectation and realization . . . . In the very finest of soccer matches the ball for long periods is in places where it is impossible to expect any definite alteration in the relative position of the two sides. In lawn tennis the duration of the rally is entirely dependent upon the subjective skill of the players. In baseball alone does the encounter between the two representative protagonists approach the definitiveness of the individual series of episodes in cricket which together constitute the whole. (*B.B.*, 193)

Even baseball, however, cannot quite match the structural complexity of cricket's mode of representation. Like many games, James observes, "[c]ricket is first and foremost a dramatic spectacle. It belongs with the theatre, ballet, opera and the dance" (*B.B.*, 192). Cricket's uniqueness, in these terms, consists not solely in its spectacularity but in the manner in which its enactment of competition and struggle is conducted at the level of representative individuals – bowler and batsman – whose individual performances emerge sustainedly and uninterruptedly as allegories of the situation of their team's. James distinguishes cricket specifically from baseball in this respect:

> the baseball-batter . . . may and often does find himself after a fine hit standing on one of the bases, where he is now dependent upon others. The [cricket] batsman facing the ball does not merely represent his side. For that moment, to all intents and purposes,

he is his side. This fundamental relation of the One and the Many, Individual and Social, Individual and Universal, leader and followers, representative and ranks, the part and the whole, is structurally imposed on the players of cricket. What other sports . . . have to aim at, [cricket] . . . players are given to start with, they cannot depart from it. Thus the game is founded upon a dramatic, a human relation which is universally recognized as the most objectively pervasive and psychologically stimulating in life and therefore in that artificial representation of it which is drama. (*B.B.*, 193)

In speaking of cricket as a form of dramatic art, James does not mean that cricket *resembles* drama. He means that it *is* drama. Indeed, it is drama of a distinctly orthodox and historic kind. On numerous occasions throughout *Beyond a Boundary*, he draws an analogy between the spectacle of cricket in the West Indies and the spectacle of drama in classical Greek society: "Once every year for four days the tens of thousands of Athenian citizens sat in the open air on the stone seats at the side of the Acropolis and from sunrise to sunset watched the plays of the competing dramatists. All that we have to correspond is a Test match" (156).[7]

The consequences that follow from this association of cricket and classical Greek drama are significant. Inasmuch as cricket's spectacularity emerges as an integral aspect of its esthetic being, so, too, does its popularity. The role of the crowd is, in James's view, positively constitutive of cricket's meaning as a cultural form. In a brilliant passage in *Beyond a Boundary*, he exposes the elitism of the famous cricket commentator Neville Cardus, who represented the game as an art form readily enough, but who insisted at the same time that its meaning as art was unavailable to the majority of those who made up its audience. On the one hand, James notes, "all [Cardus's] work is eloquent with the aesthetic appeal of cricket" (191).[8] On the other hand, even as Cardus moved to grapple with this "aesthetic appeal" of cricket, he shied away from its democratic implications. Although cricket was a form of art to him, he would not allow that it might be so too for the millions who followed the game throughout the world. Art was not for the masses: "I do not believe that anything fine in music or in anything else can be truly understood or truly felt by the crowd." To the extent that cricket was an art, therefore, its true meaning necessarily remained inaccessible to the overwhelming majority of those who watched and played it. James takes strong exception to this sentiment:

Neville Cardus . . . often introduces music into his cricket writing. Never once has Neville Cardus . . . introduced cricket into his writing on music. He finds this "a curious point." It is much more than a point, it is not curious. Cardus is a victim of that categorization and specialization, that division of the human personality, which is the greatest curse of our time. Cricket has suffered, but not only cricket. The aestheticians have scorned to take notice of popular sports and games – to their own detriment. The aridity and confusion of which they so mournfully complain will continue until they include organized games *and the people who watch them* as an integral part of their data. (*B.B.*,191–2)[9]

James writes not only against the Neville Carduses of his world, exponents of a frankly confessed conservatism in cultural criticism, but also, implicitly, against such influential Marxist theorists as T.W. Adorno and Herbert Marcuse, who insist upon the "autonomy" of art from life. Adorno, for instance, argues that it is only by virtue of this autonomy (achieved at the price of art's innocence) that art is capable of withstanding the imperatives of commodification in the capitalist era. In his view, only that cultural labor that risks incomprehensibility is today able to resist recuperation by the "culture industry." Sport is specifically listed by Adorno, along with film and mass music, as a wholly fetishistic cultural practice, disclosive only of regressive social values.[10]

James would have refused to concede the validity either of the Adornian principle of art's autonomy, or of the conception that, in Adorno's thought, makes that principle necessary – that life itself has become totalitarian, has been reduced to "the sphere of private existence and now of mere consumption" and as such, is "dragged along as an appendage of the process of material production, without autonomy or substance of its own."[11] This is not to suggest that James is insensitive to the reified quality of everyday life in the era of multinational capitalism. On the contrary, he both acknowledges "the violence and ferocity of our age" (*B B.*, 193) and traces the effects of this violence upon the ways in which cricket is played. At no stage, however, does he commit himself to the hypostatized romantic conception of art as that which, in the words of the early Lukács, "always says 'And yet!' to life."[12]

Within the context of twentieth-century esthetic theory, this romantic conception has typically been mobilized in the service of an irreducibly Eurocentric anticapitalism. Even where – as in the problematic of Western Marxism – this anticapitalism has been insistently radical in tendency, it has invariably been sketched against the backdrop of "civilization." While culture has tended to be theorized as that which opposed the consolidation and extension of this civilization (that is, of capitalist hegemony), so, too, and paradoxically, the much heralded "decline of the West" has tended to be theorized not as the death rattle of imperialism but as the end of history. Auschwitz, Adorno has written, "demonstrated irrefutably that culture has failed . . . . All post-Auschwitz culture including its urgent critique, is garbage."[13]

James is never disposed to think in such terms. Against those conservative cultural critics who complain about "the envy, the hatred, the malice and the uncharitableness" of the modern form of cricket, he points out that it is not in cricket alone that a new ethic has come to prevail, but in "modern society" at large: "Modern society took a turn downwards in 1929 and 'It isn't cricket' is one of the casualties. There is no need to despair of cricket. Much, much more than cricket is at stake. If and when society regenerates itself, cricket will do the same . . . . The owl of Minerva flies only at dusk. And it cannot get much darker without becoming night impenetrable" (*B.B.*, 190). At first glance this might seem to support the Adornian reading of culture and society, but against such a reading, in turn, James would protest that it is only from a vantage point within "modern society" – that is, from the centers of the capitalist world system – that the darkness seems all-encompassing. In James's view, this darkness is not, in fact, the darkness of "night impenetrable," but rather of a world-historical eclipse signalled, in the world of politics, by the rising tide of anti-imperialism and, more narrowly in one sphere of the world of culture, by the emergence, the sudden explosion in the late 1950s and the 1960s, of West Indian cricket.

Hence the indispensability, for James, of a *sociopoetics* of cricket, an approach to the game that will make neither the mistake of supposing it to be less than a form of art, nor the mistake of supposing it, as a form of art, to be autonomous. In the trenchant "Introduction" to a selection of his writings on cricket that appeared in 1986, he notes that "An artistic, a social event does not reflect the age. It is the age. Cricket, I want to say most clearly, is not an addition or a decoration or some specific unit that one adds to what really constitutes the history of a period. Cricket is as much part of the history as books written are part of the history" (*C.*, xi).

Elsewhere, his tone is even more insistent – as when, in *Beyond a Boundary* (70), he asserts that "cricket and football were the greatest cultural influences in nineteenth century Britain, leaving far behind Tennyson's poems, Beardsley's drawings and concerts of the Philharmonic Society. These filled space in print but not in minds." The point is, however, that as James understands cricket, it is not merely as a form of culture, but concretely and materially as a form of *national* culture. It is for this reason that James can maintain that a biography of Donald Bradman will need, at the same time, to be "a history of Australia in the same period" (*B.B.*, 180). Similarly, no one ignorant of the historical trajectory of West Indian society over the course of the past hundred years will, in his view, be able to grasp the meaning of the play of Wilton St Hill, Learie Constantine, or Rohan Kanhai.

In order for us to understand why this should be so – to appreciate the extent to which (and the different manners in which) cricket has figured as a constituent of national consciousness in England, Australia, and the West Indies – it is necessary to examine James's social history of the game. He locates its institutionalization in the years between 1780 and 1840. Cricket was created, he writes,

> by the yeoman farmer, the gamekeeper, the potter, the tinker, the Nottingham coal-miner, the Yorkshire factory hand. These artisans made it, men of hand and eye. Rich and idle young noblemen and some substantial city people contributed money, organization and prestige. Between them, by 1837 they had evolved a highly complicated game with all the typical characteristics of a genuinely national art form: founded on elements long present in the nation, profoundly popular in origin, yet attracting to it disinterested elements of the leisured and educated classes. Confined to areas and numbers which were relatively small, it contained all the premises of rapid growth. There was nothing in the slightest degree Victorian about it. At their matches cricketers ate and drank with the gusto of the time, sang songs and played for large sums of money. Bookies sat before the pavilion at Lord's[14] openly taking bets. The unscrupulous nobleman and the poor but dishonest commoner alike bought and sold matches. (*B.B.*, 158–9)

No sooner had cricket been consolidated in these terms, as a game essentially outside the realm of bourgeois social relations, than it became, during the Victorian era, the site of an ideological struggle. It was not, James writes, that the English national bourgeoisie, the "solid Victorian middle class" (*B.B.*, 159), consciously set out to appropriate the game, to lift it from its artisanal, regional, and predominantly rural roots and to make it over in their own image. Yet it was precisely such an appropriation that was effected, and James describes it as "unerring" (163). Cricket was transformed from a game expressing the social ethos of a residual and increasingly marginal combination of class fractions into a "moral discipline," disseminated above all in such public schools as Thomas Arnold's Rugby and serving the interests of the middle-class rise to hegemony:

> The Victorians made it compulsory for their children, and all the evidence points to the fact that they valued competence in it and respect for what it came to signify more than they did intellectual accomplishment of any kind. The only word that I know for this is culture. The proof of its validity is its success, first of all at home and then almost as rapidly abroad, in the most diverse effects and among peoples living lives which were poles removed from that whence it originally came. This signifies, as so often in any deeply national movement, that it contained elements of universality that went beyond the bounds of the originating nation. (*B.B.*, 164)

If this transformation of cricket must, retrospectively, be viewed in the light of an ideological struggle, it must be acknowledged that the struggle was not always recognized as such. Indeed, in the person of W.G. Grace, the greatest exponent of cricket in the Victorian era and one of the greatest players who ever lived, James identifies a figure whose astonishing aptitude for the game derived from the seemingly uncomplicated (if compound) presence within him of residual and emergent elements of the national culture. Grace, he writes (and I do not apologize for the length of the quotation, for James's formulation could neither be improved upon nor adequately summarized)

> seems to have been one of those men in whom the characteristics of life as lived by many generations seemed to meet for the last, in a complete and perfectly blended whole. His personality was sufficiently wide and firm to include a strong Victorian streak without being inhibited. That I would say was his greatest strength. He was not in any way inhibited. What he lacked he would not need. All that he had he could use. In tune with his inheritance and his environment, he was not in any way repressed. All his physical and spiritual force was at his disposal to do what he wanted to do. He is said on all sides to have been one of the most typical of Englishmen, to have symbolized John Bull, and so on and so forth. To this, it is claimed, as well as to his deeds, he owed his enormous popularity. I take leave to doubt it. The man usually hailed as representative is never quite typical, is more subtly compounded than the plain up-and-down figure of the stock characteristics. Looking on from outside and at a distance it seems to me that Grace gives a more complex impression than is usually attributed to him. He was English undoubtedly, very much so. But he was typical of an England that was being superseded. He was the yeoman, the country doctor, the squire, the England of yesterday. But he was no relic nor historical or nostalgic curiosity. He was pre-Victorian in the Victorian age but a pre-Victorian militant. (*B.B.*, 175–6)

On the domestic stage – and, by osmosis, in Australia – cricket was refunctioned by the Victorian middle classes as an instrument of moral discipline. Yet it proved sufficiently pliable as a cultural form to withstand several further refunctionings. James offers a sociopoetical analysis of some of these: the glittering back foot-batting of Kumar Shri Ranjitsinhji in England and Victor Trumper in Australia in the Edwardian years, for example; and the reorganization of batting in the interests of aggression and efficiency on the part of the Australians, led by Ponsford and Bradman, in the 1920s and 1930s. Above all, however, he is interested in chronicling the social history of cricket in the West Indies in the years before and after decolonization in the 1960s.

Here, a somewhat different canvas must be used. Cricket was not introduced to the West Indies under the rubric of moral discipline alone. The social space of the West Indies was marked out as a *colonial* space, and cricket, imposed there as it never was in Australia, New Zealand, or South Africa upon a subject people from without had a specific role to play in the maintenance of colonial authority. To James, the special wonder of cricket is that even in the face of these unpromising originary circumstances, it proved possible to transform the game into "a means of [West Indian] national expression" (*C.*, 171). West Indians have, over the years of this century, been able to pull cricket across the Manichean divide of colonialism; they have been able to force it to carry the weight of *their* social desires and to speak *their* language, whether of emergent anticolonialism, nationalist affirmation, or, since decolonization, of international self-presence. In *Beyond a Boundary*, James remarks on "the grandeur of a game which, in lands far from that which gave it birth, could encompass so much of social reality and still remain a game" (97).

The "indigenization" of cricket in the West Indies could never have taken place beneath the level of popular consciousness as, arguably, its "Victorianization" did in nineteenth-century England. James describes the ideologically resonant but psychologically unproblematical confluence of the old and the new in the person of W.G. Grace. Writing of himself, by contrast, he notes that while he was a colonial subject, "a British intellectual long before I was ten," this subject position contrived to render him "an alien in my own environment among my own people, even my own family" (*B.B.*, 28). Where nativist intellectuals have tended to lament this sort of "alienation," however, regarding it as the ground of a "loss of self" from which they have never been able to recover, James suggests that its ideological implications were not fixed but volatile. Colonial subjection did not always produce obedient colonial subjects: "[I] found [myself] and came to maturity within a system that was the result of centuries of development in another land, was transplanted as a hot-house flower is transplanted and bore some strange fruit" (*B.B.*, 50).

What was true of the "system" was true, too, of at least one of its elements: cricket. Introduced to the West Indies as part and parcel of colonial governance – part and parcel of an ensemble that included "English Puritanism, English literature and cricket" – it was fought for and fought over, made to vibrate with "the realism of West Indian life" (*B.B.*, 30). Because, in order to make cricket their own, the West Indian masses had to prise it loose from British culture; because British culture was precisely what, as a colonized population, they struggled against; and because, by virtue of the specificity of the circumstances of their colonization, they had comparatively few institutionalized forms of cultural practice of their own, they bestowed a privileged position upon cricket. At the risk of oversimplification, one might say that in the West Indies, cricket became culture. Thus, James, citing E.W. Swanton's 1957 observation to the effect that "'in the West Indies the cricket ethic has shaped not only the cricketers but social life as a whole,'" comments that

> [i]t is an understatement. There is a whole generation of us, and perhaps two genera-
> tions, who have been formed by it not only in social attitudes but in our most intimate
> lives, in fact there more than anywhere else. The social attitudes we could to some
> degree alter if we wished. For the inner self the die was cast. (*B.B.*, 49)

In the colonial West Indies, cricket emerged as the cultural form most expressive of popular West Indian social aspirations. If, in being introduced to the West Indies, the game had seemed a perfect ideological foil for colonialism, it now began to rep-resent a remarkably different sensibility. This sensibility was not a revolutionary one. It could not have been, in the absence of a revolutionary social movement. The ideological protocols of cricket were refashioned, not overthrown. West Indian cricket emerged entirely within the constraints of the rules of the colonial game. However, where the predominant characteristics of the colonial game had consisted in orderliness, discipline, resolution, and puritanism, the West Indian game reflected a different rationality. The social significance of this rationality was, nat-urally enough, misrecognized by English commentators. They could see in the emergent West Indian style of play only indiscipline, excess, and irresponsibility. Thus a correspondent for *The Times* reported in 1928 about the West Indian batsman Wilton St Hill:

> W.H. St Hill . . . can be relied upon to provide the entertainment of the side. He is very
> supple, has a beautifully erect stance and, having lifted his bat, performs amazing
> apparently double-jointed tricks with his wrists and arms. Some of those contortions
> are graceful and remunerative, such as his gliding to leg, but some are unsound and
> dangerous, such as an exaggerated turn of the wrist in cutting. He will certainly play
> some big and attractive innings, but some others may be easily curtailed by his exotic
> fancy in dealing with balls on the off-side. (quoted in *B.B.*, 102–3)[15]

James turns to Wilton St Hill in discussing the emergence of West Indian cricket because the Trinidadian was one of the truly decisive – and, for James, truly *repre-sentative* – figures in the game in the years before 1939. It was on the strength of batting of the quality and style of St Hill's that cricket in the West Indies was able to shoulder the political burden of its popularity. I have already cited James's comment to the effect that "the cricket field was a stage on which selected individ-uals played representative roles which were charged with social significance" (*B.B.*, 72). The role St Hill played, in these terms, was tragic because, as a batsman, he carried all before him except for one season. This one season – with the visiting

West Indian side in England in 1928 – was historic, however. Not only did it become the yardstick by which the English public measured his play, but it was also read by St Hill's devoted followers back in Trinidad as a comprehensive setback for the kind of cricket he played, and for the social vision embryonically prefigured in such cricket. For the Trinidadian crowds, James writes,

> the unquestioned glory of St Hill's batting [in the years prior to 1928] conveyed the sensation that here was one of us, performing *in excelsis* in a sphere where competition was open. It was a demonstration that atoned for a pervading humiliation, and nourished pride and hope. Jimmy Durante, the famous American comedian, has popularized a phrase in the United States: "That's my boy." I am told that its popularity originates in the heart of the immigrant, struggling with the new language, baffled by the new customs . . . Wilton St Hill was our boy. (*B.B.*, 99)

For years, St Hill batted brilliantly against any opposition. He was left out of the West Indian side to England in 1923 solely on racial grounds; he persevered and, in 1926, when the English side visited the West Indies, he was outstanding. When, finally, in 1928, he simply could not be left off the touring West Indian team to England, he left with the expectations of all Trinidad hanging on his performance. "We [were] . . . convinced in our own minds," James writes, "that St Hill was the greatest of all West Indian batsmen and on English wickets this coloured man would infallibly put all white rivals in the shade" (*B.B.*, 100). The responsibility proved to be too much for St Hill. Not only did he fail in England, but he failed miserably: "He was a horrible, a disastrous, an incredible, failure, the greatest failure to come out of the West Indies" (101). This collapse must be read in ideological terms: St Hill failed because no one person could have succeeded, at that time, in doing what he was asked to do. Although he never overcame the blow of this failure, it was not his alone, but that of all Trinidadians whose social desires his batting represented. James concludes that St Hill's "spirit was untameable, perhaps too much so" (103). Only when it is understood historically is this conclusion fully intelligible. It suggests that St Hill's tragedy lay in the fact that although he played cricket as it would come to be played, and in such a way as to articulate the aspirations of the masses who adored him, he could not represent himself on the stage of the world when it mattered most.

To raise the issue of self-representation in the colonial context is to raise the issue of nationalism. In the history of West Indian cricket it is to move from Wilton St Hill to Learie Constantine. James argues that St Hill's failure was not his alone, but a representative failure reflecting a certain prematurity, a certain lack of cohesion in the social consciousness of the classes whose aspirations were expressed in St Hill's batting. This argument can be cast counterfactually as a question, What would it have taken for St Hill to succeed? The question finds its answer, for James, in the career of Constantine, who succeeded – spectacularly – where St Hill could not. Where St Hill failed so desperately in 1928, Constantine, his near contemporary and fellow Trinidadian, took England by storm. "He took 100 wickets, made 1000 runs and laid claim to being the finest fieldsman yet known" (*B.B.*, 110).

James locates the difference between St Hill and Constantine in class terms. St

Hill was born in 1893, into the Trinidadian lower middle class. He worked all his life as a salesman in a department store. His experiences as a cricketer simply underscored his experiences as a "brownish" (*B.B.*, 93) subject of a colonial order. With Constantine, it was different. Born a few years later than St Hill, he was a member of a cricketing family universally respected in the West Indies:

> "From the time young Constantine knew himself he knew his father as the most loved and most famous cricketer in the island. His mother's brother, Victor Pascall, was the West Indies slow left-hander, a most charming person and a great popular favourite with all classes. We cannot overestimate the influence of all this on young Constantine. He was born to the purple, and in cricket circles never saw himself as inferior to anyone or dependent for anything on anyone. (107)

Constantine received a good elementary education but found himself incapable of securing a job commensurate with his qualifications. On the cricket field, he was first among equals; off it, and despite his family's reputation, he was black in a colonial society in which a strict color bar reserved preferential jobs for whites. In St Hill's case, the encounter with discrimination in the social sphere was expected and, partly because of this, met with resignation. In Constantine's case, it was unexpected and bitterly resisted. James reads Constantine's success in England in 1928 in the light of a strike against colonialism: "Constantine, the heir-apparent, the happy warrior, the darling of the crowd, prize pupil of the captain of the West Indies . . . revolted against the revolting contrast between his first-class status as a cricketer and his third-class status as a man" (*B.B.*, 110).

If the tour to England in 1928 was a crushing defeat for St Hill, it allowed Constantine to emerge as a national hero. In this fact, James locates the fundamental difference between the two players. St Hill was idolized, revered by his followers, but he could never have been spoken of as a "national hero." The social aspirations to which his batting gave eloquent voice were those of the populace, and they would come in due course to serve centrally as constituents of West Indian national consciousness. They were not – or not yet – *national* in scope or tendency. Constantine, however, was a properly national hero. The irony was that as Trinidad was then constituted it was a colony and not a nation. Constantine's success on the cricket field, James argues, was therefore as instrumental as any other factor in laying the ground for the emergence of a national consciousness in Trinidad and for that matter the West Indies.

It is testimony to his extraordinary timeliness that Constantine recognized this. He recognized it, in fact, at a time – the late 1920s – when even James himself did not do so. In *Beyond a Boundary*, James records some of his conversations with Constantine during these years, when both men lived and worked in the north of England, Constantine as a professional cricketer, James as a writer, journalist, and political activist. James recalls Constantine's insistence that despite the fact that West Indian teams seemed invariably to lose important matches to English teams, the standard of West Indian cricket was as high as that of English cricket.

Constantine's repeated "They are no better than we" was already a political demand. "It was a slogan and a banner. It was politics, the politics of nationalism" (*B.B.*, 117). It was such because Constantine's proposed solution to the problem was so demonstrably nationalist in tenor:

> They are no better than we, he used to say: we can bat and bowl and field as well as any of them. To my – as I thought – devastating query, "Why do we always lose and make such a poor show?" he would reply: "We need a black man as captain". I was stupid enough to believe that he was dealing with the question of race. I should have known that it was not so . . . . What he used to tell me was that the West Indian players were not a team and to become a team they needed a captain who had the respect of the players and was able to get the best out of the team. Not too far from his argument was the sentiment that a good captain would respect all the men. (*C.*, 257)

The fact that this quotation is extracted from a 1970 essay on Sir Frank Worrell points to the direction assumed by James's social history of cricket in the West Indies. If the space between Wilton St Hill and Learie Constantine is the space through which the problematic of nationalism entered West Indian cricket, that between Constantine and Worrell marks the moment of decolonization. What Constantine was prescient enough to be able to imagine, Worrell was able to make real, but not before conditions were ripe. Worrell's captaincy of the West Indian team in the late 1950s and early 1960s – like the play of individuals such as Garfield Sobers, Rohan Kanhai, Lance Gibbs, and Wesley Hall on this team – had everything to do with the current of West Indian politics. James, in a passage I have already cited, speaks of Kanhai's batting at this time as expressive of the "West Indian quest for identity," after all.

It would be possible to extend James's examination of West Indian cricket as "national allegory"[16] almost indefinitely. James himself has written extensively on Worrell, Sobers, and Kanhai. It would not be difficult to apply his analytical methods to the eras of Clive Lloyd and Vivian Richards – a period of more than a decade in which the West Indies never came close to losing a test series – although it would be impossible to match his insights, generated, as he points out, from a lifetime's *study* of cricket.

> I did not merely play cricket. I studied it. I analysed strokes, I studied types, I read its history, its beginnings, how and when it changed from period to period, I read about it in Australia and in South Africa. I read and compared statistics, I made clippings, I talked to all cricketers! particularly the inter-colonial cricketers and those who had gone abroad. I compared what they told me with what I read in old copies of *Wisden*. I looked up the play of the men who had done well or badly against the West Indies. I read and appreciated the phraseology of laws. (*B.B.*, 41–2)

Two passages, for me at least, represent James's cultural criticism at its most illuminating and expansive. The first is just two sentences long: "Garfield Sobers, I shall show, is a West Indian cricketer, not merely a cricketer from the West Indies. He is the most typical West Indian cricketer that it is possible to imagine" (*F.P.*,

113). In order to understand this formulation, it is necessary to cite the second passage, drawn from *Beyond a Boundary* (225):

> What do they know of cricket who only cricket know? West Indians crowding to Tests bring with them the whole past history and future hopes of the islands. English people, for example, have a conception of themselves breathed from birth. Drake and mighty Nelson, Shakespeare, Waterloo, the Charge of the Light Brigade, the few who did so much for so many, the success of parliamentary democracy, those and such as those constitute a national tradition. Underdeveloped countries have to go back centuries to rebuild one. We of the West Indies have none at all, none that we know of. To such people the three W's, Ram and Val wrecking English batting, help to fill a huge gap in their consciousness and in their needs. In one of the sheds on the Port of Spain wharf is a painted sign: 365 Garfield Sobers.

"365 Garfield Sobers": the reference is to the highest score made by any batsman in a test match (until 1994, when Brian Lara scored 375 against England) and to Sobers, who made it. Two features of these passages seem to me momentous in their implications. First is James's argument, to which I have already alluded, that in the West Indies cricket is not only *also* culture, that is, one cultural form among several, but culture itself. It was not only the rare cricket critic who, watching Sobers send a good length ball skimming to the cover boundary, felt himself to be in the presence of a national cultural treasure. Rather, this was the experience of the West Indian crowd as a whole, as explained by the fact that a popular phrase was coined to describe this very stroke: "Not a man move" (*F.P.*, 215). Could it be that all followers of cricket in the West Indies are then to be understood as intellectuals, the knowing possessors of national culture? The second texture follows from the first, James's restatement of the category of genius. For James, Sobers is unquestionably a genius, where "genius" does not describe an individual who transcends temporal or geographical situation, but one who most succinctly, "unerringly," represents it in its compound and overdetermined tendencies. It is an index of the achievement of James's writing on cricket that he is able, in an entirely compelling way and in a single passage, to cover all the ground between the exceptionality of genius and the typicality of national culture.

Notes

1 E.P. Thompson, "C.L.R. James at 80," *Urgent Tasks*, No. 12 (Summer 1981): back cover.
2 C.L.R. James, *Beyond a Boundary* (London: Hutchinson, 1963), Preface. Further references to this book (*B.B.*) will be given parenthetically.
3 Hazel V. Carby, "Proletarian or Revolutionary Literature: C.L.R James and the Politics of Trinidadian Renaissance," *South Atlantic Quarterly*, No. 87 (Winter 1988): 51.
4 C.L.R. James, "Garfield Sobers," in *The Future in the Present: Selected Writings* (London: Allison and Busby, 1977), 214. Further references to this work (*F.P.*) will be given parenthetically.
5 C.L.R. James, "Kanhai: A Study in Confidence," in *Cricket*, ed. Anna Grimshaw (London: Allison & Busby, 1986), 165–6. Further references to this book (*C.*) will be given parenthetically.

6 Walter Benjamin, "The Image of Proust," in *Illuminations*, trans. Harry Zohn, ed. Hannah Arendt (New York: Schocken, 1969), 201. The more relevant comparison, from James's own point of view, would be to the writings about prize boxing, chess, or the game of fives by the early nineteenth-century English essayist William Hazlitt. James refers admiringly to Hazlitt on several occasions in *Beyond a Boundary*.

7 A test match is a match between representative teams of two nations. The duration of such a match is five days (occasionally six days are allotted). Test-match cricket is the highest form at which the game is played.

8 James cites with approval the following comment of Cardus: "Why do we deny the art of a cricketer, and rank it lower than a vocalist's or a fiddler's? If anybody tells me that R.H. Spooner did not compel a pleasure as aesthetic as any compelled by thc most cultivated Italian tenor that ever lived I will write him down a purist and an ass" (quoted in *B.B.*, 191).

9 James continues, in a move that I confess I have never fully understood, to concede that "Sir Donald Bradman's technical accomplishments are not on the same plane as those of Yehudi Menuhin. Sir John Gielgud in three hours can express adventures and shades in human personality which are not approached in three years of Denis Compton at the wicket" (*B.B.*, 192). It is difficult to know what to make of this concession because James immediately undermines it by his insistence that cricket is "not a bastard or a poor relation, but a full member of the community" of the arts. Certainly, James's point against Cardus is made: cricket is an art, not for the one or two "sensitive" souls among its viewers alone, but in its fundamental reality as it is conventionally played and watched. Beyond this, it seems contradictory to maintain simultaneously that cricket is not a "poor relation" of the other arts and that the technique of Sir Donald Bradman – the most proficient batsman who ever lived – is "not on the same plane" as that of Yehudi Menuhin. The thrust of James's work as a whole is along the lines of the affirmation – that cricket is indeed a fully articulated form of art – rather than of the concession. (See for instance, his comments in an essay on "The 1963 West Indians," published just one year later than *Beyond a Boundary*, and reprinted in *Cricket*, 134–46). This, accordingly, is the tendency I have chosen to emphasize.

10 See Theodor W. Adorno, "On the Fetish-Character in Music and the Regression of Listening," in *The Essential Frankfurt School*, eds Andrew Amto and Eike Gebhanlt (Oxford: Basil Blackwell, 1978), 270–99.

11 Theodor Adorno, *Minima Moralia: Reflections from Damaged Life*, trans. E.F.N. Tephcott (London: Verso, 1978), 15.

12 Georg Lukás, *The Theory of the Novel: a Historico-Philosophical Essay on the Forms of Great Epic Literature*, trans. Anna Bostock (Cambridge: MIT Press, 1983), 72.

13 Theodor W. Adorno, *Negative Dialectics*, trans. E.B. Ashton (New York: Continuum, 1973), 366–7.

14 Lord's is a famous cricket ground in London, home of the Marylebone Cricket Club, and headquarters of cricket worldwide.

15 The scarcely disguised racism of this report does not, of course, escape James. Throughout his writings he has attempted to combat the still pervasive stereotypes about "natural" black athleticism. For an extended treatment of this question, see his "Cricket and Race" (1975), reprinted in *Cricket*, 278–9.

16 The term is Fredric Jameson's. See "Third-World Literature in the Era of Multinational Capitalism," *Social Text*, No. 15 (Fall 1986): 65–88.

21

Cricket, literature and the politics of de-colonisation: the case of C.L.R. James

Helen Tiffin

In a chapter in *Sport in History,* Richard Cashman, writing on 'The phenomenon of Indian Cricket' noted that:

> The historical relationship between cricket and Indian national identity differs from that of other colonial societies, such as Australia. Whereas the game provided a natural vehicle for the expression of an emerging nationalism in the antipodes, an interest in the game had first to be created in India by the colonial government. The continuation of this element of colonial culture after 1947 attests to the thorough job done by the British. There were a number of stated reasons for the official encouragement of cricket. The game would further the process of anglicization . . . Indian players would develop the traits of 'manliness' . . . and teamwork which would be character-building.[1]

This century, the idea of cricket as a vehicle for the perpetration of certain British moral values throughout the Empire is accepted as axiomatic and needs no further elaboration here. But I have quoted at length from this chapter not just to make this point, but to introduce the West Indian background which lies somewhere between the Indian and Australian circumstances alluded to here.

Columbus discovered the West Indies in 1492, and within a hundred years the native Carib and Arawak Indians were virtually exterminated.[2] Since then the population has been a population in exile: European adventurers and planters; African slaves; and, with the abolition of the slave trade and the system of slavery in the nineteenth century, indentured labourers from China and India. In contrast to the Indian situation then, the significant facts are that the black West Indian population was not on home ground, and its traditions, cohesive social structures and languages had been destroyed or dissipated. Secondly, the violently close contact between Briton and African spanned almost four centuries, and with African culture in exile and disarray, there was an inextricable interweaving of European cultural and psychic influences with the African personality.

Initially there was a typically ambivalent attitude to this interpretation on the part of the slave owners. African-language groups had been deliberately broken up to lessen the chance of slave rebellion, so a *lingua franca* for the slaves themselves and between slave and master was obviously necessary. Initially, however, planters were reluctant to allow slaves to learn the language of the master, just as in the French islands men of colour were prohibited from participating in French sports;[3] but in time it became clear that not only *would* the slaves learn the language, but that in doing so they would inevitably absorb the morals, culture and values of the dominant group. With the widespread use of the language in the English islands, African deracination and concomitant anglicisation was well underway.

With the rise of national feeling and the re-establishment of race consciousness in this century, we have come to see that the operation of language in such a situation is rather like the workings of sport. It has frequently been noted that cricket provided the white Commonwealth with a safety valve for rising national sentiment, within the confines of a 'gentlemanly' set of rules. On the other hand, of course, it attested to the superiority of English cultural *mores*, and inculcated the very comfortable belief (from a British viewpoint) that the best way for a colonial to assert a national identity was to beat the British at their own game.

After four centuries of the complex cultural interweaving undergone by the mixed populations of the British West Indian islands, the boundaries between 'them' and 'us' had become very complex and blurred. Moreover, the absorption of white middle-class values by a black population had artificially created in the islands a European class situation complicated by a colour caste one. The emancipation of millions of slaves in the nineteenth century created a mass of the black poor, the so-called dwellers of 'the yard'[4] whose economic circumstances forbade their participation in the white middle-class life-style they had come to regard as the only acceptable one.

In his article on the sociology of West Indian cricket, Maurice St Pierre puts this succinctly:

> Differentiation in West Indian society along lines of race, colour, class and power had a number of important consequences for the darker skinned members, nurtured as they inescapably were in a system characterised by violence – white master to slave.
>
> At the same time the cultural emphasis in West Indian society upon things 'white' and de-emphasis on things 'non-white', buttressed the European slant of West Indian society by slavish emulation of whites by non-white West Indians. Such emulation was not, however, rewarded by upward mobility in West Indian society. The result was frustration which bespoke aggression and violence.
>
> Non-whites set out to out-perform whites in all facets of European culture. There was the dress, the speech, the culinary habits – and there was cricket! The thirst for recognition produced non-white cricketers superior to white cricketers in every department of the game, but as in every other walk of West Indian life, these West Indians were denied entrance into the top echelons of West Indian Cricket Society.[5]

The dilemma of this divided consciousness – European and African – in the contemporary West Indian, is stressed in the poems of the St Lucian, Derek Walcott:

> I who am poisoned with the blood of both
> Where shall I turn, divided to the vein?

357

I who have cursed
The drunken officer of British rule, how choose
Between this Africa and the English tongue I love?
Betray them both, or give back what they give?[6]

It is against this complex historical background that the achievements of C.L.R. James must be considered. In almost every field of twentieth-century West Indian life James was innovator and initiator; in history, in literature, in politics. His association with *The Beacon* magazine (1931–33) places him at the very beginnings of a West Indian literature, while his own novel, *Minty Alley* (1936) established the importance of the folk in the Caribbean literary tradition which followed him. In his revision of Caribbean history, *The Black Jacobins*, (1938, revised 1963) James redressed the wrongs done to fact and race by the previously European-written, centred, and biased accounts of Toussaint L'Ouverture and the San Domingo revolution. In *The Case for West Indian Self-Government* (1933) James grappled with the concepts of a West Indian freedom in a world irretrievably Europeanised and divided within itself along colour caste lines engendered by slave history and deracination. The James of *Beyond A Boundary* (1966) is thus no stranger to social complexity and irony and, like his earlier works, *Beyond A Boundary* assesses the contemporary legacy of this history. But though James does go – as he always did – beyond some boundaries, one might be justified in asking, with Maurice St Pierre, why, 'at a time when West Indians are in the throes of shedding the various vestiges of colonialism . . . the game of cricket, which is a manifestation *par excellence* of colonial legacy, still features very prominently in the West Indian cultural and sporting scene'.[7]

What is surprising is that while *Beyond a Boundary* tentatively explores this question, it is itself in orientation and direction the best example in James's writing, of the problems encountered in viewing a traditionally British institution from the 'divided' West Indian perspective. In it James rightly jokes and assesses the combined influences of literature, politics and sport; but his own life and works demonstrate that, of the three, cricket is the least susceptible of extension and adaptation, the most insidiously influential, and the most problematic area in which to isolate what is (in James's own terms) 'West Indian, *sui generis*'.

Revolutionary developments in any post-colonial situation are necessarily in a curious position. On the one hand, the writer, politician, historian or political activist supports and asserts what is national and local, and opposes this to the values imported and/or imposed by the colonising power. But there is here the fundamental irony that, by the very nature of colonialism, the colonist never remains untouched by the values of that imperial power. Moreover, de-culturisation and deracination have usually meant that rising nationalist expressions of difference and dissent must be made in the language of the coloniser, and frequently too, must adopt (for want of any alternative) the imported forms of expression – forms often evolved over centuries in an at least half-alien culture. The novel, the history, the political system, the games available as vehicles of self-expression and self-assertion are often, as in the West Indian case, those of the overlord. There is then, always a tension between the writer's, politician's and sometimes (in the case of cricket) player's motive, and the form through which his or her dissent is being expressed. So when, as in the Caribbean, the contemporary population is 'divided to the vein', a very complex situation results.

In the preface to *Beyond a Boundary* James states that 'This book is neither cricket reminiscences nor autobiography. It poses the question: *What do they know of cricket who only cricket know?* To answer involves ideas as well as facts',[8] and James' earlier works had always engaged with both.

In *Minty Alley, The Black Jacobins,* and in writing the case for West Indian self-government, James, as he had done as a cricketer, is working within European forms and ideas.[9] The novel, the history, even nationalist moves towards independence have their roots in Europe and European ideas. It cannot be stressed too much that in spite of de-colonisation and the various 'back to Africa' movements, West Indian identity is still substantially and irretrievably European. Nevertheless, in *Minty Alley, The Black Jacobins* and in both *The Case for West Indian Self-Government* and his own political activities, James is (as he is to a lesser extent in *Beyond a Boundary*) aware of the conflict between idiom and intention, and of the 'divided to the vein' aspect of the West Indian psyche. But within the terms of this problem, the stance he must take is clearer for James in the literary and political arenas than it can be in either his overall attitude to cricket or in his assessment of it in *Beyond a Boundary.*

I want firstly to look at James's awareness and use of this general social complexity in *Minty Alley* and, more briefly, in *The Black Jacobins,* and then compare these with *Beyond a Boundary.* What James has striven for in his life and works,[10] is the establishment of a Caribbean identity along the lines of that to which he refers in his 'Appendix' to *The Black Jacobins:*

> Castro's revolution is of the twentieth century as much as Toussaint's was of the eighteenth. But despite the distance of over a century and a half, both are West Indian. The people who made them, the problems and the attempts to solve them, are peculiarly West Indian, the product of a peculiar origin and a peculiar history. West Indians first became aware of themselves as a people in the Haitian revolution. Whatever its ultimate fate, the Cuban revolution marks the ultimate stage of a Caribbean quest for national identity. In a scattered series of disparate islands the process consists of a series of unco-ordinated periods of drift, punctuated by spurts, leaps and catastrophes. But the inherent movement is clear and strong.
>
> The history of the West Indies is governed by two factors, the sugar plantation and 'Negro' slavery . . . Wherever the sugar plantation and slavery existed, they imposed a pattern. It is an original pattern, not European, not African, not a part of the American main, not native in any conceivable sense of that word, but West Indian *sui generis* with no parallel anywhere else. [11]

James's historic, literary and political works are a search for and often the expression of this pattern. It is my contention that it is only in *Beyond A Boundary* that he fails to really engage with the problem, though he does hint at its parameters.

With Albert Gomes and Alfred Mendes, James was instrumental in establishing the first successful Caribbean literary magazine, *The Beacon,* which, like the BBC's *Caribbean Voices* programme, represented the beginnings of a local outlet and audience for writers in West Indies. James and Mendes had earlier produced the only issues of a magazine called *Trinidad,* in 1929 and 1930, and the degree to which the anglicised West Indian middle-class had to be re-educated to an acceptance of local reality is easily gauged by the response to James's own story, 'Triumph' in the 1929 issue. 'Triumph' like the later *Minty Alley,* dealt with slum life in Trinidad, with the people of 'the yard', their poverty, jealousies, their loves. The 'cultural cringe' response of the reading public is familiar. 'Letters protesting against the obscenities of the magazine', Mendes reported in the next issue (1930) of *Trinidad,* 'have been pouring into the *Guardian* office during the past week. One is from a Boy Scout who says: "Its disagreeable implications cast unwarrantable aspersions on the fair name of our beautiful island"'.[12]

Behind the entertaining image of the irate 'Boy Scout' strangled by his English vocabulary and class assumptions, can be seen the more general and serious problem. The depiction of this aspect of West Indian social reality will not mirror and thus will not meet English middle-class standards. Hence that reality is to be avoided. James and the Jamaican novelist, Claude McKay, set out to wage war on these attitudes. As early as *Banana Bottom* (1933) and *Minty Alley* (1936), they deliberately dealt with the dwellers of the 'yard' and with their restorative vitality, their passions, their spontaneity, their communality, and the depth of their engagement with life, in the midst of poverty and dreadful physical conditions. In so doing they set the tradition for the West Indian novel. From then on, it might be argued, it was almost impossible for a writer whose work was not grounded in the values of the folk to find recognition. In a sense James is at the very root of both the establishment of the folk as fit subject for fictional treatment, and the establishment of the novel of 'the yard' as the only acceptable path for a literary tradition *sui generis,* to follow. After James, McKay, and Roger Mais, recognition of white or coloured middle-class novels as a valid part of the tradition was precluded. (The novels of John Hearne, excluded from the mainstream in this way, remain unrecognised.) One can easily see parallels with the 'bush versus city' ethos in the Australian tradition, I think.

But to accuse James of (or credit him with) the establishment of all *exclusively* 'folk' reality for West Indian literature is to deny the complexity of his own novel, *Minty Alley.* James, true to his search for a West Indian identity, carefully structured his novel to acknowledge the existence of both the folk *and* the middle classes. In *Minty Alley,* the middle-class narrator, Haynes, is forced, because of reduced economic circumstances, to take up board and lodging with Mrs Rouse in Minty Alley, an area of experience to which his own 'caste' path would never under normal circumstances have led him. Haynes's account of the tempestuous relationship between Benoit, Mrs Rouse and the Nurse is one of intensity, passion, jealousy, warmth and communality in which he, better educated, more detached, more generally Europeanised, can only vicariously participate. Although his affair with

Maisie indicates the deep attraction the torrid but very real life of the yard has for the bookish Haynes, it is necessarily a brief romance. James saw that, at the time at which he was writing, the gulf between the classes in the West Indies had become almost unbridgeable.

The form of *Minty Alley* (its real subject the vitality of yard life, but this portrayed through the eyes of a middle-class narrator) allowed James to bring together, as a distinctively West Indian reality, the two classes artificially separated by the history of white oppression and to anatomise the depth of the gulf between them. His use of West Indian 'dialect' is, like Claude McKay's, also pioneering, and heralded the slow twentieth-century erosion of the concept of a correct standard form of English expression.

In *The Black Jacobins*, James states his aim clearly in his preface:

In 1789 the French West Indian colony of San Domingo supplied two-thirds of the overseas trade of France and was the greatest individual market for the European slave-trade. It was an integral part of the economic life of the age, the greatest colony in the world, the pride of France, and the envy of every other imperialist nation. The whole structure rested on the labour of half-a-million slaves.

In August 1791, after two years of the French Revolution and its repercussions in San Domingo, the slaves revolted. The struggle lasted for 12 years. The slaves defeated in turn the local whites and the soldiers of the French monarchy, a Spanish invasion, a British expedition of some 60,000 men, and a French expedition of similar size under Bonaparte's brother-in-law. The defeat of Bonaparte's expedition in 1803 resulted in the establishment of the Negro state of Haiti which has lasted to this day.

The revolt is the only successful slave revolt in history, and the odds it had to overcome is evidence of the magnitude of the interests that were involved. The transformation of slaves, trembling in hundreds before a single white man, into a people able to organise themselves and defeat the most powerful European nations of their day, is one of the great epics of revolutionary struggle and achievement. Why and how this happened is the theme of this book.[13]

In *Minty Alley*, the intention and achievement are reasonably clear-cut. In *The Black Jacobins* the situation is more complicated. James's sympathy with the people of the yard, in spite of his own middle-class background had inevitably led him, especially in the general international climate of the 1930s, towards socialism.[14] The problem with any formalisation of the general socialist tendency – into party, school, or theory – is that, given the European nature and origins of socialism, its ideals must to some degree always complicate or compromise local nationalist black interests.[15] *The Black Jacobins* is interesting for what was to happen later in *Beyond a Boundary* in two particular ways. Firstly, in analysing the class interests involved in the slave trade in Revolutionary France, and the interests of the slaves in Haiti, James, (though very much redressing the deliberately horrific post-revolution European depictions of Haiti and the Haitian revolution) is led into some rather odd historical gymnastics in order to square class revolution in Europe with race-slave interests in the Caribbean. The triumphant:

San Domingo was allowed only six deputies. In less than five minutes the great liberal orator [Mirabeau] had placed the case of the Friends of the Negro squarely before the whole of France in unforgettable words. The San Domingo representatives realised at last what they had done; they had tied the fortunes of San Domingo to the assembly of a people, the revolution and thenceforth the history of liberty in France and of slave emancipation in San Domingo is one and indivisible.[16]

is just a little too tidy. Race, colonial interests, revolutionary and bourgeois interests in France, were not to be as well tidied away as this suggests.

Secondly, James is able to simplify in *The Black Jacobins* a problem that arises in terms of *Beyond a Boundary*. As a product of a *British* slave history, now, after centuries 'divided to the vein', James would find attack on British civilisation and British values difficult without also confronting its implications for West Indian culture and character. This complication is to some extent eliminated by the European overlord being in this case France, though, where British middle-class liberal interests in connection with Haiti are mentioned, James is uncompromising:

The British bourgeoisie investigated the new situation in the West Indies and on the basis of what it saw, prepared a bombshell for its rivals. Without slaves San Domingo was doomed. The British colonies had enough slaves for all the trade they were ever likely to do. With the tears rolling down their cheeks for the poor suffering blacks, those British bourgeois who had no West Indian interests set up a great howl for the abolition of the slave trade.[17]

But later, true to the ideal of an international brotherhood of the worker, the class ideology now natural to him, James depicts the British and French peasant populations as unanimously supporting Haitian slaves in a brotherhood of the oppressed:[18] a rather aberrant excursion out of probability into the ideal.

Nevertheless, *The Black Jacobins* was, like *Minty Alley*, record-breakingly revolutionary in its assessment of Caribbean history from the black slave point of view. The happenings in revolutionary France are shown to have their legitimate relevance only in terms of Haiti, not *vice versa* as European historians had always presented them. Thus it is, firstly, the orientation of outlook (the historical European material related to the periphery rather than to the European 'centre') that is revolutionary, and secondly, the uncompromising assessment of the atrocities of the European slave past, *vis-à-vis* the reports of Europeans like Spencer St John, whose horrific account of child-eating and occult practices in Haiti accelerated and reinforced the European horror of a free black state, which the name of Haiti still conjures. Although James used English forms and the English language in *Minty Alley* and *The Black Jacobin*, he nevertheless managed to *create* a profoundly West Indian history and literature, and it is an astounding achievement. James's use of the language and form in both works tested their elasticity against the Caribbean experience, and in so doing extended and altered immeasurably the moral range available to subsequent novelists and historians. *Beyond a Boundary* attempts to do the same, but is less successful.

In *Beyond a Boundary* James establishes at the outset the connection between literature and cricket, and by implication the politics of de-colonisation which he had explored in fictional form in *Minty Alley*. The section is entitled 'A Window to the World' and hints at the 'boundaries' James has overcome in his earlier works and those he intends to reach beyond here.

> By standing on a chair a small boy of six could watch practice every afternoon and matches on Saturdays. . . . From the chair also he could mount on to the window-sill and so stretch a groping hand for the books on top of the wardrobe. Thus the early pattern of my life was set.[19]

Literature and cricket are coupled as ways of looking at the world outside from a world inside the house. It is impossible not to expect that James's examination of cricket and society in the following pages will be as stringent, as grounded in social realism, and as record-breakingly creative as *Minty Alley*. This seems further indicated when he writes:

> In reality my life up to ten had laid the powder for a war which lasted without respite for eight years, and intermittently for sometime afterwards – a war between English Puritanism, English literature and cricket and the realism of West Indian life.[20]

Minty Alley and *Beyond a Boundary* are products of this war, but the outcomes in the two skirmishes are rather different. To win acceptance for the characters of *Minty Alley*, James had to look away from an imposed white middle-class value system that had for centuries denied, first, the slaves and, then, the people of the yard a human identity and value. The lower-class blacks were seen as an unpalatable aspect of the West Indian reality that threatened the maintenance of English 'standards'. James made a direct assault on this notion in 'Triumph' and *Minty Alley*, making the moral values behind the later West Indian novel home based, not British middle class oriented. Though the novel *form* was European, its application here entirely local, except in so far as the gulfs within local society were a product of the English value importation. Only by not denying the local – the West Indian – reality, could these gulfs ever be bridged. In *The Black Jacobins* James had written a West-Indian oriented history, where the events of Europe are seen to impinge on Haitian life and not *vice versa*. Nevertheless, James, committed to the solidarity of the working class across race and colonial lines, was occasionally led away from the Caribbean reality towards an ideal with which that reality might eventually have conflicted, but which was here generally low key enough to remain unobtrusive.

But in *Beyond a Boundary* the problem of the divided West Indian sensibility is more fully exposed. James, in the passage quoted above, seems to promise all examination of the clash between English imported ideal forms and values and West Indian reality. Though this remains implicit throughout, the strength of cricket as the most insidiously influential of all imperial cultural forms is attested in James's failure to ever really extricate the Caribbean reality from the English ideal.

Moreover, this attachment to the notion of solidarity of working men across race and colonial lines this time bedevils his intention to examine the clash of values directly. Part of the problem was that attempted equations of underdogs in European society and underdogs in post-colonial and post-slave societies are always problematical. Frequently the dominant Europeans in colonial areas were from the ranks of the lower middle class at home, and cross-colonial class metamorphosis of this kind denies the ideal in empire practice.[21] Cricket, even if (in James's view) a working man's game in England, was a game of white privilege at the periphery of empire. But, if by chance and time the black cricketer could 'arrive', he was really only being offered the opportunity to be as good as his master; he had little chance of redefining the moral assumptions behind the game. A fair deal for West Indian social reality in fictional and historical terms meant a moral re-definition of value and a new perspective. Cricket in Trinidad, on the other hand, is gradually shown by James to reach *English* moral standards by the circuitous route of ousting the white Trinidadian hegemony so that black West Indian and white Englishman could meet on fair and equal (English) terms.

James avoids the head-on clash between the morality of *Tom Brown's Schooldays* (the ethics of Empire) and the de-colonisation of West Indian reality by dividing *Beyond a Boundary* into two main sections. The first deals with the social niceties and lack thereof in the conditions for black cricket in Trinidad. Here, very slowly, political colonisation is mirrored in cricket, with the eventual appointment of a black captain and the choice of players on the grounds of ability, not colour.[22] Wilton St Hill's omission from the team to tour England in 1923 is deplored, and the difficulties of choosing a cricket club of the correct skin shading between Queen's Park, Constabulary, Shamrock, Maple, Shannon and Stingo is dealt with entertainingly. Thus James does not avoid the issues of race, culture and colonialism in Trinidad, but by laying the blame at the feet of the white *West Indians*, avoids a head-on confrontation with the British ideal. Though it is an unfair comment on James's general attitudes, it is difficult not to be reminded of Fanon's dictum that the colonial will always attack fellow colonial, rather than the imperial power.

The frustration of the black cricketing audience (and some players) is anatomised and the local white hegemonies eventually defeated, but nowhere does James really confront the meaning of English cricket with its uncomfortable West Indian reality. Instead he shows how the values implicit in cricket were distorted in the West Indies; he never examines those values or their appropriateness in a colonial, post-slave society, or suggests that values implicit in the game might continue to hinder the recognition of that purely local value he strove so successfully to establish in his earlier works.

Orlando Patterson's 'The Ritual of Cricket'[23] published six years after *Beyond a Boundary* points some interesting contrasts. In this article Patterson analyses a particular England versus West Indies match in Jamaica for the light it throws on cricket in the West Indies generally, and for the essential significance of this meeting ground of the two cultures. Like James, Patterson agrees that one must look behind the surface of the game to its social ramifications and he agrees on its fundamental importance;[24]

> In the West Indies the test match is not so much a game as a collective ritual – a social drama in which almost all of the basic tensions and conflicts within the Society are played out symbolically.[25]

Patterson goes on to consider, as James does, the 'cultural dualism peculiar to West Indian Societies' and its cricketing implications:

> On the one hand there is the culture of the elite group, essentially British in orientation, the creolised version of the culture of the former colonial masters. On the other hand there is the culture of the masses, which, in its traditional form, is a tenuous syncretism of the fragments of African culture which survived slavery and the local adjustments to the demands of the plantation system . . . The 'superior' culture of the white master was accepted with all its implications of lowly conception of things black and Afro-Jamaican. The way one spoke, the way one behaved were negatively evaluated. The black lower-class Jamaican accepted this and despised himself for having to accept it. While accepting the superiority of British culture the Jamaican also hated it for what it had made of his own culture and of him. It was in short, a deep-seated love–hate relationship.[26]

Although the Sabina Park (Jamaica) riot of 12 February 1968 provides the occasion for Patterson's analysis of the West Indian social background and the meaning of cricket in such a context, he also links the earlier 1953–54 riots at the Bourda Ground (Guyana) and the 1959–60 riot at Queens Park Oval (Trinidad) to the Sabina Park incident. In all cases, Patterson notes, the riot occurred during a test against England; in all cases the same history of slavery and colonialism had resulted in major social stratification of these West Indian communities; and everywhere the complicated history of the West Indian had produced in him a peculiar love–hate relationship with all things English. Noting that cricket emphasises 'order',[27] Patterson sums up its ritual significance in such a context, accounting for the riots by going beyond

> the superficial explanations offered by socially unsophisticated sports commentators – the weather, the fact that the home side was losing, just plain lack of discipline and so on. These simply beg the question. . . . Cricket is the Englishman's game *par excellence.* The very term 'cricket' has become a byword for all that is most English in the British way of life. The vocabulary of cricket is a standard *pool* of stock images for Tory statesmen. No better symbol of English culture could be found. Yet, this is the game which West Indians have usurped, have come to master. What the former colonial subject has done is to literally beat the master at his own game. . . . Cricket is the game we love for it is the only game we can play well, the only activity which gives us some international prestige. But it is the game, deep down, which we must hate – the game of the master. Hence it becomes on the symbolic level the English culture we have been forced to love, for it is the only real one we have, but the culture we must despise for what it has done to us, for what it has made of the hopeless cultural shambles, the incoherent social patchwork, that we have called Afro-Jamaican culture.[28]

It is on this last point that James seems to differ from Patterson and, by implication, from the Jamaican crowds with whose recognition of the symbolic ritual of cricket Patterson identifies. James, with an unshakable love of the game itself, its art, its skill and toughness, will only go historically and symbolically speaking, as far as seeing it as an opportunity for the West Indian to beat the master at his own, beautiful game.

Where Patterson sees the class divisions and tensions within contemporary Jamaican society both reflected and exacerbated by the setting – the masses behind chicken wire in the bleachers, the lower middle class in the covered stands, the upper, (and generally lighter) sections in the Grandstand and the Pavilion – as well as in the meaning of the game itself, James in his article on Sobers, sees instead a meeting ground for all classes:

> The local masses of the population, Sobers' ancestors and mine, at first looked on; they knew nothing about the game. Then they began to bowl at the nets, producing at that stage fine fast bowlers. Here more than anywhere else, all the classes of the population learnt to have an interest in common.[29]

Patterson does seem to have taken a closer look at why the different classes were there and at how they were still radically divided.

The second aspect of *Beyond a Boundary* which militates against James's confronting the meaning of cricket in the West Indies is his more general argument for it to be taken seriously as an art form. It is difficult to support this on the one hand, and deride the values implicit in the game on the other. Hence, the second section of the book begs the West Indian social question, in order to deal convincingly with cricket as art. To do this, James shifts the emphasis away from the West Indian social complications he had promised to tease out and turns, instead, to the origin and values of cricket in an almost exclusively English context. The perpetration and projection of these values in the structure of the British empire remains unexamined: the argument, instead, ranges backwards, to Greece and Rome and to the historical justification for James' point that sport *is* culture, the truly popular culture. Woven into these two basic sections – cricket in the West Indies, and the history and meaning of cricket in nineteenth-century Britain and of sport generally in classical Greece – is an examination of the individual performances of West Indian and English cricketers. The careful, but seemingly spontaneous reminiscent structure here has the effect of placing the performances of the 'best' West Indians *on a par* with English idols like W.G. Grace. Cricket, James proves, is just as legitimate an art form as literature, painting or sculpture; cricket cannot be separate in its origins and direction from its social surroundings; and Jack is as good as his master, in his master's terms. (But he has not changed the terms.) Once these conclusions are put together in the politics of colony and empire, the result is confusing. James, sensing this, keeps his examination of the moralities exclusively local. By going to England himself, by detailing Constantine's successes and failures in England, he only *seems* to bridge the old gulf of the middle passage.

Though James dismisses the racial stereotypes often foisted on West Indian cricketers (the spontaneous, happy-go-lucky careless 'native'), he never really attempts to argue for a genuine Caribbean metamorphosis of the sport. Individuals have creative moments which lift them, with one stroke or ball out of the realm of social reality and into art. On balance, in *Beyond a Boundary*, James is more interested in arguing a case for cricket as art, than for any creative extension of the form into a West Indian identity, or a West Indian identity into the form. In *Minty Alley* and *The Black Jacobins*, the periphery was magically metamorphosed into the centre – an extraordinary feat of psychic de-colonisation. But, in *Beyond a Boundary*, the centre remains in England. Mahomet still goes to the mountain.

Cricket seemed to offer the colonial the chance to strike back. Hence, the temptation for the colonial to see cricket as an opportunity to prove himself to the 'master' is, even to as perceptive a politician as C.L.R. James, irresistible. The problem is that in cricket the colonial simply proves he can abide by the rules and the morality of the British game. He does not and has not in any significant sense altered the assumptions behind it. For this reason I find *Beyond a Boundary* a frustrating book. It makes its case for cricket as an art form; it makes its case for the necessity of considering the social milieu out of which cricket comes; but it fails to examine, while tantalisingly raising the question, the implications of the transfer of the game from its English origins to colonial soil. Moreover, the problem here is exacerbated by James's devotion to the European socialist notion of international working class solidarity.

In effect, *Beyond a Boundary*, interesting and provocative though it is, fails to engage with the real issue of empire – colonial cricket, partly because West Indian society, even more than our own, is divided to the vein. The values of cricket, and the strike-back it seemingly offered, have proved too seductive. James notes with horror the values of a society that had managed to discard the moral apparatus of British public school sport and he is too honest a writer not to record his reactions to it.[30] But the answer to his disagreement with these alien American sporting values, and his quarrel with Trotsky's view,[31] is his statement 'I was British'.[32] To be West Indian was and is, in a sense, to be British, but to be something else as well. *Minty Alley* and *The Black Jacobins* gave a deracinated people an identity that took account of this complex history. *Beyond a Boundary*, though it promises to investigate the roots of the divided West Indian psyche, in the end opts out of the social present in favour of an empire ideal.

In his 1970 introduction to Rowland Bowen's *Cricket: a History*, James is still committed to the true notion of history as being that of the worker, and to the idea of cricket as 'an integral part of British Civilisation'. But he also notes Hegel's observation that 'the owl of Minerva flies only at dusk. That is to say, one seriously examines and explores a situation, a totality, only when it is in the stage of its decline'.[33] The implication of this and of the rest of James's introduction here is that while the *heyday* of British civilisation and of cricket is passing, neither that civilisation nor the game which so effectively expressed its values can ever really disappear. A remarkable West Indian writer, nationalist and revolutionary thinker, James proves in all his works that that which is West Indian, *sui generis*, will always be partly British. That 'part' is noticeably more prominent in his book on cricket than in any other of his writings.

Notes

1 R.I. Cashman and M. McKernan, eds, *Sport in History* (University of Queensland Press, 1979), pp. 188–90.
2 See any West Indian history, or Louis James, *The Islands in Between* (OUP, 1968).
3 See for instance, C.L.R. James, *The Black Jacobins* (Knopf, 1963), p. 21.
4 James introduces readers unfamiliar with the West Indian 'yard' to it at the beginning of his short story, 'Triumph': 'Where people in England and America say "slums", Trinidadians say "barrack-yards". Probably the word is a relic of the days when England relied as much on garrisons of soldiers as on her fleet to protect her valuable sugar-producing colonies. Every street in Port of Spain proper could show you numerous examples of the type: a narrow gateway leading into a fairly big yard, on either side of which run long, low buildings, consisting of anything from four to eighteen rooms'. 'Triumph' is reprinted in Andrew Salkey, ed., *Stories from the Caribbean* (Elek, 1965), p. 133.
5 Maurice St Pierre, 'West Indian Cricket – A Socio-Historical Appraisal'. Part I, *Caribbean Quarterly*, 19, 2 (1973): 12.
6 Derek Walcott, *Selected Poems* (Farrer, Straus, 1962), p. 14.
7 Maurice St Pierre, 'West Indian Cricket', p. 7.
8 C.L.R. James, *Beyond a Boundary* (Hutchinson, 1963), Preface.
9 C.L.R. James, *The Case for West Indian Self-Government* (Hogarth Press, 1933). Reprinted in C.L.R. James, *The Future in the Past* (Lawrence Hill, 1977), p. 25; 'Cut off from all contact with Africa for a century and a quarter, they [descendants of African slaves in the West Indies] present today the extraordinary spectacle of a people who, in language and social customs, religion, education and outlook, are essentially Western and, indeed, far more advanced in Western culture than many a European community'.
10 Not all James's works have been explicitly concerned with the Caribbean. For a selected bibliography see Munro and Sander, eds, *Kas-Kas* (African and Afro-American Research Institute, Texas, 1972).
11 *The Black Jacobins*, pp. 391–2.
12 *Trinidad Guardian*, 22 December 1929, quoted in Kenneth Ramchand's introduction to *Minty Alley* (New Beacon, 1971), p. 9.
13 *The Black Jacobins*, p. ix.
14 In an interview James states: 'I have been a member of the Revolutionary Socialist Party since 1934, and that's how I think'. *Kas-Kas*, p. 38.
15 In an interview with *Afras Review* in 1976, James does seem aware of this potential conflict: 'I am for the international struggle for socialism, but I am not going to tell the African that he must forget he is an African. I say that this is what you have to remember'. 'Afras Review talks to C.L.R. James', *Afras Review*, 2 (1976): 7.
16 *The Black Jacobins*, pp. 60–1.
17 *Ibid.*, p. 51.

18 *Ibid.*, p. 139.
19 *Beyond a Boundary*, p. 13.
20 *Ibid.*, p. 30.
21 See C.L.R. James, *The Future in the Past*, pp. 29ff. on this British colonial class meta-morphosis: 'His antecedents have not been helpful. Bourgeois at home, he has found himself after a few weeks at sea suddenly exalted into membership of a ruling class'.
22 See Maurice St Pierre, 'West Indian Cricket', p. 7ff.
23 Orlando Patterson, 'The Ritual of Cricket', *Jamaica Journal* 3, 1 (March 1969): 22–5.
24 Patterson notes that, in 1969, 'Cricket, outside of test matches, is rapidly losing ground both as a participant and spectator sport in the West Indies, the one exception being Barbados' (*ibid.*, p. 23). Barbados has always been regarded as the 'most English' of West Indian islands.
25 *Ibid.*
26 *Ibid.*
27 *Ibid.*, p. 25. 'The most striking thing about cricket as a game is its emphasis on order. All games . . . involve some acceptance of rules and cease to exist when such rules are neglected. But cricket is exceptional both for its complexity and its almost consciously articulated ideology of obedience and authority, the latter being symbolised in the person of the umpire. Nor is it an accident that cricket is one of the few games that requires two umpires'.
28 *Ibid.*, pp. 23–4.
29 C.L.R. James, 'Garfield Sobers', in *The Future in the Past*, p. 219.
30 *Beyond a Boundary*, pp. 52–3.
31 *Ibid.*, p. 151.
32 *Ibid.*, p. 152.
33 Rowland Bowen, *Cricket: A History* (Eyre & Spottiswood, 1970), pp. 22–3.

22

Redemption sounds: music, literature and the popular ideology of West Indian cricket crowds

Hilary McD. Beckles and Harclyde Walcott

Cricket, like Protestant Christianity, was introduced into English West Indian society and promoted as part of the ideological armour of an aggressive English cultural imperialism. Neither were intended for the social consumption of the politically disenfranchised and materially impoverished black communities. Both were instruments of Empire imported and imposed upon colonial society by English officials and the resident white elite who valued above all the political importance of formally organised social institutions.

The early nineteenth century, however, was a significant social moment for both cricket and Christianity advocates. While non-conformist missionaries, in particular, were traversing the region feverishly seeking a mass (black) membership for their churches, the colonial elite was doing all within its power to protect their cricket culture from the social effects of ideological egalitarianism released by anti-slavery politics. By the mid-century whites were satisfied, at least moderately so, that there was still one social institution whose doors remained closed to the lower orders, and in which 'gentlemen' could enjoy exclusively the social pleasures and privileges associated with their oligarchical ownership of private property.

There is nothing particularly phenomenal about these early ideological positions adopted by the Anglo-colonial elite with respect to the politics of Christianity and cricket. A sophisticated appreciation of the value system of cricket, whites argued, was beyond the intellectual reach of blacks, whose participation was seen as detrimental to its development. In the ideological sphere, 'high' moral and aesthetical expression were appropriated monopolistically by this ruling elite, while concepts that denoted crudity and primitivism were levelled against the labouring classes. The eurocentrism and racism of creole whites, then, functioned as an ideological boundary that separated colonial social groups, within the established church as well as on the cricket field.

During the late nineteenth century, however, Afro-West Indians confronted the 'imported/imposed' Englishness of the plantation-based cricket world with precise and sensitive cosmological demands that had the effect of changing forever the social trajectory and meaning of the game.[1] Within this process of cultural domestication and class appropriation black creoles sculptured unique and distinct methodological and aesthetical forms that reflected and promoted their social identity and ideological concerns. In their varied roles as players, spectators and commentators, blacks succeeded in determining and defining the popular images, politics, and social considerations of this activity which was soon to gain hegemonic cultural dimensions.[2]

In the West Indies while Englishmen and their creole progeny sought to imitate and fossilise cricketing images and behavioural patterns that originated with the Victorian gentry, blacks surrounded and infused the game with an aura and ethos derived from their popular struggles and residual African cultural norms. Even before 1928, when the West Indies cricket team gained 'test' status, observers were keen to point out that blacks brought to the game a unique, dynamic, celebratory, theatrical presence. With reference to the early period, for example, Algernon Aspinall, historian of the English in the nineteenth century West Indies, commented on the 'sheer excitement' and 'demonstrative' expressions of 'the black spectator'. 'It is not unusual', he tells us, 'to see many of them rush out on the ground and leap and roll about from sheer excitement when a wicket falls on the side which they do not favour, or when a brilliant catch is made'. Also, A.F. Somerset, who toured the West Indies in 1895 with the Slade Lucas team, states while comparing the verbalist, participatory 'playing' of the West Indian crowd with its less verbose, more quietly consumerist English counterpart:

> A good ball dealt with brings a shout of 'played!' all around the ground, and to stop a 'yorker' evokes a yell that would not be given for a hit out of the ground in England. When that comes off a large part of the crowd spring on to the ground, throw their hands and umbrellas in the air, perform fantastic dances, and some of them are occasionally arrested by the police.[3]

In the Barbados vs England match of that tour, he stated, the England captain was forced to use a whistle to get the attention of his fieldsmen, so noisy and festive was the crowd.

This expressive physical and oral appreciation of performance had hardly changed a century later. In fact, it has been consolidated into that realm of popular recognition generally referred to as custom. Poet, Edward Brathwaite, captured the language and sound of the Barbados cricket crowd:

> Clyde back pun de backfoot an' prax!
> is through extra cover an' four red runs all de way.
> 'You see dat shot?' the people was shoutin';
> 'Jesus Chrise, man, wanna see dat shot?'
> All over de groun' fellers shakin' hands wid each other
> An' in front o' where I was sittin',
> One ball-headed sceptic snatch hat off he head
> as if he did crazy
> an' pointin' he finger at Wardle [the bowler]
> he jump up an' down

371

like a sun-shatter daisy an' bawl
out; 'B . . L . . O . . O . . D, B . . I . . G . . . B . . O . . Y .
bring me he 'B . . L . . O . . O . . D '.[4]

This tradition of language, dance and sound 'speaks' directly to the variety of issues central to an ontological understanding of what is West Indianness. That the West Indian voice is clearly heard in the sound of the cricket crowd should indicate the basic truth of C.L.R. James's assertion that spectators take with them through the gates the full weight of their history and visions of the future. No one requires a sophisticated literacy to comprehend this reality once the first ball is bowled. This 'sound' of gathered West Indians, like the talking drums of their ancestors, is a secret code which is very easily misconceived and misunderstood by those not perfectly tuned to its transmission. It is a sound that fills the air and unites those whose mission it is to put together fragments of an old world in new, more resistant forms.

The oral and scribal literature, music, and dance of the West Indian cricket crowd, then, are cultural missiles that emanate from a complex command centre which is ideology and race/class consciousness. The inherent beliefs of the common people with respect to past and current achievements and injustices, as well as everyday fears and expectations, are often displayed at moment of 'play', and in ways which support Brathwaite's and Naipaul's view that cricket for many constitutes a level of consciousness and existence located somewhere above mundane matters of economics and politics. It is this historically informed matrix of consciousness, actions and ideology that continues to engage the creative art forms of West Indians. Cricket as the principal popular cultural occupation of the region, therefore, engages these artists in a dialectical and symbiotic relation, that has allowed for some of the finest expressions of music, art and literature.

The language employed by the West Indian voice within the cricket arena, furthermore, is not only authentic, but perhaps more importantly, it is pure in that it remains spontaneous in its creative form and insists upon being uncensored. Its linguistic code is no different in meaning from the drum beat call to arms by the enslaved on the plantation in an earlier era. At the same time it is also the infrastructure for a sophisticated literary play on the pressing socio–political issues 'beyond the boundary'. All together, as a discursive practice, they constitute a compelling element of an indigenous literary canon that rejects notions of the region as 'other' by the imperial centre and insists upon the existence of plurality in style and genre. The voice of the cricket crowd as heard, and interpreted, to which generations of artists have responded, is therefore rooted in popular ideology and echoes levels of consciousness within the fragmented West Indian nation.

The oral and scribal text of the West Indian cricket culture, then, constitutes a store house of information on the native tongue, sound, and senses. In terms of content this text has been fiercely anti-colonial, and at a time when such an ideological position had not taken shape in the form of organised political activity. The cricket crowd said as much about English colonialism as political leaders on their soap boxes; working-class calypsonians send as many potent messages to Whitehall

372

in their cricket songs as scholars did in their written texts. The metaphoric cricket poems, songs, and prose of the regions, then, represent an innovative literary and artistic style of communication that reinforces the significance of the game within mass society. It is this sporting activity that has given the multi-national region its only mass heroes. While political or intellectual leaders may attain popularity within single territories, only the following of cricket heroes transcends national, ideological, and generational boundaries. This reality provides a unique terrain for artists and intellectuals to speak to the region as one about itself as a unified civilisation.

Such an opportunity was not to be missed by an artist as penetrating and perceptive as Trinidad's Errol John. In his play, *Moon on a Rainbow Shawl*, the quintessential classic of contemporary Caribbean theatre, John speaks of the racial injustices within early twentieth century colonial society that found fertile soil in its cricket fields. In the playscript, Charlie Adams, who just by an analysis of his name, is a 'regular' common kind of being – if not the first man in terms of biblical text – has a decidedly promising career ahead of him as a cricketer, possessing in his physical and mental faculties an abundance of skills and power of application. While on tour of Jamaica, however, he expressed some measure of disgust at the discriminatory treatment meted out to dark skinned members of his team by the hosts. For this social 'indiscretion' his cricketing career came to a cataclysmic end, with the consequence of his being unemployable, alcoholic, abjectly depressed and finally, a convicted criminal. Broken dreams and a shattered life led to Adams's social death in a colonial community that offered him 'recognition' on condition of self-negation and denial. What is important about this scenario from our view point is not the written text, but the fact that John's father was himself a 'recognised potential' who, during the 1930s had experienced considerable frustration and humiliation at the hands of the 'white' cricketing authorities.[5]

Charlie's dream was no different from that of most black working class West Indian boys from the 1930s to present; to escape the poverty and racial oppression of their little world aboard the cricket vehicle – the one which took the most passengers from the ghettoes to the suburbs and beyond. He tells his story of hope, struggle and despair, and finally defeat by the white and brown 'savannah' colonial upper class of the Queens Park Cricket Club:

> *Charlie.* In my day, EPF – I use to get my bats second-hand. An' sometimes they had to last me from season to season, but my big talent was with the ball.
>
> I used to trundle down to that wicket – an' send them down red hot! They don't make them that fast these days. The boys don't keep in condition. Today they send down a couple of overs – they are on their knees.
>
> But in my time, John, Old Constantine, Francis, them fellas was fast! Fast! Up in England them so help put the Indies on the map.
>
> *EPF.* I only saw you once on the green, Charlie. Yer was kind of past yer prime. But the ole brain was there! And batsman was seein' trouble! Trouble, man! And I say this to you now, papa – You was class!

Charlie. In them days, boy – The Savannah Club crowd was running most everything. People like me either had to lump it or leave it.

EPF. It ent much different now, Charlie.

Charlie. Is different – a whole lot different. In them times so when we went Barbados or Jamaica to play cricket they used to treat us like hogs, boy. When we went on tours they put we in any ole kind of boarding-house. The best hotels was fer them and the half-scald members of the team – So in twenty-seven when we was on tour in Jamaica I cause a stink, boy. I had had enough of them dirty little boarding-house rooms. I said either they treat me decent or they send me back. The stink I made got into the newspapers. They didn't send me back. But that was the last intercolony series I ever play. They broke me, boy.

EPF. [quietly] Fer that?

Charlie. I should of known mey place. If I had known mey place, EPF, I'd a made the team to England the following year. And in them days, boy – the English County clubs was outbidding each other fer bowlers like me. But the Big Ones here strangled my future, boy'.

The collective memory of the cricket 'crowd' has in store cases by the dozens of 'potentials' who dried and died on the cricket vine on account of such social injustices. Popular awareness of these individual experiences have provided inspiration for the sound and voice of protest as well as success. Bruce St John, 'nation-poet' of Barbados, understood the tragic drama that lurks in the dark corners of the cricket culture. He urges the player, however, to be optimistic and to persevere against all adversity since, in the final instance, the crowd, like Christ of the New Testament, is understanding and sympathetic. Cricket, St John tells us, has assumed quasi-religious proportions for the Barbadian masses:

Le' muh tell yuh somet'ing Boyse boy,
De Lord got somet'ing to do wid cricket.
De wicket does remin' me o' de Trinity
God in de centre of de three,
Holy Ghost pun de lef' and Jesus
Pun de right an' de bails like a crown
Joinin' dem an' mekkin' dem Three in One.
De pitch like an altar north and south
Wid de sun transfigurin' de scene
And de umpires like two high priests
Wid de groundsmen as de sextons, Yes, Yes. . . .
Cricket is de game o' de Lord
Cricket is de game o' de Master
Play de game right, Boysie boy
An' you stan' a good chance hereafter.[6]

St John's utopian 'hereafter' refers less to the social honour and economic betterment dreamt of by Charlie Adams, and more to a perception that the moral values of the game if properly applied to social life lend toward the making of a Christian character that is readily embraced by the society.

St John's optimism and generosity, however, did not find its way into Edward Brathwaite's use of the cricket metaphor in his clinical (for some cynical) assessment of the West Indian personality. Brathwaite seems to share Wilson Harris's criticism of the West Indian mind as disunited, consumed in apathy and unwilling to be disciplined into taking responsibility for its destiny: In 'Rites', the famous poem in which these themes are explored, Brathwaite confronts the question of ill-discipline and irresponsibility:

> I tole him over an' over
> agen : *watch de ball, man*, watch
> de ball like it hook to your eye
>
> when you first goes in an' you doan know de pitch.
> Uh doan mean to poke
> but you jes got to *watch what you doin'*;
>
> this isn't no time for playin'
> the fool nor making no sport; this is cricket!
> But Gullstone too deaf:
> mudder doan clean out de wax in 'e ear!
> Firs' ball from Cass an' he fishin':
> secon' ball an' he missin', swishin'
>
> he bat like he wishin'
> to catch butterfly; though the all Gullstone ever could
> catch
> pun this beach was a cole!
>
> But is always the trouble wid me;
> too fraid an' too frighten.
> Is all very well when it rosy an' sweet,
>
> but leh murder start an' bruggalungdung!
> you cahn fine a man to hole up de side.[7]

On this matter, if not on any other, Brathwaite and Naipaul agree.

For Naipaul, West Indian cricketers, like the politicians, lacked the kind of mental preparation necessary for the attainment of creative accomplishments. For him, colonials are generally imitators and flippant in manner – nation builders are not. With reference to the 1963 West Indies tour of England, one of his fictional characters says:

> You know what's wrong with our West Indians? No damn discipline. Look at this business this morning. That Hall and Trueman nonsense, Kya-kya, very funny. But that is not the way the Aussies won Tests. I tell you, what we need is *conscription*. Put every one of the idlers in the army. Give them discipline.[8]

If Brathwaite saw in cricket characteristic features of an unfit West Indian personality – one not yet ready for serious survival concerns – and was therefore unwilling to celebrate and savour the 'highs' of the game on account of the 'lows' that were sure to follow, calypsonians from the earliest days had no such reservations. They composed and performed melodies that captured the essence of historic moments in a way that newspaper reporters could not. In the first West Indies Test match at Lords, against England, which was played in 1928, Learie Constantine, at age 26, took 4 wickets and took 2 catches. To mark the occasion, Trinidadian calypsonian, Lord Beginner (Egbert Moore) composed the song:

> Joe Small and Griffith was
> excellent
> was magnificent
> And our cricketer, great Wilton St Hill
> Did not do well because he was
> ill
> He made a name for the West
> Indies
> Who he was? Learie Constantine
> That old pal of mine.[9]

This calypso, notes Kim Johnson, is the first celebration in song of a West Indies cricket hero. Many more have been written since then, but none, perhaps, has been as memorable as Beginner's 1950 'Cricket Lovely Cricket'.[10]

The 1950 West Indies tour of England was special in many ways. But the most significant feature was that thousands of West Indians had recently emigrated to England and represented for the first time a significant 'home crowd' within the English crowd cheering on the West Indies. The vocal support they offered the West Indies team during tests strengthened its resolve to the same degree as it disturbed English supporters now faced with a new and novel circumstance. The tensions of race relations in England, and the 'blues' of the migrant communities, meant that the psychological profiles of West Indian spectators had also been reconfigured. Anti-black racism has long been an endemic feature of West Indian societies, but there was something different and unfamiliar about the English brand of racism. Perhaps it was the absence of cultural space that prevented West Indians from creating their own world, in spite of racism, that heightened anxieties and produced the besieged consciousness.

The first test was played at Old Trafford, and England won by 202 runs. The second test at Lords, however, produced the long sought after result – West Indies won by 326 runs on account of the brilliance of young mystery spinners Sonny Ramadhin and Alf Valentine. England received a thrashing that broke their resolve, and the West Indies romped home to a 3–1 historic test victory after winning the third and fourth test by 10 wickets and an innings and 56 runs respectively.

The Lords test was the scene of the first 'cricket carnival' in England. The ground exploded in dance, song and bacchanal, West Indian style, and signalled the beginning of a tradition that was to shape the culture of cricket crowds in England. Lord Kitchener and Lord Beginner were at Lords for the pivotal test, and already known as legendary artists, they led jubilant West Indians across the field in a procession of improvised singing. The well known photograph of these two Lords of calypso at Lords, surrounded by chanting melody makers, says more about that moment in the hearts of West Indians than match reports ever could. Kitchener, with guitar in hand, and Beginner leading the vocals produced for the cricket world the song 'Cricket, Lovely Cricket':[11]

> Cricket, lovely cricket
> At Lord's where I saw it
> (repeat)
> Yardley tried his best
> But Goddard won the test
> They gave the crowd plenty fun
> Second Test and
> West Indies won
>
> With those two little pals of mine
> Ramadhin and Valentine
> The king was well attired
> So they started with Rae and
> Stollmeyer
> Stolly was hitting balls around
> the boundary
> But Wardle stopped him at
> twenty
> Rae had confidence
> So he put up a strong defence
> He saw the King was waiting
> to see
> So he gave him a century

For West Indians, even those who came of age (in the cricketing sense) after the 1950 test, this was their redemption song.

Lord Beginner, then, was critical in the establishment of a literary and musical tradition that is, ironically, perhaps more West Indian than the cricket itself. Kitchener, notes Kim Johnson, built upon and deepened this art form in ways that enhanced the standing of cricket for West Indians as 'de Lord's game'. According to Johnson: in 1965 Kitchener sang 'The Cricket Song' about the 1964 series, telling the story in his beautiful couplets alongside an old-time call-and-response chorus:

> (Bowl Griffith) Bowl, don't
> stop at all
> (Bowl Griffith) Give him
> back the ball
> (Bowl Griffith) Sobers and
> Hall
> (Bowl Griffith) Bring Gibbs
> and all.

And then in 1967 he sang 'Cricket Champions' about the 1966 series in England when West Indies, led by Sobers, won three, drew one and lost one test:

> England must understand
> We are the champions
> Sobers carray and hit them
> potow! potow! – two four
> Holford come back and hit
> them bodow! bodow! – two more.

But in between these two gems by Kitchener something had changed, Sparrow sang 'Sir Garfield Sobers' (1966) about 'the greatest cricketer on Earth, or Mars' and the victory over Australia, and narrative ball-by-ball calypso commentaries went out of fashion. Thereafter, in the 1970s, Relator penned the marvellous 'Gavaskar'. Although this was structured in an old-time narrative mode and made fun of the names of the Indian cricketers, Relator was not only singing humorously about serious cricket – not no Chinese match – but also commentating the first West Indian Test defeat at the hands of India:

> and its Gavaskar
> We real master
> Just like a wall
> We couldn't out Gavaskar at all.

Short Shirt sent 'Viv Richards' from Antigua in 1975, Maestro gave us 'World Cup'. And Sparrow sang 'Kerry Packer' which in 1978 savagely tore down the final myth of cricketing heroism;

> I eh negotiating ah told them
> If they got money we can't control them
> A West Indian cricketer must always be broke
> Is then he does bowl fast and make pretty stroke.[12]

These songs reflect both the celebratory and commemorative values of the wider society, and are rooted in the cultural bedrock of their 'call and response', 'praise song' and 'judgemental' oral traditions. They also chronicle the history of West Indies cricket, the successes and failures. But, more importantly, they articulate national political concerns and popular ideologies. David Rudder's 'Rally Round the West Indies' calls for firm support for the West Indies team during the difficult years that followed the retirement of several players from the extraordinarily victorious Clive Lloyd team. But Rudder is also concerned with the wider geo-political issues involved in West Indies survival when he beckons:

> Soon we must take a side or be left in the rubble
> In a divided world that don't need islands no more
> Are we doomed for ever to be at somebody's mercy
> Little keys can open up mighty doors
> Rally round the West Indies now and forever.

378

The West Indies cricket crowd, of course, provides the inspiration and ideological parameters for this musical tradition. It is common indeed for the crowd to call upon known musical talents to take the lead and improvise songs to suit the occasion and mood of the game. What happens in the recording studios is but a refashioning of forms and ideas already ventilated by the cricket crowd. It is the crowd that provides the interpretation of events to which the artist responds, and within the creativity of the moment history is preserved in sound.

A classic 'character' in the musical tradition of the West Indies cricket crowd is the Barbadian calypsonian, Mac Fingall, a school teacher by profession, and also popular comedian. He loves cricket as much as he cares for the popular theatre, and blends the two to magical effect much to the delight of spectators at Kensington Oval. Fingall enters the Oval with his trumpet under his arm, and big bass drum around his neck. Soon he is accompanied by persons unknown to himself who had arrived with conch shells, kettle drums, flutes, fifes and other instruments. The 'band', somehow, is assembled, the crowd calls the tune, and Fingall's trumpet rings out. By this time, 8,000 people within the stand are rocking, swaying, and nodding to the pulsating song.

The music, of course, reflects the mood of the moment. When West Indies batsmen are in trouble, the music ceases. When West Indies batsmen are punishing the opposition's bowlers, the silence erupts into carnival. When, however, West Indies fast bowlers are not making the required impression on the opposition's batsmen, Fingall puts away the trumpet and seeks to inspire them with a drumming solo that heats the blood, quickens the heartbeat, and energises the muscles. The quickening rhythmic sound of drums drives the fast bowlers on, unnerves the batsman, and all too often wickets begin to tumble.

During the recent tours of England and Australia to the West Indies complaints were lodged to West Indian officials by the tourists with respect to the musical scores of crowds. In response, an attempt was made in Barbados to outlaw the taking of musical instruments, the drum in particular, into the Oval. This resulted in a heated national debate in which spectators vowed to boycott 'matches' unless the 'sounds' were allowed. References were made to the persistent attempts, before and after slavery, by white colonials and their recent black allies, to criminalise the drum, star of the African musical cosmology. Any attack upon the drum, they said, is an attack upon the 'souls of black folks'.

Viv Richards, West Indies captain, responded to a decision of the Barbados cricket authorities to ban the drum by stating that it was shortsighted, anti-social, and disrespectful of black people whose cricket culture has long been characterised by the presence of sound. The drums, he said in addition, had inspired his bowlers and fieldsmen, and should be treated with respect. The crowd would have none of it. They won this battle, and officials were left to plead for a sound level consistent with the cultural norms of tourists.

Familiarity with the display of West Indian social culture, furthermore, would indicate that wherever there is 'sound', there are sights to behold. It is here that we enter the psychological world of the saturnalia, mask, maskerade, and make belief of everyday life. At this time, the two most well known 'crowd' characters carry the names King Dyall (Barbados) and Gravey (Antigua). King Dyal, as his alias indicates, assumes to derive his royal bearing from an ancient pedigree. He is the most well known member of the Barbados cricket crowd, and announces his arrival at the gates with the waving of his walking cane, the tipping of his derby, and the installation of his pipe. A tailor by trade, he wears brightly coloured three piece suits, with matching shoes, hat and gloves, and rides an old bicycle which has been variously painted yellow, white and pink. As a member of the inner city black working class, the 'King' as he is known, has no time for black people and preaches at cricket his love for all things English. He is not a supporter of the West Indies team, and makes much of his preference for the English team. For him, the 'gods' of cricket are Peter May, Colin Cowdrey and Len Hutton. Black spectators around him he describes as 'monkey', 'ignorant sheep' and 'primitives'.

The 'king' of the Oval verbally abusing his subject with language not far removed from that used by Kipling brings tremendous comic relief to spectators during less exciting cricket moments. The king represents the imperial mask that 'upward' looking blacks were forced to wear under the colonial regime. The mask in time became a cultural norm which now stands in a dichotomous relation to the liberating cricket culture. While the king at the Oval is symbolic of the nineteenth century white, colonial gentleman spectator, the tackiness of his attire portrays his class position, and reveals the self-contemptuousness endemic to the colonised mind. The king, therefore, in his maskerade, is a reminder of the values and practices black cricketers fought against, and at the same time his presence represents a confirmation of popular admiration for the pomp and regalia of graceful gait and carriage.

Antigua's Gravey is a different kind of cricket character. His is the maskerade associated with dance, song and flamboyant costume. He dresses, more often than not, in women's clothing – wigs, earrings, make-up and handbag included – and dances, some would say immorally – throughout the game in front of amused crowds. The sexual connotations of his dances entertain spectators who call upon him to show them what he can 'do'. His dances and other athletic antics are popular with the Antiguan cricket crowd, which has developed a reputation in the region for its musical character. Gravey's intention is to mock the ascribed effeminacy of English cricketers, and his dance suggests that they are being assaulted by West Indian macho. It is a dance of triumph and conquest, well understood by the West Indian masses – particularly in terms of the subliminal sexuality of the experience.

The West Indian cricket aesthetic, then, is shaped fundamentally by cultural expression in the form of colour, song and dance, which dictate that cricket looks best if played on a clear bright day. Fielders, of course, ought to be clothed in sparkling white flannels and the field should be green with a pitch Barbadian fans would refer to as 'shining like dog stones', meaning flat, shiny and glass-like. This is the perfect setting for the first day of a test match. The requirements for the spectators are largely visual, in terms of mass and colour, and the pleasures are maximised when moments of tension and tautness are mixed with periods of excitement and relaxation. This is the arena of action, the theatrical environment. The centre of good theatre is conflict and this begins long before the first ball is delivered. The objectives of the opposing teams are clear. Bat must dominate ball or vice versa; and after five days only West Indian cricket can end in the fashion Paul Keens-Douglas describes in his 'performance' poem 'Tanti [Auntie] at the Oval':

> Islands need seven runs with nine balls to bowl an' one wicket to fall.
> Dis time I forget 'bout Tanti Merle,
> Excitement in de Oval like you never seen in ya life,
> Gore come into bat an' is den de action start
> Nine balls seven runs to go . . . noise in de place
> Eight balls six runs to go . . . Tanti start waving de basket
> Seven balls six runs to go . . . Tanti on top de seat
> Six balls five runs to go . . . Tanti fall off de seat
> Five balls five runs to go . . . Tanti wavin' de parasol
> Four balls four runs to go . . . Police cautionin' Tanti
> Three balls three runs to go . . . I can't see Tanti
> Two balls three runs to go . . . Tanti climbing de fence
> One ball three runs to go . . . Tanti on the field
> Gore hit de ball an' Finlay pelt down de wicket for two runs
> And is then de bachanal start[13]

The Afro–West Indian also demands from cricket what he seeks in every form of art – a sense of style. This special quality cannot be defined. It can be perceived by senses well trained for the task, and the sensation is unmistakable. Quality drama must promote high art, and in West Indian society an important cultural residue of the African ancestry is the centrality of style to all ontological expressions. Some batsmen can be very prolific, consistent and reliable, but are never in the West Indies defined as 'great' unless they meet the popular criterion of style. This special quality – essence if you like – is considered endemic to West Indian cricket culture, and does not occupy centre stage in other cultures. As Sobers walked to the wicket, the evidence of this 'thing' is witnessed and celebrated. Something in the way he moved satisfied some spectators who readily confess that they paid to see Sobers, not to see him score runs.

The question of cricket style, or 'class', has occupied literary aestheticists for some time. V.S. Naipaul in a letter to C.L.R. James indicated that cricket in the West Indies 'represents style, grace and other elements of culture in a society which had little else of the kind'.[14] This quality which is celebrated and deified by West Indians within the cricket culture is defended in the most uncompromising manner, and is indicative of the popular refusal to be liberal on the matter of 'artistic purity'. C.L.R. James concludes:

> I submit finally that without the intervention of any artist the spectator at cricket extracts the significance of movement and of tactile valves. He experiences the heightened sense of capacity. Furthermore, however, the purely human element, the

literature, the frustration, in cricket may enhance the purely artistic appeal, the significant form at its most unadulterated is permanently present. It is known, expected, recognised and enjoyed by tens of thousands of spectators. Cricketers call it style.[15]

This visual impression, West Indians would suggest, is expressive of individual confidence that by extension indicates a mastery of form that allows the game to transcend the mundane and to be elevated into the category of art. And, it is this rare quality that occasionally solicits from West Indian crowds another kind of 'sound' – that of stone silence – which indicates a sudden neutralisation of the central nervous system. Extreme beauty, they say, can only be understood, experienced and appreciated within the total freedom of a vacuum or the cluttered anarchy of sensual abandonment and madness.

The West Indian cricket crowd, then, has made its distinctive contribution to the artistic tradition in the forms of music, dance, theatre, and oral and scribal literature. It is a special contribution that requires careful attention lest its value is lost within a haze of elitist value assumptions about the culture of the 'lower orders'. This, of course, can easily happen in the West Indies where such groups who attend cricket matches dressed in jacket and tie in spite of the heat (96° F in the shade) commonly refer to popular culture as expressions of the 'mob', or 'rabble'. The 'sounds' of the crowd, they consider, are the result of a lack of domestic manners and breeding, an attitude that reflects the traditional world view of the colonial white community.

But the redemption 'sounds' of the crowd are indicative of a deeper cultural search for authenticity and cultural freedom. That you must make your own sound in order to have an independent voice is pretty well understood. What needs to be further understood is the relationship between social life as 'activated' consciousness and the reproduction of the creative process. Understanding how social attitudes and mentalities are translated into performing art – on the field in the case of players – and 'sounds' in the case of the crowd cannot be fully understood in the absence of an indigenous anthropology. What seems clear, furthermore, is the manner in which the cricket crowd continues to be both transmitter and receiver of artistic forms and practices that go to the centre of any definition of the term 'West Indian'.

Notes

1 Algernon E. Aspinall, *The British West Indies: Their History, Resource and Progess* (London, Isaac Pitman, 1912), pp. 153–4.
2 *Ibid.*
3 *Ibid.*, p. 154.
4 Edward Brathwaite, *The Arrivants: a New World Trilogy* (London, Oxford University Press, 1981), 'Rites' p. 200.
5 Errol John, *Moon on a Rainbow Shawl* (London, Faber and Faber, 1958), pp. 61–2.

6 Bruce St John, 'Cricket', in *Bumbatuk* 1, (Cedar Press, Bridgetown, 1982) pp. 17, 19.

7 Brathwaite, *The Arrivants*, p. 198.

8 V.S. Naipaul, 'England v. West Indies (1963)'. Cited in Michael and Simon Davie (eds), *The Faber Book of Cricket* (London, Faber and Faber, 1987), p. 187.

9 Cited in Kim Johnson, 'Calypso Cricket', *Sunday Express* (Trinidad and Tobago), 4 April 1993.

10 *Ibid.*

11 *Ibid.*

12 *Ibid.*

13 Paul Keens-Douglas, 'Tanti Merle'.

14 Ana Grimshaw (ed.), *C.L.R. James: Cricket* (London, Allison & Busby, 1986), p. 131.

15 C.L.R. James, *Beyond a Boundary* (London, Hutchinson, 1963), p. 198.

23

C.L.R. James: a remembrance

Brian Stoddart

Cyril Lionel Robert ("Nello") James died at his home in the London suburb of Brixton on May 31, 1989, at the age of 88, and was buried at his birthplace of Tunapuna, Trinidad, 12 days later. It is doubtful whether any other person connected with the social analysis of sport, or ever likely to be, will live a life as full as the man once dubbed by *The Times* as the "Black Plato of our generation" *(Sunday Sun,* 1989).

When his magisterial book, *Beyond a Boundary,* appeared in 1963, it was immediately declared the greatest book ever written on cricket and established James as the game's most eminent intellectual. The book predated the rise of modern sports history and sociology and, except for those scholars working on the social construction of cricket, it remained relatively unknown to other sports analysts until it was reprinted in 1984 (Balliett, 1984; Walcott, 1984). James then became, somewhat belatedly, more widely recognized as a major figure in the field (Metcalfe, 1987).

At the risk of oversimplifying the theses in *Beyond a Boundary,* James argued that the potent combination of cricket and an education derived from the English public school system (particularly in English literature) marked his evolution as a political thinker and activist while growing up in Trinidad. From there, he argued that such cultural consciences produced a remarkable Caribbean conservatism, despite the prevailing economic and social deprivation that should have made the region a classic revolutionary site. James, then, was something of an intellectual contemporary (almost certainly unknowingly) of the Italian theorist Antonio Gramsci, who stressed the cultural themes initially explored by Marx – themes that were largely overlooked because of the emphasis on economic strands by other analysts (Femia, 1981). Throughout this book, then, James stressed how cricket either helped to form or supplemented the social practices based in the intersecting lines of color and class which, in the Caribbean, produced an infinitely graded and persistent social hierarchy.

From that platform constructed by James have sprung a series of works on Caribbean cricket that arguably constitute, both qualitatively and collectively, the best literature on any sport and its social context (Burton, 1985; Marshall, 1965;

384

Patterson, 1969; Sandiford, 1986; Stoddart, 1987, 1988a; St Pierre, 1973; Thompson, 1983). As Orlando Patterson put it, the ultimate power of cricket in the Caribbean is that because the game was the creation of the former white masters, it should have been rejected by the black masses; yet it was not and, to the contrary, it flourished (Patterson, 1969). The search for reasons underlying that paradox have prompted the efforts of all researchers in the field.

The depths of that search initiated by James were important enough in the specific cultural context; but in his breadth of interest, intellectual curiosity, and awareness of the multifaceted nature of the human condition, James provided an object model of how those who probe the social contours of sport might approach their tasks. This is summed up in one line from *Beyond a Boundary:* "What do they know of cricket who only cricket know?" In other words, a game cannot be fully understood simply in its own terms without consideration of its cultural environment.

Similarly, to *really* understand his cricket book, historians and sociologists would benefit appreciably from a knowledge of James' other interests and writings. Throughout an admirably productive life James wrote – among a host of other things – a novel on Trinidadian working-class life; the first coherent case for West Indian self-government; *The Black Jacobins,* a brilliant work about the slave revolt in Haiti in the late eighteenth century; a book on the Communist International; works on Africanism and the black struggle; several works on Marxist theory; and of course innumerable essays on cricket. The James bibliography is vast, varied, and fascinating, so it is little wonder that the impact of his life work had already begun to be reviewed before his death (Anderson, 1985; Buhle, 1986, 1989).

During his life he worked as a teacher in Trinidad; as a cricket writer (with Neville Cardus at the *Manchester Guardian)* and Caribbean activist (with the great cricketer-politician Learie Constantine) in Britain; as a spokesman for the Socialist Workers Party in the US (resulting in his arrest, imprisonment, and deportation during the McCarthy era); as a strategist for pro-independence in Africa; as an organizer and newspaper editor for Dr Eric Williams's People's National Party which came to constitute the government in Trinidad until the mid-1980s; and finally as a father figure for Afro-Caribbean radicalism amidst the racial tension of Britain in the Thatcherite period.

In the course of his writings, travel, and work, James met a bewildering array of important twentieth-century figures: Leon Trotsky, Paul Robeson, George Headley, Frank Worrell, Kwame Nkrumah, Bob Marley, Julius Nyerere, Michael Manley, Stokely Carmichael, Walter Rodney, Martin Luther King, and countless others. For most if not all of these people, James's stature was such that he became a cult figure, a leading father figure in black activism. Edward Said, something of a late twentieth-century counterpart of James through his scholarship, Middle Eastern origins, pro-Palestinian views, and attacks on Western cultural domination, succinctly sums up the Trinidadian's life purpose as reaffirming "the value of the epic struggle for human emancipation and enlightenment" (Said, 1989).

There were victories along the way, such as engineering the election of Frank

Worrell as the first regular black captain of the West Indies cricket team in 1959, an important cultural victory over the white elite on the eve of Caribbean political independence. James knew that cultural empowerment was just as important, if not more so, than political enrichment. But in so full a life there were inevitably disappointments, none more bitter than the failure of the shortlived West Indian Federation whose collapse represented for James a major blow to Pan-Africanism. It was ironic and symbolic that after the demise of the Federation, something called "West Indies" existed only in the regional cricket team and the regional university, the two principal origins of James's dilemma.

In the assessment and reassessment of James's work (of which this short remembrance is, in one sense, a part), it is important to recognize that there were blind spots and weaknesses, not all of which James was aware. Several years ago, Caribbean literature expert Helen Tiffin pointed to several inconsistencies between his literary and cricket assertions (Tiffin, 1981). But even within *Beyond a Boundary* itself there were flaws in the analysis of the condition of Caribbean cricket. It was, for example, about Trinidadian rather than West Indian cricket, in the same way that Michael Manley's book is Jamaican rather than West Indian (Manley, 1988). But James projected his view to the West Indian level, thereby smoothing out several social characteristics unique to the other Caribbean cricket cultures.

And even in the case of Trinidad itself, James devoted little real space to the role of cricket among the black masses and none to the plight of the East Indian population descended from indentured laborers. It is a particularist, albeit brilliant and evocative, view of cultural discrimination through cricket, involving the white elite's suppression of a tiny, articulate, and intelligent nonwhite elite. To evoke Gramsci again, it is reminiscent of his emphasis on the role of the intellectual cadres (Gramsci, 1957).

In turn, the idea of *acceptance* of class segmentation permeates James's work on cricket but is rarely confronted. As in the long history of Caribbean slavery itself, of which cricket arose in the wake (Stoddart, 1988a), there were remarkably few rebellions against the prevailing social order even though we know that quite sophisticated and politicized networks existed in most settings (Beckles, 1984; Craton, 1982). What appears in James, that is, are some compelling reasons for *why* rebellious and resistant behavior should have occurred within cricket, but very little on why such behavior did *not* emerge.

It might even be argued that in constantly referring to "West Indian" cricket, James was accepting a colonialist structure that arose from the long-term British presence in the area, and the short-term attempt at Pan-West Indianism. What has emerged after independence is a series of separate small states whose social and political cultures are distinctively diverse, the natural result of long periods during which their colonial cultures were quite different. In attempting to override that reality for a romantic view of Afro-Caribbeanism, James overlooked the fact that Trinis, Bajans, and Jamaicans saw each other as distinctive populations, and that radically opposed political traditions and quite different ones were developing in, say, Barbados and Guyana even though, superficially, conditions seemed to be quite similar (Stoddart, 1988b).

But if James did not have all the answers and even failed to ask some of the questions, his position as inspirationalist for the "thick description" (Geertz, 1973) of sport is unquestioned. If anything, from the perspective of the lesser developed world, his work needs to be much better known at a time when developed world theories are applied too readily to inappropriate locations (Stoddart, 1989). And if a reading of his now aging but timeless classic on Caribbean cricket could convince a few readers that it is possible to convey complex ideas in an elegant style based on a rich multidisciplinary background, rather than through convoluted jargon grounded in one-dimensional viewpoints, then so much the better.

It is highly likely that in the years to come C.L.R. James will be recognized as a really major intellectual and activist figure in a bewildering array of human affairs and geographical locations. After all, anyone whose death can cause the appearance of obituaries in such a range of publications as *The Times* of London, the *New Left Review* (editorial), the Barbados *Daily Nation* (Cozier, 1989), the St Louis *Post-Dispatch* (Pollack, 1989), and this journal, was clearly no ordinary person.

References

Anderson, J. (1985, Summer). Cricket and beyond: the career of C.L.R. James, *The American Scholar*, pp. 345–9.

Balliett, W. (1984, June 25). Mr James and Captain Worrell, *New Yorker*, pp. 106–7.

Beckles, H. (1984). *Black Rebellion in Barbados: the struggle against slavery, 1627–1838*. Bridgetown: Antilles.

Buhle, P. (ed.) (1986). *C.L.R. James: his life and work*. London: Allison & Busby.

Buhle, P. (1989). *C.L.R. James: the artist as revolutionary*. London: Verso.

Burton, R.D.E. (1985, September). Cricket, carnival and street culture in the Caribbean. *British Journal of Sports History*, pp. 179–97.

Cozier, T. (1989, June 1). C.L.R. James, *Sun Nation* (Barbados), p. 5.

Craton, M. (1982). *Testing the Chains: resistance to slavery in the British West Indies*. Ithaca, NY: Mouvement.

Femia, J.V. (1981). *Gramsci's Political Thought: hegemony, consciousness and the revolutionary process*. Oxford: Oxford University Press.

Geertz, C. (1973). *The Interpretation of Cultures*. New York: Basic.

Gramsci, A. (1957). *The Modern Prince and Other Writings* (trans. Louis Marks). New York: International.

James, C.L.R. (1963). *Beyond a Boundary*. London: Hutchinson.

Manley, M. (1988). *A History of West Indian Cricket*. London: Deutsch.

Marshall, W.K. (1965). Gary Sobers and the Brisbane Revolution, *New World Quarterly*, 2, pp. 35–42.

Metcalfe, A. (1987). C.L.R. James' contribution to the history of sport, *Canadian Journal of History of Sport*, 18, 2, 52–7.

New Left Review. (1989, May–June). (Editorial), p. 175.

Patterson, O. (1969, March). The ritual of cricket, *Jamaica Journal*, pp. 23–5.

Pollack, J. (1989, June 25). Reflections on C.L.R. James, *St Louis Post Dispatch*, p. 12.

Said, E. (1989, May–June). Review of Buhle, *New Left Review*, p. 175.

Sandiford, K.A.P. (1986, December). Cricket and the Barbadian society, *Canadian Journal of History*, pp. 421–36.

Stoddart, B. (1987, Winter). Cricket, social formation and cultural continuity in Barbados: A preliminary ethnohistory, *Journal of Sport History*, pp. 317–40.

Stoddart, B. (1988a). Cricket and colonialism in the English-speaking Caribbean to 1914: Towards a cultural analysis. In J.A. Mangan (ed.), *Pleasure, Profit, Proselytism: British culture and sport at home and abroad, 1700–1914* (pp. 231–57). London: Cass.

Stoddart, B. (1988b, Fall). Caribbean cricket: The role of sport in emerging small nation politics, *International Journal*, pp. 618–42.

Stoddart, B. (1989). Sport in the social construct of the lesser developed world: A commentary, *Sociology of Sport Journal*, 6, 125–35.

St Pierre, M. (1973, June and September). West Indian cricket, *Caribbean Quarterly*, Parts I and II, pp. 7–27; 20–35.

Sunday Sun (Barbados) (1989, June 4). Report on death of C.L.R. James, p. 3.

Thompson, L. O'B. (1983). How cricket is West Indian cricket: Class, racial and colour conflict. *Caribbean Review*, 12, pp. 23–5, 50–3.

Tiffin, H. (1981). Cricket, literature and the politics of decolonisation: The case of C.L.R. James. In R. Cashman and M. McKernan (eds), *Sport: Money, Morality and the Media* (pp. 177–193). Sydney: University of New South Wales.

Walcott, D. (1984, March 25). A classic of cricket, *New York Times Book Review*, 1, pp. 36–7.

Lares and penates

Brian Stoddart

Given the intellectual debt owed to C.L.R. James by contributors to this volume, it is singularly appropriate that this summary should draw upon some themes established in *Beyond A Boundary*. The book itself, of course, is among the magical few which grow in stature as they age. While the republished and original essays here add detail, heighten intellectual sophistication and broaden the debate, the central generative process is still that created by James. That influence has helped make Caribbean cricket unique in more than its playing form, because the game has unquestioningly been seen as having a key social role in the culture (or cultures) of the region. In so doing, the literature created about Caribbean cricket has become the best in the rapidly expanding field of sports cultural analysis, and its analytical dimensions have been felt in all sports fields.

Because of this, 'Nello' James can rest easy that his twin pantheon of cricket and literature are still seen not only as intertwined and present in the Caribbean, but that their potency is now recognised more widely. It is not that he always got it right, was unchallengeable or totally unblinkered, as I have suggested here. Rather, it is that in deconstructing Caribbean cricket he pinpointed many of the leading impulses in the growing enthusiasm for sport which have emerged around the world from the middle of the nineteenth century onwards. One of his most instructive insights was into the very social complexity of people devoted to cricket (and, by extension, sport).

What do men live by?

For any historian or sociologist of sport or culture, James's most significant observation was also perhaps his simplest: that cricket had the power to raise passionate partisanship to the point of obsession. The essays here confirm that at two levels.

In the direct sense, a hallmark of Caribbean life is that the deeds/misdeeds of cricketers have aroused furious and detailed discussions centred on performance statistics. As a collective, Caribbean people constitute one of the greatest sources of cricket records and general knowledge. English and Australian visitors, for example, are always surprised to discover that 'their' cricket is invariably better known by 'outsider' Caribbean devotees than it is by themselves.

Indirectly, the permeation of cricket into other areas of regional life has been remarkable. Cricketers have become political figures (Grantley Adams to Wesley Hall, to follow the Bajan example) while politicians themselves have seen the game as deeply symbolic and significant (Michael Manley most prominently but preceded by Eric Williams and matched by Tom Adams among several others). Cricket has featured in George Lamming novels, Kamau Brathwaite poems, Kitchener calypsos and folklore of many varieties.

What James knew, instinctively, was that it all had to mean something and that it had to be linked to other social phenomena. In that, his ideas have been well developed here by Burton, Tiffin and Beckles/Walcott, in particular, because they all in their own ways see cricket as *performance*: in the playing of and responding to cricket, what is it that Caribbeans reveal about the roles taken in their lives by what is, after all, an acquired taste and a rather odd form of physical activity? From that point it is but a short step to the enlightening works of Geertz, Gluckman, Turner and the other social anthropologists concerned with social drama.

There has been a downside to this passion dimension, however. Many outside observers mistook passion, in both playing and spectating, for frivolity, leading directly to the idea of 'calypso cricket' in its perjorative sense with the emphasis on wasted opportunities, happy-go-lucky players, parties, gambling and short-term gratification at the expense of long-term solidarity. If it was not sugar and calypso, it was rum and reggae.

The irony is that nothing could have been further from reality. As with so much else in the Caribbean story, image supplanted reality at the expense of analysis (provocative commentators might want to point to Caribbean cricket as an early victim of post-modernist thinking!). Most if not all the papers here reveal the deep-seated seriousness of a game which became a contested site for cultural control in the immediate aftermath of slavery, through the struggle for political independence and into the post-independence search for meaning. At every step, cricket was there hence the political significance of Constantine, Ramadhin/Valentine, Worrell, Sobers, Richards *et al.*

Consequently, individual players such as these have always taken on more important roles than simply those occupied on the field. The writers here have pointed to this both explicitly and inferentially, and it is important to note that the players themselves might not necessarily have appreciated fully the emotional capital invested in them – Sobers in Rhodesia is perhaps the most spectacular case study here, but there are others such as the 1980s rebel tourists to South Africa.

An associated point needs to be made here. Such role models have not necessarily been all high profile players or even in the Caribbean itself. One major aspect of the story untold here concerns the hundreds of players who have performed in English league cricket since the late 1920s and in the counties since the late 1960s.

Against the background of post-World War Two migration patterns, these cricketers helped focus cultural continuity in a new environment and to provide aspiration in an often hostile climate. This is an important issue which requires further attention.

All this attention to people raises a glaring question – what about the women? As Hilary Beckles hints here, this is a most complex issue which also deserves a great deal more investigation. As most observational reports indicate, women have long been present at matches as spectators but, in the Caribbean, rarely as players. At club level in some locations, at least, women provide support roles: preparing food for club nights, organising entertainment, taking care of children. Where clubs are multisport in nature, women might be found playing hockey, say, but still preparing food for cricketers.

That Caribbean cricket participation is highly gendered is obvious, but the reasons are not quite so transparent. It has something to do with the gendering process in slave and post-slave relations, with the associated working out of Afro-Caribbean social/cultural roles in new circumstances, with questions about emerging sexual mores and practices, with child-rearing customs, and with ongoing patriarchal dominance. Again, the simplest point to make is that we know far too little about this and that it needs full exploration – as C.L.R. James might have suggested had he considered women's roles (remarkably few women feature in his book), the presence of women in the stands has to mean something.

And that is one of the key points, of course: everything in the Caribbean cricket pageant has a place, a purpose and a meaning.

All the world's a stage

As one or two writers point out in these essays, cricket has probably been *the* one major and enduring means by which Caribbean messages have been relayed to the world. With the possible exceptions of Bob Marley, Peter Tosh and one or two other limited examples, Caribbean music has remained encapsulated within the culture itself, either at home or within expatriate communities. Caribbean writers like Derek Walcott have won acclaim but not mass appeal at the international level. Cultural performers in other spheres like dance and art display similar features. Expatriate athletes like Patrick Ewing, Ben Johnson and Merlene Ottey have won applause in their fields. In all these cases, however, and in intellectual fields as well, there has never been established the deep-seated, powerful international impact as seen in cricket.

Were it not for cricket, the region would be little known in the British post-colonial worlds of Australia, New Zealand, South Africa, India, Pakistan and the rest. My father grew up in New Zealand and never once left its shores, yet he instilled in me a knowledge of and enthusiasm for the Caribbean (West Indies was the ubiquitous term – it was a long, long way 'west' of New Zealand, but such was the power of the British colonial mind and global view). That arose from the memories created by watching Everton Weekes *et al.* when they toured New Zealand in the early 1950s. The consciousness of things Caribbean, it needs be underlined, was caused neither by politics nor economics but by cricket.

It is for that reason, probably, that the Caribbean's role on the world stage has been dictated by cricket. As I have pointed out in one of my essays here, the combined power of the island states was most significant in halting white cricket powers from defying international sentiment and re-engaging with South Africa well before the early 1990s. In its own way, the Caribbean cricket power has had a role in inflicting the momentous changes which have overtaken apartheid South Africa.

While that is the most spectacular success it is also the easiest to recognise. In other spheres it is difficult to gauge how much real knowledge of Caribbean matters was taken on by foreign cricket audiences. In Australia and New Zealand, for example, there is little, almost no, Caribbean material taught in schools and universities, covered in the media outlets, canvassed in economic forums or engaged at the highest political levels. There is a residual awareness that the region sprang from slavery with an appropriate abhorrence of that practice. For the most part the images are those that come from popular music (ranging from Harry Belafonte to 10CC's 'We Don't Like Cricket' and Billy Ocean) or film and television images which are inevitably of beach bars, luxury hotels, beaches and dumb or sinister locals.

Even so, the images created by Caribbean cricketers in Australia and elsewhere have (mostly) been positive despite all the talk of fast-bowling assassins and the like. We could still do with a lot more investigation into this point of impact. When Australia toured the Caribbean in 1992 it was the first time Australian cricket fans had *seen* (via television) what the conditions were like – previously they had relied on the word pictures of the print journalists or the radio commentators. Now they could *see* the tiny islands, grounds and populations, marvel at the cultural practices recounted here by Beckles and Walcott, and many resolved to go when Australia next tours in 1995. Perhaps the resonances will alter consequently and so broaden the world stage perception.

There is another stage, however, and one dealt with here in a largely indirect way. It is a smaller, often less obvious stage but one with an enormous significance: administration and, by definition, power. From studies in the histories of many colonial and post-colonial conditions it is clear that the conservatising role of institutions has been highly significant in dampening the pace of change, even in situations where the signs for change have been propitious. More precisely, it is clear that the administrative structures of institutions have been important preservers of dominant cultural values. Nowhere is this more significant than in cultural institutions of which cricket, in this case, is part.

From these essays it is clear that we now need to find out a lot more about these structures of power because in them reside many of the origins of the social practices so challenged here. To state an obvious point: at a time when Caribbean politics was moving towards independence and some semblance of equal rights across colour divisions, the same was not necessarily happening in so important a social organism as cricket. The construction of cricket power, then, became an art form in continuing patterns of domination, with liberation coming from other parallel art forms.

What is art?

It has long been my contention that the analysis of Caribbean cricket has produced the single best set of intellectual literature about any sport anywhere in the world. Consider, in a comparative sense, the relative paucity of the works on cricket elsewhere in the world and the point is substantiated. In part that has to do with the recognised centrality of cricket in the culture, the growing concerns with all forms of colonial domination, the very passion generated by the Caribbean game. Whatever the origins, the results are as impressive as the contributors themselves.

The debt to James is obvious, as mentioned throughout this book. Orlando Patterson perhaps best personifies the realisation of cricket's power in that his work was written en route to a Harvard position (where his principal concerns have been with slavery and freedom) via activist positions on site, as it were. Hilary Beckles, too, has come to cricket via a study of slavery marked by his training in the leftist traditions of Hull. The twinning of slavery and cricket immediately sets the social significance of what can be treated as a mere game. Sociologists like Thompson and St Pierre demonstrate these aspects in their work as well.

'Outsiders' like Manning, Yelvington, Burton and myself reflect related concerns: a relationship between theories of power and colonial practice, the structuration of inequality historically and anthropologically, the forces of change/continuity, and the power of comparative example. Frank Manning was doubly interesting in that not only was he a cultural outsider but also a cricketing one as well, coming from a background outside C. Wright Mills' 'cultural baggage', in this case, cricket.

Collectively, this group of analysts has made an enormous contribution to this specific subject, and to the broader world of sports history. That academic subculture has been overwhelmingly empirical in outlook until very recently when European analysts have begun to turn their attention to sport as a social phenomenon. The origins of this empiricism are complex, but in the British and North American settings proceed from the fact that sports history began life in schools of physical education rather than sociology, history or anthropology. Given that such was not the case in the Caribbean, the analytical edge was honed early.

Strangely, or perhaps not so, the significance of this body of work has been recognised but slowly – in North America and Europe because few scholars read about cricket, in the British and British-related world because James and his successors were not the normal stuff of physical education courses. That situation, happily, has begun to turn as the importance of sport as a social site looms ever more large in the late twentieth century heading to the twenty-first. If nothing else, by gathering these essays together the collection establishes the combined power of the work and also points to future directions.

If this art of analysis is evidently significant from this work, so is the influence of the image, most particularly as portrayed through the word pictures of press/radio and the visual pictures of television and film. One obvious avenue of further research to emerge from this collection is the importance of the media in creating the atmospherics of Caribbean cricket. The images conveyed 'Home' by the early cricket tourists were just as important in creating the concept of the 'Caribbean' tradition as are those more recently conveyed by television. We now know enough about the power of representation to know that the symbolism of Caribbean cricket has as much power as its physical reality. This has been particularly the case since 1975 when Caribbean sides have relied heavily on the 'four quicks' mode of attack. If earlier images were of carefree and careless batsmen, more recent ones have been of sinister, relentless, heartless, vicious fast bowlers – Michael 'Whispering Death' Holding is an excellent image here.

The point is simple enough, if we accept the idea of the social construction of reality – in many respects Caribbean cricket has been analysed in the eye of the beholder, with most beholders having their views mediated by information agents. Tour books are wonderful in this respect. With rare exceptions they make little or no concession to the idea that the games recounted have a social context. The essays here, then, put the spotlight on these information sources and demand further artistic interpretation.

Of course, the real artists are the players themselves (too often the forgotten characters in sports history) and it is clear that the more their roles change the more they stay the same. From the late nineteenth century onwards, poor black men have used cricket to get on in life either economically or socially or, as in the case of Herman Griffith, as a complex way of lashing out at how things were. For many of them it was a tough battle, and it is chilling to think that the talents of Everton Weekes and Gary Sobers (to name just two Barbadian examples) might never have been seen around the world but for social manipulations which allowed them into mainstream cricket.

The money now is infinitely better, the price being limited appearances by international players in the nurturing environments which produced them in the first place. Besides which, cricket may be losing its power to education, migration and alternative sporting success – a naive way, but a telling one, to look at this concerns the number of young black men who have played for England in recent years but who in other circumstances might have played for West Indies.

One thing remains, though – whatever else changes, Caribbean players will always retain an almost undefinably dynamic quality which guarantees anticipation.

Lares and penates

Wherefore are those things hid?

A leap from those players to the world of intellectual theory is an enormous one, indeed, but one made constantly in these essays. As Kenneth Surin shows, it is possible to 'read' a great many things into the simple state of cricket. Some readers may find such theorising unconvincing, others will find it unlocks the puzzle. Either way, the role of theory in defining the ultimate social status of cricket, along with its social dimensions, cannot be stressed highly enough. We might learn more details of the cricketing past, but will make nothing of them without turning to social analysts to help interpret them. The roll call here is impressive (from Marx to James and Gramsci, from Hegel to Bourdieu and numerous others), but will need to grow if analytical progress is to be made. As Edward Said and others increasingly recognise the power of culture, perhaps they will turn more to sports as a post-colonial artefact and, in this specific case, to cricket as a powerful social agent.

What we need to know, then, is not so much about the game itself as about its deep layering – and C.L.R. James knew that many years ago.

The future in the past

Something else that James pointed to was the idea that just as most of life's niches are in a state of constant flux so, too, is cricket, especially in its Caribbean mode. The pressures within Caribbean cricket now derive directly from social change, just as did the pressures of the past. It grew in the aftermath of slavery, spread in the economic and social discrimination which replaced that more direct form of subjugation, broke the mould in the midst of political freedom and finally rose to power as fuller freedoms spread.

Yet, as Orlando Patterson points out so forcefully, Caribbean cricket essentially remains a cultural contradiction: a beloved game which is redolent of an alien and dominant ideology.

That contradiction runs through all these essays, either directly or indirectly, and the challenge that remains is to explain fully the collective psychological force of that condition. C.L.R. James would have understood that, because it has much to do with life imitating art: the contours of the modern game as played and conveyed by Caribbean people are still essentially about struggle in one form or another, and therein lies the ultimate message.

Index